DRAMA
for Students

Advisors

Erik France: Adjunct Instructor of English, Macomb Community College, Warren, Michigan. B.A. and M.S.L.S. from University of North Carolina, Chapel Hill; Ph.D. from Temple University.

Kate Hamill: Grade 12 English Teacher, Catonsville High School, Catonsville, Maryland.

Joseph McGeary: English Teacher, Germantown Friends School, Philadelphia, Pennsylvania. Ph.D. in English from Duke University.

Timothy Showalter: English Department Chair, Franklin High School, Reisterstown, Maryland. Certified teacher by the Maryland State Department of Education. Member of the National Council of Teachers of English.

Amy Spade Silverman: English Department Chair, Kehillah Jewish High School, Palo Alto, California. Member of National Council of Teachers of English (NCTE), Teachers and Writers, and NCTE Opinion Panel. Exam Reader, Advanced Placement Literature and Composition. Poet, published in *North American Review, Nimrod,* and *Michigan Quarterly Review,* among other publications.

Jody Stefansson: Director of Boswell Library and Study Center and Upper School Learning Specialist, Polytechnic School, Pasadena, California. Board member, Children's Literature Council of Southern California. Member of American Library Association, Association of Independent School Librarians, and Association of Educational Therapists.

Laura Jean Waters: Certified School Library Media Specialist, Wilton High School, Wilton, Connecticut. B.A. from Fordham University; M.A. from Fairfield University.

DRAMA
for Students

**Presenting Analysis, Context, and Criticism
on Commonly Studied Dramas**

VOLUME 27

Sara Constantakis, Project Editor

Foreword by Carole L. Hamilton

GALE
CENGAGE Learning™

Detroit • New York • San Francisco • New Haven, Conn • Waterville, Maine • London

Drama for Students, Volume 27

Project Editor: Sara Constantakis

Rights Acquisition and Management: Mardell Glinski Schultz, Barb McNeil, Tracie Richardson, Robyn Young

Composition: Evi Abou-El-Seoud

Manufacturing: Drew Kalasky

Imaging: John Watkins

Product Design: Pamela A. E. Galbreath, Jennifer Wahi

Content Conversion: Katrina Coach

Product Manager: Meggin Condino

For product information and technology assistance, contact us at **Gale Customer Support, 1-800-877-4253.** For permission to use material from this text or product, submit all requests online at **www.cengage.com/permissions.** Further permissions questions can be emailed to **permissionrequest@cengage.com**

While every effort has been made to ensure the reliability of the information presented in this publication, Gale, a part of Cengage Learning, does not guarantee the accuracy of the data contained herein. Gale accepts no payment for listing; and inclusion in the publication of any organization, agency, institution, publication, service, or individual does not imply endorsement of the editors or publisher. Errors brought to the attention of the publisher and verified to the satisfaction of the publisher will be corrected in future editions.

Gale
27500 Drake Rd.
Farmington Hills, MI, 48331-3535

ISBN-13: 978-0-7876-8123-4
ISBN-10: 0-7876-8123-7

ISSN 1094-9232

This title is also available as an e-book.
ISBN-13: 978-1-4144-4939-5
ISBN-10: 1-4144-4939-9
Contact your Gale, a part of Cengage Learning sales representative for ordering information.

Printed in the United States of America
1 2 3 4 5 6 7 14 13 12 11 10

Table of Contents

ADVISORS ii

THE STUDY OF DRAMA
(by Carole L. Hamilton). ix

INTRODUCTION xi

LITERARY CHRONOLOGY xv

ACKNOWLEDGMENTS xvii

CONTRIBUTORS xix

ARIA DA CAPO
(by Edna St. Vincent Millay) 1
  Author Biography 2
  Plot Summary 2
  Characters 4
  Themes 6
  Style 9
  Historical Context 10
  Critical Overview 12
  Criticism 13
  Sources 24
  Further Reading 24

THE CRUCIBLE 25
  Plot Summary 26
  Characters 30
  Themes 34
  Style 36

Cultural Context 38
Critical Overview 40
Criticism 40
Sources 47

DESIRE UNDER THE ELMS
(by Eugene O'Neill) 49
   Author Biography 50
   Plot Summary 51
   Characters 55
   Themes 56
   Style 58
   Historical Context 59
   Critical Overview 61
   Criticism 61
   Sources 72
   Further Reading 73

THE GOVERNESS
(by Neil Simon) 74
   Author Biography 75
   Plot Summary 76
   Characters 78
   Themes 78
   Style 80
   Historical Context 81
   Critical Overview 83
   Criticism 84
   Sources 93
   Further Reading 94

HEATHER RAFFO'S 9 PARTS OF DESIRE
(by Heather Raffo) 95
   Author Biography 95
   Plot Summary 96
   Characters 99
   Themes 101
   Style 102
   Historical Context 103
   Critical Overview 104
   Criticism 105
   Sources 114
   Further Reading 115

HENRIETTA
(by Karen Jones Meadows) 116
   Author Biography 117
   Plot Summary 117
   Characters 120
   Themes 122
   Style 124
   Historical Context 125
   Critical Overview 126
   Criticism 127

Sources 132
Further Reading 132

I NEVER SAW ANOTHER BUTTERFLY
(by Celeste Raspanti) 134
   Author Biography 135
   Plot Summary 135
   Characters 137
   Themes 139
   Style 140
   Historical Context 140
   Critical Overview 142
   Criticism 142
   Sources 149
   Further Reading 149

LIGHT SHINING IN BUCKINGHAMSHIRE
(by Caryl Churchill) 151
   Author Biography 152
   Plot Summary 152
   Characters 155
   Themes 158
   Style 159
   Historical Context 159
   Critical Overview 161
   Criticism 162
   Sources 169
   Further Reading 169

ROBERT JOHNSON: TRICK THE DEVIL
(by Bill Harris) 170
   Author Biography 171
   Plot Summary 171
   Characters 173
   Themes 175
   Style 177
   Historical Context 178
   Critical Overview 180
   Criticism 181
   Sources 191
   Further Reading 191

THE SERVANT OF TWO MASTERS
(by Carlo Goldoni) 193
   Author Biography 194
   Plot Summary 194
   Characters 197
   Themes 199
   Style 200
   Historical Context 202
   Critical Overview 203
   Criticism 203
   Sources 208
   Further Reading 208

A STREETCAR NAMED DESIRE 209
   Plot Summary 210
   Characters 215
   Themes 217
   Style 219
   Cultural Context 220
   Critical Overview 221
   Criticism 221
   Sources 229

THE TROJAN WOMEN
(by Euripides) 231
   Author Biography 232
   Plot Summary 232
   Characters 235
   Themes 238
   Style 240
   Historical Context 241
   Critical Overview 244
   Criticism 245
   Sources 257
   Further Reading 257

URINETOWN
(by Greg Kotis and Mark Hollmann) 259
   Author Biography 260
   Plot Summary 261
   Characters 263
   Themes 265

   Style 267
   Historical Context 267
   Critical Overview 269
   Criticism 270
   Sources 278
   Further Reading 278

WEST SIDE STORY
(by Arthur Laurents, Stephen Sondheim,
Leonard Bernstein, and Jerome Robbins) . . . 280
   Author Biography 281
   Plot Summary 282
   Characters 284
   Themes 287
   Style 289
   Historical Context 290
   Critical Overview 291
   Criticism 292
   Sources 300
   Further Reading 301

GLOSSARY OF LITERARY TERMS 303

CUMULATIVE AUTHOR/TITLE INDEX . . 341

CUMULATIVE NATIONALITY/ETHNICITY
INDEX 349

SUBJECT/THEME INDEX 355

The Study of Drama

We study drama in order to learn what meaning others have made of life, to comprehend what it takes to produce a work of art, and to glean some understanding of ourselves. Drama produces in a separate, aesthetic world, a moment of being for the audience to experience, while maintaining the detachment of a reflective observer.

Drama is a representational art, a visible and audible narrative presenting virtual, fictional characters within a virtual, fictional universe. Dramatic realizations may pretend to approximate reality or else stubbornly defy, distort, and deform reality into an artistic statement. From this separate universe that is obviously not "real life" we expect a valid reflection upon reality, yet drama never is mistaken for reality—the methods of theater are integral to its form and meaning. Theater is art, and art's appeal lies in its ability both to approximate life and to depart from it. For in intruding its distorted version of life into our consciousness, art gives us a new perspective and appreciation of life and reality. Although all aesthetic experiences perform this service, theater does it most effectively by creating a separate, cohesive universe that freely acknowledges its status as an art form.

And what is the purpose of the aesthetic universe of drama? The potential answers to such a question are nearly as many and varied as there are plays written, performed, and enjoyed. Dramatic texts can be problems posed, answers asserted, or moments portrayed. Dramas (tragedies as well as comedies) may serve strictly "to ease the anguish of a torturing hour" (as stated in William Shakespeare's *A Midsummer Night's Dream*)—to divert and entertain—or aspire to move the viewer to action with social issues. Whether to entertain or to instruct, affirm or influence, pacify or shock, dramatic art wraps us in the spell of its imaginary world for the length of the work and then dispenses us back to the real world, entertained, purged, as Aristotle said, of pity and fear, and edified—or at least weary enough to sleep peacefully.

It is commonly thought that theater, being an art of performance, must be experienced—seen—in order to be appreciated fully. However, to view a production of a dramatic text is to be limited to a single interpretation of that text—all other interpretations are for the moment closed off, inaccessible. In the process of producing a play, the director, stage designer, and performers interpret and transform the script into a work of art that always departs in some measure from the author's original conception. Novelist and critic Umberto Eco, in his *The Role of the Reader: Explorations in the Semiotics of Texts* (Indiana University Press, 1979), explained, "In short, we can say that every performance offers us a complete and satisfying version of the work, but at the same time makes it incomplete for us, because it cannot simultaneously give all the other artistic solutions which the work may admit."

Thus Laurence Olivier's coldly formal and neurotic film presentation of Shakespeare's *Hamlet* (in which he played the title character as well as directed) shows marked differences from subsequent adaptations. While Olivier's Hamlet is clearly entangled in a Freudian relationship with his mother Gertrude, he would be incapable of shushing her with the impassioned kiss that Mel Gibson's mercurial Hamlet (in director Franco Zeffirelli's 1990 film) does. Although each of performances rings true to Shakespeare's text, each is also a mutually exclusive work of art. Also important to consider are the time periods in which each of these films was produced: Olivier made his film in 1948, a time in which overt references to sexuality (especially incest) were frowned upon. Gibson and Zeffirelli made their film in a culture more relaxed and comfortable with these issues. Just as actors and directors can influence the presentation of drama, so too can the time period of the production affect what the audience will see.

A play script is an open text from which an infinity of specific realizations may be derived. Dramatic scripts that are more open to interpretive creativity (such as those of Ntozake Shange and Tomson Highway) actually require the creative improvisation of the production troupe in order to complete the text. Even the most prescriptive scripts (those of Neil Simon, Lillian Hellman, and Robert Bolt, for example), can never fully control the actualization of live performance, and circumstantial events, including the attitude and receptivity of the audience, make every performance a unique event. Thus, while it is important to view a production of a dramatic piece, if one wants to understand a drama fully it is equally important to read the original dramatic text.

The reader of a dramatic text or script is not limited by either the specific interpretation of a given production or by the unstoppable action of a moving spectacle. The reader of a dramatic text may discover the nuances of the play's language, structure, and events at their own pace. Yet studied alone, the author's blueprint for artistic production does not tell the whole story of a play's life and significance. One also needs to assess the play's critical reviews to discover how it resonated to cultural themes at the time of its debut and how the shifting tides of cultural interest have revised its interpretation and impact on audiences. And to do this, one needs to know a little about the culture of the times which produced the play as well as the author who penned it.

Drama for Students supplies this material in a useful compendium for the student of dramatic theater. Covering a range of dramatic works that span from 442 BCE to the 1990s, this book focuses on significant theatrical works whose themes and form transcend the uncertainty of dramatic fads. These are plays that have proven to be both memorable and teachable. *Drama for Students* seeks to enhance appreciation of these dramatic texts by providing scholarly materials written with the secondary and college/university student in mind. It provides for each play a concise summary of the plot and characters as well as a detailed explanation of its themes. In addition, background material on the historical context of the play, its critical reception, and the author's life help the student to understand the work's position in the chronicle of dramatic history. For each play entry a new work of scholarly criticism is also included, as well as segments of other significant critical works for handy reference. A thorough bibliography provides a starting point for further research.

This series offers comprehensive educational resources for students of drama. *Drama for Students* is a vital book for dramatic interpretation and a valuable addition to any reference library.

Sources

Eco, Umberto, *The Role of the Reader: Explorations in the Semiotics of Texts*, Indiana University Press, 1979.

Carole L. Hamilton
Author and Instructor of English at Cary Academy, Cary, North Carolina

Introduction

Purpose of the Book

The purpose of *Drama for Students* (*DfS*) is to provide readers with a guide to understanding, enjoying, and studying dramas by giving them easy access to information about the work. Part of Gale's "For Students" literature line, *DfS* is specifically designed to meet the curricular needs of high school and undergraduate college students and their teachers, as well as the interests of general readers and researchers considering specific plays. While each volume contains entries on "classic" dramas frequently studied in classrooms, there are also entries containing hard-to-find information on contemporary plays, including works by multicultural, international, and women playwrights. Entries profiling film versions of plays not only diversify the study of drama but support alternate learning styles, media literacy, and film studies curricula as well.

The information covered in each entry includes an introduction to the play and the work's author; a plot summary, to help readers unravel and understand the events in a drama; descriptions of important characters, including explanation of a given character's role in the drama as well as discussion about that character's relationship to other characters in the play; analysis of important themes in the drama; and an explanation of important literary techniques and movements as they are demonstrated in the play.

In addition to this material, which helps the readers analyze the play itself, students are also provided with important information on the literary and historical background informing each work. This includes a historical context essay, a box comparing the time or place the drama was written to modern Western culture, a critical essay, and excerpts from critical essays on the play. A unique feature of *DfS* is a specially commissioned critical essay on each drama, targeted toward the student reader.

The "literature to film" entries on plays vary slightly in form, providing background on film technique and comparison to the original, literary version of the work. These entries open with an introduction to the film, which leads directly into the plot summary. The summary highlights plot changes from the play, key cinematic moments, and/or examples of key film techniques. As in standard entries, there are character profiles (noting omissions or additions, and identifying the actors), analysis of themes and how they are illustrated in the film, and an explanation of the cinematic style and structure of the film. A cultural context section notes any time period or setting differences from that of the original work, as well as cultural differences between the time in which the original work was written and the time in which the film adaptation was made. A film entry concludes with a critical overview and critical essays on the film.

To further help today's student in studying and enjoying each play or film, information on audiobooks and other media adaptations is provided (if available), as well as suggestions for works of fiction, nonfiction, or film on similar themes and topics. Classroom aids include ideas for research papers and lists of critical and reference sources that provide additional material on each drama. Film entries also highlight signature film techniques demonstrated, as well as suggesting media literacy activities and prompts to use during or after viewing a film.

Selection Criteria

The titles for each volume of *DfS* are selected by surveying numerous sources on notable literary works and analyzing course curricula for various schools, school districts, and states. Some of the sources surveyed include: high school and undergraduate literature anthologies and textbooks; lists of award-winners, and recommended titles, including the Young Adult Library Services Association (YALSA) list of best books for young adults. Films are selected both for the literary importance of the original work and the merits of the adaptation (including official awards and widespread public recognition).

Input solicited from our expert advisory board—consisting of educators and librarians—guides us to maintain a mix of "classic" and contemporary literary works, a mix of challenging and engaging works (including genre titles that are commonly studied) appropriate for different age levels, and a mix of international, multicultural and women authors. These advisors also consult on each volume's entry list, advising on which titles are most studied, most appropriate, and meet the broadest interests across secondary (grades 7–12) curricula and undergraduate literature studies.

How Each Entry Is Organized

Each entry, or chapter, in *DfS* focuses on one play. Each entry heading lists the full name of the play, the author's name, and the date of the play's publication. The following elements are contained in each entry:

Introduction: a brief overview of the drama which provides information about its first appearance, its literary standing, any controversies surrounding the work, and major conflicts or themes within the work. Film entries identify the original play and provide understanding of the film's reception and reputation, along with that of the director.

Author Biography: in play entries, this section includes basic facts about the author's life, and focuses on events and times in the author's life that inspired the drama in question.

Plot Summary: a description of the major events in the play. Subheads demarcate the play's various acts or scenes. Plot summaries of films are used to uncover plot differences from the original play, and to note the use of certain film angles or techniques.

Characters: an alphabetical listing of major characters in the play. Each character name is followed by a brief to an extensive description of the character's role in the play, as well as discussion of the character's actions, relationships, and possible motivation. In film entries, omissions or changes to the cast of characters of the film adaptation are mentioned here, and the actors' names—and any awards they may have received—are also included.

Characters are listed alphabetically by last name. If a character is unnamed—for instance, the Stage Manager in *Our Town*—the character is listed as "The Stage Manager" and alphabetized as "Stage Manager." If a character's first name is the only one given, the name will appear alphabetically by the first name. Variant names are also included for each character. Thus, the nickname "Babe" would head the listing for a character in *Crimes of the Heart,* but below that listing would be her less-mentioned married name "Rebecca Botrelle."

Themes: a thorough overview of how the major topics, themes, and issues are addressed within the play. Each theme discussed appears in a separate subhead. While the key themes often remain the same or similar when a play is adapted into a film, film entries demonstrate how the themes are conveyed cinematically, along with any changes in the portrayal of the themes.

Style: this section addresses important style elements of the drama, such as setting, point of view, and narration; important literary devices used, such as imagery, foreshadowing, symbolism; and, if applicable, genres to which the work might have belonged, such as Gothicism or Romanticism. Literary terms are explained within the entry, but can also be found in the Glossary. Film entries cover how the director conveyed the meaning, message, and mood of the work using film in comparison to the author's use of language, literary device, etc., in the original work.

Historical Context: in play entries, this section outlines the social, political, and cultural climate in which the author lived and the play was created. This section may include descriptions of related historical events, pertinent aspects of daily life in the culture, and the artistic and literary sensibilities of the time in which the work was written. If the play is a historical work, information regarding the time in which the play is set is also included. Each section is broken down with helpful subheads. Film entries contain a similar Cultural Context section, because the film adaptation might explore an entirely different time period or culture than the original work, and may also be influenced by the traditions and views of a time period much different than that of the original author.

Critical Overview: this section provides background on the critical reputation of the play or film, including bannings or any other public controversies surrounding the work. For older plays, this section includes a history of how the drama or film was first received and how perceptions of it may have changed over the years; for more recent plays, direct quotes from early reviews may also be included.

Criticism: an essay commissioned by *DfS* which specifically deals with the play or film and is written specifically for the student audience, as well as excerpts from previously published criticism on the work (if available).

Sources: an alphabetical list of critical material used in compiling the entry, with full bibliographical information.

Further Reading: an alphabetical list of other critical sources which may prove useful for the student. It includes full bibliographical information and a brief annotation.

In addition, each entry contains the following highlighted sections, set apart from the main text as sidebars:

Media Adaptations: if available, a list of audiobooks and important film and television adaptations of the play, including source information. The list may also include such variations on the work as musical adaptations and other stage interpretations.

Topics for Further Study: a list of potential study questions or research topics dealing with the play. This section includes questions related to other disciplines the student may be studying, such as American history, world history, science, math, government, business, geography, economics, psychology, etc.

Compare and Contrast: an "at-a-glance" comparison of the cultural and historical differences between the author's time and culture and late twentieth century or early twenty-first century Western culture. This box includes pertinent parallels between the major scientific, political, and cultural movements of the time or place the drama was written, the time or place the play was set (if a historical work), and modern Western culture. Works written after 1990 may not have this box.

What Do I Read Next?: a list of works that might give a reader points of entry into a classic work (e.g., YA or multicultural titles) and/ or complement the featured play or serve as a contrast to it. This includes works by the same author and others, works from various genres, YA works, and works from various cultures and eras.

The film entries provide sidebars more targeted to the study of film, including:

Film Technique: a listing and explanation of four to six key techniques used in the film, including shot styles, use of transitions, lighting, sound or music, etc.

Read, Watch, Write: media literacy prompts and/or suggestions for viewing log prompts.

What Do I See Next?: a list of films based on the same or similar works or of films similar in directing style, technique, etc.

Other Features

DfS includes "The Study of Drama," a foreword by Carole Hamilton, an educator and author who specializes in dramatic works. This essay examines the basis for drama in societies and what drives people to study such work. The essay also discusses how *DfS* can help teachers show students how to enrich their own reading/ viewing experiences.

A Cumulative Author/Title Index lists the authors and titles covered in each volume of the *DfS* series.

A Cumulative Nationality/Ethnicity Index breaks down the authors and titles covered in each volume of the *DfS* series by nationality and ethnicity.

A Subject/Theme Index, specific to each volume, provides easy reference for users who may be studying a particular subject or theme rather than a single work. Significant subjects from events to broad themes are included.

Each entry may include illustrations, including photo of the author, stills from stage productions, and stills from film adaptations, if available.

Citing Drama for Students

When writing papers, students who quote directly from any volume of *DfS* may use the following general forms. These examples are based on MLA style; teachers may request that students adhere to a different style, so the following examples may be adapted as needed.

When citing text from *DfS* that is not attributed to a particular author (i.e., the Themes, Style, Historical Context sections, etc.), the following format should be used in the bibliography section:

"*Our Town.*" *Drama for Students.* Vol. 1. Ed. David Galens and Lynn Spampinato. Detroit: Gale, 1998. 227–30.

When quoting the specially commissioned essay from *DfS* (usually the first piece under the "Criticism" subhead), the following format should be used:

Fiero, John. Critical Essay on *Twilight: Los Angeles, 1992. Drama for Students.* Vol. 2. Ed. David Galens and Lynn Spampinato. Detroit: Gale, 1998. 247–49.

When quoting a journal or newspaper essay that is reprinted in a volume of *DfS*, the following form may be used:

Rich, Frank. "Theatre: A Mamet Play, *Glengarry Glen Ross.*" *New York Theatre Critics' Review* 45.4 (March 5, 1984): 5–7. Excerpted and reprinted in *Drama for Students.* Vol. 2. Ed. David Galens and Lynn Spampinato. Detroit: Gale, 1998. 51–53.

When quoting material reprinted from a book that appears in a volume of *DfS*, the following form may be used:

Kerr, Walter. "*The Miracle Worker.*" *The Theatre in Spite of Itself.* Simon & Schuster, 1963. 255–57. Excerpted and reprinted in *Drama for Students.* Vol. 2. Ed. David Galens and Lynn Spampinato. Detroit: Gale, 1998. 123–24.

We Welcome Your Suggestions

The editorial staff of *Drama for Students* welcomes your comments and ideas. Readers who wish to suggest dramas to appear in future volumes, or who have other suggestions, are cordially invited to contact the editor. You may contact the editor via e-mail at: **ForStudentsEditors@cengage.com.** Or write to the editor at:

Editor, *Drama for Students*
Gale
27500 Drake Road
Farmington Hills, MI 48331-3535

Literary Chronology

480 BCE: Euripides is born on September 23 on the island of Salamis, off the coast of Greece.

415 BCE: Euripides's play *The Trojan Women* is produced.

406 BCE: Euripides dies in Macedonia, a region within Greece.

1707: Carlo Goldoni is born February 25 in Venice, Italy.

c. 1745: Carlo Goldoni's play *The Servant of Two Masters* is published in Italian and will be published in English later.

1793: Carlo Goldoni dies on February 6 or 7 in Paris, France.

1888: Eugene O'Neill is born on October 16 in New York, New York.

1892: Edna St. Vincent Millay is born on February 22 in Rockland, Maine.

1915: Arthur Miller is born on October 17 in New York, New York.

1918: Arthur Laurents is born July 14 in New York, New York.

1918: Leonard Bernstein is born August 25 in Boston, Massachusetts.

1918: Jerome Rabinowitz (later Jerome Robbins) is born October 11 in New York, New York.

1919: Edna St. Vincent Millay's play *Aria da Capo* is produced. It will be published in 1920.

1923: Edna St. Vincent Millay is awarded the Pulitzer Prize for Poetry for *The Harp-Weaver, and Other Poems*.

1924: Eugene O'Neill's play *Desire under the Elms* is produced. It will be published a year later.

1927: Neil Simon is born July 4 in Bronx, New York.

1928: Celeste Raspanti is born in Chicago, Illinois.

1930: Stephen Sondheim is born March 22 in New York, New York.

1936: Eugene O'Neill is awarded the Nobel Prize for Literature.

1938: Caryl Churchill is born on September 3 in London, England.

1941: Bill Harris is born in Anniston, Alabama.

1947: Tennessee Williams's play *A Streetcar Named Desire* is published.

1948: Tennessee Williams is awarded the Pulitzer Prize for Drama for *A Streetcar Named Desire*.

1950: Edna St. Vincent Millay dies of heart failure on October 19 in Austerlitz, New York.

1951: The film *A Streetcar Named Desire* is released.

1952: *A Streetcar Named Desire* wins Academy Awards for Best Actress, Best Supporting Actress, Best Supporting Actor, and Best Art Direction-Set Decoration, Black-and-White.

1953: Arthur Miller's play *The Crucible* is produced and published.

1953: Eugene O'Neill dies of pneumonia on November 27.

1953: Karen Jones Meadows is born in New York, New York.

1957: Laurents, Bernstein, Sondheim, and Robbins's *West Side Story* is produced.

1963: Mark Hollman is born in Belleville, Illinois.

1970: Heather Raffo is born in Michigan.

1971: Celeste Raspanti's play *I Never Saw Another Butterfly* is published.

1973: Neil Simon's play *The Governess* is written and produced.

1976: Caryl Churchill's play *Light Shining in Buckinghamshire* is published.

1983: Tennessee Williams dies on February 24 in New York, New York.

1985: Karen Jones Meadows's play *Henrietta* is produced.

1990: Leonard Bernstein dies of a heart attack brought on by lung disease on October 14 in New York, New York.

1991: Neil Simon is awarded the Pulitzer Prize for Drama for *Lost in Yonkers*.

1993: Bill Harris's play *Robert Johnson: Trick the Devil* is produced. It will be published in 1995.

1996: The film *The Crucible* is released.

1998: Jerome Robbins dies of a stroke on July 29, in New York, New York.

2001: Greg Kotis and Mark Hollmann's play *Urinetown* is produced.

2002: Greg Kotis and Mark Hollmann are awarded the Tony Award for Best Original Score for *Urinetown*.

2002: Greg Kotis is awarded the Tony Award for Best Book of a Musical for *Urinetown*.

2003: Heather Raffo's play *Heather Raffo's 9 Parts of Desire* is produced. It will be published in 2006.

2005: Arthur Miller dies of heart failure on February 10 in Roxbury, Connecticut.

Acknowledgments

The editors wish to thank the copyright holders of the excerpted criticism included in this volume and the permissions managers of many book and magazine publishing companies for assisting us in securing reproduction rights. We are also grateful to the staffs of the Detroit Public Library, the Library of Congress, the University of Detroit Mercy Library, Wayne State University Purdy/Kresge Library Complex, and the University of Michigan Libraries for making their resources available to us. Following is a list of the copyright holders who have granted us permission to reproduce material in this volume of *NfS*. Every effort has been made to trace copyright, but if omissions have been made, please let us know.

COPYRIGHTED EXCERPTS IN *DfS*, VOLUME 27, WERE REPRODUCED FROM THE FOLLOWING PERIODICALS:

American Theatre, v. 22, April, 2005. Copyright © 2005 Theatre Communications Group. All rights reserved. Reproduced by permission.—*Austin Chronicle*, April 25, 2008. Reproduced by permission of the author.—*Back Stage*, v. 45, October 29, 2004. Copyright © 2004 VNU Business Media, Inc. All rights reserved. Reproduced by permission.—*Birmingham Post*, April 15, 2009. Reproduced by permission.—*Business World*, May 2, 1997. Copyright © Financial Times Information Limited 1997. Reproduced by permission.—*Canberra Times*, August 22, 2007. Copyright © 2007 Rural Press Limited. Reproduced by permission.—*Christian Science Monitor*, February 4, 1985. Copyright © 1985 The Christian Science Publishing Society. All rights reserved. Reproduced by permission from *Christian Science Monitor* (www.csmonitor.com).—*Cleveland Jewish News*, v. 88, April 4, 2003. Copyright © 2003 *Cleveland Jewish News*. Reproduced by permission.—*The Drama Review: TDR*, v. 18, December, 1974 for "'The Trojan Women' at LaMama" by B. E. Copyright © 1974 *The Drama Review*. Reproduced by permission of the publisher and the author.—*Educational Theatre Journal*, v. 21, December, 1969. Copyright © 1969 The Johns Hopkins University Press. Reproduced by permission.—*Eugene O'Neill Newsletter*, v. 10, summer-fall, 1986; v. 11, summer-fall, 1987. Copyright © 1986, 1987 Suffolk University. Both reproduced by permission.—*Genre*, v. 20, summer, 1987 for "The Unwarranted Discourse: Sentimental Community, Modernist Women, and the Case of Millay" by Suzanne Clark. Copyright © 1987 by the University of Oklahoma. Reproduced by permission of *Genre*, the University of Oklahoma and the author.—*Herald Sun* (Australia), August 14, 2007. Reproduced by permission.—*Independent* (London), April 19, 1997. Copyright © 1997 Independent Newspapers (UK) Ltd. Reproduced by permission.—*Jewish Bulletin of Northern California*, v. 102, September 25, 1998. Copyright © 1998 San Francisco Jewish

Contributors

Bryan Aubrey: Aubrey holds a Ph.D. in English. Entry on *A Streetcar named Desire*. Original essay on *A Streetcar Named Desire*.

Cynthia A. Bily: Bily is a freelance writer and editor. Entry on *Aria da Capo*. Original essay on *Aria da Capo*.

Catherine Dominic: Dominic is a novelist, freelance writer, and editor. Entry on *Robert Johnson: Trick the Devil*. Original essay on *Robert Johnson: Trick the Devil*.

Sheldon Goldfarb: Goldfarb is a specialist in Victorian literature who has published two academic books on William Makepeace Thackeray as well as a novel for young adults set in Victorian times. Entry on *West Side Story*. Original essay on *West Side Story*.

Joyce Hart: Hart is a published author and creative writing teacher. Entry on *Henrietta*. Original essay on *Henrietta*.

Sheri Metzger Karmiol: Karmiol teaches literature and drama at the University of New Mexico,where she is a lecturer in the University Honors Program. Entry on *The Governess*. Original essay on *The Governess*.

David Kelly: Kelly is a writer and an instructor of creative writing and literature. Entry on *Urinetown*. Original essay on *Urinetown*.

Claire Robinson: Robinson holds a master's degree in English. Entry on *The Crucible*. Original essay on *The Crucible*.

Bradley A. Skeen: Skeen is a classics professor. Entry on *The Trojan Women*. Original essay on *The Trojan Women*.

Leah Tieger: Tieger is a freelance writer and editor. Entries on *Desire under the Elms* and *The Servant of Two Masters*. Original essays on *Desire under the Elms* and *The Servant of Two Masters*.

Carol Ullmann: Ullmann is a freelance writer and editor. Entry on *Heather Raffo's 9 Parts of Desire*. Original essay on *Heather Raffo's 9 Parts of Desire*.

Rebecca Valentine: Valentine is a writer who holds a bachelor's degree in English. Entries on *I Never Saw another Butterfly* and *Light Shining in Buckinghamshire*. Original essays on *I Never Saw Another Butterfly* and *Light Shining in Buckinghamshire*.

Aria da Capo

EDNA ST. VINCENT MILLAY

1919

Edna St. Vincent Millay's one-act play *Aria da Capo*, written at the end of World War I, has often been called an antiwar play. It features a central allegorical story of two innocent shepherds, good friends who are driven to suspicion and then to killing each other. Their tragic story is framed by scenes of two comic characters whose trivial dialogue highlights the indifference that humans feel toward conflict and death. Though Millay is better known for her poetry than for her drama, *Aria da Capo* is generally considered her most important play. Written early in her career, it demonstrates the command of meter and form, the understanding of music and of theater history, and the social and political concerns that would reappear throughout her work.

The play was first produced by the Provincetown Players on December 5, 1919, in the New York City acting company's small theater on Macdougal Street in Greenwich Village. It was a simple, low-budget production, with Millay's sister Norma and Norma's future husband playing two of the five roles. By the time it closed two weeks later, the play was recognized as one of the best the small company had put on, and when Millay issued the script as a book in 1920, *Aria da Capo* had already been performed in several other small theaters. It has been produced steadily ever since, on college campuses and in theater festivals, typically as part of a program of one-act plays. The text is available in a 2009 edition from Dodo Press.

Edna St. Vincent Millay (The Library of Congress)

AUTHOR BIOGRAPHY

Millay was born on February 22, 1892, in Rockland, Maine. Her middle name, St. Vincent, was the name of a hospital where her uncle had been treated well, and the girl was always called "Vincent" within the family. Her parents divorced when Millay was eight, and she and her two sisters were raised by their mother, Cora Buzzelle Millay, who encouraged them to be independent, to appreciate art and music, and to read. As a young child Millay began writing poetry, and it was her mother who suggested she submit her long poem "Renascence" to a literary contest. The poem was published in the 1912 edition of the anthology *The Lyric Year*, leading to praise, to mentoring from more experienced writers, and to a scholarship to Vassar College.

At Vassar, a college for intelligent and free-thinking women, Millay continued to write poetry, and also wrote and acted in plays. She studied literature and languages, finding ideas,

forms and images in classical and world literatures that she would draw on throughout her career. After graduating in 1917 she moved with her sisters to Greenwich Village in New York City, entering a world of liberal politics, feminism, and sexual and artistic freedom. That year she published her first book of poems, *Renascence and Other Poems*, and began acting with the New York "Little Theatre" company the Provincetown Players. She also wrote plays for the company, the most significant of which was *Aria da Capo*, first performed by the Provincetown Players on December 5, 1919. Over the next few years she published the play and more volumes of poetry, gaining a wide readership who eagerly accepted her work's provocative and frank descriptions of female sexuality. She spent most of 1921–23 traveling through Europe on assignment for *Vanity Fair* magazine, and publishing more poetry and plays. Millay was generally better known for her poetry than for her plays, and she was also celebrated for her unconventional bisexual lifestyle.

Returning to the United States in poor health in 1923, Millay was awarded the Pulitzer Prize for Poetry for *The Harp-Weaver, and Other Poems*. She was the first woman to win the prize. Later that year she married Eugen Jan Boissevain, who encouraged and supported Millay's writing and took care of her business and domestic responsibilities so she could focus on her work, while both also pursued other relationships. Millay was intensely involved in political causes: *Aria da Capo* is often considered an antiwar play, and Millay joined with other artists to protest the trial and execution of the anarchists Nicola Sacco and Bartolomeo Vanzetti in 1927. In the early years of World War II she wrote propaganda poetry supporting the Allies. A nervous breakdown in 1944 left her unable to write for two years, and she and her husband retreated to their farm in Austerlitz, New York. After his death from lung cancer in 1949, she lived reclusively until her own death, apparently from heart failure, on October 19, 1950.

PLOT SUMMARY

Echoing the form of musical composition that gives it its title, *Aria da Capo* is structured in three parts, with its third section a variation of the first. It is a one-act play in one scene, written

MEDIA ADAPTATIONS

- *Aria da Capo* was adapted as a one-act opera by Larry Alan Smith, performed for the first time by the American Chamber Opera Company in 1986. The opera is not available as a recording.

in blank verse, or unrhymed iambic pentameter. As the play opens, a man and a woman, Pierrot and Columbine, are seated at a banquet table on a stage (the stage directions indicate that the setting is "A Stage," not "A Dining Room"). Columbine's first line, which opens the play, demonstrates her character's level of intelligence and the depth of her concerns immediately: "Pierrot, a macaroon! I cannot *live* without a macaroon!" She is remarkably stupid and incurious, focused on macaroons or artichokes or wine or vinaigrette, or whatever she happens to see at any given moment. She reveals that she is unable to count her own fingers, because she needs her fingers to count. Her dining companion, Pierrot, is somewhat more intelligent, but he has had too much to drink, and when he declares his love for Columbine, neither Columbine nor the audience takes it seriously.

As the two chatter away, Pierrot abruptly announces new identities for himself. "I am become / A pianist," he says, and a few lines later, "I am become a socialist." A moment later he is a philanthropist, and then he asks Columbine whether she would like to be an actress (after all, he says, she is blond and uneducated), because he is now her manager. Columbine responds to it all with confusion, and with more talk of increasingly exotic food, including peacock livers, caviar, and persimmons.

This absurd conversation is interrupted with the entrance of Cothurnus, a large man in a toga and the traditional mask of tragedy. Pierrot, breaking character, orders Cothurnus to get off stage because it is not yet time for his scene. But Cothurnus, tired of waiting, insists on staying, so

Columbine and Pierrot leave the stage, and he summons Thyrsis and Corydon, two rustic shepherds, to come on stage and perform their scene. The two shepherds appear and complain mildly that it is too early and the stage is not set for their scene, but as Cothurnus takes his place on a chair at the back of the stage with a prompt-book, Thyrsis and Corydon move the banquet furniture out of the way, recline on the floor, and begin a conversation about their sheep and the clouds.

The language of Thyrsis and Corydon is formal and flowery, reminiscent of the pastoral poetry of the nineteenth century. But this is clearly a *scene* performed by two actors, and when they occasionally forget their lines, they pause until Cothurnus prompts them. When Corydon proposes the traditional pastoral activity of composing a song about sheep, Thyrsis suggests another game: they should build a wall between them, and not allow each other to cross it. Using the dining room chairs from the earlier banquet as posts, and a supply of crepe paper ribbons as weaving material, they make a low fence down the center of the stage and sit down on their respective sides. Thyrsis, who suggested the game in the beginning, decides almost immediately that he does not like it and does not want to forbid Corydon from coming to his side. "It is a silly game," he says, and proposes that they compose a song after all. But Corydon, believing that Thyrsis may simply be plotting to come over and steal his land, refuses to reunite with his friend.

Now Corydon realizes that while he and some of the sheep are on his side of the wall, the water is on Thyrsis's side. He points this out to Thyrsis and reminds him that both groups of sheep were recently all one herd, but Thyrsis has become suspicious himself and now refuses to let Corydon and his sheep come across. This makes Corydon suspect that Thyrsis suggested the wall in the first place because he was planning to take the water, and anger escalates on both sides. At one point Corydon remembers that they are supposed to be playing a game. The two friends reach for each other over the wall and attempt to smooth things over, but they dissolve into suspicion again. Occasionally throughout this scene the shepherds are interrupted by Columbine and Pierrot, who argue offstage, come onstage to fetch props, and continue their irrelevant and unimportant dialogue. During these interruptions, Thyrsis and Corydon stop all talk and action, but they soon pick up again where they had left off.

Corydon comes upon a bowl of jewels (actually, according to the stage directions, a bowl of confetti and ribbons), and he realizes that, because of the wall, the jewels are his and he does not have to share them with his friend. Thyrsis offers to exchange some water for some gems, but Corydon has lost interest in the sheep and is now willing to let them die of thirst. He gloats over his newfound wealth and imagines what he can buy with it. Looking for jewels on his own side of the wall, Thyrsis comes upon a black weed that he recognizes as poisonous. He chops it and mixes it in a bowl of water and offers the water to Corydon. Meanwhile, Corydon has strung together a necklace, which he offers to Thyrsis. They meet at the wall, where Thyrsis poisons Corydon, who strangles him with the necklace. The friends remember again that they were only playing a game, but it is too late. Breaking through the wall, Corydon finds his friend, and they die in each other's arms.

Cothurnus closes his prompt-book, covers the shepherds' bodies with the banquet table from the opening of the play, and calls "Strike the scene!" He exits, and Pierrot and Columbine reappear. Columbine discovers that there is something under the table, and Pierrot identifies it casually as "the bodies / Of the two shepherds from the other play." For a moment Pierrot worries that the audience will not accept the sight of them resuming their meal with two dead men under the table, but Cothurnus tells them to move the tablecloth to cover the bodies and assures them that "The audience will forget." The two take their seats and begin their scene again, repeating the first lines of the play.

CHARACTERS

Columbine

Columbine is a young woman, blonde, pretty and charming, who shares a meal and a conversation with Pierrot. Like the other characters in *Aria da Capo*, Columbine is modeled on a conventional or stock character found in literature. Columbine and Pierrot are characters that appear and reappear in the plays of *Commedia dell'Arte* ("the comedy of art or improvisation"), originating in Italy in the fifteenth and sixteenth centuries. Plays from the Commedia dell'Arte were still written and performed into the twenty-first century; in fact, Millay herself played the role of Columbine in a Commedia dell'Arte production by the Provincetown Players.

In this play, Columbine is recognized at the outset for her stock character. According to the stage direction, when the curtain rises she and Pierrot are "dressed according to the tradition." In Columbine's case, this means a dress with a tight bodice and a full skirt of many shades of pink. She also wears a hat, which she leaves behind when she exits the stage at the end of the first scene and retrieves in the middle of the shepherds' scene. Columbine appears to be rather stupid: she talks on and on about food, naming small delicacies that she "cannot *live* without." She coaxes Pierrot to declare his love for her, but ignores him when he does. She is vain and foolish and is unable to follow Pierrot's rambling conversation. In an Author's Note that Millay included in the original publication of the play, she gives detailed instructions about the set, the costumes, and the characters. In the playwright's conception, Columbine exaggerates her empty-headedness, "because she believes men prefer women to be useless and extravagant; if left to herself she would be a domestic and capable person." However, there is little evidence of this duplicity in the text itself.

Columbine, like the other characters, exists on two levels in the play: she is Columbine, the vacuous partner of Pierrot, and she is an actress playing the part of Columbine. Throughout the first banquet scene she remains in character, as she does offstage when she is overheard arguing with Pierrot during the shepherds' scene. But at one point she bursts onstage looking for her hat, interrupting the shepherds and asking Cothurnus, "Is this my scene, or not?" When she and Pierrot return to the stage after the death of the shepherds, she appears as the actress, fussing about to rearrange the furniture and props for their scene and discovering the bodies of Thyrsis and Corydon before she steps back into character.

Corydon

Corydon, a shepherd like his partner Thyrsis, is a stock character from classical Greek pastoral poetry and stories. Pastoral literature deals with shepherds and their flocks moving about the countryside, enjoying an idyllic life of peace and beauty. In the Renaissance, Italian poets revived the pastoral, and the conventions—including the traditional Greek names for characters—appeared in English poetry and drama until the eighteenth century. In *Aria da Capo*, therefore, the audience is expected to know as soon as Cothurnus interrupts Pierrot and Columbine for the next scene and calls "You, Thyrsis! Corydon! / Where are you?" that the next scene will feature two shepherds.

When Corydon and Thyrsis first come on stage, however, it is not in their roles as shepherds but in their roles as actors about to play shepherds. They argue with Cothurnus about whether it is time for their scene and whether the stage, which has been set up for the farce played by Pierrot and Columbine, can be properly used for their upcoming tragedy. Corydon points out that they need a wall for their scene and complains that they "cannot build / A wall of tissue-paper"—which, as it turns out, is exactly what they do. At Cothurnus's urging, they move the dining room table out of the way and begin their scene.

Corydon is, at heart, trusting and honest, a simple soul who genuinely loves his friend Thyrsis. For a few lines, Corydon and Thyrsis recline and watch their sheep grazing. They utter fanciful similes in poetic language, echoing the conventions of pastoral poetry. After a while, Corydon suggests that the two compose a song about a lamb, but he goes along with Thyrsis's idea that they build a wall instead. When the two tire of the wall game, it is Corydon who becomes suspicious first, but it is not a deep-seated suspicion: the actor playing Corydon forgets his line and has to be prompted by Cothurnus to say "How do I know this isn't a trick?," undercutting the force of Corydon's doubt. Later, it is Corydon who has been cut off from the water and has to remind Thyrsis that the sheep were only recently a single flock, the responsibility of both of them. He acknowledges the reason for Thyrsis's suspicions, but says, "one of us has to take a risk, or else." However, when Thyrsis invites him over to get some water, he fears his friend, who has become a stranger.

He turns greedy quickly when he finds the gold and jewels, making sarcastic remarks to Thyrsis and ignoring his flock's need of water. Not until he is thirsty himself is he ready to make a deal—a bowl of water in exchange for a bowl of jewels—but as soon as the deal is made, he finds he cannot give up even a portion of his jewels, and he plots instead to strangle Thyrsis with a necklace. He does not realize until he is dying that he has let his greed and suspicion

separate him from Thyrsis, and he breaks through the wall to die with his friend.

Cothurnus, Masque of Tragedy

Cothurnus is an imposing stage manager, directing the actors to begin and end their scenes and prompting them when they forget their lines. The name "Cothurnus" comes from the Greek word *kothornos*, referring to a kind of thick-soled boot that was a conventional part of the costume in Greek and Roman tragic theater. The boots were made to different heights, emphasizing the relative importance of the roles in these tragedies. In *Aria da Capo*, the appearance of Cothurnus is a signal that the farce is over, and the next scene will be a tragedy. However, while he is named in the Cast of Characters, his name is not said aloud in the play until nearly the end; Millay's instructions in her Author's Note indicate that he should wear a toga and "heavy boots . . . as nearly as possible like the tragic Roman buskin" to indicate his role.

Cothurnus makes his first appearance abruptly, while Columbine and Pierrot are talking, and Pierrot breaks character to ask him why he has come onstage. Cothurnus replies that he is tired of waiting, and his presence is so commanding that the others do what he tells them. He orders Thyrsis and Corydon to come out and do their scene, and he discounts their concerns that the stage is not set properly for a tragedy. It does not matter, he says, whether the props are right or not, just as it does not matter whether they are prepared to say their lines well. Cothurnus, it seems, has seen these scenes many times before and knows that "One wall is like another." He takes a seat on a chair or elevated platform at the back of the stage, and orders the shepherds to begin.

Occasionally, as the shepherds move through their scene, the actors forget their next lines, and Cothurnus, using a prompt-book, gets them going again. At times, it seems that the shepherds—or the actors playing them—forget that they are angry and suspicious, and Cothurnus has to remind each of them to ask, "How do I know this isn't a trick?" Although he appears to force the shepherds to act out feelings of hatred and suspicion that do not arise from within them, the words and the actions played out in front of him have no effect on Cothurnus, and when the shepherds are dead, he simply closes his prompt-book and calls for the next scene. Pierrot and Columbine have no need to worry about staging a farce on a tragic set littered with dead bodies, he says, for "The audience will forget."

Pierrot

Pierrot is a cynical man who dines and flirts with Columbine. Like his partner, he is a stock character from the Commedia dell'Arte, and is expected to be recognized as soon as the curtain goes up. Pierrot traditionally dresses in white silk smock and pants, with a ruff around his neck and a cap on his head; often he has his face painted white and a single teardrop painted on his cheek. The stage directions for *Aria da Capo* indicate that is he "dressed according to the tradition" except that he wears lilac instead of white.

Following the convention, Pierrot repeatedly declares his love for Columbine, and she rebuffs him. Typically, he is rather stupid and she is smarter; in this play, those roles are reversed. Pierrot is world-weary but cheerful. He has seen it all, and he is bored with the world, but rather than being depressed or angry he is simply indifferent. While Columbine revels in one food after another, Pierrot simply asks for more wine. Pierrot comes the closest to openly stating the themes or the lessons of the play, when he says that he is always wanting "a little more" than what he has, or "a little less," or when he mocks the pretentiousness of modern art and music. At one point he declares himself a socialist, saying, "I love / Humanity; but I hate people." Nothing Pierrot says seems to matter to him or to Columbine.

Like the other characters, Pierrot speaks onstage both in character and also as the actor playing Pierrot. When Cothurnus interrupts his scene, Pierrot even changes his way of speaking, dropping the formal poetic language he has been speaking to ask, "Say, whadda you mean?" He shows no surprise or interest in finding two dead bodies onstage when he returns, and he agrees readily when Cothurnus argues that the audience will soon forget about the bodies if a tablecloth is drawn over them. Showing no concern, he sits down with Columbine and begins the scene again.

Thyrsis

Thyrsis is a shepherd who watches over a flock with his partner Corydon. The name "Thyrsis" comes from a book of pastoral poems by the Roman poet Virgil (70–90 BCE), whose poems known as the *Eclogues* include a singing contest between two shepherds named Thyrsis and Corydon.

In *Aria da Capo*, Thyrsis and Corydon are alike in their simplicity and in their affection for each other. In her Author's Note, Millay observes,

"The personalities of Thyrsis and Corydon are not essentially different." Their actions are slightly different: it is Thyrsis who first suggests they build a wall as a game, and it is he who is the first to regret the separation once the wall is built. But when Corydon asks for water, he begins to think of the water as his, and to think of the sheep on his wide of the wall as his, until his feelings of longing for his friend return and he cries, "It is an ugly game. / I hated it from the first. . . . How did it start?" In the end, his fear and doubt overcome his affection, and he poisons Corydon.

THEMES

Struggle and Conflict

While *Aria da Capo* is frequently discussed as an antiwar play, the struggle and conflict explored in the play need not be identified so specifically. True, in 1919 and 1920, when the play was written and first performed, the United States and Europe were still reeling from the horrors of World War I—a war with so many deaths and catastrophic injuries that for many people it shook the foundations of belief in human decency. But it is not only war that the play argues against. Rather, it demonstrates how easily untempered greed and suspicion can separate friends, coworkers, neighbors and, yes, nations.

When Thyrsis and Corydon begin their scene, their affection for each other is obvious. They refer to the large flock as "Our sheep," they speak the same flowery language, they finish each other's thoughts, they notice the same things. Only minutes after he suggests that they build the wall, Thyrsis misses his friend and regrets his game, and through the scene the shepherds take turns being suspicious or saying "let's drop this." But they are unable to drop it, pushed along by a force they cannot control. At the end, they seem surprised by what they have done to each other, by how the game has gotten out of hand, and even after murdering his friend, Corydon's dying words to Thyrsis include "I want to be near you."

The play demonstrates in several ways that the animosity between the two shepherds is superficial, unimportant. The wall dividing them, after all, is made of crepe paper, and the jewels they fight over are only pieces of confetti. The men are rather simple-minded, clearly not scheming or

TOPICS FOR FURTHER STUDY

- Research the Commedia dell'Arte characters Pierrot and Columbine. How are these characters typically dressed? How do they behave? Prepare a presentation for your classmates showing how these characters have been depicted on the stage, in film, or in the other visual arts. Alternately, prepare a similar presentation about Cothurnus, Masque of Tragedy, or about shepherds in pastoral art and literature.

- Research the Provincetown Players of Greenwich Village in New York City. What was distinctive about the plays they produced? How would the company's various locations have affected the sets, costumes, props, and casts of the plays? Write a paper in which you explain how *Aria da Capo* fits in with the other works of this theater company.

- Watch the 1968 video biography of Millay, *Millay at Steepletop*, which includes archival film footage and interviews with Millay's sister, Norma, who played Columbine in the original production of *Aria da Capo*, directed by Millay in 1919. Prepare a presentation in which you show a short excerpt from the documentary and explain to your classmates how this excerpt helps you understand the playwright and the play.

- Imagine that, instead of using conventional shepherd characters from pastoral literature for the middle section of the play, Millay had used two characters from the twenty-first century, perhaps from another part of the world. Write your own scene based on Thyrsis and Corydon, but more overtly related to a contemporary conflict.

- Identify an antiwar story, song, or movie from the twenty-first century. Write a paper in which you compare and contrast your selection with *Aria da Capo*, in terms of language, imagery, or another quality.

- Examine the book *Talking Peace: A Vision for the Next Generation* (1993) by former President Jimmy Carter, which addresses conflicts that might affect teen readers, from interpersonal disagreements to international war. Write an essay in which you speculate on advice Carter might offer to Thyrsis and Corydon to settle their conflict, quoting from Carter's book where appropriate.

- Listen to one or more of the famous da capo arias from George Frideric Handel's *Messiah*: "Rejoice Greatly," "He Was Despised," or "The Trumpet Shall Sound." Prepare a presentation in which you play a recording of the aria for your class and analyze its three-part structure.

- Read young-adult novel *How Young They Die: A Novel about the First World War* (1969) by Stuart Cloete. Compare the author's approaches to portraying the horrors of war in an essay.

---

malicious, and they are shepherds—symbols of peace and tranquility. Neither feels his anger very deeply; in fact, each actor forgets the line "How do I know this isn't a trick?" and has to be prompted by Cothurnus, emphasizing that they are playing roles, that the lines are artificial, and that the suspicion is imposed from without. As the two remember and forget again, they are only easily recognizable stock characters playing a "silly game," and that game occurs within a scene-within-the-play. As it plays out, of course, it becomes "a pretty serious game," a deadly game. The impression left on the audience is that while the threat feels very real and important at times to Corydon and Thyrsis, it is trivial and not worth the cost of human lives—as is the case generally with the struggle and conflict that divides humanity. Rather than propose a solution for human conflict, the play simply demonstrates its power to destroy.

Original Provincetown Theatre in Provincetown, MA (*The Library of Congress*)

Apathy

Perhaps more horrifying than the destruction brought about by struggle and conflict is an apathetic response. People feel sorrow or anger, they die of starvation or preventable illnesses, they kill each other in battle, and yet few people take action to stop it, or even pause to contemplate the destruction. This is the case with Columbine and Pierrot in *Aria da Capo*; their minds are so filled with the most trivial of things that they barely notice that Thyrsis and Corydon are dead.

As the play opens, Columbine and Pierrot are dining and chattering about artichokes and wine and dresses and persimmons. Columbine never raises a single important issue or idea (she can barely keep track of her own conversation about food), and Pierrot raises them only to mock them. His suggestion "let us drink some wine and lose our heads" sums up his philosophy

neatly: rather than engaging with the world, he prefers to distance himself from it. For a brief moment he declares himself a student, ready to "search into all matters," but he moves on almost immediately to another temporary identity. Soon he is a pianist, playing empty, meaningless music *"Vivace senza tempo senza tutto"* ("lively, without tempo, without anything"), and then a socialist who loves humanity and hates people, a philanthropist, a manager, and a critic who says, "there is nothing / I can enjoy." In every one of his roles, he is ineffectual and detached. He does not take himself seriously when he says serious things, and of course he cannot be taken seriously by Columbine or by the audience, because he is Pierrot, a man in a clown suit.

Cothurnus, the closest thing this play has to a God-like figure (when Corydon says that his scene is not ready, Cothurnus replies, "I am the scene"), is another example of detachment. He sees the world as just a series of scenes, and when he tires of one he calls for the next one. He rejects Thyrsis's complaint that a tissue-paper wall will not suffice, replying that "One wall is like another." As soon as Thyrsis and Corydon are dead, according to the stage directions, "Cothurnus closes the prompt-book with a bang" and "arises matter-of-factly." With no show of emotion, he covers the bodies with a table, and calls for the next scene. The deaths mean nothing to him.

Columbine and Pierrot are also largely unaffected by the deaths. Columbine screams when she sees something unexpected, but once Pierrot has calmly explained that it is simply the dead men, she finds it only "curious" that Thyrsis has been strangled with ribbons. Their detachment is again made clear. But the audience cannot sit back and shake their heads over the characters' callousness: they, too, are implicated. Cothurnus has hinted at this earlier when telling Thyrsis that "One wall is like another," and that the actors' feeling behind their lines does not matter so much as the fact of the lines and gestures being delivered. As is made clear at the end of the play, he is describing what matters *to the audience*. Near the end of the play, almost ready to begin the scene again, Pierrot asks for the bodies to be removed: "We can't / Sit down and eat with two dead bodies lying / Under the table! . . . The audience wouldn't stand for it!" But he is wrong, as Cothurnus points out, and as Pierrot realizes. The audience cares as little as the actors do: "The audience will forget." So the play includes everyone—not just the characters—in its condemnation of the apathy that allows suffering to continue, year after year, scene after scene.

STYLE

da Capo Aria Form
Although it is a one-act play without separate divisions called scenes, *Aria da Capo* is structured in the same way that a form of vocal music called the *da capo aria* is structured. The da capo aria, popular during the Baroque period, roughly 1600 to 1750, was a song generally performed as part of an opera; often, an aria contains an opera's most beautiful and dramatic material, much like a soliloquy in tragic theater. The *da capo aria* was constructed in three parts.

After an opening section that was often a complete song that might have stood on its own, the middle section was in a different key, with different instruments, and a different dramatic tone. The third section was not written down in detail by the composer; rather, the performers returned to the first section and created ornamented variations on it *da capo*, or from their heads, showing their ability to improvise and to use their full range of vocal expression.

Millay, who studied music as a child and once considered a career as a classical pianist, constructs her play after the musical form that gives it its name. Thus, the play opens with the farcical dialogue between Pierrot and Columbine, moves abruptly on Cothurnus's command into the tragedy of Thyrsis and Corydon, and then returns to a variation of the Pierrot and Columbine scene. Millay's use of traditional forms is a hallmark of her work. She wrote nearly two hundred sonnets, a fourteen-line form introduced in Italy, mastered by poets including William Shakespeare and John Donne, and largely out of fashion by the time Millay was writing. In addition to *Aria da Capo* she wrote four other verse plays, or plays written in poetic lines, a form dating back to the ancient Greeks, also used by Shakespeare and his contemporaries, and little used in the twentieth century.

Commedia dell'Arte
The opening and closing sections of *Aria da Capo*, featuring Pierrot and Columbine, are based on the Italian dramatic form Commedia dell'Arte, an improvisational form popular in the fifteenth and sixteenth centuries. The Commedia dell'Arte was performed by troupes of players who performed on street corners and in public squares; they might begin a performance whenever a large enough crowd was at hand. The plays were improvised, but they had several characters called "stock characters" who appeared again and again: Harlequin the clown, Pierrot and Columbine the servants, a miser, a shopkeeper, a braggart, and others, each with a distinctive way of dressing and talking. The audiences knew these characters and how they might behave, and the fun was in seeing what new conflicts or love affairs the actors could dream up, and what references to local people and news they could weave in.

When the curtain goes up to begin *Aria da Capo*, the audience is meant to know at once that it is about to see Commedia dell'Arte. Pierrot and Columbine are "dressed according to the tradition," so that will be recognized at a glance. The stage directions explain that the stage is set for a Harlequinade, a particularly silly variation on the Commedia dell'Arte that was performed indoors with "a merry black and white interior." This is what Pierrot is referring to when he complains to Cothurnus, "The scene is set for me!" and what Corydon means when he says, "this is the setting for a farce." The absurdity of the dialogue between Pierrot and Columbine, their conventional set design, and the history of the Commedia dell'Arte from which they come, emphasize the contrast between the first and third sections of the play and the story of betrayal and murder between Thyrsis and Corydon, both heightening the tragedy and mocking it.

Blank Verse

Aria da Capo is a verse drama, or a play written in verse. In this case, Millay has adopted blank verse, or unrhymed iambic pentameter, as the form for her lines, following the model set by Shakespeare, Christopher Marlowe, and other important English-language playwrights. All of the speech in Millay's play is in iambic pentameter, or lines of ten syllables, alternating stressed and unstressed. Iambic pentameter is also the meter used by many of the greatest works of English-language poetry, including John Milton's *Paradise Lost*, the *Lyrical Ballads* of William Wordsworth, and the sonnets. Some of the play's lines are quite regular, falling naturally into a perfect stressed-unstressed pattern ("I'll teach you how to cry, and how to die"), while others approximate the pattern ("You would be dead by now. And if I were a parrot"). Some of the lines are in what is thought of as poetic language ("What say you, Thyrsis, shall we make a song"), while others are not ("Say, whadda you mean?—get off the stage, my friend"). Whatever the demands of the different characters and sections, the play holds to its blank verse throughout, participating in a rich tradition that reaches back centuries.

In Shakespeare's plays, the high and noble characters, including kings, princes, and warriors, typically speak in iambic pentameter, while commoners, including servants, merchants, and the "rude mechanicals" in *A Midsummer Night's Dream*, speak in prose. Millay breaks from this convention in *Aria da Capo*, having not just Cothurnus, the Masque of Tragedy, speak in verse, but also her clown, servant, and shepherds. This serves the twin purposes of elevating their dialogue, demonstrating the

underlying seriousness of the play, while mocking their importance, reinforcing the message that humanity is generally indifferent to the type of conflict being played out on the stage.

HISTORICAL CONTEXT

In 1919, as Millay was writing *Aria da Capo*, the United States and Europe were just emerging from World War I, which had begun with the assassination of Austrian Archduke Franz Ferdinand on June 28, 1914. What started as a conflict between Ferdinand's homeland, Austria-Hungary, and Serbia, the home of his assassin, quickly drew in allies on both sides until most of the larger European countries were involved, and fighting occurred throughout Europe. The United States, which at first was determined to remain isolationist, or to stay out of the war, joined the conflict in 1917, declaring war on Germany after German submarines had sunk seven American merchant ships and a British liner with American passengers aboard.

It would be hard to overstate the devastating effects of World War I on the survivors. Put simply, no one before this war had imagined how terrible warfare could be. New inventions, including airplanes, armored vehicles, submarines, machine guns, long-range artillery, chemical weapons, and flame throwers, made it possible to injure or kill many people at one time, and from great distances. In the five years of the war, more than seventy million people fought, and more than fifteen million were killed. In Europe, millions more were seriously injured, many of them with missing limbs or with disfiguring burns from mustard gas and phosgene gas attacks. Millions also suffered from post-traumatic stress disorder, which was then referred to as "shell shock." Germany, which suffered six million deaths and injuries in battle, had also lost more than half a million civilians to starvation when the British blockaded the country. The Ottoman Empire (occupying what is now Turkey) lost as much as 25 percent of its population during the war, including more than 600,000 Armenians who were killed by the Empire in what is generally considered either an ethnic cleansing or a genocide. People took to referring to World War I as "the war to end all wars," because they believed—or wanted to believe—that humankind would never again

COMPARE
&
CONTRAST

- **1919–1920:** The Treaty of Versailles, ending involvement in World War I between Germany and the Allies, is signed on June 28, 1919. The United States enters a period of relative peace.

  Today: The United States and its allies have been involved in armed conflict in Afghanistan since 2001 and in Iraq since 2003. Both wars are controversial, and support from the American public wavers.

- **1919–1920:** The Eighteenth Amendment to the U.S. Constitution goes into effect on January 16, 1919, making it illegal to make, sell, or transport any alcoholic beverages, including the wine shared by Pierrot and Columbine. The so-called Noble Experiment ends in 1933, and alcohol sales resume.

  Today: Alcohol sales in the United States have a value of more than 100 billion dollars each year.

- **1919–1920:** Millay and others campaign for women's suffrage, or the right of women to vote in American elections. The Nineteenth Amendment to the U.S. Constitution is ratified on August 26, 1920, eight months after the first performances of *Aria da Capo*.

  Today: Women make up more than half of the eligible voters in the United States, and of the eligible voters the percentage of women who actually vote is higher than that of men.

- **1919–1920:** The wall erected by Thyrsis and Corydon is largely viewed as metaphorical by Millay's contemporary audiences. There are no well-known human-constructed physical barriers separating people or nations.

  Today: The United States is building a series of fences and walls along the southern border of the country, to prevent illegal immigration through Mexico. In the Middle East, the Israeli–West Bank barrier, also under construction, is a network of fences restricting the movements of Palestinians. Both projects draw international controversy.

engage in anything so destructive. They referred to the millions of dead and wounded as the "Lost Generation."

From the beginning, there were people opposed to the war, including religious pacifists, many of whom declared themselves conscientious objectors and served time in prison rather than fight, and various socialist and labor groups, who did not wish to see oppressed workers in different countries fighting each other. In the United States, those opposed to the country entering the war staged public demonstrations, wrote editorials, and created posters and slogans. Once the United States entered the war, opponents were looked at with renewed suspicion, and even prosecuted under new laws intended to prevent anyone from encouraging others not to participate in the war effort. In the world of art and literature, a new pessimism about the human capacity for moral growth emerged, along with a new suspicion of nationalism and of technology as an agent for good, particularly just after the war. The sense that the world was irrational and unknowable led to new artistic movements including Dadaism and surrealism, which were grounded in antiwar sentiment and which used strange juxtapositions and seemingly ridiculous images, tones, and dialogue in an attempt to capture the chaos and disillusionment of the times.

Millay was in college at Vassar during the first years of the war and, according to her biographer Nancy Milford's *Savage Beauty*, she paid little attention to it. After she moved to New York and after the United States entered the war, and as she came to know people who were

Many of Edna St. Vincent Millay's works involved the theme of the liberated woman.
(© *Mary Evans Picture Library / Alamy*)

involved in fighting the war or in opposing it, Millay learned more about the conflict and its destructiveness. Millay began writing *Aria da Capo* in 1919, after the armistice that ended fighting on the war's Western front was signed in November 1918. By the time the play was first staged, in December 1919, the Treaty of Versailles had been signed, formally ending conflict between the Allies and Germany.

CRITICAL OVERVIEW

As a one-act play, *Aria da Capo* is often performed, particularly on college campuses, but it has not been reviewed or analyzed as frequently as full-length plays typically are, and none of Millay's drama has received as much attention as her poetry. The Provincetown Players were important enough, however, that Alexander Woollcott reviewed the play in the *New York Times* shortly after its opening in 1919, calling it "the most beautiful and most interesting play

in the English language now to be seen in New York." Woollcott acknowledges that the play might be difficult for "the average unthinking audience" to understand, but points out that no mother who has lost a son in the war could miss the play's antiwar message. Although the play ran for only two weeks in its original production, so many other theater companies began performing the play that when Millay published the play in book form in 1920, she included production notes to answer the questions she was receiving from directors. The first major review of the book, however, seemed to have been based on only a cursory reading: William Lyon Phelps, in a 1921 combined review of *Aria da Capo* and four other books of Millay's poetry, describes it as a play "in prose," and writes that he wishes he had seen it performed because "the prose dialogue is just what it should be, and the dramatic movement admirable." In a 1924 essay in Poetry, Harriet Monroe calls the play a "masterpiece of irony," saying that Millay "stabs the war-god to the heart with a stroke as clean, as deft, as ever the most skillfully murderous swordsman bestowed upon his enemy." While reviews were generally positive, not all critics have liked the play. In 1937, the poet John Crowe Ransom mocked it as being no more mature than Millay's college plays, or than "the prize-winning skit on the Senior Girls' Stunt Night of an unusually good year," in an essay for *The Southern Review*.

Later critical analysis of the play has often focused on the structure and techniques Millay used to convey meaning. Mary J. McKee examines the influence of Commedia dell'Arte on *Aria da Capo*, citing in particular the "spontaneity" and "incongruity" of the Pierrot-Columbine scenes, in a 1966 essay in *Modern Drama*. Millay's varying levels of language inform a 1985 essay from *Tamarack* by John J. Patton. Pierrot and Columbine, he notes, speak with a light and contemporary diction that helps the audience understand that "we cannot take these two characters with any degree of seriousness," while the shepherds speak in "a more deliberate measure and more formal level of diction," highlighting the seriousness of their scene. More recently, Barbara Ozieblo explains the allusions to popular culture that inform some of the jokes in the opening scene, and traces the ways the play blurs "the edges between 'reality' and 'theatricality'" in a 2004 essay in the *Journal of American Drama and Theatre*.

Millay went largely unnoticed by critics through the middle decades of the twentieth century, but she was rediscovered toward the end of the century. Many critics in this new wave have looked at Millay's work, including her plays, through a feminist lens. Agreeing with the common understanding that the shepherds Thyrsis and Corydon are forced by Cothurnus to act out their scene of war, Will Brantley, in a 1991 essay in *Colby Quarterly* sees a "feminist scorn" in the way the tragic deaths are framed by Pierrot and Columbine, and argues that Millay saw war and conflict as "male destructiveness." In a 1997 essay titled "Millay's Big Book, or the Feminist Formalist as Modern," Joseph Aimone describes the dialogue between Pierrot and Columbine as "gendered byplay" and Millay's task as "working out the gendered politics of the modern."

CRITICISM

Cynthia A. Bily

Bily is a freelance writer and editor. In this essay on Aria da Capo, *she considers how Marxist theory explains the changes that come over Thyrsis and Corydon.*

Thyrsis and Corydon, the two shepherds in Edna St. Vincent Millay's *Aria da Capo*, seem to have an idyllic life. As they begin their scene, Thyrsis's opening line captures this feeling: "How gently in the silence, Corydon, / Our sheep go up the bank." They contemplate the flock and the landscape for a moment, even noticing the passing of the clouds and the effect of the changing light on the grass, until Corydon suggests, "What say you, Thyrsis, shall we make a song." The idealized image of innocent shepherds reclining on a hillside, making rustic but pretty music as they watch peaceful sheep grazing in the meadow, is at the heart of pastoral literature and art dating back to the ancient Greeks. Writers including the Greek Theocritus (3rd century BCE), the Roman Virgil (70–19 BCE), the British poet and playwright Christopher Marlowe (1564–1593), and the American John Greenleaf Whittier (1807–1892) have used pastoral settings to hearken back to a simpler time. The characters in pastoral literature live, as Thyrsis and Corydon do, in harmony with their animals and their landscape, and though they may appear innocent and naïve, they are also cheerful and content.

THEY ARE CONTENT TO LIVE PEACEFUL LIVES AS SIMPLE SHEPHERDS UNTIL THE DESTRUCTIVE FORCES OF CAPITALISM LEAD THEM ASTRAY."

But it does not take long for the idyll to be disrupted. The "game" of building a wall turns deadly serious, and soon the two friends are suspicious and fearful, gradually becoming killers. Only as death approaches do they remember their fondness for each other, and they die as they began, reclining together. What could make two beloved companions turn against each other this way? What makes them forget their fondness for each other, and for their flock? Why do they build the wall, and why is it so difficult for them to share their water and their wealth?

The German economist and political theorist Karl Marx (1818–1883) raised similar questions in the nineteenth century, most famously in his book the *Communist Manifesto* (1848), written with the economist Friedrich Engels (1820–1895). Observing how the Industrial Revolution was creating large groups of factory workers who worked long hours for low wages and a small group of factory owners who earned substantially more, Marx and Engels (and their followers, who came to be known as "Marxists") wondered why poor people around the world—who greatly outnumber people of wealth—did not band together in revolution to improve their lives. Did factory workers not see that a few owners were getting wealthy from the labor of the workers?

Marx argued that a capitalist economic system compelled people to compete with each other instead of working cooperatively. Because capitalist societies use "capital," that is, money and other symbols of wealth instead of relying on most families creating their own useful goods like food or clothing, people start to see everything in terms of monetary value (its "exchange value") instead of looking at whether an item actually helps them or their neighbors live (its "use value"). Instead of using any surplus to help

WHAT
DO I READ
NEXT?

- *The Harp-Weaver and Other Poems* (1923) is Millay's Pulitzer Prize–winning book of poetry, and includes poems about women in the throes of love and loss, generally in a tone of sorrow and grim resignation. The strongest of these poems are those in traditional forms, including "Sonnets from an Ungrafted Tree," a narrative sonnet sequence about a woman facing the death of a husband she does not love.

- By the time she published *Make Bright the Arrows: 1940 Notebook* (1940), Millay had refined her attitude toward war. The poems in this collection, written after Germany had invaded the Netherlands, were intended to inspire American readers to prepare for war in defense of England and France. They were generally received as inferior poems and as ineffective propaganda.

- Terence Rattigan's *Harlequinade* (1948) is a one-act play using elements of Commedia dell'Arte. It is about a traveling theater company whose performance of Shakespeare's *Romeo and Juliet* is marred by its elderly actors' struggles to play the teenage characters, and by a disruption caused by a member of the audience.

- Hillary DePiano's *The Love of Three Oranges: A Play for the Theatre That Takes the Commedia dell'Arte of Carlo Gozzi and Updates It for the New Millennium* (2003) is a full-length contemporary comedy based on an earlier work by an eighteenth-century Venetian playwright. It tells the story of the melancholy Prince Tartaglia, who falls in love with three giant oranges after being cursed by a witch and sets out on a quest that leads him across the paths of many of the stock characters of Commedia dell'Arte.

- *The Eclogues*, by the Latin poet Virgil, is a book of ten sections, called "Eclogues" or "Bucolics," featuring shepherds and cattle herdsmen conversing on various social and political subjects. In the seventh eclogue, two shepherds named Thyrsis and Corydon engage in a singing competition. It is available in a 1984 Penguin Classics edition.

- *Habibi* (1997), by Naomi Shihab Nye, is a novel about Liyana, a fourteen-year-old Palestinian American girl who moves with her family from St. Louis, Missouri, to Jerusalem in Israel. There she experiences the effects of separation and intolerance when she falls in love with Omer, a Jewish boy.

- *War Is a Force That Gives Us Meaning* (2002), by the *New York Times* reporter Chris Hedges, explores why the human psyche is attracted to war. Based on literary works and on his own reporting in regions of conflict around the world, the book highlights the devastations of war while acknowledging its uses.

others, people in capitalist societies tend to hoard their wealth for themselves. And in an economy in which people do not grow their own food or make their own tools or clothing, people become materialistic and increasingly use their capital to buy useless items that serve only to increase their status.

Although they are not living in an industrialized society, even Thyrsis and Corydon are led to internalize the toxic values that Marxist theorists warn against. They are content to live peaceful lives as simple shepherds until the destructive forces of capitalism lead them astray. One might point out, however, that shepherds do not typically own the sheep they tend; Thyrsis and Corydon are apparently doing a low-paying but sometimes dangerous task to protect someone else's sheep. The first sign that capitalist values are at play in the scene comes when Corydon suggests making up a song and Thyrsis replies, "I know a game worth two of that." On the literal level, the reply is ridiculous: There is no logical way in which a game is "worth" two songs, or worth twice as much as a song. Of course, it is clear that Thyrsis simply means that his game would be more fun than the song, but it is significant that he uses such language. To a Marxist, this is an example of "commodification," or assigning an economic value to an abstract thing or quality not generally thought of as being part of the marketplace, and it is a sign that Thyrsis lives in a world where capitalist values are at least in the background.

For a short time after the wall ("a wall a man may see across, / But not attempt to scale") is built, Corydon remembers that he and Thyrsis were friends, and that the flock of sheep, divided into two by the wall, was once one. He still cares about the flock's well-being and begs Thyrsis for water for the sheep, but Thyrsis refuses. Though he did nothing special to earn it, now that Thyrsis has all of the water on his side of the wall (Marxists would say he controls the means of production) he will not share it, even though he has more than he needs, even though it is his friend asking, even though the sheep that are thirsty were recently under his care. Corydon is horrified by Thyrsis's change in attitude—until he, too, acquires a resource. Once Corydon finds the gold and jewels (items that have no use value for a shepherd) he immediately becomes greedy and selfish, celebrating that "the wall / Was up before I found them!—Otherwise, / I should have had to share them." Ignoring the fact that his sheep are dying of thirst, he imagines wasteful and vainglorious ways to spend his money: building a city full of women, erecting a bridge in his own honor. Both men are devoted to each other and to their flock until they are divided irrevocably by the idea of wealth.

Aria da Capo is a one-act play, and the downfall of the two shepherds happens very quickly. It seems illogical that they would turn against each other so easily, just as it seems illogical that very poor people would accept a society in which some people are able to buy expensive cars and watches and vacation homes while others have little or nothing. Marxism describes various internalized belief systems, or "ideologies," that keep poor people content with less, and keep them separated from each other. Why do men and women with below-average income and education join their country's military to fight against relatively low-income people from other countries, instead of

joining together to overthrow both governments and seize control of the wealth? Because they have accepted ideologies called "patriotism" and "nationalism"; they believe that their primary loyalty should be to their country, not to other people of their socioeconomic class. Even though many soldiers in many wars do not understand fully what a particular conflict is about, they stand willing to fight and die.

Why, Marx asked, do so many poor people accept their poverty during peace time instead of challenging the system that keeps them poor? He believed it was because members of the working class have internalized another ideology— religion—that teaches them that God is in control, that they will find a greater wealth in Heaven. One of Marx's most famous lines appeared in his book *Critique of the Hegelian Philosophy of Right* (1844), in which he said that religion was the "opiate of the masses." He meant that religion worked like the drug opium, and that believers acted like opium addicts, living in a cloud of calm acceptance. In the twenty-first century, the author and journalist Thomas Frank looked at another form of ideology in his book *What's the Matter with Kansas? How Conservatives Won the Heart of America* (2004), in which he asks why low-income Kansans—and people throughout the United States—consistently vote for Republican candidates, even though, he says, the Republican agenda tends to help wealthy people at the expense of the working class. Working-class voters, he argues, have accepted an ideology of cultural solidarity that blinds them to their own interests. In all of these instances, people are not seen as naturally violent or greedy; rather, they behave the way they do because they have absorbed false values from those who have greater wealth and power.

In a similar way, the play emphasizes repeatedly that the destructive actions of Thyrsis and Corydon do not come from within them; rather, they come from forces larger than the two—in this case, from Cothurnus, Masque of Tragedy. From the beginning, the shepherds (or the actors playing the shepherds, or the actors playing the actors playing the shepherds) forget their lines and have to be prompted by Cothurnus before they can continue. When Corydon first suggests that the two make a song, Thyrsis's initial response is to agree eagerly. But he stumbles over his line, and Cothurnus reminds him to suggest the wall game instead. When Thyrsis quickly tires of the game and suggests they sing the song, Corydon forgets *his* line, and has to be prompted by Cothurnus to say, "How do I know this isn't a trick?" Still later, Corydon suggests they drop the game, and this time it is Thyrsis who has to be reminded to say, "But how do I know this isn't a trick...?" In each case, the instinct of the shepherds is to sit together and sing together, and they are prodded apart by the larger forces that Cothurnus represents. Finally, they internalize the fear and suspicion and are driven to kill.

The structure of the play-within-the-play reinforces the play's rejection of capitalist values. By framing the shepherds' tragic scene with the farcical scene with Pierrot and Columbine, by using colored bits of paper to represent of a bowl of jewels, by having Cothurnus insist that a wall of tissue-paper is just as good as one made of rocks, the play emphasizes the flimsiness of the tragedy. In this play, the deaths of two shepherds are no more important than a dialogue about macaroons, gold and jewels have no more value than a bowl of confetti, and the wall that separates the shepherds—the ideologies like nationalism or religion that keep the lower classes at war with each other—have no real substance. Marx and his followers believed that one day the working class would rise up and take control of the factories, mines, power plants, and other means of production. When that day came, they believed, the workers would establish a new order in which people would work as hard as they could, take only as much wealth as they needed, and look after the weak and the sick who could not work. *Aria da Capo* does not reflect this optimism. The conflict between Thyrsis and Corydon, like the conflicts created to keep the working classes from uniting, is just "a silly game." But by the time Corydon asks, "Why do we play it?—let's not play this game," it is too late.

Source: Cynthia A. Bily, Critical Essay on *Aria da Capo*, in *Drama for Students*, Gale, Cengage Learning, 2010.

Suzanne Clark

In the following excerpt, Clark examines a number of Millay's poems dealing with broad issues, including women.

> It is a dangerous lot, that of the charming, romantic public poet, especially if it falls to a woman.
>
> Louise Bogan, "Edna Millay (1939)"

Women writers in the age of modernism discovered a cruel paradox: the more successfully they wrote, both to appeal to a feminized

> MILLAY'S POETIC STYLE IS FOUNDED ON COMMONALITY: IN THIS IT IS CLASSIC RATHER THAN MODERN. SHE MAY SHOCK HER AUDIENCE, BUT SHE DOES NOT SEPARATE HERSELF FROM THEM."

community of readers and to help readers feel part of the literary community, the less they could be considered serious writers. The more clearly they appealed to the shared feelings of a popular community, the more they risked being labeled "sentimental," or merely popular. In the years of the great modernists—Eliot, Pound, Stevens, H.D., Williams—the project of poetry was to turn away from a mass culture, to establish a distance between literature and all other forms of writing. But, as Sandra Gilbert suggests, women writers may have had a different task than men writers in the early twentieth century, involving not alienation from history but the building of agreement, not the tragic vision but the dialogue of human exchange. Furthermore, as Sherry O'Donnell taught me to see, women have long made poetry part of their community-building practice. Embedded in the processes of middle-class history, women's writing has looked different. In the first decades of this century, what was recognizably women's writing was not at all like the new work of writers like Eliot or Stevens. But it was a difference that had no warrant in the project of modernism. This was not a matter of specific cases. Modernist poetics excluded female poets at the level of theory.

Feminist critics today write in a moment of critical history which seems to value difference and marginality and even feminist criticism itself, but our efforts may have some troublesome affinities with the problems of women writers in the heyday of modernist poetry—writers like H.D., Louise Bogan, and even Marianne Moore, as well as the woman Harriet Monroe hailed as the Sappho of our times, Edna St. Vincent Millay. We should not accept without careful distinction modernist claims about the connection of revolution and the new word, the revolution of language. At a moment when the culture produces the separation of disciplines and the commodification of value, alienation is not novel. Then, as Baudrillard wants to assert: "He is truly a revolutionary who speaks of the world as non-separated."

Modernism offers its own forms of repression: where will we draw the boundaries of literariness, the definitions of "interesting" texts? Sentimentality has no warrant in the literary history of modernism; whatever is called sentimental has been excluded from the serious, the literary, the tough, the interesting. And the sentimental in the annals of twentieth century criticism turns out to have an uncanny relationship to writing by women. The seemingly ahistorical critical term "sentimental" represses its historicity, its rejection of a literary history dominated by women. In the following examination of women's situation in literary modernism, I will suggest that we must face the question of the sentimental and its relationship to the history of writing by women. What is at issue, I will argue, in the question of the sentimental is the relationship of literary daughter to literary mother—the very possibility of a female tradition.

I

In the twentieth century, the horror of the "sentimental" helps define the good male poet much as the prostitute once defined the good woman. When a female literary history arises out of the generations of women writers, it appears as a reviled past: the anxiety of influence appears as the threat of the Mother (nature, love, tongue, muse), powerful in several guises. If the strong male poet may be said to rewrite his literary fathers in a Bloomian act of "misprision," what of the poet's literary mothers? He—and the disguised she—rejects the female literary ancestors altogether, making literary history the legends of warring kings, not a genealogy. Like the principle of the sentimental, the mother is constructed as powerful and dominant, but only in the very gesture of repudiation required for males to define themselves as "different." A woman poet is a contradiction in this history. So, perhaps, is a woman critic. A woman poet is *created by* this history as a poet-within-history, powerful, and so not really literary. Women's power is separated from poetry, domesticated.

Maturity for modernist critics like John Crowe Ransom as for Freud involved a separation from the sentimental (m)Other. Therefore when Ransom evaluated the work of Edna St. Vincent Millay, he found her immature, all too womanly, "fixed in her famous attitudes." The

story of the male mind which he rehearses in an essay on Millay seems to him so obvious he needs no argument. It has for him become a matter of biology, not culture or history.

Ransom writes:

> The minds of man and woman grow apart, and how shall we express their differentiation? In this way, I think: man, at best, is an intellectualized woman. Or, man distinguishes himself from woman by intellect, but it should be well feminized. He knows he should not abandon sensibility and tenderness, though perhaps he has generally done so, but now that he is so far removed from the world of the simple senses, he does not like to impeach his own integrity and leave his business in order to recover it; going back, as he is often directed, to first objects, the true and tried, like the moon, or the grass, or the dead girl. He would much prefer if it is possible to find poetry in his study, or even in his office, and not have to sit under the syringa bush. Sensibility and tenderness might qualify the general content of his mind, if he but knew the technique, however "mental" or self-constructed some of that content looks. But his problem does not arise for a woman. Less pliant, safer, as a biological organism, she remains fixed in her famous attitudes, and is indifferent to intellectuality. I mean, of course, comparatively indifferent; more so than a man. Miss Millay is rarely and barely very intellectual, and I think everybody knows it.

(784)

At the same time that Ransom would seem to deny that a woman could be anything more than "indifferent to intellectuality," he maintains that a man at his best is "an intellectualized woman." The woman, precisely, is in-different, incapable of entering into the play of differences. Ransom's interests in the feminine seem the reverse of the post-modernist view. In fact, however, they have disturbing resemblances to the interests of Derrida, for example, or Lyotard. To the extent that Postmodernism takes up the modernist move, it defines "difference" as what is interesting. In order to qualify for the avant-garde, the woman must be defined as something new, marginal, other, subversive—different. The woman must not be moralizing and sentimental.

My research on the sentimental has grown out of this historical situation governing our reading as well as our writing. The sentimental, we can probably all agree, is what I call an "unwarranted discourse." Recent work on the sentimental novel, notably Tompkins' *Sensational Designs,* has argued strongly for the literary importance of the genre. Nevertheless, to call writing "sentimental" is still to criticize it severely—whether the writing is rhetorical or literary, novel or poetry. But the sentimental is a tradition, a set of conventions and writing practices, and not just a failure to do something else. The very word "sentimental" came into being in eighteenth-century England, together with the sentimental novel, as a term of approval. It is connected to the pathetic appeal—the appeal to emotions, especially pity, as a means of persuasion.

In his *Philosophy of Rhetoric,* first published in 1776, George Campbell endorses the sentimental at the same time that he recognizes its connection to ideology, to "the moral powers of the mind." According to Campbell, the sentimental "occupies, so to speak, the middle place between the pathetic and that which is addressed to the imagination, and partakes of both, adding to the warmth of the former the grace and attractions of the latter." Campbell, like Hugh Blair, assumes the importance of appeals to passion. The pathetic works best, he says, "by some secret, sudden, and inexplicable association, awakening all the tenderest emotions of the heart...it will not permit the hearers even a moment's leisure for making the comparison, but as it were by some magical spell, hurries them, ere they are aware, into love, pity, grief, terror." Campbell was the dominant rhetorical text for much of the nineteenth century in America. It was not so bad to be sentimental then. What has happened to the once-positive connotation of the word? Campbell joined two things together that were firmly separated by modernism: he considered poetics to be a "particular mode" of rhetoric, and he considered both reason and passion to be legitimate parts of persuasion. A quick glance at the evening news will confirm our guess that the sentimental has not vanished—that it has pride of place, indeed, in journalism—a persuasive appeal in a genre supposed to be without persuasion. But when we apply the word "sentimental" to a piece of writing, we usually mean something pejorative. In his introduction to *A Lover's Discourse,* Roland Barthes writes:

> Discredited by modern opinion, love's senti-
> mentality must be assumed by the amorous
> subject as a powerful transgression which
> leaves him alone and exposed: by a reversal of
> values, then, it is this sentimentality which
> today constitutes love's obscenity.

Episodes of love, like eruptions of the imaginary, appear in the modern, rational conversation, the discourse of our times, as something to be gotten over, grown out of, unwarranted. As Foucault has pointed out, it is sex, not love, which has been connected to freedom, subversion, and critical discourses in our time (5). The appeal to feeling has become increasingly suspect, more distant from the rational.

Paradoxically, in an age of elite poetry such as modernism, the poet who writes within conventions shared by bourgeois culture practices a version of difference. Marginality then is a version of the obscurity-in-plain-view women know so well. For women have long been writing in a well-populated solitude, "warranted," as Barthes says, "by no one." And modernist women poets were read with an eye to the gap between popular culture and serious writing. Tompkins has pointed this out in her work on Stowe. The sentimental tradition of women writers is connected to women's power—but also collides with modernist expectations. Ann Douglas, arguing for the "feminization" of American culture, associated this sentimental with the hegemony of consumer culture. But recently critics including Radway, Modleski, and Rabine have taught us to look again at the possibilities of popular fiction by women, arguing in various ways that the love story has been read too narrowly. *The Lover's Discourse* suggests a stronger adversity: if sentiment is the modern "obscene," has it not suffered the oppression of censorship and disapproval once arrayed against sexual obscenity?

In spite of their dramatic presence at the birth of modernism, the women writers of the moment did not establish an authoritative place for women in modernist literature. There were many women, from Sara Teasdale to Gertrude Stein to Kay Boyle, appearing in modernist magazines and anthologies, and women were powerful editors too: Harriet Monroe of *Poetry,* Margaret Anderson and Jane Heap of *The Little Review,* H.D. of *The Egoist,* Marianne Moore of *The Dial.* Yet a list of names resists our collecting and abstracting: the case of Sara Teasdale seems quite unlike that of Gertrude Stein; Edna St. Vincent Millay and Marianne Moore seem to have little in common even if we wish to say both practice versions of subversion—or compliance. No sense of a women's tradition emerges. The powerful old domestic tradition is denied.

The fact is that for many woman writers in the twenties, poets and novelists alike, the woman's tradition was all too coherent. Kay Boyle, whose stories are filled with female heroines, refuses to this day to identify herself as a woman writer and rejects feminist criticism. Like Millay, she early established a reputation for independence of spirit. Boyle has characterized herself as "a dangerous 'radical' disguised as a perfect lady" (Spanier Illustration 32). She seems, that is, to want to keep her credentials as a revolutionary modernist—but she also seems to believe that revolution has a problematic relationship to the community of women.

Louise Bogan, writing both as poet and critic, marked her love poetry with the bitter loss of authority, of the very warrant for her subject: woman, love, the lyric. Adopting modernist attitudes, she wrote critically of the sentimental past: "Women, it is true, contributed in large measure to the general leveling, dilution, and sentimentalization of verse, as well as of prose, during the nineteenth century" (*Achievement* [*Achievement in American Poetry*] 20). At the same time she argued that "the wave of poetic intensity which wavers and fades out and often completely fails in poetry written by men, on the feminine side moves on unbroken" (*Achievement* 19). The scorn of Bogan's critical modernism seems more harshly directed against her own work (and the volume of what she accepted is slender) than against the poetry she reviewed as critic for *The New Yorker* for so many years.

Perhaps this reflexivity itself, this self-wounding, has to do with the "feminine" in her work. She understood that the woman's place as imaginary object of the lyric (stopped, still) became terrible, "dreadful," Medusa-like, if fixed as the mirror image of the self. Her poetry rejected this imaginary. Bogan seemed at once to cite the rejected tradition and to inscribe the feminine into language as estrangement. On the cover of *The Blue Estuaries,* Roethke approves her "scorn" of what he calls the usual lyric "caterwauling," and Adrienne Rich praises her for committing a "female sensibility" to language. Bogan both constitutes and distances an ideology that is female, situating herself within the contradiction of asserting a lover's discourse which is at the same time a forsaken language. By refusing the "caterwaul," she also accedes to male standards, male codes, male criticism. Like Marianne Moore, Bogan was severe with her own work, pruning mercilessly, and perhaps giving the critical spirit so large a scope that she curtailed her own productivity, unbalancing the relationship between

the critical and the assertive. Edna St. Vincent Millay, too middle-class, too "public," may have served her as an emblem of what could go wrong.

When a woman poet like Edna St. Vincent Millay defied the laws of modesty, obscurity, and constraint to reach out for her woman readers, she earned the contempt of critics. It's risky for a writer to appeal to a community of readers that identifies her with the feminine. How in the world, we might ask, could it possibly be a daring political gesture to write "O world, I cannot hold thee close enough?" But the popular appeal was precisely what was risky. Millay had grown so hugely popular by the late 1920's that her kitchen was featured in *Ladies Home Journal* ("Polished as a sonnet...Light as a lyric... Must be the kitchen for EDNA ST. VINCENT MILLAY." Only late in the article, at the back of the magazine, did they admit that her husband was really the cook of the household.) I want to argue that the risk of shame is especially daunting when the female readership is middle-class, bourgeois, and sentimental, and when the values affirmed have to do with love and motherhood. That feminine community, however populous, is non-literary and non-authoritative by definition. Therefore what Millay risked by writing poetry of inclusion rather than of exclusion—risked and perhaps lost—was poetry itself.

In certain ways too much the daughters of that bourgeois patriarchy which generated their mythologies, the women poets who wrote and were read in the first decades of the twentieth century, were perhaps also too much the mothers of ourselves as readers. Like our mothers they served to give us the texts for the first rush of poetic feeling ("O world, I cannot hold thee close enough."), the heat of romantic rebelliousness ("I've burned my candle at both ends"), the encounter with "poetic" language ("Little faces looking up / Holding wonder like a cup"), and even the first idea of poem as "image" ("Whirl up, sea—/ Whirl your pointed pines"). Women quickly became textbook poets, schools texts, and they are still there, in the books for school children from elementary through high school: Millay, Wylie, Teasdale, H. D., Moore. The critical history of these women poets, then, has been shaped by the sentimental reader—by indulgent admirers who simply endorse motherhood, country, and Edna St. Vincent Millay, but also by ambitious critics who want to be mature and interesting, who feel they have to cast off their youthful memories of poetry in order to grow up.

In the literary world defined by modernism, however, the writer who wrote for women, whose audience included "the ladies," opened herself to the most terrible critical scorn. Morton D. Zabel characterized the awfulness of what he called "Popular Support" for the arts in a "Comment" for *Poetry* in 1930. Subtitled "Cattle in the Garden," Zabel's piece makes the connection between bad taste and writing for the ladies. An example of "Popular Support" are items from the Herald-Tribune Books, where "week after week, poetry is plucked from every bush that grows by the effusive Miss Taggard, that energetic specialist in Immortality" whose "style (and incidentally her critical standards) derive largely from Queen Marie's testimonials for Pond's Facial Creams" (269). But far worse is the General Federation of Womens' Clubs' fifth annual Poetry week. Zabel quotes from Mrs. Anita Browne, Founder-Organizer:

> To the rhythmic beat of humming presses that puncture the air with their poetic metre as each revolution imprints a page of this Poetry Week Magazine, it seems a happy singing, as though the presses sense the harmonies within the printed program of the Poetry Week activities.... The marvel of the printing press! The pillar of education; the historian of all time; the etcher of the poet ... the Monarch: the printed Word! So these pages proclaim the fifth annual celebration of Poetry Week, in which the whole nation joins.

(274)

There is a terrible innocence on the part of Browne about the great distance between her aims—"happy singing," "harmonies," a poetry "in which the whole nation joins"—and the ambitions of modernist criticism for toughness and excellence. But Zabel knows, and he drives the point home:

> But while Mrs. Browne and her loyal cohorts celebrate their victories, "certain of us by nature more sardonic than these: will probably pause to wonder ... where meanwhile Poetry was keeping herself ... from the uproar and ribaldry while the cattle stampeded the flowers, fruit, and vines of her no-longer sacred-and-unprofaned gardens."

(276)

In fact, the scorn heaped on the ladies and their sentimental taste has been so very thick one wonders what it has been at work to create. Clearly, much literature in our century has been written with the idea of refusal, of offense, of violating the readers' expectations. We have grown used to the stories of the heroic author—

D. H. Lawrence, for example—who offends the public (the women guarding public morality) with his exposes of love and adultery, his ever-more-graphic representation of sexuality. Refusals like those of Eliot or Williams or Stevens are less obviously gendered. Nevertheless, their rejection of the rhetorical and poetic conventions that might help readers gain access to their work is a rejection of the mass audience and a refusal to meet readerly expectations. The teachers and the cultivated ladies who made it their practice to translate the canon of great literature for children and for the unlettered—the community-building women—were disenfranchised by the practices of modernism, which required a more academic priesthood.

This context helps us to understand the antagonistic critical reception given Edna St. Vincent Millay as she grew in popularity during the '30s and '40s. John Crowe Ransom criticized Millay for her sensibility: "Miss Millay is rarely and barely very intellectual, and I think everybody knows it" (784). Allen Tate said "Miss Millay's success with stock symbolism is precariously won; I have said that she is not an intellect but a sensibility: if she were capable of a profound analysis of her imagery, she might not use it" (335–36). And Cleanth Brooks simply picked up Ransom's theme to conclude that Millay was "immature." She failed to be a major poet because she lacked irony: "Miss Millay has not grown up" (2).

In the age of Eliot, defined by the failure of relationship and the anti-heroics of the poetic loner, Millay was writing most of all about love, and her sentimental subject was only the beginning of her crime: more than that, she was writing in a way that is easily understood, that invites the reader in, that makes community with the reader and tries to heal alienation. Millay was of course flagrantly engaged during the twenties in the Bohemian leftish lifestyle of Greenwich village, with its tenets of free love and support for the working masses. But her radical lifestyle never put off her readers the way a radical poetics might have. Millay's poetic style is founded on commonality: in this it is classic rather than modern. She may shock her audience, but she does not separate herself from them. The accessibility of her work seems from the beginning of her career more important to her readers than her Bohemian attitudes. In Millay, we see that the gestures of social revolt don't always sever ties. She can write "My candle burns at both ends" and take a flippant attitude about her lovers, but the fact that she does it in sonnet form kept her credentials as a member of the American middle-class consensus in order. The epithet "bourgeois" or "middle-class" in the mouth of a modernist critic was meant to be as devastating as the charge of sentimentality. But some continuity with the middle class was for Millay as for many other women writers a prerequisite for maintaining a woman's tradition and for creating a community with women readers.

Source: Suzanne Clark, "The Unwarranted Discourse: Sentimental Community, Modernist Women, and the Case of Millay," in *Genre*, Vol. 20, No. 2, Summer 1987, pp. 133–52.

John Crowe Ransom

In the following essay, Ransom, himself a poet, laments the lack of intellectual interest in Millay's work.

Miss Millay is an artist of considerable accomplishments. She is the best of the poets who are "popular" and loved by Circles, Leagues, Lyceums, and Round Tables; perhaps as good a combination as we can ever expect of the "literary" poet and the poet who is loyal to the "human interest" of the common reader. She can nearly always be cited for the virtues of clarity, firmness of outline, consistency of tone within the unit poem, and melodiousness. Her career has been one of dignity and poetic sincerity. She is an artist. . . .

[The limitation of Miss Millay] is her lack of intellectual interest. It is that which the male reader misses in her poetry, even though he may acknowledge the authenticity of the interest which is there. . . . It is true that some male poets are about as deficient; not necessarily that they are undeveloped intellectually, but they conceive poetry as a sentimental or feminine exercise. Not deficient in it are some female poets, I suppose, like Miss Marianne Moore; and doubtless many women are personally developed in intellect without having any idea that poetry can master and use what the intellect is prepared to furnish. . . .

Such are Miss Millay's limits. . . . We come finally to her quite positive talent or, if anybody quarrels with that term, genius. But I still have to identify by restriction the field in which I find it displayed.

The formal, reflective, or "literary" poems fall for the most part outside this field. She is not a good conventional or formalist poet, and I

think I have already suggested why: because she allows the forms to bother her and to push her into absurdities. . . .

Then, the young-girl poems fall outside it; and I am afraid I refer to more poems than were composed in the years of her minority. This charming lady found it unusually difficult, poetically speaking, to come of age. "Renascence" is genuine, in the sense that it is the right kind of religious poem for an actual young girl of New England, with much rapture, a naive order of images, and a dash of hell-fire vindictiveness. . . . But the volume *A Few Figs from Thistles* is well known as a series of antireligious and Bohemian shockers, and that stage should have been far behind her when she published the work at the age of twenty-eight. The college plays were exactly right for their occasions, but *Aria da Capo* comes long afterward and still suggests the prize-winning skit on the Senior Girls' Stunt Night of an unusually good year. And then come the poems of *Second April*, whose author at twenty-nine is not consistently grown up. . . . [Grandually] the affectations of girlhood in Miss Millay disappear.

When they are absent, she has a vein of poetry which is spontaneous, straightforward in diction, and excitingly womanlike; a distinguished objective record of a natural woman's mind. The structures are transparently simple and the effects are immediate. There are few poems, I think, that do not fumble the least bit, unless they are very short, but she has the right to be measured as a workman by her excellent best. Her best subjects are death, which she declines like an absolute antiphilosopher to accept or gloze, a case of indomitable feminine principle; personal moods, which she indulges without apology, in the kind of integrity that is granted to the kind of mind that has no direction nor modulation except by its natural health; and natural objects which call up her love or pity. I have to except from this list the love of a woman for a man, because, in her maturity at least, she has reserved that subject for the sonnets, and they are rather unconventional in sentiment, but literary, and corrupted by verbal insincerities. . . .

The most ambitious single work of Miss Millay's would be her operatic play, *The King's Henchman;* ambitious, but suited to her powers, and entirely successful. . . . Operatic drama lends itself to Miss Millay's scope. Its action is a little brief and simple, and it permits the maximum number of lyrical moments and really suits Poe's idea of the long poem as a series of short poems rather than a single consecutive whole. The work does not prove Miss Millay to be a dramatist, but it shows what an incessant fountain of poetry is a woman's sensibility in the midst of simple human and natural situations. It should be remarked that, being tenth century, the properties have the advantage of being a little picturesque, and the tone of the language slightly foreign, like a Scottish or Irish idiom perhaps. But these are the arrangements of the artist, of whom it cannot so fairly be said that she is in luck as that she is a competent designer.

Source: John Crowe Ransom, "The Poet as Woman," in *Southern Review*, Vol. 2, No. 4, Spring 1937, pp. 783–806.

Edward Davison

In the following excerpt, Davison contrasts Millay's plays with her poetry.

... Miss Millay's definitely dramatic work deserves a fuller treatment than the scope of this essay permits. Of the four plays, *Aria da Capo* and *The King's Henchman* are the most successful. *Two Slatterns and a King,* though slight, is delicately wrought and fulfils its description as "a moral interlude." But Miss Millay never wrote anything more rounded and poignant than *Aria da Capo,* a miniature tragedy whose lyrical irony helps to contradict Mr. Robert Frost's thesis about good fences making good neighbors. It would be an offense to attempt to analyze her tender mingling of poetry and parable, for this ingenious and skilfully wrought little play justifies its author from first to last and will make a friend of every reader.

The King's Henchman, Miss Millay's most recent work, has lately been written about almost *ad nauseam* in the newspapers and weekly reviews. Considered merely as an opera libretto it has never been matched in English. But on no account must it be considered primarily as an opera libretto. Viewed on its own intended merits as a three-act play, written chiefly in irregular verse, it is curiously unique, a sort of changeling child of poetry. The author treats an exceptionally beautiful story (one that had already served that now forgotten poet William Mason as the theme of a choric tragedy) in a manner that restricts her rather unnecessarily. What is gained in the way of atmosphere, by means of her skilful use of a vocabulary predominatingly Anglo-Saxon, is lost again to a great extent by the persistence of such infelicities (to modern ears) as

Aelfrida: I do not know thy name.
Aethelwold: Nor I thy name. "Aetholwold," I hight.

and later

Aelfrida: I must be gone! "Aelfrida," I hight.

It is not altogether just to find fault with an imitation of the archaic because it succeeds in being archaic. But archaism has no particular virtue in itself; and there are many passages in *The King's Henchman* where poetry as well as drama is sacrificed to the consistency of the style. On the whole the play is admirable, though chiefly for its merits as a *tour de force.* Considering all the difficulties it is literally amazing that Miss Millay contrived to sustain its lyrical pulse. That the author set herself such a tough artistic task suggests that she is not now content with the relatively fortuitous triumphs of her earlier work. She is prepared to face the vital problems concerning the intellectual organization of her poetic impulse, prepared obviously to forget some of her lyric facility for a time while she learns to rule it with a firmer head than before. This is the first major means whereby a poet whose work suggests a general drift changes himself into a poet with an attitude. So far, Miss Millay has not evolved an attitude. Her work is not the poetic expression of some more or less consistent scheme of values, like the work of Mr. A. E. Housman, Mr. Robert Frost, Mrs. Browning, Shelley, Keats, Milton, Shakespeare. It has no scale to measure the world. Lacking that, a poet cannot even approach greatness.

Source: Edward Davison, "Edna St. Vincent Millay," in *English Journal*, Vol. 16, No. 9, November 1927, p. 681.

Harriet Monroe

In the following essay, Monroe contends that Millay is "the greatest woman poet since Sappho."

Long ago... I used to think how fine it would be to be the greatest woman poet since Sappho....

I am reminded by that old dream to wonder whether we may not raise a point worthy of discussion in claiming that a certain living lady may perhaps be the greatest woman poet since Sappho....

[The] woman-poets seem to have written almost exclusively in the English language. Emily Bronte, Elizabeth Barrett Browning, Christina Rossetti, Emily Dickinson—these four names bring us to 1900....

Emily Bronte—austere, heroic, solitary—is of course the greatest woman in literature. Not even Sappho's *Hymn to Aphrodite* . . . can surpass *Wuthering Heights* for sheer depth and power of beauty, or match it for the compassing of human experience in a single masterpiece. But *Wuthering Heights,* though poetic in motive and essence, classes as a novel rather than a poem. . . . As a poet, she has not the scope, the variety, of Edna St. Vincent Millay, whose claim to pre-eminence we are considering. . . .

"Renascence" remains the poem of largest sweep which Miss Millay has achieved as yet—the most comprehensive expression of her philosophy, so to speak, her sense of miracle in life and death—yet she has been lavish with details of experience, of emotion, and her agile and penetrating mind has leapt through spaces of thought rarely traversed by women, or by men either for that matter.

For in the lightest of her briefest lyrics there is always more than appears. In [*A Few Figs from Thistles*], for example, in "Thursday," "The Penitent," "To the Not Impossible He" and other witty ironies, and in more serious poems like "The Betrothal," how neatly she upsets the carefully built walls of convention which men have set up around their Ideal Woman, even while they fought, bled and died for all the Helens and Cleopatras they happened to encounter! And in *Aria da Capo,* a masterpiece of irony sharp as Toledo steel, she stabs the war-god to the heart with a stroke as clean, as deft, as ever the most skilfully murderous swordsman bestowed upon his enemy. Harangues have been made, volumes have been written, for the outlawry of war, but who else has put its preposterous unreasonableness into a nutshell like this girl who brings to bear upon the problem the luminous creative insight of genius?

Thus on the most serious subjects there is always the keen swift touch. Beauty blows upon them and is gone before one can catch one's breath; and lo and behold, we have a poem too lovely to perish, a song out of the blue which will ring in the ears of time. Such are the "little elegies" which will make the poet's Vassar friend, "D.C." of the wonderful voice, a legend of imperishable beauty even though "her singing days are done." Thousands of stay-at-home women speak wistfully in "Departure" and "ament"—where can one find deep grief and its futility expressed with such agonizing grace?

Indeed, though love and death and the swift passing of beauty have haunted this poet as much as others, she is rarely specific and descriptive. Her thought is transformed into imagery, into symbol, and it flashes back at us as from the facets of a jewel.

And the thing is so simply done. One weeps, not over D.C.'s death, but over her narrow shoes and blue gowns empty in the closet. In "Renascence" the sky, the earth, the infinite, no longer abstractions, come close, as tangible as a tree. "The Harp-Weaver," presenting the protective power of enveloping love—power which enwraps the beloved even after death has robbed him, is a kind of fairy-tale ballad, sweetly told as for a child. Even more in "The Curse" emotion becomes sheer magic of imagery and sound, as clear and keen as frost in sunlight. Always one feels the poet's complete and unabashed sincerity. She says neither the expected thing nor the "daring" thing, but she says the incisive true thing as she has discovered it and feels it.

Miss Millay's most confessional lyrics are in sonnet form, and among them are a number which can hardly be forgotten so long as English literature endures, and one or two which will rank among the best of a language extremely rich in beautiful sonnets. . . .

Beyond these, outside the love-sequence, the "Euclid" sonnet stands in a place apart, of a beauty hardly to be matched for sculpturesque austerity, for detachment from the body and the physical universe. Other minds, searching the higher mathematics, have divined the central structural beauty on which all other beauty is founded, but if any other poet has expressed it I have yet to see the proof. That a young woman should have put this fundamental law into a sonnet is one of the inexplicable divinations of genius. . . . If Miss Millay had done nothing else, she could hardly be forgotten.

But she has done much else. Wilful, moody, whimsical, loving and forgetting, a creature of quick and keen emotions, she has followed her own way and sung her own songs. Taken as a whole, her poems present an utterly feminine personality of singular charm and power; and the best of them, a group of lyrics ineffably lovely, will probably be cherished as the richest, most precious gift of song which any woman since the immortal Lesbian has offered to the world.

Source: Harriet Monroe, "Edna St. Vincent Millay," in *World Literature Criticism Supplement*, Vol. 24, No. 5, August 1924, pp. 260–67.

SOURCES

Aimone, Joseph, "Millay's Big Book, or the Feminist Formalist as Modern," in *Unmanning Modernism: Gendered Re-Readings*, edited by Elizabeth Jane Harrison and Shirley Peterson, University of Tennessee Press, 1997, pp. 1–13.

Brantley, Will, "The Force of Flippancy: Edna Millay's Satiric Sketches of the Early 1920s," in *Colby Quarterly*, Vol. 27, No. 3, September 1991, pp. 132–47.

Frank, Thomas, *What's the Matter with Kansas? How Conservatives Won the Heart of America*, Metropolitan Books, 2004.

Marx, Karl, *Critique of Hegel's Philosophy of Right*, 1843, translated by Annette Jolin and Joseph O'Malley, edited by Joseph O'Malley, Cambridge University Press, 1970.

Marx, Karl, and Friedrich Engels, *The Communist Manifesto*, 1848, translated by Samuel Moore, 1888, edited by David McClellan, Oxford University Press, 2008.

McKee, Mary J., "Millay's *Aria da Capo*: Form and Meaning," in *Modern Drama*, Vol. 9, September 1966, pp. 165–69.

Millay, Edna St. Vincent, *Aria da Capo*, Harper and Brothers, 1920.

———, "Author's Note," in *Aria da Capo*, Harper and Brothers, 1920, pp. 44, 47–49.

Milford, Nancy, *Savage Beauty: The Life of Edna St. Vincent Millay*, Random House, 2001, pp. 125, 132.

Monroe, Harriet, "Edna St. Vincent Millay," in *Poetry*, Vol. 24, No. 5, August 1924, pp. 260–67.

Ozieblo, Barbara, "Avante-Garde and Modernist Women Dramatists of the Provincetown Players: Bryant, Davies and Millay," in *Journal of American Drama and Theatre*, Vol. 16, No. 2, Spring 2004, pp. 1–16.

Patton, John J., "The Variety of Language in Millay's Verse Plays," in *Tamarack: Journal of the Edna St. Vincent Millay Society*, Vol. 3, No. 1, Fall 1985, pp. 8–16.

Phelps, William Lyon, "Edna St. Vincent Millay, Poet and Dramatist," in *New York Times Book Review and Magazine*, October 16, 1921, p. 10.

Ransom, John Crowe, "The Poet As Woman," in *Southern Review*, Vol. 2, No. 4, Spring 1937, pp. 783–806.

Woollcott, Alexander, "Second Thoughts on First Night," in *New York Times*, December 14, 1919, sec. 8, p. 2.

FURTHER READING

Britten, Norman A., *Edna St. Vincent Millay*, Twayne Publishers, 1967.

Part of the Twayne Publisher's United States Author Series, this volume is an excellent introduction to Millay's life and work for the general reader, although it is somewhat out of date and somewhat coy about sexual matters. The book includes a brief analysis of all of the major works, a critical biography, a chronology, and an annotated bibliography.

Cheney, Anne, *Millay in Greenwich Village*, University of Alabama Press, 1975.

This volume, which the author calls a "psychological biography," examines Millay's years in Greenwich Village just after she graduated from college as her period of initiation and maturation. Cheney devotes particular attention to Millay's changing views of art, religion, and sexuality during this period.

Freedman, Diane P., ed., *Millay at 100: A Critical Reappraisal*, Southern Illinois University Press, 1995.

Many of the twelve essays in this collection, published in the one hundredth year after Millay's birth, focus on her poetry, but her dramatic works are also discussed as the writers analyze Millay's approach to four central themes: modernism, love, the female body, and masquerade.

Green, Martin Burgess, and John Swan, *The Triumph of Pierrot: Commedia dell'Arte and Modern Imagination*, Macmillan, 1986.

This volume explores why so many artists of the early part of the twentieth century turned to Commedia dell'Arte—particularly to images of Columbine and Pierrot and their colleague Harlequin. Painter Pablo Picasso, composer Igor Stravinsky, and filmmaker Charlie Chaplin are among the artists studied.

Meade, Marion, *Bobbed Hair and Bathtub Gin: Writers Running Wild in the Twenties*, Nan A. Talese/Doubleday, 2004.

A lively account of the 1920s as lived and described by four unconventional women: Millay, Zelda Fitzgerald, Dorothy Parker, and Edna Ferber. This entertaining book focuses on the women's intersecting social lives more than on their writing.

Milford, Nancy, *Savage Beauty: The Life of Edna St. Vincent Millay*, Random House, 2001.

Savage Beauty is the definitive biography of Millay, written by an accomplished author with full access to Millay's letters and papers and with the support of Millay's sister Norma. The volume is an unflinching look at an important, self-destructive talent.

The Crucible

1996

The Crucible, a film released in 1996, was based on the play of the same title by Arthur Miller, which was first performed and published in 1953. The play is based on historical events known as the Salem witch trials, which took place in Massachusetts in 1692. In the trials, more than 150 people were arrested and imprisoned for witchcraft, nineteen of whom were hanged. The play's events are set in motion when a young girl who is infatuated with a married man accuses his innocent wife of witchcraft.

Miller wrote the play at a time in American history characterized by an intense anticommunist suspicion that came to be known as McCarthyism. The events of *The Crucible* are symbolic of the so-called Red Hunts perpetuated by U.S. Senator Joseph McCarthy and his colleagues. More generally, the play is an indictment of intolerance. It quickly became a classic of American literature and is widely studied in schools and colleges. It won an Antoinette Perry (Tony) Award and a Donaldson Award in 1953, an Obie Award from *Village Voice* in 1958, and a Tony Award nomination for best play revival in 2002.

Miller adapted his play into the screenplay of *The Crucible*. The film, directed by Nicholas Hytner and starring Daniel Day-Lewis as John Proctor and Winona Ryder as Abigail Williams, is true to the story line of the play, with much of the dialog repeated word-for-word. The film met with a largely positive critical response, though it

fared poorly at the box office. Miller was nominated for an Academy Award for Best Adapted Screenplay.

The film contains brief scenes of nudity and portrays the aftermath of an adulterous relationship.

PLOT SUMMARY

The Crucible opens in Salem, Massachusetts, in 1692. It is night. The girls of the village creep out of their houses and meet in the woods. The slave Tituba leads them in a voodoo ritual to make the men that they wish to marry fall in love with them. Abigail Williams, who has brought a cockerel to the ritual, does not want to reveal the name of the man she is thinking about. The other girls say she is thinking of the married John Proctor. Abigail whispers to Tituba. Tituba, shocked, rebukes Abigail. Abigail grabs the cockerel, smashes it against the ground, and drinks the blood. The girls are hysterical and dance. The meeting is broken up by the unexpected arrival of the Reverend Parris, Abigail's uncle. The girls run off screaming. Parris's daughter, Betty, falls unconscious. This scene is not included in the play.

In Parris's house, Abigail tries in vain to wake Betty Parris, who has gone into a coma-like state. Ruth Putnam also cannot wake since the ritual. The girl's mother, Ann Putnam, is terrified that she may lose her one surviving child, whom she believes has fallen victim to the devil. Her husband, Thomas Putnam, shares her belief, as do some villagers.

Parris demands of Abigail whether the girls were conjuring spirits, but Abigail insists that they only danced. Parris, suspicious, asks Abigail why Elizabeth Proctor, for whom Abigail used to work, fired her. He asks Abigail whether rumors that she had an affair with John Proctor are true. Abigail accuses Elizabeth of spreading lies.

Parris announces that he has invited the Reverend Hale, an expert on witchcraft, to Salem to investigate recent events. Abigail runs with the other girls to Parris's home. They know that people convicted of witchcraft can be hanged. Abigail tries again to wake Betty. Betty wakes and, under the delusion that she can fly, tries to jump out of the window. She accuses Abigail of drinking blood, an activity associated with devil worship,

and of making a charm to kill Elizabeth Proctor. Abigail threatens to kill the girls if they tell anyone that they did anything in the woods except dance. Betty goes into convulsions.

Rebecca Nurse arrives and calms Betty just by sitting with her. She believes that the girls are playing a silly game and will soon tire of it. Ann Putnam says that witchcraft must be responsible for the fact that she only has one surviving child left out of eight, but Rebecca believes that only God has the answer to this.

Abigail waits for John Proctor and they talk. Skeptical about the claims of witchcraft, he is amused to hear about her escapades, which she says involved only dancing. Abigail begs him for a kind word and reminds him that he loved her once, before his wife found out about their affair and dismissed her. Proctor insists that their affair is over. He even denies that it happened, but Abigail insists that it did, and she kisses him. He pushes her away. Abigail bitterly complains that Elizabeth is blackening her name. As Proctor walks away, Abigail says that she knows he loves her.

Hale arrives in Salem with a pile of books on witchcraft. Rebecca warns Hale that seeking out evil spirits is dangerous. Hale examines Betty and Ruth for the marks of the devil.

Parris admits to Hale that he found Abigail dancing in the woods (dancing was forbidden by the Puritans). Hale questions Abigail and finds out that at the dance there was a cauldron and a "witches' stew" with a live frog in it. Hale summons all the girls who danced and tells them that they can save themselves by telling him who invoked the devil. When a girl points to Abigail, Abigail accuses Tituba.

Tituba is whipped to force a confession from her. Abigail accuses Tituba of sending her spirit into her and forcing her into devil-worship. Hale asks Tituba when she compacted with the devil. Tituba protests innocence, but as the whipping continues, she breaks down and gives the men the confession they require. Hale and Parris ask Tituba whom she saw with the devil, and Tituba names some village women. Abigail and the girls then call out the names of women whom they say they saw with the devil. The arrests begin.

Judge Danforth is invited from Boston to take charge of the witchcraft trials. Judge Hathorne imprisons and condemns fourteen people to death unless they confess to bewitching the children.

FILM TECHNIQUE

The Crucible has a realistic, almost documentary appearance. The setting of late seventeenth-century Salem is faithfully recreated. The buildings and costumes look authentic, and Miller has attempted in the dialog of his screenplay to accurately represent the speech of the time.

There is a stark contrast in the film between the brightly lit exterior shots showing the unspoiled, open, and the Edenic landscape of the newly settled Massachusetts and the dimly lit and monochromatic interior shots. The interior shots, with their brown and black color palette, create a claustrophobic and oppressive feeling that reflects the spiritual and emotional repression of the austere Puritan society of Salem. The message is that the Puritan settlers have arrived in Eden and caused a second fall of man through their narrow and mistaken theology. Paradise has been lost for a second time (the first loss having taken place in the biblical Garden of Eden, when Adam and Eve disobeyed God and ate fruit from the tree of knowledge of good and evil).

This polarity between the Edenic landscape and the miniature hell that the new inhabitants create within it is reflected in the different types of camera shots. The open countryside is frequently shown in establishing shots and extreme long shots, enabling the viewer to sense the broad possibilities and freedom open to the settlers. The scenes concerned with accusations of witchcraft, including the courtroom scenes, mostly use medium shots and close-ups, creating a more enclosed atmosphere. These closer shots also allow the viewer to focus on the characters' emotions or, more usually, their strained attempts to control their emotions.

In one pivotal scene, a zoom shot is used to great effect. Zoom shots are shots in which the camera focuses in closer on a subject or moves back from a subject. A zoom shot is used in a court scene just before Danforth is confronted by Elizabeth. This confrontation has been set up as laden with significance by Danforth's avowed determination to get to the truth and Proctor's assertion that Elizabeth is an honest woman who cannot lie. The camera moves in on Danforth as if from the point of view of the approaching Elizabeth (though this is before she actually arrives, adding to the sense of suspense). The slow zoom conveys a sense of some significant event approaching and implies that Danforth is meeting his nemesis: If Elizabeth confirms her husband's story, this will throw Abigail's claims of witchcraft into doubt and end the trials.

The zoom also changes the focus from the initial long shot that gives a more general sense of the court to the final close-up that focuses in on Danforth's face, encouraging the viewer to seek signs of doubt and fear. So subtle is Paul Scofield's performance as Danforth that the question of how much emotion has percolated through the self-control at the center of his personality is open to interpretation. However, this in itself makes a powerful point about the repression that governed Puritan society of the time: It is difficult to know what people truly feel because they are so much under the control of duty, convention, and expectation.

This suspense-filled introduction to the encounter between Danforth and Elizabeth makes the outcome all the more heartbreaking. Elizabeth lies, for the first time in her life, out of loyalty to her husband's reputation. It becomes clear that nothing will prevent the tragedy that is unfolding.

Elizabeth encourages Proctor to tell the court that Abigail told him that what happened in the woods had nothing to do with witchcraft. He is reluctant to denounce Abigail as a fraud because he fears that their affair will be revealed.

Elizabeth learns that her husband spoke to Abigail alone, and is suspicious that they are continuing their affair. John is angry that Elizabeth judges him, but she replies that the judge is within his own heart.

20th Century Fox / The Kobal Collection / Wetcher, Barry / The Picture Desk, Inc.

Judge Danforth arrives in Salem, and the trials begin. Sarah Osborne is brought into court. She is told that Sarah Good has confessed and so will not be sentenced to death. Sarah Osborne accuses Abigail of making up stories. Ruth Putnam accuses her neighbor, George Jacobs, of being in league with the devil.

Proctor rebukes his servant, Mary Warren, for attending the trials when he forbade her to do so. Mary gives Elizabeth the gift of a doll that she has made. She tells Proctor that she cannot work in the house for a while because she is now an official of the court. She adds that Elizabeth has been accused, but that she defended her. She refuses to name Elizabeth's accuser. Mary informs Proctor that she will not be ordered around. Elizabeth believes her accuser was Abigail, who wants her dead.

Proctor meets Abigail in the forest and tells her to inform the court that her accusations of witchcraft are lies. Abigail accuses Elizabeth of sending her spirit to attack her. Proctor tells Abigail that if she accuses Elizabeth in court, it will be the end of her.

Hale calls on the Proctors and says that Rebecca Nurse is suspected. He questions the Proctors to find out if they are properly Christian. He accuses Proctor of infrequent church attendance and of not baptizing his youngest son. Proctor replies that he does not like Parris's greedy behavior. Hale asks Proctor to recite the Ten Commandments. Proctor forgets one: the prohibition against adultery. Proctor tells Hale that Abigail told him that the children's afflictions are nothing to do with witchcraft. Hale replies that they have already confessed, but Proctor points out that they would be hanged if they did not confess.

Giles Corey and Francis Nurse arrive and tell Proctor that their wives, Martha and Rebecca, have been arrested. Rebecca is charged with the supernatural murder of Ann Putnam's babies. Proctor is incredulous and asks Hale if he still believes these accusations.

Ezekiel Cheever arrives with a warrant for Elizabeth's arrest. Abigail has accused her in court. For the first time, Hale seems doubtful. Cheever asks to see any dolls that Elizabeth keeps, but she says she has not kept dolls since she was a child. Cheever sees the doll that Mary Warren made for Elizabeth. It has a pin stuck in its abdomen. Cheever says that Abigail fell to the floor earlier that day. A needle was found in her abdomen, and she claimed that Elizabeth had sent out her spirit to stick it into Abigail. Proctor asks Mary how the doll came to be in his house. Mary says that she made it for Elizabeth and put her sewing needle into the doll for safekeeping. Proctor orders Hale out of his house, demanding to know why the accusers are always assumed to be innocent. Proctor says they are merely settling old scores and vows not to give his wife up to vengeance. Elizabeth is led away.

Proctor orders Mary to tell the court that she made the doll and stuck the needle in it. Mary says if she does, Abigail will turn on her and accuse Proctor of adultery.

In court, Martha Corey is accused of bewitching some pigs that she sold to a man and that had died. Martha says that the pigs died because the man did not feed them. Suddenly, Proctor, Giles Corey, Francis Nurse, and Mary Warren enter. Corey says they have evidence to prove the girls are frauds and that Mary will tell the court the truth. Danforth asks Proctor whether he is trying to disrupt the court, but Proctor says he is only trying to save his innocent wife and friends. Danforth says Proctor need not worry about Elizabeth's immediate execution because she is pregnant and by law cannot be hanged until she has given birth. Proctor shows Danforth a deposition signed by many villagers testifying to the good characters of Elizabeth, Martha, and Rebecca. Danforth responds by ordering the arrest of all those who signed so that they can be examined.

Thomas Putnam is summoned to answer Corey's claim that Putnam praised his daughter Ruth for accusing George Jacobs of witchery because this would win him some land. If Jacobs were hanged, his land would be forfeit, and Putnam would be able to buy the land. Corey says that an unnamed man heard Putnam say this. Corey refuses to name the man, and Danforth arrests him for contempt of court.

Proctor gives Danforth Mary's deposition swearing that she and the other girls lied about the witchcraft. Danforth summons Abigail and the other girls into court. While Proctor and Mary look on, Danforth tells the girls that Mary has sworn that she and the other girls were only pretending about the witchcraft. Abigail says Mary is lying about this and about how the doll came to be in the Proctors' home.

Abigail repeats her claim that Elizabeth sent her spirit out to stab her. Danforth says if Abigail is lying, it can only be because she wants Elizabeth to be hanged. Proctor says Abigail does want this.

Judge Hathorne challenges Mary: If she was pretending before, can she pretend to faint now, for the court? Mary cannot, saying that she has no sense of it now. Danforth suggests that this might be because there are no spirits loose at the moment, whereas there had been before. He asks Abigail to look into her heart and say whether she is lying about the witchcraft. Abigail begins to shiver and accuses Mary of bewitching them all. The other girls hysterically join Abigail in shivering. Abigail prays to God for help. Proctor confesses to their affair and tells how Elizabeth dismissed her when she found out. He says Abigail's stories of witchcraft are a whore's vengeance and that she means to replace Elizabeth in Proctor's home.

Danforth summons Elizabeth to confirm or deny the truth of Proctor's assertion. Proctor has told Danforth that Elizabeth has never lied. Danforth orders Proctor and Abigail to turn their backs so that they cannot signal to Elizabeth how she should reply. Elizabeth is brought in and Danforth asks her why she dismissed Abigail. Elizabeth does not know that her husband has already confessed to his affair. She says only that she felt that he fancied Abigail and so fired her. Danforth asks her if Proctor committed adultery. For the first time in her life, Elizabeth lies. Trying to save her husband's reputation, she says no. Proctor tells Elizabeth that he has already confessed to the affair. Elizabeth realizes that she has vindicated Abigail and condemned herself and the other accused persons. Hale tells Danforth that Elizabeth has understandably lied, that private vengeances are behind the accusations of witchcraft, and that Abigail is lying.

Abigail screams, pretending that Mary has sent out her spirit in the form of a yellow bird that is sitting on the ceiling rafter. The girls join in the drama, screaming and running from the courtroom into the river. Mary recants her testimony, claiming that Proctor came to her in spirit form and threatened to murder her if his wife was hanged, forcing her to bear false testimony. Hale says that Mary has lost her reason, but Danforth believes her and says that Proctor is in league with the devil. Proctor shouts out that

God is dead. Proctor means that good and evil have become confused in the witchcraft saga, but Danforth interprets his words as a sign that Proctor has renounced God for the devil. Proctor is arrested.

Parris announces from the pulpit that all those convicted of witchcraft by the court, including Sarah Osborne, Rebecca Nurse, George Jacobs, Martha Corey, and John and Elizabeth Proctor, are excommunicated from the church.

Some of the supposed witches are hanged publicly, watched by a mob that includes an exultant Abigail and the other girls. Corey is tortured by being pressed under a pile of stones but refuses to give the name of the man who accused Putnam. He asks his torturers to pile on more stones and is pressed to death. This and all the other executions by hanging are shown in the film but not the play, in which they are reported by other characters as having taken place.

The next round of hangings is greeted with silence from the crowd and seems to subdue even Abigail.

Abigail complains to Danforth that Hale's wife is sending out her spirit to attack her. This is too much even for Danforth, who says that the wife of a minister is too pure to do such things. Many villagers have turned against Abigail and the hangings because respected people have refused to confess to witchcraft, thereby saving themselves.

In a scene that does not exist in the play, Abigail visits Proctor in prison and begs him to run away with her to Barbados. She says she only acted out of desire for him and adds that the jailer will let him escape. She asks him to meet her on the ship. Proctor replies that they will meet in hell, and Abigail runs off alone.

Parris tells Danforth that Abigail stole all his money before running away. Parris asks Danforth to postpone the executions of Proctor, Martha, and Rebecca, as they are well respected and the people might take revenge upon Danforth. Danforth realizes that Proctor must confess to witchcraft. Hale begs Elizabeth to persuade her husband to confess and save his life. Hale feels that life may be more important in God's eyes than any principle.

Elizabeth asks to be allowed to speak with her husband alone. In a final, loving meeting, Proctor asks Elizabeth what she thinks of his idea of giving the court the confession they want. Elizabeth

replies that she cannot judge him but that she wants him alive. Proctor says that now his affair is publicly known, he has little to lose in the way of reputation. He asks Elizabeth's forgiveness, but she replies that it is he who must forgive himself. Whatever he does, she knows he is a good man. She blames her own coldness for prompting his adultery, saying that it stemmed from her feeling that she was so plain that no man could truly love her. She asks him to forgive her.

Proctor, overcome with love for his wife, shouts to the waiting men that he wants to live. Danforth asks him to write his confession so that it can be posted on the church door as an example to Rebecca and Martha, who have not confessed. Proctor gives a verbal false confession of binding himself to the devil but will not admit to seeing anyone else with the devil. He signs a prewritten confession but then rips it up. He has decided that he cannot, after all, bear the public shame of his name being posted on the church door. He has chosen death over dishonor. Proctor and Elizabeth kiss, and he is led away. Hale asks Elizabeth to go after him and persuade him to recant, but she says he knows that he is good and she will not take that from him.

Proctor, Martha, and Rebecca ascend the scaffold. The crowd is silent, and some people are weeping. The three condemned prisoners recite the Lord's Prayer. Proctor is the last to hang; his recitation of the prayer is missing only the final word, Amen. This scene is not in the play, which ends with Elizabeth Proctor's gratitude for her husband's knowledge of his goodness and does not show his execution. The inclusion of the execution scene reinforces the sense of injustice that is one of the themes of the play and film.

A note before the final credits says that the Salem witch trials ended after nineteen people were hanged, as more and more people refused to give false confessions.

CHARACTERS

Ezekiel Cheever

Ezekiel Cheever (played by John Griesemer) is a resident of Salem who acts as a clerk of the court.

Giles Corey

Giles Corey (Peter Vaughan) is the husband of Martha Corey. He is the first to voice suspicion to Hale about his wife involving herself in witch-craft, though his fears stem from ignorance: He blames his wife's reading of books other than the Bible for his own difficulty in praying. He later comes to regret his words when Martha is arrested as a witch.

Corey is a litigious man who has successfully launched several lawsuits and prides himself on his knowledge of law. He says that someone told him he heard Thomas Putnam praising his daughter Ruth for accusing George Jacobs of witchery, an accusation that allowed Putnam to buy up Jacobs's land. However, Corey refuses to name the man who told him this, and he is there-fore held in contempt of court and pressed to death under a heap of stones.

Martha Corey

Martha Corey (Mary Pat Gleason) is the wife of Giles Corey. Giles raises suspicions about Mar-tha when he unwisely asks Hale about her habit of reading books that are not the Bible, which he says prevents him from praying. She is accused of witchcraft after she sells some pigs that later die. Martha becomes an example of how the most innocent activities, such as reading and selling pigs, became traps in the hysterical atmosphere of Salem. Along with Rebecca Nurse and John Proctor, Martha is hanged for witchcraft in the final scene of the film because she courageously refuses to confess to a crime she did not commit.

Judge Danforth

Judge Danforth (played by Paul Scofield, who received an Academy Award nomination for Best Supporting Actor and won the British Academy of Film and Television Arts award for Best Supporting Actor) is the deputy gover-nor of Massachusetts and the presiding judge at the witch trials. He prides himself on his scrupu-lous and thorough commitment to correct judi-cial procedure and to uncovering the truth. However, his bias becomes evident when he gen-erally assumes the accusers to be telling the truth and their victims to be liars. He is unrepentant to the end, perhaps suppressing any doubts about the truth of the accusations in order to save face.

Reverend Hale

Reverend Hale (Rob Campbell) is a learned young minister who is invited to Salem to ascertain whether there is witchcraft going on. He arrives with an enormous pile of books on witchcraft and

evidently prides himself on his precise knowledge of the subject, which he is keen to distinguish from mere superstition. He undertakes his task with zeal, examining Betty and Ruth for marks of the devil, questioning Abigail and her troop of girls, and even interrogating people of good reputation like the Proctors. He begins to doubt the reliability of the accusations of witchcraft when Rebecca and Elizabeth are arrested: He knows them to be good people. His keen intellect cannot support the clear foolishness and hysteria that drive the trials.

As people begin to hang as a result of the trials, he turns against the process and tries to save the lives of the condemned. He decides finally that life is more important than principle, and for that reason vainly tries to persuade Eliz-abeth to talk Proctor into giving a false confes-sion and saving his life.

Judge Hathorne

Judge Hathorne (Robert Breuler) is a judge who assists Danforth in presiding over the witch tri-als. He delights in catching out accused people by twisting their words against them.

Marshal Herrick

Marshal Herrick (Michael Gaston) is a marshal (law enforcement official) in Salem.

George Jacobs

George Jacobs (William Preston) is an old man and a major landowner who is accused of witch-craft by Ruth Putnam. Giles Corey accuses Tho-mas Putnam of prompting his daughter to falsely accuse Jacobs of witchcraft so that he can buy up Jacobs's land after he has been hanged. Putnam is the only person in Salem who is wealthy enough to buy such a large tract of land.

Jacobs reveals the absurdity of the girls' accusations of witchcraft because he is obviously too old and infirm to enter Ruth Putnam's bed-room through the window and attack her, as she claims. However, this objection is evaded by the introduction of spectral evidence, in which it is assumed that someone can send out their spirit to attack someone through supernatural means.

Francis Nurse

Francis Nurse (Tom McDermott) is the husband of Rebecca Nurse and a wealthy and respected resident of Salem. He is disliked by Thomas and Ann Putnam on the grounds of land disputes and because the two families disagreed on the choice of minister for Salem.

Rebecca Nurse

Rebecca Nurse (Elizabeth Lawrence) is an elderly woman who enjoys great respect in Salem society. Rebecca is a wise and pious woman who, along with John Proctor, is the voice of reason in the film. She believes that seeking loose spirits is dangerous and disapproves of Hale's being brought in to lead the witch hunt; she correctly feels it will cause divisions in local society. She is proved right about this and everything else on which she expresses a view.

A mother and grandmother many times over, she takes a practical attitude to the behavior of Betty Parris and Ruth Putnam. She believes that the girls are indulging in silly games that they will soon tire of, a belief that is borne out by the fact that she is able to calm the hysterical Betty simply by sitting quietly with her. This suggests that she may occupy the role of a healer in Salem society, though Ann Putnam takes it as evidence of evil at work.

The fact that even someone as well liked and respected as Rebecca can be accused of witchcraft shows how extreme and hysterical the prevailing culture in Salem has become. This is emphasized in Hale's first glimmerings of disbelief when he hears that Rebecca has been arrested as a witch.

With Martha Corey and John Proctor, Rebecca is hanged in the final scene because she refuses to make a false confession.

Goody Osborne

See Sarah Osborne

Sarah Osborne

Sarah Osborne (Ruth Maleczech), also called Goody (short for *Goodwife*, a title that was used in the same way as the modern *Mrs.*) Osborne in the film, is a resident of Salem who is accused by the girls of witchcraft. She refuses to confess and is hanged.

Betty Parris

Betty Parris (Rachael Bella) is the daughter of the Reverend Parris. She is one of the two girls who fall into a coma-like state after attending the voodoo ritual in the woods and being caught by her father.

Reverend Parris

Reverend Parris (Bruce Davison) is the minister of the church in Salem. A faction in the village opposes him as minister. This fact adds to his sensitivity over the implications that his daughter Betty and niece Abigail have involved themselves in witchcraft: it is bad enough, for a Puritan minister, even to believe that they danced, as dancing was forbidden. His defensiveness fuels his zeal to join in the witch hunt with Hale and Danforth.

Proctor dislikes Parris because he views him as a worldly and greedy man who is concerned more with ownership of the minister's house and having gold candlesticks in the church than with God.

Elizabeth Proctor

Elizabeth Proctor (played by Joan Allen, who was nominated for an Academy Award for Best Supporting Actress and won a Best Supporting Actress award from the Broadcast Film Critics Association) is the wife of John Proctor. She dismissed Abigail Williams from her job working in the Proctor household when she found out about her affair with her husband. She sometimes appears cold, a quality remarked upon with some frustration by her husband.

Elizabeth, unlike her husband, is as virtuous at the beginning of the film as she is at the end. However, she goes through her own journey of self-discovery. At the film's end, she realizes that her husband genuinely loves her. For the first time, she is able to overcome her insecurity, which she realizes has been the source of her seeming coldness. She was always convinced that she was plain and that no man could honestly love her. She expresses her love for her husband and tells him that she knows he is a good man. She is fulfilled by the fact that he also knows himself to be a good man, doing the right thing in standing by the truth and refusing to make a false confession.

John Proctor

The farmer John Proctor (Daniel Day-Lewis) is the protagonist and hero of the film. He is honest and plain-speaking, and he dislikes hypocrisy in all forms. However, he has a dark secret that drives much of the film's action. Before the film opens, Proctor gave way to lust and had an affair with Abigail Williams when she was working in the Proctor household. He now regrets this and feels he made a mistake. Initially, he tries to deny to Abigail that the affair happened, though she will not accept his fabrication. Subsequently, he realizes that he can stop Abigail from ruining any more innocent people by exposing her as a fraud—but this strategy will likely bring his affair to public knowledge. He holds back from telling the truth because he wants to protect his reputation.

Proctor's maturation and redemption are shown when he eventually faces up to his sin of adultery and then admits it publicly. His personal drama parallels the public and societal drama of the witchcraft accusations and trials.

Proctor loves his virtuous wife, Elizabeth, but at the same time he feels judged by her for his transgression. He tries to please her but becomes frustrated when she reminds him of his affair. This creates a tension between the two that is resolved only in the film's final scenes, when she acknowledges the unparalleled good that she sees in him. Paradoxically, though on the surface he has lost his public good name by open admission of his adultery, he has gained something far more precious: his conviction of his inherent goodness and truthfulness. Consistent with this alliance with goodness and truth is his final refusal to sign the false confession of witchcraft, even though doing so would save his life and enable him to live on with Elizabeth and the child she is carrying.

Proctor is a flawed hero: he has done wrong, but he tries hard to be a good man and finally succeeds.

Ann Putnam

Ann Putnam (Frances Conroy) is the wife of Thomas Putnam. She is an angry and embittered woman who dwells upon the fact that seven of her eight babies died soon after birth. She chooses to blame witchcraft for her misfortune and specifically accuses Rebecca Nurse of supernaturally murdering her babies. Her main motivation is jealousy, as Rebecca has many living children and grandchildren. A secondary motivation is the hostility that simmers between the Putnam and Nurse families.

Ruth Putnam

Ruth Putnam (Ashley Peldon) is the sole surviving child of Thomas and Ann Putnam. She is one of the two girls who fall into a coma-like state after the voodoo ritual in the woods. She accuses other residents, including George Jacobs, of witchcraft, leading Giles Corey to claim that she is being manipulated by Thomas Putnam to serve his own ends.

Thomas Putnam

Thomas Putnam (Jeffrey Jones) is a wealthy landowner in Salem. He is engaged in a land dispute with Francis Nurse and also has a grudge against Nurse for preventing his brother-in-law from being appointed minister of the church. He and his family therefore have a vested interest in accusing people such as Rebecca Nurse of witchcraft. According to Giles Corey, Putnam thanks his daughter for accusing George Jacobs because he plans to buy up Jacobs's land once he has been convicted and hanged. Putnam's greed and materialism prompt him to use the witch trials to enrich himself.

Judge Sewall

Judge Sewall (George Gaynes) is one of the judges who preside over the witch trials. He expresses doubts about the reliability of the accusations of witchcraft.

Tituba

Tituba (Charlayne Woodard) is a black slave from Barbados who belongs to Reverend Parris. She leads the voodoo ritual in the woods for Abigail and her troop of girls.

Mary Warren

Mary Warren (Karron Graves) is a servant in the Proctors' household. She is weak and easily influenced. She is one of the girls who took part in the voodoo ritual and is terrified when the talk of witchcraft begins, as she knows people who are convicted of being witches are hanged. She goes to the witch trials in defiance of Proctor's order that she stay in the house. As one of the girls who accuse others of witchcraft, she quickly becomes full of her own importance when she tells Proctor that she is now an official of the court and will no longer be ordered around by him. Proctor temporarily wins her over to the idea of telling the court truthfully that the girls are frauds. However, in court, she cannot stand up to Abigail's attacks and changes sides, retracting her testimony.

Abigail Williams

Abigail Williams (Winona Ryder) is Reverend Parris's niece and the villain of the film. Duplicitous and vindictive, she initiates the accusations of witchcraft as a way of deflecting blame from herself for the voodoo ritual in the woods. She is motivated by her desire for John Proctor, following their affair when she was working in his house, and her accompanying jealousy of his wife, Elizabeth Proctor. She wants to take Elizabeth's place in their house.

Abigail is an intelligent and manipulative opportunist, who is repeatedly able to turn events to her own advantage. An example of this is the scene in which Mary Warren testifies that Abigail and the other girls are frauds. Abigail pretends convincingly that Mary is at that moment bewitching the court.

The characters in the film are all fictionalized versions of historical characters who were involved in the Salem witch trials. There is one character in the play who does not appear in the film, though her role in the play is insignificant. This is Susanna Walcott, a younger companion of Abigail. A character who appears in the film but not the play is Judge Sewall, a fictionalized version of a historical figure who helped preside over the Salem witch trials and later recanted and apologized for his part in them.

THEMES

Temptation
While the play of *The Crucible* had as its main theme the injustice of the McCarthy Red Hunts of the 1950s, by the time the film was made in 1996 these events had faded from public awareness. The film shifts the emphasis toward the theme of temptation and illicit sexual desire. As Shannon M. Clark points out in her essay "The Floating Paranoia in American Society," Bob Miller, the son of Arthur Miller and one of the producers of the film, said, "The story is really about sex. It's about relationships, it's about betrayal, it's about forgiveness."

This shift in emphasis is marked by several additions to the film that are not in the play. The opening scene of the film shows a group of girls driven to the edge of hysteria by their desire for certain men in the community. Their excitement rises as each girl names the man of her dreams. Abigail is unable to name her beloved, John Proctor, as he is married. After Abigail smashes the cockerel to the ground and drinks the blood, some of the girls begin to take off their clothes and dance.

This scene is not in the play. Its addition in the film enables viewers to judge for themselves the extent and nature of the girls' involvement in forbidden activities of dancing and witchcraft rituals. Many modern viewers will conclude that this is a trivial incident in the time-honored

tradition of amateur witchcraft with which countless children experiment, and that it has more to do with an obsession with men than an obsession with devils.

The scene frames repressed and thwarted sexual desire as a chief motivation of the film's action. This is confirmed by the addition toward the end of the film of a scene not in the play between Abigail and John Proctor. Abigail visits Proctor in prison and begs him to run away with her. Clearly in love with him, she explicitly states the motivation for her behavior: She wanted him.

Similarly, the final scene between John and Elizabeth Proctor has an extra emotional dimension in the film that is not in the play. In the play, after Elizabeth unexpectedly asks her husband to forgive her for her coldness, Proctor tells his accusers that he chooses to have his life and confess. The stage direction says that he makes this statement in a "hollow" voice and that he is "off the earth," in other words, that he belongs more to death than life. Perhaps his decision to confess comes from a realization of his duty to his wife and family, even if this means losing his good name. The sense is that he has murdered his spiritual integrity in order to keep his bodily life.

In the film, the motivation for Proctor's decision is presented quite differently. Proctor is so moved by his wife's revelations about the reasons for her coldness that his shouted declaration to his accusers that he wants to live becomes an ecstatic celebration of the couple's newfound love. Though he does not explicitly answer Elizabeth's request for forgiveness, he does not need to. Love has filled the gap that guilt and suspicion had opened up between them. When Proctor changes his mind, tears up his false confession, and submits to execution, there is a sense that he has sacrificed his bodily life in order to save his spiritual integrity.

Madness
The film shows how easily and quickly a society can lose rationality and descend into hysteria and madness. In this crazed atmosphere, whatever nonsense Abigail and her troop dream up is taken as divinely inspired truth. Conversely, any rational defense that an accused person puts up is assumed to be lies.

This hysteria is at the opposite pole to the repression of Puritan society, and it is tempting to blame the ease with which that hysteria takes over on the extremity of the repression. Perhaps if the inhabitants of Salem were not such

READ.
WATCH.
WRITE.

- Consider Miller's characterization of Elizabeth Proctor in the play and the film versions of *The Crucible*. Are there any differences? Joan Allen received high praise for her portrayal of the character in the film. Analyze Allen's performance and consider how she makes the character convincing. Give an oral presentation to the class on your findings.

- John Proctor is often described as a flawed hero, but one with whom it is easy to sympathize and identify. Hold a class discussion on this proposition, considering the way that the film character is written by Miller, performed by Daniel Day-Lewis, and directed by Nicholas Hytner. For the direction part of this question, consider any elements of the film that are within the director's control, such as lighting, setting, camera shots, editing techniques, visual symbolism, use of color, and so on.

- Research the topic of the Salem witch trials. Identify a historical or modern parallel to the witch hunts. Note any similarities and differences between the two events. What lessons can be drawn from these events? Write an essay on your findings.

- The historical figure Tituba was probably not as she is portrayed in the play and film of *The Crucible*, an African Caribbean woman, but a Native American, possibly from the Arawak peoples of South America. She was referred to in the Salem records as Tituba Indian. Using the contemporary records of the Salem witch trials (http://etext.virginia.edu/salem/witchcraft) and other sources, research what is known about Tituba and her role in the Salem witch hunt. As you do so, bear in mind her position as a slave with the Reverend Parris's household and as a woman from a different country, culture, and religion living in a white European Puritan settlement. Make notes on what relevance these factors may have had to the events that unfolded in Salem. Imagining that you are Tituba, write a diary of your life around the period of the witch trials, using your notes as a basis. Read or perform a selection of diary entries to the class.

- Research key cases in the day-care abuse trials of the 1980s and 1990s in which verdicts were subsequently overturned on appeal. Look at issues such as the reliability of witnesses, modes of investigation by the prosecution, the type of evidence that was given and accepted, and the role of judges. Why have these cases been likened to the Salem witch hunt and the McCarthy Red Scare Communist Hunts? Was any reliable evidence involved? In addition, consider at least one case in which abuse was found to have taken place and the verdict stood. What differences do you notice between this case and the cases in which verdicts were overturned? Write a report or give a class presentation on your findings.

- Research the activities of the House Committee on Un-American Activities (1938–1975). Choose a category of people investigated by the committee: for example, artists and writers, Hollywood motion picture workers, immigrants and ethnic minorities, labor union members, or government employees. Consider the arguments from both sides of the issue. Write a report or make an audio recording of your findings.

strangers to the more earthy, sensual, and irrational aspects of human nature, they would be less susceptible to believing the girls' foolish utterances.

This interpretation is backed up by the two voices of common sense, John Proctor and Rebecca Nurse. The former has given way to lust and had an affair; the second has had many

20th Century Fox | The Kobal Collection | Wetcher, Barry | The Picture Desk, Inc.

children and gained wisdom from the experience. Perhaps partly as a result of their experiences, both are more fully human than the rigid Puritans such as Danforth and Parris, who are appalled even at the possibility that the village girls danced. Neither Rebecca nor Proctor takes the accusations of witchcraft seriously, and both maintain an accurate moral compass. Although Proctor falls short of his own and society's moral standards, he is aware of what he has done wrong and struggles successfully to set his path straight. Proctor and Rebecca have a balanced view of what it means to be human, lending them an immunity to the hysteria of the witch hunt.

STYLE

Opening Montage

The opening credit sequence is a montage consisting of many close-up and blurred motion shots of the Salem girls rushing out of their houses in the night to attend Tituba's ritual. The effect is of hurried movement, effectively

conveying the girls' excitement. The low lighting of this scene is symbolic of secrecy and of occult matters.

Lighting and Setting

In the opening sequence, the low lighting makes it hard to make out faces and reflects the furtive nature of the girls' activities. Darkness also symbolizes the way the witch hunters are trying to peer into hidden, mysterious, and forbidden activities. In a wider sense, it also comments on the darkness of the worldview of the Puritans of Salem, who chose to see witches and devilry in places where it did not exist. Darkness often symbolizes ignorance, whereas light symbolizes reason and knowledge, as is shown by its incorporation into our word *enlightenment*.

The lighting is increased slightly in subsequent scenes of the interiors of the houses and church of the Salem residents, but it is still low, and the color palette is somber, dominated by browns and black. As the people's clothes and the buildings share the same dull colors, the effect is that the people merge into their surroundings. This reflects the repressive Puritan society, which emphasized modesty and disapproved of sensuality, individual expression, and standing out. The latter behavior was linked in the Puritan mind with the sins of vanity and pride.

A more brightly lit exterior scene is the one in which Abigail and John Proctor talk privately. The brighter lighting and more open setting reflect the brief period of sensual exploration and breaking of boundaries that the two experienced before their affair turned sour.

The lighting is brighter still in the scene that shows John Proctor working in his hay field. A wide horizon and an expanse of golden corn are shown under a brilliant blue sky. The effect on the viewer is like the proverbial breath of fresh air. The setting reflects the commonsense, enlightened attitude of Proctor, who is a voice of reason in the film. Unlike many of the residents of Salem, he does not naturally inhabit dark and claustrophobic interiors. While the tense scene between him and his wife takes place in the dark interior of their house, Proctor is not at ease. He complains to his wife that it still feels like winter in the house and says he will cut some flowers to bring inside. This remark allies him with the blue sky and golden corn of the previous brightly lit exterior shots rather than with the dark interior.

The scene in which Proctor stands in the river like the biblical prophet John the Baptist, amid a crowd of accusers, also uses lighting and setting to make a point. Here, the dark obsession with witchcraft and devilry, in the form of a baying mob of witch-obsessed girls and men, has invaded an Edenic landscape, with its purifying water. Notably, however, Proctor is left standing in the river while the hysterical girls and judges scream from the banks. They do not quite belong in the purity of the river, but Proctor does, with the bright blue sky illuminating his figure.

A setting including water is also used in the reconciliation scene between Proctor and his wife, which takes place against the well-lit background of the sea. The unsullied vastness of the ocean reflects the expansion that has taken place in the awareness of these two characters. For the first time, they accept and love one another for who they truly are, with no suspicion or jealousy polluting their perception.

It is fitting that the final execution scene, in which Proctor, Martha, and Rebecca are martyred for their adherence to the truth, is shot against a bright and clear blue sky. The three are also elevated above their accusers because they are standing on the scaffold. The effect is to show that their perceptions are unclouded and that they stand for truth and purity.

The play does not make use of the contrast between interiors and exteriors in the same way as the film because it is entirely set in interiors. Symbolic effects using lighting may be used by theater directors, but the Edenic settings of the Massachusetts landscape would be harder to reproduce or suggest in a theater.

Christian Symbolism

After Elizabeth Proctor perjures herself in court to save her husband's reputation, Abigail whips up the girls into a frenzy over her pretence that Mary is bewitching them, and they all run to the river and plunge in. Danforth accuses Proctor of being in league with the devil. The visual symbolism shows the truth, however. At this point, Proctor is the only person still in the river. The image symbolically recalls the biblical image of John the Baptist, who predicted the coming of the Messiah (later interpreted in the Gospels as Jesus Christ), promised God's justice, and baptized people in the river to purify them of sin.

Proctor's choice of this moment to proclaim that God is dead underlines the biblical symbolism and creates situational irony. This is a literary device in which the outcome of events proves to be opposite to the one that was intended, expected, or deserved. Whereas John the Baptist promised God's justice, Proctor is lamenting the apparent absence of God's justice in a world turned upside down by hysteria. A further ironic twist lies in the fact that Danforth and the hysterical girls take Proctor's words to confirm their notion that he is in league with the devil, whereas to the viewer, his words testify to his alliance with the truth.

Christian symbolism recurs in the scene of Proctor's execution. Proctor's position on the scaffold between Martha and Rebecca symbolically recalls the crucifixion of Jesus Christ between two other people. This symbolic connection with Christ gives Proctor an aura of holy innocence. The fact that he recites the Lord's Prayer shows his alliance with God rather than the devil. The fact that he hangs before he can finish the prayer symbolically shows the tragedy of a life brutally cut short. It also strikes the viewer as sacrilegious, as to cut people short before they finish a prayer shows disrespect for their religion and for the god to whom they pray. It tells the viewer that the true lover of God (Proctor) has died on the scaffold, while those who persecuted him have done evil in God's name.

The portrayal of Proctor as the Christ figure makes a moral point. Proctor was tortured, during his life, by the knowledge of his sinful affair. His persecutors, on the other hand, believe that they are on the side of purity and truth. The symbolism cuts through such delusions and draws the moral landscape precisely for the viewer, showing who is right and who is wrong.

CULTURAL CONTEXT

Spectral Evidence and Other Legal Anomalies

In the film *The Crucible*, most of the accusations of witchcraft depend upon spectral evidence. Spectral evidence is evidence based on dreams and visions. A person giving spectral evidence might testify that the alleged witch had sent out his or her spirit in the form of a bird, animal, or other creature. Spectral evidence is impossible to disprove because no witnesses are required and the accused does not even have to be physically present at the scene of the alleged crime. Because the spirit can take any form, it does not even have to look like the alleged witch.

All that is required in the way of spectral evidence is for someone to denounce someone else. As is pointed out in the film of *The Crucible* by several characters, this opens the door for people who wish to take revenge on people against whom they harbor grudges. For example, Rebecca Nurse is accused by the Putnams due to bad feeling over the minister, land, and Ann Putnam's dead babies.

In the historical Salem witch trials, spectral evidence was allowed in a court of law by the presiding judge, William Stoughton. A precedent was cited from a 1662 witch trial in Bury St. Edmunds, Suffolk, England. Stoughton does not appear as a character in Miller's play or film, though many of his questionable legal decisions are transferred to the character of Judge Danforth.

According to Stoughton's biography on the University of Missouri-Kansas City School of Law Web site, Stoughton had no formal legal training, and his degree was in theology. The biography notes that he "allowed many deviations from normal courtroom procedure during the witchcraft trials. In addition to admitting spectral evidence, the court allowed private conversations between accusers and judges, permitted spectators to interrupt the procedures with personal remarks, [forbade] defense counsel for the accused, and placed judges in the role of prosecutors and interrogators of witnesses."

The main legal problem with the Salem witch trials was that once people had been accused of being witches, it was difficult for them prove their innocence and be set free. The penalty for witchcraft was hanging, and the only way to escape hanging was to confess to being a witch. Therefore, an accused person had the choice between denying the charge and being hanged, or confessing and living with the stigma of being a self-confessed witch.

Senator Joe McCarthy and the Red Hunts

Miller wrote the play *The Crucible* as an indictment of the anticommunist hysteria that gripped the United States in the 1950s. Its most prominent proponent and public face was U.S. Senator Joseph McCarthy. Because of the Cold War (the tensions between the United States and the Soviet Union that grew after World War II), some Americans in government and elsewhere feared that communists were infiltrating and attempting to subvert American society. A large number of politicians, artists, writers, actors, intellectuals, government employees, and other Americans were interrogated by government and private industry committees and investigated for alleged communist sympathies. People lost their jobs, and some were even imprisoned, frequently on the basis of flimsy evidence and dubious legal procedures.

The hearings later came to be known as Red Hunts and subsequently as witch hunts, in reference to the Salem witch trials. The term McCarthyism has passed into the language to describe any reckless and unsubstantiated allegations against a set of people.

Many of Miller's friends and colleagues were summoned to testify before the House Committee on Un-American Activities (HUAC), a Congressional committee that investigated alleged communists and fascists. This committee, which was not directly connected with McCarthy, began its activities in 1947. Among those who were called to testify before the HUAC was the theater director Elia Kazan, who had directed many of Miller's plays. Kazan appeared before the committee in 1952. In an attempt to avoid being blacklisted

The Kobal Collection. Reproduced by permission.

and banned from working in Hollywood, he named eight people as one-time members of the Communist Party. Miller spoke to Kazan about his testimony immediately before traveling to Salem to research *The Crucible*. In 1956, Miller himself was called to testify before the HUAC but refused to name names. As a result, in 1957 he was convicted of contempt of Congress, though the ruling was overturned in 1958.

Public Outrage in Modern Society

By the time Miller adapted his play as a film in 1996, Soviet communism had collapsed and McCarthy's Red Hunts had faded from public awareness. However, prurient interest in other sorts of behavior commonly thought to be deviant from the cultural norm was lively. Media reports proliferated about the sex scandal involving President Bill Clinton and Paula Jones, which went to court in January 1997, two months after the film's release. The focus of public outrage at this time was not witchcraft or communism but extramarital affairs. Reflecting this cultural shift, the theme of illicit sexual desire is more to the forefront in the film of *The Crucible* than it is in the play.

Modern Witch Hunts

While fear of communists has receded, fear of the devil has not vanished from contemporary society. Thus the film *The Crucible* is able to tap into this lingering fear. In the 1980s and 1990s, in the United States and other countries, there was a rash of child abuse trials in which children and adults accused day-care center workers, parents, and others of crimes from molestation to Satanic ritual abuse. The phenomenon came to be known as day-care abuse hysteria. Some of the accused were given long prison sentences on flimsy evidence. In many cases, their convictions were subsequently overturned when aspects of the trials were questioned.

Legal anomalies in these cases included the acceptance of hearsay evidence; the acceptance of evidence from unreliable witnesses, including mentally ill and alcoholic people; the assumption of the truth of the psychological theory of repressed memory, in which traumatic events become unavailable to recall until they surface under certain circumstances; the assumption that any child who said that abuse had not taken place was in denial and therefore wrong; interviewer bias; and coercive questioning and leading of witnesses by the prosecution.

CRITICAL OVERVIEW

The Crucible was in general well received by film reviewers. James Berardinelli, writing for *Reel-Views*, notes that the universality of the play makes it particularly suitable for adaptation to film at this later date. He writes that although the play was written as an allegory on the McCarthy period, "its true power lies in its ability to be re-interpreted to fit any time period." Berardinelli explains that its themes—"the lure of power, the gullibility of those who believe they have a moral imperative, the need to accept responsibility for the consequences of all actions, and the nature of truth—are universal in scope." As proof of this thesis, Berardinelli adds that events such as those depicted in the play "have recurred with alarming predictability throughout human history."

Berardinelli singles out the performances of Daniel Day-Lewis (John Proctor), Karron Graves (Mary Warren), Joan Allen (Elizabeth Proctor), and Paul Scofield (Judge Danforth) for praise. He sums up the film as "a motion picture of surprising emotional and intellectual impact."

Jeff Strickler, reviewing the film for the *Star Tribune*, agrees that it has much contemporary relevance: "While the 17th century and the Red Menace are long gone, Miller and director Nicholas Hytner have had no trouble finding other contemporary veins. This is a story about fear, the corrosive power of bigotry and the abuse of power."

A reviewer for *Rolling Stone* calls *The Crucible* "a seductively exciting film that crackles with visual energy, passionate provocation and incendiary acting." The reviewer writes that Miller's screenplay is "a model of adventurous film adaptation, showing a master eager to mine his most-performed play for fresh insights instead of embalming it." The reviewer considers the standout performances to be those of Ryder, Day-Lewis, Scofield, and Allen.

Victor Navasky, writing in the *New York Times*, believes that the Salem witch hunts provide the basis of a film with great contemporary relevance: "As I think about the sex, supernatural religion, politics and paranoia that boil and bubble in the Miller and Hytner brew, it occurs to me that *The Crucible* was probably destined for Hollywood all along."

THE WITCHCRAFT HYSTERIA IN *THE CRUCIBLE* TURNS SALEM'S RIGID POWER STRUCTURE ON ITS HEAD."

CRITICISM

Claire Robinson

Robinson holds a master's degree in English. In this essay on The Crucible, *she examines how the film and play explore the relationship between power, responsibility, and intolerance, and she discusses the relevance of these topics today.*

Although the Puritans who founded Salem were fleeing religious persecution in England, they established a society that was equally intolerant. This time, their society was in line with their beliefs. The oppressed became the oppressors. The play and film of *The Crucible* show how the rigidity built into every level of Puritan Salem society gave birth to the witchcraft hysteria that destroyed it.

The new society of Salem was a theocracy. A theocracy is a government that claims to rule by divine authority, as opposed to a secular state, in which the state and religion are separate. Anyone who disagreed with elements of Salem's governance was thus seen as opposing God and supporting the devil. Similarly, anyone who disagreed with the theology laid down by the governing authorities was seen as a subversive who threatened the social order.

In Salem, things were seen in terms of right or wrong, good or evil. As Danforth says of the witch trials in the film of *The Crucible*, a person is either with the court or against it: there is no road in-between. People could be tried in court and executed for having the wrong ideas or transgressing against the edicts of the officially sanctioned religion. The authorities claimed that they ruled with divine sanction, and their power was absolute. The individual had little say in how society was run.

Rigidity of belief was reflected in strict rules for behavior. Any deviation from correct behavior was viewed as a sin against God, as well as an act against local authority. The Puritans viewed

WHAT DO I SEE NEXT?

- *The Scarlet Letter* is an indictment of intolerance in seventeenth-century Puritan New England, based on the novel of the same name by Nathaniel Hawthorne (who was a descendant of John Hathorne, one of the judges who presided over the Salem witch trials). In the film, a woman has an adulterous affair and is forced to wear a scarlet letter as a public sign of her sin. The four-episode television adaptation made by WGBH in 1979 is more highly rated by reviewers and more faithful to the novel than the 1995 film version, which starred Demi Moore and Gary Oldman and was directed by Roland Joffé. The WGBH version, starring Meg Foster and Josef Sommer, was directed by Rick Hauer. The DVD of this version was released in 2003.

- *Cromwell* (1970; DVD version released in 2003) is a fictionalized film biography of Oliver Cromwell (played in this movie by Richard Harris), the Puritan military leader who led the anti-Royalist, pro-Parliament Roundhead forces in the English Civil War (1641–1651). In the Civil War, King Charles I was executed, and Cromwell became the head of the new Commonwealth of England. The film shows how at this point in history and in this place, the Puritans were the force for freedom of religion and of the individual. This movie was directed by Ken Hughes.

- *The New Puritans: The Sikhs of Yuba City* is a critically acclaimed 1985 documentary film about the Indian Sikh immigrants who came to Yuba City, California, to live in the early 1900s, creating a rural life that mirrored the one they had left in India. The film was made by the Center for Asian American Media and focuses on the generational conflicts between traditional value systems and the growing influence of American ways. It was directed by Tenzing Sonam Ritu Sarin. The DVD version was released in 2008.

- *A Man for All Seasons* (1966) is a film adaptation of the 1954 play of the same name by Robert Bolt, who also wrote the screenplay. Set in sixteenth-century England, it tells the story of the standoff between King Henry VIII and Sir Thomas More, who refused as a matter of conscience to approve the king's divorce. The story has parallels with that of John Proctor in *The Crucible*. The film, directed by Fred Zinnemann, won six Academy Awards, including Best Picture, with Paul Scofield winning the Award for Best Actor for his portrayal of More. The DVD version was released in 2007.

- *The Children's Hour* (1961) is a classic film adaptation of Lillian Hellman's 1934 play of the same name. It is the story of two head-mistresses of an exclusive school for girls who are falsely accused by a malicious child of having a lesbian relationship. The film stars Audrey Hepburn and Shirley MacLaine, and it was directed by William Wyler. The DVD was released in 2002.

- *12 Angry Men* (1957), directed by Sidney Lumet, is a courtroom thriller about a young Puerto Rican accused of murdering his father. Eleven members of an all-white, all-male jury are convinced that the boy is guilty, but one (played by Henry Fonda) has doubts. It falls to him to convince the others of his point of view. The film is a critically acclaimed examination of racial prejudice and cultural differences. The DVD was released in 2008.

---

material and sensual desires and individuality of thought with suspicion, believing that they were the devil's work. Children, and to a great extent

women, were expected to be seen and not heard. They were expected to dress modestly, to walk along the street with eyes downcast and arms demurely by their sides, and not to speak unless asked. Dancing and any hint of lascivious or flirtatious behavior was forbidden. Dabbling in witchcraft rituals was seen as deliberately invoking the devil himself. Thus, in the eyes of Salem's authorities, the girls who dance are doubly guilty, and Abigail is thrice guilty: her adulterous affair, if known, would mark her as an outcast.

The social structure, too, in a Puritan society such as Salem was highly stratified, with almost all the power concentrated at the top and the rest of society relatively powerless. Near the bottom of the social hierarchy were unmarried girls like Abigail and her companions. The girls who become the accusers in *The Crucible* are both children and female, and so are doubly powerless. Below the unmarried girls were slaves like Tituba, who had no power or rights. A person could not do much to change his or her position in the hierarchy. Marriage would marginally improve a woman's social position, but generally speaking, this would mark the limit of social mobility.

The witchcraft hysteria in *The Crucible* turns Salem's rigid power structure on its head. When the girls are discovered dancing in the woods and dabbling in witchcraft, the full force of society's disapproval is set to descend upon them. Like all Salem residents, they are aware that they face disproportionately severe punishments for relatively minor transgressions. By accusing others of witchcraft, the girls escape punishment for their own transgressions and make others appear to be the sinners. In a wider sense, they are able to off-load responsibility for their actions. If witches and the devil, acting through apparently respectable members of society, are to blame for the forbidden voodoo ritual—not to mention for many of the everyday misfortunes of Salem residents—then the girls are innocent. Accused of any transgression, they can simply say that the devil made them do it.

Furthermore, because the girls claim to be able to see spirits, they are instantly elevated to the privileged position of holy prophets or seers who have direct communication with the divine. It is perceived that their word is identical with God's word, and those who defend the people accused of witchcraft ally themselves with the devil. The girls are able to enjoy a sense of great power over others, perhaps for the first and last time. As their leader, Abigail has gone from outcast adulteress to God's representative on earth in one ingenious stroke.

Other characters also evade responsibility for their actions through accusing others of being witches. Ann Putnam is able to shift responsibility for her inability to bear healthy children or to keep them alive once born by accusing Rebecca Nurse of murdering them. Abigail is able to avoid answering Mary Warren's testimony that she is making fraudulent claims about witchcraft by pretending that Mary is bewitching the court. Thomas Putnam is able to avoid the effort of acquiring land by honest means when his family accuses landowners like George Jacobs and the Nurses of witchcraft: They will be executed, their land will be forfeit, and he will be able to buy it.

Accusing others thus becomes an attractive option with no downsides except bad conscience—and this can be silenced by the prevailing ideology that the accusers are aligned with God whereas the accused are aligned with the devil.

As a black woman, a foreigner, a person brought up in a non-Christian religion, and a slave, Tituba occupies the lowest position in the social hierarchy of a seventeenth-century white Puritan town such as Salem. It would be natural for her to relish the temporary increase in status and power that she would enjoy as priestess of the voodoo ritual.

Tituba's relatively innocent foray into a powerful role takes a tragic turn when she is made a scapegoat by Abigail. Abigail shifts suspicion of witchcraft from herself by accusing Tituba of summoning the devil. Tituba is whipped mercilessly until she begins naming names of supposed witches.

In the play, Tituba is interrogated but not whipped. This difference in the film strengthens the theme of racial and class prejudice and makes clear the psychological process through which she becomes a false informer. When she tells the truth and protests her own or others' innocence, she is tortured. When she lies and begins denouncing others as witches, the whipping stops and she is praised and blessed. By contributing to the witch frenzy, she is able to transform herself from a powerless victim to someone who wields the power of life and death over others.

If less rigid people—for instance, John Proctor or Rebecca Nurse—had been in charge in the Salem of the film, things would have turned out differently. Proctor and Nurse take a realistic and practical view of things. Realistically viewed, even to the present day, occult rituals have provided a fertile field of experimentation for young people who want to attract the attention of a member of the opposite sex. For example, many women alive today will remember childhood adventures such as staring into a mirror flanked by two candles on the eve of May Day (May 1) in the hope that their future husband's face will be revealed to them, or consulting a Ouija board for the name of a future lover. The girls of Salem, if spared the fear of being whipped or hanged for dancing and taking part in a love ritual, would have moved on from experimenting with the occult to other ways of attracting lovers, just as millions of young people of all historical periods have done.

The written coda at the end of the film of *The Crucible* explains that as fewer people were willing to give false confessions, the witch trials died out. Thus, the scene was set for a more liberal society to take form in the United States, complete with constitutional safeguards on freedom of belief and expression. The witch trials, a suppression of individuality with few historical precedents, helped lay the groundwork for an age in which individuality is prized and defended.

Because of these developments, it is tempting to assume that the modern secular and democratic state is free from the intolerance that afflicted Salem. However, this assumption is not borne out by the evidence. As many commentators point out, the message of *The Crucible* has as much relevance today as it ever did.

On matters of religion and belief, in theory, the secular state is neutral. It guarantees freedom of religion and belief and treats all people the same regardless of their beliefs. Nevertheless, most officially secular states do involve themselves to some extent in the religious affairs of the individual. For example, since President George W. Bush pronounced that the United States was involved in a war on terrorism following the attacks of September 11, 2001, there has been increased state surveillance of people and operations identified with what are described as extreme forms of Islam. In some situations, people do not have to have been convicted of a crime to be placed under surveillance. It can be argued that this development has led to certain religious beliefs becoming criminalized and that the old

assumption that a person is innocent until proven guilty has been set aside.

States also attempt to stamp out radical and unorthodox ideas and activities. In the United States, in the wake of the war on terrorism came the concept of the domestic extremist. According to a report by FOXNews.com, in March 2009 the Department of Homeland Security (DHS) released the "Domestic Extremism Lexicon," which details activist groups working in areas as diverse as animal rights, environment, tax resistance, alternative media, antiabortion, and Cuban independence, and analyzes "the nature and scope of the threat" that they pose. The report draws a link between so-called extremism and terrorism. FOXNews.com says the report was withdrawn within hours of its release and the DHS claimed that a "maverick" division of the agency had released it without authorization. As laws already exist against acts of terrorism and violence, placing such groups under surveillance based on the possibility that they might commit such illegal acts would appear to criminalize unorthodox ideas.

In a review of the film of *The Crucible* in the *New York Times*, Navasky writes: "The old nativist impulse that identified the foreign with the radical and the immoral is ever present in *The Crucible* and speaks to a theme in American history that includes not only Salem and McCarthyism but the Alien and Sedition Acts, the Palmer raids and countless other mobilizations grand and mini—in the face of the unfamiliar." Navasky adds, "There may not be any more domestic Communist menace, but 'Arab' is in too many quarters a code word for 'terrorist.'"

The film's director, Nicholas Hytner (quoted by Edward Rothstein in a review for the *New York Times*), also finds no shortage of contemporary subjects that the drama speaks about: "the bigotry of religious fundamentalists across the globe," "communities torn apart by accusations of child abuse," and "the rigid intellectual orthodoxies of college campuses."

Miller gives his own explanation for the universality of *The Crucible* in an interview with Navasky in the same *New York Times* review: "I have had immense confidence in the applicability of the play to almost any time, the reason being it's dealing with a paranoid situation. But that situation doesn't depend on any particular political or sociological development. I wrote it blind to the world. The enemy is within, and within stays within, and we can't get out of within. It's always on the edge of our minds that behind what we see is a nefarious plot."

Source: Claire Robinson, Critical Essay on *The Crucible*, in *Drama for Students*, Gale, Cengage Learning, 2010.

Marie Morgan

In the following review, the 1996 film is described as a "play that actively invites transformation into a film."

"[O]ne of the strangest and most awful chapters in human history" is how the playwright Arthur Miller describes the Salem, Massachusetts, witchcraft persecution, that profoundly disturbing moment in our early history which many Americans today perceive entirely through the medium of *The Crucible*. This is a play that actively invites transformation into a film. It is a classic courtroom drama. There are subtly drawn characters whose imperfections and manipulability are displayed on every hand, characters engaged moreover in bringing about reversals of fortune: the humble drag down the proud; children humiliate parents; women strip men of power; persons of mean intellect bamboozle learned jurists and clergymen. Belief in supernaturalism cuts a wide swath through the drama, contesting every scene with its opposite number—social psychology. And, like all theatre of the bench and bar, it raises fundamental questions of fairness and propriety in the cumbersome mechanisms of the legal system and the blinkered men sworn to uphold it.

The setting—Hog Island, a nature preserve off the coast of Ipswich, where the film's makers threw up a convincing replica of a Puritan village—is a study in chiaroscuro. Ubiquitous pigs and goats, bristly creatures with spindly shanks, are animals now seen only in the turf-and-byre settings of farm parks devoted to endangered livestock. Four-square buildings with intricately laid stone foundations and handsomely thatched roofs are so comely in their spartan appointments as to take one's breath away. Gardens abound with the herbs and roots that would have been used by Puritans to physick themselves. Complexions are careworn, marred by smuts and scars; fingernails are begrimed, teeth stained and snaggled. Rubbed garments are handstitched and vegetable-dyed to reproduce a New England boiled dinner palette, varied a little by faded crimson and Prussian blue. Only men in authority are garbed in black, with steeple-crowned hats and Geneva bands.

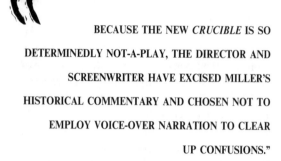

BECAUSE THE NEW *CRUCIBLE* IS SO DETERMINEDLY NOT-A-PLAY, THE DIRECTOR AND SCREENWRITER HAVE EXCISED MILLER'S HISTORICAL COMMENTARY AND CHOSEN NOT TO EMPLOY VOICE-OVER NARRATION TO CLEAR UP CONFUSIONS."

To say that this is a sumptuous undertaking hardly does justice to the production values of *The Crucible*. To say that this is repertory acting of a high calibre cannot convey the emotional richness and intelligence of the performances. Daniel Day-Lewis, Rob Campbell, Winona Ryder, and Jeffrey Jones lend the film resonance and honesty. It is, however, Paul Scofield, playing Deputy Governor Danforth, Joan Allen as Elizabeth Proctor, and Karron Graves as the dim maidservant who give truly impressive performances. Scofield's Danforth is a man resolute for truth, having to ransack his intellect and learning in circumstances where testimony is bogged in credulity and extra-legal procedures in a community wracked by vendettas, land grabs, and the litigious strife we have come to associate with New England Puritanism. As Proctor's wife, Joan Allen, with silences more reproachful than speech and glances in which blame and pity are terribly mingled, makes us understand how the bond between man and wife, strained through sexual infidelity, can withstand every test placed on it by a vengeful community. Grave's handling of the difficult role of reluctant recruit to Abigail Williams's cadre of accusers is the most convincing detail in what is shown to be a reign of terror.

Comparison of the text of the 1953 play with the screenplay finds the author opening up his story. How he re-conceives the play is made clear from the outset. Repressed sexuality breaking out of bounds will drive the action of the film more explicitly than it did the play. A nocturnal gathering of Salem's adolescent females in the forest sets the tone for the new *Crucible*. Gleefully entreating the slave Tituba to distribute charms and work spells to draw in their intended lovers, the girls appear to be out for a heathenish good time. The Reverend Samuel Parris bursts in upon the revelers just as Abigail slashes the throat of a cock, sending Parris's daughter into a mysterious swoon. This new scene replaces the play's first commentary. There Miller explains that "the virgin forest was the Devil's last preserve" and goes on to assert that "for good purposes, even high purposes, the people of Salem developed a theocracy, a combine of state and religious power" (*The Crucible: A Play in Four Acts* [New York, 1953], pp. 3, 5)—a gross misconception of remarkable staying power. This fateful, and lethal, intermingling of worldly and otherworldly power is central to Miller's vision of a society badly out of joint and peculiarly prone to catastrophic imaginings.

Given sufficient ambiguity, indeterminacy, and the kind of ironies historians delight in, any drama will crash of its own intellectual weight. Miller and Hytner have not encumbered the film in this fashion. They telescope the witchcraft hysteria into (apparently) a few weeks and misrepresent the legalities of the case—John Hale is made by Miller to serve double duty in the roles of clergyman, expert witness, and special prosecutor. This tightens up the play and film considerably, sparing us *longueurs* of exposition. Even so, a historian is bound to ask what is going on when filmmakers creatively develop a notorious historical episode as a means of interpreting, and explicitly universalizing, the American psyche and character. Because the new *Crucible* is so determinedly not-a-play, the director and screenwriter have excised Miller's historical commentary and chosen not to employ voice-over narration to clear up confusions. To the extent that the actors' intelligence convinces us of the calamitous destruction of trust, the result is all to the good. And yet, insofar as we are meant to see the Salem episode whole, the film creates its own puzzles, mysteries that are not resolved by recourse to the screenplay. To choose one example, why is Samuel Sewall—absent from the play—inserted into the film? He seems peripheral to the proceedings, a whingeing spectator, not the honest man of God who would later offer public contrition for his role in the witchcraft hysteria. And what of the Reverend Hale, a man who begins as a case-hardened witch-smeller but emerges as the sole clerical dissenter from the fell work of Governor Danforth? His conversion to the role of critic is based on scattered indications that the accusers are not

what they say they are and on a palpable fear of being on deck when the cannon tears loose from its carriage. What are we to make of poor Giles Corey, here depicted as a somewhat addle-pated bruiser, addicted to litigation and sufficiently cunning in the law to dig a pit for himself? The pseudo-legal justification given by Danforth in the film for subjecting Corey to pressing under slabs of granite makes nonsense of the historical Corey's principled refusal to plead before the Court of Oyer and Terminer. Instead, Miller has Danforth kill Corey because he refuses to name the villager whose hearsay testimony Corey cites in hopes of discrediting Thomas Putnam, whose grasping ways and excessive influence with the inquisitors are shown to fuel the tragedy.

The storyline of *The Crucible* is as straightforward as anyone could ask. Indeed, some plot devices that are meant to move the story along smack of contrivance. We are shown a proud Tituba screaming defiance at Samuel Parris, who plies a rope to her back to coerce the initial confession of dealings with the devil. But then, like Sewall, Tituba does a fast fade. Despite the filmmakers' insistence that this is a film about sexuality seeking dark outlets, what we are shown of the accusers' gabblings and posturings does little to convey sexual or erotic yearnings. The sexuality on view here is that of Abigail Williams, who instigates and artfully channels the rantings of her girlish coterie as a means of punishing John Proctor. And lest anyone be inclined to think that the Salemites have a plausible reason for their wholesale scape-goatings of the unpopular and unhinged amongst them, Williams, who has defamed dozens so as to secure the conviction of Proctor's wife, conveniently declares herself false. She flees the jurisdiction after rifling her master's money box to steal the fare for a ship making for Barbados, the very place from which Tituba was carried away a slave years before.

Though we are to imagine ourselves in a world where superstition presses in upon the steady practices and rigorous mentality of these Puritans, the sources of the fears rousting the phlegmatic yeomen and sanctimonious notables remain obscure. We see that the people are scared, but the orchestrated howls and twitches that make up the bewitchment scenes, while unseemly, are far from terrifying. The intent is to demonstrate the malleability of people in the mass, bent on working off the old grudges of an insular community. This is because the cards are stacked so heavily in favor of rationalism and empiricism, specifically, social psychological models of crowd behavior. We are meant to think not only of the Army-McCarthy hearings but also of the McMartin child molestation trials. Or perhaps the Tawana Brawley incident will come to mind.

Tellingly, what there is of God in the Salem of witchcraft times is formal and pat. The clergy are shown as self-deluded and cowardly, while the accusers are prompt to invoke God and his blessings upon their vaporings and caperings. A climactic scene presents a "mass exodus" where "unbounded hysteria sweeps the CROWD of people who ... run after the GIRLS" into the sea, a kind of parody of group baptism. Mary Warren, the house servant whom Proctor is counting on to expose the accusers' fakery, shrieks, "You're the Devil's man! I go your way no more, I love God," while the villagers chant their approval of her pious expostulations. Her master, seeing how easily swayed his people are, proclaims, "I say you are pulling Heaven down and raising up a whore! I say God is dead!" (*The Crucible: Screenplay* [New York, 1996], pp. 78–79). Downright blasphemy, as this speech plainly is, would have shaken and angered the Puritans of Salem as much as, if not more than, vague allegations of witchcraft. Yet Proctor's shocking declaration goes unpunished, though he is hanged on the other charge.

This declaration of the death of God is the ultimate message of *The Crucible*. Proctor, having snatched at freedom through a lie, tears up the confession that would have blackened his name. He is left in the end only with personal loyalty, loyalty to his good name and to the married love he shares with Elizabeth. That he, and the women who share the gallows with him, die with the Lord's Prayer on their lips does not prove that God is, after all, alive in Salem. The Miller-Hytner collaboration is an absorbing film framed around a whole-souled secularism. We are brought, through the glamour of exceptional acting and direction, to see what a given community, in the throes of a given hysteria, can be cozened into believing, repudiating in the process any notions of propriety, safety, or the right of private judgment. Over against the paranoia, the mob mentality, and the colorable arguments for perverting justice, Miller and Hytner give us

not the redemptive power of faith but the refusal to purchase freedom with a lie.

Source: Marie Morgan, Review of *The Crucible*, in *New England Quarterly*, Vol. 70, No. 1, March 1997, pp. 125–29.

Alicia A. Herrera
In the following review, Herrera believes that Miller's play plot makes The Crucible *a successful film.*

After the debacle of the completely rewritten Demi Moore film, *The Scarlet Letter*, the idea of Hollywood presenting yet another historical drama focusing on intolerance and set in the time of the Puritans is somewhat unpleasant to contemplate. But *The Crucible* has a very powerful plus on its side—the screenplay was written by Arthur Miller based on his own powerful play, and thus the story was saved from the possibility of suddenly getting a happy ending just to satisfy the ideas of studio honchos on what makes a good story.

The Crucible tells the tale of the Salem witch trials. It starts with a group of girls going into the woods in the dead of night to dance and brew up love spells. Things go bad when they are seen by the town's preacher, who catches his daughter and niece participating in the illicit activities.

The following day, two of the youngest girls become "afflicted," and do not wake up. The idea that they are bewitched gains credence, and the whole mess escalates when the girls as a group start accusing townspeople of consorting with the devil—as victims of bewitchment, they are safe from prosecution of witchcraft for which they could be hanged. This quickly degenerates into an orgy of accusations as greed and revenge start to color the proceedings and accusations. And in the perverse logic of witch hunting, those who confess to being witches are released while those who profess their innocence are killed.

The main accuser, Abigail Williams (Winona Ryder), is the parson's niece and is deeply in love with John Procter (Daniel Day-Lewis), an upstanding and God-fearing farmer for whose family she used to work and with whom she had a short affair. She was dismissed by his sickly wife, Elizabeth (Joan Allen), when this was discovered. Abigail accuses Elizabeth of witchcraft, hoping to gain John if his wife is no longer in the way, but he quickly becomes implicated himself.

He finds himself faced with a dilemma—lie, confess and live, or be truthful, keep his good name and die.

Arthur Miller wrote the play in the '50s as a reaction to the McCarthy witch hunt for communists which he equated with those of Salem centuries earlier—all it took was an accusation without evidence to do the damage.

The film is less powerful than the play on which it is based. While being faithful to the original, the very setting of the movie works against it. The play is claustrophobic, set in the closed tight rooms of Salem, focusing attention on the conflict between truth and the lie. Simply by having so much of the film outside in the open, this claustrophobic atmosphere, which heightened the paranoia of the story, is weakened.

Miller also shows what happened in the woods, a scene which is talked about in the play but which is not shown. Simply by not being shown in the play, it keeps an air of the mysterious—nobody really knows what happened and this makes the subsequent accusations more frightening. But showing it in the film, the mystery is erased, leaving the audience less of an understanding of how terrified people at that time were of the devil and his associates.

And somehow the focus of the film, instead of being on the community's frightened reaction to having witches in its midst, is moved to the personal conflict between John, Abigail and Elizabeth. But this does not really detract from the story, unless one has seen the play done beforehand.

Daniel Day-Lewis does a fine job as Proctor, giving his patented tortured passionate act which he does so well (think of *My Left Foot* and *In the Name of the Father*). Winona Ryder takes the antagonist's role in the film and shows that her reputation as the finest actress in her generation is deserved. But again, this is not a stretch for her.

Outstanding is Joan Allen as Elizabeth. Giving a much more subdued performance compared to the other two, she comes out the stronger presence. Just by standing quietly erect in the background of a scene, she draws the audience's attention.

Director Nicholas Hytner, in his Hollywood film debut (he is well-known in the Philippines as the director of the Cameron Mackintosh musical *Miss Saigon*), shows a definite talent for filmmaking. His powerful visuals move the story along and heighten the tension in a tale that to the thinking person is much more frightening than any slasher film.

Source: Alicia A. Herrera, "Arthur Miller's Play Gets Hollywood Nod: *The Crucible*," in *Business World*, May 2, 1997.

SOURCES

"1958: Arthur Miller Cleared of Contempt," in *On This Day: 1950–2005*, British Broadcasting Corporation (BBC), http://news.bbc.co.uk/onthisday/hi/dates/stories/august/7/newsid_2946000/2946420.stm (accessed July 1, 2009).

Berardinelli, James, Review of *The Crucible*, in *ReelViews*, 1996, http://www.reelviews.net/movies/c/crucible.html (accessed July 2, 2009).

Chira, Susan, "Recovered Reputations," in *New York Times*, April 6, 2003, http://www.nytimes.com/2003/04/06/books/recovered-reputations.html (accessed July 2, 2009).

Clark, Shannon M., "The Floating Paranoia in American Society," in *Paper to Flesh: Explorations of Performance*, Senior Seminar, State University of West Georgia, Spring 2001, p. 24, http://www.westga.edu/~engdept/dp/AnthSS/hartleyanth_s01.pdf (accessed July 1, 2009).

Frank, Reuven, "'I Have Here in My Hand a List...,'" in *New Leader*, Vol. 86, No. 6, November-December 2003, pp. 47–49.

Latner, Richard, "The Long and Short of Salem Witchcraft: Chronology and Collective Violence in 1692," in *Journal of Social History*, Vol. 42, No. 1, Fall 2008, pp. 137–56.

Marino, Steven A., "Arthur Miller," in *Dictionary of Literary Biography*, Vol. 266, *Twentieth-Century American Dramatists, Fourth Series*, edited by Christopher J. Wheatley, Thomson Gale, 2003, pp. 185–209.

"'Maverick' DHS Office Issues Glossary of Domestic Extremist Groups," in *FOXNews.com*, May 5, 2009, http://www.foxnews.com/politics/2009/05/05/maverick-dhs-office-issues-dictionary-domestic-ex tremist-groups/ (accessed July 2, 2009).

Miller, Arthur, *The Crucible*, Penguin Classics, 2000.

Navasky, Victor, "The Demons of Salem, with Us Still," in *New York Times*, September 8, 1996, http://movies.nytimes.com/movie/review?res=940CE0DB1038F93BA3575AC0A960958260 (accessed July 2, 2009).

Norton, May Beth, "Finding the Devil in the Details of the Salem Witchcraft Trials," in *Chronicle of Higher Education*, Vol. 46, No. 20, January 21, 2000, p. B4.

Review of *The Crucible*, in *Rolling Stone*, December 12, 1996, http://www.rollingstone.com/reviews/movie/5948849/review/5948850/the_crucible (accessed July 2, 2009).

Rothstein, Edward, "On Naming the Names, in Life and Art," in *New York Times*, January 27, 1997, http://theater2.nytimes.com/mem/theater/treview.html?res = 9F00E3DA 133AF934A15752C0A96 1958260 (accessed July 2, 2009).

Steyn, Mark, "The Crucible of Hollywood's Guilt: Elia Kazan (1909–2003)," in *Atlantic*, Vol. 292, No. 5, December 2003, pp. 38–39.

Strickler, Jeff, "Everywitchway; When Arthur Miller Wrote *The Crucible* 45 Years Ago, He Used the Witch Hunts of Salem, Mass., as an Allegory of Sen. Joseph McCarthy's Rabid Anti-Communist Purge of the '50s. With That Era Long Gone, Miller Has Adapted His Play to Explore Some of Its Contemporary References," in *Star Tribune* (Minneapolis, MN), December 20, 1996, p. 1E.

Tucker, Veta Smith, "Purloined Identity: The Racial Metamorphosis of Tituba of Salem Village," in *Journal of Black Studies*, Vol. 30, No. 4, March 2000, p. 624–34.

"William Stoughton," in *University of Missouri-Kansas City School of Law*, http://www.law.umkc.edu/faculty/projects/ftrials/salem/SAL_BSTO.HTM (July 1, 2009).

Desire under the Elms

EUGENE O'NEILL

1924

Eugene O'Neill's *Desire under the Elms* is considered a classic play by one of the twentieth century's leading dramatists. Indeed, no study of American playwrights is complete without the inclusion of O'Neill and his work. *Desire under the Elms* premiered in New York City at the Greenwich Village Theatre on November 11, 1924, shocking critics and censors alike. (The plot features an affair between stepmother and stepson, as well as the murder of their infant son.) The play was nevertheless a popular success, enjoying a run of 208 performances upon its initial production. In 1925, *Desire under the Elms* first appeared in print in *The Complete Works of Eugene O'Neill*. The play itself portrays the highly dysfunctional Cabot family, pitting father and son against one another as they battle not only for possession of the land they farm together, but also for the love of Abbie, the Cabot patriarch's third wife. The small cast of characters is largely isolated on their New England farm, thus heightening the drama and urgency of their situation as each character in turn betrays the other. A thematically rich drama that explores the nature of love, desire, and greed, *Desire under the Elms* remains a popular performance piece almost a century after its initial premiere. The play is also widely available in book form; as of 2009, the 1995 edition of *Three Plays* (which includes *Desire under the Elms*, *Strange Interlude*, and *Mourning Becomes Electra*) remained in print.

Eugene O'Neill (*The Library of Congress*)

AUTHOR BIOGRAPHY

O'Neill was born in New York, New York, on October 16, 1888, the third son of Ella Quinlan O'Neill and famed actor James O'Neill. He was their only child to survive infancy. O'Neill's parents provided only an unstable home life, and many of his plays reflect this, as they explore the workings of dysfunctional families. The only stability O'Neill experienced in his young life was found at the family's summer cottage in New London, Connecticut. The O'Neill family was devoutly Catholic, and they traveled in support of James's acting career. Notably, O'Neill was raised predominantly by the nurse who traveled with them; his own mother developed an addiction to morphine and was thus largely unable to care for him. At the age of seven, O'Neill was sent to boarding school.

As a teenager, O'Neill renounced his family's faith and forever after viewed religion with suspicion and disgust. In fact, themes of men who fight against fate or God appear in several of his works. In 1906, O'Neill began attending Princeton University, but he failed most of his freshman classes and then dropped out. For the next six years, he

worked as a sailor and traveled the world. In 1909, he married Kathleen Jenkins. The couple had a son, Eugene O'Neill, Jr., but divorced in 1912. O'Neill did not take part in the boy's life until he was almost eleven. (Eugene O'Neill, Jr., committed suicide when he was forty years old.) Following his own failed suicide attempt around 1912, O'Neill returned to New London and began publishing poetry in the local newspaper. Shortly after his return, O'Neill relocated to the Gaylord Farm Sanitarium in Wallingford, Connecticut, where he spent a year recovering from tuberculosis. In 1914, he attended a playwriting workshop at Harvard University, but he was largely dissatisfied with the experience.

O'Neill continued writing, however, and he staged his first one-act play, *Bound East for Cardiff*, in 1916 in Provincetown, Massachusetts. The play was a success, launching both O'Neill's career and the Provincetown Players acting troupe. In 1918, he married his second wife, writer Agnes Boulton. The couple's son, Shane, was born in 1919, and their daughter, Oona, was born in 1925. O'Neill and Boulton divorced in 1928. Once again, O'Neill had little to do with his children after the divorce. Nevertheless, the years of his unsuccessful marriage to Boulton were his most prolific and successful. In 1920, O'Neill's first full-length play, *Beyond the Horizon*, was produced on Broadway, garnering O'Neill his first Pulitzer Prize. His play *Anna Christie* was produced the following year and earned O'Neill his second Pulitzer. Several plays followed, most notably *Desire under the Elms* in 1924. The play features the themes of Greek tragedy and underlying Freudian influence that later became a hallmark of O'Neill's work. *Strange Interlude*, first performed in 1928, also features Freudian themes. That play was an immense success, earning O'Neill his third Pulitzer and launching him into international fame.

On July 22, 1929, not long after divorcing Boulton, O'Neill married his third wife, Carlota Monterey. The couple soon went to live in France, and O'Neill began working on his epic play, *Mourning Becomes Electra* (1931). Following the release of the play, O'Neill and Monterey kept to themselves, traveling to and living in mostly remote locations in a state of semiretirement. He was awarded the Nobel Prize for Literature in 1936. However, by his early fifties, O'Neill was suffering from a neurological disease similar to Parkinson's (it was actually misdiagnosed as Parkinson's at the time). Despite suffering frompain and uncontrollable muscle tremors, he continued to write by hand. In fact, this period signaled the onset of the second phase of O'Neill's career, in which he produced some of his best-known and best-loved plays. These include *The Iceman Cometh* and *Long Day's Journey into Night*. The former play was written in 1939, although it was not produced until 1946. The latter, perhaps O'Neill's greatest dramatic achievement, was completed in 1941, but it was not produced until 1956 (three years after O'Neill's death). The work received a Pulitzer Prize (O'Neill's fourth).

O'Neill wrote his final play, *A Moon for the Misbegotten*, in 1943. The work is a sequel to *Long Day's Journey into Night*. His nerve disorder had left him largely incapacitated by then, and O'Neill was no longer able to write. He lived in constant pain until his death from pneumonia on November 27, 1953. O'Neill was buried in a private ceremony at Forest Hills Cemetery in Boston, Massachusetts, on December 2, 1953.

MEDIA ADAPTATIONS

- In 1928, *Desire under the Elms* was adapted as a silent film released in the Soviet Union as *Qali bazrobidan*.

- *Desire under the Elms* was adapted as a feature film of the same title in 1958. The movie stars Sophia Loren as Abbie and Anthony Perkins as Eben, and it was directed by Delbert Mann. It is considered an American film classic and is available on DVD.

- In 1976, the play was adapted in Belgium as a Dutch-language television movie under the title *Liefde onder de olmen*.

- *Desire under the Elms* was adapted as an audiobook by L.A. Theatre Works in 2004. Another audiobook adaptation, narrated by Amy Brenneman, was released in 2009 by Playaway.

PLOT SUMMARY

Act 1, Scene 1

It is the summer of 1850 at the Cabot farmhouse in rural New England. The farmhouse is dwarfed by the two giant elm trees on either side of it. Twenty-five-year-old Eben comes out onto the porch and looks up at the evening sky. He comments on its beauty, spits, and then goes back inside. Simeon and Peter, Eben's half brothers (ages thirty-nine and thirty-seven, respectively) come in from working in the fields. They also comment on the beautiful sky. The two men discuss the gold rush in California and how working on the farm only serves to make their father, Ephraim, rich. They discuss Ephraim's leaving the farm two months ago. Having had no word from him since, the brothers wonder if he is dead. Eben eavesdrops from the kitchen window. It is clear that all three are waiting for their father to die so they can inherit the farm. Eben joins the conversation, startling his brothers. He then tells them that dinner is ready.

Act 1, Scene 2

The brothers are eating dinner. Eben expresses his resentment for his father and declares that he is not his son because they have nothing in common. He mentions his mother, a kind woman whom Ephraim worked to death. Eben also says the farm rightfully belonged to his mother. Because of this, he claims that the farm should belong to him, and not to his father or even his half brothers. Peter and Simeon only laugh. Eben accuses them of not protecting his mother from Ephraim. He also blames himself and says that he is haunted by his mother's ghost. He states that she will not rest in peace until he confronts Ephraim.

Eben plans to go to town to see his sweetheart, Minnie. She is an older woman with a bad reputation. According to Peter and Simeon, she once dated Ephraim, and they tease Eben about it. He storms out of the room. After he leaves, the brothers say that he is almost an exact replica of their father.

Act 1, Scene 3

Eben stumbles in the next morning, waking his brothers just before dawn. He tells them that last night in town, he learned that Ephraim has taken a third wife. The men curse and say that now she will inherit the farm. Peter and Simeon decide that they might as well set off for California right away. Eben offers them three hundred dollars each to aid them on their journey if they agree to sign over their inheritance claims. He knows where Ephraim has hidden his profits from the farm, and he intends to pay them with the money. Eben believes the money is rightfully his in any case. Peter and Simeon agree to think it over. Eben goes to cook breakfast.

Alone, Peter and Simeon consider Eben's offer and decide wait to see the new wife with their own eyes in case their brother is trying to trick them. They also decide not to do any more farm work until their father arrives, and they hope that Ephraim's new wife is a mean woman who brings their father nothing but sorrow.

Act 1, Scene 4

The three brothers are eating breakfast. They inform Eben that he will have to run the farm alone. Rather than being angry, Eben is pleased, taking this as a sign that they intend to sign over their claim on the farm. He rushes off to work, and his bothers again comment that he is exactly like their father. On the porch, Eben looks out at the farm and comments on its beauty, gloating in the fact that it belongs to him.

Peter and Simeon are too restless to sit still; they wander outside and marvel at the farm's beauty. Then, they decide they should probably go help Eben, at least for old time's sake. Eben rushes up and says that Ephraim is coming up the road with his new wife. Simeon declares that he and Peter might as well leave now, and they agree to sign over their shares. After the deal is done, they awkwardly say goodbye.

On the road, Peter and Simeon see their seventy-five-year-old father and his new wife, thirty-five-year-old Abbie Putnam. Abbie sees the house for the first time and marvels at its beauty and at her ownership of it. Ephraim says the farm belongs to him, but then corrects himself and says it belongs to both of them. Ephraim notices his sons and asks why they are not working. He introduces Abbie, and both brothers spit on the ground. Abbie glares at them and then goes inside to look at 'her' new home.

Ephraim tells the brothers to get to work, but they tell him they are leaving for California. They joke and dance and celebrate their new-found freedom. Their father curses them, but they only laugh harder. Abbie finds Eben in the kitchen and is immediately attracted to him. She

flirts with him and tries to make peace, but he will have none of it. He is attracted to her as well but is too angry to care. Abbie tells Eben that she married his father for his farm, but when Eben threatens to tell his father, Abbie remarks that Ephraim will not believe him and will probably run him off the farm for spreading such an evil lie. Eben calls her a witch and a devil, but Abbie continues to flirt with him. For a moment, Eben begins to soften, but then he remembers himself and storms out.

Outside, Eben encounters Ephraim, who is calling on God to curse his ungrateful sons. Eben ridicules Ephraim and his angry God. The two bicker and then set off to work on the farm. Ephraim declares that despite his age, he is still a better farmhand than his son.

Act 2, Scene 1

Two months have passed, and it is a hot Sunday afternoon in summer. Abbie sits on the porch and teases Eben about Minnie as he heads off to town. She says it is clear that she and Eben are meant to be together and it is only a matter of time before he gives in. Eben hopes that Ephraim will hear her and throw her out. They play out an argument almost identical to the one they had two months ago, then declare their mutual hate. Eben storms off.

Ephraim comes along, and it is clear that he has mellowed as of late. He is clearly in love with his new wife, though she can barely contain her disgust. He sees that she and Eben have been fighting again, despite her denial. He tells her Eben is soft, like his mother, but Abbie laughs and says that Eben is just like Ephraim. She notes that Ephraim is the one who is getting soft. He says that since he cannot take the farm with him when he dies, he would like to set the livestock free and burn everything to the ground before he dies so no on can inherit it. However, since he realizes that this will not happen, he says that he is growing fonder of Eben, if only because he has stayed when his brothers have left.

Growing jealous, Abbie tells Ephraim that Eben is trying seduce her. Ephraim flies into a rage and threatens to kill his son. Frightened for Eben, Abbie takes it back and says she was only worried that Eben would inherit the farm instead of her. Ephraim offers to run Eben off the farm to please her, but she notes that they need him to help work the land. Still, Ephraim says that he would like to leave the farm to his own flesh and blood, which is the closest he can come to keeping the farm when he dies. Abbie then suggests that they have a son together. Ephraim is overjoyed at the thought and promises to leave the farm to her if she bears him a son.

Act 2, Scene 2

Eben is alone, pacing in his bedroom. Abbie and Ephraim are in their bedroom, and Ephraim is telling her all of his secret hopes. He explains why he works so hard and says how lonely he was until she came. He says that God is hard and wants him to be hard. He tells Abbie that Eben's mother's family tried to claim legal rights to the farm, which is why Eben believes that the farm is rightfully his. He declares his love for her. Abbie is not listening. When Ephraim realizes this, he grows hurt and angry. He says that she, like everyone else, will never understand him and that the only way she can ever redeem herself is to have a son. Ephraim decides to go sleep in the barn; he says something in the house makes him feel cold and unsettled and that he feels peace only in the barn.

Outside, Ephraim falters and calls out to God. When he receives no answer, he continues on his way to the barn.

Abbie and Eben sit alone, stewing, in their respective rooms. Finally, Abbie can take no more and rushes into Eben's room. They kiss, but Eben pushes her away. Abbie declares her love but ultimately grows frustrated and angry at Eben's rejection. She then demands that Eben meet her in the parlor. The room has been sealed since Eben's mother died.

Act 2, Scene 3

Abbie is sitting apprehensively in the parlor. When Eben arrives, she says there is a spirit in the room. Eben says it is his mother. Abbie feels that the spirit loves her since it knows she loves Eben. He is surprised that the spirit does not hate her for trying to steal the farm, but he realizes that Abbie is right. After speaking of his mother, Abbie offers to be like a mother to Eben, but the two soon begin kissing passionately. At first, Eben resists, but he can feel his mother's spirit urging him on. He does not understand this, but then he realizes that his love for his father's wife is his mother's "vengeance on him [Ephraim]—so's she kin rest quiet in her grave." Abbie and Eben then give in to temptation.

Act 2, Scene 4

The next morning, Eben heads out to begin his chores. Abbie pokes her head out the window,

and the lovers talk sweetly and kiss. Soon after, Eben encounters his father and says that he can feel that his mother's spirit has left the house and gone back to her grave in peace. Because of this, he says, he and his father are no longer enemies. Ephraim is confused by this speech and notes again that Eben is soft.

Act 3, Scene 1

It is now spring of the following year, and Eben is sitting alone in his room, clearly upset. Downstairs, a party is being held to celebrate the birth of Abbie's son. Ephraim is beside himself with joy, but Abbie is preoccupied by Eben's absence. The other partygoers, mostly from neighboring farms, all seem to suspect the affair and make insinuating remarks that Ephraim does not notice. Instead, he boasts of his strength and vitality.

Upstairs, Eben goes into the master bedroom and looks at the baby in his crib. Abbie senses something and goes upstairs. Ephraim tenderly offers to help her but she rebuffs him. The partygoers freeze, but Ephraim remains oblivious. Abbie then joins Eben in the bedroom. He says of his son, "I don't like lettin' on what's mine's is his'n. I been doin' that all my life." Abbie declares her love and begs Eben to be patient.

Outside, Ephraim catches his breath, tired from all the dancing. His celebratory mood falters, and he says that there is something restless in the house that seems to be dripping from the elm trees that watch over it. He decides to go to the barn. When he leaves, the party finally becomes festive, and the other partygoers begin to have a good time.

Act 3, Scene 2

Half an hour later, Eben is moping outside the house. Ephraim is moping on his way back from the barn. However, when he sees Eben, he becomes jolly and gloats. He tells Eben that the farm now belongs to Abbie and her son, that this was why Abbie had the baby in the first place. Eben realizes that Abbie has used and betrayed him, and he vows to kill her. Ephraim blocks his way, and the two begin fighting furiously. Abbie rushes out and tries to stop them.

Ephraim throws Eben to the ground, crows over having bested him, and goes back inside. Abbie rushes to Eben to check on him but he pushes her away. He accuses her of using him to have a baby so she could steal the farm. Abbie swears that she loves Eben, that she made that plan before they were lovers, and that she does not want the farm, only Eben's love. Eben does not believe her. He says he wishes he had never loved her and that their son had never been born. He now plans to join Peter and Simeon in California. He also plans to call his mother back from the grave to haunt the farm and to tell Ephraim the truth about the baby.

Abbie says she hates her son if his existence has killed Eben's love for her. She asks whether he would still love her if she could find a way to take everything back and to prove that she does not want the farm. Eben says he probably would, but that what is done cannot be undone. He goes back into the house to pack.

Act 3, Scene 3

The next morning, Eben sits at the kitchen table with his bags. Ephraim is upstairs sleeping. Abbie is also upstairs; she is standing, horrified, by the baby's cradle. She rushes downstairs and tries to kiss Eben, but he is unmoved. He tells her he is still leaving them to be haunted but that he will not tell Ephraim about the baby's true paternity lest the old man take out his anger on the child. He says he will come back one day to claim his son. Abbie responds that Eben does not need to leave because she has killed him. Eben assumes that she means she has killed Ephraim and is overjoyed at the news. When Abbie says that she has killed the baby, Eben falls to his knees in horror.

Abbie says she did not want to kill the baby, but she did it so that Eben would love her again. Eben does not believe her. He says she only did it to steal from him again, taking what was rightfully his. He then decides to go for the sheriff before leaving for California. He wants her locked up because although she is "a murderer an' thicf," she still tempts him. Abbie says she does not care about going to jail; she only wants Eben to love her again.

Act 3, Scene 4

An hour has passed. Abbie is sitting at the kitchen table, dejected. Upstairs, Ephraim wakes with a start, surprised to have slept in. He looks at the baby and thinks he is sleeping soundly. Then he goes downstairs, but when he sees Abbie, he tenderly asks if she is ill. He suggests she lie down and gather her strength so she can care for the baby when he wakes. Abbie says the baby is dead—she killed him. Ephraim does not believe her, and he rushes upstairs to see for himself. He rushes back and

shakes Abbie, demanding to know how she could do such a thing.

Abbie screams that the baby was Eben', that she has always hated Ephraim. She says that she should have killed Ephraim and not the baby. Ephraim realizes that the haunting feeling that kept driving him from the house was his subconscious knowledge of the affair. Although the baby was not his, he expresses genuine pity and sadness at his death. He recovers himself and vows to go for the sheriff, but then he learns that Eben has already gone. He tells Abbie that if she had loved him, nothing she could do would ever make him go to the sheriff.

Eben comes back in, and Ephraim tells Eben he ought to leave the farm or risk being arrested as an accomplice. Then he leaves them both in disgust. Eben goes to Abbie and begs her forgiveness for going to the sheriff. He declares his renewed love for her and suggests that they run away together. Abbie says she must face justice, but that she can bear it because she has Eben's love. Eben intends to tell the sheriff that he killed the baby with her, stating that he put the idea in her head and says, "I'm as guilty as yew be. He was the child o' our sin." Abbie protests, but Eben says he wants to be with her, even if that means going to prison.

Ephraim comes back into the house and tells them they both ought to hang for what they have done. He says he is leaving the farm to rot and that he has let the livestock loose. He plans to burn everything to the ground, take his savings, and head to California. However, when he goes to get his savings, he finds there is nothing left, and Eben tells him he gave the money to Peter and Simeon. Ephraim replies that it is God's will that he stay on the farm. He is getting old, he says, and will be more lonely now than ever before, but "God's hard an' lonesome" as well.

The sheriff enters with his men. Eben confesses to killing the baby as well, and the sheriff arrests him and Abbie. Eben and Abbie simply say goodbye to Ephraim, who turns his back on them and leaves the house. Eben and Abbie declare their love for one another, hold hands, and walk out of the house. They both stop to admire the sky one last time. The sheriff also admires the view, commenting that the Cabot farm is beautiful and that he wished it was his.

CHARACTERS

Eben Cabot

Eben Cabot is the twenty-five-year-old son of Ephraim and the younger half brother of Peter and Simeon. He professes that he is not like his father, but other characters say that he is exactly like him. Eben hates his father, believing that Ephraim worked his mother to death on the farm and that her restless spirit remains in the house. Eben also believes that the Cabot farm rightfully belonged to his mother and that as his mother's heir he has the only true claim to it. Ephraim legally owns the farm and profits by Eben's work on it, so Eben resents his father and stays only in the hope of inheriting the farm in the future. Indeed, Eben even steals his father's savings to buy out his brothers' claims on the farm. To Eben, however, this act is not stealing, since he believes that the money belongs to him.

At the beginning of the play, Eben is dating an older woman named Minnie, and he is unperturbed by her previous relationship with his father. Indeed, Eben implies a sense of triumph in possessing what used to belong to his father. He also declares that he does not believe in love. This belief, however, is overturned by Abbie Putnam, Ephraim's third wife. Abbie and Eben are instantly attracted to one another, but Eben resists Abbie's charms because he sees her as a threat to his inheritance. However, he finally gives in to temptation when he comes to believe that his mother's spirit will be pleased by the affair. He notes that his and Abbie's love will be his mother's "vengeance" on Ephraim. In fact, after Eben and Abbie have consummated their affair, Eben says that his mother's spirit has finally gone to rest in peace. Thus, Eben's love for Abbie is motivated by his desire for revenge, not by his desire for Abbie. Once Eben believes that his mother's spirit is at rest, he even tells his father that he no longer bears him any ill will.

Later, when Abbie bears Eben's son and passes the infant off as Ephraim's, Eben must again struggle with his sense of injustice: "I don't like lettin' on what's mine's is his'n. I been doin' that all my life." When Eben learns that Abbie extracted Ephraim's promise to will her the farm should she bear him a son, Eben feels used and betrayed and wishes that his son had never been born. This statement, coupled with his renewed hate for Abbie, spurs her to kill the baby in a desperate attempt to prove the purity of her love

for him. Eben is at first disgusted by this act and informs the sheriff of Abbie's crime. However, soon after, he regrets this and acknowledges his hand in the baby's death (however unwitting). Eben again declares his love for Abbie and willingly stands to face charges with her. At the beginning of the play, Eben comments on the beauty of the sky; as he leaves with Abbie and the sheriff, his last words are also in praise of the sky.

Ephraim Cabot

Seventy-five-year-old Ephraim Cabot is the father of Peter, Simeon, and Eben, and he is hated and resented by all who know him, including his own wife and sons. Ephraim is proud and strong, and he is constantly stating that everyone else is weak in comparison. His boastful behavior and his pride in ownership of his farm are largely to blame for the hate his family bears him. Indeed, Ephraim would like to take the farm with him when he dies; failing that, he would like to burn it to the ground so no one else can have it. Though it turns out that the farm is indeed rightfully his, he works others to the bone in order to maintain it and reap the profits. Ephraim also reveals a softer side, however. He claims that God is hard and also lonesome and that all he has ever done is follow God's will for him. When he reveals his loneliness and innermost thoughts to Abbie, he becomes a more sympathetic character. His dismay at her rejection of him as he bares his soul to her is poignant, as are his private moments of sadness and self-doubt. Thus, beneath his hard and boastful exterior, a sensitive and lonely soul is revealed. He even expresses pity for the dead baby despite learning that the child was not his. Nevertheless, he is not blameless, and his rude behavior plays a large hand in sowing the seeds of discord that ultimately prove to be his and the other characters' undoing.

Peter Cabot

Peter Cabot is the thirty-seven-year-old son of Ephraim, Simeon's younger brother and Eben's older half brother. He and Simeon often hold the same opinions and appear almost as two parts of one character. They tend to speak in turns, embellishing or completing the other's thoughts. Like Eben, Peter hates his father and believes the farm should belong to him. However, he and his brother would rather travel to California and join the gold rush than stay and work for their inheritance. This is especially true when Peter learns of his father's new wife. Because Abbie's presence represents another obstacle to their inheritance, the brothers decide to leave for California as soon as she arrives. Thus, what was once merely a dream of escape becomes an active plan. Peter is also shrewd. He suspects that Eben may be trying to trick him into leaving and therefore waits to confirm Ephraim's marriage rather than take Eben's word for it. Ultimately, Peter and Simeon willingly sign over their shares in the farm in return for their father's stolen savings.

Although Peter is sad to leave the farm he clearly loves, he is also overjoyed at his newfound sense of freedom. Because his inheritance no longer holds any power over him, he is able to ridicule his father with impunity, laughing and dancing as he leaves the farm forever.

Simeon Cabot

Simeon Cabot is the thirty-nine-year-old son of Ephraim, Peter's older brother and Eben's older half brother. He and Peter are inseparable, sharing the same thoughts and ideas and often speaking together. Simeon hates his father as much as his brothers do, and he is working on the farm only in hopes of inheriting it someday. However, he also dreams of joining the gold rush in California and would probably do so if he had any money. This problem is solved, however, when Eben offers him his father's stolen savings in return for relinquishing his claim on the farm. Although it appears that Simeon would not normally consider this offer, the introduction of Ephraim's new wife makes him more inclined to accept. Indeed, Abbie's arrival presents another obstacle to his possible inheritance, and thus Simeon and his brother decide to cut their losses and set out for California. Still, he is smart enough to wait for Abbie's arrival rather than believe Eben, who, he suspects, may be trying to trick him.

Simeon loves the farm, but he also experiences a manic sense of joy at his sudden freedom from it. He pesters his father, dances, and sings as he leaves the Cabot farm, never to be seen or heard from again.

Abbie Putnam

Thirty-five-year-old Abbie Putnam is Ephraim's third wife and is forty years younger than her husband. She is both stepmother and lover to Eben, who is only ten years younger than her. Abbie's arrival acts as a catalyst for Simeon and

Peter's departure, and it also fuels Eben's hate for her and his father. When Abbie comes to the farm, she is as obsessed with taking ownership of it as the other characters. She tells Eben that she was an orphan and forced to work for others at an early age. When she married her first husband, she thought she had escaped that life. However, he was an alcoholic, and both he and their baby died, forcing Abbie to begin working for others again. Thus, to her, the farm represents an opportunity to work for herself. She even tells Eben that she married Ephraim only for his farm. This statement is underscored by her clear and constant disgust for her husband. However, despite Abbie's eagerness to own the farm, its beauty is mostly lost on her. Abbie has eyes only for Eben, whom she truly loves.

Abbie's love for Eben is not motivated by a desire for gain or for vengeance. Although she arrives with a desire to own the farm, her desire for Eben's love becomes more pressing, and she no longer cares about the farm or who possesses it. In fact, Abbie is compelled to prove this when Eben retracts his love upon learning that her infant son has secured her inheritance. To demonstrate her priorities, she kills the infant. Eben's horror at the murder compels him to turn her in to the sheriff. Abbie, however, is unconcerned at her imprisonment and likely hanging; she cares only for Eben's love. When Eben renews his love for her, she willingly relinquishes herself to the authorities, stating that she can bear anything as long as she has Eben's affection. At the end of the play, as she leaves the Cabot homestead hand in hand with her lover, she finally stops (at Eben's bidding) to admire the beauty surrounding her.

THEMES

Desire

Desire is an overriding theme in the play, and it is no coincidence that the word appears in the title of O'Neill's masterpiece. From the very first scene, it is clear that Eben, Simeon, and Peter all desire the farm. However, Peter and Simeon's desire to take part in the gold rush ultimately asserts itself over their desire to own the farm. Eben desires Minnie, and his desire is undiminished when he learns that she used to date his father. In fact, it seems to be inflamed all the more because Eben enjoys the idea of possessing

TOPICS FOR FURTHER STUDY

- Peter and Simeon abandon their inheritance and travel to California to mine gold. At the end of the play, Ephraim considers doing the same. Use the Internet to research the California gold rush. Create a PowerPoint presentation in which you relate your findings.

- The Cabot farm is largely isolated from the outside world, and this isolation both underscores and fuels the intense relationships of the farm's inhabitants. For a more modern exploration of the result of an isolated upbringing, read Christina Meldrum's young-adult novel *Madapple*. In an essay, compare and contrast the themes of isolation as they are treated in that novel and in O'Neill's play.

- Do you believe that the play could have ended differently? If so, how? Rewrite the final scenes of *Desire under the Elms* and explain how the plot would have to change in order to support your revision.

- Lead a debate in which one side argues for Eben's guilt and complicity in his son's murder and the other argues for his innocence. Be sure to cite examples from the text in support of your arguments.

what once belonged to his father. This is, after all, exactly the scenario he hopes to see played out in regard to his ownership of the farm. Ephraim is motivated by his desire to find a wife, a woman he can love and who will alleviate his loneliness. He also desires the farm, despite already possessing it. This is shown in his wish to take the farm with him when he dies or to burn everything so no one else can have it. Even though he grudgingly plans to will the farm to a son, he does so only because it is the closest he can come to continuing to possess it.

At first, Abbie also desires the farm, but her desire for Eben becomes more important. She ultimately renounces her claim on the farm because of this. Both Abbie and Eben desire

one another, although Eben initially fights his desire. Abbie tells him, "nature'll beat ye, Eben. Ye might's well own up t' it fust 's last." However, Eben only gives in to his desire for Abbie when he feels that his mother's spirit encourages him to do so (and to do so in order to avenge her death). Thus, Eben's desire for vengeance is more pressing than his desire for Abbie. Notably, as the characters act on their given (and conflicting) desires, they each contribute to the tragedies that ensue.

Religion

O'Neill's rejection of God and religion can often be seen in his work, and *Desire under the Elms* is no exception. In fact, it is one of his first plays in which the theme is fully formed. Ephraim is constantly calling out to God for guidance, though mostly to curse his ungrateful sons. The other characters take no stock in Ephraim's faith, and they never speak of God or invoke him. The only time Eben mentions religion is when he ridicules Ephraim for beseeching God. In one scene, Ephraim calls out to God in pain and seems to wait for an answer. The ensuing silence seems to speak for itself; Ephraim's loneliness is underscored, and he wanders off to seek safe haven in the barn. Indeed, the cows offer him more comfort than God does. Ephraim believes, however, that God has called him to the farm and sentenced him to be hard and live a hard life. He even tells Abbie that he once left the farm and could have become a rich man in the Midwest, where the soil is better. However, he notes that God wanted him to return to the farm because God is not pleased by easy success. He also believes that God told him to go find another wife, which is why he has married Abbie. Like all of the things God has instructed Ephraim to do, marrying Abbie brings Ephraim only unhappiness. At the end of the play, when Ephraim decides to abandon the farm and travel to California, he learns that Eben has given his savings away and that he will be unable to leave. Once again, Ephraim states that it is God's will for him and that although he will be more lonesome than ever before, "God's hard an' lonesome" as well.

Ephraim identifies with God, but he is ultimately consigned to endless suffering because of it. He constantly describes himself as hard and God as hard. He acts accordingly and thus alienates everyone around him. This results in his loneliness, the second trait he claims to share with

A scene from a 1994 production of Desire Under the Elms *at the Palace Theatre in Watford, U.K.*
(© Donald Cooper / Photostage)

God. In essence, O'Neill portrays Ephraim as a man whose unhappiness stems from his faith.

STYLE

Dialect

All of the characters in *Desire under the Elms* speak in dialect, a stylized form of nonstandard speech. The dialect in the play is characterized by swallowed consonants, as in "an'" for *and* or "doin'" for *doing*. The use of the word "ye" for *you* is another example of dialect. Nonstandard grammar abounds, as when Abbie declares that "nature'll beat ye, Eben. Ye might's well own up t' it fust 's last" or when Eben states "I don't like lettin' on what's mine's is his'n."

Dialect varies by region but also indicates the class or origins of its speaker. Indeed, the nonstandard speech in the play speaks to the Cabots' rural roots and likely lack of any formal education. In essence, the characters' style of speech reveals them to be little more than ignorant country bumpkins. Their intrigues, too, are as small-minded as their speech.

Circularity and Repetition

The play both opens and closes with Eben commenting on how "purty" the farm is. This device gives the play a sense of circularity, as if little has changed. This circularity is further underscored by the sheriff's comment that he wishes the farm belonged to him. In the beginning of the play, these sentiments were expressed by Eben and his brothers. The play also features a great deal of repetition throughout, including comments about the farm's beauty. Other repeating comments or actions include arguments over who owns the farm, God's hardness, Ephraim's loneliness, the haunting spirit of Eben's mother, Abbie's repeated declarations of love for Eben, and her repeated displays of disgust toward Ephraim. Ephraim frequently comments that there is something in the house driving him to the barn, the only place he can seem to find peace. Ephraim repeatedly asserts his ownership of the farm and mentions his desire to own it forever

COMPARE
&
CONTRAST

- **1850s:** Farming is one of the main sources of employment in the United States and almost the only occupation in rural areas. Farms are often small, owned and operated by the families who live on them. Farm work is largely achieved through manual labor.

  1920s: Following the industrial revolution, farming is no longer quite as prominent an economic power in the United States. However, it remains a significant form of income and livelihood. Farming has also become more profitable as a result of the increasing mechanization of the agricultural process.

  Today: Working family farms are largely a thing of the past, having given way to large, industrialized farms that are run by corporations and that rely heavily on machinery in order to succeed. However, smaller farms devoted to organic or sustainable farming are becoming more popular.

- **1850s:** The California gold rush is in full swing, beginning in 1848 and ending in 1855. The discovery of gold in the state incites roughly three hundred thousand prospectors to travel to California in the hopes of making their fortune through mining gold.

  1920s: By the 1920s, many of the boom towns that had been built during the height of the gold rush have been abandoned, transformed into ghost towns. Other settlements, however, have flourished, growing into industrial centers.

  Today: Gold mining today is largely undertaken by mining corporations, although some individual prospectors persist, particularly in Alaska.

- **1850s:** Women are only just beginning to gain the right to own property outside their husbands' control. In 1848, New York passed the Married Women's Property Act, becoming the first state to grant this right. Thus, Abbie's attempts to possess the farm, as well as her scheme to bear a son to do so, are in line with social attitudes regarding the rights of women.

  1920s: The women's suffrage movement, which began in the 1850s, finally reaches fruition with the passage of the Nineteenth Amendment in 1920. The amendment grants adult women who are citizens of the United States the right to vote.

  Today: For the most part, women are granted the same legal rights as men. However, economic disparities persist; as of 2007, women still earn seventy-seven cents for every dollar that is paid to men.

(regardless of how unrealistic that desire may be). Even his references to God remain the same; God is spoken of throughout the play in almost identical terms. Ephraim's boastfulness is similarly repetitive in nature. This repetition serves to show us that the characters essentially do not change throughout the course of the play. Abbie is the only character who changes, replacing her lust for the farm with her lust for Eben. This stylistic device, then, shows that although everything has changed on the surface, everything (or almost everything) remains the same on a deeper level.

HISTORICAL CONTEXT

Greek Tragedy

Desire under the Elms is based firmly in the historical tradition of Greek tragedy. Greek tragedies are some of the earliest recorded plays, and they influence all drama that has been written since. In particular, O'Neill's play draws on the tragedies of *Oedipus Rex* and *Medea*. *Oedipus Rex* portrays a hero who unwittingly kills his father and marries his own mother. Eben is essentially doing the same with his stepmother, a parallel that is underscored by her offers to act

An elm-lined road evokes the theme of Desire Under the Elms. *(Image copyright Joe Gough, 2009. Used under license from Shutterstock.com)*

as a mother to him. Although Eben does not actually kill his father, a near-murderous intent seems to cloud his every action. It is important to note, however, that Eben's actions are not unwitting. *Medea* features a mother who kills her children as an act of revenge against her husband, who has betrayed her. Although Abbie commits infanticide not as an act of revenge, but as an act of conciliation (apology), the comparison is nevertheless apt. The Oedipus myth was first portrayed in tragic form in Sophocles' *Oedipus Rex*, first produced around 429 BCE. *Medea* was first produced as a tragedy by Euripides around 431 BCE.

In general, tragedies are serious, sad, or morbid, and they often include a series of events that end in death. The events and resulting death are also often based on the tragic flaw or fatal flaw of one or more of the characters. All of these principles apply to *Desire under the Elms*. Greek tragedy also features the hero's reversal of fortune (and given the nature of tragedy, this is usually a progression from good to bad). This reversal is also affected by the hero's tragic flaws. If Eben is the hero, then his fortune progresses not from good to bad, but from bad to worse. The context of O'Neill's play is firmly rooted in Greek tragedy.

Sigmund Freud and Psychoanalysis

Interestingly, *Desire under the Elms* is influenced by Sigmund Freud in much the same way that it is influenced by Greek tragedy. This is because Freud largely drew upon Greek myths and archetypes when forming his theories. Indeed, he is responsible for coining the term *Oedipus complex* to describe the situation of a man being in love with or desiring his mother. (The opposite phenomenon—a woman in love with her father—is known as the *Electra complex*, a term also drawn from a Greek myth.) Indeed, on a very basic level, Freud posited that basic archetypes (such as those found in the Greek myths) largely motivate the human psyche. Often termed the father of modern psychology, Freud lived from 1856 to 1939. He was quite famous during his lifetime, and it is highly likely that O'Neill was familiar with the psychologist's work. Freud largely posited that personality was formed via childhood experience; Eben's desire for Abbie is largely motivated by revenge for the mother he lost at a young age. Freud also suggested that males are afraid of losing their power to other males, a principle clearly at work in the oppositional relationship between Ephraim and Eben.

In addition, Freud popularized the idea of a conscious and subconscious, as well as the resulting theory that actions are largely dictated by the subconscious. This theory was later refined in Freud's work on the id, ego, and super-ego. These three elements of the psyche, according to Freud, dictate human behavior. The id represents instinctual behavior, the ego represents the conscious behavior aimed toward pleasing or appeasing the id, and the super-ego is the largely unconscious organizing principle that creates a basic personality structure. In general, much of the literature of the early twentieth century (and beyond) was influenced by Freud's work. His ideas inspired writers to portray characters' actions according to a psychological framework. O'Neill's plays are no exception.

CRITICAL OVERVIEW

Although *Desire under the Elms* was deemed shocking and controversial by critics and censors upon its initial production in 1924, the play was a popular and commercial success. It enjoyed a lengthy first run and has been regularly revived ever since. The play's initial popularity may have been based on its controversy. As a contributor for the *Nation* noted in a 1925 article, the play's notoriety began to draw an audience interested

only in being titillated, people "who clearly had not heard of [the play] before the censors began to discuss its morals." For this reason, the contributor finds that "here is proof that censorship of literature is both pernicious and stupid." In another 1925 review of the play, also published in the *Nation*, Joseph Wood Krutch calls it "powerfully original" and declares that "no other play could stir us to so warm an admiration or so passionate a dislike."

Despite the initial controversy, though, *Desire under the Elms.* has mostly received critical praise for almost a century. Take for instance, two reviews from 1984 and 1994, respectively. According to Frank R. Cunningham in *Critical Essays on Eugene O'Neill*, "In O'Neill's most mature play of his early career, *Desire under the Elms*, Romantic myth and motif are raised to the pinnacle of dramatic expression and psychological power." Ruby Cohn, writing in the third edition of the *Reference Guide to American Literature*, notes that the play is "not only frequently revived" but has an interesting place in the playwright's development: "it set O'Neill's feet firmly on hard realistic ground." She adds that "in O'Neill's hands . . . these characters loom large." Furthermore, Cohn states that "although marred by turgid dialogue and abuse of repetition, *Desire under the Elms* nevertheless achieves moments of passionate intensity which predict O'Neill's wholly functional final tragedies."

CRITICISM

Leah Tieger

Tieger is a freelance writer and editor. In the following essay, she discusses the elements of Greek tragedy and Freudian psychology that can be found in Desire under the Elms.

O'Neill's *Desire under the Elms* remains relevant almost a hundred years after its initial production largely because it deals with the unchanging aspects of human nature. The same aspects are set down in archetypal roles and conflicts, such as those portrayed through Greek myth and tragedy. In the early twentieth century, interest in such archetypes was renewed when Freud used them as the basis for his psychoanalytic theories. Thus, no discussion of *Desire under the Elms* is complete without an examination of both Greek tragedy and Freudian theories. O'Neill's play draws on plot elements from two specific Greek tragedies, *Oedipus Rex* and *Medea*,

WHAT DO I READ NEXT?

- Hillary Jordan's 2008 novel *Mudbound* received a 2009 Alex Award honoring adult books that are recommended for young adults. The book bears similar plot points to O'Neill's play. Set in 1946 on an isolated farm in the Mississippi Delta, the story portrays Laura; her husband, Henry; and their two young daughters. Henry's father, Pappy, is an unpleasant old man who moves in with them. When Henry's brother, Jamie, returns from fighting in World War II, Laura and Jamie fall in love.

- For another story of a son who struggles in the shadow of his overbearing father, read Lensey Namioka's *Yang the Youngest and His Terrible Ear*. This young-adult novel, published in 1992, features young Yingtao. He and his family have just immigrated to Seattle, Washington, from China, and although Yingtao is not musically inclined, his father, a music teacher, forces him to play the violin. Yingtao must then give a recital in the hopes of attracting new students for his father.

- O'Neill's best-known play, *Long Day's Journey into Night*, was written in 1941, though it was not performed until 1956, three years after the author's death. The play features a highly dysfunctional family and its morphine-addicted matriarch and is autobiographical in nature, given that O'Neill's own mother was a morphine addict.

- H.W. Brands's *The Age of Gold: The California Gold Rush and the New American Dream* was published in 2003. A scholarly exploration of the California gold rush and its aftermath, this book explores how the gold rush transformed not only California but all of America.

- Another great playwright, and O'Neill's contemporary, was George Bernard Shaw. Where O'Neill's *Desire under the Elms* references Greek tragedies, Shaw's *Pygmalion* (first produced in German in 1913) alludes to Greek mythology. Shaw's play was also adapted as the classic American film *My Fair Lady*.

- To learn more about the Freudian theories at work in *Desire under the Elms*, read *The Ego and the Id: The Standard Edition of the Complete Psychological Works of Sigmund Freud*. This compendium of Sigmund Freud's writings was edited by Peter Gay and published in 1990.

---

yet it also exhibits elements characteristic of Greek tragedy as a whole. Tragedies often end in death or loss, particularly a loss resulting from a series of events set in motion by the internal flaws of one or more of the characters. This series of events ending in tragedy often represents a turn for the worse, as is the case in O'Neill's play.

Greek tragedy, in general, also references the power of the gods and a sense of immutable fate, references that are also made (by Ephraim) in *Desire under the Elms*. This sense of spiritual bondage is also inherent in the tragic or fatal flaw that brings about a character's downfall. Discussing the intersection between these two

elements in the *Eugene O'Neill Newsletter*, Preston Fambrough notes that *Desire under the Elms*

> is charged with an uncompromisingly mystical view of the forces at work in and through human beings, forces which may manifest themselves in forms recognizable by the science of psychoanalysis...but which ultimately transcend scientific or rational explanation.

Fambrough goes on to note that

> in Greek tragedy, action appears to proceed naturally from a given quantity called 'character,' ... in ways that reflect universal 'laws' of the human experience. At the same time, the action appears as the product of supernatural forces, a reaction against some breach of the cosmic order.

Similarly, the critic finds that "in [*Desire under the Elms*], we are made cognizant simultaneously of the dark, only partly knowable forces of the individual subconscious and of a superhuman cosmic principle working itself out through the action of the tragedy."

Next, it is important to examine the specific tragedies that inspired O'Neill's play. The lesser of the two, Euripides' *Medea*, was first produced around 431 BCE. It portrays a woman who kills her children in order to exact revenge on their father, a man who has shunned her for another woman. Notably, O'Neill introduces significant changes in his treatment of this myth. Abbie does not kill her son as an act of revenge, but instead as an act of peace. Rather than anger or hurt her lover, Abbie hopes to win his love again through the act of murder. The second, and more essential, tragedy informing *Desire under the Elms* is Sophocles' *Oedipus Rex*, first produced around 429 BCE. The play finds Oedipus unintentionally killing his father and marrying his mother. The act is unintentional simply because Oedipus does not know who his parents are. However, the essential act, of overtaking one's father and usurping his place with the mother, is mirrored strongly in O'Neill's play.

In fact, it is the Oedipus myth that informs Sigmund Freud's theories regarding the Oedipus complex: the universal unconscious desire to overthrow paternal power and to take on the father's role as husband. This is the primary Freudian idea influencing *Desire under the Elms*, but it is not the only one. For instance, Eben's loss of his mother at an early age brings about his need to replace her, and it speaks to Freud's belief that childhood experiences, especially traumatic ones, shape one's personality. This latter idea, that past experiences forever inform present and future actions, is also espoused by Freud's contemporary Carl Jung. Commenting on this psychological theory in the *Selcuk University Social Sciences Institute Journal*, Cumhur Yilmaz Madran observes that

> one of the tragic elements O'Neill used in *Desire under the Elms* is the haunting past. The past in the play determines and controls the tragic action. In the play the past controls the present and creates the future.

According to Madran, the play also "reflects certain facets of the ambivalence of love and hate described by Freud."

Discussing the Oedipus complex at work in O'Neill's play, Madran remarks that Ephraim's youngest son "suffers from Freud's Oedipus complex. It derives from Eben's unconscious rivalry with his father for the love of his stepmother." He then notes that "O'Neill adopts the ancient 'Oedipus myth' to structure his play.... It is the tragedy of desire as it appears in the play, human desire." In service to this tragedy, elements of projection and transference are also at work. Both projection and transference are theories originally set forth by Freud. The former term describes when a person projects an internal desire, thought, or flaw onto an external person or object, thus effecting a disassociation from the desire, thought, or flaw. With transference, a person allows another being or object to act as a stand in for the actual person or object that is desired (but is, generally, unattainable). In a deeply Freudian sense, Abbie is merely an object of transference, as Eben transfers his feelings for his mother onto his stepmother. Madran notes that

> Eben's internal conflict is not to be missed, for it goes to the psychological core of O'Neill's play. The exploration of Eben's personality must be based on his relationship with his mother. The main source of Eben's tragedy must be sought in his psychological quest for a mother figure.

This mother figure, then, must replace the dead mother whose spirit Eben believes inhabits the house (a spirit he frequently addresses in the present tense). In fact, Abbie is not the first figure whom Eben attempts to use in fulfillment of this role. Minnie, an older woman Ephraim once dated, embodies Eben's first attempt at this particular transference. However, Eben reaches a more absolute fulfillment in his attachment to Abbie. Madran states that "the existence of the mother is sensed most strongly at the moment of Eben's sin.... The mysterious presence of the mother is felt in the parlour in which the ... desires of Eben and Abbie are fulfilled." Even more pointedly, the spirit of Eben's mother is allowed to rest in peace once the transference is complete. True to Freudian form, Madran finds that "Eben carries with him the eternal image of his mother. Since his mother's image is unconscious, it is unconsciously projected upon Abbie." However, whereas Eben's role in this projection and transference may be unconscious, Abbie's role is just the opposite. According to Madran, she takes on the "double roles in the play as a mother and as a lover."

Notably, she does so consciously and willingly. She offers to act as a mother to her stepson when she first meets him and does so again when she finally succeeds in seducing him.

Source: Leah Tieger, Critical Essay on *Desire under the Elms*, in *Drama for Students*, Gale, Cengage Learning, 2010.

Bette Mandl

In the following essay, Mandl considers the role of women and nature in Desire under the Elms.

In the famous stage directions for the first act of *Desire under the Elms*, O'Neill describes the trees of the title:

> Two enormous elms are on each side of the house. They bend their trailing branches down over the roof. They appear to protect and at the same time subdue. There is a sinister maternity in their aspect, a crushing, jealous absorption. They have developed from their intimate contact with the life of man in the house an appalling humaneness. They brood oppressively over the house. They are like exhausted women resting their sagging breasts and hands and hair on its roof, and when it rains their tears trickle down monotonously and rot on the shingles.

Travis Bogard praises O'Neill's restraint in imposing these elms as symbols on an essentially realistic play: "the novelistic rhetoric that links the elms with Eben's dead mother and with an exhausted life force holds no meaning beyond the printed page" (205). While this prelude may have its theatrical limitations, however, it does, as Normand Berlin suggests, have its resonance in the play (55). The description of the elms, which O'Neill referred to as "characters, almost" (Chothia 40), initiates a metaphoric pattern that O'Neill works with throughout. In linking the maternal—here "a sinister maternity" compounded of opposites—to the natural world, to the landscape, he prepares us for the projection of the intensities of the Freudian "family romance" onto the terrain of the Cabot farm.

O'Neill claimed to have dreamed *Desire under the Elms* in its entirety. As Louis Sheaffer has pointed out, O'Neill did some borrowing—particularly from Sidney Howard's *They Knew What They Wanted*—as well as dreaming (126). However, O'Neill certainly drew on *collective* dream, on an enduring tradition of mythic and psychological fantasy, when he identified woman, and particularly the mother, with the land. Theorists who have recently focused on

> HIS PRIDE DERIVES FROM HIS MASTERY OF THE LAND AND HIS SENSE OF SUPERIORITY OVER THE WOMEN. HOWEVER, HIS SATISFACTION WITH HIS WAY OF BEING IN THE WORLD IS FLAWED. HE SUFFERS FROM A PERSISTENT UNEASE AND LONELINESS."

such imagery provide us with a context in which to consider its centrality to the play. In a celebrated essay entitled "Is Female to Male as Nature Is to Culture?" Sherry Ortner suggests that for a variety of reasons, biological, social, and psychological, "women are . . . identified or symbolically associated with nature, . . . [while] men . . . are identified with culture" (73). Women, that is, are seen as co-extensive with, or at least much closer to, the natural world. Men, on the other hand, have traditionally felt compelled to master and transcend nature in order to create and maintain culture. This division, Ortner argues, gives rise to a seemingly universal hierarchical structure that places culture and man *over* nature and woman. Ortner is concerned with the ways in which this analogy derives from and influences our experience. As Annette Kolodny points out in her study of the imagery that links woman and the land in American writing about the new world, "language . . . contains verbal cues to underlying psychological patterns" and can therefore "be examined as a repository of internal experience and external expression" (73). Kolodny discusses the tension, fraught with suggestions of oedipal ambivalence, "between the initial urge to . . . join passively with . . . a maternal landscape and the consequent impulse to master and act upon that same femininity" (270). The conceptual fusion of woman and nature tends to put both in jeopardy. Kolodny's work, like that of Ortner, is a vivid reminder of the risk of metaphor.

The power of *Desire under the Elms* is, in large measure, contingent on such imagery as these theorists hold up to scrutiny. O'Neill could be said to have collaborated in the imaginative tradition whose problematic implications they identify. However, while *Desire* tends to illustrate the conjunction of landscape and gender that Ortner and Kolodny describe, the play also has a distinct affinity with their critique. In 1925, O'Neill called *Desire* "a tragedy of the possessive—the pitiful longing of man to build his own heaven here on earth by glutting his sense of power with ownership of land, people, money" (Sheaffer 441). While O'Neill maps out his dramatic territory using the quintessential equation "woman equals nature," he also illuminates the overweening desire to possess and to dominate that is its corollary.

Striking congruities emerge in the play as it becomes apparent that land and woman are at the heart of the struggle between Eben Cabot and his father. Blaming Ephraim for having exhausted, and thereby killed, his mother, Eben is determined to wrest from him the farm she claimed as her own. He believes that only then will her soul finally be at peace. Eben resents his father for the hardness Cabot is so proud of, and insists, "I'm Maw—every drop o' blood." He claims to have learned from doing the arduous domestic tasks she used to do, to "know her, suffer he sufferin'." He is in revolt against the way of life on the Cabot farm, "makin' walls—stone atop o' stone—makin' walls till yer heart's a stone...."

Eben's brothers, Simeon and Peter, the older sons of Cabot's first marriage, are somewhat removed from the primary intensities of the play. They had felt kindly toward Eben's mother, but refuse to blame their father for her death. "No one never kills nobody," Simeon says. "It's allus somethin'. That's the murderer...." Peter agrees: "He's slaved himself t'death. He's slaved Sim 'n' me 'n' yet t' death—on'y none o' us hain't died—yit." They decide to leave rather than fight over the farm when they learn that their father has married and they are likely to lose their inheritance. Likened in O'Neill's description to "friendly oxen" and "beasts of the field." Simeon and Peter say of the farm animals that they "know us like brothers—an' like us." Eben's brothers are not linked with the mother; nor do they aspire to the drive for mastery of the father. It seems appropriate, then, that they do not figure significantly in the highly polarized world of *Desire*.

It is Eben, seeing himself as his mother's heir, who engages most fully in the struggle with the father for power and possession. He has his first sexual experience with Min after he learns that both his father and his brothers had been with her. In a simile characteristic of the drama, Eben says that Min "smells like a wa'm plowed field, she's purty" and later declares to his brothers: "Yes, siree! I tuk her. She may've been his'n—an' your'n, too—but she's mine now!" He uses the money his mother told him Cabot had hidden, to buy their shares of the farm from his brothers. After the transaction is completed, Eben talks with "queer excitement": "It's my farm! Them's my cows!" Simeon and Peter see their father in him: "Dead spit 'n' image!" O'Neill tells us that Eben "stares around him with glowing, possessive eyes. He takes in the whole farm with his embracing glance of desire" and says, "It's purty! It's damned purty! It's mine!" The restricted vocabulary (Chothia 79), appropriate to the "inexpressiveness" (O'Neill quoted in Sheaffer 159) that was a focus for O'Neill in this work, reveals all the more transparently the overlap of landscape and gender that is crucial to its realization.

That there will be a contest between Eben and his father over Abbie, Cabot's new wife, is anticipated even by Simeon, who is slow and plodding. Before we meet Abbie or know what her own intentions are, we sense that her principal role will be to mediate the relationship between father and son. Shortly after Abbie arrives at the farm, Simeon and Peter take off for California to search for gold, choosing, in Cabot's terms, an easy life, which at times tempts even the harsh, scripture-quoting patriarch himself. They leave Cabot, Abbie and Eben on the farm, which itself figures so significantly in the intensely oedipal configuration.

Abbie is a compelling character. O'Neill describes her as thirty-five, and "full of vitality." She has "about her whole personality the same unsettled, untamed, desperate quality which is so apparent in Eben." Like Eben, she wants the farm. An orphan who has already endured a difficult marriage, and whose child and first husband have died, she married the 75-year old Ephraim Cabot in order to have a home. Without exonerating her, O'Neill represents her desire for the farm as different in kind from that of the men. As she says to Eben defiantly, "Waal—what if I did need a hum?" Her relation to nature as a generative force is also different from theirs. She speaks of "Nature—makin' thin's grow—bigger 'n' bigger—burnin' inside ye—makin' ye want t' grow—into somethin' else—till ye're jined with it—and it's your'n but it owns ye, too—and makes ye grow bigger—like a tree—like them elums—." She envisions a mutuality of possession which is conspicuously absent on the Cabot farm. And she taunts Cabot when he talks of the sky as "purty" and like a "wa'm field up thar," asking him, "Air yew aimin' t' buy up over the farm too?"

Jealous when Eben goes off to see Min, Abbie tells Cabot that her stepson tried to make love to her. Here she becomes linked with Phaedra, as she has been with Iocasta. In spite of the dramatic stature the mythic dimension adds to her role, however, she remains, like the land, essentially an object of contention between father and son. Ephraim wouldn't consider letting her inherit the farm even though all his sons have disappointed him. "Ye're on'y a woman." When she reminds him that she is his wife, he says, "That hain't me. A son is me—my blood—mine. Mine ought t' get mine. An' then it's still—mine—even though I be six foot under."

Abbie decides to conceive a child who could inherit the farm for her. Cabot, not knowing that she has Eben in mind as the father, is ecstatic at the possibility of a new son. His reflections at this point provide the clearest indication of the kind of symbol system that O'Neill employs with consistency throughout *Desire under the Elms*. Cabot says to Abbie, "Sometimes ye air the farm an' sometimes the farm be yew. That's why I clove t' ye in my lonesomeness.... Me an' the farm has got t' beget a son!" Abbie, hearing what appears to be a barely conscious admission, tells him he's "gittin' thin's all mixed." Cabot insists, "No, I hain't. My mind's clear's a well. Ye don't know me, that's it." Cabot envisions having Abbie *as* the farm produce a son who would guarantee him an eternity of ownership. As Abbie says, he is getting things "all mixed." The confusion he articulates, however, is a primal one.

As Cabot goes on to explain himself to his wife, whose thoughts are actually with Eben, he reveals more fully what Simeon had referred to as the "somethin'—drivin' him—t'drive us!" Cabot describes himself in his youth as having been "the strongest an' hardest ye ever seen—ten times as strong an' fifty times as hard as Eben." Boasting of his achievement in making "corn sprout out o' stones," he speaks of the God he worships, insisting: "God's hard, not easy! God's in the stones!" He projects, as Frederick Wilkins

has said, "his own hardness onto his conception of the deity."

Ephraim's battle with the stony soil and his disdain for the softness of the mother of Simeon and Peter, and the mother of Eben, suggest the hierarchy that Sherry Ortner discerns. His pride derives from his mastery of the land and his sense of superiority over the women. However, his satisfaction with his way of being in the world is flawed. He suffers from a persistent unease and loneliness.

In the book, *Woman and Nature: The Roaring Inside Her,* Susan Griffin suggests that man's efforts to distance himself from the feminine and from the natural world contribute to his sense of exile and homelessness. Her prologue is a meditation on man: "He says that woman speaks with nature.... But for him this dialogue is over. He says he is not part of this world, that he was set on this world as a stranger. He sets himself apart from woman and nature." This passage seems to echo the revelation of Cabot's "lonesomeness," which is prefaced by his conflation of Abbie and the farm. The sequence of his reflections seems to suggest, as the theorists do, a profound connection between man's conception of landscape and gender, and the experience of alienation.

Cabot is uncomfortable in the house, the sphere of the feminine: "It's oneasy. They's thin's pokin' about in the dark—in the corners." At home, he is troubled by "somethin'," which he feels "droppin' off the elums"—the symbols of a "sinister," but violated maternity. His grueling work on the land, bound up as it is with assertion and control, affords him no comfort either. He would try to console himself by remembering what he possessed: "It was all mine! When I thought of that I didn't feel lonesome." But neither his periodic efforts to conjure up the exaltation of ownership, nor his attempts to seek temporary refuge in the barn with the cows, alleviate his essential isolation.

The attraction of Abbie and Eben thwarts Cabot's hope for a new heir. With thoughts of a child, and with increasing love for Eben, Abbie re-opens the parlor of Eben's mother and insists that he court her there. When with trepidation they sit together in the parlor, both Eben and Abbie sense the approval of the maternal spirit, and the easing of her cares. Eben decides that his mother accepts his union with Abbie, who insists on her similarity to the mother, because it would serve as revenge against Cabot.

After Abbie bears the child he believes is his own, Cabot arranges a celebration. His neighbors easily guess who the child's father really is. But Cabot outdoes everyone there with his age-defying dance, performing one of what John Henry Raleigh calls his "legendary feats" (55). O'Neill once said, "I have always loved Epraim so much! He is so autobiographical" (Sheaffer 130). But while Ephraim Cabot is permitted a dazzling display of endurance, it is Eben who is granted a release from what O'Neill, in another reference to the play, called "old man Cabotism" (Sheaffer 250).

Eben, finding it difficult to respond to his newborn son, tells Abbie, "I don't like this. I don't like lettin' on what's mine's his'n. I been doin' that all my life. I'm gittin' t' the end of b'arin' it!" He is ready for the ultimate confrontation with the father, which is precipitated by Cabot's disclosure that Abbie wanted a son in order to get the farm for herself. When Abbie fears that she will lose Eben, she makes a desperate effort to prove her love for him above all else, by murdering their baby. It is through the appalling act of infanticide that O'Neill resolves the violent tensions of the Cabot household. The death of the baby interrupts a bitter cycle of succession that threatens to stretch into a future where the sins of the fathers—and brother—are visited upon the children. It also shocks Eben into a transformation.

After he reports Abbie to the sheriff, Eben acknowledges his own unwitting complicity in her crime. He says, "I want t' share with ye, Abbie—prison 'r death 'r hell 'r anythin'!... If I'm sharin' with ye, I won't feel lonesome, leastways." Eben's lines suggest that he is no longer in the throes of an oedipal obsession with Abbie, or with the farm. Newly able to love Abbie, he has moved beyond his father's relation to woman and the land, and the loneliness it engendered. By having the son break free from its influence, O'Neill seems to subvert the imagery that has informed the play. The son is rewarded for his renunciation of the paradigm his father had glorified. Having made it possible for his mother's spirit to rest, Eben now manages, through his determination to stand by Abbie, to earn the father's "grudging admiration," a reconciliation of sorts. When the sheriff looks around the farm "enviously," and says, "It's a jim-dandy farm, no denyin'. Wished I owned it!" we are able to gauge the distance Eben has travelled from the imperatives that shape the "tragedy of the possessive."

Source: Bette Mandl, "Family Ties: Landscape and Gender in *Desire under the Elms*," in *Eugene O'Neill Newsletter*, Vol. 11, No. 2, Summer–Fall 1987, pp. 19–35.

Preston Fambrough

In the following essay, Fambrough investigates the mystical aspects of Desire under the Elms *and the influences of Greek tragedy.*

A notion which recurs continually in modern attempts to define tragedy is that of "mystery." According to Richard Sewell, tragedy "sees man as a questioner, naked, unaccommodated, alone, facing mysterious, demonic forces in his own nature and outside" (4–5). George Steiner locates the uniqueness of the form in the "inexplicable" (128) nature of the forces that destroy the protagonist, forces "which can neither be fully understood nor overcome by rational prudence" (8); while Richmond Y. Hathorn defines tragedy as "a work of literature which has as its chief emphasis the revelation of a mystery" (223).

The admission of an irreducible core of mystery at the center of the human experience runs counter to the prevailing intellectual current of the past two centuries—the rationalism of the Enlightenment followed by the reductive positivism of its successors. And just as Nietzsche traced the decline of Attic tragedy to the advent of Socratic rationalism, so George Steiner attributes the eclipse of the form after the French classical period to modern faith in reason and science to reveal all truth and resolve every human dilemma (8). Joseph Mandel is wide of the mark in asserting that nineteenth-century naturalistic determinism is "tragic" (5104-A): fate ceases to be tragic the moment it can be reduced to knowable forces amenable to scientific analysis and control. As Steiner explains, the antithesis of tragedy lies not necessarily in comedy but in didacticism, naturalism and the literature of social criticism, a literature which reduces man's nature and experience to knowable quantities and hence views all his ills, individual and social, as remediable (8).

In his deliberate and sustained effort to revive Tragedy on the modern stage, Eugene O'Neill, while paying lip service to the modern science of psychology, repeatedly insisted on mystery as the essence of his vision of human destiny. In 1919 he wrote to Barrett Clark, "Perhaps I can explain the nature of my feeling for the impelling, inscrutable forces behind life which it is my ambition to at least faintly shadow at their work in my plays" (qtd. in Cargill 100).

> THE PRINCIPAL CHARACTERS ARE MOTIVATED DIRECTLY BY DEMONIC ELEMENTS—THE GHOST, EPHRAIM'S GOD, THE 'DESIRE' OF THE TITLE—WHICH, THOUGH BEYOND THE KEN OF SCIENCE AND REASON, ARE IN SOME WAY APPREHENSIBLE AND IDENTIFIABLE."

Elsewhere he asserted that his interest lay in the relationship between man and God, rather than between man and man (qtd. in Krutch, *Nine Plays* xvii). In interpreting the latter remark, Törnqvist explains that O'Neill thought of himself as a religious playwright, not "in the strict sense that such a designation can be bestowed on Eliot or Claudel...but in the wide sense, that what chiefly concerns him are ultimate, transcendental phenomena" (11).

There are a number of oft-quoted remarks of O'Neill's which might seem, in isolation, to indicate a conventional positivist scepticism toward the transcendental or supernatural, a rejection of mystery in favor of the science of psychology. In the manuscript version of his foreword to *The Great God Brown*, the playwright affirms that "if we have no Gods, [sic] or heroes to portray we have the subconscious, the mother of all gods and heroes." Repeatedly, in his working diary notes for *Mourning Becomes Electra*, he speaks of the necessity for finding a "modern psychological approximation of the Greek conception of fate from without, from the supernatural" (qtd. in Clark 534); and he explicitly denies the existence of any supernatural element in *Electra* (Clark 536).

But thoughtful critics have always discerned an element of intransigent mysticism beneath this surface allegiance to positivism. Asselineau cautions that, the playwright's disclaimers notwithstanding, the psychological view of fate at work in *Electra* does not "entirely supersede the traditional belief in an external fate" ("*MBE* as Tragedy" 147). Törnqvist explains that while O'Neill shares the naturalist's preoccupation with heredity and environment as determinants of human destiny, "positivism was foreign to O'Neill's antirationalistic, mystical mind" (29).

And he points to the curious mingling of scientific and metaphysical language in such expressions as the following: "I'm always acutely conscious of the Force behind—(Fate, God, our biological past creating our present, whatever one calls it—Mystery certainly)" (qtd. in Gelb 4 and Törnqvist 17). Chabrowe sees in *Desire, Strange Interlude, Electra*, and *Long Day's Journey into Night* "attempts to reveal man's struggle against the mysterious force that shapes his existence and limits him" (xvi). And Krutch contends that "at a time when naturalism was the literary norm, he wrote plays that were symbolic in method and mystical in intention" ("O'Neill Revolutionary" 29).

Desire under the Elms, "the first of O'Neill's works in which the influence of Greek tragedy is clearly manifest" (Gelb 539), is charged with an uncompromisingly mystical view of the forces at work in and through human beings, forces which may *manifest* themselves in forms recognizable by the science of psychoanalysis—e.g. Eben's Oedipus complex—but which ultimately transcend scientific or rational explanation. And whether or not O'Neill's emphasis shifts in the course of his career from an "external" to an "internal" concept of fate, as Chabrowe suggests (102), in this play the two coincide and fuse much as they do in O'Neill's ancient models. In Greek tragedy, action appears to proceed naturally from a given quantity called "character," a complex of distinguishable human traits usually seen in part as having been shaped by past experience and perhaps even by heredity (e.g. Antigone, Hippolytus) in ways that reflect universal "laws" of the human experience. At the same time, the action appears as the product of supernatural forces, a reaction against some breach of the cosmic order. As Kitto explains, "the gods are not directing events as if from outside; they work *in* the events" (128, Kitto's emphasis); "the action is seen on two planes at once, human and divine" (133). Similarly, in *Desire*, we are made cognizant simultaneously of the dark, only partly knowable forces of the individual subconscious and of a superhuman cosmic principle working itself out through the action of the tragedy.

In *Desire* the leitmotif "thin'" functions to reveal at every turn of the action the transcendent, inscrutable force working through the multiplicity of identifiable human motives in the play. The motif is established in scene two where it recurs several times in quick succession. When Eben bitterly accuses Ephraim of having killed his mother, Simeon replies, "No one never kills nobody. It's allus some thin'. That's the murderer." When Eben inquires "What's somethin'?" his brother replies "dunno." In this exchange, the basic significance of the motif is already revealed. Simeon contends not merely that people are the pawns of a force beyond their control, but that this force can only be identified as a "thin'." This recourse to the indefinite pronoun establishes from the outset the essential inscrutability of the fate at work in the play. Of course we are tempted to supply an explanation—Ephraim's grimly irrational Puritan work ethic, perhaps a function of sexual guilt or repression. But it is not his inarticulateness that makes Simeon hesitate to oversimplify the old man's motivation by naming it. And this cryptic generalization echoes throughout the play in characters' attempts to account for their own or each other's actions and to articulate the mysterious influences they sense at work around them.

Still in the second scene Simeon, in asking Eben to explain his long-standing grudge against the elder brothers, remarks that "Year after year it's skulked in yer eye—somethin'." Later in the play Ephraim, recounting to Abbie how he once left his stony New England farm for a rich and easy life in Ohio, only to abandon his crop and return home, explains, "I could 'o been a rich man—but somethin' in me fit me and fit me—the voice of God sayin': 'This hain't wuth nothin' t'Me. Get ye back t'hum!'" (2.2). The tone of wonder in which he exclaims "I actooly give up what was rightful mine!" (2.2) underscores the profoundly incalculable nature of a force that could drive the intensely covetous Ephraim to such an uncongenial act.

The old man, throughout the play, is conscious of a hostile presence in the house: "They's thin's pokin' about in the dark, in the corners" (2.2). "Even the music can't drive it out," he exclaims during the festivities in honor of the baby, "somethin'" (3.1). And finally, after he learns the truth about Eben and Abbie's relationship and the child's paternity: "That was it—what I felt—pokin' around the corners—while ye lied—holdin' yerself from me—sayin' ye'd already conceived.... I felt they was somethin' onnateral—somewhars—the house got so lonesome—an' cold—drivin' me down to the barn—t'the beasts o' the field" (3.4).

The mysterious influence at work on Eben and his father can be identified, at one level, with the avenging spirit of Eben's mother. Having driven Ephraim out of the house, the same "onnateral" force seems to impel Eben toward Abbie in spite of the young man's fierce resistance and to preside over their union in the parlor that is sacred to the dead woman's memory:

Abbie: When I first come in—in the dark—
    they seemed somethin' here.
Eben: (*simply*) Maw.
Abbie: I kin still feel—somethin'....
Eben: It's Maw. (2.3)

Yet to equate the supernatural element of the play absolutely with the mother's ghost, as Racey does (44), oversimplifies O'Neill's tragic cosmology. Eben himself, baffled at first that his mother's ghost should seem to favor a union between him and Abbie, her rival for the land, at last thinks he discerns the spirit's purpose: "I see it! I see why. It's her vengeance on him—so's she can rest quiet in her grave!" (2.3). But we know that in fact this love, while punishing Ephraim, will also destroy the dead woman's beloved son as well as his child. The tragic catastrophe clearly transcends what could conceivably be the will of Eben's mother's ghost. I believe Abbie's frantic rejoinder here, "Vengeance o' God on the hull o' us!" (2.3), provides a clue to the underlying cosmology of the play. As often seems the case in Greek and Elizabethan tragedy, there appear to be at least two levels of superhuman forces at work here. First there are the immediate and circumscribed influences impinging directly on the characters—Cabot's Old Testament god, the ghost, the darkly irrational "Desire" of the title. But apparently these fragmentary forces partake of a larger, more remote, more inhuman and inscrutable will. This is what Abbie intimates in emending Eben's explanation of their passion as retribution on Cabot for his cruelty to the dead woman. The deity she evokes here is something much vaster than the petty tyrant Ephraim serves: it is Moira, the ultimate will of the universe itself.

When Eben learns that Abbie has murdered their child, he cries "Maw, where was ye, why didn't ye stop her?" (3.3). Again, it is Abbie who senses the truth: "She went back t'her grave that night we first done it, remember? I hain't felt her about since" (3.3). This observation not only reveals the limited scope of the ghost's influence within the larger cosmic design; it adumbrates something of the relationship between this cosmic design and human justice or morality. Kitto has explained, in analyzing Greek tragedy, that while the logos of the tragic universe includes principles we recognize as "just"—the wicked seldom if ever go unpunished—there are uncharted realms of the cosmic law which transcend human justice (148). In *Desire under the Elms*, as in most tragedies, the innocent suffer with the guilty.

In the *Iliad*, the anthropomorphic gods, even the mightiest of them, are usually seen to be clearly subordinate to Moira. Zeus himself bows to this inexorable force at least twice in relinquishing his determination first to save the life of his son Sarpendon and later the life of Hector. Steiner maintains that the Greek Pantheon, representing the partly intelligible elements of man's destiny, serves as a "reassuring mask" between us and Fate (5–6). O'Neill's tragedy reveals a similar cosmology. The principal characters are motivated directly by demonic elements—the ghost, Ephraim's god, the "desire" of the title—which, though beyond the ken of science and reason, are in some way apprehensible and identifiable. The ubiquitous leitmotif "thin'" emerges as the common denominator linking these half-knowable forces and pointing to the ineffable mystery beyond.

Source: Preston Fambrough, "The Tragic Cosmology of *Desire under the Elms*," in *Eugene O'Neill Newsletter*, Vol. 10, No. 2, Summer-Fall 1986, pp. 25–29.

Hollis L. Cate

In the following essay, Cate argues that the poetic language of Ephraim Cabot provides insight into his character.

My contention...is not only that Eugene O'Neill's character Ephraim Cabot is a spontaneous poet but also that the old man's total character cannot possibly be understood if his poetic nature is not taken into account. With all his faults old Cabot does have at least one inherently redeeming side.

O'Neill once wrote Professor A. H. Quinn: "But where I feel myself most neglected is just where I set most store by myself—as a bit of a poet, who has labored with the spoken word to evolve original rhythms of beauty, where beauty apparently isn't." In making the statement O'Neill mentions *Desire under the Elms* among other of his plays, and well he should have, for old Ephraim Cabot, now generally considered the protagonist of the play, is one of O'Neill's most forceful poets. Professor Quinn in 1926, two years after the appearance of *Desire,* published an article in *Scribner's Magazine* dealing

> BUT IF HE IS A MAN OF TRAGIC STATURE AS SEVERAL CRITICS HAVE SAID OR IMPLIED, THEN ONE MUST CONSIDER CAREFULLY, IN REACHING SUCH A CONCLUSION, THE OLD MAN'S SPEECH AS AN INTEGRAL PART OF HIS NATURE."

with O'Neill as poet and mystic. Though the article seems to be gathering a little dust these days, anyone making an approach to *Desire under the Elms* in particular should give it his attention; O'Neill certainly shows his poetic side in creating the speeches of Ephraim Cabot. The old man comes to mind as one reads Mr. Quinn's observation: "Even in the most degraded man, O'Neill recognizes the saving grace that comes from his divine origin." If Cabot is given to degradation on the one hand, his poetry is a "saving grace" on the other. Further, Professor Quinn was speaking boldly, at the time, to several critics in saying "it is a pitiful stupidity of criticism that sees only the repellent...in *Desire Under the Elms*." O'Neill himself had a tender feeling for Cabot. He said in a letter: "I have always loved Ephraim so much! He's so autobiographical!" Although O'Neill was, no doubt, referring to his sleeping in the barn as Cabot does, there is no denying that Ephraim, like his creator, is "a bit of a poet." Clearly, one redeeming feature of *Desire* and of Cabot himself is his role as spontaneous poet, a "maker" who turns again and again for his images to the mysterious world of Nature about him.

The role of Nature itself in the play is highly significant. [In his *Eugene O'Neill*] Frederick Carpenter says that in the final analysis the spirit of Nature is the hero of the play. Cabot certainly seems to agree. Nature is for the old man the one true abiding force, God's revelation of Himself to man; and, further, in the Romantic tradition it is a solace, an escape from the encroachments of the everyday world. Ephraim, in his closeness to its presence, habitually looks to Nature for his metaphors and similes. In part he is an Emersonian man who senses that "every natural fact is a symbol of some spiritual fact" and who uses spontaneous images in his speech. No other character in the play even approaches him in his use of poetic diction because no other character longs as he does to have at least a glimpse through Nature of that mysterious sphere beyond temporality. With all his shortcomings Cabot at least recognizes the beauty and harmony of Nature. It is a mistake to assume that Ephraim thinks that God is *only* in the stones, contrary to S.K. Winther's observation that Cabot reads the lessons of the stones as the true symbol of God's reality. Mr. Winther's statement that Cabot "listens to the voice of nature" and is "exalted by her beauty" is to be stressed as much as, if not more than, the point that the old man is preoccupied with identifying the stones with the Deity.

There has been a great deal of critical comment on Cabot's attitude toward God, the crux of it being that Ephraim has created God in his own image, that is, God is hard, isolated, lonesome, and unsympathetic. But there is more to Cabot's nature than what these adjectives describe, despite the fact that he always refers to himself as "tough" and "hard." O'Neill on one occasion describes Cabot's eyes as taking "on a strange, incongruous dreamy quality." Here we get a glimpse of the introspective Cabot whom the other characters fail to see and whom Cabot himself is not fully cognizant of, a man whose vision, from time to time, transcends the external, material world. When he says, "The sky. Feels like a wa'm field up thar", he reveals a sensitivity which is congruous with eyes of "dreamy quality." Later he refers to the sky again in a conversation with Eben:

> CABOT. Purty, hain't it?
> EBEN. (*looking around him possessively*) It's a durned purty farm.
> CABOT. I mean the sky.
> EBEN. (*grinning*) How d'ye know? Them eyes o'your'n can't see that fur.

Again Cabot looks upward, comments on the sky, and is typically misunderstood. Eben's remark about the old man's eyesight is, of course, ironic. Cabot "sees" in a spiritual way far more effectively than any other character in the play. Ephraim, like Oedipus and Gloucester in *King Lear,* doesn't see and yet he does. [In his *A Poet's Quest*] Richard Dana Skinner describes him as "the nearsighted one, of narrow vision and narrow pride, imperious, yet in many ways completely identifying himself with a lonesome and hard God." [In her *Eugene O'Neill and the Tragic Tension*] Doris Falk similarly points out

that God to Cabot is an image of his own ego. His poetic diction, however, indicates that he carries on an intuitive search for the Deity's true revelation through Nature; and we must remember that he has a poetic side that one can easily identify with a God not hard and lonesome. Neither of the observations above takes into account the old man's recognition of an aesthetic in Nature. Indeed, there was more of God to be found by Cabot's staying on the farm than by going to the West in search of gold. Another view is that "the harsh, loveless, and covetous Puritanical religion practiced by Ephraim Cabot is a perversion of religion that cripples love and destroys man" [Peter L. Hays, "Biblical Perversion in *Desire Under the Elms*"]. But the spirit of beauty and harmony is within him, as him poetry shows; unfortunately, however, he fails to grasp its full essence or develop its potential and therein lies the heart of the old man's tragedy.

Cabot's reliance on poetic diction is evident in almost every scene in which he appears. At one point he says, "When ye kin make corn sprout out o'stones, God's livin' in ye!" In a sense Cabot's corn is his poetry, which is prompted by a muse at least partially divine, for he draws spiritual strength through his recognition of man's dependence on Nature and, thus, on God for a language which expresses the harmony of existence itself, a language made up of forceful figures of speech: metaphors, similes, personification, and synecdoche.

Cabot's metaphors and similes include references to familiar objects as well as to animals. In the first place he describes himself as he, in part, sees himself and as *he knows* the other characters see him, but his total being, as stated earlier, goes far beyond his own descriptive terms. He says that he is as "sound'n tough as hickory!", "a hard nut t' crack", "hard as iron yet!", and "like a stone—a rock o' judgment". Several times he says he is getting old, "ripe on the bough." Revealing a side of his nature seldom seen, Ephraim recalls the Song of Solomon and is very much carried away in a well-known poetic speech addressed to Abbie: "Yew air my Rose o' Sharon!...yer eyes air doves; yer lips air like scarlet; yer two breasts air like two fawns; yer navel be like..." and so on. Later he says to those who have come to the dance: "What're ye all bleatin' about—like a flock o'goats?...thar ye set cacklin' like a lot o' wet hens with the pip! Ye've swilled my likker an' guzzled my vittles like hogs, hain't ye?" His hearers dictate his imagery, and "doves" and "fawns" used in his speech to Abbie are replaced with "goats," "hens," and "hogs," with the appropriately descriptive words "bleatin'," "cacklin'," "swilled," and "guzzled." Cabot, forever the poet, even spontaneously uses onomatopoeia. He later, in typical fashion, tells the others that they are "all hoofs!" and their "veins is full o'mud and water." Quite often in heated moments he reaches for his figurative language. Such is the case when he berates Eben: "It's ye that's blind—blind as a mole underground.... They's nothin' in that thick skull o' your'n but noise—like a empty keg it be!" Rarely is there a simple statement without the figurative analogy for driving home the point. Speaking to Eben again the old man says, "A prime chip o' yer ye be!" In addition to the metaphor itself there is internal rhyme, as well as an emphasis on labial formations which Cabot bites off in grim, tight-lipped fashion. His final figure comes late in the play after the death of Abbie and Eben's child and after he has learned of their affair: "Ye make a slick pair o' murderin' turtle doves!:" He is the unrelenting poet to the end.

Cabot, as a spontaneous image-maker, uses both personification and synecdoche. When he describes the mysterious "something'" that pervades the house, he says: "Ye kin feel it droppin' off the elums, climbin' up the roof, sneakin' down the chimney, pokin' in the corners!" Cabot conveys the personified movement he wishes to convey with well-balanced participial phrases. In speaking to Abbie and Eben at the end of the play, he tells them that young fools like them should "hobble their lust," which, in the image, become an animal of vice that should be restrained. Finally, in saying to Eben, "An' the farm's her'n Abbie's! An' the dust o' the road —that's your'n!", Ephraim makes his point by using a part for the whole, significantly, an unpleasant part.

This...is not an attempt to vindicate Ephraim Cabot; several critics have enumerated his faults and shortcomings, making telling points against him. But if he is a man of tragic stature as several critics have said or implied, then one must consider carefully, in reaching such a conclusion, the old man's speech as an integral part of his nature. O'Neill once said in a letter: "...I'm always, always, trying to interpret Life in terms of lives, never just lives in terms of character. I'm always actually conscious of the Force behind—(Fate, God, our biological past creating

our present, whatever one calls it—Mystery certainly)—and of the eternal tragedy of Man in his glorious, self destructive struggle to make the Force express him instead of being as an animal is, an infinitesimal incident in its expression." Cabot, in his effort to catch a glimpse of the true Force, seems determined not to be an "infinitesimal incident in its expression." O'Neill leaves us with the impression that Cabot, with all his vitality, robustness, and strength, is living yet somewhere on that rocky New England land because we see him as a part of Nature, the partial essence of which he spontaneously expresses out of his poetic consciousness and because we are secure in the truth that Nature is still there, as both O'Neill and Cabot knew it would be.

Source: Hollis L. Cate, "Ephraim Cabot: O'Neill's Spontaneous Poet," in *Markham Review*, Vol. 2, No. 5, February 1971, pp. 115–17.

SOURCES

"The Censored Audience," in *Nation*, Vol. 120, No. 3117, April 1, 1925, p. 346.

Cohn, Ruby, "Eugene O'Neill: Overview," in *Reference Guide to American Literature*, 3rd ed., edited by Jim Kamp, St. James Press, 1994.

Conkin, Paul K., *A Revolution Down on the Farm: The Transformation of American Agriculture since 1929*, University Press of Kentucky, 2008.

Cunningham, Frank R., "Romantic Elements in Early O'Neill," in *Critical Essays on Eugene O'Neill*, edited by James J. Martine, G. K. Hall, 1984, pp. 65–72.

Easterling, P. E., *The Cambridge Companion to Greek Tragedy*, Cambridge University Press, 1997.

Fambrough, Preston, "The Tragic Cosmology of *Desire under the Elms*," in *Eugene O'Neill Newsletter*, Vol. 10, No. 2, Summer-Fall, 1986, pp. 25–29.

Freud, Sigmund, *The Basic Writings of Sigmund Freud*, translated and edited by A. A. Brill, Modern Library, 1995.

Gelb, Barbara, "Eugene O'Neill," in *Dictionary of American Biography*, Supplement 5: 1951–1955, American Council of Learned Societies, 1977.

Harper, Douglas, *Changing Works: Visions of a Lost Agriculture*, University of Chicago Press, 2001.

Heberden, Melodee, Maria McCracken, and Dave McCracken, *Gold Mining in the 21st Century*, New Era Publications, 2005.

Holliday, J. S., *Rush for Riches: Gold Fever and the Making of California*, University of California Press, 1999.

"It's Time for Working Women to Earn Equal Pay," *American Federation of Labor and Congress of Industrial*

Organizations, http://www.aflcio.org/issues/jobseconomy/women/equalpay/ (accessed June 22, 2009).

Krutch, Joseph Wood, "Drama," in *Nation*, Vol. 120, No. 3129, June 24, 1925, pp. 714–24.

Madran, Cumhur Yilmaz, "The Ambivalence of Love and Hate in *Desire under the Elms*: A Psychological and Mythological Approach," in *Selcuk University Social Sciences Institute Journal*, Vol. 16, 2006, pp. 449–58.

McMillen, Sally, *Seneca Falls and the Origins of the Women's Rights Movement*, Oxford University Press, 2008.

O'Neill, Eugene, *Desire under the Elms*, in *Three Plays: Desire under the Elms, Strange Interlude, Mourning Becomes Electra*, Vintage Books, 1959, pp. 1–58.

Sklar, Kathryn Kish, *Women's Rights Emerges within the Anti-Slavery Movement, 1830–1870: A Brief History with Documents*, Palgrave Macmillan, 2000.

Stilling, Roger J., "Eugene O'Neill," in *Dictionary of Literary Biography*, Vol. 331, *Nobel Prize Laureates in Literature, Part 3: Lagerkvist-Pontoppidan*, Gale, 2007, pp. 373–95.

FURTHER READING

Black, Stephen A., *Eugene O'Neill: Beyond Mourning and Tragedy*, Yale University Press, 2002.

    Black's literary biography provides insight into O'Neill's life and work. In particular, it traces the autobiographical elements in the dramatist's plays.

Dutta, Shomit, ed., *Greek Tragedy*, Penguin Classics, 2009.

    This anthology of classical Greek tragedies includes works by Aeschylus, Euripides, and Sophocles. The plays in this volume influenced not only O'Neill's work but nearly all dramatic works ever produced. Indeed, Greek tragedies are some of the first recorded plays, and they lay the foundation for the art of drama and the theater.

Findling, John E., and Frank W. Thackeray, *Events That Changed America in the Nineteenth Century*, Greenwood Press, 1997.

    This interesting history provides a context for the Cabot farmhouse and its inhabitants in 1850. Given the book's scope, it also covers the early twentieth century and thus the context of the era in which O'Neill was living and writing.

Kramer, Peter D., *Freud: Inventor of the Modern Mind*, Eminent Lives, 2006.

    This biography of Sigmund Freud presents a straightforward account of the psychoanalyst's life and work. It will add not only to any student's understanding of Freud's basic principles, but also to the themes underpinning much of the literature produced in the early twentieth century.

The Governess

NEIL SIMON

1973

The Governess, a one-act play by Neil Simon, was written in 1973. The play consists of a brief scene taken from another Simon play, *The Good Doctor*. Strictly speaking, *The Good Doctor* is not a play but a series of vignettes or short sketches, and thus, *The Governess* is able to stand alone as a one-act play. *The Good Doctor* is sometimes labeled a musical, but strictly speaking, the play has only some musical accompaniment, rather being a musical itself. *The Governess* contains no music.

The Governess is based on a short story, "A Nincompoop," by the nineteenth-century Russian writer Anton Chekhov. The play is a satire on innocence, trickery, and money and involves the interaction between two characters, the mistress and the family governess, whose innocence the mistress fails to appreciate as an important value. The action takes place in Russia at the turn of the century. Simon's use of Chekhov was a departure from his previous plays, since *The Governess* is not set in contemporary New York and does not focus on New York life.

The Governess first opened on Broadway at the Eugene O'Neill Theater on November 27, 1973, as part of the *The Good Doctor*. The play ran for 208 performances and received several Tony Award nominations, including Best Featured Actress in a Play (a win for Frances Sternhagen, playing the mistress), Best Featured Actor in a Play, Best Original Score, and Best Lighting

Neil Simon (AP Images)

design. *The Governess* is available as act 1, scene 3 of *The Good Doctor*, which is included in *The Collected Plays of Neil Simon, Volume II*, published in 1979 by Random House.

AUTHOR BIOGRAPHY

Marvin Neil Simon was born on July 4, 1927, in the Bronx in New York City. He is the youngest son of Irving, a garment salesman, and Mamie, who worked a series of part-time jobs to help with family finances while her husband traveled for his job. Simon graduated from DeWitt Clinton High School in 1944, at age sixteen, and began taking classes at New York University, where he joined the Army Air Force Reserve program. The following year, Simon was sent to Colorado for military training at Lowry Field, where he also attended the University of Denver and where he taught himself to write comedy by watching comedians. When he received a discharge from the military in 1946, Simon returned to New York and began writing

television comedy sketches with his brother, Danny, for Goodman Ace at CBS. In 1953, Simon married Joan Baim. The couple would eventually have two daughters, Ellen and Nancy. In 1956, the writing partnership ended when Danny chose to change careers and begin directing television shows. Simon continued to write for comedy shows and received Emmy Award nominations for comedy writing in 1956, 1957, and 1959. By 1957, Simon had decided to try playwriting and began writing his first play, *Come Blow Your Horn*, which proved to be a success on Broadway in 1961.

Simon's second play, *Barefoot in the Park*, was even more successful when it premiered on Broadway in 1963; it was quickly followed by *The Odd Couple* (1965), which received Tony Awards for acting and directing and for Simon as author. Simon was a success as a playwright and soon had several plays on Broadway at one time. *Sweet Charity* (1966), *Plaza Suite* (1968), and *The Sunshine Boys* (1972) were also huge successes and quickly found their way to film, as had Simon's earlier works. Simon's wife died in 1973, leaving him with two daughters, ten-year-old Nancy and fifteen-year-old Ellen. That same year, Simon married Marsha Mason only a few months after they met, when she auditioned for a part in *The Good Doctor*. In the years that followed, Simon continued to write successful plays, including *California Suite* (1976) and *Chapter Two* (1977), as well as screenplays, such as *The Goodbye Girl* (1977). Simon and Mason, who starred in several of Simon's plays and in the films he wrote, were divorced in 1982.

The autobiographical trilogy *Brighton Beach Memoirs* (1982), *Biloxi Blues* (1984), and *Broadway Bound* (1986) earned Simon several awards, but most important, finally established Simon as a success with the critics, who had previously provided mixed reviews of his work. In 1987, Simon married Diane Lander. They were divorced the following year, but remarried in 1990. Simon was awarded a Pulitzer Prize for *Lost in Yonkers* in 1991. In 1995, he was a Kennedy Center Honoree and in 1997 received the William Inge Theater Festival Award for Distinguished Achievement in the American Theater. Simon and Lander were divorced a second time in 1998. They have one adopted daughter, Bryn. Simon married Elaine Joyce in 1999. He has continued to write plays and screenplays, including *The Dinner Party* in 2000 and *Rose's Dilemma* in

2003. During his career, Simon has written more than thirty plays and nearly as many screenplays.

PLOT SUMMARY

The Governess opens with a brief statement from the writer, who addresses the audience with a few comments about the previous scene in *The Good Doctor*. The writer than makes a few remarks about the scene that is to appear next, *The Governess*. The writer explains that the stories he is telling are not intended to paint a harsh picture of the world, at least no harsher than life really is, but he does note that some people are trapped in a harsh reality. The writer suggests that the story of the mistress and the governess is just such a story—one of harshness.

After the writer provides his few comments, the play begins with the mistress sitting at a desk on stage, her account book open in front of her. She calls for Julia, the children's governess. At Julia's name, the writer interjects the word "trapped," which recalls his earlier remarks about people who are trapped in a harsh world. The audience immediately understands that the governess is one of those trapped people. When Julia appears, she is told by the mistress not to look down but to look her mistress in the eyes. Although Julia looks up at the mistress as instructed, her head immediately drops down again. She has learned the respectful and subservient position that is required of the servant class.

The mistress begins by asking Julia how the children are doing in French and mathematics, but it is clear that the mistress is not really interested in the answers that Julia provides. Julia is again asked twice in quick succession to lift up her eyes and look at her mistress. After the second request, Julia lifts her eyes and is told that she does not need to be afraid to look people in the eye. The mistress also tells Julia that if she thinks she is inferior, that is how people will treat her. Julia is deferential and exceedingly polite to her mistress, providing short answers to all of the mistress's questions and instructions. In response, the mistress simply remarks that the governess seems a quiet girl, but something in the mistress's manner suggests that being quiet is not really a compliment but rather a character flaw.

The mistress tells the governess that she has been called to meet with her to settle the family account: she is to be paid. When the mistress

MEDIA ADAPTATIONS

- *The Good Doctor*, from which *The Governess* is taken, was filmed in 1978 and is part of the Broadway Theatre Archive collection. The film was directed by Jack O'Brien and starred Edward Asner, Richard Chamberlain, Marsha Mason, and Lee Grant. It is available on DVD.

- *The Governess*, staged at the KKT Theatre in Chicago in the late 1980s can be seen online at http://TubeQ.com/view/786091.

reminds Julia that the family agreed to pay her thirty rubles a month, Julia is surprised and says she was promised forty rubles. In response, the mistress claims that the usual fee is thirty and that if Julia kept her head up and looked people in the eye, she would hear more accurately. The mistress insists that Julia heard incorrectly; when the mistress again says thirty rubles, as if speaking to someone of low intelligence, Julia simply agrees that the mistress is correct. The mistress tells Julia that she has been employed for two months, but Julia disputes that accounting and claims she has been employed for two months and five days. The mistress again insists that she is correct and that Julia should write things down and keep better records. Once again, the governess agrees.

When Julia has agreed to the revised length of her employment, the mistress begins deducting days of salary. First nine Sundays are deducted, but of course, Julia did not agree to not being paid on Sunday. When instructed to think of the Sunday agreement, Julia still cannot recall that particular agreement. At this point, the mistress tells Julia to look up at the mistress, as if doing so will help her recall the memory. When Julia looks at her mistress, she simply agrees that she is not to be paid on Sunday. Next the mistress deducts three holidays, Christmas, New Year's Day, and Julia's birthday, but Julia insists that she worked on her birthday.

The mistress replies that Julia did not need to work on her birthday, but if she insists that she did work, then she will be paid. When asked by the mistress if she insists on being paid, Julia backs down yet again.

Next the mistress deducts for the four days one of the children was sick, but Julia replies that she still taught the second child, who was not sick. The mistress reminds Julia that she was hired to teach two children, and asks if she is supposed to be paid her full salary for doing only half the work. Julia says no, and the four days are deducted. Next are the three days that Julia had a toothache and was told she could quit at noon, but Julia insists she worked until four in the afternoon. However, as she has since the very beginning of their conversation, the mistress looks at her accounting book and insists that Julia did not work after lunch. Julia agrees once again with her mistress and even thanks her, although for what exactly is not clear. The next deduction is for a broken teacup and saucer. Julia responds that she only broke the saucer, but the mistress says a cup is no good without the saucer. In a condescending tone, the mistress says that the teacup and saucer were heirlooms, but she is willing to only deduct two rubles. Julia once again thanks her mistress.

The next deduction is for ten rubles for a jacket one child tore while climbing a tree. Although Julia told him not to climb the tree, ultimately she is still responsible, according to the mistress. Julia is also responsible for the children's shoes that were stolen by a maid who was discharged for the theft. When Julia insists she is not responsible for this loss, she is told that she was hired to keep her eyes open, and they were apparently on the clouds that day. Earlier the complaint was that Julia looked down at the floor and not at her mistress; now the complaint is that she looks at the clouds and daydreams. The mistress deducts another five rubles. Another ten rubles are deducted for money that was advanced to Julia previously. Julia insists she did not receive an advance on her salary, but the mistress says she wrote it down. Why would she write it down if it did not happen? Julia responds by saying she does not know why the mistress would write down something that did not happen, and when challenged again by her mistress, the governess quietly agrees to the reduction. After all of the deductions, the governess is to receive fourteen of the eighty rubles owed to her for working two months and five days.

When she hears the total, Julia turns away crying but still agrees with her mistress's total accounting. The mistress claims to be sensitive to tears, which cause her pain, and she asks why Julia is crying. Julia tells her mistress that the only money given to her was three rubles for her birthday, which were given to her by the mistress's husband. Immediately, the mistress exclaims that the three rubles were not entered into the accounting book and promptly deducts them from the money owed to Julia. Now she is to receive eleven rubles. When the mistress asks if Julia wishes to check her accounts, Julia says there is no need. The mistress places eleven coins on the desk, and Julia is told to count the money. When she says it is not necessary, the mistress insists. Julia counts the coins, and only ten are present. However, the mistress insists that Julia must have dropped one coin. She is told to keep the ten coins and if the eleventh is not found, they can discuss it next month. Julia agrees, thanks her mistress, and tells her she is kind.

In the concluding lines of *The Governess*, the mistress asks Julia why she thanked her. Julia replies that she thanked her mistress for paying her the money owed to her. The mistress is incredulous and asks if Julia did not realize that she was being cheated. There were no notes in her accounting book. Indeed, the mistress made it all up, deducting rubles for whatever reason she could find. The mistress admits she was cheating Julia and yet she continued to thank her. She wants to know why. Julia responds that in previous jobs, she was not paid at all. The mistress is incensed and says that Julia was cheated in the past and that the mistress was just playing a joke on her governess. Although it was a cruel lesson, the mistress claims that Julia is too trusting, which is dangerous. She then hands Julia an envelope with the remainder of the eighty rubles owed to her. Julia simply agrees with her mistress again and turns to leave the room. The mistress stops her and asks if she is really as spineless as she appears. The mistress asks why Julia does not protest or stand up for herself. The mistress also asks if it is possible to be so simple and innocent. At this point the mistress's words are cruel and she intends them to be, as if she is trying to awaken Julia to the dangers she faces in her innocence. The plays ends when Julia turns back to the mistress with a slight smile and says yes, it is possible for a person to be as innocent as the governess appears.

CHARACTERS

Julia, the Governess

When the audience is introduced to the governess, she is responding to a summons from her mistress. In fact, the governess has rushed into the room, since she knows that a summons is not to be ignored. Julia remains standing while the mistress sits. From her stance, with downcast eyes, the governess appears to be a quiet, unassuming, subservient member of the staff. She keeps her eyes on the ground, does not look at all at her mistress, and patiently waits for her mistress to speak to her. The governess knows her place in the household and her role in this society. Julia quietly acquiesces to everything her mistress says, regardless of how obvious it is that the woman is wrong. Although the governess questions the injustice she faces, it is not because she does not know she is being exploited. Julia does question her employer's words, but she is not in a position to protest. Julia is a member of the servant class. She is a domestic in a wealthy household, and she understands that her role is to accept whatever is given to her. She tells her mistress that in previous households, she was not paid anything for her work. The exploitation of the working class is something Julia understands and has faced before. The governess is not stupid, nor is she unaware that the mistress is cheating her, but because of her position in the household, she is unable to demand justice.

The Mistress

When the play opens, the mistress is seated at a desk with an accounting book open in front of her. It is clear from her position and the open book that she is the person in the position of authority in this dialogue. The mistress has summoned the governess, who rushes into the room. Julia's rushing into the room suggests that the mistress demands a prompt response when a servant is summoned. The mistress is a bully. She holds a position of authority and uses it to harass the governess. The mistress devises a joke, as she calls it, which is intended to teach a lesson to her governess that if she is so trusting of people, she will be cheated. However, the mistress is incapable of realizing that the governess is not trusting or innocent; because of her position in the household, she is unable to protest when she is cheated. Whether the governess is trusting or not does not matter, but the mistress is so unaware of the ramifications of social

stratification in her society that she thinks tormenting the governess is an acceptable way to teach her a lesson. Interestingly, the mistress is completely unaware that she is cruel or unjust to the governess. When the governess tells the mistress that she had not been paid anything in her previous places of employment, the mistress says that Julia was cheated. Julia knows this, of course, but she is unable to do anything about it. The mistress is so insulated from the struggle of the lower classes that she thinks they are unaware when they are cheated. It is the mistress who is an innocent about the ways of the world, not the governess.

The Writer, Kuryatin

The writer's role is very brief. At the beginning of the play, he comments on the previous scene and then provides a few words about the action that is to follow. In a sense, the writer functions similarly to a chorus in a Greek tragedy. He comments on what has occurred and provides a preview of what is to occur next. The writer is sometimes identified as Simon by critics, although the part is not played by the playwright on stage.

THEMES

Oppression

The Governess opens with comments from the writer about the harshness of the world for those who are trapped. The governess is one of those trapped individuals who exists in a dependent state. She is dependent on the honesty and good will of her employer. The governess is the object of her employer's "lesson," which is designed, according to the mistress, to teach the governess that she needs to assert herself if she is to avoid being exploited. The irony is that it is the employer who is exploiting the governess. What the mistress does not grasp is that Julia is not allowed to protest or to demand justice. As a household servant in a wealthy household, she is entirely at the mercy of her employers. In her rush to teach Julia a lesson, the mistress exploits Julia's innocence, and in doing so, she treats the governess harshly. The governess is indeed trapped. She reveals at the end of the conversation that her previous employers have not always paid her as promised. She is, accordingly, grateful that the mistress is going to pay her anything

TOPICS FOR FURTHER STUDY

- Drama is meant to be seen and heard and not simply read. With one other student from your class, choose a section of dialogue from *The Governess* to memorize and then present to your classmates. After you have completed your mini-performance, ask each of your classmates to write down at least one thing that they learned from hearing and seeing your performance of the play that they did not know just from reading it. Have students share their thoughts with the rest of the class.

- Tom Stoppard, David Ives, Harvey Fierstein, and Tony Kushner are also playwrights and contemporaries of Simon. Choose one of these writers to research in some depth, and then write a report in which you outline the kinds of plays this playwright composes, the themes he addresses, characters he creates, and why he chooses to write.

- *The Governess* is based on an Anton Chekhov short story. Read at least three of Chekhov's short stories, and write a paper in which you discuss recurring themes that you observe in his stories.

- Staging is important in bringing the images of a written play to life for a theatrical audience. Draw or illustrate in some way one of the images that Simon's play created in your mind as you were reading. You may also use photography. Or create a PowerPoint presentation that explains how you chose the images and what you think the images add to your understanding of this drama.

- Imagine for a moment that you are a producer who plans to stage this play on Broadway. Prepare an oral report in which you explain which contemporary actors you would choose to play the two roles and why you would select them. Pay special attention to the characterizations that you will be creating and how these actors would portray these two characters. Give examples of other characters played by the chosen actors and describe how your expectations for the roles would demand similar or different performances from the actors. Your analysis of the characters and actors should include enough information to support your choices.

- Simon's play is based on a short story. Read one of the short stories in *No Easy Answers*, edited by Donald R. Gallo, a collection of stories for young adults, and rewrite the story as a one-act play. Prepare an evaluation of the changes you made to the story as you converted it to a play and present your findings as an oral report to your classmates.

at all, even though she is entitled to much more. This episode reveals the oppression and helplessness of the governess, who needs a job desperately enough that she is forced to agree to deductions from her salary that she knows to be wrong. The mistress finds the oppression of her children's governess entertaining. She knows that she is in control and that the governess cannot object, and she makes that point several times when she asks the governess if she disagrees with the many deductions from her salary. The mistress and her accounting book are the ultimate authority, and the ultimate oppressor.

Perception

Much of the story of *The Governess* is based on the ability of the mistress and the governess to see and understand what is happening during their conversation. The mistress repeatedly tells the governess to lift up her eyes and look at her mistress. The governess keeps her eyes cast down toward the floor; but in truth, she actually sees what the mistress does not see—the cruelty of her employer. At the end of the play, the mistress justifies her cruelty by explaining that she had hoped to teach the governess the lesson that she should not be so trusting of other people. The mistress explains that the world is a very dangerous place for people who are so trusting. When Julia does not protest the injustice of the lesson inflicted by her mistress, who easily admits that she has been cruel, the mistress asks if it is possible for a human being to be treated so badly and not protest the treatment. She wonders if it is possible for someone to be so innocent. The governess responds that it is possible. In the original Chekhov short story, "The Nincompoop," on which Simon based *The Governess*, the mistress refers to the governess as a nincompoop, which is a slang term referring to a foolish person or a simpleton. Although the mistress thinks that her governess is spineless and foolish, or perhaps a simpleton, for allowing herself to be exploited, the play reveals that it is the mistress who is doing the exploiting. It is the mistress who is the foolish one. She does not see this, of course, but the governess does understand. The small smile on Julia's face as she exits the stage reveals that she understands the irony of the lesson that the mistress was trying to teach, even though the mistress lacks any understanding herself. Although the mistress spent much of her time with the governess instructing her to look up and look at her mistress, it was the mistress who did not see the cruelty of the lesson being taught.

The mistress also fails to see that the structure of the household puts the governess at a disadvantage in any dialogue with her employer. The governess never forgets that she is an employee and that she has no authority and no possibility of achieving justice in a dispute with her employer. The mistress's constant instructions to look at her reveal that it is the mistress who is ignoring her position. Simple fairness and a position of authority suggest that the mistress is entrusted with treating her employee with kindness, but the mistress does not see or understand that it is she who violates Julia's trust. However, Julia clearly sees that she is being cheated. She does not see until the end of the conversation that the mistress perceives the entire interview as a joke, but she does see the unfairness and cruelty in the actions of her employer. Her employer never sees that her actions have been unkind.

19th-century Russian woman (Image copyright Kateryna Potrokhova, 2009. Used under license from Shutterstock.com)

STYLE

Farce

The term "farce" is used to describe a particular form of dramatic comedy that relies upon elaborate word play or physical action to make the audience laugh. The plot of a farce moves quite quickly, not giving the audience much time to dissect the action or to consider it in depth. Farce is also characterized by absurdity, as in the case with Simon's play, in which the mounting deductions from Julia's salary, which the mistress itemizes, quickly reach a level where they no longer make sense. The situation is improbable, which is another characteristic of the farce. Justice is not an element of the farce although it may have a happy ending rather than a tragic one. The governess is paid what she is owed at the end of Simon's play, but she has been tortured emotionally, and for that, there is no justice. Since a farce tends to rely upon stereotypical characters, *The Governess* also fits that description. The audience easily recognizes the mistress as a rich autocratic woman who is used to having her own way, while the governess is the easily cowed victim who is smarter than the mistress is willing to acknowledge. Farce relies upon the use of stock characters to make the humor work.

Irony

Irony is used to describe a situation in which reality is different from appearance. In some cases, irony refers to verbal irony, in which a character says something but means something that is exactly the opposite of what the words actually mean. In verbal irony the words are often humorous and are sometimes confused with sarcasm, but irony is less cruel than sarcasm. However, in drama, irony often refers to knowledge that the audience has but that the characters on stage lack. In *The Governess*, the mistress thinks that she is the wise one who is trying to teach her governess a lesson to protect her. The irony is that the mistress is the one posing the threat. Rather than teaching her governess a lesson that will protect her, the governess learns a lesson about the cruelty of her mistress. The greater irony is that the mistress is in fact the cruel person she describes to her governess. The mistress is the one who cannot be trusted.

One-Act Dramatic Structure

The Governess is a one-act play with prose dialogue, stage directions, and no interior dialogue. There are no soliloquies, and thus, the thoughts of the characters are reflected in their speeches, and all action occurs on stage. The actors address one another and not the audience. Although ancient Greek tragedies usually had five components, beginning with the *prologos* and ending with the *exodos*, they were not actually divided into acts (Greek comedies sometimes had six components). Editors in ancient Rome divided some Roman plays into five acts, but others were not divided until the Renaissance. The five-act dramatic structure began in the Renaissance and is found in the works of the Elizabethan playwrights such as William Shakespeare. The five acts denote the structure of dramatic action: exposition, complication or rising action, climax, falling action, and catastrophe or resolution. The five-act structure was followed until the nineteenth century when the Norwegian playwright Henrik Ibsen combined the last two acts into one act, as he did with *Hedda Gabler*, which has four acts. Ibsen found the rigidity of

the five acts paradigm too limiting and so wrote plays with two acts, four acts, and even the traditional five acts. During the twentieth century, audiences became more accustomed to three-act plays. Since the end of the nineteenth century, however, one-act plays have been more widespread. Early in the twentieth century they were associated with vaudeville and comedy, but more recently one-act plays have featured serious themes and are often presented with other one-act plays at a single performance.

Simon's one-act play mostly follows the traditional structure of dramatic action. The exposition is at the beginning of the play when the audience learns that the governess has been summoned by her mistress so that an accounting of her wages may be made. The complication, or rising action, occurs when the mistress begins to deduct money from Julia's salary. The climax is the point of a drama when the action takes a dramatic turn. In this case, it occurs when the audience realizes that the mistress is deducting money unjustly and cheating her employee. The falling action signals the resolution of the plot. This occurs when the mistress admits that the entire scene was a cruel joke to teach the governess a lesson. The catastrophe is usually the death of the hero, but there is no formal catastrophe in this play. Instead, the play ends when it is revealed through Julia's smile that she has always understood that she was being cheated but was unable to protest the unjust treatment by her mistress.

HISTORICAL CONTEXT

An Atmosphere of Protest

In the early 1970s news in the United States was consumed by demonstrations against the Vietnam War. *The Governess* was a departure for Simon, who typically wrote plays that were autobiographical in nature and that were generally situated in New York City or that involved a world that could be identified as similar to New York. However, the years during which Simon was reading Chekhov were years of dramatic protests against the war, when demonstrators filled the streets. These demonstrations sometimes turned violent; people were killed and buildings were bombed. Many of the protests were centered on college campuses and led by college students. In May 1970, the tone of the

COMPARE
&
CONTRAST

- **1900s:** In Russia, which is still under the capitalist tsarist regime, conditions are harsh for workers, who live in poverty even though they often work eleven-hour days, six days a week. Wages are low and hours are long. The situation is very similar to that of workers in the United States at the turn of the century.

  1970s: In the United States, 25.5 million people live below the poverty level, which is 3,908 dollars per year for a family of four. In addition, more than ten million people live barely above the poverty line. The situation in the Soviet Union is worse. Poverty has increased, along with industrial and agricultural shortages. In some parts of the Soviet Union, 57 percent of the population live below the poverty line.

  Today: Poverty in both Russia and in the United States continues to be a problem for large segments of the population. In 2004, it is estimated that the number of Russians living in poverty has decreased although a significant percentage of the population lives barely above the recognized poverty level of 1,500 rubles per family members (about 60 dollars). In the United States, the number of people living below the federally estimated poverty level of just over twenty-one thousand dollars for a family of four, has increased to more than 37 million in 2007, up from 36.5 million in 2006.

- **1900s:** In Russia, the tsar and the nobility, whose lives are those of privilege, maintain power over the lower classes. By some estimates, the peasant class makes up 80 to 85 percent of the Russian population. Most peasants live in the rural countryside and survive by working in agriculture.

  1970s: In what is now the Soviet Union, only 8.5 percent of the population live in large urban areas. The majority of the population continues to live in rural areas, earning their living through farming. The disparity between the privileged class and the working class continues even after the revolution of 1917.

  Today: Only about 25 percent of Russians now live in rural areas, but the rural population accounts for about 40 percent of Russia's poverty. People who earn their living through farming are more likely to suffer from poverty since agriculture is easily disrupted by weather, droughts, market prices, and so forth.

- **1900s:** The Russian Orthodox Church is the primary center of religion. The church is very influential, and while those in the upper echelons of the church leadership enjoy comfortable and even wealthy lives, parish priests are very poor and lead lives that are comparable to those of the peasants who make up such a large part of Russian society. In the Russian Revolution of 1917, many of the church leaders will be murdered and the church will never again be as powerful as in the early days of the twentieth century.

  1970s: In Russia, churches are actively oppressed by the government and have little authority and little influence on government actions. In contrast, in the United States, much of the opposition to the Vietnam War is led by religious leaders. Both Protestant ministers and Roman Catholic priests take an active role in opposing the war. Church leaders also take an active role in pushing the U.S. government to take action to combat poverty and racial discrimination.

  Today: In Russia, a series of laws passed in the late 1990s ensures greater religious freedoms. Virtually all religious groups are now represented in Russian society; however, religious leaders have no political influence. In the United States, religious leaders are active partners with politicians in political discourse. Much of the discussion in recent years, however, has focused on religious extremists and terrorism and the threat they pose to peace.

protests changed dramatically when four college students were shot and killed by national guardsmen at Kent State University in Ohio. The civilian massacre of villagers by U.S. soldiers at My Lai, which had become public during the spring of 1970, and the American invasion of Cambodia, also in the spring of 1970, further increased opposition to the war and led to even more demonstrations. In response to these events, a national student strike shut down more than 500 colleges and universities. An April 1971 demonstration in Washington, D.C., drew more than 500,000 protestors. The effect of several years of public demonstrations increased pressure on the Nixon Administration to end the war and withdraw the troops. In using Chekhov's short stories as a source for *The Governess*, Simon was moving from the memories of the Great Depression of his childhood in New York City to a country where poverty and economic injustice were even more pronounced than in the United States. Poverty in Russia eventually led to a revolution that changed the political picture in Russia and led to a revolution that destroyed the tsars and the aristocracy and resulted in the creation of the Communist Soviet Union. In the 1970s, the people's opposition to the war changed the United States and helped to end a war. Large public protests made clear that people wanted an end to the war. Past public protests had proven effective and were instrumental in changing society as part of the civil rights and women's rights movements.

Economic Turmoil

While the opposition to the Vietnam War was the focus for many people, that was not the only cause of turmoil in 1973. The early 1970s were a time of economic recession in the United States. The Arab oil embargo of 1973, a punishment directed at the United States for its support of Israel during the October 1973 Yom Kippur War, caused the price of gasoline to hit a new high. In 1972, gasoline prices were at about 30¢ a gallon. During the oil embargo, gas was rationed, long lines formed at gas stations, and the price of gas quadrupled to about $1.20 at the worst part of the recession. In some areas of the United States people waited in line for hours to buy ten gallons of gas. Gasoline sales on Sundays were stopped, oil to heat homes was sharply curtailed, and Congress lowered national speed limits to 55 mph. The oil embargo contributed to the fall of the Dow Jones Industrial Index from a

A good doctor *(Image copyright Emin Kuliyev, 2009. Used under license from Shutterstock.com)*

high of 1051 in January 1973 to 577 by December 1974, a drop of 45 percent during those two years. In addition, the Vietnam War was costly, and government spending for the war was much higher than expected. As a result, inflation hovered at 10 percent, interest rates climbed, and unemployment increased. The increase in fuel prices had a ripple effect on the entire economy, not just in the United States, but throughout the world. Questions about the Watergate political scandal and concerns about recession filled the news. Simon's play reflects many of those same themes.

CRITICAL OVERVIEW

Even before *The Governess* premiered on Broadway in November 1973 as a scene in *The Good Doctor*, Simon was a successful playwright. However, *The Good Doctor* was not considered by critics to be one of his better plays, and the reviews were generally mixed in their evaluation of the different sketches. However, it is worth noting that *The Good Doctor* in spite of poor reviews, received several Tony Award nominations and even received a Tony Award for Best Featured Actress in a Play.

One of the more positive reviews of *The Good Doctor* was written by Clive Barnes, a New York theater critic. In his review for the *New York Times*, Barnes acknowledges the problems in this pairing of Simon and Chekhov. When the pairing works well, the results "are droll and enchanting," when it does not work, the results "are labored." Barnes notes that the character of the writer is designed to link the many sketches together, which provides some unity. The problem, suggests Barnes, is that some of the sketches, including that of *The Governess*, are "slender, one-dimensional character sketches"; and yet, some of the sketches "have more depth." According to Barnes, there is "much fun" to be found in *The Good Doctor*, "at least here and there." Calling Simon's use of Chekhov, "admirable," Barnes also admits that there are places "where the deft dialogue sounds out of joint with the period," and where Simon's modern approach does not work with Chekhov's characters.

In his review of the *The Good Doctor* for the *New York Times*, Walter Kerr is much less positive than Barnes. Kerr points out that *The Good Doctor* is neither the best of Chekhov nor the best of Simon. Kerr observes that the Chekhov stories that Simon chose for this play lack the necessary "stage energy" to work well. The stories are "brief to the point of cursoriness" and are meant to be briefly read. These stories lack the "living detail that makes for theatrical growth, theatrical suspense." In spite of the mixed reviews, *The Good Doctor* has continued to be staged since its 1973 debut; it is therefore useful to look at a more recent staging, such as the one in 2004 at the Arena Players Repertory Theatre in Long Island, New York. In a review for *Newsday*, Steve Parks notes many of the same issues that Barnes and Kerr mentioned more than thirty years earlier. Parks refers to the pairing of Chekhov and Simon as the pairing of an odd couple. Although Parks refers specifically to the staging as a major fault in this production, where Simon's humor is transformed into "a decorous corruption of vaudeville," Parks still places blame for the play's failure on Simon's use of sketches by Chekhov, for whom laughter "was not the best medicine." In spite of several generally mixed and quite often negative reviews, *The Good Doctor* is still frequently staged in theaters, as is *The Governess*.

CRITICISM

Sheri Metzger Karmiol

Karmiol teaches literature and drama at the University of New Mexico, where she is a lecturer in the University Honors Program. In this essay, she discusses social class and hierarchy in The Governess.

Even in a democratic society, such as that of the United States, class hierarchy, the division of wealth, and access to the means to improve one's life are often unattainable for all people. Imagine, then, life in a world in which a few wealthy people control the lives of the poor, who cannot escape their fate. This is the world created by Simon in *The Governess*. In this very brief one-act play, two characters hold center stage; one has power and one is powerless. The characterizations are brief and not well defined. In fact, both characters are little more than stereotypes who represent the rich oppressor and the poor victim, and yet, this brief drama raises important questions about honesty and justice and reveals the helplessness of those for whom there is no escape from oppression. *The Governess* is a critical examination of social hierarchy and the cruelty inherent in a system of social stratification that allows employers to exploit employees. Although classified as a farce, *The Governess* lacks the content that would make it a comedy. In spite of the fact that a farce generally refers to a drama that contains comedic elements, there is little humor to be found in this play. Instead, Simon transforms a Chekhov short story into a brief piece of social commentary that forces the audience to think about the economics that govern social hierarchy, role-playing, and truth.

Although based on Chekhov's short story, "A Nincompoop," Simon's transformation of the story into *The Governess* contains several changes that are important in understanding the underlying themes of social stratification and oppression. In Chekhov's story, the governess is immediately told to sit down upon entering the room. She is never told to look up or not to look at the floor. The deductions to her salary

WHAT DO I READ NEXT?

- *Brighton Beach Memoirs* (1982) is generally considered to be one of Simon's finest plays. It is the semi-autobiographical coming-of-age story of Simon's childhood.

- *The Collected Plays of Neil Simon*, in four volumes (1971–1998), contains all of Simon's plays.

- Simon has written two memoirs, *ReWrites: A Memoir* (1996) and *The Play Goes On: A Memoir* (1999). Both memoirs are chatty and easy to read, and each provides a great deal of personal information about the author's life.

- *The Essential Tales of Chekhov* (1998) is a collection of many of Chekhov's best short stories.

- Mary Lou Belli and Dinah Lenney's *Acting for Young Actors: The Ultimate Teen Guide* (2006) is a how-to guide for teenagers or young adults who might be interesting in acting. The author includes information about acting classes and finding an agent as well as a listing of unions to join and Web sites that might be helpful in getting started in an acting career.

- *Ten-Minute Plays for Middle School Performers: Plays for a Variety of Cast Sizes* (2008) by Rebecca Young is a theater book of plays for teenagers. The topics of the plays focus on issues that concern teenagers, including being popular, jealousy, and shoplifting.

---

are very quickly listed, and Julia expresses little opposition to the deductions. When she does object, the objections are voiced in a whisper. Perhaps the most significant change is in making the male master a female mistress. In changing the master in Chekhov's short story to a mistress in his play, Simon removes an important dynamic in the play—that of gender oppression. Julia is no longer a woman oppressed by a man.

> INSTEAD, SIMON TRANSFORMS A CHEKHOV SHORT STORY INTO A BRIEF PIECE OF SOCIAL COMMENTARY THAT FORCES THE AUDIENCE TO THINK ABOUT THE ECONOMICS THAT GOVERN SOCIAL HIERARCHY, ROLE-PLAYING, AND TRUTH."

Instead, she is a woman oppressed by economics and social class.

The focus on Julia's eyes and where she directs her vision is another significant change that Simon incorporates into his adaptation of Chekhov's story. Chekhov never mentions Julia's eyes or where she happens to look. In contrast, Simon emphasizes Julia's ability to see the injustice perpetrated upon her. Throughout the play, there are many references to Julia's choosing not to look at her mistress. When called to a meeting by the mistress, Julia is especially deferential, looking down at the floor in a humble and unassuming manner. When told to look up at her mistress, Julia does so only for a brief moment and quickly looks down at the floor again. The mistress repeatedly asks Julia to look at her, but looking at her mistress is not something Julia does easily. At first the mistress equates Julia's not looking at her with thinking herself inferior, but the mistress also uses Julia's submissive stance as a way to take advantage of her, by making obviously outrageous deductions from Julia's salary and forcing her to agree to the deductions. At one point, the mistress demands that Julia look at her, as if looking at her mistress will help her recall an agreement that never existed. The mistress equates Julia's inability to "see" with guileless innocence, but in reality, Julia can see quite well. Rather than being naive, Julia's vision is based on knowledge. She has seen this kind of behavior before and knows that she has no recourse. Chekhov was critical of social stratification and of a world in which class designations allowed a small group of people to exploit the working poor, and these are criticisms that Simon also adopts and emphasizes in *The Governess*.

The mistress is a vain woman who thinks that her social position entitles her to be a bully and to harass her employee, which she disguises as teaching the governess a lesson. The mistress is a shallow, thoughtless woman, more fixated on her superiority than on the feelings of those she employs. When she reduces the governess to tears, she is less concerned about Julia's feelings than her own. Although the mistress quickly demands the reason for Julia's tears, the purpose of her inquiry is not to express compassion or concern for the governess. Indeed, the mistress explains that she is sensitive to tears. The mistress is focused on how Julia's tears make her feel, and not what they represent to the governess. Julia's tears are important signifiers for the audience, since they allow the audience to fully appreciate the depth of her pain. Any desire to laugh at the extremity of the mistress's actions in deducting part of Julia's salary is erased when Julia cries. While the listing of deductions seems incredible, and even for a brief moment so unbelievable as to be humorous, Julia's tears remind the audience that the actions of the mistress are not funny.

Julia's tears have another purpose as well. In his essay "Liquid Politics: Toward a Theorization of 'Bourgeois' Tragic drama," Tom McCall argues that tears are an important manifestation of the physiological ability to identify with the suffering of others. In other words, when the audience sees Julia cry, they should be so touched by her suffering that they might also cry in sympathy. McCall explains that "'the human heart' has been touched if there are tears." Those who do not cry, suggests McCall, and remain unmoved at the tears and suffering of others are "virtual villains," since "villains have dry eyes." While the audience is unlikely to cry at Julia's tears, that is not because they do not sympathize with the governess. Instead, her character is not well defined or explored in Simon's play, which makes it harder for the audience to identify with her pain. However, as McCall suggests, "for virtuous characters, externalized sentiment remains grounded in feelings represented onstage as authentically felt." In other words, the audience knows that the pain the governess feels is authentic because her tears reveal the truth of her feelings. The mistress ignores those authentic feelings and forgets that the wealthy have a responsibility for those who are less fortunate and an obligation not to exploit people who are in need of help. Julia's tears are meant to remind the audience that the mistress has failed in this obligation. The lack of tears from the mistress signals to the audience that she has an inability to feel the pain of those who work for her and a lack of compassion for those in need.

The mistress is selfish and, despite her avowed reason for the cruel lesson she plays on the governess, she acts in this manner because it provides entertainment and a chance to demonstrate to the governess the superiority of her mistress. The governess is not as naive as the mistress thinks. Nor is she as guileless or as spineless as the mistress suggests. Instead, she is a victim of the mistress, who uses economics both to harass her employee and to control her response. The mistress never grasps that what she has done is cruel or hurtful. She cannot understand Julia's point of view because she does not understand what it means to be the victim of social inequity. Communication between these two different social hierarchies is hampered by the wide gulf between the women's experiences. The governess has worked before without being paid what she has been promised, and the mistress initially appears to be no different from these past employers. The mistress is willing to cheat her governess, and the governess is accepting of this because it repeats a previous experience.

At the beginning of the play, the writer mentions the harshness of the world for those who are trapped, and he insinuates that it is Julia who is trapped. The mistress's actions are dehumanizing, and the audience is meant to wonder at the deference the governess accords her mistress. Initially, it certainly seems as if Julia is the one trapped. She is a victim of her employer's choice whether to pay a salary or not. Since Julia mentions that she has not been paid in the past, it is clear that there is no justice for the lower classes. An employer can choose not to pay an employee if he or she so desires. In a sense, then, Julia is trapped in a social hierarchy that devalues her work. She understands the lesson that the mistress is teaching only too well. Interestingly, though, it appears that the mistress is also trapped in a world where she is incapable of understanding or respecting the feelings of another human being.

Good drama can expose injustice, engage the audience in a dialogue with the characters, and reveal the conflict that exists between the poor and weaker members of a society and those with greater economic and political power. In *The Governess*, Simon emphasizes the emotional and financial burdens placed upon the lower class by the wealthier class who control the world in which they all must live. Neither Chekhov's short story nor Simon's play presents an ideological argument against either injustice or exploitation, but the story and play do illuminate the problems of social hierarchy and expose the cruelty of the upper class. By using a play that lasts less than ten minutes on stage, Simon forces his audience to use their own imaginations and powers of analysis to probe the complexities of the hierarchical relationship between these two women. In *The Governess*, Simon reveals the flaws of the society in which the mistress and governess live. By the end of the play, the audience is able to understand that it is not the governess who must see what she is like; it is the mistress who does not see her own cruelty. That is the truth that lies at the heart of Simon's play.

Source: Sheri Metzger Karmiol, Critical Essay on *The Governess*, in *Drama for Students*, Gale, Cengage Learning, 2010.

Simon Plant

In the following interview, Plant asks Simon about revamping an old project, Little Me.

In a rehearsal room at the top end of town, Debra Byrne, Adam Murphy and Mitchell Butel are savoring the wicked words Neil Simon supplied for *Little Me,* in preparation for next week's opening night at the State Theatre.

Over in California, the 80-year-old author of this slap-happy 1962 musical is crafting another play.

"I will not speak about that," Simon says flatly.

Little Me is a different matter. Simon was in good company when he signed on for this sly comedy about a murderous Southern gal named Belle Poitrine. Cy Coleman penned the score, Bob Fosse did the dance numbers, the great TV comic Sid Caesar got to play all the men in Belle's life, and Simon is happy to reminisce about that glorious conjunction:

Herald Sun: Little Me *was only your second Broadway show. What kind of writer were you back then?*

Neil Simon: Well, I didn't know anything about writing a musical. I just had to listen to what everyone was telling me.

HS: But you earned a Tony nomination . . .

Simon: Yeah. I had a good time doing *Little Me.* I thought it was a fun kind of show.

HS: Casting Sid Caesar was your idea, wasn't it?

Simon: There was only person I knew who could do it and that was Sid. He was still very much stuck to television—looking to see where the camera was—but he was an enormously funny actor. He did pretty well for us, I think.

HS: Strangely, Little Me *was never adapted to the big screen. Did that disappoint you?*

Simon: No, I expected that. I didn't think it was for film.

HS: When was the last time you had a belly-laugh in the theatre?

Simon: Spamalot was wonderful. Anything (director) Mike Nichols does is brilliant. I go to see musicals for the fun of it and I go to see plays to see what's going on. What people are liking, what they're not liking. When it comes down to it, I write what I like.

HS: Which is?

Simon: Families, relationships, getting on in the world.

HS: Just like Chekhov.

Simon: Oh, thank you for putting me in his company.

HS: Is he a hero of yours?

Simon: Of course. Brilliant. I think what happened a lot of times with his plays was that the critics in Russia weren't sure if they were serious or comedies.

HS: A lot of contemporary plays dispense with storylines. Does that bother you?

Simon: Can't say I have an opinion. They're just writing about today and what they think the world is like. I'm writing a play at the moment and I'm not thinking, 'What is TODAY?' I'm thinking about something that will endure.

HS: Like The Odd Couple *(1965)?*

Simon: That play, I think, works better than most of the things I've written.

HS: Did Nathan Lane and Matthew Broderick do The Odd Couple *justice in 2005?*

Simon: Yeah, they were really wonderful. It was good to see the play again in such good hands.

HS: Ten years ago you were quoted as saying, "I have no reason to write another play except that I'm alive and I like to do it". Still applies?

Simon: Oh yes. I'll keep doing it as long as I think I can. Doesn't mean anybody will put them on, but I hope they will.

HS: Do you follow a daily routine?

Simon: I work five or six days a week. Start pretty early in the morning, break for lunch and go as far as I can in the afternoon. At six or seven o'clock, I'll have a drink.

HS: Do you have to earn that?

Simon: No, no. I deserve it anyway.

HS: At home, are you Oscar Madison or Felix Unger?

Simon: I don't think I'm either one. Maybe I have a little of both in me.

HS: How does it feel when things are going well with a project?

Simon: You get very excited, it feels good, but you never know when it's going to fall apart. When it does, you put it in the drawer and go on to the next one.

HS: Got many scripts in the drawer?

Simon: I don't want to bend over and see. It hurts my back.

Source: Simon Plant, "All Neil at His Feet," in *Herald Sun* (Australia), August 14, 2007, p. 51.

Daniel Walden

In the following essay, Walden profiles Simon's works, life, successes, and failures.

Even before World War II, the theatrical and musical scene in the United States was strongly influenced by Jewish talent. Names like Jack Benny, Eddie Cantor, George Jessel, Henny Youngman, Irving Berlin, George Gershwin, Richard Rodgers, and Oscar Hammerstein were among those most respected and admired in the entertainment world. However, it is only in post-World War II America that the American Jew has emerged as a significant literary influence on television and the stage.

American Jewish writers growing up after World War II were comfortable enough within their identity as Americans, who were Jews, to feel free to express themselves, and they found an audience that was ready to listen. To those innumerable Americans who yearned for a safe niche in the midst of an increasingly depersonalized and alienated society, it seemed that Jewishness symbolized the human condition. But to be mature, to understand that condition, was to

> IN HIS HUMAN CONCERNS, THROUGH HIS ABILITY TO SMILE THROUGH THE TEARS, SIMON DEALS WITH PEOPLE HE KNOWS. HIS CHARACTERS ARE OFTEN BUT NOT ALWAYS JEWISH."

wrestle with the angel, as Jacob did, as playwright Neil Simon is trying to do.

There is little doubt that Neil Simon is one of the most prolific, productive, and successful playwrights the United States has ever produced. Although his work does not always revolve around specifically Jewish characters or themes, he has not forgotten either his roots or his aspiration to be evaluated as a serious playwright. Always he obeys the drive "to put down on paper the human condition and what it's up against," and he has also followed the need to confront his own past, his burden of guilt, together with his perception of the contradiction between shoddiness of values and the stereotyped image of absolute morality.

In a little over two decades, Simon has had at least twenty shows produced and has turned most of them into successful films. Yet, having pursued success and caught it, he's learned that "up close the American Dream is a vulgarity, that people love you or hate you simply because you've made a lot of money." The conflict between Simon's sensitivity to pain and suffering and his extraordinary talent and success is central to understanding his plays.

In the late 1950s, in Hollywood with a few weeks on his hands, Neil Simon began writing *Come Blow Your Horn,* a play based on the experiences and feelings he and his brother Danny had in trying to move away from their parental Jewish home. The play took eight weeks to write, three years to rewrite, and had at least eight producers before it appeared on a stage. After a tryout at the Bucks County Playhouse in August, 1960, it opened in New York on February 22, 1961, where it ran for two years but was only semi-successful. "That's when I started *Barefoot in the Park,* which turned out to be a smash," Simon remembered. Both *Barefoot* and *Come Blow Your Horn,* like much of Simon's early work, were based on his family and his personal experiences.

Barefoot is a light play, a soufflé, while the meatier *Come Blow Your Horn* deals more seriously with Jewish family life; rich in humor and small tragedies, it is based in large part on the relationship between Simon's parents. "I grew up in a family that split up dozens of times," he recalled. "My father would leave home, be gone for a few months and then come back, and I felt that our life was like a yo-yo! We'd be spinning along pretty good, and then—zap, the string would break and he was gone." The string broke five times, and, according to Danny Simon, who tried to shield Neil from the brunt of it all, his brother "must have felt pain that he didn't show. He saved it for his writing." Simon's childhood, from which he later pulled so much material, was "funny, but it wasn't funny when we were living through it."

The Odd Couple also came from life, but not from Neil's. Danny Simon says that after his own divorce he wanted to write a play about his experience but after writing fourteen pages he couldn't go on. It was the germ of a work "about two divorced men living together, and the same problems they had with their wives repeat with each other." When Neil took over the idea he wrote a play about two guys he knew; he thought he was writing a black comedy about two men who were basically unhappy. The characters, however, are believable, they are real, for Neil Simon's genius, as Mike Nichols notes, is for "comedy and reality; extremely distorted but recognizable, not zany behavior." The question is whether art was imitating life or vice versa. As Neil Simon has admitted, "I suppose you could practically trace my life through my plays...they always come out of what I'm thinking about and what I am as a person."

Between 1961 and 1970 Neil Simon had a succession of hits. *Come Blow Your Horn* opened in 1961, *Barefoot in the Park* in 1963, *The Odd Couple* in 1965, *The Star-Spangled Girl* in 1966, *Plaza Suite* in 1968, and *The Last of the Red Hot Lovers* in 1969. Simon became the first playwright since Avery Hapgood, in 1920, to have four plays running simultaneously on Broadway; when *The Star-Spangled Girl* opened, *Barefoot*, *The Odd Couple* and *Sweet Charity* were still in production. Alongside all the kudos, however, ran an undercurrent of criticism proposing that Simon take more chances with his material. Of

Plaza Suite, Brendan Gill wrote that he regretted that "the greater Mr. Simon's success in the world, the fewer the chances he seems willing to take with his considerable talent." Of *The Last of the Red Hot Lovers*, Gill said that "Simon's so-called seriousness has a banality of insight not easily to be distinguished from that of soap opera." And the reviewer for *Time* magazine wrote that "Simon ought to risk more seriousness. The wine of wisdom is in him, and he ought to let it breathe longer between the gags."

Simon was whipsawed between those who wanted him to take a risk, and those who wanted him to continue doing what they thought he had been doing. Known as a surefire gagwriter, as a manufacturer of machine gun humor, he had created a kind of monster. There was always the question whether a serious play of his, unleavened by humor, would be accorded fair treatment. It was just as reasonable to suppose that a departure from his customary product would garner brickbats as it was to suppose that it might draw applause. Yet Simon kept trying for that mix of elements that would both represent him at his best and also lead to commercial success and general approbation.

With *The Last of the Red Hot Lovers,* he began moving in that direction. In this play his protagonist, Barney Cashman, searching for decency and beauty while trying hard to be "the last of the red hot lovers," begins to despair, but is then convinced that decent and beautiful people do exist. In this play, Simon commented both on the values of our society and on the problems of married couples. But his next play, *The Gingerbread Lady,* was his first major attempt at a serious work.

The Gingerbread Lady promised to be Simon's first completely serious and successful play. Put into rehearsal in October 1970, it opened its pre-Broadway run in New Haven. The story line concerns Evy Meara, a middle-aged alcoholic, ex-supper club singer, who is involved with Lou Tanner, a macho non-talent; Jimmy Perry, an unsuccessful homosexual actor; Toby Landau, a forty-year-old, fading beauty; and Evy's daughter Polly, a bright seventeen-year-old. Evy is a compulsively filthy talker who finds love almost anywhere she can but is determined to destroy herself. In Toby's words, summing up the characters' interactions, "We all hold each other up because none of us has the strength to do it alone." With no reinforcement from outside, they use substitute props: makeup, alcohol, heterosexuality, homosexuality. At the end, goaded by her daughter to try once again to relate to her, Evy sends Polly away; having been beaten up by Lou, she can no longer struggle against the odds. Evy is alone, drinking, as the curtain falls.

Very early in the run, it became apparent to the play company that something was wrong. After the first preview Maureen Stapleton, who played Evy, said: "I thought everybody out front had taken a suicide pact." Neil Simon, the next night, just before the New Haven opening, said: "There's a crisis." He was right. The *New Haven Register* called it an "uncomfortable play." The *West Hartford News* wrote that "we don't care much about these people." After the Boston opening, Simon summarized the reviews with the words, "They just felt I didn't write a very good play. . . . It's simple. When people leave the theatre they are filled with despair—despite the fact that they are filled with truth. They say, 'I paid $9 and I don't want to be filled with despair.'" That is, "People want to be told to fight on; you can win. I'm telling them if you fight on, there's nothing but crap."

Convinced that so much of the play simply didn't work, Simon decided to close the production after the Boston run. A few days later, however, realizing how much of the play *did* work, he reversed himself and decided to rewrite, to try to find out how he could lighten the play without compromising his standards. He made Evy a more sympathetic woman, he cut down on the vulgarity, he allowed Toby to see a brighter future before her, and he revised the ending so that the audience would feel that the possibility of strength and improvement for Evy might be ahead. Gradually the changes were incorporated into the play. Ahead was the New York opening.

After the New York opening, Simon carefully weighed the reviews. The *New York Post* spoke of his "distinction as a playwright." The *New York Times* dwelt on "the dialogue between a great actress and a playwright who has suddenly discovered the way to express the emptiness beneath the smart remark and the shy compassion that can be smothered by a wisecrack." But *The Post* also pointed out that the contrast between the sadness and the humor weakened the play, while Walter Kerr of the *Sunday Times* lamented the weakness of Evy as a character. Even Mel Brooks, with whom

Simon had worked years before as a writer, commented that, "Doc [Simon] is going to have a long, hard road. He's got to have his papers stamped. He doesn't have his credentials and he will not be allowed into Serious Land. I think it is very important that he launch this deeper side of his talent. The best thing Doc could do to make that transition would be to dip his pen in the blood of his heart and write for an Off-Broadway 199-seat house a total tragedy. The easiest thing Doc could do is just obliquely to insinuate there's more to life than one laugh after another." To Simon himself, *The Gingerbreak Lady* was, in many ways, "the most satisfactory play I've ever written."

Like much of Simon's work, this play seems to have been drawn in large part from the grief and guilt he feels over his past, his childhood. By the playwright's own admission, he dealt with some of the really ugly, painful things in his youth by blocking them out and later relating to them through humor. To Simon, the ideal play is one where the audience laughs all night but in the last few minutes is touched by a sense of tragedy.

The success of *The Odd Couple,* produced in 1965, had convinced Simon that he could make people laugh. Having learned that he had that capability, he no longer felt compelled to produce non-stop amusement, but worked to protect the serious moments within his plays. *The Sunshine Boys,* for instance, produced in 1973, is a very serious production that deals with old age and its problems. It is also a very funny play; through the attention-grab of its laughs, the playwright was able to get his message across. For Simon, who sees humor in every situation, can't write a play totally devoid of it. For example, in *The Visitor From London,* the third of the four one-act plays in *California Suite,* we meet a woman who is married to a man who turns out to be a practising homosexual. That they love each other and love will somehow continue is apparent. To Simon, it's a serious piece, but the laughs throw the audience off. Yet they are necessary; as Simon says, "It's like a political speech—when you hear one filled with bromides that you've heard over and over again, you turn off. But if there's a bit of humor injected into it, you might listen, and you still get the point."

Today Neil Simon, seemingly at the height of his fame and success, is passing through a difficult period. Transferred from New York to

California, he is trying to find a middle ground, to explore his new terrain through a play like *California Suite,* to reexamine his past in New York through a play like the earlier *Chapter Two.* In *Chapter Two,* he entrusted his past and his present to George Schneider, the play's protagonist. Married to his first wife, Barbara, for twelve years, George is crushed by her death. When he first hears of Jennie Malone, a recently divorced woman, he is not particularly interested; like any good New Yorker, he has his friends, the Knicks, the Giants, the Mets, his jogging, and his watercolors. But, pushed by his brother Leo, as Jennie is pushed by her friend Faye, they talk, look each other over, and like what they hear and see. Within two weeks they decide to marry. Leo, who loves his brother and has his interests in mind, tries to get George and Jennie to delay the marriage for a few weeks; however, after a long talk with Jennie, during which he explains to her how George went to pieces after Barbara's death, he reverses himself, saying he doesn't know why George waited so long. "I was born to be a Jewish mother," Leo moans.

There is an undercurrent of Jewishness that runs through the play. George and Leo are obviously Jewish. (Jennie and Faye are just as obviously not.) George's mother, a stereotypically Jewish mother, calls him from Florida, the haven for many retired, well-off Jews, wanting to know who Jennie is, what does her father do, and so on. Similarly, when George cuts himself shaving on the morning of the ceremony, he asks Leo, "Was there any royalty in our family?" and, predictably, hears Leo answer: "Yeah. King Irving from White Plains."

What was an undercurrent surfaces to become a main force late in the second act when George and Jennie return from their honeymoon. It had been a beautiful five days and a terrible last two days. George has not been able to forget Barbara; he hasn't been ready for a full commitment. In fact, in a truth-telling outburst, he tells Jennie that he resents her for everything, mostly because he couldn't tell her that he missed Barbara so much. Jennie, trying desperately to understand, is at first confused. But after George packs his bags and announces that he's off to Los Angeles, presumably for business, she finally gets angry. In a moment of justifiable rage she tells him of her love and devotion, and she criticizes him for his guilt complex. "I don't

know what you expect to find out there," she says, "except a larger audience for your two shows a day of suffering." If Jennie knows anything, it is that she knows how to feel. She also is able to tell George directly that what ails him is George, and his inability to break with certain aspects of his tradition, no longer compatible or appropriate to the American present.

Jennie's outburt, her insightful remarks, are the medicine George needs. He has been wearing his heart on his sleeve, indulging in suffering, in the way many Russian Jews did in the *shtetlach.* Breaking through, he can now concede that Jennie is one of the healthiest people he knows. At last, he understands that he's been holding on to self-pity; he sees that he was afraid of being happy. Though he's committed to going to Los Angeles, he almost immediately decides to return. He finishes his book, whose title, *Falling Into Place,* describes what has happened with the pieces of their lives. George, of course, is still Jewish, but he has traded the archaic reliance on suffering that marred his health for the refreshing outlook of a metropolitan-oriented Jennie Malone, a woman who is Jewish, in the sense that Lennie Bruce defined Jewishness, even if she's *goyish.*

Neil Simon has freely admitted that *Chapter Two* is autobiographical, that it is about the trauma he experienced at the death of his first wife and the rage he felt over that loss. In my judgment, *Chapter Two* is mature Simon, an *almost* excellent play. The romantic sequences are beautifully, warmly written. The anger is especially well portrayed in Act II, and Jenny's long speech in that act, full of shifts and shadings, is an interesting breakthrough. The characterization is magnificent, although Brendan Gill in the *New Yorker* calls Simon-like characters "automata" and the hero in *Chapter Two* a "zombie." The obvious strengths of *Chapter Two* were pointed out by the *New York Times, Newsweek* and *Time,* all of which gave it strong reviews. But, again, Brendan Gill accused Simon of "having mistaken earnestness for seriousness," *Time* revealed another flaw, one common to much of Simon's work. As T. E. Kalem put it: "The play ends happily—a pact Simon always keeps with his audience. When will he choose to keep the compact he seems to want to make with himself—to plunge in deep-bold instead of toe-deep-scared into the consciousness stream of the real Neil Simon?" In short, this is an almost excellent play—but the promise of perfection is still unfulfilled.

Of all the media for which Simon produces—the stage, the screen, television, and the musical theatre—the stage remains the forum that affords him the most satisfaction. Yet he goes into new territories to keep interested in the work. The desire for new challenges drew him to write the book of his first original musical, *They're Playing Our Song,* for which the music and words were produced by Marvin Hamlisch and Carol Bayer Sager. Previously, Simon had adapted several other works from musicals and he's constantly being asked to do more. According to Walter Kerr, the music for *They're Playing Our Song* is "irrepressible," but it's as though someone went to Simon with a non-existent plot, two agreeably efficient principals, and some baggage cars full of beautiful scenery and "asked him to give the principals something, *anything,* to say. Which is what he has done..." But, Kerr added, Simon was never a mere manufacturer of one or two line gags. "He's always needed a situation to suggest what the laugh's going to be about, needed a character idiosyncrasy to prod him into phrasing responses that will explode." In short, "middle-of-the-road tepid it is, with Mr. Simon uncharacteristically boxed in. Next time let's hope they'll play *his* song." The reviewer for the *Village Voice* agreed in most respects, adding that Simon appeared to think that Hamlisch's music was as good as that of Mozart and Beethoven, saying he was "as important to our time as they were to theirs." He asked: "Wouldn't the show be better off if the author didn't compare himself with Aristophanes, Moliere or Chekhov? Why mix genres and ambitions quite so vengefully? It is one thing to tell jokes all the way to the bank, quite another to believe that the bank confers distinction or immortality."

After almost two decades of criticism, it appears that the critics only partly understand Neil Simon. Walter Kerr is surely right in noting that Simon creates character and is not just a gagman. And the *Village Voice's* Gordon Rogoff is surely right in pointing out that telling jokes does not confer distinction or immortality. But it might be stressed that what fascinated Simon, what made up the challenge for his first musical, was the relationship between Vernon and Sonia. What cried out for analysis, dissection, explanation, enlargement, humor, was the way in which a male composer and a female lyricist related to each other. Whether the result

was successful or not is a separate question. It is possible that Marvin Hamlisch's music, along with that of Richard Rodgers, Irving Berlin, Steven Sondheim, et al, may be as important in our time as Mozart's and Beethoven's were in theirs. History's verdict has yet to be heard. But where, in what play, in what interview, has Simon pretended to equality with Aristophanes, Moliere and Chekhov? True, he was happy when someone once referred to him as a "distinguished" playwright, and another called him a playwright of distinction. But he has never forgotten that it is history that confers distinction and immortality. Embedded in an ages-long tradition, he has never given up thinking of himself as a kid who grew up in the Bronx, as a Jewish kid whose childhood was traumatic, as one of those buffeted by external forces for so long.

In interview after interview over the years, Neil Simon has reminded himself and his readers that he and his brother Danny came from the Bronx, and that his childhood experiences were very important. As a result, he said: "The humor itself is often self-deprecating and usually sees life from the grimmest point of view. Much of that, I think, comes from my childhood." What was left unsaid, however, was that this style of humor comes right out of the Eastern European experience, is consistent with the humor in the stories of Mendele, Sholom Aleichem, and Peretz, and is part of a tradition that includes Abraham Cahan, Saul Bellow, Bernard Malamud and Philip Roth. For Simon, writing plays rather than short stories is the best form of self-expression for himself. It is the healthiest outlet he can find for his neuroses and frustrations. It is the best way he knows to share his joys.

In the only book on Neil Simon, Edythe McGovern argues that among Neil Simon's strengths are his great compassion for his fellow human beings which precludes his soliciting laughter in direct proportion to the hurt suffered by his "people"; a basic regard and respect for the family; an awareness of human limitation; his sensitivity to language; and his theory of plots, in that he never relies on subplots but stays with the story line as the characters live out their scenes naturally. In addition Simon, respecting conventional moral behavior, allows his characters great latitude in moral fallibility. Above all, "his plays, which may appear simple to those who never look beyond the fact that they are amusing are, in fact, frequently more perceptive and revealing of the human condition than many plays labeled complex dramas." Perhaps Simon's perspective can be pinpointed in what Barney Cashman said in *Last of the Red Hot Lovers:* "We're not indecent, we're not unloving, we're human. That's what we are, human."

In his human concerns, through his ability to smile through the tears, Simon deals with people he knows. His characters are often but not always Jewish. Yet, coming from a Jewish and metropolitan background, he understands Lenny Bruce's words: "If you live in New York, or any other big city, you are Jewish"; and he realizes that Leopold Bloom, James Joyce's hero in *Ulysses,* the Jew with his hang-up, his self-doubt, his self-hate and his awkward alienated stance, is a twentieth-century symbol for Everyman.

These very concrete terms embody what Neil Simon and Woody Allen and many others have put more artistically. The style and content of Jewish humor strike a deep responsive chord in post-World War II America. Alienation, acculturation and assimilation, allegedly Jewish diseases, belong to all, just as the humor that emanates from the tensions is universal. For the Jew, the conflict is real. For the others, the conflict is more diffused but powerful nonetheless; for most Americans are caught between the nostalgic yearning for a safe, comfortable, well-defined past and the difficult challenge of adapting to an increasingly and frighteningly depersonalized society. It is this tension, this conflict, these concerns which form the heart of Neil Simon's plays. Simon has given us warm and believable characters; he has given us people for whom there is hope, strugglers like George Schneider of *Chapter Two,* like the woman married to the homosexual in *California Suite.* Being Jewish, being very human, through his plays Simon also transmits the sense of Horace Walpole's admonition: "Life is a comedy to a man who thinks, a tragedy to a man who feels." Or, as Edythe McGovern said, "To Neil Simon, who thinks and feels, the comic form provides a means to present serious subjects so that audiences may laugh to avoid weeping."

Source: Daniel Walden, "Neil Simon: Toward Act III?," in *MELUS*, Vol. 7, No. 2, Summer 1980, pp. 77–86.

SOURCES

"1970s Oil Crisis," in *Recession.org*, http://recession.org/ history/1970s-oil-crisis (accessed June 25, 2009).

"American Masters: Neil Simon," in *Public Broadcasting System (PBS)*, http://www.pbs.org/wnet/americanma sters/database/simon_n.html (accessed June 10, 2009).

Barnes, Clive, Review of *The Good Doctor*, in *New York Times*, November 28, 1973, p. 36.

Barranger, Mark, "The Anti-War Movement in the United States," in *Modern American Poetry*, http://www. english.illinois.edu/maps/vietnam/antiwar.html (accessed June 25, 2009).

"Biography of Neil Simon," in *The Kennedy Center*, http://www.kennedy-center.org/calendar/index.cfm? fuseaction = showIndividual&entitY_id = 3523 &source_ type = A (accessed June 10, 2009).

Chekhov, Anton, "The Nincompoop," in *Selected Stories*, Signet, 1969, pp. 20–22.

Courtney-Thompson, Fiona, and Kate Phelps, eds., *The 20th Century Year by Year*, Barnes & Noble, 1998, pp. 256–71.

Davis, Jessica Milner, "Farce," in *Farce*, Methuen, 1978, pp. 1–24.

Harmon, William, and Hugh Holman, *A Handbook to Literature*, 11th ed., Prentice Hall, 2008, pp. 178–79, 224, 298–99.

Jennings, Peter, and Todd Brewster, eds., *The Century*, Doubleday, 1998, pp. 424–34.

Johnson, David, "What Is Poverty for Russians," April 27, 2004, http://www.cdi.org/russia/johnson/8184-3.cfm (accessed June 25, 2009).

Kerr, Walter, Review of *The Good Doctor*, in the *New York Times*, December 9, 1973.

Matthews, Mervyn, *Poverty in the Soviet Union*, Cambridge University Press, 1986, p. 24.

McCall, Tom, "Liquid Politics: Toward a Theorization of 'Bourgeois' Tragic Drama," in *South Atlantic Quarterly*, Vol. 98, No. 3, 1999, pp. 593–622.

"Number of Americans in Poverty Up Slightly," in *CBSNews.com*, August 26, 2008, http://www.cbsnews. com/stories/2008/08/26/national/main4384762.shtml (accessed June 24, 2009).

Parks, Steve, Review of *The Good Doctor*, in *Newsday*, July 7, 2004.

"Poverty Thresholds for 2007 by Size of Family and Number of Related Children under 18 Years," in *U.S. Census Bureau.gov*, http://www.census.gov/hhes/www/ poverty/threshld/thresh07.html (accessed June 25, 2009).

"Religion in Russia," in *Embassy of the Russian Federation*, http://www.russianembassy.org/RUSSIA/religion. htm (accessed July 23, 2009).

"Russian Poverty," in *icepoverty.pbworks.com*, http://icepo verty.pbworks.com/f/Russian + Poverty + Brochure.pdf (accessed June 25, 2009).

Simon, Neil, *The Collected Plays of Neil Simon*, Vol. 2, Random House, 1979, pp. 432–39.

Trager, James, *The People's Chronology*, Henry Holt, 1992, pp. 1027– 44.

Trumbore, Brian, "The Arab Oil Embargo of 1973–74," in *BUYandHOLD: A Division of Freedom Investments*, http://www.buyandhold.com/bh/en/education/history/2002/arab.html (accessed June 25, 2009).

The Unofficial Neil Simon Homepage, https://www.msu.edu/~pelowsk1/neilsimon/ (accessed June 10, 2009).

White, Stephen, and Ian McAllister, "Orthodoxy and Political Behavior in Postcommunist Russia," in *Review of Religious Research*, Vol. 41, No. 3, March 2000, pp. 359–72.

Wolf, Richard, "1.1 Million Americans Joined Ranks of the Poor in 2004," in *USA Today*, August 30, 2005, http://www.usatoday.com/news/washington/2005-08-30-census-poverty_x.htm (accessed June 24, 2009).

FURTHER READING

Bryer, Jackson R., *The Playwright's Art: Conversation with Contemporary American Dramatists*, Rutgers University Press, 1995.

    This book contains interviews with many playwrights, including Simon.

Critchley, Simon, *On Humour*, Routledge, 2002.

    This book is a philosophical study of what makes people laugh. The author discusses humor as it reflects on the human condition, including why people laugh at inappropriate moments and why racist and sexist jokes are sometimes considered funny.

Engel, Barbara Alpern, *Women in Russia, 1700–2000*, Cambridge University Press, 2004.

    This book is a comprehensive history of the lives of Russian women. The author provides very readable histories of individual women, as well as a more generalized history of women's lives.

Frank, Stephen P., *Crime, Cultural Conflict, and Justice in Rural Russia, 1856–1914*, University of California Press, 1999.

    In this book, the author examines the conflict between the peasant class and local governments. Frank uses primary documents as his sources, which reveal that social class issues were an important facet of the justice system in tsarist Russia.

Hischak, Thomas S., *American Theatre: A Chronicle of Comedy and Drama, 1969–2000*, Oxford University Press, 2001.

    This book contains information about every play produced on the New York stage between 1969 and 2000. More than 2,000 plays are included. The author groups the plays according to topical issues.

Koprince, Susan, *Understanding Neil Simon*, University of South Carolina Press, 2002.

    This book provides an overview of Simon's career and an analysis of sixteen of his major plays.

Heather Raffo's 9 Parts of Desire

HEATHER RAFFO

2003

Heather Raffo's 9 Parts of Desire is a one-act, one-woman play that expresses the collective experiences and identities of Iraqi women in the context of Iraq's troubled history. Over the course of an hour and a half, nine characters tell their stories, share secrets, and divulge politics, all expressed by a single actress on a set littered with props used interchangeably by the characters. Raffo, an Iraqi American woman, was inspired to write this play following a visit to family in Iraq in 1993. She spent the next ten years interviewing Iraqi women. This work eventually coalesced into *Heather Raffo's 9 Parts of Desire*.

Raffo's title comes from Geraldine Brooks's nonfiction book about Islamic women, *Nine Parts of Desire: The Hidden World of Islamic Women*, which in turn draws its title from a recently recovered text by Imam Ali, an important Islamic leader from the seventh century. He wrote, "God created sexual desire in ten parts; then he gave nine parts to women and one to men." *Heather Raffo's 9 Parts of Desire* was first produced in August 2003, with Raffo performing, at the Traverse Theatre in Edinburgh, Scotland, and has since been produced in London, New York, and Washington, DC. It is available in a 2006 edition from Northwestern University Press.

AUTHOR BIOGRAPHY

Raffo was born in Michigan in the early 1970s to a Christian Iraqi father and an Irish Catholic

Heather Raffo (AP Images)

moved to the Bush Theatre in London, England, later that year. In October 2004, it was produced at the Manhattan Ensemble Theatre in New York and thereafter toured the United States. For her work on *Heather Raffo's 9 Parts of Desire*, Raffo was awarded the Lucille Lortel Award for best solo show, the Blackburn Prize Special Commendation, and the Martin Seldes-Garson Kanin Fellowship, all in 2005.

In 2006, Raffo joined five other playwrights and actors in writing *The Middle East, in Pieces*. Her contribution was an excerpt from *Heather Raffo's 9 Parts of Desire*; the work was read at Cherry Lane Theatre in New York as part of the Reading Series produced by Back House Productions.

Raffo considers herself more an actress than a writer and continues to perform on the stage, in films, and in television commercials. She lives in New York and Los Angeles.

PLOT SUMMARY

Heather Raffo's 9 Parts of Desire opens with the dawn call to prayer. The first character the audience meets is the *mullaya*, or professional mourner. She is singing a traditional Iraqi song, "Che Mali Wali" ("Because I Have No Ruler") and throwing shoes into a river onstage. In her poetic monologue, the mullaya talks about the river as the source of life, both the beginning and the end. Over and over, she uses the word "sole," which when spoken to an audience also sounds like "soul." An additional layer of meaning comes from the fact that in Middle Eastern cultures, the bottom of one's shoes or feet, the soles, are considered to be unclean. The mullaya mourns what has been lost, referring in particular to the Marsh Arabs displaced after Saddam Hussein dammed and diverted the Tigris and Euphrates Rivers. The mullaya herself is a Marsh Arab and mourns for the loss of the life she once lived, but she concludes, "Now the river has developed an appetite for us."

The mullaya transforms into the next character, Layal the artist. Layal comments that many artists and intellectuals, including her sister, have left Iraq. She stays because she is not sure she would be as good an artist outside Iraq. She paints nudes and is the curator at the Saddam Art Center, a post many think she attained by sleeping with a government official, although

mother. In 1974, at the age of four, Raffo traveled with her parents to Iraq to visit her father's family, a trip that she recalls as being full of magic and wonder. She graduated from the University of Michigan in 1993 with a bachelor's degree in English and spent that summer backpacking around Europe before making her way to her relatives in Baghdad, Iraq. It took her seventeen hours by bus to reach Iraq from Jordan, but once she arrived, she was warmly embraced and entertained by her family. Her experiences there, including a trip to the Saddam Art Center, where she saw Layla al-Attar's inspiring painting *Savagery*, were the inspiration for *Heather Raffo's 9 Parts of Desire*, which she began writing in 1998 as part of her thesis for her master of fine arts degree in acting performance at the University of San Diego. Raffo also credits American playwright Ntozake Shange and her play *For Colored Girls Who Have Considered Suicide When the Rainbow Is Enuf* as inspiration. Raffo's play premiered at the Traverse Theatre in Edinburgh, Scotland, in August 2003 and then she denies this. She tells of a college woman brutalized by Saddam's son Uday and how she immortalized this woman in a painting of a blossom hanging from a branch, unreachable by hungry dogs. "I fear it here / and I love it here" Layal admits.

Layal becomes Amal, an intense Bedouin woman. Amal is looking for answers. She tells how she left her Saudi Bedouin husband, a plastic surgeon, in London after she caught him sleeping with one of her friends. She next moved to Israel and married a fellow tribesman who promised to move her somewhere else, but she was only the second wife, and the first wife would not allow them to move. She leaves him also and begins a long-distance relationship over the telephone with Sa'ad, a friend of her first ex-husband. After a year, they decide to marry. They meet for the first time in Dubai and have dinner, and then Sa'ad calls off the marriage, saying "you are not the Amal I love." He tells her he is not worthy, but Amal is heartbroken and ashamed. Amal is a woman of deep passion and love but believes that Sa'ad rejected her for being fat and not pretty enough, not fashionable enough. Now she fears running into Sa'ad in London, where her children visit with their father. She feels free finally, but not at peace.

Amal transforms into Huda, an Iraqi exile living in London. A lifelong political protestor, she talks about the war in Iraq. Huda hates Saddam Hussein, Iraq's president, so much that she cannot protest this war because that would ally herself with his supporters. "[T]his war was against all my beliefs / and yet I wanted it."

Huda then becomes the doctor, who is vomiting from a terrible stench and then washing her hands. She has just lost a patient, a mother giving birth. However, the baby, who has two heads, has survived. She talks about the horrors she has seen here in Basra, including children affected by radiation poisoning. Her husband has lost his legs and cannot work. Although she is Western-trained, the doctor returned to Iraq to work in the best hospitals, which are now reduced by radiation and cancer to a horrible experiment. Feeling nauseous, she admits to the audience that she is pregnant.

The doctor then becomes an Iraqi girl, dancing to American pop music. She is angry at her mother, who will not let her out of the house since the U.S. soldiers arrived. The Iraqi girl tells how her grandparents had their house run over with a tank because they did not understand the English spoken by the soldiers who came to their house. Her father was taken away for speaking against Saddam to his daughter, who had repeated his words at school. Her brothers are also gone, and she and her mother do not leave the house without a male escort now, for fear of kidnapping. The girl is so adapted to life in a war zone that she can identify different bombs by the sounds they make as they pass overhead. On some level, she understands her role in her father's disappearance and feels "stupid," as her mother calls her.

The Iraqi girl becomes Umm Ghada. Umm Ghada, or Mother of Tomorrow, is a woman without a name. She is a survivor of the destruction of the Amiriyya bomb shelter during the Gulf War and calls herself Umm Ghada after her daughter, Ghada, the only body she was able to identify. She now lives in a trailer at the site and has dedicated her life to keeping alive the memory of what happened to more than four hundred innocent people. The shelter was mistaken for a military communications center and targeted for the trial of a new, two-part bomb. The first bomb drilled through the shelter, and the second bomb went in the hole and detonated. Four hundred three people died; Umm Ghada was the only survivor. She asks the audience to sign her witness book.

Layal returns, paintbrush in hand. She tells a proverb about a restaurant where one can eat free of charge and one's grandson will pay the bill later. A man goes in, eats, and is surprised when the waiter brings him a bill. It is from his grandfather. Layal is living with her sister because her house, in the upscale neighborhood of Mansur in Baghdad, was bombed while she was away. She laughs to think someone thought her dangerous enough to try to kill her and destroy her paintings. Layal then talks about falling in love with another art student and having an affair with him. Her husband shot her when he found out, but she did not die. She sees herself as having so much hunger for love and flesh that she cannot control herself. "I tell you / when you're this way / so attached / always loving like you will die without something— / you love like an Iraqi woman!" She describes Americans as loving freedom and being "passionate, selfish, charming," whereas the Iraqis want to be attached, protected, to "love like you cannot breathe."

Layal transforms into the American. She is glued to the scenes of war on her television set. She talks about her father, who recognizes the neighborhoods where his family lives in this footage. They are looking for familiar faces, beloved family, aching for knowledge of what is happening to them. She says their names over and over, like a prayer, trying to call them on the phone but the lines are down. Like Layal, the American relates how her Iraqi relatives are attached to each other and to their past.

Huda takes Layal's place. She says she cannot leave London because this is where her husband died. She is done moving, although many people she knows have gone back to Iraq. She sees that the young women who should be stepping up to fill her shoes are giving up their education and wearing the veil. "Their grandmothers are more liberated than them." Huda also talks about the attachments between Iraqis: her family is a mix of Kurd, Shi'a, and other ethnicities and lived together comfortably. Huda recalls how Saddam should have been removed from power during the Gulf War. The Iraqi people were counting on the United States to help, but the United States turned its back on them, and Saddam killed ten of thousands of people. The United States embargoes, which had been intended to cripple his dictatorship, ended up only strengthening it. Huda now believes that the way to change is by gradual development, not revolution.

Huda becomes Nanna, an old woman selling things on the street. The third call to prayer sounds. She says that the looting Iraqis had been spurred on by Americans. "It's freedom to have!" Nanna feels her life has been spared and she owes a debt for that. She confides to the audience that the burning of the National Archives and the Qur'anic Library was not an accident, and now their history has been erased. Nanna believes this is a punishment from God because the Iraqis did not do away with Saddam themselves. She remembers a time in school when she drew a picture of her mother and was chastised by the teacher because it was only proper to draw the men in one's family. So Nanna erased her mother.

Nanna now becomes the American. She scorns the media attention given to seven people trapped underground in the United States, as compared with the millions of lives threatened by the war that the United States has engaged in

on Iraqi soil. She worries about her Iraqi relatives and keeps saying their names. She knows she needs to go on with her life, but she cannot do mundane things without being disgusted with herself. The American is consumed with worry. She still cannot call her family in Iraq. She is angered and embarrassed by the images and words of American supremacy. "Why don't we count the number of Iraqi dead?" she cries out.

Layal returns and says that she has been called a whore for choosing to paint herself nude, for painting Saddam, for installing a mosaic of U.S. president George H. W. Bush on the floor of the lobby of the Rashid Hotel. She knows that despite these criticisms, she is more free to express herself than the Americans are. She has been used by her government and needs them as much as they need her. She wishes she were afraid and knows she cannot escape complicity.

Huda abruptly takes over, mid-sentence. She is remembering the coup in 1963, when she was among one hundred eighty thousand people who were rounded up for their leftist politics and held in prison for months. Conditions in the prison were terrible, and treatment was inhumane. Huda says the people need only empowerment to help them accomplish their dream of liberation.

The character changes back to Layal, who is in the middle of a bomb raid. It is near the end of the Gulf War in the early 1990s. She is on the phone, asking someone to do something about the bombing. She lives in a rich neighborhood and cannot believe this would happen, even by accident. The person on the line is asking her to do a mosaic and then to meet with him privately tomorrow. Layal reluctantly agrees.

The scene switches now to the American, who is listening to a message from her uncle in Iraq, asking her if she is okay. It is immediately after the terrorist attacks in the United States on September 11, 2001. Her family loves her very much, and they do not stop calling until they hear her voice.

Layal takes over, answering the phone. It is her daughter Sabah, whom she clearly misses and worries about. Layal tells her to stay away from Baghdad, that it is too hot for her to come home, which has a double meaning: both the temperature of summer in the desert and the political condition of the city. Their line cuts out and Layal drops her phone.

The American's uncle leaves another message for her, after the September 11 attacks. He asks her to visit and bring her family because it is hard for them to get to her. Now, in 2003, it is the American's turn to desperately try to call her family overseas. She finally connects with her Aunt Ramza in Iraq, who speaks very little English but tells her to pray and that she loves her. The American recites the names of forty-six of her Iraqi relatives as a prayer for their safety.

Layal declares that she will never leave Iraq and that she does not believe in the American idea of freedom. She is now amused at the idea of creating this mosaic of President Bush, because she is not afraid of the consequences. She starts smashing things in her studio to make pieces for the mosaic. Her next speech is ecstatic, hysterical, and mournful, blending together dialogue from the other women the audience has heard from. The fourth call to prayer sounds, and Layal ends with, "I'm dead."

The mullaya takes over Layal's pacing but speaks with ease rather than volatility. Her dialogue is full of warnings, such as, "To the well one day you'll return / thirsty, assured it will be there / but you'll not find—spring, nor river / so beware of throwing a stone / into the well." The mullaya steps into the river to wash, gradually becoming fully immersed in the water. A professional mourner, the mullaya uses the dialogue of all the women to mourn with them, for them.

The last call to prayer is heard, and the mullaya becomes Nanna, still selling things on the street. She has Layal's painting, *Savagery.* Nanna tells the audience that Layal died when a bomb fell on her sister's house. The painting is worth more because of her tragic end. "I give you secret," Nanna confides, "some trees are womans / this one, little one, is me / I let her paint me / *aa*, she see me / shhh / don't say / my husband he thinks it's just a tree."

CHARACTERS

Amal
Amal is a thirty-eight-year-old Bedouin woman who is full-figured and vibrantly inquisitive. Her name means "hope." Bedouins are traditionally desert-dwelling nomads. Amal has been married and divorced twice and has a fourteen-year-old son, Omar, and an eight-year-old daughter, Tala,

MEDIA ADAPTATIONS

- An audio performance of *Heather Raffo's 9 Parts of Desire* is available on compact disc. Performed by Raffo, the production was recorded at Ark Sound Studios and is available for sale on the playwright's Web site, http://www.heatherraffo.com. It also includes music by American and Iraqi musicians.

from her first marriage. She left her first husband, a Saudi Bedouin plastic surgeon based in London, after she found him sleeping with one of her friends. She also left her second husband, an Israeli Bedouin, when he did not keep his promise to take her out of the Middle East. Her true heartbreak comes from Sa'ad, a friend of her first husband, with whom she strikes up a long-distance romance. He breaks off their relationship shortly after they meet in person for the first time. Amal cannot understand why she has been rejected. Her love and loyalty, as well as her independent spirit, are a refreshing take on Middle Eastern women for the Western viewer.

The American
The American is the first of Raffo's three main characters and is loosely based on Raffo herself. The American lives in New York City and is half-Iraqi; however, because she is blonde, people do not see her as someone of Middle Eastern descent. As war descends on Baghdad, she is gripped with fear for her extended family and driven to frustrated anger by the cavalier attitudes of the other Americans around her, who either cheer for the war—which could mean the deaths of her innocent relatives—or cannot stand to watch news coverage of the war, which is a denial of what is happening. The American recites the names of her relatives—Raffo's cousins, aunts, and uncles—as if to stay attached to them, to keep them alive. More than any of the other characters, the American is struggling to reconcile the halves of her identity. She is safe compared with the others, but she is the least at peace.

The Doctor

The doctor is Western trained, but she returned to work in one of the best hospitals in the Middle East in the city of Basra. The war has brought cancers and birth defects to Basra, caused by radiation, taking her job far beyond normal health care. Her daily life and work are full of horrors now, and she is barely coping. She is also suffering from morning sickness because she is pregnant, a condition that should bring joy but for the Doctor is fraught with worry because of the high risk of birth defects in her region.

Huda

Huda is an intellectual Iraqi exile living in London; she is the second of Raffo's three main characters. She is in her seventies, drinks whiskey, and chain smokes. Huda is the most political character, denouncing Saddam Hussein for specific acts of inhumanity. She hates Saddam so much that she cannot help but want this war, since it means he may finally be deposed. Her name means "enlightenment," a fitting description for an academic who has spent her life protesting the dictatorship in Iraq. Her enlightenment has come at a hard price. She spent several months in prison following the 1963 Ba'ath coup and has been unable to return home permanently. She has lived in London for a long time; her husband died and was buried there, and she feels she cannot part with the life they built in London. Huda leaves the future to the younger women, despairing that they take up the veil and give up their educations. However, she now believes that change must come slowly if it is to endure.

Iraqi Girl

The Iraqi girl, named Sammura, is about nine years old. She is trapped at home with her mother because the streets have become unsafe for women to walk alone. Her three older brothers have disappeared and are presumed dead; her father was taken away after the Iraqi girl repeated at school something he said against Saddam Hussein. Since the war began, her mother will not let her go to school. She loves to watch American television shows, such as *Oprah*, and dances along with American pop music. Her mother calls her "stupid" because Sammura appears naive about the war and its implications; in fact, though, she can tell the difference between Kalashnikov and M16 gunfire, and she speaks English better than anyone else in her family. The Iraqi girl knows

that she is smart, but she understands she has made a mistake regarding her father and for that feels stupid.

Layal

Layal is an Iraqi artist and Raffo's third main character. Her name means "nights," and is a variation on the name Layla. Layal is loosely based on the famous Iraqi artist and painter Layla al-Attar, who, like Layal, was curator of the Saddam Art Center and was favored by Saddam's government. In the play, Layal exudes confidence, but her life has not been easy. She was shot by her husband when he discovered her having an affair, but she miraculously survived. She has had to sleep with men to maintain her position of political favor, and she has had to take on work that she did not want, such as the mosaic of President George H. W. Bush at the Rashid Hotel. In exchange, she has been able to express herself in unexpected ways without challenge, including the creation of the painting *Savagery* and its incongruous display at the heart of the Saddam Art Center. This artwork corresponds to a real painting of the same name by al-Attar, which provided the inspiration for Raffo to write *Heather Raffo's 9 Parts of Desire*. At the end of the play, Layal begs her daughter not to come home, an allusion to the death of al-Attar, who died in a 1993 bomb raid ordered by the administration of U.S. President Bill Clinton following an assassination attempt on former President Bush. Al-Attar's husband and housekeeper also died, and her daughter was blinded in one eye.

Mullaya

The mullaya is a professional mourner; in this play, she is a mythic figure, tying together past and present. She is seen at the beginning, dropping the shoes of dead people into a river, which symbolizes ushering the dead into the next realm. She is a Marsh Arab, an ethnic group that lived in the marshlands at the junction of the Tigris and Euphrates Rivers in southern Iraq for five thousand years until they were displaced in the early 1990s, when Saddam ordered the rivers dammed and diverted. Saddam thus turned the marshlands into desert as punishment against the Marsh Arabs for rising up against him and harboring defecting soldiers. Having lost their livelihood, the Marsh Arabs dispersed throughout Iraq and Iran. The mullaya, a member of an ancient profession and an ancient ethnic group, is in mourning herself. At the end of the play, she brings together all the voices of Raffo's nine characters in a monologue that is part eulogy and part song of love and survival.

Nanna

Nanna is Arabic for "Granny." Nanna is an old woman peddling found objects on the street to buy necessities. She has seen a lot in her life and speaks of the burning of libraries and the loss of history. She holds secrets and memories but appears willing to give up almost anything for money to buy food, as when she tries to sell Layal's painting at the end of the play. Nanna represents the past and the immediate future of Iraq, as its people struggle for stability and identity.

Sammura

See Iraqi girl

Umm Ghada

Umm Ghada is the sole survivor of the destruction of the Amiriyya bomb shelter on February 13, 1991. This civilian installation was mistaken for a military communications center and thus targeted. She lost her nine family members among the 403 dead; she calls herself Umm Ghada, or "mother of tomorrow," after her daughter Ghada, the only body she could identify. Umm Ghada lives in a trailer next to the destroyed shelter, keeping alive the memory of what happened and acting as a witness of its existence to other people. The character of Umm Ghada is loosely based on the real person of Umm Greyda, a woman who lost eight children in the bombing and lives on-site to serve as a guide.

THEMES

Survival

Survival is a central theme in *Heather Raffo's 9 Parts of Desire*. Raffo's nine portrayals of different Iraqi women describe a culture that is still full of hope and love despite decades of oppression under Saddam Hussein. These women are not victims but survivors—survivors of both the war and their individual tragedies. Layal has had the freedom to seek the full extent of her expression as an artist and survives despite indignities that she must suffer as a woman in the realm of politics. Through her art, she is able to save women who have been victimized, such as the college student whom Uday murders and whom

TOPICS FOR FURTHER STUDY

- Write an additional scene for *Heather Raffo's 9 Parts of Desire*, using one or more of the nine characters Raffo created. You can choose to add to Raffo's themes or include new information about the Iraq War. In small groups, create a video recording of your scene being performed, and use computer software to edit the recording. Show your film to your class.

- Choose a period of time in the history of Iraq to read about in depth: any period from ancient times to the present day. Write a research paper about the period you chose. Discuss what you have learned and how it relates to Raffo's play.

- Create a work of visual art that is inspired by Raffo's play. Use the medium of your choice—paint, collage, or photography, for example—and make sure to include your artistic interpretation of the nine characters and who they represent to you. Give your work a title and write out a brief explanation of how you created it and what it represents. Share your work in a class art show.

- Imagine that ten years have passed and the Iraqi girl is approximately eighteen years old. Write a story describing what she is now doing with her life, what happened to the other members of her family, and how her experience as a young girl during Saddam's overthrow affected her. Read Lois Lowry's *Number the Stars*, about best friends who help each other survive World War II, for ideas on how young girls deal with hardship and tragedy and still persevere.

she secretly memorializes as an unreachable blossoming branch in one of her paintings. Layal dies in a U.S. bomb raid, but her message lives on in her paintings.

The Iraqi girl is an unlikely survivor because, being young, she seems so fragile against the mechanisms of war. However, she shows herself to be clever and leaves the audience with the sense that she will grow up to be the sort of woman Huda envisions as a leader in Iraq's future. Huda is a survivor in a very literal sense: imprisoned for several months after the Ba'ath Party takeover in the 1960s, she has lived in exile from Iraq all her life but has never given up hope of return, or at least the reform of Iraq and the downfall of Saddam. The doctor, who like Layal has chosen to stay in Iraq and work, faces the horrors of birth defects and cancer in children on a daily basis. Her despair is tangible and her survival seems tenuous, yet she is full of hope when she reveals that she is pregnant. Nanna, who has lived a long life and survived revolution after revolution, feels that her life has been spared for some reason and that she must owe a debt for that. She is a mouthpiece for history, representative of cultural survival, but she feels that the Iraqi people are being punished by God for not getting rid of Saddam sooner. Raffo's theme of survival in this play maintains a sense of hope, rather than the despair of a victim. The mullaya, a professional mourner, is speaking of hope and renewal when she says "I cannot choose to leave / throw our arms wide / sing to my mother / I am home again."

Love

Love is a theme echoed by all the characters in this play, in different ways. For Amal, love is loyalty, and those who are not loyal to her will lose her; however, when she is on the receiving end of rejection, Amal cannot understand what went wrong or how her lover saw her as anything other than herself. Layal, sexy and confident, paints nudes of herself and conducts affairs that she barely conceals from her husband. Her love is very physical, but it also takes shape in her paintings, where she preserves the dignity of women in general, despite the politics she must take part in. She loves her attachment to people, scorning the American idea of freedom. Umm Ghada's love for her murdered family has shaped her present life as a survivor and witness to their senseless deaths. She has given up her individuality, calling herself simply Mother of Ghada. The American, who loves her relatives in Iraq, is desperate to hear that they are safe. She is caught between two worlds, watching footage unfold and praying for their lives.

The title of this play is derived from a hadith (a story) of Imam Ali, an important Muslim leader from the seventh century. He said, "God

Heather Raffo performs 9 Parts of Desire *at the Manhattan Ensemble Theater in New York.* (AP Images)

created sexual desire in ten parts; then he gave nine parts to women and one to men." Raffo's title, *Heather Raffo's 9 Parts of Desire*, is an allusion to this hadith and to the complexity of love that women feel. All of the women in Raffo's play are passionate and torn, but their love buoys them and helps them to survive.

STYLE

Symbols

Symbols are objects, marks, or sounds that represent something else. Symbols are quick and effective ways to communicate meaning without extended explanation. Raffo's one-act, one-woman play relies on symbols to fill in meaning surrounding the actress's monologue. For example, the water on stage that represents the two rivers of Mesopotamia's landscape, the Tigris and the Euphrates, also symbolizes life and death. This meaning is drawn out by the mullaya's use of the water, because she is a professional mourner. The doctor, whose profession also deals with life and death, also uses the water on stage.

Another important symbol is the *abaya*. The abaya is a square overgarment that is usually black and worn loosely at the shoulders or from the top of the head. It is a symbol of Iraqi identity in this play, distinguishing the actress from her audience. The actress performing in this play uses her abaya to effect the transformation between characters. Through use of the abaya, which is as much prop as clothing throughout the play, Raffo illustrates the range of personalities and of stories of Iraqi women.

Dramatic Monologue

Dramatic monologue is a narrative style used in plays wherein the character is communicating information with another person not obviously present on stage, such as the audience. Traditionally, dramatic monologues are given in verse; in *Heather Raffo's 9 Parts of Desire*, the characters all speak in free verse, a type of poetry that does not follow any specific rules for rhyme or meter. Raffo's characters, speaking in dramatic monologues, share themselves with the audience, establishing an emotional journey that is more meaningful for both the characters and the audience than if the characters were speaking to themselves, unaware of being observed. Amal, for example, says, "I have never talked this before / nobody here knows this thing about me." She is excited to share herself with outsiders.

HISTORICAL CONTEXT

Founding of Modern Iraq

Modern Iraq was shaped after the dissolution of the Ottoman Empire following World War I. The region, known by its ancient name of Mesopotamia, was under British control until the United Kingdom granted independence, and the Kingdom of Iraq was formed in 1932. In July 1958, after decades of instability and British intervention to maintain oil supplies, a military coup successfully overthrew the monarchy and established the Republic of Iraq. The republic was first led by General Abdul Karim Qassim.

Qassim was friendly with the Soviet Union, then a communist nation, which prompted the anti-communist governments of the United Kingdom and the United States to support his overthrow. Qassim was ousted and killed in February 1963, and by 1968, the Ba'ath Socialist Party controlled Iraq. Saddam Hussein, a Ba'ath Party leader, took the offices of president and prime minister in July 1979 in a bloody purge of government officials that claimed more than five hundred lives.

Iraq under Saddam Hussein

Saddam Hussein was president of Iraq from 1979 to 2003. He maintained his rule through brutal suppression of opposition. His secular government was unusual for a Middle Eastern country, and in 1980, Saddam began a war with neighboring Iran, which had recently come under Islamic rule. Suspicious that insurgency was developing in the Kurdish village of Halabja in Iraq, in March 1988, Saddam ordered poison gas to be dropped, killing five thousand people and wounding ten thousand more—an act classed as genocide by Human Rights Watch. Iraq's economy and thus its people were devastated by the war, which ended in a stalemate in August 1988. In 1990, Saddam invaded Kuwait, a small nation south of Iraq on the Persian Gulf, hoping to take control of its rich oil resources and thus repay some of Iraq's war debt. Kuwait repelled Iraq with the support of U.S. military forces in a conflict that became known as the Gulf War. Saddam was nearly overthrown during the Gulf War; however, the U.S. military withheld support at the crucial time and Saddam successfully quelled the rebellion.

For all that Saddam was a dictator and an inept military commander, Iraq had some of the best universities and hospitals in the Middle East and generously supported its artists, musicians, and writers. However, people lived in fear of coming under Saddam's scrutiny. Many people, suspected of being dissidents, simply disappeared, like the Iraqi girl's father in Raffo's play.

The Iraq War

On March 20, 2003, a coalition of forces sent by the United States, the United Kingdom, and other countries invaded Baghdad to oust Saddam from power, following reports that he had weapons of mass destruction, which posed a threat to security around the world. Baghdad and other cities were bombed, and the Ba'ath

Iraqi Shite women, the focus of 9 Parts of Desire *(Ali Yussef | AFP | Getty Images)*

CRITICAL OVERVIEW

Party was unseated. Saddam was captured in December 2003; after a lengthy trial, he was executed for crimes against the Iraqi people on December 30, 2006. Meanwhile, religious and political groups struggle for control of Baghdad and the rest of Iraq while the United States tries to hand over sovereignty to the unstable nation.

Heather Raffo's 9 Parts of Desire premiered in August 2003, five months after the United States invaded Baghdad, seeking to overthrow Iraqi president Saddam Hussein. Public consciousness and curiosity about Iraqis was high at this time, bringing her production greater attention. Jackie McGlone, reviewing the original show at the Traverse Theatre in Edinburgh, Scotland, for the *Scotsman*, calls it a "powerful drama," whereas Joyce McMillan, writing for the same publication, is more critical. "Neither a slightly confusing script, nor Raffo's deeply-felt but poorly differentiated performance, quite rise to

the challenge posed by this huge theme." Michael Billington, reviewing the same production for the London *Guardian*, finds small technical faults with Raffo's performance but sees tremendous value in what her play has to say. He writes, "The effect of her show is to challenge the audience's comfortable moral certainties and to make manifest the daily sufferings of Iraqi women and the people at large."

Raffo next performed her show at the Bush Theater in London. Reviewer Fiona Mountford describes it in the *Evening Standard* as "unstructured sprawl" and an "underwhelming Production." According to Simi Horwitz in "Face to Face: Heather Raffo; Exploring the Complexity of Identity," in *Back Stage*, both the London *Times* and the *Independent* selected *Heather Raffo's 9 Parts of Desire* as a best play for 2003.

The play then moved to the Manhattan Ensemble Theatre in New York City. Writing for the *New York Times*, Charles Isherwood concedes, in a generally positive review, that "the play may not be particularly distinguished as a dramatic text, but it is effective as humanistic journalism."

Raffo's play went on to tour the country and be performed by other actresses. She occasionally made small updates to keep the text relevant. In 2008, Chris Jones reviewed Raffo's performance at the Museum of Contemporary Art for the *Chicago Tribune*, noting, "It's probably fair to say that this piece had more impact in 2003 than it does today." However, Jones still finds value in the play, which he describes as "highly absorbing... with equal parts intellectual heft and raw human compassion."

CRITICISM

Carol Ullmann

Ullmann is a freelance writer and editor. In the following essay, she examines Western misperceptions of Iraqi women and how Raffo dispels these misperceptions in her play Heather Raffo's 9 Parts of Desire.

Heather Raffo's 9 Parts of Desire was inspired by the playwright's experiences with real Iraqi women after she traveled to Iraq to visit her father's family in her early twenties. "When I returned to the U.S., people would say, 'Oh, you're an Arab—and you went to Baghdad, so did you wear a veil?'" Raffo told McGlone in an interview for Edinburgh's *Scotsman*.

In the United States, many people believe that women in the Middle East are uneducated, unemployed, robed from head to foot, often veiled, and kept by men as if they were property. They are thought to be voiceless and modest. It is a very stimulating image for a nation where men and women freely argue the finer points of equality. Western misperceptions of women in Middle Eastern countries come from a combination of sources, but primarily news media, television shows, and films. When the war in Afghanistan began in 2001, images sent back to the United States by reporters and photographers showed Afghani women veiled and robed from head to foot in a garment called a burqa. Intentionally or not, these women were considered by Western reporters and their viewers to be helpless victims of both the war and the culture of which they were part.

Afghanistan, which is located in south-central Asia, between Iran and Pakistan, was unusual compared with other countries in the Middle East and southwest Asia because it was governed by the Taliban. The Taliban is a fundamentalist

> DESPITE SADDAM'S HARSH METHODS OF CONTROLLING HIS PEOPLE, ALL WERE ENCOURAGED TO GET AN EDUCATION, INCLUDING WOMEN."

group that interprets the Sharia, or Islamic religious law, very conservatively. The Taliban ruled in Afghanistan from 1996 until 2001, when it was overthrown by North Atlantic Treaty Organization forces in an effort to stem terrorist activities abroad, believed to be supported by the Taliban. While in power, the Taliban required women to dress in burqas and travel only with a male escort, and it forbade them to attend public school or hold jobs in most sectors. This extreme conservatism became a standard image, to Westerners, of what was wrong in the Middle East.

The war in Afghanistan immediately preceded the United States-led invasion of Iraq in 2003. Iraq and Afghanistan could not be more different culturally, but media coverage at the outset of the war in Iraq was vague about Iraq's possible connections to Islamic terrorists, which thematically tied Afghanistan and Iraq together. Afghanistan is largely inhabited by Sunni Muslims, whereas Shi'a Muslims dominate in Iraq. Iraq was a secular nation under Saddam Hussein, and it was unusual for women there to be veiled. Despite Saddam's harsh methods of controlling his people, all were encouraged to get an education, including women. Women held jobs, owned businesses, and participated in politics. Iraq was, in some ways, more socially progressive than many other Middle Eastern countries, where theocracies or democracies failed to give women opportunities equal to those of men. Iraq had the best universities and the best hospitals in the region, and Saddam's government was a strong supporter of the arts. This is what Raffo saw when she visited Baghdad in 1993. Raffo told McGlone, "There are no images of Iraqi women out there that aren't flat, one-dimensional and somewhat victimised. The real Iraqi woman does not exist in western culture."

Raffo shows the many faces of Iraqi women through the characters in her play. Some wear an abaya, a long, loose overgarment, but none of Raffo's women are veiled. In Raffo's play, the

WHAT DO I READ NEXT?

- *Reading "Lolita" in Tehran* (2003) by Azar Nafisi is a memoir about Nafisi's life as a professor of literature in Iran. She lived there from the late 1970s, when Iran came under Islamic rule, until she emigrated in 1997. The story of her difficult life in Iran is interwoven with interpretations of books that Nafisi assigns to her students.

- *The Orange Trees of Baghdad: In Search of My Lost Family* (2007) by British Iraqi Leilah Nadir tells the family history of her Iraqi relatives as they live through the British occupation, the revolution of the 1960s, the Iran-Iraq War, the Gulf War, and the overthrow of Saddam Hussein.

- Farrah Sarafa's *Mediterranean Lattice: Eastern Shadows over Western Mirage* (2008) is a poetic exploration of her identity—her mother is a Muslim Palestinian and her father is a Christian Iraqi—as she travels through Europe alone one summer.

- *The Big Empty* (2004) by J. B. Stephens is a young-adult novel set in the near future. Seven teenagers search for hope in the form of an underground liberal society within a United States that has come under military

rule after a virus kills more than half the human population on planet Earth.

- The 1989 novel *The Joy Luck Club*, by Amy Tan, tells the secret past of four mothers who escaped China during the war with Japan and the revolution that followed. Interwoven with the mothers' stories are the tales of their four daughters—eight very different women who have all loved and lost.

- A 2009 collection of plays, edited by Holly Hill and Dina Amin, *Salaam: Peace; An Anthology of Middle-Eastern American Drama*, explores Middle Eastern identity by American playwrights from a variety of backgrounds. This anthology includes *Heather Raffo's 9 Parts of Desire*.

- *The Handmaid's Tale* (1985), by Margaret Atwood, is a novel about a near-future society in which the United States comes under theocratic (religious government) rule, and the rights of women are severely restricted. The narrator of the story, a woman whose only job is to produce children and turn them over to caregivers, remembers how things used to be and how and why they changed.

---

abaya is practical desert clothing rather than a symbol of overzealous protection of femininity. It is also used as a prop to represent long hair, a baby, a painting, and more. All nine women are vibrantly alive—angry, hurt, confused, impassioned. Layal, a famous painter, and the doctor have made the choice to live in Iraq despite pressures to live and work elsewhere. Layal asks, "Who will be left to inspire the people if all the / artists and intellectuals run?" and "What's to paint outside Iraq? / Maybe I am not so good artist outside Iraq." The doctor despairs at what her country has become after the Gulf Wars. There is so much radiation from depleted uranium used in munitions that babies

are born with grotesque birth defects, and young children suffer from cancer at alarming rates. The doctor is an intellectual, suffering for love of her country.

Umm Ghada, survivor of the destruction of the Amiriyya bomb shelter, lives to bear witness to the world of the senseless murder of more than four hundred civilians. She is calm and peaceful, but she will not let Amiriyya be forgotten lest it happen again. Nanna is a witness to history, having lived in Iraq throughout its transformation from British mandate to kingdom to republic. "I see things / I see everything." Huda is also a witness to the past but lives in exile. She has spent her whole life fighting from the outside, in the form of political protests, to have Saddam removed from power and make Iraq a safe place to live again. She drinks alcohol, something an observant Muslim would never do. The Iraqi girl, Sammura, is energetic and modern. She knows English better than the rest of her family. She can distinguish, by sound, between the firing of different weapons and know how far away the shooting is. She seems to be a silly girl obsessed with American television at first but truly struggles with the deaths and disappearances of her grandparents, brothers, and father. She hopes to study and be smarter for her father when he returns, if he returns.

Amal is an Iraqi Bedouin woman who has been married and divorced twice. She is not modest, and her forthright expressions of love are surprisingly frank. Amal's tale of divorce and heartbreak, her concern about her weight and her children could be the story of many women all over the world. The American, like many Americans, is obsessed with news coverage over the war, but unlike others, she is desperately seeking knowledge that her family members in Iraq are safe. Like Huda, the American lives outside Iraq, where it is supposedly safe, but this safety also renders her powerless to do anything but watch the war unfold.

The mullaya is the most mythic and traditional figure in the play. She defines herself as a Marsh Arab, an ethnic group whose way of life was destroyed by Saddam when he diverted the Tigris and Euphrates Rivers, causing the marshes to dry out. She is outcast, like Huda and the American, but in her own country. At the conclusion of the play, she becomes an amalgamation of all nine characters, channeling them as if to usher them to another realm:

> I fear it here
> and I love it here
> I cannot stop what I am here
> either I shall die
> or I shall live a ransom for all the daughters
> of savagery.

In *Heather Raffo's 9 Parts of Desire*, Raffo shows the audience nine very different, very Iraqi women, none of whom are veiled, modest, or ignorant. They are of different ethnicities, religions, ages, education, and professions, but are united by a shared culture and history. "I knew I had to tell the stories I'd heard because they're funny, sexy, radical and deeply emotional," she explained to McGlone. Raffo's play is important for Western audiences to see because it dispels the myth of the silently suffering, burqa-wearing woman in a dusty hovel. Raffo writes, as the mullaya, "life did choose to root / here in this grave / all my family is here / . . . / always it is life and death / and life and death." The love and suffering of these women are not only universal to people the world around but also across time. With these lines, Raffo acknowledges that which is past, reaching far back into ancient Mesopotamia but also forward into the future.

Source: Carol Ullmann, Critical Essay on *Heather Raffo's 9 Parts of Desire*, in *Drama for Students*, Gale, Cengage Learning, 2010.

Pat McDonnell Twair

In the following review, Twair documents the production history and Raffo's strong characterization in Heather Raffo's 9 Parts of Desire.

In a one-woman show which has drawn an enthusiastic response from critics wherever it has played, Heather Raffo, the daughter of an Iraqi immigrant to the United States, tells the story of Iraqi women under siege.

A caretaker at the Amariyeh bomb shelter, a Scotch-drinking intellectual in London, a twice-divorced Bedouin looking for a new husband, a pre-teen gyrating to 'N Sync who hasn't been allowed to go to school since the GIs arrived in Iraq. These characters represent just a few of the Iraqi women Heather Raffo portrays in *Nine Parts of Desire*.

Her subjects are composites of Iraqis Raffo met when she visited her father's family in 1993. She has been developing the characters ever since as her conversations continued through the second Gulf War and resulting occupation.

One of them may even be Raffo herself I thought, as I watched her portrayal of an Iraqi American woman in Manhattan who impatiently filed her fingernails while viewing news coverage of Iraq: "Why don't they count the number of Iraqi dead," the agitated woman asks of no one in particular.

Ironically, Raffo says she didn't appreciate her paternal Iraqi heritage while growing up in Michigan, where her civil engineer father emigrated to in the 1960s and later married her American mother. But everything changed with Desert Storm. Suddenly the University of Michigan graduate was desperate to see her father's homeland.

No one was happy with her mission to view the war-torn land of her ancestors. But in 1993,

Raffo crossed one border after another until she was in the arms of her nine uncles and aunts in sanction-impoverished Baghdad. The visit was to change her life.

During a month long run of *Nine Parts of Desire,* Raffo played to a full house at the prestigious Geffen Playhouse in Los Angeles. There are no costume changes in her one-act performance but Raffo does astonishing things with an abaya as she transforms herself into a series of remarkably different women.

Although she does not speak Arabic, the broken English accents of her characters reveal regional and class distinctions. Take for instance, the high-pitched singsong voice of the Bedouin woman who divorced her Saudi husband in London and left her second husband, a Bedouin from Israel, before striking up a correspondence with a third potential spouse.

Instantaneously, Raffo morphs into Hooda, who speaks the king's English albeit with a smoker's hoarseness. A chandelier illuminates the pampered woman who has fled to London where she ruminates: "This war is against all my beliefs, yet I wanted it."

This single act tribute to the spirit of survival in Iraqi women developed out of a 20-minute performance Raffo made at San Diego's Old Globe theatre in California, for her MFA acting thesis at the city's university. The title *Nine Parts of Desire* is borrowed from an Islamic adage that god bestowed nine parts of sexual desire to women, and only one to men.

Raffo premiered *Nine Parts of Desire* in August 2003 in Scotland, at Edinburgh's Traverse Theatre. It then moved to the Bush Theatre in London's off-West End where critics praised it as one of the best five plays in the London September 2003 season. New Yorkers viewed the show from October 2004 to May 2005 at the Manhattan Theatre Ensemble.

The play opens with Mulaya, a homeless crone who tosses shoes into a river as she mourns the lost soles/souls of the dead. Her lament is poetry:

> When the grandson of Genghis Khan
> Burned all the books in Baghdad
> The river ran black with ink
> What colour is the river now?
> It runs the colour of old shoes
> The colour of distances
> The colour of soles torn and worn
> This river is the colour of worn shoes.

With a few magical twists of the abaya, Mulaya is transformed into a blonde artist, Layal, who performed favours for Saddam Hussein and his sons. As she works at her easel, she comments that she could have escaped the war and moved to London with her sister. "But what happens if all the intellectuals go? Here, I am a good artist, I may not be in London."

Raffo passionately portrays a physician desperate over the disintegrating condition of her hospital and the smell of raw sewage that makes her retch. She decries the effects of depleted uranium weapons that have left radiation in the air, water and soil.

"Iraq had the best hospitals in the Middle East," she shouts, now it has been cast into the Dark Ages. The desperate doctor curses radiation that causes infants to be born with no heads or two heads and creates breast cancers in toddlers who play on battle-sites alive with depleted chemical waste.

Perhaps the most tragic is Um Rudha, who lives in a yellow trailer next to the site of the Amariyeh bomb shelter where 403 Iraqis were immolated in 1991 when a US bomb destroyed it. All the members of Um Rudha's family were incinerated in the air strike leaving her alone, to feed and clothe herself by guiding visitors through the ghastly memorial

"Now you sign the witness book," she tells the audience, "your name will be a witness too."

How do Iraqi Americans react to *Nine Parts of Desire?*

Following her performances at the Geffen, Raffo met with Arab psychologist Dr. Ilham Sarraf who enthused: "You have told our stories. This is my fourth viewing and I identify more of my sisters each time I come."

Up close to this commanding talent, Raffo proves to be not a larger-than-life Medea-like figure, but a petite young woman who graciously accepts praise for her remarkable portrayal of women under fire.

Source: Pat McDonnell Twair, Review of *Nine Parts of Desire,* in *Middle East,* No. 362, December 2005, pp. 56–59.

Pamela Renner

In the following review of Heather Raffo's 9 Parts of Desire, *Renner follows the success of the original production run and provides an account of Raffo's early life.*

" AS *NINE PARTS OF DESIRE* ILLUMINATES A HIDDEN, FEMALE WORLD, RAFFO EFFECTIVELY EXTENDS THAT IMMIGRATION OFFICIAL'S GALLANT INVITATION TO ALL OF US, WELCOMING US TO AN IRAQI FAMILY WE DIDN'T KNOW WE HAD."

In 1974, a curious and lively four-year-old girl from Michigan went with her family to visit her father's homeland, Iraq. To this day, Heather Raffo—creator and performer of the Off-Broadway hit *Nine Parts of Desire*—remembers every detail of that visit. She can still see her grandmother's house in her mind's eye; she can feel the warmth of the desert land that gave the ancient world its first code of civil law under Hammurabi, the priest king of Babylonia. When she went back as an adult in 1993, just after the first Gulf War, so much had changed, and yet her family was in many ways the same: embracing of the exotic cousin with her blonde hair and American ways who had come all the way from the U.S. to tell them, "We're sorry, and we love you and are thinking about you."

"I think that young people are especially influenced by their first war," Raffo reflects. "If you came of age during Vietnam, that event helped shape you. My coming of age was the first Gulf War—although it wasn't very long in time frame and didn't seem to affect Americans that much, it affected me hugely."

The war played out on television screens as a triumph of American airpower, with a mostly invisible enemy. The name of Saddam Hussein grew to such emblematic proportions that it seemed to fill the sun-bleached spaces of the country from border to border.

The launch of the war in 1991 marked Raffo's political awakening, and in many ways it also divided her life in two. Raffo realized, "Oh, I'm not just from Michigan—I'm living in Michigan with a big family in Iraq. I'm not on one side of this war. I can't sit in a bar with people cheering as bombs are going off. My body, blood and psyche want my family to live. What if I never see them again? What if they're just in the wrong place in the wrong time?"

In *Nine Parts of Desire,* her solo evocation of contemporary Iraqi womanhood, Raffo doesn't let us forget the savagery of Saddam's regime; neither does she ignore the way that violence, occupation and insurgency have trampled law to dust. At the same time, there are no soldiers in sight on the small stage. Instead, Raffo trains us to see—as if for the first time—those women in black abaya who peer out from the margins of newspaper photographs, the mothers and daughters of Iraq's scarred contemporary world, whose power to love is, in many ways, heightened by the tumult of their lives.

Nine Parts of Desire is Off Broadway's dark-horse hit of the season, with gorgeous reviews and a matching enthusiasm from audiences, who have turned a limited engagement—directed by Joanna Settle and produced by the not-for-profit Manhattan Ensemble Theater—into an open-ended run. The play premiered in 2003 at the Edinburgh Fringe Festival, and later played London's Bush Theatre. In England, Raffo garnered critical plaudits from *The Times* of London and *The Guardian*. She returned to New York City last spring for a reading at the Public Theater's New Work Now! festival.

MET's artistic director David Fishelson got word of a one-woman show dealing with Iraqi womanhood from an English colleague, and his curiosity was piqued. He invited Raffo to do an informal reading at MET's theatre in Soho, and the moment she finished performing, he walked on stage and optioned the play. Fishelson's instincts have been borne out by the intimate production's luminous reception. With glowing reviews in *The New Yorker, New York Times, Wall Street Journal* and other publications, *Nine Parts* is now on its fourth extension. Additional engagements are in the works for the 2005–06 season at the Geffen Playhouse in Los Angeles and in Washington, D.C., San Francisco, Chicago, Seattle and Philadelphia. The play is also in the running for a number of literary prizes.

While many of theatre's established playwrights have remained silent to date about the ongoing Iraqi war and its casualties, Raffo has jumped into the vacuum with a work of experiential and poetic resonance. Alone on stage, she summons a chorus of resolutely individual Iraqi women. Some are far from the eye of the storm; others embody it. Umm Gheda, whose entire family was incinerated by an American "smart bomb" during the first Gulf War, survives as a witness to atrocity, having lost all other identity in the chaos:

I named my daughter Gheda
Gheda means tomorrow.
So I am Umm Gheda, "mother of Gheda"
it is a sign of joy and respect to call a parent
    by their kunya.

In Baghdad, I am famous now as Umm
    Gheda
because I do live here in yellow trailer
outside Amiriya bomb shelter
since the bombing
13 February 1991.

Yes I was inside
with nine from my family
talking laughing
then such a pounding shaking
everything is fire
I couldn't find my children [. . .]

In the whole day later [. . .]
the only body I did recognize
is my daughter—Gheda
so I did take her name.

There are other women in Raffo's group who desperately hold on to a name, a story, any shred of individuality. Among the characters are a woman physician, struggling against the cancers caused by environmental poisons unleashed by the bombings; a painter who collaborated with Saddam's regime, yet filled his museums with forbidden images of female nakedness; a robust Bedouin mother who has left two husbands behind and lost the love of a man she idealized; an Iraqi girl who dances to *NSYNC and wishes she could befriend the American soldiers; a hard-drinking expatriate in her fifties who lives in London and deplores the persecution of civilians under Saddam; a professional mourner who immerses herself in the grief of a whole people; and a young American woman who has an Iraqi family and can hardly tear herself away from the daily news reports on television—so deep is her fear for those who might end up as unnamed casualties of a CNN news feed. Their words rain down in torrents, changing us as we listen.

Raffo remembers that first 1974 trip to Iraq as a childhood interlude of enchantment—the voices of cousins who chattered, hugged and teased her, the intricate stories her uncle told the children as they slept out on the roof, enjoying the clear desert sky with its canopy of stars.

As Raffo grew up, the family was forced to grow apart. In the '70s, there were still aunts and uncles who popped in to visit the family in Michigan. Their vivacity stirred Heather's imagination, and they brought gifts of sandals or spices that smelled like the place she remembered. Why she identified so strongly with these ties of blood is still a bit of an enigma for Raffo.

In 1980, when Iraq went to war with Iran, the borders shut tight. In the midst of American sanctions and embargoes and a devastating collapse of Iraq's economy that left even the middle classes starving, Raffo felt drawn to return to the Iraqi family she remembered with a child's clear eyes.

She finally did, in 1993. To approach Iraq at that time required a 20-hour bus ride across the desert, only to arrive at a closed border. It took Raffo five hours to get through the checkpoint. Border patrol divided up the bus's passengers into lines, one for returning Iraqis, one for people from other Arab states. The third line, for designated "others," was empty; Raffo stood alone. With her American passport, flowing blonde hair and limited Arabic, she expected a long bureaucratic tussle.

Raffo told the officer in charge that she had an Iraqi father. "This guy sitting at a big desk looked like trouble," says Raffo. But, to her surprise, the official got up, walked all the way across the room to greet her, and stamped her passport for entry. "He had the warmest twinkly eyes you ever saw," she recalls. "He said, 'Welcome to your father's country.'"

It was as if a wall had parted, and suddenly she was on the inside: "I was the daughter—the daughter of a whole country. They could not see me as anything different." Her Baghdad family, by now grown to 60 or 70 people, had amiable shouting matches in Arabic concerning whose house she'd visit first for dinner, until her eldest uncle, Behnam, intervened, devised a social calendar for his visiting niece. (Years later, he was also the first to reach her after 9/11 devastated New York, having become almost like a second father during her 1993 stay.)

She continues, "There was an inner seed in me that felt this connection to Iraq. It had a lot to do with my femininity—I don't know why. When I started working on this play and meeting Iraqi women and really talking to them, I realized how similar we were, and they would laugh, 'Oh, you're Iraqi!' They wouldn't give me any room to be American, too."

Their instinctive acceptance helped Raffo conquer her sense of fracture and self-division. Her personal family story is also the story of the two nations that have formed her bloodline, and it's no longer just hers.

As *Nine Parts of Desire* illuminates a hidden, female world, Raffo effectively extends that immigration official's gallant invitation to all of us, welcoming us to an Iraqi family we didn't know we had.

Among Raffo's gallery of characters is a painter named Layal, based on a woman artist named Layal Al-Attar who once filled the palaces and museums of Saddam with flattering portraits and lush nudes. "She was already dead in 1993, when I first saw her artwork in Iraq," Raffo notes. Was Layal a voluptuary without conscience or a prisoner of the regime? Raffo wasn't certain, and everything she learned in her research only deepened the paradox. "Layal was like the Marilyn Monroe of Baghdad. Everything about her was steeped in rumor. She was this complicated woman who was possibly very tied to the regime. Maybe she was forced to be; maybe she liked it."

Layal's nude portraits also bear the metaphoric burden of explicating other female lives. Her canvases always transform her subjects, sometimes in the Ovidian sense, making raped and murdered girls into slender trees rebounding with blossoms. In her monologue, Layal says: "Always I paint them as me / or as trees sometimes like I was telling you / I do not want to expose exactly another woman's body / so I paint my body / but her body / herself inside me. / So it is not me alone / it is all of us / but I am the body that takes the experience."

An actress by training and vocation, Raffo acknowledges the parallels to her own methodology: "Those lines were absolutely the way the play shifts my psyche into their psyche." Critics have labeled her a chameleon, and some have marveled at her ability to change not only voice but tempo, as she performs her interconnected soliloquies. Before our eyes, she seems to grow gaunt or fat, young or aged, exuberant or sorrowful with the burden of remembering.

Raffo says, "It is only my body on stage, and it's a way to give an audience the flesh of Iraqi women, the thoughts of Iraqi women, while protecting them as well. The hardest thing for Iraqi women to do is put themselves out there in that way. Even Layal, who is very

sexy and loves attention—even her nature is to be very coy about what she's going to reveal and how. So I felt that the gift I was given as a creator and artist was an ability to be emotionally and spiritually naked. Maybe that's my gift as a writer, too."

In terms of her literary influences, there's really only one that feeds this play: Ntozake Shange's *for colored girls who have considered suicide/when the rainbow is enuf*. Raffo discovered Shange's poetic drama about African-American women in an undergraduate theatre class, and its form opened a vein of deep identification. "Reading it, I just felt like the women were speaking from inside me, and speaking something so central and truthful," Raffo says. "They were finding words that I'd wished I had at the time. I wasn't an African American or Puerto Rican; I'd never been discriminated against; I didn't have these experiences, but the raw current of need and desire and emotion and femininity, and the ability to articulate it as it moves through the world, was absolute."

Raffo's women are also witnesses to loneliness, savagery and the desolation of love—in short, they are not so very different from Shange's characters in their hearts. They speak of the desire for friendship, the pain of rejection, the need to memorialize the murdered and to absolve the living.

When Saddam lost the first Gulf War and the provinces of Iraq began to rise up against the Baathist regime, many felt that the CIA had made promises that it then failed to keep. American forces could have toppled Saddam, but didn't. "The biggest crime for me is that we chose as a world community to go to war with Iraq in 1991, and there were lots of groups, already established, that were anti-Saddam. Something like 18 out of 20 provinces fell after the war, and we saw Saddam going in with helicopters to put down the uprisings—and we let him do it! In a no-fly zone!

"They rise up, and we don't do anything. What we're doing now could have been done in 1991, without us going to Baghdad. Instead, we have given them 13 years of the worst oppression they've ever had: all the intellectuals leaving, the middle class starving, doctors making $4 a month! So when they say that this war was to liberate human beings, I say, 'No. That was your chance. That's when we would have gotten the roses in the street.'"

When Raffo began writing *Nine Parts of Desire* in 1998 for a thesis project, she recognized that she needed more research, more testimony, to draw upon. "Americans were hungry for this human face of Iraq," she says. "They only knew Saddam. They wanted me to tell them everything. I think that was one of the reasons why I knew a play could be worthwhile." Her subsequent interviews included a circle of Iraqi expatriates in London as well as her Iraqi relations. The play is not a literal transcription of Raffo's interviews any more than it is a polemical antiwar tirade. At a recent talkback, Raffo sat in shiny purple sweatpants, her hair still damp from the evening's onstage immersion in a river that could be the Tigris or Euphrates, an immersion that stands in for the river of voices, gradually merging, and the flow of measureless history.

Her chair faced her Manhattan Ensemble Theater audience, an audience hungry to know how much of the play was "real." All of it was real, Raffo gently explained, but almost nothing was literal. "I liken it to writing a song," she said. "I went and lived with them, and then I came home and wrote it, and said, 'This song's for you.'

"Their history is our history," she continued. "I mean, that was the cradle of civilization; aren't we all tied together from our beginnings?"

In the play, it's Nanna, a street vendor and scavenger who sells what she finds to keep from starving, who addresses the audience directly in these words:

I have too much existence
I have lived through 23
revolutions
my life has been spared
if my life has been spared
to whom do I owe my debt?
I have so much to repay.
To whom do I owe my debt?

THE AMERICAN

She hasn't left her apartment in New York
    City for days; she is glued to the TV.

Now they're digging through mass graves
    with their bare hands.
and one guy on tv I saw him
he found a pack of cigarettes
and he said my brother smoked
this kind of cigarette
so this is my brother's body
and he took the bones
so he could bury them / what

he thought
was his brother.

I've never seen men cry like that.

I watch my dad
try not to cry
because when he's watching tv
and it's green
nighttime footage of
bombs
he can recognize the street and
the neighborhoods
where all his family
lives
still.

I watch tv
looking for
faces
of my family
so all I do is cry.
But my dad
he ends up choking and making himself
sick
and
he's lived here in the US
for 40 years
he plays golf
5 times a week.
he's just sad / but
contained
because you
can't
you just can't
watch it
on tv.
I'm on my knees
in the middle of my apartment
with my mom
on the phone
watching
I'm holding a rosary
watching
CNN
and I want to pray
but I don't have
words
so I say their names
out-loud
Sarta,
Zuhair,
Behnam,
Zuhira
over and over trying
to see them

alive
and we don't know if—
anything
and we can't call
we can't get through on the phones
still
and
now
now people are burying their dead in their
     backyard
in the garden
the football field
its everyday
a police station
my uncle Sarta lives next to a police station
Amo Zuhair lives next to the airport
Ama Hooda / the Palestine Hotel
Ama Zuhira / in Karada / Mount Lebanon
Maysoon she used to work for the UN—
the whole face got blown off / I'm reading on
     the bus—

They never forget ever.
They carry everything with them /
I mean everything they are / they're so
     attached / like
great-grandparents, parents, children /
it lives in them, walks with them
they can't let go
of anything
they hold inside them.
So when they cry
it's lifetimes
I've never seen anything like it.

—From *Nine Parts of Desire*

Source: Pamela Renner, "Iraq Through the Eyes of Its Women," in *American Theatre*, Vol. 22, No. 4, April 2005, pp. 20, 71.

Simi Horwitz

In the following interview, Horwitz asks Raffo about her motivation for creating the one-woman show.

Actor Heather Raffo asserts she did not write her one-person show, *Nine Parts of Desire,* in which she stars, as a vehicle for herself. Its creation emerged from a much deeper place: her identity— and pain—as a woman of Iraqi heritage.

"I'm an American, but I became aware of myself as an Iraqi—had a sense of myself as 'the other'—for the first time during the Gulf War," Raffo recalls.... "I realized from that point on that my cousins in Iraq—family whom I loved— would be viewed by many Americans as dark and dirty. I also realized that the only difference

between my cousins and myself was the accident of where we were born. That was my loss of innocence and, in a way, the beginning of this piece, although I didn't start writing it until I was in graduate school at the University of San Diego. It was my master's thesis."

Nine Parts of Desire, which bowed Off-Broadway at the Manhattan Ensemble Theater on Wed., Oct. 13, presents a portrait of nine Iraqi women from all Walks of life—from the most traditional (indeed, some are awash in mythic beliefs) to the most modern, calculating, and cynical; from those who feel anyone in power is an improvement over the brutality of Saddam Hussein to those who feel that President Bush brought only chaos to the region and ulti-mately betrayed the Iraqis.

The play is based on a series of interviews Raffo conducted with Iraqi women and inspired by an aphorism from a Muslim text: "God cre-ated sexual desire in 10 parts, then gave nine parts to women and one to men." Raffo, who inhabits each persona fully, moving from char-acter to character seamlessly, says that whatever their differences, "all the women are united by their desire to live fully. I chose the title because it has a certain resonance. It points to the com-plexity of these women."

A highly animated, 34-year-old native of Oke-mos, Mich., Raffo, who punctuates her thoughts with a flurry of hand motions, meets with me in a Back Stage conference room, eager to talk about her worldview, politics, and the evolution of her show, which played in England last season and was selected as the best show in London by *The Times* and as one of the five best plays in London in December 2003 by *The Independent.*

"I would love audiences to find these women—many of whom may be alien—familiar in some way," notes Raffo. "I'd love to hear an American say, 'That Bedouin woman is just like my aunt.' But at the same time, I want American audiences to walk out a little confused, not able to say, 'Oh, I get it,' but rather [to] understand how difficult it is to grasp the psyche of people who have lived under Saddam for 30 years with American support, then had a war with Iran, resulting in 1.5 million deaths, followed by 13 years of sanctions and two wars under American firepower."

Still, in an effort not to create characters who are too foreign to Westerners, Raffo admits presenting the most secular, educated women, "softening the religious aspects, although many Iraqis are Christian, not Muslim." Indeed, Raffo was raised a Roman Catholic. Her American-born mother and Iraqi-born father, who came here as a young man to work as a civil engineer, are both Christian.

Perhaps not surprisingly, Arab-American audiences have been the most responsive, Raffo reports: "They come to me at the end of the show with tears running down their faces. They recognize the women I'm portraying. One young man told me he lost eight members of his family because they didn't have a picture of Saddam Hussein on their wall. I had an Iraqi father and daughter come backstage with very different politics. The father kept saying, 'Bush is a miracle, Bush is a miracle.' The daughter didn't feel that at all, but they both loved the show. I don't know what Americans feel," Raffo continues. "They're less vocal, but I think they're enjoying it, with the exception of some middle-aged Republicans who saw it in Edinburgh, didn't get it, and were obviously turned off."

PERTINENCE IN A DEEP WAY

Raffo wanted to act from the outset. She earned her undergraduate degree from the University of Michigan in Ann Arbor, where she majored in literature, before heading off to the University of San Diego, where she received her M.F.A. Short of a brief dry period, Raffo has worked steadily as an actor in commercials ("which pays the rent") and in theatre. Some of her recent acting credits include an Off-Broadway production of *Over the River and Through the Woods*, along with *Macbeth* (as Lady Macbeth), *The Merry Wives of Windsor* (Mistress Page), and *The Rivals*, all with the Acting Company. Under the auspices of the Old Globe Theatre, Raffo acted in *Othello* (directed by Jack O'Brien), *Romeo and Juliet* (directed by Daniel Sullivan), *As You Like It* (directed by Stephen Wadsworth), and *The Comedy of Errors* (directed by John Rando).

Raffo credits her acting experience in classical theatre as a significant—albeit unwitting—influence on her development as a writer: "It has allowed me to think mythically, poetically, and out of the box. There's nothing that prepared me more for writing than acting. Acting is about sympathizing and feeling with your whole body. And when I write, I'm in my bones, just like an actor."

She adds that her acting background helped her with interviewing Iraqi women—that and

being an Iraqi, "which got me in the door, and being an American, which, oddly enough, made it possible for the women to trust me. They felt they could say things to me, as an American, that they wouldn't allow themselves to say to another Iraqi."

Raffo insists that while she defines herself as an Iraqi-American (equally American and Iraqi), being a woman is what most shapes her.

"What's missing in the world is the feminine balance," Raffo suggests. "I'm not talking about female empowerment, but rather the combined energy of the male and female in everybody."

Raffo's most significant artistic influence is Ntozake Shange, a feminist playwright: "When I first read *For Colored Girls Who Have Considered Suicide/When the Rainbow Is Enuf*, I felt I could write too. I felt it came from my blood. If I ever meet Ntozake, I'm going to hug her."

Raffo continues to view herself essentially as an actor, but writing has given her a chance to "integrate my voice in the process. I wish that were true for me as an actor, where only a part of me is used. Acting in my own one-person show is the best way to go for integrating all aspects of me. But, truthfully, I don't really care for solo shows, unless they really enhance the material."

Raffo is not entirely sure what she'll do next: "My real ambition is to appear in movies. I never really wanted to do theatre, although I believe the best training is in theatre. And before I did this piece, I dreamed about doing all the great classic roles. I no longer feel that need. In fact, I'm angry when I think about some of the classics. Why is everyone suddenly doing Greek plays to talk about Iraq? Why don't we go to the Iraqi artists when we talk about Iraq? Or unearth our own stories—new stories—that deal with Iraq?" She adds, "I'm not talking about topicality, but pertinence in a deep way."

"What's missing in the world is the feminine balance. I'm not talking about female empowerment, but rather the combined energy of the male and female in everybody."

Source: Simi Horwitz, "Exploring the Complexity of Identity," in *Back Stage*, Vol. 45, No. 44, October 29, 2004, pp. 7, 44.

SOURCES

Billington, Michael, Review of *Heather Raffo's 9 Parts of Desire*, in *Guardian* (London, England), August 5, 2003, p. 24.

Dear, John, S. J., "Iraq Journal: Notes from a Peace Delegation to a Ravaged Land," in *Sojourners Magazine*, Vol. 28, No. 4, July-August 1999, p. 13.

Hirst, David, "Obituary: Saddam Hussein," in *Guardian* (London, England), December 30, 2006, http://www.guardian.co.uk/world/2006/dec/30/iraq.guardianobituaries (accessed July 5, 2009).

Horwitz, Simi, "Face to Face: Heather Raffo; Exploring the Complexity of Identity," in *Back Stage*, October 29, 2004, pp. 7, 44.

Isherwood, Charles, Review of *Heather Raffo's 9 Parts of Desire*, in *New York Times*, October 14, 2004, p. E1.

Jones, Chris, Review of *Heather Raffo's 9 Parts of Desire*, in *Chicago Tribune*, May 8, 2008, http://leisureblogs.chicagotribune.com/the_theater_loop/2008/05/9-parts-of-desi.html (accessed July 5, 2009).

Kinsley, Susan F., "Whatever Happened to the Iraqi Kurds?," in *Human Rights Watch Report*, March 11, 1991, http://www.hrw.org/legacy/reports/1991/IRAQ913.htm (accessed July 5, 2009).

MacFarquhar, Neil, "Saddam Hussein, Defiant Dictator Who Ruled Iraq with Violence and Fear, Dies," in *New York Times*, December 30, 2003, http://www.nytimes.com/2006/12/30/world/middleeast/30saddam.html (accessed July 5, 2009).

McGlone, Jackie, "Looking for Layla," in *Scotsman*, July 24, 2003, http://news.scotsman.com/ViewArticle.aspx?articleid=2446194 (accessed July 5, 2009).

McMillan, Joyce, Review of *Heather Raffo's 9 Parts of Desire*, in *Scotsman*, August 4, 2003, p. 11.

Mountford, Fiona, Review of *Heather Raffo's 9 Parts of Desire*, in *Evening Standard*, September 25, 2003, p. 52.

"The Taliban's War on Women: A Health and Human Rights Crisis in Afghanistan," in *Physicians for Human Rights*, 1998, pp. 29–31.

Raffo, Heather, *Heather Raffo's 9 Parts of Desire*, Northwestern University Press, 2006.

Renner, Pamela, "Iraq Through the Eyes of Its Women," in *American Theatre*, April 2005, No. 2204, pp. 20–22, 70–71.

Sandler, Lauren, "An American and Her Nine Iraqi Sisters," in *New York Times*, October 17, 2004, Arts, p. 7.

FURTHER READING

Ali, Imam, *The 2500 Adages of Imam Ali*, Forgotten Books, 2008.
Imam Ali, son-in-law of Mohammed and founder of the Shi'a sect of Islam, is credited with these adages, or hadiths, which are respected as Muslim teachings. The title of Raffo's play comes from a hadith by Imam Ali.

Brooks, Geraldine, *Nine Parts of Desire: The Hidden World of Islamic Women*, Doubleday, 1994.
Brooks, an Australian journalist and correspondent for the *Wall Street Journal*, draws on her experience as Middle East correspondent and draws a modern portrait of Muslim women behind the veil.

Kelly, Michael J., *Ghosts of Halabja: Saddam Hussein and the Kurdish Genocide*, Praeger, 2008.
Kelly writes about Saddam's senseless murder of thousands of Kurds and his trial by the Iraqi High Tribunal. He examines Saddam's motivations, as well as the lack of response from the rest of the world to this genocide.

Polk, William R., *Understanding Iraq: The Whole Sweep of Iraqi History, from Genghis Khan's Mongols to the Ottoman Turks to the British Mandate to the American Occupation*, Harper Perennial, 2006.
Polk, a diplomat and an academic, examines Iraq's troubled history of war, occupation, and revolution and makes recommendations for a peaceful future.

Henrietta

KAREN JONES MEADOWS

1985

Karen Jones Meadows's play *Henrietta* (1985) emphasizes several of the social issues of the 1980s, including homelessness and lack of aid for people who have mental health and drug problems. Henrietta, the main character of the drama, makes a very minimal amount of money selling fruit. She spends most of her days sitting on a crate on a busy sidewalk criticizing people who pass by. Not all of the passers-by ignore her. Sheleeah, a twenty-something, somewhat successful accountant, notices Henrietta and wishes she would go away. Henrietta embarrasses Sheleeah. In spite of her frustration with the woman, there is something about Henrietta that Sheleeah is attracted to. Sheleeah believes Henrietta has found a way to beat the system. Henrietta does not have to spend her days in a downtown office with a boss applying constant pressure to get her work done. This makes Sheleeah think that Henrietta enjoys a freedom that Sheleeah does not have.

As the play progresses, the audience discovers the flaws in Sheleeah's conclusions as well as the flaws in Henrietta's personality. The play concludes on a less-than-happy note. However, the characters decide that no matter how much they might complain, they each like the paths they have chosen for themselves.

Henrietta made its debut at the Negro Ensemble Company stage in New York in 1985 and has since been staged on the East Coast, West Coast, and places in between, receiving mixed reviews. This was the playwright's first full-length stage play for adults.

AUTHOR BIOGRAPHY

Jones Meadows was born in 1953 and grew up in the Bronx in New York City. She attended Wheelock College in Boston, Massachusetts. As an adult, she has lived, from time to time, in Charlotte, North Carolina, the state her parents were from. In an interview with Anthony C. Davis, a writer for the *Philadelphia Tribune*, Jones Meadows stated that it was in North Carolina that she first saw a different way in which "Black people lived." She added: "I hadn't experienced a situation where we had our own stores and properties until I went to North Carolina." Living in North Carolina may have enhanced her view of the lives of African Americans in the south.

In addition to *Henrietta* (1985), Jones Meadows has written *Tapman* (1988), which tells the story of a down-on-his-luck blues musician, and her most critically acclaimed play to date, *Harriet's Return* (1995 and significantly revised in 2003), which chronicles the life of Harriet Tubman, who devoted her life to helping slaves find freedom through the Underground Railroad.

Jones Meadows has also written plays for youth, such as her *Sala Cinderella* (1996), which is based on the themes of self-identity, as in the classic fairytale "Cinderella," but with an African twist. This play has been popular for elementary schools' drama productions.

Besides writing plays, Jones Meadows also acted in a small role as an emergency room nurse in the 1987 movie *Critical Condition*. She has also appeared in many television commercials. Jones Meadows performed the one-woman role of Harriet Tubman in her own play *Harriet's Return*. She has produced shows for Comedy Central and Fox Television. In 1995, Jones Meadows was appointed the McGee Professor of writing at Davidson College in Davidson, North Carolina. She has one son and lives in Albuquerque, New Mexico.

PLOT SUMMARY

Act 1, Scene 1

Jones Meadows's stage play *Henrietta* opens with the title character, Henrietta, sitting on a crate outside an apartment building. The setting is somewhere in New York City. It is a weekday in late September. As Henrietta watches people passing by, she taunts them with insulting remarks.

She comments on their clothes and the way they look as if she were talking to herself. However, she says everything out loud. She also criticizes people for not paying any attention to her. To gain more attention, Henrietta blows into small paper bags and then pops them.

Henrietta pays special attention to twenty-eight-year-old Sheleeah Hampton, who walks by. Henrietta tells Sheleeah that she does not have to stop and talk to her because Henrietta is used to being ignored. She says that it is better not to talk to people. She uses the example of Malcolm X, the African American human rights activist. Henrietta states that Malcolm talked to people, and she insinuates that he was killed because of this. Of course, Henrietta is contradicting herself because she is sitting out on the sidewalk attempting to start up conversations with the people who are walking past her.

Sheleeah is at first irritated. She asks Henrietta why she always bothers her. Sheleeah adds that she is tired of Henrietta's heckling. Henrietta defends herself, telling Sheleeah that her role is that of a teacher. She merely points out things that people should know about themselves. For example, Henrietta tells Sheleeah that the wild colors she is wearing that day do not look good on her. The bright colors make Sheleeah look like a showoff. Henrietta adds that by her wearing the bright colors, Sheleeah must be seeking attention. Henrietta then says that by her heckling, Sheleeah also gets more attention, if that is what she wants. Sheleeah walks away, and the first scene ends.

Act 1, Scene 2

It is Saturday evening when the second scene opens. In this very short scene, the audience sees Sheleeah walk by Henrietta. Sheleeah is dressed in black. Henrietta tells Sheleeah that black does not suit her at all. As a matter of fact, Henrietta states, black makes Sheleeah look like she is in mourning.

Act 1, Scene 3

Henrietta is again sitting on a crate on the sidewalk. She has a bowl pressed into her lap and is cutting fruit. Sheleeah appears and tells Henrietta that she wants to talk with her. Henrietta comments that because it is Sunday, Sheleeah must not be very busy. Henrietta takes the time to examine Sheleeah closely when the younger woman sits down next to her. Henrietta asks Sheleeah if she has been trying to bleach her skin. Sheleeah quickly denies this. Henrietta points out that people do not like to admit that they do this nowadays. Then she changes the subject and asks Sheleeah where she works. Sheleeah attempts to answer, but Henrietta corrects her. She does not want to know what Sheleeah does, she wants to know the address. Henrietta is thinking of meeting Sheleeah for lunch. When she learns where Sheleeah works, Henrietta decides it is too far away.

Henrietta changes the topic again, this time asking Sheleeah about her boyfriends. Henrietta has noticed that one of the men who comes to visit Sheleeah drives a fancy car. Sheleeah responds by telling Henrietta that she is not used to discussing her private affairs with a stranger. Henrietta laughs at this comment. She points out the uselessness of this sentiment. After all, everyone in the neighborhood is talking about Sheleeah and her men friends, Henrietta tells Sheleeah. Henrietta continues to talk about Sheleeah's boyfriends. The one with the fancy car is too feminine, Henrietta tells Sheleeah. Sheleeah disagrees and describes him in masculine terms. Henrietta does not listen. Instead, she tells Sheleeah that she likes Sheleeah's other boyfriend better. Sheleeah tells Henrietta that the other man is too boring. Henrietta says Sheleeah could work on the second boyfriend and make him stronger. Henrietta asks which man has the most money. They both make a lot of money, Sheleeah replies.

Sheleeah says she has to leave. Henrietta tells Sheleeah that she needs some empty jars and Sheleeah can drop them by on Thursday. Sheleeah says she has no idea where to find empty jars. Henrietta pays no attention to her. Instead, she tells Sheleeah what size jars to look for. She adds that if Sheleeah cannot bring them to her, Henrietta will go over to Sheleeah's apartment and get them. Sheleeah does not want Henrietta coming to her place, so she tells her she will bring them on Thursday. Henrietta senses that Sheleeah is embarrassed by her, and her feelings are hurt. So she criticizes Sheleeah, calling the young woman a sinner for sleeping with two men.

Act 1, Scene 4

It is Sunday, one week later. Sheleeah arrives on the street with jars for Henrietta, later than she had promised. Henrietta admits that she has been shouting out obscenities directed at Sheleeah, hoping that the name-calling would embarrass

her enough to bring Henrietta the jars. Sheleeah warns Henrietta that someone is going to hurt her one day for all the degrading remarks she makes. Sheleeah then refers to Henrietta as a derelict, a homeless person with no money. Henrietta disagrees. She points out that she does not fit the usual description of a derelict. She is clean and does not stink. Sheleeah defines a derelict as "a person who doesn't take care of themselves... and doesn't have the guts to face life...uh, is weak and preys on the emotions of others."

After hearing this, Henrietta says that Sheleeah might be right. "I am a derelict," she says. But she accuses Sheleeah of having the wrong definition. Henrietta believes a derelict is anyone who is down on his or her luck and has been discarded by society, "not necessarily by any fault of their own." Furthermore, Henrietta says that derelicts exist because of people like Sheleeah, "who call yourself better." Then Sheleeah leaves.

The character Thomas Boston is introduced as he brings Henrietta a copy of the Sunday newspaper. Sheleeah returns, and she and Thomas introduce themselves to one another. Thomas leaves to go to church, and Henrietta begs Sheleeah to sit down and talk with her. Henrietta says she is trying to be more humble but then she adds that being humble "Makes me want to throw up." She also tells Sheleeah that Thomas steals the Sunday paper for her every week. It makes him feel useful, Henrietta says.

Henrietta invites Sheleeah to come to her house. This surprises Sheleeah. It is insinuated that Sheleeah thought Henrietta lived on the street. Henrietta says she has a room she stays in. Then she asks Sheleeah if she wants to come for lunch. Sheleeah reminds Henrietta that she once said that she had no food. Henrietta responds, telling Sheleeah that she will have to bring the food.

Act 1, Scene 5

The last scene of Act One takes place inside the room Henrietta stays in. As Henrietta cooks some very old beans, Sheleeah looks around Henrietta's place. She sees photographs and asks who the people are. One is Henrietta's daughter. Sheleeah is surprised that Henrietta is a mother. Another photograph is Henrietta's son. Henrietta confesses that she has three children: one daughter, Tootie, and two sons, Keith and Frazier. Henrietta is reluctant to provide any details about her children, and she finally tells Sheleeah that they are all dead. Henrietta points out the pictures of her two husbands, Henry and Laney.

Henrietta tells Sheleeah that the jars she asked for are to hold the fruit salad she makes and sells. That is how Henrietta makes money. Thomas shows up again, and Henrietta tells Sheleeah that Thomas is her landlord. When Henrietta tells Sheleeah that she does favors for Thomas, Sheleeah thinks Henrietta is referring to sexual favors. Henrietta says it is nothing like that. She does Thomas's laundry in exchange for cheap rent. Sheleeah admits that she once used sex to earn money, because there was a time when she had no other way of making a living.

Henrietta and Sheleeah proceed to get drunk on a bottle of very cheap and very old sherry. The more they drink, the more they open up to one another. In some ways, Sheleeah says she would like to be more like Henrietta. Sheleeah believes that Henrietta's lifestyle is attractive because Henrietta seems to have so much freedom to do whatever she wants. Sheleeah also thinks that Henrietta is very clever in the way she controls other people, making them do what she wants them to do. Sheleeah also insinuates that she believes Henrietta fakes being mentally unstable.

The conversation between Henrietta and Sheleeah becomes more irrational as the scene closes. Henrietta asks Sheleeah to be her friend, then tells her she does not need anyone. By the end, however, Henrietta admits that she would like to call Sheleeah "Tootie." As Sheleeah is about to leave, Henrietta suggests that if Sheleeah loves her, "This time I'll be better. I'll be so much better." It is through this statement that Henrietta lets the audience know that she believes Sheleeah is her daughter who has come back home to her.

Act 2, Scene 1

When act two opens, it is late October, a few weeks later. Thomas and Sheleeah are sitting outside the building in which Henrietta lives. Thomas is attempting to tell Sheleeah a story, but she is too distracted to sit still. Sheleeah wants to leave and asks Thomas to tell Henrietta that she has stopped by. As soon as Sheleeah leaves, Henrietta appears. She is carrying a big bag of fruit and is nicely dressed. Henrietta tells Thomas she is tired but insists that she must "get ready for Tootie."

Thomas tells Henrietta that he is thinking of inviting Sheleeah to a church function. Henrietta warns Thomas that he is not Sheleeah's type of

date. Thomas says he would rather Sheleeah be like a sister. When Henrietta explains that she took down the clothes line inside her apartment but puts it back up when Sheleeah is not around, Thomas comments that Henrietta is not being totally honest. "Holding out on her, huh? Not like you and me—we trust each other."

After Thomas and Henrietta go inside the building, Sheleeah appears. She boasts of having gotten away with pretending she was "a little off." She says she has learned how to do this from watching Henrietta. Thomas takes offense at this statement, claiming that Henrietta is not crazy as Sheleeah has insinuated. Sheleeah defends herself, saying, "OFF was probably a poor choice of words, FREE. I was free instead of appropriate." As the conversation continues, Sheleeah brushes all of Thomas's comments to the side. Sheleeah makes it evident that she is there to talk only to Henrietta. However, Henrietta tells Sheleeah that they cannot talk in front of Thomas unless they include him in their conversation. Sheleeah becomes angry and leaves.

Act 2, Scene 2

The next scene takes place a month later. Sheleeah is trying to enter Henrietta's apartment, but Thomas is blocking her way. He has noticed how often Sheleeah has been coming by and wants to know what Sheleeah and Henrietta are doing. Thomas accuses Sheleeah of taking Henrietta away from him. He tries to scare Sheleeah by telling her that he was in jail once for killing someone. Sheleeah pays little attention to him, leaving him outside as she finally makes it to Henrietta's room.

Sheleeah has been making plans for Henrietta. She wants to turn Henrietta's fruit selling into a bigger business. She also wants Henrietta to move. Henrietta is reluctant about both ideas. She is not used to working with someone else, and Sheleeah definitely talks as if she is a business partner. Sheleeah is also very bossy, telling Henrietta she has to make big changes in her life. She has to dress better, write down her recipes, and make more money. Henrietta fights against those changes, but Sheleeah does not listen to her. Where once Sheleeah was trying to be more like Henrietta, she is now trying to make Henrietta more like her.

Henrietta asks Sheleeah to find her a man. Henrietta describes the man she wants: someone who has all his teeth, a car, a good job, and a decent place to live. Sheleeah is surprised that

Henrietta would consider a relationship with a man. But Henrietta has set her mind on it and tells Sheleeah to bring a man around in two weeks.

Thomas enters Henrietta's place and asks her not to leave. He accuses Sheleeah of wanting to take Henrietta away from him. The conversation among the three of them becomes very confused. Henrietta begins calling Sheleeah "Tootie" again and referring to her as her daughter. Sheleeah asks Henrietta to control herself. She wants Henrietta to go back to being as rational as she was a few minutes before. Then Sheleeah and Thomas shout at one another. Sheleeah calls Thomas "a moron." At this point Henrietta tells Thomas and Sheleeah to stop screaming. She also tells Sheleeah she should not call Thomas names. Sheleeah insists that Henrietta make a choice between her and Thomas. Henrietta tells Sheleeah that Thomas is family, and she could never leave him. With everyone yelling, Henrietta becomes very confused. The scene ends with Henrietta shouting "DON'T TAKE MY FAMILY!!!!!"

Act 2, Scene 3
Scene 3 takes place two weeks later. Thomas and Henrietta are talking outside of their building. Henrietta tells Thomas she has not seen Sheleeah (she calls her "Tootie") for two days. Thomas tells Henrietta that he saw her. He went by her apartment and found out that she was moving. Some men were there with a truck. Thomas helped Sheleeah pack. He has no idea where she is going. Henrietta accuses Thomas of lying to her. Henrietta cries because she feels Sheleeah has lied to her.

Act 2, Scene 4
The last scene of the play is very short. Henrietta is back on the street, sitting on her crate. She is calling out to strangers as they pass by. She criticizes how people look. Then she tells them that Sheleeah was too attached to her. She says Sheleeah "tried to get" her. She says Sheleeah had "lots of expectations and attachments. That's what messes you up," Henrietta says.

CHARACTERS

Henrietta Mabeline Barthalamew
Henrietta is the fifty-to-sixty-year-old protagonist of this play. It is around her that most of the action occurs. She is not homeless, but nearly so.

She lives by her wits, begging for food and making enough money to supplement her diet. Most of her time is spent sitting on the sidewalk outside the building where she lives in a one-room apartment. Henrietta's favorite pastime is making comments to people who pass by, telling them how they look, criticizing the colors they are wearing, or otherwise making fun of them. She believes it is through her comments that she teaches others how to live.

Henrietta has been married twice and had three children. Both of her husbands and all three children are dead. This makes her feel very unlucky. She makes vile comments about her sister, whom Henrietta believes is not as good a person as she is. Henrietta admits that she is jealous of her sister, though, because her husband and children are still alive. Sometimes, Henrietta's thoughts can be very rational. She knows what she has to do every day to keep clean and fed, for example. However, if things happen too fast around her, she quickly becomes confused. She also often contradicts herself. At one moment she says she needs no one but herself. At other times, she acts very lonesome and dependent on others.

Though she attempts to hide her emotions, Henrietta has moments when her feelings are completely exposed. In particular, she misses having a family. She feels cursed for having lost her husbands, her sons, and her daughter. When Sheleeah befriends her, Henrietta imagines that Sheleeah is her daughter Tootie. Henrietta acts as if the presence of Sheleeah has given her a second chance to prove that she is a good mother. If she can open up to Sheleeah, then maybe the curse would be lifted, and she would be happy again. In the end, after Sheleeah abandons her, Henrietta comments that it is much better to be unattached to everything and everyone around her. It is better to keep her emotions to herself and to keep quiet.

Thomas Boston
Thomas owns the building in which Henrietta lives. Therefore Thomas is Henrietta's landlord. He inherited the building when his mother died. Thomas, a man in his forties, is rather slow-witted. Henrietta describes him like this: "He'd a been a hood, if he hadn't been so stupid." Sheleeah calls Thomas "a moron." Henrietta reprimands Sheleeah for saying this to Thomas's face, although Henrietta secretly agrees. Thomas, on the other hand, thinks of himself as a killer. It is not clear

whether Thomas really has a criminal record or he just claims to have murdered someone to make him sound powerful and mean. Sometimes Thomas likes to scare people so they will take him seriously.

Thomas takes care of Henrietta in small ways. He steals the Sunday newspaper for her each week. He gives her a special financial break on the rent and lets her use his bathroom. He also looks in on her to make sure that she has food and is feeling well. Thomas also needs Henrietta. She provides him with a sense of family. He becomes jealous and feels threatened when Sheleeah makes plans to take Henrietta away. He cannot stand the idea of Henrietta not living across the hall from him. He tells Henrietta, at the end of the play, that Sheleeah has moved away. He helped her move, he tells Henrietta. This is never verified, and at one point, Henrietta is concerned that Thomas might have killed Sheleeah to get rid of her. This issue is not resolved by the end of the last scene.

Frazier

Frazier was Henrietta's oldest son. He appears in this play only through a photograph. Henrietta describes him as "hell on wheels." Henrietta insinuates that Frazier died while in the military. At one point, Henrietta says: "Frazier had fifty more days in active duty, then he would have been home."

Sheleeah Hampton

Though Henrietta first calls her "Shelra" and later calls her "Tootie," her real name is Sheleeah. She is a twenty-eight-year-old businesswoman who lives near Henrietta. Henrietta sees Sheleeah walk by almost every day and taunts her with insults about the way she dresses and the men she dates. Eventually Sheleeah tries to make friends with Henrietta, hoping that will stop Henrietta from picking on her. The more Sheleeah learns about Henrietta the more she is attracted to her. Because Sheleeah believes that Henrietta has more freedom than she does, she wants to be more like her. So Sheleeah begins to practice being somewhat off, mentally, as she imagines Henrietta is. There are times throughout the play when Sheleeah believes Henrietta is only pretending to have mental issues in order to control the people around her.

At first, because Henrietta does not have to work, Sheleeah thinks Henrietta has a better life. However, Sheleeah turns things around once

Henrietta starts calling her Tootie, Henrietta's dead daughter's name. As her relationship with Henrietta grows closer, Sheleeah wants to make Henrietta become more like her, a businesswoman with a lot of money. She wants to change Henrietta's life. When Henrietta understands what Sheleeah is attempting to do, she stops her. In response, Sheleeah runs away. She eventually leaves the neighborhood without telling Henrietta where she is going. The last time Sheleeah and Henrietta are together, Henrietta says that Sheleeah thinks she is better than Henrietta. "You want me to rise to your level. That's it! But I won't. It ain't up! It's even!" This observation by Henrietta might have been too difficult for Sheleeah to face. Immediately after this, Sheleeah disappears from Henrietta's life and two scenes later, the play ends.

Henrietta's Sister

Henrietta's sister is mentioned a few times in the play but she never makes an appearance. Henrietta describes her sister as being "hateful" and a "child abuser." Henrietta expresses jealousy caused by her sister's children still being alive, though Henrietta's children are all dead.

Henry

Henry is Henrietta's first husband. He is dead by the time of the play. Henrietta tells Sheleeah a little bit about him. Henry was "kind of firm and stiff" Henrietta says. He was also the father of Henrietta's three children.

Keith

Keith was Henrietta's second-born son. He does not appear in the play except through a photograph; he died without Henrietta knowing about it immediately. Henrietta describes Keith as being "sickly the whole time."

Laney

Laney was Henrietta's second husband, who is dead. Henrietta compares Laney to her first husband, finding Laney to be kinder and "a good time man." However, Henrietta also states that Laney "died of meanness." After Henrietta's first husband left her, Laney helped raise Henrietta's three children.

George Murray

George is a man who works with Sheleeah. He never makes an appearance in this play, but Sheleeah mentions him when Henrietta begins to talk about wanting a man in her life. Sheleeah believes George would make a perfect match for Henrietta.

Tootie

Henrietta's daughter, Tootie, never makes an appearance in this play except through a photograph. Sheleeah asks questions about her when she visits Henrietta's apartment. Tootie's father was Henry, Henrietta's first husband. Tootie left home when she was a teen because she did not get along well with Henrietta's second husband, Laney. Henrietta feels responsible for her daughter's death. Later, Henrietta states that Tootie had a drug problem. She also says that Tootie was a "girl thug, with a knife and everything." Henrietta begins to call Sheleeah "Tootie" later on in the play. Henrietta imagines that Tootie has come back to give Henrietta a second chance at being a better mother.

THEMES

Freedom

One of the main themes of Jones Meadows's play *Henrietta* is freedom of choice. Although the character Sheleeah believes that Henrietta exemplifies this theme, both female characters exercise this freedom.

Henrietta sets her own pace throughout the day. She sits on her crate on the sidewalk when she wants to. She either reads the paper while she sits there, cuts up fruit to sell, or badgers people who walk by. Though she has some restraints in her life, she is the character who could easily be seen as the most free.

In the middle of the play, Sheleeah offers Henrietta a chance to change her life. Sheleeah buys new clothes for Henrietta and offers guidance in how Henrietta could improve her fruit-selling business so she can make more money. Sheleeah is also willing to help Henrietta find a better place to live and a new man-friend. But Henrietta chooses to turn these offers down. She realizes how much of her personal freedom she would have to sacrifice in order to improve her life, based on Sheleeah's interpretation of success. In the end, Henrietta decides that financial success is too confining. She exercises her freedom of choice by choosing not to change.

Sheleeah also has freedom of choice. Sheleeah has enough money to make her life more

comfortable than Henrietta's. She has a nicer apartment, pretty clothes, and two boyfriends. By some definitions, Sheleeah is a success. But Sheleeah does not like the confinement of having to go to work each day and having to deal with people she does not like. For a while, Sheleeah thinks Henrietta is happier and luckier than she is. But the better Sheleeah comes to know Henrietta, the more she discovers the flaws in Henrietta's life. For Sheleeah, Henrietta is not much better off than a homeless person. She compares her life with Henrietta's and comes to the conclusion that she is much better off than she had originally thought.

When Henrietta realizes that Sheleeah is trying to change her, she challenges Sheleeah, telling her that they are equals. Sheleeah then uses her freedom of choice to turn her back on Henrietta and return to the world she had previously created.

Jealousy

The theme of jealousy plays out in three different instances. First, Henrietta admits she wants what her sister has. Henrietta says despite the fact that her sister is a mean-spirited woman, she has not lost her husband or any of her children. In contrast, Henrietta has lost everyone. Henrietta does not want to model her sister's behavior, but she does envy her sister's luck in keeping her family together.

Thomas displays jealousy about the budding relationship between Sheleeah and Henrietta. He is fearful that Sheleeah will replace him in Henrietta's life. For her part, Sheleeah is also jealous of Thomas. She makes Henrietta choose between her and Thomas, insinuating that Henrietta cannot maintain relationships with both of them. Through these acts of jealousy, the playwright suggests how devastating and limiting this negative emotion can be. In Henrietta's case, her jealousy can blind her to the beauty of her life and her memories of her family. Her jealousy might also be preventing her from seeing the positive aspects of her sister. Thomas's and Sheleeah's jealousy prevents them from gaining new friendships.

Punishment

Henrietta believes she must have done something wrong in her life, and that is why she has lost both of her husbands and her three children. She thinks she is being punished. This causes her to reexamine her life, wondering what she did to

TOPICS FOR FURTHER STUDY

- Conduct research on the problems of homelessness. Provide information concerning how people living on the street (or in the countryside outside of cities) were dealt with in the early part of the twentieth century. When was the term *homeless* coined and how did this change the way people looked at people who could not afford a roof over their heads? Who provides help for the homeless? Are there particular cities that have more homeless people than others? What are the problems involved in making accurate counts on how many people are homeless? Present your findings to your class. Use visuals (photographs, charts, etc.) to enhance your prepared remarks.

- The playwright offers very few details about what her three characters look like. Create portraits of Henrietta, Sheleeah, and Thomas based on how they act, what they say, and how they interact with one another. Display the portraits in your class while discussing the play and ask your classmates to describe how they think the characters look.

- The play provides a little information about Tootie, Henrietta's daughter. The audience knows that she was streetwise, did drugs, and ran away from home as a teenager. Imagine that Tootie is still alive and wants to reunite with her mother. She is seventeen and tells her mother she is dying from AIDS and wants to die at home. Write a letter Tootie might have composed in her attempt to help her mother understand why she ran away and why she now wants to come home. Be as specific as you can about how Tootie might feel. Remember that Tootie is probably desperate, scared, and sick. She is seeking nurturing, love, and forgiveness.

- In this play, Henrietta mentions Malcolm X, stating that he was killed because he told everyone what he was thinking. Read a biography of Malcolm X, such as Arnold Adoff's *Malcolm X* (2000). Prepare a speech about Malcolm X. Provide some important details of his life as well as some of his ideas about race and how black people should live. Include some of the Malcolm X's ideas that might have made someone angry enough to kill him. Make your speech approximately ten minutes long. You do not have to memorize it. You can use notes. Practice what you are going to say several times, while standing in front of a mirror, before you make your presentation to your classmates.

- Read a book about what it is like to be homeless as a child or teen, such as *No Place to Be: Voices of Homeless Children* (1992) or *Under the Overpass: A Journey of Faith on the Streets of America* (2005). Compare the experiences of the young people to the experiences Sheleeah and Henrietta describe in learning how to get by without any money. Describe to your class some of the things you have learned and discuss the similarities and differences with your classmates.

make her less fortunate than her sister, even though Henrietta believes she is better than her sister. Henrietta also tries to figure out why Tootie, her daughter, ran away and turned to drugs, which might have been what killed her. The issue of punishment drives Henrietta to want to call Sheleeah by her daughter's name. In the back of her mind, Henrietta wants to believe that Tootie has come back to her, giving her a second chance to be a better mother. If Henrietta can improve, maybe her wrongdoings (whatever they might be) will be forgiven and her life improve.

The idea of punishment implies a spiritual belief, faith in a higher power. Though Henrietta does not go to church on Sundays as Thomas does, her conviction of punishment insinuates that some power is watching over her, judging

The title character, Henrietta, is homeless.
(Image copyright Anne Kitzman, 2009. Used under license from
Shutterstock.com)

her actions and providing punishments when she does wrong. In Henrietta's case, her punishment is to live with loneliness.

STYLE

Internal Conflict

In any fictional art—plays, novels, short stories—authors use conflict to build interest and complexity in their work. Sometimes the conflict is external, such as when a character must confront a great sea storm or a competitor. However, another form of conflict is one that is found inside one or more of the main characters as they struggle with their own thoughts and feelings.

In Jones Meadows's play, all three characters have internal conflicts, some more subtle than others. One of Henrietta's conflicts involves the loss of her family. Throughout the play, she attempts to resolve the emotions she battles in having lost her husbands and her children. The greatest of these is the loss of her daughter, Tootie. More subtle internal conflict that Henrietta faces is her ambivalence about whether she is comfortable living alone, if she enjoys communicating with people, and whether she truly likes her somewhat deviant lifestyle.

Sheleeah and Thomas also have internal conflicts, such as jealousy and insecurities about their identities and their place in life. A playwright exposes internal conflicts through the characters' dialogues—what they say to one another, their tone of voice, their choice of words, and their body language. By bringing the conflicts to light, the characters are given more than one dimension. Thomas, for instance, is not just a dim-witted bungler. He also needs companionship. He wants to help Henrietta and also wants her to help him. Sheleeah is not just a meddling neighbor; she wants to bring Henrietta happiness and is in need of a mother's love. As the characters attempt to resolve their internal conflicts, the audience watches them develop, which makes the characters feel more real and allows the audience to identify with them.

Open Ending

Jones Meadows's play ends without an obvious resolution, a dramatic style that is called open ending. In fact, the play ends very similarly to how it began. Henrietta is sitting on her crate on the sidewalk, basically talking to herself. Though Henrietta has been on a journey, building a relationship with Sheleeah and then losing it, her life has not really changed. Thomas has been forced to expose his feelings toward Henrietta, but his life also remains much the same as it was in the beginning of the play.

The audience is left unsure about what has happened to Sheleeah. Thomas attempts to inform Henrietta, but Henrietta is unsure of Thomas's credibility. This leaves the audience to make conclusions of their own. Has Sheleeah really moved away? Is she going to make an appearance later? Did Thomas kill her to be rid of her? Audiences might also wonder if Henrietta or Thomas have been affected by Sheleeah's appearance in their lives. Though it appears that their lives are unchanged on the outside, what do they feel? Sheleeah stirred their emotions, but to what effect? None of these questions are answered by the playwright by the end of the play.

COMPARE & CONTRAST

- **1980s:** Recession affects the U.S. economy, creating an unemployment rate above 10 percent.

  Today: Two decades later, recession hits the U.S. economy again with the unemployment rate slowly climbing over 10 percent.

- **1980s:** The U.S. Department of Housing and Urban Development estimates that there are between 250,000 and 350,000 homeless people in the United States.

  Today: In the Annual Homeless Assessment Report to Congress in 2007, it is estimated

that the number of people living in shelters or on the streets in the United States equals at least 754,000. According to the National Law Center on Homelessness and Poverty (2007) the estimate of homeless people could be much worse, as high as 3.5 million people.

- **1980s:** The U.S. Census Bureau calculates that there are nearly 35 million people living in poverty in 1980.

  Today: The number of people living in poverty has dropped in the past two decades and is calculated at 31.3 million, as of the 2000 census.

HISTORICAL CONTEXT

Malcolm X (1925–1965)

In Jones Meadows's play, Henrietta says: "I don't talk to nobody that listens. Get you in trouble. Look at Malcolm . . . how they shot him down. Know why don't you?—Cause he talked too much. To be smart, he was a ignorant sucker." In these statements, Henrietta is referring to Malcolm X.

Malcolm X was born in Omaha, Nebraska, on May 19, 1925. His father, Earl Little, was an outspoken minister who encouraged his congregation to stand up for their civil rights. When Malcolm was six years old, his father's tortured body was found on the town's train tracks. Malcolm's mother had a mental breakdown after that, and Malcolm grew up in foster homes and orphanages. As a young adult, he spent seven years in jail, where he became interested in a Black Muslim religion referred to as the Nation of Islam. Upon his release from prison, it was through this organization that Malcolm began to encourage African Americans to band together and demand a separate state of their own, believing they would never get ahead in America as long as they allowed white people to dominate them. Malcolm was an eloquent speaker and had a charismatic

personality. Crowds of people showed up wherever he spoke.

In 1964, Malcolm became disillusioned with the Nation of Islam and left that organization and created his own, the Muslim Mosque. His earlier beliefs about blacks living separate from white people were tempered, and he began preaching the benefits of all races living in peace together. His comments irritated the members of the Nation of Islam, and according to FBI reports, Malcolm was marked for assassination. On February 21, 1965, three gunmen from the Nation of Islam rushed the stage where Malcolm was speaking at the Manhattan Audubon Ballroom and shot him to death.

History of Modern Social Welfare in the United States

The concept of the federal government assisting the poor did not really occur until the Great Depression. In the 1930s, under President Franklin D. Roosevelt and his New Deal policies, several programs, such as social security, unemployment insurance, and other relief programs were enacted to help U.S. citizens during very difficult economic times.

During the 1960s, as part of President Lyndon B. Johnson's Great Society program and the War on Poverty, social welfare programs were

The Harlem district of New York City, the setting for Henrietta *(Image copyright Pozzo di Borgo Thomas, 2009. Used under license from Shutterstock.com)*

enhanced to help decrease poverty, homelessness, and hunger, and to help pay for treatments for people who suffered from physical and mental problems. Programs such as food stamps, which helped to eliminate hunger for the poor, and Medicaid and Medicare, which helped to pay for the medical needs of senior citizens as well as disadvantaged people, were established.

In the 1970s, though, critics of the welfare program became more vocal. By that time, the number of people on welfare increased dramatically. As the welfare programs expanded, critics of the program pointed out that neither unemployment nor poverty were being eradicated. They claimed that poor people were becoming dependent on welfare checks and had lost interest in improving their lives. So during the 1980s both the federal and state governments attempted to reform the welfare system. Programs were cut, leaving many homeless people and those with mental problems to fend for themselves.

By the 1990s, many of those who studied the welfare programs realized that the reforms that had been implemented in the 1980s were not working. Then in 1996, under President Bill Clinton, an overhaul of the system was created. On August 22, 1996, Clinton signed a reform bill that limited welfare benefits in many ways. One way was to limit the time a person could receive assistance and encouraged recipients to find work. In 1994, before the Clinton act, there were over five million families enlisted in welfare programs in the United States. Ten years after Clinton's reforms, that number had dropped to just a little under two million.

CRITICAL OVERVIEW

Henrietta was first produced in 1985 by the Negro Ensemble Company in New York City. The play has not garnered a lot of critical attention through the years, but overall, those who do comment offer favorable reflections. Frank Rich from the *New York Times* saw the first production of *Henrietta* in 1985, and begins his review with the words: "Any character actress in her right mind would probably kill to play the title role." Rich goes on to describe the lead character of this play as "the most unforgettable character anyone has ever met." However, Rich also points out that the play itself "is thin." Rich credits this to the playwright's lack of experience and her obvious "desire to say something trenchant about the values of contemporary black women."

In a more recent article, David Hannah, writing for the *Philadelphia Tribune*, after Jones Meadows's play was stage at the city's Bushfire Theatre, describes the drama as "a combination of good chemistry with well placed humor." Hannah adds that the play is "worth watching." Lynda Lane, also writing for the *Philadelphia Tribune* for the same 1995 production of *Henrietta*, states that Jones Meadows "directs a message through the three characters that speak of freedom of choice."

Elizabeth Maupin, writing for the *Orlando Sentinel* in 2002, describes the protagonist of Jones Meadows's play like someone who "waddles in and out, talks a blue streak and laughs uproariously at her own aphorisms." For this particular production, Maupin faults the actress who had the lead role for dampening down the effect of Jones Meadows's work rather than faulting the writing. Another production of *Henrietta* was staged in Sacramento, California in 2006. In reviewing the play, Antonio R. Harvey, writing for the *Sacramento Observer* finds the drama to be "entertaining, humorous and compassionate."

CRITICISM

Joyce Hart

Hart is a published author and creative writing teacher. In this essay, she captures a clear picture of Henrietta, the lead character in Jones Meadows's play Henrietta *despite the contradictions the character presents.*

The potency of Jones Meadows's drama *Henrietta* is played out in full through the play's leading character. Despite, or maybe because of, her ambiguities, Henrietta brings not only strength to

> WITH HER DOUBTS AND CONFUSION, HENRIETTA DEMONSTRATES THAT SHE IS A COMPLEX BEING, LIKE EVERYONE ELSE."

the play but also humor, interest, complexity, and unity. Though the audience witnesses little change in the character of Henrietta from beginning to end of the play, this complicated woman offers multiple versions of herself throughout the play, sometimes changing her ideas of herself even in the middle of an utterance. It might make the audience wonder what message Jones Meadows is attempting to deliver in presenting such a baffling leading character.

Henrietta spends most of her time out on the sidewalk talking to no one in particular. She yells out comments as if she wants to be heard, but at the same time she tells the strangers who pass her that she does not like to talk to people who listen to her. She also declares that their lack of interest in her does not hurt her feelings. So from the beginning, Henrietta's statements are suspect. Why, for instance, would she even mention hurt feelings if she were not thinking about them? With this comment, the author signals that the audience needs to pay attention to what Henrietta says and weigh the veracity of her words, because Henrietta often says things she does not really mean. The truth of Henrietta is often found somewhere in the middle of what she says and how she contradicts herself.

This ambiguity continues in the next series of scenes, in which Henrietta insults the bright colors of Sheleeah's clothes. Sheleeah brushes Henrietta's comments off as if they meant nothing to her and walks away. Henrietta tells Sheleeah that she should listen to her. Other people, Henrietta insinuates, respect what she has to say. But as Sheleeah disappears, Henrietta alters her comment to: "Well, I use to command respect." Here Henrietta brings humor into the play as she offhandedly makes fun of herself. However, when Sheleeah next appears, instead of the bright colors she wore the day before, she is dressed in black. But Henrietta finds this drastic change just as ridiculous and tells Sheleeah what she thinks. Again Sheleeah appears to slough off

WHAT DO I READ NEXT?

- Jones Meadows's *Harriet's Return* (1995) chronicles the private and public life of Harriet Tubman, an activist who helped runaway slaves flee the South. In this one-woman play, Tubman's childhood, her activist adulthood, and the final moments of her life are portrayed.

- A classic African American play written by a female playwright is Lorraine Hansberry's 1959 Broadway hit *A Raisin in the Sun*. This was the first play written by a black female to be produced on Broadway. The play, suitable for young-adult audiences, is set in Chicago in the 1950s and explores tensions both within an African family of the times as well as conflicts with the surrounding white society.

- *For Colored Girls Who Have Considered Suicide When the Rainbow Is Enuf*, the 1975 Obie Award-winning play, was written by Ntozake Shange, who is both a poet and a playwright. The play is written through a series of poems and covers challenging everyday situations that black women face.

- Brenda Wilkinson has collected the stories of twenty-four prominent African American females in her book *African American Women Writers* (1999). Authors such as Phillis Wheatley, Zora Neale Hurston, Lorraine Hansberry, Octavia Butler, and Terry McMillan are presented. This book offers an introduction to the lives and the works of these important writers.

- James Baldwin, famed author of several novels and books of essays, also wrote plays. One of his more famous was *Blues for Mister Charlie*, published in 1964 at the climax of the civil rights movement. The play is about Medgar Evers, a civil rights activist from Mississippi, who was murdered in 1963.

- August Wilson, one of the most prominent black dramatists in the United States, wrote *Joe Turner's Come and Gone* in 1988. The setting of the play is Pittsburgh in 1911 and it focuses on African Americans who have recently moved from the South and are attempting to restructure their lives and their identities.

- In another production of August Wilson's work, *Fences* (1983), the playwright explores race relations during the 1950s. This play won the 1983 Pulitzer Prize for Drama.

- William S. Yellow Robe is a noted Native American playwright. In his 2000 collection *Where the Pavement Ends: Five Native American Plays*, the author provides a realistic representation of contemporary day-to-day life on an American Indian Reservation. His plays are written with subtle humor and include an exploration of issues such as ecology, relationships with the outside white world, and the search for Native identity.

- Errol Hill has collected a series of essays on the history of black stage productions in his book *The Theatre of Black Americans: A Collection of Critical Essays* (2000). These essays begin with the performance of Negro spirituals and continue through the Harlem Renaissance and on into the national black theater movement in the twentieth century.

- In the young-adult novel *The First Part Last* (2003) by Angela Johnson, teenage father Bobby is left to raise his daughter as a single parent when his girlfriend dies. Though Bobby is surrounded by a family support system, he struggles with what it means to be a single parent as a sixteen-year-old.

Henrietta's comments. But on the third day, when Sheleeah appears, she is dressed "very nicely" according to the stage directions. Through these scenes, the author points out that even though Henrietta might be delusional, she has influenced Sheleeah. So in part, Henrietta's opinions of herself are at least partially correct. Though she might not command respect through her appearance and anti-social behavior, she has influenced Sheleeah. This signals that there is more to Henrietta than meets the eye.

In act one, scene three, Henrietta repeats a reference to someone hurting her feelings. Sheleeah is hesitant about finding empty jars for Henrietta, and Henrietta takes this personally. At least, that is what Henrietta wants Sheleeah to believe. When Henrietta senses that Sheleeah does not want to help her, she gives Sheleeah a lecture, one with confusing advice. First she tells Sheleeah that people are supposed to look out for one another by doing "all in your power to help them." But by the end of her short speech, Henrietta says that she is finished with "being nice to people. I know better." Here the audience has to look below the surface of her words and try to understand Henrietta, which is difficult to do. Is she merely manipulating Sheleeah, trying to make Sheleeah feel sorry for her and help her? Or was Henrietta hurt so profoundly in her past that she is afraid to be nice to other people because she does not want to be hurt again? Does Henrietta understand that it is good to be nice to others, or is she full of hot air, merely using the concept of social support so she can get sympathy and the jars she needs? The definition of who Henrietta truly is remains a mystery.

In act one, scene five, Henrietta makes another confusing statement. She talks about her insanity, describing her state of mind to Sheleeah. This happens as Sheleeah is looking at the photographs of Henrietta's family, making the surprising discovery that not only was Henrietta twice married but that she is also a mother. As Henrietta recalls the hardships of her marriages and the loss of her children, she stops and asks Sheleeah, "Know why I left my mind?" She does not give Sheleeah any time to speculate and immediately explains that she was forced out of her mind. It was too crowded because she had all those thoughts about the people she had lost. Henrietta then says, "you can separate your mind, you know that." She also declares that she is not really crazy, "just out of my mind." Trying to make sense of this is a challenge. If someone were out of their mind, would they know it? Could they explain it? Is Henrietta really out of her mind or is she just acting like that so she can slip into a world where she does not have to think? But she does think. She talks

about her husbands and children, at least to Sheleeah. Can a person control their insanity, losing their mind when they want to? These are more questions that the author does not answer. She presents these questions through Henrietta but leaves her audience to answer them.

In scene two in act two, Henrietta describes how she learned to be a street person. For her, it was a charade. She says "I had to study months to learn how to get things free." She learned from three other street people while she apprenticed herself to them. She learned how to walk and talk like she was a derelict. She learned how to beg. She did not like the part of street life that included stealing or sleeping on sidewalks, so that was why she started selling fruit, to make enough money so she would not have to do that. But she did act out the role of looking broken down and destitute so others would feel sorry for her when she begged. She admits that she also knew how to manipulate the police so they would not arrest her. With this admission, Henrietta becomes more suspicious. She definitely has chosen this path, all the aspects of it—the mental breakdown, the poverty, the distance from those around her. She claims to love the life she has created, though she has moments when she blames others for her poverty. At one point she tells Sheleeah that it is people like her, who look down on Henrietta, that are at the root of the poor quality of her life.

By the end of the play, Henrietta is all over the place. She wants Sheleeah to come back. Then she convinces herself that Sheleeah has gone home to her family because Henrietta pushed her in that direction. Then she says she does not need Sheleeah. She also tries to push Thomas away and then panics when she thinks he has left her. In the closing moments, Henrietta is calmer, but that peace has come at a cost. Once again, she has closed herself off from the world. She claims she needs no one. She declares that Sheleeah is the one with a messed up mind, not her. And then Henrietta says she knows she is right because "I excel in being . . . correct." If the audience attempted to find one word that would describe Henrietta, it might be the word "confused."

The author might have used the theme of human perceptions to tie this play together. The first hint of this is Henrietta's perception that she is always correct, no matter what she says or how she contradicts herself. This comment could be

Sheelah is a confident accountant. *(Image copyright Demid, 2009. Used under license from Shutterstock.com)*

pointing out that other people's perceptions might be just as off kilter. What are people's perceptions of Henrietta? Is she a derelict as Sheleeah once thought of her? Is she mentally off, as Henrietta refers to herself? With the barrage of insults that Henrietta throws out at the crowds, is Henrietta a mean person? Or is she softhearted deep down, using the vile verbiage to throw people offtrack, to encourage people to keep their distance from her, despite the fact that some part of Henrietta wants to be close to them?

Most people would look at Henrietta and call her poor. But Henrietta says she does not want more money. She looks at Sheleeah, who has money, and feels sorry for her. Sheleeah's pursuit of money, Henrietta implies, makes her feel superior to those who do not have it. For most of time in this play, Henrietta does not want for anything; but Sheleeah's desires for more material things drive her life, always making her feel as if she does not have enough. So between Henrietta and Sheleeah, which of them is more at peace, or happier, or has a richer experience?

All these questions that Jones Meadows leaves unanswered are what provide depth to this play. The audience has to work through their own feelings and perceptions in order to understand Henrietta. By creating an ambiguous character to lead the play, the author could be saying that it is not good to pigeon-hole anyone. Stereotyping people is the easy way out. The play points out that Henrietta is not what she seems. Typical perceptions do not define her. With her doubts and confusion, Henrietta demonstrates that she is a complex being, like everyone else.

Source: Joyce Hart, Critical Essay on *Henrietta*, in *Drama for Students*, Gale, Cengage Learning, 2010.

Jeff Hudson

In the following review, Hudson summarizes the role of Sheleeah in a local production of Henrietta.

Henrietta was first produced in New York about 21 years ago. The script by Karen Jones-Meadows introduces us to a spunky Harlem bag lady in her 50s, with a penchant for loudly announcing exactly what's on her mind. She is boldly assertive yet humorous and often warm. She has more than one screw loose, but sometimes her remarks cut close to the bone.

Like many derelicts, Henrietta has a touch of lunacy, and we gradually learn that she's endured losses that would test anyone's sanity. But Henrietta's madness (like Hamlet's) is deliberate to a degree. She appreciates that being "crazy" also allows her a degree of personal freedom, and even protection.

The play describes the arc of Henrietta's unlikely friendship with Sheleeah, a sexy, well-dressed, young professional woman. Henrietta and Sheleeah have utterly different lifestyles and goals, and yet, in a strange way, they need each other.

Henrietta, as produced locally by Celebration Arts, is at times effective but at other times quite uneven. Actress Coni Taylor (as Henrietta) does the street lady with aplomb, focusing her intense, unpredictable demands on Sheleeah and occasionally on members of the audience. Actress Cecily J. (as Sheleeah) develops a credible relationship with Henrietta. Gregory Jolivette rounds out the cast as Henrietta's landlord. But the production (directed by Linda Barton White) moves awkwardly, with pauses between scenes, occasional lapses of momentum and continuity, and glitches with sound and lighting.

Henrietta is an interesting piece, with some good acting, but this production comes up short in several areas. At the same time, *Henrietta* has more to say than several glossier, more mainstream shows about town. We recommend *Henrietta,* notwithstanding its shortcomings, while simultaneously hoping for more consistency and polish in the next effort from Celebration Arts.

Source: Jeff Hudson, Review of *Henrietta,* in *Sacramento News & Review,* Arts & Culture section, September 14, 2006.

John Beaufort

In the following review of the Negro Ensemble Company's production of Henrietta, *Beaufort discusses the poignancy of the work despite the forced dramatic action.*

Henrietta sits astride a box in front of a dilapidated Harlem brownstone, heckling passers-by. "I don't talk to nobody that listens," she proclaims cheerfully. But Henrietta definitely wants to be heard. She is a bag lady with a difference. She blows up small paper bags and explodes them to punctuate her fusillades of words. Add to the foregoing that Henrietta is played with gusto and a gambit of emotions by the wonderful Frances Foster and you will get the general impression of the unpretentious new comedy being presented by the Negro Ensemble Company at Theatre Four.

Karen Jones-Meadows has written *Henrietta* with genuine affection for her scruffy monologuist. Henrietta's humor and irrepressible audacity are almost always a match for the dark demons that might drive her across the line that distinguishes harmless eccentricity from a more seriously disturbed mental state. "I'm not crazy," Henrietta tells her new friend Sheleeah, "just out of my mind." To Henrietta, the troubles she's seen eminently qualify her to deal with the problems of the world. "That's what I'm here for," she informs the skeptical Sheleeah (Elain Graham).

Having established the dimensions for her character portrait (with subordinate figures), the playwright unfolds a slender tale of a fragile relationship. After a few rounds of verbal hostilities, Henrietta and Sheleeah become friends. Admitted to Henrietta's riotously cluttered tenement room, Sheleeah learns about the men she married and the children she lost or from whom she has been estranged. Henrietta's account of a checkered past occasionally gives way to a momentary outburst of desperate inner rage.

Henrietta is in fact a study of loneliness and the human need for interdependent relationships. As the relationship between the two women develops, Henrietta assumes the role of surrogate mother and even begins imagining that Sheleeah is her daughter. For her part, the younger woman sees financial possibilities in Henrietta's fruit-salad concoction and wants to move her out of her shabby quarters. The latter project is furiously opposed by Henrietta's indulgent landlord-neighbor (William Jay). The confrontation ends predictably.

With Miss Foster to fill out all the dimensions of the central character, her depths as well as her surfaces, *Henrietta* comes off best as a beguiling and touching stage portrait. Miss Graham's crisp Sheleeah and Mr. Jay's bewildered landlord contribute to the development of what becomes a three-way relationship. The author's problem emerges in the development itself, the increasing sense of contrivance in the attempts to intensify the dramatic situation.

Samuel P. Barton's staging faithfully responds to the common humanity and the human comedy of the extending vignettes. Llewellyn Harrison's setting handily encompasses the three principal sectors of action. The production was lighted by Sylvester N. Weaver and costumed by Karen Perry. The tender, incidental tones of "Sometimes I feel like a motherless child..." underscore the feeling of this poignant stage miniature.

Source: John Beaufort, "Gusto and Unpretentiousness from the Negro Ensemble Company: *Henrietta*," in *Christian Science Monitor*, February 4, 1985, p. 32.

SOURCES

Davis, Anthony C., "Play Examines the Philosophies of DuBois, Booker T.", in *Philadelphia Tribune*, April 4, 1997, Sect. C, p. 1.

"The Eighties in American, Homelessness," in *Salem Press*, https://salempress.com/Store/samples/eighties_in_america/eighties_in_america_homelessness.ht m (accessed July 1, 2009).

Gussow, Mel, "Stage: 'Tapman,' with Moses Gunn," in *New York Times*, March 1, 1988, Sect. C, p. 17.

Hannah, David, Review of *Henrietta*, in *Philadelphia Tribune*, October 27, 1995, Sect. E, p. 9.

Harvey, Antonio R., Review of *Henrietta*, in *Sacramento Observer*, September 28–October 4, 2006, Sect. E, p. 2.

"How Many People Experience Homelessness?," in *National Coalition for the Homeless*, http://www.nationalhomeless.org/factsheets/How_Many.html (accessed August 2, 2008).

Katz, Michael B., *In the Shadow of the Poorhouse: A Social History of Welfare in America*, Basic Books, 1996.

King, Woodie, Jr., ed., "Henrietta," in *National Black Drama Anthology*, Applause, 1995, pp. 200–38.

Lane, Lynda, Review of *Henrietta*, in *Philadelphia Tribune*, October 17, 1995, Sect. C, p. 3.

Maupin, Elizabeth, Review of *Henrietta*, in *Orlando Sentinel,* June 1, 2002, Sect. E, p. 1.

Peterson, Jane R., and Suzanne Bennett, *Women Playwrights of Diversity: A Bio-Bibliographical Sourcebook*, Greenwood Press, 1997, p. 1637.

"Poverty in the United States: 2000," in *U.S. Census Bureau*, http://www.census.gov/prod/2001pubs/p60-214.pdf (September 2001).

Rich, Frank, Review of *Henrietta*, in the *New York Times*, January 29, 1985, Sect. C, p. 13.

Stoker, Robert Phillip, *When Work Is Not Enough: State and Federal Policies to Support Needy Workers*, Brookings Institution Press, 2006.

Wolf, Richard, "How Welfare Reform Changed America, in *USA Today*, http://www.usatoday.com/news/nation/2006-07-17-welfare-reform-cover_x.htm (July 18, 2006).

X, Malcolm, *The Autobiography of Malcolm X*, edited by Alex Haley, Penguin Books, 1973.

FURTHER READING

Brown-Guillory, Elizabeth, *Their Place on the Stage: Black Women Playwrights in America*, Praeger Paperback, 1990.

> This books offers an extensive background reading for anyone interested in the history of African American female playwrights, such as Lorraine Hansberry, Alice Childress, and Ntozake Shange. Besides a review of the playwrights' works, a brief history of the African origins of African American theater is explored. The author offers her interpretation of the playwrights' major plays as well as an analysis of the theme and images that the dramatists offer.

Elam, Harry, Jr., *The Fire This Time: African-American Plays for the 21st Century*, Theatre Communications Group, 2002.

> For a more contemporary experience of African American drama, this anthology offers plays by August Wilson, Suzan-Lori Parks, Lynn Nottage, Robert O'Hara, Robert Alexander, Kamilah Forbes and the Hip Hop Junction, and Stephen Sapp, to name a few of the included writers.

Henderson, Mary, *The City and the Theatre: The History of New York Playhouses: A 250 Year Journey from Bowling Green to Times Square*, Back Stage Books, 2004.

> Extensively researched, Henderson's book offers readers a comprehensive history of how the theater districts of New York were formed. The book begins in 1699, when the first petition was made for a license to perform plays in Manhattan, and ends with the end of the twentieth century and the making (and re-making) of Times Square. Photographs and a list of historic buildings are also included.

Krasner, David, *A Beautiful Pageant: African American Theatre, Drama, and Performance in the Harlem Renaissance, 1910–1927*, Palgrave Macmillan, 2002.

> The Harlem Renaissance refers to the first time that major publications paid serious attention to the writings of African Americans. Krasner focuses on this period but with an eye to some of the lesser-known artists from this period, such as Georgia Douglas Johnson and Willis Richardson. Krasner offers insights into this historic period, making this book a good reference for students interested in black theater and culture.

Nevius, Michelle, and James Nevius, *Inside the Apple: A Streetwise History of New York City*, Free Press, 2009.

> This is more than a tourist guidebook of New York City. The authors provide a thorough history that extends back to the time of

glaciers and goes forward to the birth of gay rights. If a major event occurred in the city, there is a good chance readers will find a story about it in this book.

Perkins, Kathy A., ed., *Black Female Playwrights: An Anthology of Plays before 1950*, Indiana University Press, 1990.

The works of seven black playwrights are the focus of this publication. They include Georgia Douglas Johnson, Mary P. Burrill, Zora Neale Hurston, Eulalie Spence, May Miller, Marita Bonner, and Shirley Graham. The styles and themes of these playwrights are diverse, giving the reader a sense of the black experience during the turn of the twentieth century.

I Never Saw Another Butterfly

CELESTE RASPANTI

1971

After coming across a book of poems and drawings created by children of the Holocaust concentration camps, Celeste Raspanti wrote the play *I Never Saw Another Butterfly* in 1967. Officially published in 1971 and presented as a one-act cutting in 1980, the drama is based on the true story of survivor Raja Englanderova.

Raja was one of 15,000 children under the age of fifteen to enter the gates of Terezin, a Nazi concentration camp located in Czechoslovakia (now divided into the two nations the Czech Republic and Slovakia). Raspanti brings to life the experiences of all those children by holding a magnifying glass to the experience of just one.

Terezin was created as a "model camp," one designed to fool outsiders—particularly the International Red Cross—into thinking the Jews were being treated humanely throughout the Holocaust. Most adults who entered the camp were intellectuals, artists, and scholars. The children of Terezin were encouraged to create. They wrote poetry, played music, drew, and painted pictures. When Terezin was liberated, six thousand poems and drawings previously hidden were discovered. Some of those works were compiled into a book called *I Never Saw Another Butterfly* by Hana Volavkova. The book inspired Raspanti to translate the children's art into drama.

The one-act play investigates the topics of death and victimization while exploring themes of the true meaning of survival and what is required to hope in the face of despair.

AUTHOR BIOGRAPHY

Raspanti was born in Chicago, Illinois, in 1928. The youngest of three children born to Italian immigrant parents, Raspanti grew up in a close extended family. After winning a writing contest in 1943 at her Catholic girls' high school, she knew she wanted to be a writer. Her plans changed when, in 1946, she entered a convent and became a nun. Though she maintained a love of writing, her focus changed to teaching.

Raspanti graduated from Milwaukee, Wisconsin's Alverno College with a bachelor's degree in English in 1950 and earned her master's degree, also in English, from Marquette University seven years later. While working on her master's degree, she taught high school in Illinois and Wisconsin until accepting a job as an English professor at Alverno, where she remained until 1969. At that time, Raspanti moved to Minnesota and earned a Ph.D. in theater arts from the University of Minnesota-Minneapolis.

In 1963, Raspanti came across a book of drawings made by children of the Terezin concentration camp from 1942 to 1944. By the end of the book, she was speechless. The last section of the book listed the names, birth dates, and transport dates of each child, as well as the date each died at Auschwitz. After reading the phrase "perished at Auschwitz" on page after page of listed names, Raspanti was startled to read "Raja Englanderova, after the liberation, returned to Prague."

In her essay "Where Does a Play Begin?" Raspanti remembers, "At that moment I knew I was committed to these children.... My first reaction to the story of the Terezin children was silence. My second reaction was the inability to keep silent." Four years later, Raspanti traveled to Prague to meet Terezin survivor Raja Englanderova. On that same trip, she visited two of the most notorious death camps, Auschwitz and Dachau.

Raspanti's travel and research resulted in the play *I Never Saw Another Butterfly*. Though not officially published until 1971, the show opened in 1967 under the title *A Place of Springs* and was produced and performed by Alverno's theater department. Milwaukee's Jewish community paid to fly Raja to Milwaukee for the premier of the play. The one-act version of that same play was published in 1980. A sequel, *The Terezin Promise*, was published in 2004.

Throughout the 1970s and 1980s, Raspanti held various teaching and consulting positions at Minnesota universities and colleges. *No Fading Star*, also about the Holocaust, was published in 1979. In 1993, she helped the Saint Paul Seminary plan and produce events to commemorate the institution's one hundredth anniversary. Raspanti retired in 1995.

Writing constituted a major part of Raspanti's life, both before and after retirement. She has published many other dramatic scripts as well, including a stage adaptation of Vera and Bill Cleaver's classic novel *Where the Lilies Bloom*. In addition to her plays, Raspanti has written and published numerous articles for academic and professional journals.

Since retirement, Raspanti has been a driving force in the Italian community of the Minneapolis-St. Paul region. In addition to serving on several civic boards, she publishes *Notizie: An E-mail Newsletter for Italian Americans, Italians and Italophiles* and belongs to numerous Italian cultural and historical organizations.

PLOT SUMMARY

I Never Saw Another Butterfly opens with a voice announcing the names, ages, and death dates of the children of Terezin. An older Raja appears and explains that all her family and friends have been murdered by the Nazis. The Loudspeaker then narrates a series of events: Nazis enter Prague on March 5, 1939. Jewish children are banned from elementary schools on December 1, 1939. Auschwitz is ready for prisoners on September 27, 1941. Terezin is set up as a walled Jewish ghetto/concentration camp on October 16, 1941.

Irena Synkova, self-appointed caretaker of the camp's children, meets twelve-year-old Raja as she first enters Terezin. They befriend one another, and Irena invites Raja to attend the makeshift school she has set up. There the children draw, paint, and write.

Various children share their visions of what they plan to do when they escape the ghetto. Their plans reveal that what they miss most are the simple things: curtains on windows, playing ball, making their beds, or staying up late. Raja sums up what every child knows, "Before, when I

MEDIA ADAPTATIONS

- *I Never Saw Another Butterfly*, adapted as a musical by Joseph Robinette with music by E. A. Alexander, was published by Dramatic Publishing in 2007.

used to live at home, / It never seemed so dear and fair."

Irena and Raja talk about Auschwitz. Raja knows those who go never come back. Her good friend Zdenka is transported to Auschwitz, as are others. Raja misses her friends and hates life inside Terezin. She cries, and Irena calms her by grabbing her hands. It is a turning point in the play, as it is the moment in time when Raja leaves behind her childhood to face the horrifying reality of her life.

Irena tells her, "You are no longer a child— this minute, you are no longer a child—and so I tell you . . ." Irena shares the fact that her own nine-year-old daughter was torn from her arms and thrown from the moving train. She wanted to die, so intense was her grief. Then Irena found purpose in Terezin, where she willingly takes responsibility for the children. Raja weeps but finds strength in Irena's story.

Raja meets Honza as both watch the train carrying Jiri, Honza's brother, out of Terezin. Raja's brother Pavel and his wife Irca are on the same train. Honza tells Raja about a newspaper he and his friends produce and distribute through the boys' side of the camp. Raja asks Honza to send over a copy to post in the girls' section. *Vedem*, their newspaper, which means "We are leading," survives for three years, and eventually the girls are allowed to publish poetry in it. The newspaper serves as the communication line between both sides of the camp.

Honza and Raja grow closer as the months pass. They meet in secret and sometimes in the work fields, where they hide small presents for one another. Honza tells Raja that the flowers growing in front of the main tower are

hers, that he's giving them to her. She gives him a poem. He sneaks a sausage from the kitchen for her.

Honza tells Raja he is going away for a few days. He's been assigned to a special detail to build something outside of Terezin. Raja worries that Honza will not return, but he does.

Raja confides in Irena that she was afraid while Honza was gone. She said if he failed to return, part of her would always be waiting. Irena tells Raja that the key to surviving is to make the waiting bearable by breaking it into small time increments. If Raja can do that, she can survive, as Irena has done. She explains, "One of us must teach the children how to sing again, to write on paper with a pencil, to do sums and draw pictures. So we survive each today. . . . "

Another train whistle blows, and a voice over the loudspeaker announces more names and ages of children who died at Auschwitz. Honza is among them. In a flashback scene, Raja talks with Honza from across the wall. They cannot see one another, and he tells her he has to report for the next transport out of Terezin. They both know what awaits him. Honza tells her he wrote her a poem and left it under the fence post.

Raja reads the poem, the last two lines of which are, "But you were too lovely, perhaps, to stay. / I loved you once. Good-bye, my love." Raja says the motto of Terezin is "good-bye," that it was, for those who lived there, freedom. "What was there to fear when you had said good-bye to everyone you ever loved?"

Irena is called to transport before she can say goodbye to Raja. She leaves a note for her instead. Accompanying the note is the last of the children's drawings and poems, which she has asked Raja to bury along with all the rest. "I have nothing else to give you but this—what you and all the children have made of Terezin— the fields, the flowers—and all the butterflies. . . . "

Raja remembers all the important things the people she loved in Terezin had told her over the years. The voices speak to her as she faces the audience one last time. This time she says, "My name is Raja—I am a Jew; I survived Terezin—*not* alone, and *not* afraid." Her experience in Terezin, as horrifying as it was, made her stronger and forged in her a will to survive.

CHARACTERS

Raja Englanderova

Raja Englanderova is the main character in the play. She enters Terezin as a twelve-year-old girl. Raja narrates the story, and the audience sees the story unfold through her eyes. In real life, Raja was one of the few children to survive Terezin.

Raja is the first character other than the Loudspeaker to speak in the play. When the first flashback occurs, she is timid and new to Terezin. As her character grows and the story unfolds, Raja is strengthened and nurtured by her relationships with Irena and Honza. By the play's end, the child Raja is alone but no longer afraid. Raja the adult narrator is defiant in her survival.

Honza

Honza is the brother of the late Jiri, who was Raja's friend. Honza and Raja grow close and fall in love. Honza gives Raja hope for a brighter future because he gives her something to hope for.

Honza brings an energy to the play no other character provides. It is he who helps publish the camp newspaper. He is the character who notices the flowers and the butterflies in the commons. Honza sneaks food to Raja. He leaves her poetry and holds secret meetings with his fellow inmates. Honza continues to find ways to actually experience life within the ghetto's walls.

Loudspeaker

The Loudspeaker is a voice that announces the names and death dates of the children of Terezin. It also provides timelines of major events pertaining to the children during the war. The Loudspeaker is used as means of providing important background information.

Irena Synkova

Irena Synkova is one of the first inhabitants of Terezin. She takes responsibility for the children and organizes them into a school. Irena's top priority is keeping each child alive both physically and spiritually.

Irena is the first person to speak to Raja at the beginning of the play, and her voice is the last one Raja hears at the end. It is Irena who draws Raja out of herself and tries to ease her fear. Irena encourages Raja to be enthusiastic about the secret school, and soon Raja credits the school and Irena with helping her heal. Irena, without trying, acts as a sort of surrogate parent, teacher, and friend for Raja.

Youth

The four youth are various children who live at Terezin. Each child has a different vision of what life will be like once he is able to return home. In the final scene of the play, the ghosts of the children speak to Raja of a memory from her time in the camp. The youth represent all the children of Terezin.

THEMES

Survival

As one of the play's major themes, survival of both the body and spirit is woven throughout the dialogue. Although Raja is the only character in the play to physically survive the imprisonment at Terezin, Irena represents the importance of spiritual survival. Having had her young daughter tossed from a moving train before her very eyes, Irena knows that in order to survive, one must find purpose. For her, that purpose involves making meaning out of horror for the children of Terezin.

Irena is the one who teaches Raja how to survive. She coaches Raja to imagine living until the morning, then, try to make it to noon. "Can you live until night?" she asks. In response to Raja's comment that she had been waiting for Honza to return from a special detail, Irena says, "Waiting days are long days, Raja. You would learn to stop thinking of tomorrow and to keep alive today. That's the secret of waiting—remember that—to keep alive today."

Late in the play, Irena speaks to Raja about the importance of someone surviving, of getting through each day, so that the children can relearn how to sing, write, and compute math facts. Key to survival at Terezin was the children's schooling. Raja says, "The singing, the reading, the learning—the poetry and the drawings—this was part of our survival." The idea that surviving goes beyond not dying, that it is achieved through spiritual nourishment, sensual experience, is clear.

Freedom

The story revolves around prisoners of a concentration camp who have had nearly every civil and personal right revoked. To outsiders, their

TOPICS FOR FURTHER STUDY

- Find a book on butterflies. Cut out the shape of a butterfly from construction paper and design and decorate it using both images from the book and themes and images from the play. Present your finished butterfly to the class and explain why you designed it the way you did.

- Imagine you are a child at Terezin, using additional research about the camp from Web sites or print sources. Together with a small group of classmates, write, illustrate, edit, and produce a four-page newspaper like *Vedem*. Do not use a computer to complete this project; everything must be done by hand. What kind of "news" would you publish? How would you decide what to include? Share the newspaper with your class.

- Read the young-adult book *Remembering Manzanar: Life in a Japanese Relocation Camp*. Both Terezin and Manzanar existed in the 1940s, one in America and one in Prague. In what ways are the camps similar? How do they differ? Make a list. Then write

a paragraph to answer this question: If you had to choose which camp to live in, which one would you choose and why?

- Research Terezin using Web sites and at least two hard-copy sources. Develop a presentation using PowerPoint or another computer program and share with the class what you learned.

- Read the full-length version of the play and write an essay explaining how it differs from the one-act version. Which version do you prefer and why?

- Read the book *I Never Saw Another Butterfly: Children's Drawings and Poems from Terezin Concentration Camp, 1942–1944*, which inspired Raspanti to write the play by the same name. Choose a favorite poem and share it with the class.

- Research Terezin and Auschwitz. Create a Venn diagram to show how they were similar and how they differed.

---

freedom appears to have been stripped away. While in one sense this is true—no one has the freedom to leave Terezin, to speak out against the way they are treated, or even to learn—in another, they are completely free.

The newspaper *Vedem*, which means "we are leading," is a form of stolen freedom. Although the boys must meet in secret to write and publish it, and it must be passed around in secret, it is a form of expression. It is a voice, many voices—voices of children who refuse to be silenced. If freedom will not be given, they will steal it. Raja explains the importance of the paper. "It was an invisible line of communication between the houses so that . . . the youth of Terezin grew up together."

Near the end of the story, Raja claims that "goodbye" is the motto of Terezin. "It was *goodbye*, not *work*, that made us free." For Raja, the

sole survivor in the play, freedom comes only when there is nothing left to lose or fear.

Memory

Memory and remembering give the prisoners of Terezin a sense of control in a lifestyle that offers very little. The purpose of concentration camps was to facilitate eradication of the Jewish race from the planet; Hitler wanted no evidence of Jewish existence left behind. By exercising their memories, sharing their stories, and writing them down, those victimized by the Holocaust created a legacy that no effort could destroy.

Memory is a powerful healing tool for Raja. She credits Irena's school with her personal healing. Months pass inside Terezin before Raja can find the courage to say anything but her name. Using paint, she commits her name to paper in

Terezin concentration camp *(Image copyright Martin D. Vonka, 2009. Used under license from Shutterstock.com)*

"crippled characters" and one day writes Irena's name. That is the sign that she is healed. "I could tell Irena the things I was remembering. I was no longer afraid to remember."

Memory as a theme is woven throughout many productions of the play in stage setting as well. In various scenes, images painted and drawn by the real children of Terezin appear on a projection screen, visible to the audience but not as a part of the actual action of the scene. The play opens with images of butterflies projected over the entire stage. It ends with yet more butterflies, this time on the screen, on the floor of the stage: everywhere. The butterflies are moving.

STYLE

Memory Play

Memory is relied upon as a narrative device to tell a non-linear (not chronologically in order) tale. Through the power of memory, characters are developed in both obvious and subtle ways.

In choosing to present Raja's story as a memory play, Raspanti has given it a more personal and immediate feel. She is not merely relating a story; she is having the character who lived the experience share her perspective of what happened. Knowing the events played out on stage truly happened to one of the characters makes the drama more powerful.

I Never Saw Another Butterfly is an inherently tragic story. Most viewers in the audience or readers of the play already understand the basic background of the Holocaust: six million Jews and members of other persecuted groups were murdered by Hitler's Nazi regime. Those who entered Terezin suffered the same fate as other Jews. That information does not need to be stressed because it is already known.

This knowledge is important to Raspanti's play because the audience brings to it a collective understanding of the general cultural and social circumstances of the time period. This allows them to focus on the memory perspective without intrusion, in essence, to remember that what is being heard and seen is one person's very distinct memory of the event. Someone else who survived Terezin might have had a very different experience and memory. The memory as structural element makes the play unique, which in turn makes it genuine.

The tragedy of the story is presented all the more powerfully because it is understated. Readers and viewers never see torture or violence, but the fact that the residents of Terezin simply disappear as a matter of daily routine illustrates the horrific conditions under which they lived. That they must sneak around in order to learn, that they cannot communicate freely with others in the compound, that privacy no longer exists—all this implies the harsh and unyielding life circumstances of the children and adults of Terezin.

Because the play is told as a memory and not a frame-by-frame narrative, Raja does not need to stress the violence. It is implied and assumed. Had the play been written to include that aspect, it might have detracted from the more intense and powerful message Raspanti wanted to convey: that people can overcome and triumph in even the most harrowing of situations.

Flashback

Raspanti makes use of flashback throughout the play as Raja speaks to the audience, narrating the story. All action except for Raja's narrative monologues are actually flashbacks in time. When the play opens, Raja speaks to the audience, explaining that she—and only she—survived Terezin. The next person to speak is Irena, who died in Terezin. So the audience understands that the action and scenes they are watching are, in reality, flashbacks.

Symbolism

The most obvious symbol in the play is the butterfly, which represents hope and freedom. The title of the play is also the title of a poem written by a child who lived in Terezin. The last butterfly this child ever saw was a dazzling yellow color, and it flew up into the sky until it could no longer be seen. Since entering Terezin, the boy could find no butterflies. The last lines of his poem say:

> Only I never saw another butterfly.
> That butterfly was the last one.
> Butterflies don't live here in the ghetto.

The way butterflies flit and flutter makes them seem carefree, the way children should be. But the children of Terezin are prisoners, and the only freedom they come to know is death.

Another symbol in the play is the act of creating. In a world where learning and creating is forbidden, to do so is an act of defiance. Amidst death and the revocation of rights, the children manage to create poetry and paintings, a symbol of their defiance against oppression. In the real Terezin, those creations were made over the course of two years, and around six thousand of them were hidden for safekeeping. In the play, the drawings depict both the world the children have left behind and the reality in which they are living.

HISTORICAL CONTEXT

The History of Terezin

Of the six million Jews put to death in the Holocaust, more than one million were children under the age of sixteen. Like their adult counterparts, these young people were tortured, starved, and worked to death in camps like Dachau, Buchenwald, and Auschwitz. Terezin was unlike these other camps. Originally built in 1780 by Emperor Joseph II of Austria, Terezin included the Big Fortress and the Small Fortress. As Hitler's troops invaded Europe, it was decided the town would be used to house Jews. The first transport arrived in November 1941.

Terezin was originally home to about seven thousand residents. The Nazis needed it to hold between 35,000 and 60,000 people. Jews were brought in to transform the town even while residents remained living there. Eventually, all residents were evicted and nearly 60,000 Jews were forced to live in cramped quarters that promoted disease.

On the outside, Terezin looked like a peaceful village, similar to those found throughout the European countryside. But behind the façade lay a concentration camp, one filled primarily with artists, intellectuals, and musicians. Inmates were separated into camps according to gender. Life in Terezin soon became focused on transports to Auschwitz; those who left never returned. Terezin did not have its own gas chambers, only a crematorium to burn the corpses of those who had died from other causes.

The first Danish Jews arrived in Terezin in October 1943. When the Danish and Swedish Red Cross began asking to know their whereabouts, Hitler permitted them to visit Terezin in an effort to prove that Jews were being treated

COMPARE
&
CONTRAST

- **1940s:** World War II and the Holocaust are in full swing, and the events depicted in Raspanti's play are taking place. The world is unaware of the concentration and death camps. Either because it is too horrible to believe or because they truly do not know, people around the world are ignorant to the plight of the Jews and other victims of the Holocaust.

  1970s: Thirty years have passed and the world acknowledges the horrors of the Holocaust. The 1970s is a decade in which sociologists begin to more fully understand the atrocities committed during World War II and the subsequent psychological impact those atrocities had, not only on individuals, but on society as a whole. "Holocaust" becomes a term written with a capital "H" in the 1970s. Publication of Holocaust literature is at an all-time high.

  Today: The atrocities of the Holocaust are no less horrific in the early twenty-first century than they were upon their discovery. Millions of people visit the Holocaust Memorial Museum in Washington, D.C., every year. More people recognize the importance of recording the personal stories of survivors of the Holocaust, because even those who were children at the time are now in their sixties and seventies. As memory becomes fuzzy with age, it is important to document the stories and preserve them.

- **1940s:** The Nuremberg trials take place in Nuremberg, Germany, from 1945 to 1946. Among others, twenty-two of the most important captured leaders of Nazi Germany are tried for war crimes. There are many trials prosecuted in Nuremberg, and the majority of them result in guilty verdicts with a sentence of life imprisonment or death.

  1970s: As they are discovered living in various countries throughout the world, Nazi war criminals continue to be tried and sentenced for their crimes.

  Today: Nazi war crimes suspect Ivan "John" Demjanjuk is found living in Ohio in May 2009. He is deported to Germany, where he will stand trial. As reported on CNN.com, this ends one of the longest-running pursuits of an alleged Holocaust criminal in history. The media is calling Demjanjuk the last Nazi war criminal.

- **1940s:** Throughout Britain and Germany, children are being evacuated, especially from cities targeted by the Allies. Millions of children are accommodated in rural regions for the duration of the war. American children are little affected by World War II except for the absence of fathers and brothers. Many mothers now work outside the home.

  1970s: East German children spend a great deal of time in state institutions because economic hardships have forced fathers and mothers into full-time work. Institutionalized children lead structured lives with strict discipline. By the end of the decade, all of Germany has outlawed spanking children in schools. American children are growing up with an anti-war movement in full stride and a mandatory busing policy to help achieve racial integration in the schools. It is a time of great social unrest.

  Today: The German government bans the use of physical punishment in child rearing. In America, spanking is still legal in some localities, although some legislators have proposed bills to change that.

humanely. To that end, he ordered the camp to be improved by adding turf, a playground, sports fields, and flowers, among other things. None of these additions were ever actually used by inmates. On the day the Red Cross visited, the Nazis made sure to line the approved route with workers who sang while they toiled. It was all a ruse.

Terezin concentration camp memorial (Image copyright Martin D. Vonka, 2009. Used under license from Shutterstock.com)

According to survivors, the community inside Terezin shared a sense of family, probably because tens of thousands of people were sharing living quarters built for only thousands. They were cramped, and they relied upon one another for their very survival. More than any other camp, Terezin developed a rich cultural life. Musicians formed symphonies and gave concerts. Actors performed plays, and writers gave lectures. Because learning itself was forbidden, adults schooled the children at night. During that time, they were encouraged to draw, paint, and write using supplies stolen by some of the adult inmates.

Despite the horrible living conditions and constant state of fear in which the prisoners of Terezin lived, they had the vision to realize the historical and cultural value of the children's artwork and poetry. Six thousand such pieces were hidden and then reclaimed after the war. Some of those works comprise the book that inspired Celeste Raspanti to write her play.

Inspiration

Raspanti joined a league of highly respected writers who contributed to the ever-growing body of Holocaust literature when she wrote her play, *I Never Saw Another Butterfly*. Although she was not a Holocaust survivor, Raspanti met Raja Englanderova and interviewed her extensively. She flew to Europe and toured the death camps. With the knowledge she gained on her travels, she was able to write a convincingly real drama of life in Terezin.

Her contribution to Holocaust literature was rather unique at the time it was written because most of what was published in the 1970s and early 1980s was from the viewpoint of adult survivors. The voices of the child victims were rarely heard.

CRITICAL OVERVIEW

I Never Saw Another Butterfly is the play for which Celeste Raspanti is best known. Although the full-length version was published first, the one-act drama is most often performed.

In her theater review for the *Orlando Sentinel*, critic Rebecca Swain praises the play for its power. "Celeste Raspanti's powerful one-act play gives the children of Terezin voice again, a strong one, and honors their brief lives."

Raspanti's personal interest in the Holocaust has been fueled by visits to the death camps and friendships with survivors. *I Never Saw Another Butterfly* is one of three dramas centered on Holocaust stories. The play is regularly performed in high schools and community theaters across the country decades after its debut. When Florida passed a law requiring all schools to teach the Holocaust, Charlotte High School theater director Ray Durkee chose *I Never Saw Another Butterfly* as a vehicle for learning. In Jay Roland's review in the *Sarasota Herald Tribune*, Durkee explains, "I like to select plays that can be integrated into the classroom and the curriculum."

CRITICISM

Rebecca Valentine

Valentine is a freelance writer who holds a B.A. in English with minors in philosophy and professional communications. In this essay, she focuses on the

WHAT DO I READ NEXT?

- *Anne Frank: The Diary of a Young Girl*, originally published in 1947, is the memoir of a Jewish teenager who goes into hiding for twenty-five months with her family and some friends. The 1993 edition contains 30 percent more text than the original, which had been edited to protect Anne's privacy. Anne died at Bergen-Belsen Concentration Camp just three months before her sixteenth birthday.

- PBS has developed a special project titled *Auschwitz: Inside the Nazi State* available at http://www.pbs.org/auschwitz. In addition to a timeline and a list of resources for educators, the site provides original maps and plans of the era's most infamous concentration camp.

- Philip Gourevitch's *We Wish to Inform You That Tomorrow We Will Be Killed with Our Families: Stories from Rwanda* (1999) is an exploration of the Rwandan genocide. This thoroughly researched investigation presents a graphic depiction of the horrors and atrocities imposed upon the Tutsi by the Hutus. Gourevitch strives to explain why this conflict should not be considered just another tribal war.

- Anne Fox and Eva Abraham-Podietz have written *Ten Thousand Children: True Stories Told by Children Who Escaped the Holocaust*

on the Kindertransport (1998). The Kindertransport rescued ten thousand Jewish children from the Nazi-occupied Europe. Only one thousand were reunited with their families. This book contains the experiences of twenty-one survivors.

- *Parallel Journeys*, written by Eleanor Ayer, Helen Waterford, and Alfons Heck and published in 2000, is the story of two youths who grew up during World War II. One is a German Jew, the other a Hitler Youth. Their stories are taken from true memoirs, and the juxtaposition of the two contrasts the perceptions of the Nazis with those of the Jews during the Holocaust experience.

- The *United States Holocaust Memorial Museum* has a Web site that features Holocaust history in various languages. Although http://www.ushmm.org/ supports the actual museum (located in Washington, D.C.), it is also a clearinghouse for information and events pertaining to the Holocaust.

- Thomas Fuchs's book *A Concise Biography of Adolf Hitler* (2000) provides insight into Hitler the man. Written in the style and format of an encyclopedia, the book dispels some of the legends surrounding Hitler and paints a well-rounded picture, not only of Hitler as a leader, but as a German citizen and fallible human.

---

role of memory as an act of resistance in Raspanti's memory play I Never Saw Another Butterfly.

After World War II, playwrights began experimenting with the concept of memory as a narrative device. In analyzing Holocaust literature collectively, many critics have explored the role of memory in reshaping individual identity. In her one-act play *I Never Saw Another Butterfly*, Celeste Raspanti uses memory not only as a narrative tool, but as a sort of character. The play is written *using* memory; it is *about* memory; it is *based* on memory.

Resistance is the willful action of opposing something. During the Holocaust, there were formal, organized resistance movements to help Jews and others escape persecution. These movements were much like the Underground Railroad used to help African Americans escape slavery in the nineteenth century. But resistance took a much more subtle—yet no less powerful—role throughout the Holocaust and beyond. *I Never Saw Another Butterfly* was written in the form of a memory play, that is, it uses memory and memories as a method of narrating the story. It mixes fact with fiction to present a version of a particular historical event.

Raspanti could have written the play without incorporating memory into its structure. She could have presented the exact same story as a simple narrative, without the use of flashback or non-linear presentation. Raja would still have been the main character, but her role as narrator would not exist. Instead, Raspanti gives power to Raja's story by constantly reminding the audience that they are viewing the authentic memories of Raja.

The play opens with Raja directly addressing the audience. She introduces herself and lets viewers know she is the only member of her family and friends to have survived Terezin. From there the audience is transported back in time to Terezin and the day Raja meets Irena Synkova. The entire play is a series of flashbacks—memories—with Raja breaking out of those flashbacks here and there to narrate or explain.

This incorporation of memory into the structure of the play is a formidable show of resistance on Raspanti's behalf. She is refusing to remain silent about the experiences of the children of Terezin. The very act of writing the play is an act of resistance; presenting it as a memory is even more so.

The characters in *I Never Saw Another Butterfly* are imprisoned, their most basic rights revoked. On the surface, they appear powerless. And on one level, they are. But on another level, they hold all the power because they possess something even the Nazis cannot take away: memory.

When Raja becomes overwhelmed with the living conditions and the knowledge that those she loves are being transported to certain death at Auschwitz, Irena tells her to remember: "Do not forget how you worked together—in this very room—and the poems, and the songs." The power and importance of memory is again emphasized when Raja laments, "There was no one who could remember me before I had come here as a child of twelve."

Memory also plays a major role in the relationship between Honza and Raja. When Honza learns he is to be transported to Auschwitz, he tells Raja of the poem he wrote for her. The poem begins, "Memory, come tell a fairy tale / About my girl who's lost and gone." Honza

knows that memory is all Raja will soon have left of the bond they shared.

In the closing scene of the play, Raja has come to understand that memory alone will keep those she loved alive in her heart. Though their lives were taken, she resists letting go completely by wrapping them in memory. "Mother, Father, Pavel, Irca. I hear you. Honza, I hear and I remember . . . Irena Synkova, I remember."

The memories the children depict in their drawings and paintings, in the poems they write—these are all acts of resistance. Though the Nazis tear them from their homes and families, memories comfort the children, and they conjure them in their minds to have strength to forge through another day of grief and desperation.

After the war, survivors returned to Terezin to collect the six thousand drawings, paintings, and poems made by the children who lived there. Someone had the amazing clarity to understand even in those horrendous circumstances that what those children created would serve as their legacy, a reminder that they had indeed existed, dreamed, remembered, and suffered. Hiding those memories and depictions of life in the ghetto was an act of resistance. By protecting those creations, the oppressed preserved memories, which in turn are now displayed in books and exhibits for the entire world to see. Those memories resisted Hitler's attempts to wipe an entire race of people from the face of the earth.

Finally, in watching a performance—or reading—Raspanti's play, the audience is acknowledging a particular set of memories of the Holocaust. By willingly exposing themselves to those memories, they are resisting the easier alternative of ignoring the abominable ugliness of history and the inhumane atrocities committed against millions of innocent people. In effect, the memories of a survivor become the memories of a current generation.

Memory is as inseparable from the Holocaust as horror. It takes on political, cultural, and social dimensions that, altogether, help develop an understanding of the psychological repercussions of the war-time tragedy. Celeste Raspanti recognized the importance of memory as resistance as she wrote her play. She insured the audience understood that importance as well by ending with a powerful scene in which Raja embraces remembrance. In that embrace lies the power to overcome.

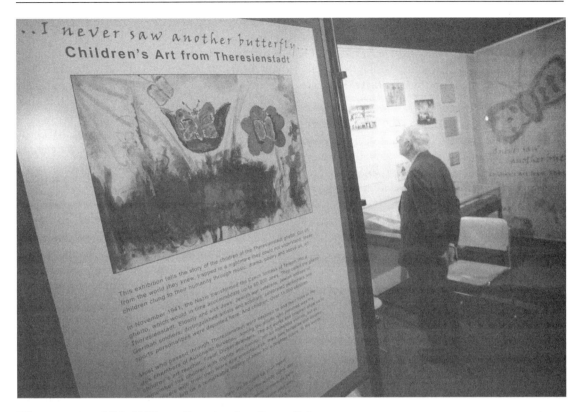

The museum exhibit "I Never Saw Another Butterfly" (Graeme Robertson / Getty Images)

Source: Rebecca Valentine, Critical Essay on *I Never Saw Another Butterfly*, in *Drama for Students*, Gale, Cengage Learning, 2010.

Douglas J. Guth

In the following review, Guth talks about the use of the play to raise funds to preserve the Terezin Museum.

College of Wooster students Lindsay Horst and Becki Dieleman both grew up in small, fairly affluent towns. Horst, 20, is a Wooster native, while Dieleman, also 20, was raised in the upper-middle class comfort of Holland, Mich.

Both young women have noticed an unfortunate side effect of small-town life: Too many people, they say, don't look beyond the borders of the United States, or even those of their hometowns. "In my high school, the world view is only what's around you—cell phones, clothes and boys," says Dieleman in a recent phone interview from her dorm.

The two friends are doing their small part to try and widen that view. They hope to increase awareness of human rights while preserving a piece of history through The Terezin Relief Project, a plan to raise $5,000 to help restore the Terezin Memorial and Museum.

The museum, located in the small town of Terezin in the Czech Republic (about 60 kilometers from Prague), suffered $2 million worth of damage during the floods that deluged Eastern Europe last year. Extensive damage to the grounds and several exhibits forced closure of portions of the museum.

During World War II, Terezin served as a Jewish ghetto and concentration camp. The ghetto was a holding place for Jews before they were sent to Auschwitz as part of Adolf Hitler's "final solution." Among these Jews were approximately 15,000 children. Of that group, only about 100 lived to see the end of the war. Terezin has since been turned into a memorial and museum that teaches visitors about the atrocities of the Holocaust and the value of human life.

The children who passed through Terezin are the subject of an upcoming production by the Wooster High School Drama Club; it's a stage adaptation of Celeste Raspanti's book, *I Never Saw Another Butterfly: Children's Drawings and Poems from Terezin Concentration Camp, 1942–1944.* The play, scheduled for April 11–12, tells their story through poems and artwork that survived the war.

Dieleman is directing *Butterfly* while Horst is busy publicizing it. The duo hopes to raise a significant portion of their $5,000 museum restoration fund through box-office sales. They have raised $900 so far through individual donations.

Raising money is only part of their plan. Neither Horst nor Dieleman is Jewish, and they believe study of the Holocaust should emphasize people over religion.

"This isn't about our religion or family backgrounds," remarks Horst, a first-year student at Wooster. "Jews were targeted and exterminated for nothing more than being Jewish, and that's what we want people to realize. Our goal is to make the audience see that people are people, no matter how different they seem."

However, "the Holocaust was not just a crime against the Jewish people, it was a crime against all humanity," Horst continues, citing the millions of non-Jewish Poles, Serbs, homosexuals and other so-called "undesirables" who perished. "We want the audience to really feel for the people portrayed, not because they share a common experience or a common background, but because they are people, too."

Butterfly focuses on a girl named Raja, who narrates the tale with flashbacks of her home life in Prague before the war, followed by her grim existence in the Terezin ghetto. "This play is a voice for people like her," taking the Shoah (Holocaust) beyond mere facts and numbers seen in history books, says Dieleman, who also directed and acted in a production of *Butterfly* at her Michigan high school.

A second-year history/pre-law major with a minor in theater, Dieleman wanted to direct the play ever since seeing an adaptation of it her junior year in high school. She traveled with her businessman father, Dale, to Prague during her senior year, and visited the Terezin site where so many suffered.

She saw the overcrowded quarters, the crematorium, and a Jewish cemetery where each marker represented the ashes of 300 people.

Even more affecting were the mixed images of hope and despair, reflected in the artwork and writings of Terezin's children, which Dieleman saw in the museum: Pencil and watercolor pictures depict work brigades, threatening guards, and deportations the children witnessed. Other drawings show a lighted menorah and figures scaling mountain peaks to liberation. Much of their children's poetry was about returning home or the bleakness of their current situation.

The innocence of these works made an impression on Dieleman. "It was all so honest—these kids were too young to be jaded," she says.

Horst had never heard of Terezin until she met Dieleman at the beginning of the school year. They became fast friends and, on a whim, they went to Wooster High School to ask if they could put on the play. To their surprise, their request was granted immediately. The time since has been spent gathering young actors from the high school, and both young women are excited about opening the show next weekend.

They know how easy it is to get angry about what went on in Terezin. But "only by appreciating what happened to people in the Holocaust can we prevent such atrocities in the future," Horst notes. "If the audience sees people just like them murdered for no other crime than being who they were, they can see why promoting tolerance and understanding is such an important cause."

Source: Douglas J. Guth, "Another *Butterfly* Taking Wing in Wooster: College Students Raise Funds for Terezin Museum, Promote Tolerance with Production of Play," in *Cleveland Jewish News*, Vol. 88, No. 1, April 4, 2003, p. 32.

Suzanne Weiss
In the following review, Weiss discusses the effect of the play on the youth involved in its production.

An estimated 15,000 Jewish children passed through the gates of the Terezin concentration camp during the Holocaust. About 100 lived to tell the tale.

Eight East Bay youths have been struggling with those statistics in recent rehearsals for the upcoming Moraga Playhouse production of *I Never Saw Another Butterfly* in Orinda.

Walking around backstage, wearing ragged coats onto which yellow stars are sewn, the young actors who have grown up in Walnut Creek, Lafayette, Orinda and Berkeley acknowledge that it's sometimes hard to relate.

"All my life I've been called Laiah and to think somebody could come in and say "Hey, Number 5074. . .," said 11-year-old Laiah Idelson of Walnut Creek, looking down at the number on the placard she wears around her neck as one of the camp's inmates.

Idelson, who is Jewish, has read a lot about the Holocaust. "But now I feel like this is more than just reading. This is all true," she said.

Playwright Celeste Raspanti based her reconstruction of life in Terezin on the true story of Raja Englanderova, one of the survivors of the Czechoslovakian camp. The script was augmented by the journals, poems and pictures that made Terezin's children famous in the book and touring exhibit *I Never Saw Another Butterfly*.

In the play, Raja journeys from childhood to adulthood, hanging onto life and her Jewish identity with courage, humor and concern for others.

Youths make up more than half the play's cast. A number of them are Jews. The playhouse specifically sought Jewish youths for the roles, sending out audition notices to synagogues, Jewish youths groups and other Jewish organizations in the East Bay.

Fourteen-year-old Alyssa Stone, who is Jewish, plays Raja. It is not an easy role for her.

"If I let myself really believe I was there, I couldn't do my lines," said Stone, of Lafayette. "I have to put this kind of transparent protective envelope around myself. I have an empathy for her, but sometimes I feel like I'm plagiarizing a pain I've only heard about."

Evan Brody, 15, of Berkeley plays Raja's boyfriend, Honza. He looks at the role with a there-but-for-the-grace-of-God attitude.

"It's hard not to let your emotions drown you out in the play," said Brody, who is Jewish. "But if my grandparents hadn't left when they did, this could have been the story of my family and I wouldn't even be here.

"It's a sad subject. But it's good in a way and happy because we can do this show for people who may never have known the stories, the poems, the songs."

One of those who might not have known is 11-year-old Josh VanLandingham of Pleasant Hill.

Josh, who is Catholic, said that studying about the Holocaust led him to audition for this show. He came to *Butterfly* from a production of *Cinderella* in Concord.

"I can relate to castles," he said. "I've seen a castle. But this is more serious."

He added that it's "kind of cool to learn about another religion though. My friend invited me to his bar mitzvah and it was good that I could go and see" what it was like.

I Never Saw Another Butterfly is Moraga Playhouse's third Holocaust-based drama in recent seasons. The playhouse, which now uses a local high school's theater for its productions, staged *Kindertransport* earlier this year and *Diary of Anne Frank* in 1995.

Playhouse founder and artistic director Cliff Beyer, however, said he isn't choosing the plays simply because they're about the Holocaust.

"It isn't necessarily so much that these are Holocaust shows but that I have a strong desire to explore man's inhumanity to man, especially in this century."

Source: Suzanne Weiss, "Young *Butterfly* Actors Grapple with Holocaust Theme," in *Jewish Bulletin of Northern California*, Vol. 102, No. 38, September 25, 1998, p. 25.

Dawn Gibeau

In the following interview, Gibeau asks two theologians, one Catholic and one Jewish, about their work to promote interfaith understanding through I Never Saw Another Butterfly.

Rabbi Max A. Shapiro and Karen Schierman, a Catholic, take turns sitting at the only desk in their shoebox of an office. Its size belies its significance, for this is the nerve center of the Center for Jewish-Christian Learning at the University of St. Thomas, and they constitute its core staff.

Theirs is the kind of enterprise that works to create understanding, to counteract ignorance and prejudice. Such ignorance and prejudice made possible a recent national report that one in five Americans is willing to believe the Holocaust never happened.

The center is unique in influencing the national and international academic sphere as well as the local community, in having a rabbi at its head and in publishing regularly.

From here, 6,000 copies of each year's Proceedings emanate to readers around the world, sharing the content of local lectures that many in the field characterize as on the cutting edge of academic dialogue. This year's topics relate to the Jewishness of Jesus. Previous topics have ranged from anti-Semitism to the novel as religious experience.

No one has ever turned down a request from the genial Shapiro to participate in the lectures—not preacher-politician Pat Robertson, not Israeli scholar-statesman Abba Eban, not Chicago Cardinal Joseph Bernardin, not Nobel Prize winner Elie Wiesel or Pulitzer Prize journalist Thomas L. Friedman, not novelist Rabbi Chaim Potok or Andrew Greeley.

The lectures are only one way the center carries out its mission, which Shapiro says is primarily to bring increased understanding of Judaism to the Christian community and secondarily to increase the Jewish community's understanding of Catholicism.

The center does not grant academic degrees or offer a Jewish studies program. However, each semester it offers classes for credit to undergraduates and students in the university's School of Divinity.

Typical courses are in basic Judaism or the Judaism of American Jews. The center also arranges for St. Thomas seminary students to study in Israel at the Hebrew Union College-Jewish Institute of Religion as well as at Catholic centers.

Locally, "people think we are the source of all wisdom," said Shapiro, so Minnesotans contemplating Jewish-Christian marriage bring their questions. So do people wondering about possibilities of employment in Jewish-Christian relations, said Schierman.

The center aims high. It is developing an interfaith library Shapiro said he hopes will become the best in the Midwest, and it sends Jewish speakers into area Catholic schools and churches as well as Catholic speakers into synagogues and temples.

Its newest project is helping to finance production next fall of the play *I Never Saw Another Butterfly*, about Jewish children's World War II experiences at Terezin transit concentration camp near Prague, in what was then Czechoslovakia. Based on a book of the same name, the play was written by Celeste Raspanti, director of special projects for the university's development office.

The center evolved from the friendship of two businessmen, the late Thomas Coughlan, and Sidney Cohen, both of whom served on the St. Thomas board.

In 1983, the friends concocted a trip for themselves, for Temple Israel's senior rabbi, who at the time was Shapiro, and for Msgr. Terrence Murphy, then president and now chancellor of St. Thomas.

Shapiro said the plan was that he would show the Catholics Jewish Jerusalem, and the Catholics would help the Jews learn more about Catholic Rome. Murphy had long hoped to establish an identifiable Jewish presence at St. Thomas.

By the time they returned to Minnesota, Coughlan and Cohen's vision was on its way to reality, for Murphy asked Shapiro to write a proposal for it. He did, and Coughlan and Cohen agreed to raise funds in their respective Catholic and Jewish communities.

Shapiro became director of the new center in 1985. However, be credits Arthur Zannoni, now a center consultant and then an associate professor of Old Testament, with working out the myriad details involved in starting the center.

Through the center, Shapiro has brought the Jewish presence Murphy sought to St. Thomas. "For Jews, it helps educate Christians about Jewish history, traditions and values," he told the university magazine. "It creates a community in which they can live as Jews with an understanding of Christianity and without apprehension."

And for Christians, he said, "the center offers the opportunity to recognize their relationship with Judaism, to understand their background and contemporary Jewish life, and to put into practice the current teachings of the Vatican about Jews and Judaism," notably that Jews did not crucify Christ.

In Washington, D.C., the Holocaust Memorial Museum was dedicated in April. The center may inaugurate a course on the Holocaust next year, and Shapiro said he hopes the St. Paul area will host the 1995 or 1996 International Conference on the Holocaust.

Shapiro, now 76, said the remembering and the dialogue are vital. Jews "couldn't possibly have the powers prejudice has endowed us with," he said.

To Rabbi Herman E. Schaalman, too, such dialogue as the center sponsors is crucial.

Schaalman, rabbi emeritus of Emanuel Congregation of Chicago, said during the center's 1991 program on the Holocaust: "If this sort of dialogue had happened in the interwar years in Germany, I would be almost willing to wager that Hitler could not have done what he finally was able to do."

Source: Dawn Gibeau, "Two Faiths Meet on Common Ground," in *National Catholic Reporter*, Vol. 29, No. 29, May 21, 1993, p. 5.

John W. Conner

In this review, Conner describes the origin and the dramatic text of I Never Saw Another Butterfly.

Current interest in drama as a form of classroom communication has created an unprecedented demand for good plays geared to the interests and concerns of adolescents. *I Never Saw Another Butterfly* is a dramatization of the lives of the Jewish children of Czechoslovakia who were temporarily interned at Terezin, a stopping-off place on the way to the gas chambers of Auschwitz. Terezin was a place of false hope for these children, but it could also have been a place of terror except for the efforts of Irena Synkova, a teacher who created a school out of sheer determination and the meager materials each child brought with him to Terezin. Irena's school provided a sense of normalcy to which her adolescent pupils could cling.

The script for *I Never Saw Another Butterfly* was created from the poems, diaries, letters, and journals of a student who was liberated at the close of the war. In many ways the script is ideal for classroom presentation: the properties required for production are simple ones, the staging is easily adapted to a schoolroom. Most important, an understanding of the characters is within the grasp of high school students. The children of Terezin are lonely, frightened, and fearful; but they are also capable of love and respect, and they are naturally curious, and usually hopeful.

I Never Saw Another Butterfly is a dramatic tribute to the depths of human faith. This reviewer feels dramatic literature in use in schools might well concern itself with this important philosophical principle.

Source: John W. Conner, Review of *I Never Saw Another Butterfly*, in *English Journal*, Vol. 62, No. 5, May 1973, pp. 828–29.

SOURCES

Bernzweig, Julie, Christina Carpenter, Sarah Mayhall, and Lorena Quintana, "History of German Children," in *Tulane University*, http://www.tulane.edu/~rouxbee/kids04/germany/_ccarpen2/history.html (accessed July 23, 2009).

Friedan, Terry, and Bill Mears, "Demjanjuk deported to Germany," in *CNN.com*, http://www.cnn.com/2009/CRIME/05/11/us.demjanjuk/ (accessed July 23, 2009).

Gillis, Charles, "American Cultural History: 1970–1979," in *Lone Star College-Kingwood Library*, http://kclibrary.lonestar.edu/decade70.html (accessed July 23, 2009).

"The Nuremberg Trials: Timeline," in *PBS: American Experience*, http://www.pbs.org/wgbh/amex/nuremberg/timeline/index.html (accessed June 15, 2009).

Raspanti, Celeste, *I Never Saw Another Butterfly*, Dramatic Publishing, 1980.

Raspanti, Celeste, "Where Does a Play Begin?," in *Dramatic Publishing*, http://www.dramaticpublishing.com/AuthorsCornerDet.php?titlelink=9775&sortorder=1 (accessed June 15, 2009).

Roland, Jay, "Play to Portray Holocaust Episode," in *Sarasota Herald Tribune*, October 29, 1996, p. 2B.

Schaefer, Margret, "German Parliament Bans Use of Corporal Punishment in Child Rearing," in *Project NoSpank*, July 24, 2000, http://www.nospank.net/deut.htm (accessed July 23, 2009).

Swain, Rebecca, "Theater Review: 'I Never Saw Another Butterfly' at Orlando Rep," in *OrlandoSentinel.com*, April 1, 2008, http://blogs.orlandosentinel.com/entertainment_stage_theat/2008/04/theater-review.html (accessed June 15, 2009).

"Theresienstadt: The 'Model' Ghetto," in *Jewish Virtual Library Online*, http://www.jewishvirtuallibrary.org/jsource/Holocaust/terezintro.html (accessed June 15, 2009).

United States Holocaust Memorial Museum, http://www.ushmm.org/ (accessed June 15, 2009).

Valentine, Rebecca, Interview with Celeste Raspanti, June 20, 2009.

FURTHER READING

Boyne, John, *The Boy In the Striped Pajamas* (movie tie-in edition), David Fickling Books, 2008.
    In 1942 Poland, nine-year-old Bruno has just moved to a new home and has no friends. Fifty feet from his home stands a barbed-wire fence that runs as far as the eye can see. Bruno watches what happens on the other side of that fence from his bedroom window and eventually befriends a young Jewish boy who lives there.

Lowry, Lois, *Number the Stars*, Laurel Leaf, 1998.
This Newbery-winning novel is the story of a
ten-year-old girl who risks her own life to save
that of her best friend in 1943 Denmark.

Schroeder, Peter W., and Dagmar Schroeder-Hilde-
brand, *Six Million Paper Clips: The Making of a Children's Holocaust Memorial*, Kar-Ben Publishing, 2004.
The all-white Whitwell Middle School in Tennessee taught ethnic and cultural diversity by
focusing on the Holocaust. In order for students
to grasp how many people were murdered by
the Nazis, they collected six million paper clips
and stored them in a railcar. This is the story of
that memorial project, complete with photographs and interviews.

Volavkova, Hana, *I Never Saw Another Butterfly*, Schocken,
1994.
Originally published in Czech, this English translation features the poetry and artwork of the
children of Terezin Concentration Camp.

Wiesel, Elie, *The Night Trilogy: Night, Dawn, Day*, Hill &
Wang, 2008.
First published in 1960, *Night* is the autobiographical account of Elie Wiesel and his father
in Auschwitz Concentration Camp. *Dawn* (1961)
tells the story of a young man who survived
World War II and becomes active in a Jewish
underground movement. In *Day*, which was
previously published as *The Accident* in 1962,
Wiesel questions the limits of the human spirit.

Light Shining in Buckinghamshire

CARYL CHURCHILL

1976

Caryl Churchill's *Light Shining in Buckingham-shire* depicts the conflicts surrounding the English Civil War (1641–1651), particularly the years 1647 to 1649. Rather than emphasize the eventual execution of King Charles I or the action of the war itself, Churchill's drama focuses on the lives and struggles of ordinary English citizens.

Light Shining in Buckinghamshire explores the themes of collective identity and what it means to be free while illustrating the multifaceted challenge to authority that fueled the English Civil War. These themes are central to Churchill's body of work, and in this particular play, she mixes historical facts and characters with fictional dialogue and characters. Her people speak as they did in seventeenth-century England, and there is sparingly used controversial language toward the end of the play.

Individualism is not important in *Light Shining in Buckinghamshire*; rather, Churchill's interest lay in the portrayal of groups of people and how they were affected by their circumstances during this major political and religious upheaval under Charles I. Because this drama is based on history, readers and viewers need a working knowledge of that time period in order to understand the significance of the dialogue and perspectives presented.

The play is available as a book published by Theatre Communications Group.

Caryl Churchill (Gemma Levine Hulton Archive / Getty Images)

AUTHOR BIOGRAPHY

Churchill was born on September 3, 1938, in London, England. After World War II, her family moved to Montreal, Quebec, Canada, where Churchill lived until the late 1950s. At that time, she returned to England to attend Oxford University, from which she graduated with a degree in English in 1960.

Churchill's first play, *Downstairs*, was written and performed in 1958, while she was still a student. That play won an award at the *Sunday Times* National Union of Students Drama Festival. She wrote two more student drama group plays before marrying lawyer David Harter in 1961. She and her husband have three sons.

In 1962, Churchill began writing radio plays for the British Broadcasting Corporation (BBC), the largest broadcasting corporation in the world. Soon she was writing television plays for the BBC as well. Most of her radio and television plays have been adapted for the stage. Her first professional stage production, *Owners*, premiered at the Royal Court Theatre in London in 1972.

Throughout the 1970s and 1980s, most of Churchill's time was spent collaborating with theater companies, such as the Joint Stock Theatre Company and the feminist Monstrous Regiment. It was during this period that she wrote *Light Shining in Buckinghamshire* (first performed in 1976, published in 1978). She spent a year as

resident dramatist at the Royal Court Theatre from 1974 to 1975.

Churchill's early plays, including *Light Shining in Buckinghamshire*, reflect her socialist views and explore historical events. She gradually became more focused on gender and feminist themes, and by the mid-1980s she was collaborating with choreographers and composers to incorporate dance-theater techniques into her plays. Churchill's willingness to experiment with dramatic form puts her in the category of postmodern playwrights.

Churchill has received numerous awards for her work, including four Obies (*Village Voice* off-Broadway Awards).

Churchill has written dozens of radio, television, and stage plays and has translated other plays. Her most recent work, a ten-minute history of Israel that ends with the Israeli attack on Gaza, is titled *Seven Jewish Children*. After debuting the play at London's Royal Court Theatre, Churchill published it online and approved free download and use as long as the producers include a collection for money to benefit the people of Gaza at the end of the event.

PLOT SUMMARY

Light Shining in Buckinghamshire differs from most stories in that it does not have a plot. Churchill wrote the drama as a series of short scenes, each one intended to be interpreted and understood on its own and without the influence of surrounding scenes.

Act 1

COBBE PRAYS

Cobbe recites a prayer out loud. He repents for feelings of lust and for swearing. Mostly, Cobbe repents for having enough to eat while so many do not, and he regrets kneeling before a "greedy, cruel, hypocritical" king.

THE VICAR TALKS TO HIS SERVANT

The vicar asks his servant how his new baby is faring, and the servant replies that the baby is very ill, no better than before. The vicar claims that suffering is part of life and is the path to heaven.

MARGARET BROTHERTON IS TRIED

Two jailers (JPs) interrogate and try the homeless Margaret Brotherton for begging in a parish other than the one in which she was born.

The JPs explain that the parish cannot provide for outside beggars, only for its own. They find her guilty and sentence her to be stripped to the waist and beaten as she leaves the parish.

STAR RECRUITS

Star presides over a prayer meeting. He gives a speech in which he declares the kingdom as belonging to the Antichrist. Star equates fighting against the king with sainthood and gives voice to the belief held by many: When parliament and the king have been defeated, Christ will come in person and rule over England.

In an attempt to recruit men to fight the government, he encourages them by saying:

> And who are the saints? You are. The poor people of this country. When Christ came, did he come to the rich? No. He came to the poor. He is coming to you again. If you prepare for him by defeating Antichrist which is the royalists. If you join in the army now, you will be one of the saints. You will rule with Jesus a thousand years.

Thomas Briggs signs up on the spot.

BROTHERTON MEETS THE MAN

Brotherton walks along with bags of things—junk, mostly—that she has collected. She meets a man who encourages her to seek warmth. Brotherton refuses, saying that the warmth will not last and so it is of no value to her. The man wishes he knew when Christ was coming; Brotherton expresses doubt that he is coming at all.

BRIGGS JOINS UP

As Briggs signs up to join the army, he asks Star how long it will be until the fighting ends. Star responds that the Royalists are the Antichrist and that the army will fight as long as it takes for men to be free and own their own land. He informs Briggs that the army values godliness. Star asks Briggs if he can take orders. Briggs states he will take orders if they do not go against God. Briggs tells him the orders cannot be against God in God's army.

HOSKINS INTERRUPTS THE PREACHER

The preacher gives a sermon in which he approves of fighting the king and asks who the saints are. Going against the rule that women do not speak out in church, Hoskins answers that everyone is a saint. The preacher says saints are those who have been chosen by God. Others are eternally damned, and no human can add to or take away from either number.

Hoskins disagrees, and soon the two are publicly arguing several of the beliefs and points that the preacher is trying to explain. When the preacher rebukes Hoskins for speaking out and recites Scripture indicating the submissive role women are expected to take, Hoskins fires back with more Scripture that proves God gives women the power to prophesy.

The preacher eventually has Hoskins thrown out of church and damns her.

CLAXTON BRINGS HOSKINS HOME

Claxton rescues Hoskins after the church people physically beat her. His wife washes her wounds, and the two women begin talking. Hoskins shares her Ranter perspective on sin and Christ's second coming, while Claxton's wife explains the traditional views of women:

> We bear children in pain. . . . And they die. For our sin, Eve's sin. That's why we have pain. We're not clean. We have to obey. The man, whatever he's like. If he beat us that's why. We have blood, we're shameful, our bodies are worse than a man's. All bodies are evil but ours is worst. That's why we can't speak.

Claxton explains that the way things are going, poor folk cannot survive. He likens life in revolutionary England to a sea of salt water. Fish can live in it; men cannot. The gentry are fish and can thrive; poor people are mere men and will die.

COBBE'S VISION

The scene opens with an actor reading actual text from a pamphlet written and published in 1649 by Abiezer Coppe, the man on whom Cobbe's character is based. It is a warning that Christ is returning to earth

TWO WOMEN LOOK IN A MIRROR

A woman comes in with a broken mirror and shows it to another woman, who is mending. The mirror was taken from the squire's (landowner's) house. His house has been ransacked by those who have worked the land for him, now that there is excitement and hope for equality among the classes.

The first woman explains to the second that there is an even bigger mirror still in the house, one in which they can see their entire bodies at once. She says, "They must know what they look like all the time. And now we do."

This is an important scene because it epitomizes (provides a good example of) the lack of self-identity women had in revolutionary England. They did not know themselves, or "see" themselves, completely; the revolution gives them hope of the opportunity to do just that.

BRIGGS RECALLS A BATTLE

Briggs remembers a battle scene in which he could not identify whom he was hitting with his musket. Was it someone from his own side or the enemy? As the smoke from all the gunfire clears, a thought occurs to him: It does not matter who is who because they were not really fighting each other, but the Antichrist, and everyone would be made free to enjoy paradise.

THE PUTNEY DEBATES

This scene marks the turning point in the play. It includes text from the actual debates and is the longest scene in the drama. Act 1 is full of hope and the promise of heaven on earth. For a brief moment, when the king is defeated, it appears as though victory has been reached. People of England were excited at the idea of taking control of their lives.

The Putney Debates were attended by soldiers, their generals and other officers, and civilians who met to negotiate terms for governing a new England. Soldiers of the New Model Army, led by Oliver Cromwell, largely embraced the beliefs and desires of the Levellers. Cromwell and other officers of the army refused to approve any compromise that would involve overthrowing King Charles. By the end of the debates, the Levellers felt betrayed by the very men who led them in battle. Act 2 reflects this sense of betrayal and disappointment.

The demands of the Levellers included universal male suffrage, meaning that every adult male would have the right to vote; the disbanding of the current parliament; an elected parliament that would hold elections every two years; a House of Commons (as opposed to a king and lords) with ultimate authority; freedom of conscience; freedom of forced servitude in the army; and full equality of all in the eyes of the law.

Upon hearing Sexby read the list, Cromwell states the obvious when he comments on the magnitude of alterations the list contains. Those in attendance debate the demands. In particular, General Ireton takes issue with the idea that all men should own land. His concern is that without constraints, people will rise up and take land that belongs to others simply because they want it. Colonel Rainborough, a Leveller, resents

Ireton's implication that freedom to own land without limits of birthright implies that the poor are in favor of anarchy. He claims that divine law—the "thou shalt not steal" of the Bible—will keep order. Ireton does not understand why Rainborough is offended. He believes there should be rights to property, but limited rights.

Rainborough wonders aloud what they have all been fighting for, if not laws and liberties. Wildman agrees and reminds everyone in the room that England's laws were made by its conquerors, a fact that led to unjust law. Ireton and Colonel Rich hold that giving all men an equal voice in representation is not in England's best interest. When Ireton continues to insist that property is given not by God or the law of nature but by human constitution, Sexby is disheartened:

> We have ventured our lives and it was all for this: to recover our birthrights as Englishmen.... There are many thousands of us soldiers that have ventured our lives; we have had little property in the kingdom.... Except a man hath a fixed estate in the kingdom, he hath no right in this kingdom. I wonder we were so much deceived.

Sexby goes further and reminds the officers that the kingdom has been preserved by the very men it has enslaved and wants to continue to enslave. Ireton wants to keep the current constitution that gives property only to a select few. Rainborough counters with the claim that the soldiers have all along, then, fought only to keep themselves enslaved.

The scene and act end with the two parties at odds; Cromwell decides to form a new committee. Those who gave years of their lives to the service of the army are left with betrayal, which sets the tone for Act 2.

Act 2

DIGGERS

This brief scene explains that for the Diggers, land equals freedom.

CLAXTON EXPLAINS

Claxton explains how he became a Ranter.

BRIGGS WRITES A LETTER

Briggs and Star talk about the new council formed by Cromwell at the end of the Putney Debates. The new council does not include anyone but officers. Star wants to see the letter Briggs is writing; it is not really a letter but a list of proposals. Despite the fact that he is no longer invited or allowed to speak at the council to represent the Levellers, he will not give up the effort toward equality. Star tells him he is wasting his time, but Briggs ignores the claim. Star reminds him that the army is executing Levellers now, and Briggs counters that this is happening because the army has given itself absolute power—it is no better than the tyrant king.

Star warns Briggs about going against God's army, and Briggs tells Star that the army is not on God's side.

THE WAR IN IRELAND

The army moves into Ireland to try to take control of its territories.

THE VICAR WELCOMES THE NEW LANDLORD

Star becomes squire of land confiscated during the war. He plans to grow crops, but he is unsure of how to get rid of the beggars and homeless people living on his land.

A WOMAN LEAVES HER BABY

Two women talk after they have journeyed far. One of them had planned to abandon her baby, who is starving to death, on the steps of a house. Now that they have walked a long distance, the woman is having second thoughts and finds she cannot leave her baby behind. The other woman tries to convince her that she is doing the right thing. The baby is dying, not even crying, and there is no food available for the woman to eat so that she can produce milk. The scene ends without the woman making a decision.

A BUTCHER TALKS TO HIS CUSTOMERS

The butcher tells his customers they have had enough meat, that they eat so much of it there is nothing left for other people who are starving. He tells them he will cut no more meat for them because "You've had your meat. You've had their meat. . . . You cram yourselves with their children's meat. You cram yourselves with their dead children."

LOCKYER'S FUNERAL

Lockyer is a Leveller leader who is executed by the army. Thousands of citizens accompany his body on the funeral march through the town. Several weeks after the funeral, the Leveller movement is crushed.

THE MEETING

Those who were betrayed by and defeated in the revolution—Cobbe, Claxton, Hoskins, Brotherton, Briggs—and a drunk meet in a pub and start drinking as they lament the events that have befallen them. During the course of conversation, each one mentions how he or she was disillusioned over the past seven years. Briggs is a broken man who no longer believes Christ is coming to create heaven on earth. Claxton argues that God will come, that man will be so perfect that the landlords will repent for stealing the land.

Brotherton has come to believe she is wicked because she is weak in the flesh. She claims to be evil and shameful, full of sin. She had a baby and killed him on the day he was born by putting him in a bag and throwing him in a ditch. Even though the bag moved, Brotherton walked away. While Cobbe and Claxton try to convince her she is not with sin, only Briggs understands the seriousness of what she has done and asks God to help her.

The drunk claims to be God.

AFTER

The final scene of the play features the same characters who were at the meeting in the previous scene. They talk about what happened to them after the Restoration (when the king was restored to the throne). The drunk stays drunk. Brotherton continues to be a beggar who steals to eat. Hoskins believes Christ really did return and nobody noticed. Cobbe laments the passing of the Blasphemy Act because he can no longer claim to be God. Briggs lives in a field and eats nothing but grass. Sometimes, people come to watch. Claxton moved to Barbados and recognizes that nothing in England has changed.

CHARACTERS

Briggs

Briggs is a regular man who joined the army for no other reason than to feed his family. He is representative of his entire social class. Initially, he is not overtly political or idealistic, but as the war drags on, he becomes increasingly aware of the underlying political and religious aspects of the conflict and joins the Leveller movement. Briggs becomes more vocal about his discontent when he realizes the New Model Army is not going to make a difference for ordinary families. (This army was formed by Parliamentarians during the war and is available to fight anywhere in the country. Unlike traditional armies, its soldiers are full-time and are not associated with any political seats in Parliament or elsewhere.)

Briggs's newfound ideology leaves him disillusioned, yet he remains in service to the army and continues to hope for a more equal distribution of wealth. By the end of the play, he has stopped eating everything but grass. He is nothing and has nothing.

Margaret Brotherton

Margaret Brotherton is a homeless woman who is tried for vagrancy and found guilty. She is beaten and forced to leave town.

Claxton

Claxton is based on a real person, Laurence Clarkson. He is a Ranter and a traveling preacher. Clarkson eventually turned his back on his Ranter beliefs and published an autobiography called *The Lost Sheep Found* in 1650. Until the end of the play, however, Claxton remains committed to his belief that human perfection is possible because God is in all things. In the play's last scene, Claxton is sorrowful that the revolution has changed nothing, and he is unwilling to admit the loss of the possibility of spiritual perfection.

Claxton's Wife

Claxton's wife represents the traditionally held idea that women are evil. She believes that women deserve the pain of childbirth, the physical abuse delivered by husbands, and the status of second-class citizens. She holds that women would not be punished so if there were not a good reason. She and Hoskins disagree as to the value of women in society.

Cobbe

Cobbe is based on a real person named Abiezer Coppe. Like Claxton, he is a Ranter. Cobbe claims to experience spiritual visions, and like many of his day, believes the moment of Christ's second coming is near.

Oliver Cromwell

Oliver Cromwell is one of the play's nonfictional characters. Cromwell was a member of Parliament and eventually the leader of the New Model Army. He participated in the Putney Debates and is largely credited with transforming England into a commonwealth (a republic in which people have an impact on the government).

In the play, Cromwell appears in the Putney Debates scene.

First Woman and Second Woman

Women had no voice and virtually no power in society. More than anyone else in the play, they are limited in speech. These two characters appear only in the scene "Two Women Look in a Mirror." The First Woman loots her former squire's home and takes items. The Second Woman is encouraged to steal a blanket for herself.

Hoskins

Hoskins is a vagrant female preacher. She is mistakenly considered by many to be a beggar, an accusation she counters by saying she gets paid in food for her preaching. Hoskins speaks out against the preacher during a sermon and is beaten up and forcibly removed from the town. This character represents the Ranter point of view: God is in everyone and everything, and all people will be saved when Christ returns to create heaven on earth.

General Ireton

Henry Ireton is based on the real Henry Ireton, the son-in-law of Oliver Cromwell and a general in the parliamentary army. He appears in the Putney Debates scene as the voice against extremist views, including the demands of the Levellers, whom he considers dangerous and impractical. Although the historical Ireton favored retaining the constitution of King, Lords, and Commons, he eventually recognized the uselessness in trying to negotiate with Charles I. Ireton signed the king's death warrant.

Preacher

The preacher represents the fire-and-brimstone religious beliefs held by most of seventeenth-century England. He claims there is no sin in fighting against an unjust king in the name of God. God has chosen those people who will be saints and those who will be damned, and no mere human can change the outcome. The preacher denounces Hoskins as eternally damned for her beliefs and for challenging him in public.

Colonel Thomas Rainborough

Thomas Rainborough is another nonfictional character who played an important role in the Putney Debates. A leading spokesman for the Levellers, Rainborough was eventually murdered by four Royalists. He appears in the play only in the Putney Debates scene.

TOPICS FOR FURTHER STUDY

- With one other person, choose sides: Digger or Ranter. Research each faction and find similarities and differences in beliefs and actions. Together, create a poster illustrating these points.

- View the fifty-minute movie *Brother against Brother: The English Civil War* from the DVD boxed set by Kultur Video (2007). Make a list comparing and contrasting how the film version of the war and those it affects differs from the play. What similarities do the two versions share?

- Pretend you are Charles I. Choose any point during the English Civil War and write a detailed diary entry. Talk about what is going on, your concerns, and the fate of England.

- Research the clothing and culture of seventeenth-century England. Draw a scene from the Putney Debates, using as much detailed accuracy as possible.

- Research the music popular in England during the Civil War. Find a copy of a piece and play it for the class on a musical instrument.

- In small groups, write, design, and produce a pamphlet written from the point of view of a Royalist or a Parliamentarian (any faction) using computer software. Make copies to share with your classmates.

- With a partner, choose to be either an interviewer or Churchill. Conduct a live interview; asking questions about this play and her other works. Why does she write about the topics she chooses? What influences her work? Research Churchill, but be creative and come up with some of your own answers so that the interview is a mix of fact and fiction.

- Create a comic strip regarding the English Civil War. The comic can be done by hand or using a computer program.

- Read *Major Sanderson's War: The Diary of a Parliamentary Cavalry Officer in the English Civil War* (2009) by P. R. Hill and J. M. Watkinson. Find evidence in the diary to illustrate which side Major Sanderson would have supported in the war. Report your findings in an essay.

Colonel Nathaniel Rich
Nathaniel Rich is based on the actual Parliamentarian army officer of the same name. In the Putney Debates, Rich was a voice of reason and compromise.

Edward Sexby
Another real-life character, Edward Sexby is a Leveller in the Parliamentarian army. During the Putney Debates, Sexby demanded immediate votes for all Englishmen and opposed any efforts of negotiation with Charles I. Sexby eventually attempted to assassinate Oliver Cromwell and died during his imprisonment for the crime. In the play, Sexby appears in the Putney Debates scene as a voice for the commoner.

Star
Star is a corn merchant whose political leanings are not known. He recruits Briggs into the army. In the second act, once Royalist lands have been confiscated, Star becomes the landlord of an estate, the land of which he wants to plow and plant. He is unsure what to do with the vagrants and beggars squatting on his land.

John Wildman
John Wildman's character is based on a real person who joined the Parliamentarian army in 1646 and helped form the Leveller party. Wildman participated in the Putney Debates and eventually tried to overthrow Oliver Cromwell. He served prison time but was released after Cromwell died. In the play, Wildman is a civilian and writes the Leveller pamphlets. His character appears only during the Putney Debates, where he argues in favor of overthrowing the king.

Winstanley
Gerrard Winstanley was a failed cloth merchant who played a key role in establishing the Digger

Women picket outside the Trico factory in Great West Road, London, during the equal pay for women dispute in 1976. (*Popperfoto / Getty Images*)

faction. Diggers believed all private property should be confiscated and divided evenly among all citizens.

THEMES

Individualism

Individual identity is important in *Light Shining in Buckinghamshire*. Churchill wants the audience or reader to believe that group identity and need are more important than individual identity and desire. She makes this point especially through characterization. Ideally, the play is performed using only six actors to portray twenty-five characters. Her goal here is not to fully develop each character but to show that individuals shared common traits, beliefs, and desires in the transitional and chaotic times of the English Civil War. In her production notes, Churchill states, "When different actors play the parts what comes over is a large event involving many people, whose characters resonate in a way they wouldn't if

they were more clearly defined." Understanding exactly who a viewer is seeing is not as important as understanding what that character represents.

Freedom

Throughout the play, discussion between characters ultimately return to what it means to be free. For some, it means having a voice and raising it when necessary. For others, it involves fair representation by those who make laws. But for everyone, freedom is equated with owning property. Through that ownership come independence and the means to provide for one's family. Only by owning land can England's working and peasant classes find freedom.

God

A common religious belief during the English Civil War was that Christ, who had left earth for heaven, was returning to prepare heaven on earth. Preachers warned of this second coming and encouraged all to repent for their sins. Women, according to common biblical interpretation of the day, were sinful, dirty, and shameful. In the play, the female preacher Hoskins portrays the beliefs of the Ranters: God is everywhere and in everything and everyone. Churchill leaves it up to the audience to decide the nature of God as she presents both sets of beliefs but does not provide any easy answers.

STYLE

Dialogue

Churchill's play includes minimal action; the entire play is performed using one table and six chairs for props. If a scene does not require a table or chairs, the actors themselves move the furniture to the sides of the stage and watch the play from there. All progression of the play relies solely on the dialogue between characters.

Epic Theater

Light Shining in Buckinghamshire was written in epic theater style. This style was popularized by the playwright Bertolt Brecht, whose works Churchill studied extensively. The play is a collage of smaller scenes, each which can be understood by itself, without the influence of other scenes in the play. In her production notes for the play, Churchill says, "Each scene can be taken as a separate event rather than part of a story. This seems to reflect better the reality of large events like war and revolution where many people share the same kind of experience." There is no climax, just a string of scenes, one following the other, but the order would not necessarily matter.

Another aspect of epic theater is simple set design. Actors play multiple roles. In Churchill's play, there are twenty-five characters, but it is suggested that only four male and two female actors play all the parts.

Realism

Churchill's characters use realistic speech common in seventeenth-century England: "we are come," "fain," "hath," and so on. In addition, she incorporates actual text and testimony from the Putney Debates in 1647 and various biblical passages. In doing so, Churchill gives a sense of realism to her play.

HISTORICAL CONTEXT

The conflict known as the English Civil War is actually a series of three wars (1642–1646; 1648–1649; 1649–1651) fought between the Parliamentarians and Royalists. It is also known as the English Revolution and the Great Rebellion.

Charles I

Earlier civil wars in England were concerned with who ruled the country; this war was more concerned with *how* the country was ruled. In 1625, England's king was Charles I. He was not well liked by Parliament (the legislative, or law-making, branch of England's government) because he was an autocrat, an absolute ruler with infinite power. He abused that power relentlessly.

By 1639, Charles had lost in the war against Spain, England's primary enemy. At the same time, the Scots rebelled against England for religious reasons and invaded the kingdom. The only way to save it was to request Parliament's help in raising money to fund the conflict. The Scots occupied most of northern England, and soon Ireland joined the revolt. Charles needed Parliament's support, but relations were so strained that Charles was forced to agree to Parliament's demands before its members would come to his rescue.

Charles had no problem with the political reforms. But when Parliament gave him its list of religious reforms, things got worse. Supporters of the king were called Royalists, or Cavaliers. The other side, those who wanted to see an end to or at least a serious reform of the Anglican Church, was called the Parliamentarians, or Roundheads. This group included most Puritans, including an extremist group called the Levellers. This faction demanded annual sessions of Parliament, payment of its members, and suffrage (right to vote) for all citizens. Basically, they wanted an end to privilege based on birthright.

Diggers and Ranters

Among this radical group was another, smaller faction made up of commoners called Diggers. They considered themselves the true Levellers because they wanted all land to belong to all people. Traditionally, only nobles and the upper class owned land; everyone else had to work that land under poor conditions and payment. Diggers were agricultural communists: they believed in equal distribution of all land to all people and an end to government.

Another radical movement of commoners was called the Ranters. Considered blasphemous by the Puritans, Ranters were self-proclaimed messiahs, prophets, and mystics who believed God is in everyone and everything. They believed they were infused with the Holy Spirit and so were removed from sin. Ranters were associated with nudity, which they embraced as a form of social protest. For them, conventional rules and norms of society did not apply. The Ranter movement, which lacked organization and leadership, was at its peak from the late 1640s through the late 1650s.

Power Struggle and the Putney Debates

By spring of 1642, Parliament and Charles struggled over power. Parliament ordered the military to report to it rather than to the king. Charles raised his own army in retaliation, and the first war began. By May 1647, each side could claim both victory and defeat, and a compromise was reached. Charles agreed to accept some of the religious reform demands and give Parliament control of the army for a specific number of years. Parliament, in turn, ordered the current army to disband. The army refused and took possession of the king. The rogue army now had all the power.

In June, the army demanded the arrest of eleven members of Parliament for the "crime" of negotiating with the king in secret. Parliament refused to turn over its members, and the army camped outside London. Members of the army debated what to do, since they were in the unique position to act against both king and Parliament. These discussions were known as the Putney Debates because they took place in the fields of Putney.

The Levellers wanted a new and improved elected Parliament that truly represented the people (with the exception of the poor and servants). Members would be voted upon by England's working class. There would be no king and no houses of lords or commons. The Diggers made clear their desire for an end to private property and the existence of government altogether.

Military and political leader Oliver Cromwell did not like the tone of the debates and ordered the Levellers back to their regiments. When they resisted, Cromwell arrested three and killed one, thus ending the Putney Debates.

The End of War

Cromwell eventually became leader of Parliament. The royalists were defeated, and Charles I was executed for treason. This event was a major turning point in England's history, as it was the first time the public authority had executed a king. The non-noble classes had grown in size and strength, and it was a clear message of the power of religion as a political force.

The Diggers were not satisfied with the beheading of the king; they revolted even more because they felt little had changed. Cromwell ordered more executions, and soon the Levellers disbanded altogether.

Light Shining in Buckinghamshire

The title of Churchill's play was taken from the title of a political pamphlet published by the Diggers in 1649. In it, they state, "You great Curmudgeons, you hang a man for stealing, when you yourselves have stolen from your brethren all land and creatures." This was the sort of emotion underlying the revolution of seventeenth-century England.

Rather than tell the story of England's war in terms of battles won and lost, Churchill chose to focus on the beliefs and hopes of the people who would be most affected by the war's outcome. Those who fought against the king believed Christ was soon returning to earth, where he would establish heaven. Every action, every thought, stemmed from that belief.

Light Shining in Buckinghamshire illustrates that exciting time when the king has been defeated and the possibilities are endless. Soon, though, the Diggers and Levellers are defeated and betrayed. Those victims turn to the other radical movement, the Ranters, who embody that last revolutionary cry before capitalism claims the kingdom.

Churchill explains in the foreword to her play:

> The simple 'Cavaliers and Roundheads' history taught at school hides the complexity of the aims and conflicts of those to the left of Parliament. We are told of a step forward on today's democracy but not of a revolution that didn't happen; we are told of Charles and Cromwell but not of the thousands of men and women who tried to change their lives. Though nobody now expects Christ to make heaven on earth, their voices are surprisingly close to us.

COMPARE
&
CONTRAST

- **1640s:** This is a major transitional time period for England. Religious and political ideologies and beliefs are colliding, and it is an era of revolution and revolt.

  1970s: Again, this is a transitional era in England's history, when citizens are at a crossroads of optimism and cynicism. It is a time of increased labor strikes, government-imposed wage freezes, and serious economic instability. England's people are feeling underrepresented and ignored. Britain finds 1976 a humiliating year, as it is forced to request a bailout from the International Monetary Fund.

  Today: A global economic crisis grips society, and England experiences a deep recession (decline in economic activity). Political parties feud over government spending issues, and the government freezes students loans and grants in the wake of the recession. England is in turmoil politically and economically.

- **1640s:** Women are relegated to traditional roles of wife and mother. Those who break away from social norms are punished severely, often in the village square.

  1970s: The women's movement is in full swing in England, as it is in America. Laws are passed to ensure that women get the same pay as men for doing the same job, but that equality never quite manifests.

  Today: Again, parallel to America, women today can be found in all fields of the business sector, though they still are not being equally compensated for the work they do. Feminist literature is enjoying a renewed interest as it connects with activists from decades ago, as well as young women.

- **1640s:** Between the 1540s and the 1640s, the cost of living in England increases a drastic 700 percent.

  1970s: The British pound is worth $2.40 in U.S. dollars. Inflation in 1972 is 7.1 percent; it jumps to an all-time high of 24 percent in 1975.

  Today: Economic experts are comparing the current economy to that of the 1970s. The British pound is worth approximately $1.65.

CRITICAL OVERVIEW

Light Shining in Buckinghamshire did not receive much attention when it first hit the stage in 1976. By the early 1990s, it was generally well received. Critic Julia M. Klein labels the play "brilliant" in her 2006 article for the *Chronicle of Higher Education*. Most critics agree with this assessment, but they also agree on the main drawback: The play makes demands on its audience.

In his theater review for the *Nation*, critic Thomas M. Disch praises the play. "As a poetic statement of the general situation of leftists living in a period of reaction, I can think of no work of comparable power." In Disch's opinion, *Light Shining in Buckinghamshire* outshines Churchill's other plays, which he heralds as "some of the finest plays of the last two decades."

That said, Disch also points out that despite good reviews of the play in 1991, the play makes intellectual demands on its audience and "even more dismayingly, it would help to know something about English history." These requirements limit the appeal of the drama.

Critic Roy Sander, in *Back Stage*, calls Churchill an "interesting writer" but considers *Light Shining in Buckinghamshire* the work of an "immature playwright, not yet versed in some of the rudiments of her craft." He dislikes the use of the same actor to portray several characters and the "tedious talk about God."

Illustration depicting the English Civil War: the storming of Bristol by Prince Rupert and his Royalist forces (Getty Images)

More than two decades after it was written and first performed, *Light Shining in Buckinghamshire* enjoyed a new sense of relevance. In a 1997 article for the London *Guardian*, British journalist Fiachra Gibbons explains:

> It's hard to imagine a play set in the aftermath of the Civil War being bang-on the moment, yet this is. . . . The play hasn't changed since 1976, but we have. The world has turned upside-down.

Gibbons is referring to the political state of England in 1976. It was an era of republicanism (in which a country is governed by an elected charter that has all official power, as opposed to a democracy, in which, theoretically, the majority rules). Parliament at the time was under heavy scrutiny for its behavior, which many Britons felt was out of sync with the desires and needs of the majority of citizens who had elected them. The overall atmosphere of England in the 1970s was one of unrest and political dissent. The ideas and beliefs of Diggers, Ranters, and

Levellers, therefore, were more easily understood by modern British people.

CRITICISM

Rebecca Valentine

Valentine is a freelance writer who holds a B.A. in English with minors in philosophy and professional communications. In this essay, she considers Churchill's Light Shining in Buckinghamshire *from a feminist perspective and questions its lack of female representation.*

The English Civil War was a time of great transition. It was a major turning point in English history as, for the first time, ordinary citizens rallied against the king's rule. More lives were lost in this war, in proportion to the population at the time, than in World War I. Some of those lives belonged to professional soldiers, some to

WHAT DO I READ NEXT?

- Christopher Hill's *The World Turned Upside Down: Radical Ideas during the English Revolution* (1984) explores the beliefs of the era's radical groups, including the Diggers and Ranters, as well as the social and emotional impulses that led to them.

- *Oliver Cromwell and the Rule of the Puritans in England* (2006) was first published in 1900. Written by Sir Charles Firth, it is the only balanced account of Cromwell's personal and professional life.

- Geoff Kennedy's 2008 book titled *Diggers, Levellers, and Agrarian Capitalism: Radical Political Thought in Seventeenth Century England* provides a detailed look into the radical movements that fed the English Civil War.

- *Civil Wars in Africa* was written by William Mark Habeeb in 2006. Written for young adults, the book analyzes past and current cultural, political, historical, ethnic, and religious conditions that have led to civil war since 1960.

- *Visionary Women: Ecstatic Prophecy in Seventeenth-Century England* is Phyllis Mack's 1995 study of radical prophecy in medieval England.

- Michael Braddick's *God's Fury, England's Fire: A New History of the English Civil Wars* (2009) is unique in that it explores not only the wars themselves but their cultural and social implications. This history volume, almost eight hundred pages long, shows how everyone, from pamphleteers to witch hunters and petitioners, was mobilized in the decade of conflict that would shape modern-day England.

- John Davenport's *The Age of Feudalism* (2007) begins with the fall of the Roman Empire and traces the history of European feudalism from the fifth century onward. Geared toward younger readers, the book contains colorful illustrations and informative sidebars.

- Author Keith Roberts and illustrator Angus McBride have published *Soldiers of the English Civil War, Volume 1: Infantry (Elite)* (1989) and *Soldiers of the English Civil War, Volume 2: Cavalry (Elite)* (1990). Rather than focus on accounts of people or events, these two volumes provide a visual reference that includes details on uniforms, military structure, and troop training; quotations from primary documents; and graphics of equipment and weaponry. The illustrations make this set appealing to all ages.

---

untrained civilians. Some belonged to women. Women, arguably more than any other subgroup, were the greatest dissenters in society during the years of the war. They broke out of traditional gender roles in nearly every conceivable way and took liberties where none were offered. Given these bold steps, women and the challenges they faced during the English Civil War are underrepresented in Churchill's *Light Shining in Buckinghamshire*.

Of the twenty-five characters in Churchill's play, only five are female. Two of those characters appear in just one scene. Churchill's goal was to present not the war itself but the lives of the ordinary citizens who would be most affected

by the conflict's outcome as well as its action. However, the play presents only a snapshot of women's lives in seventeenth-century England. Even within the limitations of the play (minimal stage props, historical fact mixed with fiction, and an emphasis on the cultural and social implications rather than the war itself), the audience and reader could be presented with more information to provide a more balanced understanding of women's role in that society at that time.

SELF-IDENTITY

The scene "Two Women Look In a Mirror" most obviously illustrates the results of the subjugation of women in rural England. For the first time, these two peasant women are seeing themselves—really seeing themselves. They have a sense of identity apart from any and all else. The first woman tells the second that there is an even bigger mirror still at the squire's house, one in which she can see her whole body. Here, the whole body is symbolic for the whole woman.

Despite their relative absence in Churchill's play, women were remarkably active in the English Civil War on a variety of levels. Some expressed their dissent by standing alongside the men in battle. They served as regular soldiers, some obviously women and others disguised as men. The situation became so threatening to the social order that King Charles banned women warriors from dressing like men.

In addition to fighting, women exacted revenge on the soldiers who threatened their families during wartime. Such dissent was not relegated to the peasantry and working class. In a *Daily Mail* article titled "Uncivil War: The English Civil War Divided Families and Proportionally Took More Lives Than World War I; As a New TV Drama Reveals, It Was Also the First War Fought Out between Spin Doctors," writer Julian Champkin reports that "highborn ladies actually commanded castles under siege while their husbands were away fighting." Nowhere in Churchill's play does the idea of dissent at such a physical level present itself.

SCANDALOUS BEHAVIOR

Churchill does show how some women chose to break out of gender restrictions in the scene titled "Hoskins Interrupts the Preacher." Hoskins has taken to preaching on the move, mobile only because no parish will allow her to stay. She was a member of the outspoken Ranter sect, which promoted free love and the idea of a sinless existence. Prior to the emergence of such sects, women had no voice, either individually or collectively. By joining with those who shared a set of values and beliefs, they gained a sense of control over their lives. Like Hoskins in the play, this already marginalized community (women) felt that the price they paid—ostracism and public damnation—was worth the benefit of no longer being overlooked and ignored.

We do not find women who practice witchcraft in the play, or at least none that claim to do so, and yet England had experienced an explosion of witch hunts as the Civil War broke out. Historians believe women claimed to be witches

for a number of reasons, some not so surprising. According to the *History Review* article "Dissent and Debauchery: Women and the English Civil War" by Alison Jones and others, some women truly believed they had magical powers, while others were simply mentally imbalanced. Still others enjoyed the power such a claim gave them. Jones and her coauthors write, "In a patriarchal society women were expected to be submissive to men; witchcraft therefore gave them a greater authority, as everyone feared them because of their powers."

Some historians believe women used a confession of witchcraft to explain their suicidal feelings or depression. In seventeenth-century England, good and bad were talked about in terms of God and the devil. Although suicidal thoughts and depression are dealt with today as symptoms of distress, back then they would have been considered the work of the devil. Many concepts we now know are normal and merely signs of something else were then believed to be unnatural. As the authors of "Dissent and Debauchery" point out,

> Many women must have looked long and hard at themselves and their roles as mothers, wives and neighbours. If they did not conform to society's views as to how they should act then some convinced themselves that they were witches.

REVOLUTION FOR ALL?

Churchill does include women in her play, and the few scenes these women occupy give the observant reader or viewer important information. But why not paint for us the whole picture? Was the omission of information deliberate? Was it considered superfluous to the point the play is supposed to make? Janelle Reinelt of Cambridge University calls Churchill "arguably the most successful and best-known socialist-feminist playwright to have emerged from Second Wave feminism." Why, then, do women receive so little attention in her cultural and social analysis of the English Civil War?

It is possible that Churchill's feminist treatment of her body of work did not flourish until after she wrote *Light Shining in Buckinghamshire*. As author, she is entitled to include whatever information she wishes in her plays. It is also quite possible that Churchill intentionally left the reader or viewer with an incomplete picture of women's lives during the English Civil War in an effort to make a point: Women, the most marginalized subset of society, remained thus throughout the English Civil War.

Although she never explicitly indicates that she empathizes with the Levellers, Diggers, or Ranters, she does make clear that even in a revolutionary atmosphere, women continue to be subjugated. In the scene "Hoskins Interrupts the Preacher," the closing line belongs to the preacher as he says, "Woman, you are certainly damned." It is up to individual interpretation to figure out whether the preacher is speaking solely to Hoskins or in general, about all women.

Given that the English Civil War was the first revolution fought by a literate population of commoners, it would have been interesting and enlightening to hear more from and about the female perspective in *Light Shining in Buckinghamshire*. Some women did keep diaries and journals. Perhaps Churchill is beseeching her audience to ask of themselves, How successful can a revolution be if its own warriors continue to subjugate its women?

Source: Rebecca Valentine, Critical Essay on *Light Shining in Buckinghamshire*, in *Drama for Students*, Gale, Cengage Learning, 2010.

David Benedict

In the following interview, Benedict talks with Churchill talk about her life after critical successes and about her body of work.

If you could stop MORI polling people about their voting intentions for a few seconds and persuade them to ask people to name this country's greatest living dramatist, most people would probably plump for Harold Pinter or David Hare. Regardless of their incontestable stature—plays as good as *Old Times* or *Racing Demon* don't fall exactly from the trees—a substantial body of opinion would place Caryl Churchill at the top of the list. Only last week, Mark Ravenhill, author of last year's surprise hit... wrote: "I read *Top Girls* at least once a year and I weep. One day, I think, one day I'll write something as good."

For those unlucky enough never to have seen Churchill's definitive play about the 1980s—a dazzlingly dramatic and politically astute analysis of what it took to rise to the top—which the *Guardian* awarded the backhanded compliment of being "the best play ever from a woman dramatist"—there's some late news just in. It's unofficial, unannounced and unbelievably overdue, but 1997 is the year of

> **THEATRE IS A MUCH MORE PUBLIC ARTFORM AND CHURCHILL HAS TAKEN THAT TO HEART, MAKING IDEAS, EMOTIONS AND STRUCTURE INDIVISIBLE."**

Caryl Churchill. Earlier this year, the National Theatre's tour of her 1976 play set around the English Civil War, *Light Shining in Buckinghamshire*, opened at the Cottesloe; *Cloud Nine*, her magnificently funny and sharp-witted modern classic about patriarchy, patriotism and sexual politics is back in a major revival at the Old Vic; *Hotel*, her latest collaborative piece for the trailblazing dance/music-theatre company Second Stride opens in London next week; and her new double-bill *Blue Heart* will open at the Edinburgh Festival in August. All of which goes some way to making up for three barren years.

Her astonishingly ambitious *The Skriker*, a vast social panorama with Kathryn Hunter as a shape-shifting underworld creature, which took Churchill years to write, opened at the National in 1994 to the bafflement of many, who were misled by the production. Others hailed it as a masterpiece. But since then, apart from her translation of Seneca's *Thyestes* for the Royal Court, the rest has been silence. You could be forgiven for thinking that she'd given up writing. You'd be right. Happily, though, she's had a change of heart; yet the playwright continues to be elusive, shying away from the media circus surrounding the business of theatre. Like much of her finest work, *Top Girls* was directed by Max Stafford-Clark. He deals with her reticence very simply: "She really wants the work to express what she's doing."

Fair enough. This isn't the disdainful aloofness of some theatrical grande dame. In fact, when she finally accedes to my request to meet during rehearsals for *Hotel*, she's thoughtful and generous and anxious to dispel any suggestion of frosty, lofty indifference. She apologises for seeming "difficult" but points out the absurdity of our meeting. "It's an odd kind of conversation," she muses, "there's more going on than just two people in a room. You're doing your job. It's going to be read by a lot of people, and when it's printed, it has a definitive quality which then gets quoted back at you 15 years later. It's also not a conversation because it's so one way. . ." And then, all of a sudden, the guarded nervousness gives way to laughter. "Never mind," she says, the shutters opening to reveal a welcoming smile leaping across her face.

She was an only child. Her father, a cartoonist, and her mother, a fashion model, moved from London to Montreal when she was 10, and she began writing short stories and producing living-room pantomimes. At 14, she wrote a full-length children and ponies book and was also improvising plays with a friend. "We would work out in some detail what was going to happen and we would play it, and, if we hadn't quite liked how it went, we would play it again." During her time at Oxford at the end of the Fifties, she won first prize at the National Student Drama Festival with her play *Downstairs.* Her first work to receive a professional production was *The Ants,* a radio play, a form which suited her because there was a market for it (and no fringe theatre in the early Sixties) and because she was raising her children.

The (then) estimable theatre journal *Plays and Players* declared *Light Shining in Buckinghamshire,* in which different actors played the same character, to be "one of the finest pieces of English playwrighting for years," but the big break came three years later in 1979 with *Cloud Nine.* Like *Light Shining,* it was written for Max Stafford-Clark's company Joint Stock and its dynamite cast (including Julie Covington, Antony Sher and Miriam Margolyes) who were wittily embracing gender-bending long before anyone dreamed of the term. Joint Stock pioneered a collaborative approach to playwriting, something which has had a marked effect on Churchill and scores of writers since. "It was very exhilarating because it was a completely different way of working." Wasn't it scary giving up authorial control? "Yes, a little bit, but there's a misconception sometimes that the actual writing process becomes collaborative. Some companies create wholly devised plays but I've never gone that far into collaboration." Joint Stock's method was based on an extended workshop / research period, after which the writer would go away and write. "And then there is more rewriting in rehearsal because you've got a group of people you work with and trust. And they trust you because you've all shared that research time.

I would be much more open to changing things than if it had been something I had written alone."

Since then, Churchill's work has split between plays created on her own and those that have grown out of collaboration, notably the dance/theatre works *The Lives of the Great Poisoners* and the forthcoming two-part *Hotel,* both written with long-term co-conspirators choreographer Ian Spink and composer Orlando Gough for Second Stride. "*Hotel* started from an idea I had of something which might work as an opera with Orlando, which was of eight lots of people in eight rooms, which would appear on stage as one room." Eyebrows might be raised at the idea of a dance company presenting an opera, but if anyone can pull it off, it's these three whose experience, versatility and sheer success rate with formal experiment is matched by no one in this country except Lloyd Newson and DV8.

"She reinvents herself every time," says Stafford-Clark, who points to Churchill's constant formal experimentation in the creation of overlapping dialogue in *Top Girls* or her comedy of City greed, *Serious Money,* written entirely in (deeply unfashionable) verse. Despite British Telecom's refusal to allow the use of its phones on stage ("This is a production with which no public company would wish to be associated"), it transferred to the West End and became a smash hit. Stafford-Clark, however, admits to finding her challenge terrifying. "She asks you to do things that haven't been done before. You think, 'Maybe it won't work, and we can't do it'." He obviously thrives on the terror, though, and you can hear the thrill in his voice as he prepares to team up again for *Blue Heart.* Other playwrights are more famous, he concedes, but then counters: "Her influence has been enormous and not just on other writers. You go into schools and you tell them 'We're doing some plays by Caryl Churchill' and that she might be involved and teachers faint and genuflect. She shaped the way they teach and think about drama."

When Churchill began writing, virtually the only other major female dramatist was Agatha Christie. Perhaps her most significant move was the shift away from the semi-autobiographical stance adopted by women novelists. Theatre is a much more public artform and Churchill has taken that to heart, making ideas, emotions and structure indivisible. I point out that almost none of her plays follow the traditional route of the journey of a single protagonist, an idea that surprises her. She mulls it over. "When I was working with Joint Stock, I think there was a strong anti-sentimental feeling about in theatre. There was an attraction to making continuities with dramatic ideas rather than going a long way down an emotional journey...which didn't mean there wouldn't be very emotional things." That's certainly borne out by the poignant final image in Tom Cairns's new production of *Cloud Nine*, where the mother confronts the ghostly image of her younger self.

With all this year's burst of dramatic activity, can it be true that, three years ago, she stopped writing? She tenses up again. Then relents. "Oh, I don't mind..." She runs a long hand through a mane of silver hair. "I just got bored with it. That feeling of 'Was I going to start thinking about another play just because I was a playwright?' I've had it before. I remember that, in 1978, I decided I definitely wasn't going to be a writer any more. It took me about four months to get out of my head the idea that I was a writer and once I'd done it, of course, I started writing again." Her laughter fills the chilly rehearsal room. She looks at me, confidingly, her gaunt, gravely beautiful head resting on one hand. "I think I wanted to wait until I missed it."

Source: David Benedict, "The Mother of Reinvention," in *Independent* (London, England), April 19, 1997, p. 4.

Helene Keyssar

In the following excerpt, Keyssar analyzes the unconventional political and gender-based aspects of Light Shining in Buckinghamshire.

...Churchill was less satisfied with [*Objections to Sex and Violence*] than with any of her other scripts. Rather than retreating to more conventional dramaturgy, however, she pressed even more firmly against the boundaries of theatrical illusion with her next play, *Traps,* in which two women and four men live in a communal relationship that has few constraints and a continually plastic structure. The title of the play is ironic, for the characters are paralyzed by the anarchy of the totally communal and therefore relativistic society they have created. The "random permutations" of the relationships are evidence of the multiplicity of simultaneously available roles so central to Churchill's vision, but the deliberately contradictory messages in the play are so unrelieved that the drama has difficulty escaping its own spinning. We are not caught within *Traps,* but remain outside it and excluded from it.

Still searching for a context for her work that would be aesthetically challenging and allow her political integrity, Caryl joined with an alternative theater company, the Joint Stock Company, in 1976 to create *Light Shining in Buckinghamshire.* Founded in 1974 by Max Stafford-Clark, William Gaskill and David Hare, Joint Stock was committed to a collective, ensemble rehearsal process and to creating a theater that was unquestionably political without being doctrinaire. Actors and designers as well as playwrights and directors were expected to think and talk about the texts and about themselves. In their first production, an adaptation of William Hinton's *Fanshen,* the company made the decision to evolve activities for rehearsal that involved the playwright with the actors in the evolution of the script. In what might seem to be an obvious gesture, but one that is decidedly rare in theater, actors were repeatedly asked to describe and then show what they thought was the political point of a scene (Itzen, p. 221). Once actors extended their interest from the conventional modern focus on what the character desires or does to the balances of power, authority and obligation in a given framework, the style of performance moved toward a Brechtian epic theater mode. Such a context was ideal for the uncompromising non-naturalistic approach of Caryl Churchill.

In her introduction to the published text of *Light Shining in Buckinghamshire,* Churchill describes how the play evolved:

First of all, Max Stafford-Clark and I read and talked till we had found a subject in the millenial movement in the civil war. There was then a three-week workshop with the actors in which, through talk, reading, games and improvisation, we tried to get closer to the issues and the people. During the next six weeks I wrote a script and went on working on it with the company during the five-week rehearsal period.

It is hard to explain exactly the relationship between the workshop and the text. The play is not improvised: it is a written text and the actors did not make up its lines. But many of the characters and scenes were based on ideas that came from improvisation at the workshop and during rehearsal....Just as important, though harder to define, was the effect on the writing of the way the actors worked, their accuracy and commitment. I worked very closely with Max, and though I wrote the text the play is something we both imagined.

Four years later, Churchill told me that this process was both exhilarating and exhausting, "much harder work in most ways than writing alone." The effort paid off, however, for both the production and the play were consistently applauded for their clarity of vision and commitment. *Light Shining in Buckinghamshire* retained many of the stylistic elements of *Owners* and *Objections to Sex and Violence*—short, self-enclosed Brechtian scenes, furniture reduced to a table and six chairs and minimal hand-props, a non-psychological depiction of characters, and company songs that interrupt and comment on the action. But it also gave its audience a coherent experience of historical change that raised serious questions about the past and the present.

Paradoxically, while both the seventeenth-century civil war setting for *Light Shining . . .* and the Joint Stock Company were male-dominated, it was with this play that Caryl was first unqualifiedly commended as a feminist. The most obvious source of this response was Churchill's emphatic attention to the sexual and political oppression of women in a historical period—the late 1640's in England—that is often described as revolutionary and liberating. In a cast of twenty-five characters, only five are women. But the women in the play ably claim their space.

The most extraordinary of these women, Hoskins, is a Ranter who believes that the millennium is at hand and that with it will come both economic and sexual freedom. Transcendent in her faith, she names falsehood and hypocrisy as she sees them in language that respects neither sexual nor social convention; her outrageous assertions repeatedly deflate the manipulative and deceiving rhetoric of the men of state. Margaret Brotherton, a vagrant beggar, functions as our reminder of what Hoskins might be without her illusory belief in the imminent arrival of Jesus Christ. And Hoskins' faith is far from orthodox; when Brotherton protests entering a holy meeting, saying, "No, I'm wicked, all women are wicked, and I'm—" Hoskins retorts, "It's a man wrote the Bible." Brotherton is a victim of poverty and her own acceptance of her servile status as a woman; Hoskins is a victim of her ideology, but, at least for a time, her commitment gives her a strength unavailable to Brotherton.

Equally striking are characters identified only as 1st Woman and 2nd Woman who reveal the particular sufferings of poor women in an emerging capitalist society; precisely because of their anonymity, these women make an unsentimental appeal to our sympathy. In contrast to other images of women during periods of war, Churchill's women do not suffer because of the deaths or defeats of their men, but because they have lost the most by the defeat of a genuinely egalitarian movement. In this play, as in *Owners,* there is no separating the evil that ensues from the ownership of property from the impoverishment of the lives of women. In Hoskins' vision of the world about to dawn, "we'll have no property in the flesh. My wife, that's property. My husband, that's property." The message is clear, more in tune with the epigrammatic assertions of other feminist plays of the seventies, and with studies of the biases of ordinary language, than with Churchill's earlier dramas.

Churchill distinguishes her feminism in the theatrical approach to this play and in its historical perspective. To emphasize the distinct angle of her vision, Churchill urged that the characters not be played by the same actors each time they appeared. In the original production presented at the Traverse Theatre in Edinburgh in 1976, six actors played all of the twenty-five roles, and characters were presented by one actor in one scene and another in the next. Churchill's most immediate intention in using this device was "to reflect better the reality of large events like war and revolution where many people share the same kind of experience (Churchill, "Note on Production"). In addition, however, the device politicizes the theatrical convention of transformations, initiated in experimental theater in the sixties and potently adapted by many feminist playwrights in the seventies. In theatrical transformations, actors paradoxically deny and reinform the magic of what Michael Goldman has called the actor-as-character by revealing rather than concealing change. In transformational exercises and episodes, actors gradually and subtly alter their facial masks, vocal tones, mimed objects. In *Light Shining . . .*, as in Ntozake Shange's *For Colored Girls . . .* or Megan Terry's *Comings and Goings,* the script requires role transformations to emphasize the commonality of the stories told and to reject the old hierarchies of theater. Theatrical transformations demand intense focus and precision and remind us that our awe of the actor derives at least in part from the confirmation that *we* can become other, that *we* can change. But transformations also assert the collective nature of theatrical performance, the interdependency of all those on stage, and undermine our often desperate desire to hook our empathy and admiration to a star, or leader. That it has been feminist theater groups and women playwrights who have sustained, explored and extended this gesture is consistent with a more widespread struggle against male authoritarianism. . . .

Source: Helene Keyssar, "The Dramas of Caryl Churchill: The Politics of Possibility," in *Massachusetts Review*, Vol. 24, No. 1, Spring 1983, p. 198.

SOURCES

Adiseshiah, Sian, "Utopian Space in Caryl Churchill's History Plays: *Light Shining in Buckinghamshire* and *Vinegar Tom*," in *Utopian Studies*, Vol. 16, No. 1, Winter 2005, pp. 3–27.

Bonner, Bill, "Ruined by Good Luck," in *HoweStreet.com*, http://www.howestreet.com/articles/index.php?article_id=9993 (accessed July 26, 2009).

Buse, Peter, "Caryl Churchill," in *ContemporaryWriters.com*, http://www.contemporarywriters.com/authors/?p=auth259 (accessed July 6, 2009).

Champkin, Julian, "Uncivil War: The English Civil War Divided Families and Proportionally Took More Lives Than World War I; As a New TV Drama Reveals, It Was Also the First War Fought Out between Spin Doctors," in *Daily Mail* (London, England), February 5, 2005, p. 13.

Churchill, Caryl, *Light Shining in Buckinghamshire*, Theatre Communications Group, 1997.

Disch, Thomas M., "Light Shining in Buckinghamshire," in *Nation*, Vol. 252, No. 13, April 8, 1991, p. 459.

Gibbons, Fiachra, "In the 1660s, They Cut the Tongues from Levellers' Mouths. Now They Just Arrest Them," in *Guardian* (London, England), January 11, 1997, p. 6.

Hackett, Douglas, "Light Shining in Buckinghamshire: A Complete Revolution?," in *English Review*, Vol. 10, No. 2, November 1999, p. 31.

Jones, Alison, Harjit Dulay, Jennifer Cobley, Joanne Hammond, Lisa Purcell, and Laura Barlow, "Dissent and Debauchery: Women and the English Civil War; A Group of Second-Year Students from Southampton University Present the Results of a Collaborative Research Project," in *History Review*, No. 47, 2003.

Klein, Julia M., "Caryl Churchill's Identity Crisis," in *Chronicle of Higher Education*, May 26, 2006.

Knox, E. L. Skip, "History of Western Civilization: English Civil War," in *Boise State University*, http://history.boisestate.edu/WESTCIV/english/ (accessed July 6, 2009).

Louth, Nick, "Back to the 1970s Economy?," July 10, 2008, in *MSN.com*, http://money.uk.msn.com/investing/articles/nicklouth/article.aspx?cp-documentid=8854840 (accessed July 26, 2009).

Reinelt, Janelle, "The Cambridge Companion to Modern British Women Playwrights, 11: Caryl Churchill and the Politics of Style," in *Cambridge Collections Online*, http://cco.cambridge.org/extract?id=ccol0521594227_CCOL0521594227A015 (accessed July 6, 2009).

Sander, Roy, Review of *Light Shining in Buckinghamshire*, in *Back Stage*, Vol. 32, No. 8, February 22, 1991, p. 44.

FURTHER READING

Bernstein, Jonathan, *Knickers in a Twist: A Dictionary of British Slang*, Canongate, 2006.

> This humorous reference book is a useful guide for Americans wanting to truly understand what the British are saying. Bernstein is a screenwriter and columnist for the *Guardian* (London) who uses his wit to tackle what could be a dry subject. Some of the selected terms date back two hundred years.

Lacey, Robert, *Great Tales from English History: A Treasury of True Stories about the Extraordinary People—Knights and Knaves, Rebels and Heroes, Queens and Commoners—Who Made Britain Great*, Back Bay Books, 2007.

> This encyclopedia-like reference book includes more than 150 stories of people both famous and not so well known. He dispels common myths surrounding time periods and people. For instance, Pilgrims did not wear shoe buckles, which did not come into fashion until the late 1660s.

Light Shining in Buckinghamshire, 1648, http://www.arxists.org/history/england/english-revolution/light-shining.htm.

> This is the text from the original pamphlet published by the Digger faction during the English Civil War.

Purkiss, Diane, *The English Civil War: Papists, Gentlewomen, Soldiers, and Witchfinders in the Birth of Modern Britain*, Basic Books, 2007.

> Like Churchill's play, this historical analysis focuses on the human, cultural, and religious perspectives of the English Civil War. It includes excerpts from letters and diaries as well as tracts from the Putney Debates and other primary sources of the era.

Robert Johnson: Trick the Devil

BILL HARRIS

1993

Bill Harris's *Robert Johnson: Trick the Devil* is a play inspired by the legend surrounding the historical blues musician Robert Johnson. According to the legend, Robert Johnson met the devil at a crossroads in the Deep South and sold his soul in exchange for unparalleled guitar-playing skills. Harris's play is set in 1938, the year the real Johnson died. Harris's character Robert Johnson, who is being pursued by a white man named Kimbrough, finds himself at a "jook joint" owned and operated by a woman named Georgia. ("Jook joint" is the term used to describe an African American bar where music, dancing, and gambling are the primary attractions. Jook joints first arose in the South during the late 1800s.) Johnson soon becomes the object of Georgia's affection, while Kimbrough confesses his desire to hear Johnson's story about the deal he made with the devil. By the play's end, Johnson has finally told his story, revealing to Kimbrough, and the others, that he tricked the devil at the crossroads, realizing as he played that he had no need of the devil's bargain after all. Johnson, however, is poisoned by Georgia's estranged husband. After Johnson's death, Kimbrough asserts that Johnson did in fact sell his soul to Satan, and that is the sole reason that Johnson was able to play guitar with such skill, thereby rejecting Johnson's own accounting of the alleged incident.

Originally staged in 1993 in New York's New Federal Theatre, Harris's play is available in the 1995 anthology *The National Black Drama Anthology:*

Eleven Plays from America's Leading African American Theaters, edited by Woodie King, Jr., and published by Applause Theatre Books.

Content Advisory Note: Harris's play contains some sexuality and violence that may be deemed objectionable for middle-grade readers.

AUTHOR BIOGRAPHY

Little has been published about Harris's life. He was born in 1941 in Anniston, Alabama, and raised in Detroit, Michigan, from the age of two. After attending Cass Technological High School as a teen, Harris later went on to study at Wayne State University. Harris received both his bachelor of art and master of art degrees (his master's in 1977) from Wayne State University. He has written plays, poems, and literary criticism. In the 1980s, Harris worked as the Production Coordinator for Jazzmobile, a non-profit organization providing free jazz concerts in New York City, and for the New Federal Theatre in New York. Three of his own plays were staged during his time in New York, including *Robert Johnson: Trick the Devil* in 1993, as well as *Stories about the Old Days* (first staged in 1986 and published in 1990), and *Every Goodbye Ain't Gone* (first staged in 1984 at the Colonnades Theater Lab and published in 1989 in *New Plays for the Black Theatre*, ed. Woodie King, Jr.). *Robert Johnson: Trick the Devil* was staged at the New Federal Theatre and directed by Woodie King, Jr. After returning to Detroit, Harris served as the Chief Curator at Detroit's Museum of African American History. Following his work as curator, Harris began working first as an associate professor, then as a professor of English at Detroit's Wayne State University. He has been awarded a Rockefeller Foundation Writer-in-Residence Grant for a comedic drama about jazz, titled *Coda* (published in 1990, with the drama *Riffs* as *Riffs and Coda*). Other awards include a Theatre Communications Collaboration Grant for Artists and the Distinguished Arts Achievement Award from Wayne State University.

PLOT SUMMARY

Prologue

In the prologue to *Robert Johnson: Trick the Devil*, two vignettes (brief scenes) play out. In the first, which the stage directions inform us takes place in

MEDIA ADAPTATIONS

- The 1986 film *Crossroads* explores the Johnson myth of meeting the devil at the crossroads, but there is only an allusion to Johnson, and the film is set in modern times. The film stars Ralph Macchio, is directed by Walter Hill, and produced by Columbia Pictures. It is available on DVD through Sony Pictures (2004).

- *The Search for Robert Johnson* (1991) is a documentary exploring the life and myth of Robert Johnson. The film is directed Chris Hunt and produced by Sony Music Corporation. It is available on DVD through Sony (2000).

- The 1997 documentary *The Life and Music of Robert Johnson: Can't You Hear the Wind Howl?* explores the life and myth of Johnson and is narrated by Danny Glover; it features Eric Clapton as himself and singer Keb Mo as Johnson. The film is directed by Peter Mayer and available on DVD through Shout Factory (2003).

- The 2000 documentary *Hellhounds on My Trail: The Afterlife of Robert Johnson*, directed by Robert Mugge, is available on DVD through Winstar.

- The 2000 film *O Brother, Where Art Thou?*, directed by Ethan and Joel Coen, stars George Clooney, John Turturro, Tim Blake Nelson, John Goodman, and Holly Hunter. It includes a reference to a young bluesman named Tommy Johnson that parallels the Robert Johnson crossroads myth. The film is available on DVD through Touchstone (2001).

- *Robert Johnson: Trick the Devil* was awarded the 1977 Silver Medal for Drama by the International Radio Programming Festival for a half-hour version that aired on the Public Broadcasting System.

1937 in Texas, Robert Johnson is singing in a hotel room that has been converted into a recording studio. The voice of a recording engineer instructs

Johnson, who does not respond but sings when he is instructed to. In the second vignette, the blind piano player, Stokes, is smoking a cigarette in Georgia's bar, "Georgia Mayberry's Colored Jook Joint," in 1938. Stokes speaks to the audience, saying that he will reveal what happened when Robert Johnson died.

Act 1, Scene 1

The first scene of the play begins with Georgia and Stokes discussing the weather and how much food Georgia needs to have prepared at the bar. When Georgia spies a man walking toward the bar, she and Stokes speculate on who it might be and what he might want. Robert Johnson enters and asks if the Greyhound bus stops at the nearby crossroads. Having already observed that he is attractive, well-dressed, and carrying a guitar, Georgia begins to flirt with Robert, who returns her interest. Robert retires to a room upstairs. In an aside (a speech delivered not to the other characters, but only to the audience), Georgia mentions her husband, a drunk who has run off, and her attraction to Robert. Recalling the day Robert arrived, Georgia mentions the arrival of a white man. Stokes also delivers an aside, in which he recalls the white man who visited Georgia's bar. The asides are removed from the linear development of the play and set the stage for the action to come. When the white man (Kimbrough) arrives, he explains to Georgia and Stokes that he is looking for someone. Knowing it is Johnson the man is seeking, Georgia and Stokes attempt to protect Johnson—they are suspicious of Kimbrough's desire to see him—by deflecting his questions with wit, humor, and general evasiveness. Kimbrough explains who Johnson is, revealing the myth that he sold his soul to the devil. Stokes and Georgia continue toying with Kimbrough, launching into a discussion about the many names an African American person can have. The exchange is intended to be humorous to them, and presumably to the audience, but to further frustrate Kimbrough, which it does. Hearing thunder, and rain, Georgia retires upstairs, suggesting to Stokes, and in an aside to the audience, that she is going to be with Robert.

Act 1, Scene 2

The second scene opens in Georgia's bedroom, where Robert is sitting on the bed, playing the guitar, when Georgia enters. Georgia tells Robert about Kimbrough, and Robert reveals that he is in fact the blues musician Kimbrough is seeking. After acknowledging that she already knew who Robert was, Georgia tells him how her husband smashed all her records of Robert's music. The discussion turns again to Kimbrough and how relentlessly he has pursued Robert, although Robert does not know why he has been followed. Georgia suggests that Kimbrough is interested in Robert because of the alleged deal he made with the devil. In reply, Robert tells her he she should not listen to what white people say, and then recounts his own experience in learning how to play the guitar, learning how to play the blues. He shares his frustration at Kimbrough's persistence, and Georgia soothes him, then joins him in bed.

Meanwhile, Kimbrough and Stokes are talking in the bar. They discuss Robert's music, and Kimbrough reveals some of his own past. Kimbrough tells Stokes of a large inheritance he has received, which enables him to live a leisurely life, and to teach English at a private women's college, as he has no skills in business to make a living any other way. Kimbrough teaches Shakespeare and makes repeated references to Shakespeare's plays. He wonders how Robert, as (he presumes) an uneducated black man can use his music to touch on the same universal themes (such as lost innocence, man's fall from grace, the need to atone for one's sins) explored in the Bible and by Shakespeare. Kimbrough compares Robert to the Greek poet-god Orpheus. Stokes informs Kimbrough that he is getting more lost the longer he looks for Robert. The conversation turns to Stokes's grandmother, Ma Ruth, who was a slave, and to Kimbrough's grandfather. As the two recollect the death of their grandparents, Lem, Georgia's husband, enters. He talks about how he had left to find work and had been employed on a government building project. The labor, he says, was worse than slavery. Kimbrough initially takes Lem to be Robert, and finding out that he is not the bluesman, proceeds to question him about Johnson. Stokes encourages Lem to leave, suggesting that Georgia will not want to see him, but Lem refuses. Lem tells the audience in an aside that some believe he poisoned Robert Johnson, but he denies it. In this aside, Lem also reveals his knowledge of and anger regarding the connection between Georgia and Robert. Comparing Kimbrough's search for Robert to trying to catch a squirrel (Robert) who is busy looking for a nut, Stokes tells Kimbrough that he has been looking for Robert the wrong way. The implication is that Robert, upstairs with Georgia, has found what he has been looking for.

Act 1, Scene 3

In the final scene of act 1, Robert, in Georgia's room, wakes from a restless sleep determined to confront Kimbrough. He is tired of being pursued. Georgia assures him that they will find a way to prevent Kimbrough from following Robert any more.

Act 2, Scene 1

Back in the bar, Kimbrough expresses his frustration at being tricked, being the object of the joke of everyone in the bar, being duped by Stokes, Georgia, Lem, and all the "servile and indifferent colored men / . . . and women" he has met as he has followed Kimbrough. He also is tired, he says "of poor whites," and of the South all together. He tells Stokes he plans on leaving on the Greyhound the next day, but insists that he will see Robert first. Certain that Stokes knows more than he is letting on, Kimbrough (using a racial slur about Robert) threatens to inform authorities that an African American who has committed horrible crimes is "on the loose." Stokes informs Kimbrough that if, upon finding Robert, Kimbrough only sees what he wants to, his search will have been fruitless anyway. Georgia appears. Not surprised to see Lem, she tells him that it is too late for him to come back to her. He insists that he still has feelings for her, that he left for the sake of work, and that it was a horrible experience, and so he returned. In the midst of their argument, Robert enters. Robert and Lem discuss Georgia. Lem is outraged, feeling usurped by Robert. Lem tells both Georgia and Kimbrough that Robert is not special, that he is just like every other bluesman. Lem tells the audience that if Robert had been in league with the devil, it did him no good as a guitar player, and it certainly did not prevent him from howling in misery when he was poisoned.

Kimbrough now begins to question Robert, and Robert, in turn, questions Kimbrough about why has been following him. As the two speak, Kimbrough asks how Robert is able to write so insightfully about "conflicts / that are central to the literature / of all civilization." Meanwhile, Lem speaks to the audience, complaining that Robert has no right to disparage him in front of his woman and a white man. According to the stage directions, he is at this

time poisoning Robert's whiskey. Robert and Kimbrough continue to talk, with Robert playing the guitar throughout the conversation. Lem interrupts periodically, and he and Robert exchange insults. Finally, Robert consents to tell Kimbrough and the others the story of how he faced Satan at the crossroads. He reveals that out of curiosity, he went to the crossroads where he was told he would find Satan. He waited, he says, and finally the devil arrived, but he "was just a ordinary white man in a suit and tie." Robert explains that he tricked the devil. By playing what he knew to be the truth and by digging deeper into his soul and his ancestry, he discovered that the music became stronger and stronger, and the devil could call "none of it a lie!" When the devil played, Robert says, he just watched him and learned all his tricks. But the devil bestowed on him no special gifts for which he had to exchange his soul. Lem accuses him of lying, and Georgia argues with Lem. Meanwhile, Robert has been sipping the drink Lem has prepared. Robert encourages Kimbrough to face his own demons, as he himself has done. Kimbrough reveals that his family had been slaveholders, and that is where their fortune, his inheritance, has stemmed from. He reveals his own tormented feelings about his past. Robert attempts to guide him through confronting his feelings about his family, but Kimbrough refuses, instead clinging to his own racism. Johnson suddenly doubles over in pain and Lem reveals the rat poison he put in Robert's drink. He tells Georgia that he killed Robert so that he, Lem, could be with her. Georgia tells him to leave, arguing that she did not ask him to commit such an act on her behalf. Robert gasps his last breath.

Epilogue

The Epilogue reveals Kimbrough, lecturing, espousing the myth that Robert denied: that in an evil pact, he sold his soul to Satan. In exchange, the devil gave Robert "unnatural insights and / musical mastery."

CHARACTERS

Georgia

Georgia operates the jook joint in which the play takes place. She is described as being in her late thirties or early forties. By virtue of her owning her own bar as an African American woman in the 1930s, her strength and independence are established immediately. Her exchanges with Stokes, the piano player, show her to be intelligent and funny. She frankly expresses her physical attraction to Robert, and is not afraid to go after what she wants. Georgia, after revealing that her husband, Lem, could be mean and petty, shows him no kindness or mercy when he returns. Horrified that Lem admits to killing Robert to be with her, she tells him to leave, to take his soul "somewhere it can't be found."

Robert Johnson

Robert Johnson is a blues singer in his mid-twenties. His character is based on a real-life figure by the same name who died in 1938 at the age of twenty-seven. The cause of death is believed to have been poisoning. In Harris's fictionalized account of Robert's last day, the playwright depicts a Robert who is confident but soft-spoken. Tired of running from Kimbrough, Robert knows he must finally confront him. The reasons he has not yet done so are only alluded to and appear to stem from the racial tension in the American South of the 1930s. At the heart of the play is Robert's revelation of what really happened at the crossroads, where he was believed to have sold his soul to the devil in exchange for unmatched skill as a blues guitarist. What he admits, however, is that whatever his intentions were in seeking out Satan that day, he walked away with his soul intact, having tricked the devil (who appears to Robert as a white man in a suit) rather than traded his soul for talent. He speaks of playing the truth, his own, and that of a people sold into slavery. The devil, he says, could not deny the truth of what he had played, nor could he best Robert. As Robert watches the Devil's attempt to outplay him, he learns new skills, just as he admits to learning from other guitarists. From this exchange, he stresses, he became an unbeatable guitar player. Robert goes on to urge Kimbrough to seek his own truth, to admit that what he has been seeking has little to do with Robert or the blues, and more to do with the way Kimbrough is haunted by his own past. Kimbrough, however, refuses to listen and fades from the scene as Robert dies.

Kimbrough

Kimbrough is a professor of English from New England, employed at a private girls' college. He is the play's only white character and the instigator,

along with Lem, of much of the play's tension. Having desperately searched for Robert Johnson, he is frustrated by the evasions of Stokes and Georgia when he questions them about the bluesman. With an increasing sense of isolation and annoyance at being the butt of their jokes, Kimbrough expresses his disgust with the South in general and with all those in it, African Americans and poor whites together, who he feels have thwarted his quest. Unlike the other characters in the play, Kimbrough speaks in blank verse (structured by unrhymed poetry), and he makes repeated references to the works of Shakespeare. Kimbrough's habit of flaunting his status as one of the East Coast academic elite, combined with the derogatory comments and racial insults he makes about southern African Americans in general, and the other characters in the play in particular, demonstrate the professor's arrogance, ignorance, and overall bad judgment: he certainly will not get any of the information he seeks by insulting those he questions. Kimbrough's shortcomings are further revealed in the play's epilogue, when he perpetuates the myth about Robert Johnson that he knows to be untrue. Throughout the play, despite the few moments in which Robert attempts to help him break free of his own past, Kimbrough remains unchanged, insisting on a version of Robert Johnson and his music that fits into his own worldview.

Lem

Lem is Georgia's husband, although the pair have been separated since Lem sought employment at a government-sponsored work program involving levee building. Despite the fact that he was being paid to work, he feels that he was driven harder than a slave. He consequently returns to his wife, who has no interest in taking him back. Lem brings with him all the frustration and anger at having attempted to find work, only to be mistreated, and upon his return, he suspects that his wife has been unfaithful. From Lem's perspective, he has been sorely used and abused first by his bosses on the government job, and then by his wife. Yet his response—poisoning Robert—is clearly unjustified. When Robert dies, Lem expresses no remorse. Rather, he tells Georgia that he killed Robert for her, so that she could now be with him. Georgia, however, wants nothing to do with her husband any longer, and, rejected, he leaves. During the play, in an aside to the audience in which Lem speaks as though the time during which the events of the play take place have already passed, he claims be innocent of the crime of poisoning Robert.

Stokes

Stokes is the blind piano player at Georgia's joint. In the listing of characters preceding the play, he is described as "a seer." As the play opens, he predicts the arrival of strangers, and of rain, and when Georgia scoffs at him, he asserts that he received such intuitive gifts from his grandmother. Despite her initial teasing, Georgia seems to place some stock in Stokes's intuitions, believing the gut reactions he expresses about the other characters in the play. In addition to being able to sense things about people, he is a skillful riddler, offering disguised information to Kimbrough about Robert, but telling him nothing directly. With Georgia, Stokes attempts a number of times to throw Kimbrough off Robert's trail. Stokes provides information to Kimbrough about African oral traditions and about his own family's history as slaves, inspiring Kimbrough to share personal information about himself and his own family. Stokes is additionally shown to be protective of Georgia, and, by extension, Robert, whom Georgia cares for. He prevents Lem from revealing too much about Georgia or her knowledge of Robert's music when Kimbrough is questioning Lem. As Robert dies, it is Stokes who comforts him and encourages him to not fight his inevitable death.

THEMES

Mythmaking

The creation of the myth of Robert Johnson functions as a driving force in Harris's *Robert Johnson: Trick the Devil*. It is Kimbrough's pursuit of Robert, and Kimbrough's desire to verify the myth that has already grown up around Robert, that serves as the play's primary conflict. Robert is weary of Kimbrough's pursuit, and Georgia and Stokes, who have some inkling of who Robert is, are driven by their motivation to protect Robert's identity from Kimbrough. Lem is as much affronted by the fact that another man has been with his wife as he is that it is this man in particular, Robert Johnson, who has been with his wife. Johnson has the reputation of being able, thanks to the gifts the devil bestowed on him, to make women desire him. Harris allows Robert to tell his own story in the play, to provide his own version of his own myth. But as Patricia R. Schroeder maintains in her 2004 book *Robert Johnson, Mythmaking, and Contemporary American Culture*, Harris himself, in the very writing of the

play, in giving Johnson his own voice, reshapes the myth of Robert Johnson.

Significantly, Harris, through his character of Robert Johnson, re-creates the Johnson myth in such a way as to transform the myth but retain some of the original elements of the myth. As the story goes, Johnson traded his soul to the devil for unmatched skills on the blues guitar. Other gifts are rumored to have been part of the deal: insights into human nature, the ability to arouse desire in women. As Harris's Johnson tells it, he tricked the devil, but he did so without selling his soul. Harris allows that Johnson's skill was his own, not a supernatural gift from an evil force, a fact that the character of Kimbrough could not accept. Kimbrough was unwilling to believe that an uneducated African American blues player could through his music speak to the universal themes of human existence explored by the literary greats such as Shakespeare. However, Harris, although he depicts the devil as a white man in a suit, suggests that this was the way the devil appeared to Robert Johnson. While this says a lot about the way African Americans in the South in the 1930s perceived white men, it also allows the supernatural element to remain. Harris seems to suggest that Robert's devil was the embodiment of the evil that whites have perpetrated against African Americans. As Johnson tells it in Harris's play, though, the devil is still the devil, despite his white human form. Harris does not allow the myth of an exchange between Johnson and the devil to be completely dismantled, but he removes from it the powerful element that robs Johnson of natural ability.

Racial Conflict

In Harris's play, the African American characters are unanimously suspicious of the white character's intentions, while the white character paints all of the southern African American he meets with the same racist brush. Much of the racial tension is due to the play's setting in the South during the 1930s, at the when time Jim Crow laws ensured that African Americans were discriminated against and were set apart from their white counterparts (see Historical Context). While this accounts to a large degree for the suspicions of Georgia, Stokes, Lem, and Robert, Kimbrough comes to the South from an elite East Coast background, and bearing with him his own racial prejudices. Kimbrough admits that he has felt a connection to Robert's blues since his grandfather's death before he explains own relatives were slaveholders, and that he refused to

TOPICS FOR FURTHER STUDY

- Harris's *Robert Johnson: Trick the Devil* takes place in the South during the Great Depression. He makes some references to race relations at that time. Using online and print resources, research the way the Great Depression impacted African Americans in particular. Did the Depression influence racial tensions? Were African Americans more or less likely than their white counterparts to participate in the government's work and relief efforts? How did segregation laws contribute to racial tensions during this time? How did segregation affect the way African Americans dealt with the struggles of the Depression? Prepare a written report on your findings.

- Robert Johnson's music gradually gained attention and appreciation after his death, and his particular style is said to be unique and powerful. Select several of Johnson's songs and compare Johnson's style, sound, and subject matter to a modern musician of your choosing. Are there similarities in the musicians' themes? Can you detect an influence of the blues in the work of the modern musician you have chosen? Prepare a report in which you compare the different artists and their works.

- In writing about Robert Johnson's last day, Harris chose the play as his literary form. In the play, the character of Robert Johnson recounts his exchange with the devil. Consider the variety of scenarios that could have occurred at the crossroads between Johnson and the devil. Write a one-act play in which you dramatize this scene with Johnson and the figure of the devil as the characters. Consider whether or not your "devil" will be a mythical embodiment of evil, a human villain, or another type of character altogether. How will the characters' speech patterns differentiate them from each other? Will they use a local dialect? Does their speech indicate how educated they are? Are any other characters present? Will the outcome uphold a mythical rendering of Johnson's guitar-playing abilities? Either film your play and show it to the class or, with another student, perform it for the class.

- Blues music has its roots in songs sung by slaves on plantations; over the years it developed into its own distinct genre. Research the origins, history, and development of the blues. Did different regions of the country have their own style of blues? Or are the differences in styles of various blues musicians more related to the time period in which they lived? Present your report orally and accompany it with selections from different styles of blues music.

- Early on in Harris's play, Kimbrough refers to Shakespeare. He compares Stokes's forecasting of rain to the predictions of the witches in Shakespeare's play *Macbeth*. Read Shakespeare's play and consider the way Shakespeare employs supernatural elements to advance his plot. (The "supernatural" refers to things that cannot be accounted for in the natural world, such as the ability to predict the future, ghosts, magic, beings with inhuman powers.) In what ways is Shakespeare's use of the supernatural similar to that of Harris? Create a PowerPoint presentation in which you compare the two dramatists' use of supernatural elements.

- Mildred Taylor's Newbery Award-winning young-adult novel *Roll of Thunder, Hear My Cry*, originally published in 1976 and available in a 1997 Penguin edition, is set in Mississippi in 1933. It is narrated by a nine-year-old girl and explores the life of an African American family during the Depression. Read Taylor's novel and compare the novel with Harris's play. Write a comparative essay in which your analysis of the two works is presented.

Robert Johnson played the blues guitar. *(Image copyright John Wollwerth, 2009. Used under license from Shutterstock.com)*

be with his slaveholding grandfather when he died. He seems haunted by guilt about his family's actions, and he has conflicted feelings about not being in the room with his grandfather when he died. Kimbrough is just as conflicted about his powerful response to the blues. When Robert urges him to acknowledge the truth—Kimbrough's own truth about his fears, and the truth about the blues being a genuine, complex, and meaningful expression of human emotion—Kimbrough's response is that he cannot stop being the "coward" and "hypocrite" that Robert accuses him of being. He cannot because he fears the blues are really just "[racial slur] mumbo jumbo." He clings to his racism, his fear, and refuses to take any responsibility for his feelings. The world, he asserts, is "not my concoction or my fault."

STYLE

Vernacular Language

The African American characters in Harris's *Robert Johnson: Trick the Devil* speak in an easy, conversational manner in the vernacular (the language or dialect of a particular region) of the rural American South of the 1930s. Their discourse includes references to African folklore (the trickster figure of the Signifying Monkey) and to African American folklore (another trickster figure, Br'er Rabbit). Such allusions are made when one character wittily insults or outsmarts another, or both, as when Stokes, knowing that Robert is upstairs, compares Robert to a fox, duped in a Br'er Rabbit story. Similarly, Stokes, possessing knowledge Lem does not have about Robert and Georgia, insults Lem by hinting at the way he is being cuckolded (that is, cheated on by Georgia, with Robert). In a similar way, Georgia and Stokes speak comfortably with one another, jesting at Kimbrough's expense, knowing how close Kimbrough really is to the man he is seeking. When Kimbrough asks the two about a man named Robert Johnson, they leisurely spend a considerable amount of time telling humorous stories about individuals with a variety of unusual names. Kimbrough becomes increasingly frustrated, and Georgia and Stokes succeed in reminding Kimbrough that he is a stranger, alone, and they are members of a separate community, one in which Kimbrough is powerless to decipher their private humor and meaning.

Blank Verse

Kimbrough sets himself up to be treated as an outsider, however. Through his demeanor, actions, and speech he isolates himself from the African American community he enters. Immediately upon setting foot in Georgia's jook joint, he draws attention to himself as a white man from the Northeast who is well educated and who demands answers to his questions. His own speech sets him distinctly apart from the other characters in the play as well. Not only does he make repeated references to Shakespeare that stand in sharp contrast to the cultural allusions made by Stokes and Georgia, but he speaks in blank verse. Blank verse is poetry that contains a regular metrical pattern, but no rhyme. It often features iambic pentameter, like many of the speeches in the Shakespearean plays so favored by Kimbrough. (Iambic pentameter is a type of metrical structure in poetry. Meter is a pattern of accented and unaccented syllables within a line of poetry. A line of verse written in iambic pentameter is one in which there are five accented syllables in the line, each preceded by an unaccented syllable. Each set of unaccented and accented syllables is referred to as a metrical foot.) Kimbrough's distinctively different speeches, and the fact that his portions of conversation often come off as academic lectures, in no way aid him in gathering information about Johnson. In contrast to the relaxed speech of the other characters, Kimbrough presents himself as formal, academic, and superior.

HISTORICAL CONTEXT

Race Relations in the South in the 1930s

In Harris's *Robert Johnson: Trick the Devil*, Lem refers to Jim Crow when he describes working on a government-sponsored works program job to be more brutal than anything related to Jim Crow laws. What Lem speaks of is the institutionalized segregation and the legal condoning of the social mindset of white superiority that occurred during this period. The term "Jim Crow" derived from the name of a character in a "minstrel show," or traveling performance troupe, featuring song, dance, and comedy. The Jim Crow character,

according to Ferris State University sociology professor David Pilgrim, was initially created by a white performer named Thomas Dartmouth "Daddy" Rice. Rice applied blackface makeup and created the Jim Crow character in the 1830s; the character embodied all the most offensive stereotypes assigned to those Africans in the United States who could not yet be called Americans, as most of them were slaves during this pre-Civil War time period. The minstrel shows such as those in which Rice performed peaked in popularity by the 1870s, when the term Jim Crow began to be viewed as a racial slur. As laws that discriminated against African Americans began to be passed in the late 1870s, they began to be called Jim Crow laws. The laws were based on the notion that whites were superior to African Americans in terms of intellectual ability and moral behavior. As Pilgrim explains, the fear at the root of the Jim Crow laws was that if African Americans were treated by whites as social equals, interracial sexual relationships would result, and the resulting mixed race would be the downfall of America. Violence was frequently used to enforce Jim Crow laws. Beatings and lynchings were common. Not only did the laws dictate that African Americans and white Americans could not eat together or sit near each other on public transportation, but anything that intimated social equality was understood by the social etiquette of the day to be off limits. An African American man, for example, could not offer to shake hands with a white man, nor was a white man ever introduced to an African American man. African Americans were introduced to whites, but never using a courtesy title such as "Mr." or "Mrs." or "Miss." Only whites were allowed such titles; African Americans were introduced by their first name alone. The segregation laws became more pervasive, and virtually all possible interactions between the two races were regulated. African Americans were relegated to separate, usually inferior, facilities, including drinking fountains, public restrooms, hospitals, schools, and prisons. While the Fourteenth and Fifteenth Amendments to the U.S. Constitution (1868 and 1870) gave African Americans citizenship and the right to vote and prohibited states from denying that right, other laws were created by the states to prevent African Americans from voting. Poll taxes were instituted in some states, as were literacy tests. A poll tax was a fee that a person had to pay in order to be allowed to vote in a national election. Such taxes essentially meant

COMPARE & CONTRAST

- **1930s:** During the 1930s, bank failures, high unemployment rates, and a massive drought all contribute to the Great Depression. Numerous government programs, called the New Deal, are instituted by President Franklin D. Roosevelt to ameliorate the suffering of countless Americans.

  1990s: In the relatively stable economic period of the 1990s, President Bill Clinton reforms various welfare and assistance programs and balances the nation's budget.

  Today: Toward the end of the first decade of the twenty-first century, a number of problems, including the risky lending practices of banks, and spending on the Iraq War, contribute to a severe economic recession. Unemployment rates are high and, under President Barack Obama's new administration in 2009, failing banks and auto companies are loaned money to help stabilize the economy. President Obama institutes the Recovery Act of 2009, which includes a re-formation of the tax code designed to benefit middle-class working families, and allows for the construction and renovation of federally owned buildings as part of a jobs creation program.

- **1930s:** Race relations are severely strained, as discriminatory Jim Crow segregation laws keep African Americans separated in all aspects of society from white Americans. Violent punishments, including beatings and lynchings, inflicted upon many innocent African Americans, contribute to growing conflicts that sometimes lead to race riots.

  1990s: While Jim Crow laws were dismantled in the mid-1960s, in the 1990s racial tensions continue to some degree. In the city of Los Angeles in 1992, for example, rioting and looting result from a jury's acquittal of four police officers who were charged in the 1991 beating of African American Rodney King following a high-speed pursuit.

Today: Race relations continue to be at the forefront of headlines in the United States. In the 2008 presidential election, Americans elect for the first time in history an African American president. Many believe that such an unprecedented event marks a turning point in race relations in America. However, according to a June 25, 2009, CNN News article ("Blacks in Survey Say Race Relations No Better with Obama"), many African Americans and white Americans alike still feel that race relations will always be an issue in the United States.

- **1930s:** The musical genre that became known as "the blues" increases in popularity during this time period, having begun to take shape during the 1920s. While the genre morphs throughout the years, a popular style in the 1930s grows out of a tradition generated from the Mississippi Delta region. Different from the brass band style blues of the earlier decade, Delta blues songs are typically played on the guitar. Some musicians record songs, travel, and play jook joints throughout the country, but, like Robert Johnson, they never achieve the success they seek during their lifetime.

  1990s: Following World War II, blues music became less of a genre unto itself. It transformed and influenced other forms of music, such as folk, rock-and-roll, and rhythm-and-blues in the 1950s and 1960s. Artists who acknowledge the influence of bluesmen like Robert Johnson include Eric Clapton and The Rolling Stones, who continue to perform during the 1990s and into the twenty-first century. Such artists have also re-recorded old blues songs.

  Today: Many modern genres attribute some of their roots to the blues of Johnson's day, including rhythm-and-blues (also known as R&B), country western, and rock.

that poor people, which included a large number of African Americans, could not vote. Poll taxes were finally banned in 1964 by the Twenty-fourth Amendment. Race riots in major cities (for example, in Detroit in 1943 and again in 1967) well into the twentieth century attest to the fact that the institutionalized dehumanization of African Americans would not be tolerated indefinitely.

Given this social structure, any interactions between African Americans and white Americans during this time period were bound to be fraught with tension, suspicion, and fear. In Harris's play, the African American characters Stokes and Georgia do their best to protect Robert, though they know little about him except that he is being followed by a white man. Robert, who knows he has done nothing wrong, is fearful and agitated by being so pursued. Yet given the atmosphere instituted by Jim Crow laws, it is not surprising that he avoided confronting Kimbrough for as long as possible.

The Great Depression

Harris's play takes place during the Great Depression, which lasted roughly a decade in America, from 1929 to the outbreak of World War II, which began in Europe in 1939. The official onset is often marked as the great stock market crash on "Black Thursday," October 24, 1929. The downward economic spiral that followed began with the massive bank failures that resulted after the stock market plummeted. Without the necessary cash flow, businesses closed, and unemployment rose dramatically. President Herbert Hoover attempted to address countless crises but with little success. In 1932 Franklin Delano Roosevelt was elected president. After taking office in 1933, he immediately began instituting measures designed to restore the banks' solvency and to get Americans working again by creating new jobs. He passed measures such as the Emergency Banking Act of 1933, which stabilized the banking system through federal government loans provided by Roosevelt's Reconstruction Finance Corporation. While Hoover had urged Americans to be self-reliant and had hoped local charities would provide for the needs of the newly homeless and hungry in their own communities, Roosevelt took another approach, establishing the Federal Emergency Relief Administration, which provided communities with funding to offer allotments of food, rent money, coal, and heating oil to Americans in need. Numerous public works programs were also instituted. The Civil

Works Administration was created to employ Americans in the construction and repair of highways, bridges, and public buildings such as schools, hospitals, and airports. Another such organization was the Civilian Conservation Corps, which provided funding for unemployed young men to work in national forests, parks, and other public lands owned by the federal government. All such programs were part of what was called the "New Deal," and when Roosevelt was re-elected, he instituted a "Second New Deal." In 1935, Roosevelt signed legislation to provide another broad work-relief organization, the Works Progress Administration (or WPA). In Harris's play, the character of Lem, seeking employment, finds it with a government-sponsored WPA position, fortifying levees. Lem finds the position to be worse than slavery, and modern sources concede that the pay for WPA jobs was minimal, but better, it was argued, than poverty and starvation. According to T. H. Watkins's *The Great Depression: America in the 1930s*, the average WPA salary was about forty-one dollars per month. When America entered World War II in 1941, the increased manufacturing needs generated by participation in the war eventually helped return the American economy to prosperity. Roosevelt, having served two terms in office and having guided the nation through the Depression, was elected at the onset of the war for an unprecedented third term in office.

CRITICAL OVERVIEW

Critical assessments of Harris's *Robert Johnson: Trick the Devil* are not numerous to date. Among the fullest examinations of his play is Patricia R. Schroeder's study in the 1989 *Robert Johnson, Mythmaking, and Contemporary American Culture*. In this exploration of the way Harris's play contributes to the re-creation of the mythology surrounding Johnson, Schroeder maintains that the work "offers an artistic deconstruction of the Robert Johnson myth because it depicts the myth being created." Schroeder demonstrates the way Harris presents a world divided: between African Americans and white Americans, between the pragmatic realism of the African American characters and the often dangerous romanticism epitomized by Kimbrough, and, within African American culture, between African influences and Western

Robert Johnson claimed to have sold his soul to the devil to play the guitar. *(Image copyright Peter Gudella, 2009. Used under license from Shutterstock.com)*

influences. Other critical responses to the play take the form of theater reviews. When the play opened in New York in 1993 under the direction of Woodie King, Jr., it was reviewed in the *New York Times* by the critic Mel Gussow, who describes Harris's play as "a high-spirited and often rhapsodic search for the musician's soul." While Gussow finds that Kimbrough's literary tangents impede the progress of the play, the critic views the work as a whole as vivid and insightful. Mia Leonin, in her review of a 2001 Florida production for the *New Times: Broward/ Palm Beach*, finds Harris's script to be "skillfully crafted" and "steeped in rural Southern vernacular, literary allusions, tall tales, song lyrics, and folklore." A 2005 production of the play in Chicago resulted in a less-than-favorable critique by Jonathan Abarbanel for *Windy City Times*. The critic describes Harris's drama as "overly poetic

but crudely structured," and argues that it lacks "biographical detail and character depth." When the play was staged in Austin, Texas, in 2008, the production was praised by Avimaan Syam, writing for *The Austin Chronicle*. Syam applauds Harris's storytelling abilities and appreciates the poetry of his script. The critic further suggests that Johnson himself is used as a metaphor by Harris.

CRITICISM

Catherine Dominic

Dominic is a novelist, freelance writer, and editor. In this essay, she maintains that while Harris's play Robert Johnson: Trick the Devil *is often studied almost exclusively for the way it interprets*

WHAT DO I READ NEXT?

- Harris's *Stories about the Old Days* is a full-length play that features two characters—one a retired factory worker (Clayborn) and one a former blues singer (Ivy), and both in their sixties—in what has been described as both a comedy and drama. The work was published by Samuel French in 1990.

- Harris's poetry collection, *Yardbird Suite: Side One: 1920–1940, A Biopoem: Fictionalized Accounts of Events Real and Imagined from the Life of Charles "Yardbird" Parker*, published by Michigan State University Press in 1997, focuses on the life and music of bluesman Charlie Parker.

- *Black Pearls: Blues Queens of the 1920s* by Daphne Harrison, published by Rutgers University Press (1988), explores the careers of female African American blues singers during the 1920s, such as Ma Rainey and Bessie Smith, some of whom would go on to experience the success Robert Johnson was unable to achieve during his lifetime.

- Lorraine Hansberry was, like Harris, an African American playwright who wrote dramas featuring African American charac-

ters, and their struggles, hopes, and dreams. Notably, she was the first African American woman to have a play produced on Broadway. *A Raisin in the Sun* premiered on Broadway in 1959. The play examines the struggles of a working-class family in Chicago. It is available in a 2004 edition by Vintage.

- Toni Cade Bambara's collection of short stories geared toward high-school-age teens *Gorilla, My Love* has been highly praised for its depiction of African American characters and the struggles they face. One story in the collection features a Mississippi blues musician. Originally published in 1972, the book is available in a 1992 Vintage edition.

- *Escaping the Delta: Robert Johnson and the Invention of the Blues* by Elijah Wald, published by HarperCollins in 2004, explores Johnson's life, his music, his lack of popularity during his lifetime, and his subsequent status as a blues legend in the years following his death. Wald additionally examines Johnson's place within the larger context of the history of the blues.

---

the historical figure of Robert Johnson, the playwright crafts a character, who, independent of the bluesman myth, is a compelling, complex figure in his own right.

Bill Harris's character of Robert Johnson, as depicted in *Robert Johnson: Trick the Devil*, has been examined by critics almost solely as the character relates to the actual bluesman Robert Johnson, who was believed to have been born in 1911, according to biographies such as Tom Graves's *Crossroads: The Life and Afterlife of Blues Legend Robert Johnson*. Certainly, the character is meant to be viewed as some representation of the actual bluesman, although one can never truly know what Harris as playwright

intended. He includes information that is reflective of the real Johnson's life, for example, that he was known for a time as Robert Spenser, and that his mother was not married to his biological father. One must not assume, however, even when considering such parallels, that a drama featuring one historically based character and a number of entirely fictional ones is intended in some way to provide accurate answers to questions about the historically based character's life. Yet the play is often discussed with the relationship between the historical and the fictional Johnsons in mind.

For example, Patricia R. Schroeder, in her analysis of the play in *Robert Johnson, Mythmaking,*

> IF HARRIS'S JOHNSON IS STUDIED AS A CHARACTER INSPIRED BY, BUT NOT A SHADOW OF, THE HISTORICAL JOHNSON, THE PLAYWRIGHT'S CREATION STANDS AS A FULLY REALIZED CHARACTER WITH HIS OWN COMPLEXITIES AND SHORTCOMINGS. HARRIS'S JOHNSON IS SOMETHING OTHER THAN, AND MORE THAN, THE RE-CREATED MAN AND MYTH OF ROBERT JOHNSON."

and Contemporary American Culture (2004) focuses her study of the character of Johnson on the way Harris re-creates the myth of the historic Johnson. In Harris's myth, she argues, Johnson encounters the devil but retains his soul. As Schroeder states, in Harris's version, Johnson's talent is the result of his natural ability and his skill at learning from other musicians, a better myth, she maintains, than that which assumes an African American man cannot naturally possess the skill and insights Johnson's music demonstrates.

Another critic, Jonathan Abarbanel, who reviewed the play for the *Windy City Times*, finds that Harris's version of Johnson lacks depth of character and excludes known biographical facts about Johnson's life. Schroeder explores Harris's new myth of Johnson, and Abarbanel complains that Harris's work lacks both biographical information and complexity of character. Such examinations are limited and do not do justice to Harris's skill and insight as a dramatist. If Harris's Johnson is studied as a character inspired by, but not a shadow of, the historical Johnson, the playwright's creation stands as a fully realized character with his own complexities and shortcomings. Harris's Johnson is something other than, and more than, the re-created man and myth of Robert Johnson.

Certainly with the many biographies of Johnson available to him, Harris could have chosen to incorporate more of the biographical facts than those few he sprinkles in throughout his drama. He chooses instead to create a character, one with very common, human traits in addition to his extraordinary guitar-playing abilities. Harris's

Johnson is a charming man with as much fear in him as confidence. Yet what makes him the most human and the most sympathetic character is his treatment of Kimbrough.

Robert walks into Georgia's jook joint and immediately begins flirting with her. His manner is easy. He teases her about the way her man's name is not listed on the sign that hangs out front above the entrance to her bar. But Johnson begins to expose his vulnerabilities when he and Georgia are alone in her room. He tells Georgia about the way Kimbrough (although he does not know Kimbrough's name) has been following him for a couple of weeks. As their talk of him continues, Robert wonders aloud, clearly frustrated and confused and perhaps frightened, "Why the hell can't he just leave me in peace!" Robert also reveals his early fascination with the blues, and again, when the conversation turns back to Kimbrough, his anger surfaces. He tells Georgia he just wants to be left alone to pursue his music, his own dream, but Kimbrough's pursuit has agitated him. He speaks of confronting him violently, but Georgia cautions him against it. After expressing his desire to chase Kimbrough "clean to hell and back," he wishes a silly, hopeful dream: that he could just go downstairs and play to a room full of appreciative people, until Georgia's whole place just floated away. Georgia's own tough demeanor softens at these words.

Later, after Georgia has left her room and has returned downstairs to find Lem, her estranged husband, waiting for her, Robert enters and is verbally assaulted by Lem. Despite Georgia's warning, Robert insults Lem, feeling that since Lem has left Georgia, he has no rights to her, nor any right to attack him. Significantly, in Robert's words to Lem, a hint of the trauma of his own past is revealed. In speaking of men who do not fight for their women and their families, he mentions the men that made his own father "sneak off from his family," that is, from a young Robert. His disdain for Lem appears to have as much to do with his own desire for Georgia as it does with his judgment of Lem as a deserter, a husband who abandons his family.

Thus far, Harris's Robert Johnson is a man whose present is infused with the past. His childhood love of the blues stands in sharp contrast to a childhood spent without a father. His present life is filled with frustration and anger at Kimbrough, whom he wishes to confront, but thus far, for whatever reason, has not. Just as easily as he imagines hurting Kimbrough, he dreams of the whole of Georgia's jook joint simply floating away. Aggressive adult anger stands side by side with childish wishes.

When Robert finally reaches the point in the play when he agrees to discuss what happened at the crossroads, it is almost a disappointment that Harris infuses Robert's tale with the supernatural figure of Satan. The Robert the reader has come to know has been an interesting, complex, human figure, but now the myth is thrust upon him, even though in Harris's version of the Robert Johnson myth, Robert retains his soul. Although Robert's tale is heavily laden with references to Satan and Robert's exchange with him, he does describe the devil as "just a ordinary white man in a suit and tie." From that reference there is perhaps latitude to view Robert's tale as a metaphor for the way white record executives attempted to capitalize on his talent. Lem's response is in some ways supportive of a metaphorical reading. He calls Robert a liar and proceeds to relate his own experiences with his version of Satan, his two bosses on the levee job, one of them African American and one of them white. Lem tells Georgia that Robert must be lying, because Robert is just a man, no better than Lem, and the devil cannot be tricked. All one can do, Lem says, is "get away." In Lem's account, the devil is more easily viewed as a metaphor for the evil that men in power inflict on those subordinate to them. His story, while referring to the devil, is not only shorter, but more realistic and less flamboyantly told than Robert's. Lem, after all, is more plain-speaking than the dreamer Robert has shown himself to be.

What fully rounds out Robert's character, myth or no myth, is his treatment of his pursuer, Kimbrough, near the end of the play. As Robert has previously revealed to Georgia, Kimbrough has hounded him. Furthermore, Kimbrough has already, through the course of the play, demonstrated his racism, having made derogatory comments about African Americans a number of times. He further confesses that his own grandfather was a slaveholder and that the inheritance on which he comfortably lives was built upon the labor of slaves. Kimbrough tells Robert how Robert's music speaks to him and has done so since his grandfather died. He is conflicted about not having stood bravely by the side of his dying grandfather's bed and about having never confronted his grandfather about having owned

slaves. Kimbrough states that he knew he was "a coward and a hypocrite," that he knew his family's money came from "lies, advantage, and misery." He admits to having made his own deal with the devil, another white man (his grandfather), in that he, Kimbrough, remained silent about his family's slaveholding past and was thereby rewarded with "comfort and leisure to teach." Kimbrough's devil is the most overtly metaphorical of the three such reference Harris depicts in the play. Robert says his devil appears to him as a well-dressed white man; Lem's is a two-faced figure—one black, one white—who metes out brutal authority over him; Kimbrough's devil is his white grandfather whom Kimbrough never confronted for fear of losing his inheritance. Intermingled with Kimbrough's confessions, Robert, like a therapist or a preacher, encourages and admonishes Robert to face his own sins of complicity and racism so that he will be able to tell the truth and move forward. Robert tells him that Kimbrough is "lost and down low" and that Kimbrough wants "to get found and rise up." Robert is suggesting here that Kimbrough is lost within his own fears and the secrets he has kept, and that Kimbrough longs to embrace truth and become a new man. Robert knows that Kimbrough was drawn to him through his music, and he encourages Kimbrough to admit this and to admit the reasons why, to confess the truth and "shame the Devil. Get out that nightmare." One of Robert's last acts on earth, as he is about to die of the poison given him by Lem, is to try and save the soul of a man to whom he owes nothing, a man tainted and tortured by his own racism, a man who has pursued Robert relentlessly. The character Harris creates is no mythological figure, although Harris does not sidestep the Johnson myth entirely. Rather, Harris's Robert Johnson is a well-crafted character, possessing the complexities and internal conflicts that make him an appealing, compelling subject of a drama, myth or no myth.

Source: Catherine Dominic, Critical Essay on *Robert Johnson: Trick the Devil*, in *Drama for Students*, Gale, Cengage Learning, 2010.

Avimaan Syam

In the following review, Syam focuses on Harris's language, imagery, and characterization in an Austin, Texas, production.

What happened when Robert Johnson went down to the crossroads? Did he best the devil

David "Honeyboy" Edwards recalls his career as the last living blues artist to play with the legendary Robert Johnson. (AP Images)

with his sensational picking skills, or did he sell his soul to get them? Depends on who you ask.

Robert Johnson is a legend, in life and death, although that legend is clouded by so many half-truths, exaggerations, lies, and speculation that the truth lives in them as much as any hard facts. The famed blues guitarist passed away in Mississippi on Aug. 16, 1938, at the age of 27. *Robert Johnson: Trick the Devil* weaves its tale through both the facts and fiction surrounding the musician's last day, making its story as much about the legend of Johnson as the man himself.

Johnson may be the title character, but *Trick the Devil* takes its time focusing on the bluesman: The story, like a guitar string, slackens and tightens over time. The ProArts Collective/Austin Community College Drama Department co-production opens in Georgia's Colored Juke Joint, where the proprietor and her blind friend, Stokes, are idly telling stories to each other. Their language is so rich and their banter so

natural that it doesn't matter that the arrival of conflict or other characters is delayed. Likewise, the action will slow down or altogether stop to allow for a monologue. You got to tell your story, no matter how long it takes.

Storytelling is at the heart of *Trick the Devil*. Characters reveal themselves through their tales, they communicate through them, their relationships change after hearing one another's accounts. The most dramatic moment in the play is not when a gun is aimed at someone's heart or when it's fired or when one of the characters dies, but when Robert Johnson tells the story of when he went down to the crossroads.

And Bill Harris' script is full of beautiful phrases, metaphors that stay with you like "run like a rabbit on a reefer breeze" or "go at each other like yard dogs over a soup bone." This is sharply in contrast with the language of Kimbrough, the white professor who's been searching for Johnson and whose every other sentence is a quote from Shakespeare.

Robert Johnson, though, may be the biggest metaphor of all. Everyone wants him to be something different. Kimbrough wants him to be the dirt-poor, cotton-pickin' emblem of the South that his records symbolize instead of the well-dressed and well-spoken man he is. Georgia, despite knowing his womanizing past, wants him as a lover. And Lem, Georgia's estranged husband, wants to prove his sufferance and manhood by besting Johnson.

So who is Robert Johnson? What do we learn about him? It's fascinating that in a play about Robert Johnson's last day, most of the conflict is created by those surrounding the legendary guitarist. Who's pulling who closer to death and destruction?

Johnson, played with slick charm by Aaron Alexander, rarely lets the characters and audience inside. Mostly he wants to be let alone—just to be himself. But the two or three moments that he does open up, that you begin to question what happened at the crossroads, say more than any of his fresh words do.

Director Marcus McQuirter's staging of *Trick the Devil* plays out like a Robert Johnson number: strong, sweet, natural, and full of longing. With some sharp performances, most notably Feliz McDonald's portrayal of Georgia, there aren't many finer ways to get the blues.

Source: Avimaan Syam, Review of *Robert Johnson: Trick the Devil*, in *Austin Chronicle*, April 25, 2008.

Orla Swift

In the following review, Swift covers a major National Black Theatre Festival in 2007 that featured Harris's Robert Johnson: Trick the Devil.

Jun. 8—Larry Leon Hamlin, founder of the National Black Theatre Festival in Winston-Salem, died Wednesday. He was 58.

Hamlin, a Reidsville native who studied at Brown University, founded the biennial festival in 1989; Maya Angelou was its first chairwoman. For black playwrights and performers, it became known as "the doorway to New York," Raleigh playwright Rudy Wallace said Thursday.

Hamlin arranged staged readings for new playwrights and booked a wide variety of performances, from musical revues to classical theater, biographical dramas, comedies and one-person shows.

Bill Harris' *Robert Johnson: Trick the Devil* went from a staged reading in 1991 to a full production in 1993 and ended up Off-Broadway. *Shoehorn,* a tap musical directed by Raleigh native Herman LeVern Jones, opened at the festival in 1995, went to New York's La MaMa Experimental Theatre and earned Jones the prestigious Audelco Award. August Wilson's *Jitney* began its pre-New York tour at the 1997 festival.

"We want the world to know that artistic excellence can be found in black theater," Hamlin said in a 2003 interview. "We want to let them know that we are alive, that we are not dying, a school of thought that some people would choose to embrace."

The festival drew ethnically mixed audiences of all ages. In 2005, more than 65,000 people attended, according to a festival press release.

Raleigh director Patricia C. Caple, who founded N.C. State University's Black Repertory Theatre, called Hamlin a visionary.

"Sometimes you can be so isolated that you can't see what's going on that's really for, by and about you," said Caple, who retired this year from NCSU. "He provided that venue for people all over the world to see the latest and greatest of black theater."

Hamlin, whose own N.C. Black Repertory Company performed at the festival, expanded the offerings beyond traditional theater. Inspired by

American Idol, he created a children's talent show. And his 2001 Midnight Poetry Jam, hosted by television star and poet Malcolm-Jamal Warner, was a huge hit.

"We thought we were doing it for young people, for the hip-hop generation, but there were four generations in the audience," he said in 2003. "My mother was there. My mother. Can you believe it? At midnight? Until 2 or 3 in the morning? And loving it? It was so beautiful to see these four generations being respectful and listening intently to one another."

Hamlin also embraced storytelling, said Beverly Fields Burnette, president of the N.C. Association of Black Storytellers.

"I e-mailed and said, 'Well, you've got poetry on the stage, how about storytelling?'" she said. "Before I knew it, it was on the schedule."

Hamlin was hardworking and friendly, Wallace said. But he relished his growing fame. By the 2005 festival, he looked like as big a celebrity as the stars he brought in.

"He was walking around with an entourage, you know?" Wallace said with a laugh. "You couldn't even get to him. He had, like, four bodyguards on each side. I don't know if that was actually necessary, but it looked good."

Hamlin died at his home in Pfafftown, near Winston-Salem, after a long illness that his family has opted not to disclose. Details about services were not available at press time.

This year's festival will go on as planned, from July 30 through Aug. 4, at venues around the city.

Source: Orla Swift, "Larry Hamlin, 58, Founded National Black Theatre Festival," in *News & Observer,* June 8, 2007.

Jonathan Abarbanel

In the following review, Abarbanel questions Harris's style and view of the myth in a Chicago production of Robert Johnson: Trick the Devil.

Now-legendary Mississippi bluesman Robert Johnson died in 1938 under mysterious circumstances close to where he was born, from poison or syphilis or both. He was 27, Black and relatively unknown even among other African-Americans of the era, so his demise was of no great official concern.

Since then, Johnson's reputation and influence have become gigantic based on his slim discography of 25 or so songs recorded 1936–1938, the sheer force of his acoustic guitar work and the unexpected poetry of his lyrics. Legend says that Johnson sold his soul to the Devil in exchange for musical prowess.

In *Robert Johnson: Trick the Devil*, playwright Bill Harris posits that Johnson kept his soul by tricking the Devil into revealing musical secrets. Harris literalizes Johnson's presumed poisoning in a backroom jook joint as revenge for Johnson's affair with another man's woman, probably true, and scatters a few other known facts, such as Johnson's first recording session in San Antonio. Otherwise, this overly poetic but crudely structured play skimps on both biographical detail and character depth, leaving one knowing no more about Robert Johnson or the blues than at the start. Harris, a poet and academic, is far more interested in a pseudo-academic discussion of the blues and recycled racial clichés than in flesh-and-blood characters. For instance, Harris ignores the death of Johnson's first wife and newborn child, which must have influenced his art.

The cast demonstrates some ability but are asked to do impossible things, especially Jason Wilson as a guilt-stricken, white, Shakespeare professor from Boston obsessed with Johnson's music. Thoroughly improbable, he's a Yankee liberal who nonetheless spouts every nasty 1930's (and later) racial cliché. You can't have it both ways, even as a comic figure which he is (though not interpreted that way by Wilson or director Ron OJ Parson). David Adams as Poisoner Lem is asked only to threaten, glare and denounce the white and black supervisors of the WPA project he's worked on. James Earl Jones II as Stokes, a blind piano player, has no relation to plot but delivers direct narration to the audience. Since the other characters narrate too, what's the point of Stokes? Throughout, characters narrate rather than dramatize thoughts and actions.

Merl Sanders as Johnson and Sidney Miller as his femme fatale fare better. Sanders has a better-looking passing resemblance to Johnson and is a gifted singer/guitar player who pulls off the musical moments with aplomb. Miller, snazzily costumed by Kaniko Sago, provides high spirits and energy until Harris turns his focus elsewhere in Act II. Everyone works on Reginald Wilson's nicely-realized unit set, book ended by a fancy brass bed and a piano. But they can't create organic dramatic life from inert matter.

Source: Jonathan Abarbanel, Review of *Robert Johnson: Trick the Devil*, in *Windy City Times*, July 6, 2005.

Patricia R. Schroeder

In the following excerpt, Schroeder describes Harris's exploration of race relations, romanticism, and the intricacies of African American culture itself.

Bill Harris's award-winning 1992 play *Robert Johnson: Trick the Devil* has some similarities to [T. Coraghessan] Boyle's story. Like "Stones in My Passway," *Trick the Devil* takes place in a southern juke joint on the day Robert Johnson is poisoned, and it echoes the story's themes of jealousy and treachery. It realistically invokes its historical era, both in the juke setting and in a wider social context, while including enough romanticism to reflect some of the same cultural bifurcations as Boyle's story. Yet Harris, an African American playwright, adds some different, specifically African American dimensions to the tale. Director Woodie King Jr. notes that in all his work, Harris is particularly interested in "giving voice to the often unheard, ignored, or misunderstood independent and creative spirit of African American males" (2). Accordingly, in *Trick the Devil* we get to hear Robert Johnson's side of his own story (at least, as Harris envisions it). But in addition to re-creating Johnson and his historical context, Harris also shows how Johnson's story came to be mythologized by cultural outsiders who glamorized Johnson and so removed him from history. According to Harris: "Every society has its indelible and embedded myths, and they're necessary to that society. One of the things that I've wanted to do is raise discussion about these myths as they apply to African-Americans, especially African-American men. The whole idea of Robert Johnson having to sell his soul in order to be able to play the way he did...that's where I start... and then examine the why of the myth, rather than just it itself. Why does America need to believe that?" (qtd. in Tysh). Examining the "why" of the myth is a crucial element of *Trick the Devil*. In so doing, the play offers an artistic deconstruction of the Robert Johnson myth because it depicts the myth being created.

The key element in this exposure of mythology as a construct is the character of Kimbrough, a pretentious northern professor and the only white character in the play. He enters "Georgia Mayberry's Colored Jook Joint" early in the play, searching for Robert Johnson, much as researchers

> **WHAT ALSO LINGERS IS THE SAD FACT THAT JOHNSON'S LEGEND AND LEGACY HAVE BEEN CO-OPTED AND DISTORTED BY THE KIMBROUGHS OF THE WORLD, PURVEYORS OF PROSCRIPTIVE 'TRUTH' WHO ARE UNABLE TO FACE TRUTHS ABOUT THEMSELVES AND THE SOURCES OF THEIR PRIVILEGE."**

from John Hammond Sr. to Alan Lomax must have done. His outsider status is immediately apparent in his language. Unlike the lively vernacular spoken by Georgia Mayberry (the juke proprietor) and Stokes (the blind piano player), Kimbrough speaks in blank verse, his dialogue replete with allusions to Shakespeare, his research specialty. Kimbrough freely admits that he is out of his element and that he is afraid. He worries about being in the Delta environment, "a world / of shadows and smoke where nothing [is] solid," a world unlike his own realm "of reason, / order and certainty." He is searching for Robert Johnson because the power of Johnson's recorded music has upset his preconceived assumptions about race and culture. Speaking directly to the audience, Kimbrough marvels that Johnson's songs remind him of the Bible and Shakespeare, that they resonate with themes of loss and atonement. He wonders: "How does he—this unschooled black Orpheus / produce songs as universal and complex / as the intellectual love of my life?" Because Kimbrough accepts the stereotype that southern black people are primitive, "superstitious," "childlike perpetrators of unrepentant, / pot-luck violence," he is unnerved that Johnson's songs echo "universal" themes. Kimbrough apparently regards the Mississippi Delta as part of some universe other than his own.

Kimbrough has also heard the legend that Johnson sold his soul for his talent, "traded something he didn't think he needed, / for what he couldn't get any other way," but he doesn't know whether this or any other story about Johnson is true. Late in the play Robert Johnson himself tells the "true" story to Kimbrough. In this version, Johnson goes to the crossroads at midnight, but the devil is "just an ordinary white man in a suit and tie," some white power broker (a recording company executive, perhaps?) trying to exploit him. Because he is particular about other people touching his guitar, Johnson refuses to allow this white devil to tune it and instead plays as ferociously as he can. His impassioned playing eventually expresses not only his own life story but all of the misery in his racial memory: "the bondage, being bid for on the block, the lash, Jim Crow, the rope, the chain gang and the Klan. . . . And *that's* what got the Devil, because he couldn't call none of it a lie!" Infuriated, the devil plays his own guitar in a sort of demonic headbutting contest, and by watching him, Johnson becomes a virtuoso. Harris's Robert Johnson thus beats the devil at his own game simply by telling—and playing—the truth.

Kimbrough, it turns out, is himself tortured by a secret: his family wealth originated from slave-holding ancestors. When Kimbrough confesses this, Robert Johnson gives him the following advice: "Face your devil, walk along with him, side by side, then go your separate ways. That's the only way. And just like me you ain't got no choice." He encourages Kimbrough: "Go back and teach, professor. Go trick the Devil and tell the truth." The truth, however, is too much for Kimbrough to face. Unwilling to give up his tainted fortune and unable to live with himself for keeping it, Kimbrough instead creates a legend about Robert Johnson that sidesteps all the issues. In the play's epilogue we see him lecturing, creating a myth about Robert Johnson that fits neatly into the worldview that Kimbrough held before his southern journey and before meeting Robert Johnson. Claiming that his "research proves that [Johnson] / was in league with Satan from the age of / seventeen," Kimbrough describes Johnson in imagery more suitable for Macbeth's witches than a Delta bluesman. He depicts Johnson and Satan this way:

> They would consort during thunder, lightning
> and rain. And when they practiced their hurly
> burly the multiplying villainies
> of nature transmuted fair to foul
> and foul to fair.

Kimbrough creates a myth about Robert Johnson that distances the truth-telling musician. He thereby preserves his "rational" worldview in the face of inexplicable musical genius and avoids acknowledging his own complicity with the hellhounds dogging Johnson and himself.

Kimbrough's willful misrepresentation is obviously an exaggeration of the ways white scholars have used the Robert Johnson story. No researcher that I know of came face to face with Johnson, heard his story firsthand, and then distorted it for personal aggrandizement. However, Harris's inclusion of Kimbrough in his reinvention of Robert Johnson—as well as his imagining the devil as a white man in a business suit—suggests that white privilege often rests upon black exploitation. In an artistic way, Harris is asking the question I asked throughout the introduction and chapter I: whose interests are served in such a representation? Harris's answer is uncompromising. During Robert Johnson's lifetime, African Americans were commodities used to shore up the personal fortunes—whether monetary, academic, or otherwise—of white people with power and media access. And if Harris uses Johnson's story as Boyle did, as "a point of departure" to comment on the present, one might assume that he is commenting on white exploitation of black talent today as well as in Johnson's era. Harris uses the story of Robert Johnson to reveal the power imbalances within American race relations and to show that myth is constructed by human beings with assumptions and agendas. By performing the construction of myth, *Trick the Devil* successfully unmasks it.

But *Robert Johnson: Trick the Devil* does more than expose the underpinnings of myth. Like Boyle's story, Harris's play is the product of a bifurcated culture, although Harris's focus is primarily on a racial divide, made apparent in the differences between Kimbrough and the other characters. Unlike Boyle, who intermingles realism and romanticism within his own narrative prose, Harris ascribes a pragmatic view of the world to his rural black characters and a naive romanticism to his more powerful white one. The realistic worldview of the black characters is best embodied by Lem, Georgia's estranged husband, who returns in mid-play from building a levee for the government. In the absence of other paying work (a reference to the Depression setting) Lem felt he had no choice but to accept the levee job, which he then found "worse than slavery." He describes long days of backbreaking labor under cruel white supervisors for small pay and with no time off. After enduring months of these conditions, Lem enters the juke enraged at Johnson's presence in Georgia's room and angry at the world: "I ain't the same as I was before I went up there moving that dirt," he warns Georgia, "so be careful, you don't know how much I can stand." Eventually, Lem poisons Robert Johnson.

Through Lem, Harris establishes the broader social context that can impel individual actions and shows the tragic psychological effects of limited opportunity.

Lem's life is most unlike the bucolic fantasies of the rural South that Kimbrough harbors, although Kimbrough soon learns that his idea of an idyllic South is a misconception. Expecting to find "the undisciplined world of soil tillers, / idlers, roaming song singers," he discovers instead "a powder keg ready to explode," his pastoral fantasy replaced by the harsh reality of a Depression-era, racist economy. His differences from the black characters are everywhere apparent, from his elevated language to his response to folk culture. When Georgia and Stokes talk about Brer Rabbit and Brer Fox—stories about betrayal and wiliness and thus relevant to the events at hand—Kimbrough dismisses them as "[n]onsense tales. . . . Diversionary, but little more." Unaware that the man he is seeking will be killed that very day in the juke joint where he sits, Kimbrough recalls a juke joint dance he once witnessed as "[j]ust darkie fun." Repeatedly the black characters observe that white people "can't see nothing but what they want to see," and Kimbrough repeatedly proves them right. The contrast is sharply etched in a fragment of dialogue near the end, when Robert is trying to help Kimbrough face his personal devils. After an intense, climactic dialogue in which Kimbrough describes the demon that haunts his dreams, we hear:

> Kimbrough: It's a metaphor.
> Robert: Metaphor my ass, it's a hellhound, fool.

In this brief exchange, Harris encapsulates the different worldviews of the two characters and emphasizes Kimbrough's dangerous romanticism. Robert faces the truth regardless of what it brings him; Kimbrough displaces it to the status of literary trope. Kimbrough's final retreat to the myth-making lecture of the epilogue is the ultimate abandonment of what he has learned, a betrayal of both Robert and himself. While imagining Johnson in league with Satan may restore his ability to function in his rational world—where poor black singers cannot be Orpheus—one wonders who has really sold his soul in this play.

In addition to the cultural fissures between black and white, realism and romanticism, Harris's play goes one step further to explore the bifurcations within African American culture itself. The scene opens on a rainy afternoon in the juke, where

Georgia and Stokes swap stories as they prepare for their evening clientele. Through their opening conversation, Harris reveals his grounding in what novelist Arthur Flowers calls the "literary hoodoo" tradition of African American literature. For Flowers, "literary hoodoo" writers are spiritually inclined heirs to a double literary tradition of western written forms and African American oral ones (75–77). Their works include elements of both western and African culture and arts and preserve the stories that are vital to "communal health and empowerment" (79). The opening dialogue between Georgia and Stokes offers a succinct example of such cultural hybridity. The blind Stokes can see the future, a gift he has inherited from his hoodoo-practicing grandmama. Yet African American culture was influenced by southern Christianity as well as by African spiritual practices, and Georgia, who knows firsthand that Stokes's predictions come true, nonetheless sees herself as someone who "went for Christian" rather than hoodoo (Harris 8). This double heritage is also reflected in the structure of Harris's play. Like most western dramas, the play proceeds in a linear, cause-and-effect manner, with characters' actions clearly motivated and plot complications leading to a climax and a denouement. The play itself thus reveals its roots in western literary traditions while it nonetheless celebrates African American oral ones.

And celebrate that oral culture it does. The play is not exactly a musical, but it includes performances of many Robert Johnson songs, and as one reviewer noted, "many of the play's speeches and sequences play like musical numbers" (Holman). The vibrancy of African American folk culture is highlighted once Kimbrough enters, his presence creating "an opportunity for the other players to reveal the ingenious language, signifying, and role-playing African Americans created to keep their real life separate from the life the white man saw" (Leonin). Georgia and Stokes invoke numerous African American folk figures, from Brer Rabbit and Brer Fox to the Signifying Monkey; they imitate black vaudevillians Butter Beans and Susie; they discuss cultural traditions like Stokes's grandmama's healing "tricks" or the significance of names to African Americans. Through their exuberant verbal facility they reveal the vitality and value of African American culture; for them, western traditions like Christianity coexist easily with African-derived cultural products and values.

Writing in *The Souls of Black Folk* in 1903, W. E. B. Du Bois famously described this duality of outlook among African Americans as "double-consciousness," or the ability of African Americans to see the world simultaneously from a majority viewpoint (as Americans) and from a marginalized one (as oppressed African Americans). He wrote:

> [T]he Negro is a sort of seventh son, born with a veil, and gifted with second-sight in this American world,—a world which yields him no true self-consciousness, but only lets him see himself through the revelation of the other world. It is a peculiar sensation, this double-consciousness, this sense of always looking at one's self through the eyes of others, of measuring one's soul by the tape of a world that looks on in amused contempt and pity. One ever feels his twoness,—an American, a Negro; two souls, two thoughts, two unreconciled strivings; two warring ideals in one dark body, whose dogged strength alone keeps it from being torn asunder. (102)

Most commentators on Du Bois's notion of double-consciousness focus on the pain of the condition, on the "twoness," the internal "war." Yet Du Bois's definition includes some decidedly positive aspects as well. He describes double-consciousness as a gift—as second sight, or the ability to see things others do not see. Elsewhere in *The Souls of Black Folk* Du Bois predicts that "the problem of the twentieth century will be the problem of the color line" (100), and one suspects that people able to assess this problem from two different viewpoints, majority and oppositional, might have some advantages in understanding the world around them. In the case of Harris's characters, at any rate, double-consciousness enables them to function smoothly in two worlds: they know how to avoid revealing themselves to Kimbrough, and they know how to survive the hardships of their own lives, often with grace and good humor. Their pragmatism is thus a result of their cultural heritage. They easily recognize and manipulate multiple frames of reference; they can see complexly in a world full of contradictions.

In this, the pragmatic African American characters contrast sharply with the bookish Kimbrough, the ivory-tower romantic with no appreciation of multiple perspectives. His worldview cannot accommodate the presence of another; all things must be shaped to fit within his singular ideas of validity and value. The poverty of this unitary vision within a bifurcated culture is emphasized in Harris's epilogue, where Stokes, not Kimbrough, has the last word. Immediately after Kimbrough's lecture on Johnson's traffic with the devil—a chilling moment, since the audience knows that Kimbrough knows better—Stokes offers a final comment. Emphasizing his own "second sight" and offering interpretive options Kimbrough could never imagine, the blind Stokes says: "Robert Johnson? He be back. He just going down to hell and ease some people's minds; maybe move some rocks around, even change the way the river run. Aw, he'll be back directly, don't you worry 'bout a thing. Just like he been here before he be back again. How I know? 'Cause it's happened before. And I seen it with my own eyes!" With this comment, an amalgam of cultural images, the play ends. The picture of Robert Johnson that lingers is of a man with supernatural insights, prodigious talent, and an ability to rise again that links him to Christ, the phoenix, High John the Conqueror, or all three, depending on your cultural frame(s) of reference. What also lingers is the sad fact that Johnson's legend and legacy have been co-opted and distorted by the Kimbroughs of the world, purveyors of proscriptive "truth" who are unable to face truths about themselves and the sources of their privilege. Perhaps, suggests Harris, the very act of myth-making is the inevitable product of our differences, of our misunderstandings and refusals to see—in short, of our quintessentially American cultural bifurcations.

Source: Patricia R. Schroeder, "The Invention of the Past," in *Robert Johnson: Mythmaking and Contemporary American Culture*, University of Illinois Press, 2004, pp. 75–81.

SOURCES

Abarbanel, Jonathan, "Theatre Reviews," in *Windy City Times*, July 6, 2005, http://www. windycitymediagroup.com/gay/lesbian/news/ARTICLE.php?AID = 8837 (accessed July 3, 2009).

"Blacks in Survey Say Race Relations No Better with Obama," in *CNN News*, June 25, 2009, http://www.cnn. com/2009/POLITICS/06/25/obama.poll/ (accessed July 3, 2009).

"Building the Recovery," in *Recovery.Gov*, http://www. recovery.gov/ (accessed July 3, 2009).

Corbett, Thomas J., "Welfare," in *MSN Encarta Online Encyclopedia*, 2009, http://encarta.msn.com/encyclopedia_761575466/welfare.html (accessed on July 3, 2009).

"During the Clinton Administration, Was the Federal Budget Balanced?," in *FactCheck.Org*, February 11, 2008, http://www.factcheck.org/askfactcheck/during_the_clinton_administration_was_the_federal.html (accessed July 3, 2009).

Graves, Tom, "Introduction: The Lowland Mississippi Delta Plantation Blues," "The Life of Robert Johnson: The Early Years," and "The Afterlife of Robert Johnson: Legend of the Crossroads," in *Crossroads: The Life and Afterlife of Blues Legend Robert Johnson*, Demers Books, 2008, pp. 1–10, 13–18, and 51–56.

Gray, Madison, "Rodney King, The LA Riots: Fifteen Years after Rodney King," in *Time*, April 7, 2007, http://www.time.com/time/specials/2007/la_riot/article/0,28804,1614117_1614084_1614831,00. html (accessed July 3, 2009).

Gussow, Mel, "Out of the Blues, a Legendary Singer," in *New York Times*, February 25, 1993, http://theater2.nytimes.com/mem/theater/treview.html?res = 9F0CE7DD123 8F936 A15751C0A96 5958260 (accessed July 3, 2009).

Harris, Bill, "*Robert Johnson: Trick the Devil*," in *The National Black Drama Anthology: Eleven Plays from America's Leading African American Theaters*, edited by Woodie King, Jr., Applause Theatre Books, 1995, pp. 4–46.

Leonin, Mia, "The Devil Is in the Details," in *New Times: Broward/Palm Beach*, March 1, 2001, http://www.browardpalmbeach.com/2001-03-01/culture/the-devil-is-in-the-details/ (accessed July 3, 2009).

"Making Work Pay," in *Recovery.Gov*, http://www.recovery.gov/ (accessed July 3, 2009).

Pilgrim, David, "What Was Jim Crow?," in *Ferris State University's Jim Crow Museum of Racist Memorabilia*, http://www.ferris.edu/htmls/news/jimcrow/what.htm (accessed July 3, 2009).

———, "Who Was Jim Crow?" in *Ferris State University's Jim Crow Museum of Racist Memorabilia*, http://www.ferris.edu/htmls/news/jimcrow/who.htm (accessed July 3, 2009).

Schroeder, Patricia, "Invention of the Past," in *Robert Johnson, Mythmaking, and Contemporary American Culture*, University of Illinois Press, 2004, pp. 58–91.

Syam, Avimaan, "*Robert Johnson: Trick the Devil*," in *Austin Chronicle*, April 25, 2008, http:www.austinchronicle.com/gyrobase/Issue/review?oid = 616083 (accessed July 20, 2009).

Watkins, T. H. "Redeeming the Hour," "The New Utopians," and "The Second New Deal," in *The Great Depression: America in the 1930s*, Little, Brown, 1993, pp. 108–37, 138–63, 242–73.

FURTHER READING

Conwill, Kinshasha, and Arthur C. Danto, *Testimony: Vernacular Art of the African-American South: The Ronald and June Shelp Collection*, Harry N. Abrams, 2001.

Conwill and Danto's book features the visual art of southern African American Vernacular artists. Vernacular artists, also sometimes called folk artists, are artists without classical training whose work is inspired by everyday, ordinary people. The images collected in this book are also accompanied by essays on the history and culture of African Americans of the Deep South.

Gioia, Ted, *Delta Blues: The Life and Times of the Mississippi Masters Who Revolutionized American Music*, W. W. Norton, 2008.

Gioia's is an exhaustive and critically acclaimed study of the genesis, development, and influence of the blues born in the Delta region of Mississippi. Much attention is paid to debunking the myths and speculations that have been attached to Robert Johnson and his career.

Greenburg, Cheryl, *To Ask for an Equal Chance: African Americans in the Great Depression*, Rowman & Littlefield, 2009.

Greenburg's book explores the daily life and struggles of African Americans during the Great Depression. She studies African American participation in New Deal programs, the particular difficulties African Americans faced in competing for jobs with white Americans, and a broader analysis of the racism prevalent during this time period.

Shine, Ted, and James V. Hatch, eds., *Black Theatre, USA: Plays by African Americans: The Recent Period, 1935–Today*, Free Press, 1996.

In this collection edited by Shine and Hatch, plays by African American dramatists are grouped according to subject matter, such as "Social Protest," "Family Life," and "Modern Women Writing on Women." A section on new plays features works by contemporaries of Harris.

The Servant of Two Masters

CARLO GOLDONI

C. 1745

Carlo Goldoni's play *The Servant of Two Masters* was first written around 1745 and then revised heavily in 1753. However, no definitive information as to its initial performance exists, and several conflicting years during the 1740s are given for the play's original composition. Despite the lack of concrete information on the origin of the work itself, the play has remained a favorite performance piece across Europe and in the United States. It was performed in 2003 at Dorset House School in Bury, Sussex, England, and a 2009 production was staged in Seattle, Washington, by the Seattle Shakespeare Company. The play has remained in print for more than two and a half centuries, and a 2006 edition was released by Broadway Play Publishers.

The Servant of Two Masters is rooted firmly in the tradition of the commedia dell'arte, a distinctly Italian form of improvisational comedy popularized in the fifteenth century. It is also a love story that hinges upon coincidences, mistaken identities, disguises, and other such intrigues. The central character, Truffaldino, is integral to the series of misunderstandings and situational comedies that ultimately end happily, though they come very close to resulting in tragedy on more than one occasion. This exciting and highly dramatic series of events takes place over the course of only one day. Notably, the play is often described as Shakespearean in its scope and construction. It thus serves beautifully as an example of classic

Carlo Goldoni (The Library of Congress)

dramatic principles, both in its resemblance to Roman comedies and to Shakespeare's plays.

AUTHOR BIOGRAPHY

Goldoni was born to an upper-middle-class family in Venice, Italy, on February 25, 1707. His father was a doctor, and his career required the family to move frequently throughout Italy. Though Goldoni initially studied medicine, he soon switched to law, ultimately graduating with his law degree from the University of Padua in 1731. However, from his teenage years, Goldoni was captivated by the theater; he even ran away from home and spent several days with an acting troupe. He also carried on a series of ill-advised love affairs during his youth, many of which even resulted in his expulsion from the various schools he attended. Despite his tumultuous youth, Goldoni began work as a lawyer in Venice as soon as he earned his degree. He also worked in several different capacities for the government, and he never held any one job for long. The romantic misadventures of his youth continued, and Goldoni was often forced to

move from city to city in order to escape the scandals he left in his wake.

In addition to his law career, Goldoni worked as a house dramatist at the San Samuele Theatre and as a librettist at the San Giovanni Grisostomo opera house. Indeed, his first libretto, *Amalasunta*, was released in 1732. Other early plays include *Belisario* (1734), *Don Giovanni Tenorio, o il dissoluto* (1736), and *El cortesan, o l'uomo di mondo* (1738). The latter play was followed by *Il servitore di due padroni* in or around 1745. It was later translated into English as *The Servant of Two Masters*. In 1747, Goldoni was employed as a dramatist for the Teatro Sant'Angelo. He worked there until 1752. By then, he had already established a reputation for experimenting with more natural forms of theater, redefining the classic but rigid form of commedia dell'arte. This groundbreaking approach incited mixed reactions at the time.

Goldoni was an extremely prolific playwright, releasing up to sixteen plays a year. Some of the plays composed during the height of his productivity included *Il padre di famiglia* (1749), translated as *The Father of the Family* in 1757; and *La bottega del caffe* (1750), translated as *The Coffee House* in 1925. Next, from 1753 to 1762, Goldoni worked as a playwright for the San Luca Theater. He moved to Paris in 1762 and served as a playwright at the Comedie-Italienne. The same year, he was also hired as the tutor to Princess Adelaide, the illegitimate daughter of King Louis XV. The king gave Goldoni a pension in 1769, and the playwright settled in France, where he worked on his plays and memoirs. His last play, *Le bourru bienfaisant*, written in French, appeared in 1771 and was translated as *The Beneficent Bear* in 1892. Goldoni died in Paris on February 6 or 7, 1793. Notably, although the facts of the playwright's life remain somewhat obscure, it is known that he married and was survived by his wife.

PLOT SUMMARY

Act 1, Scene 1
The action in *The Servant of Two Masters* takes place in Venice over the course of a single day, beginning in the home of Pantalone Dei Bisognosi. Dr. Lombardi and his son, Silvio, are arranging Silvio's marriage to Pantalone's daughter, Clarice. The innkeeper, Brighella, and Clarice's maid, Smeraldina, are also present. Clarice was previously engaged to Federigo Rasponi, Pantalone's

business partner in Turin. However, Federigo has died in a duel, and thus Clarice is free to marry her beloved Silvio.

The group is preparing to celebrate when Truffaldino, a servant, arrives and insists that Pantalone speak with his master, who is in the next room. Truffaldino's master is Federigo, and thus his assertion is quite shocking to the little group. Clarice, of course, is worried as to how this news will affect her plans to marry Silvio. When Federigo enters, it turns out to be his sister, Beatrice, in disguise. This fact, however, is apparent only to Brighella, and the others are all convinced that Beatrice is indeed Federigo. Brighella does not reveal the truth.

Confirming his daughter's worst fears, Pantalone introduces Clarice to Beatrice as "his" betrothed and says that Silvio is a nephew. Silvio does not let the lie pass and asserts his true identity and purpose. Beatrice pretends to be offended, and Pantalone apologizes for the mix-up, which occurred only because they believed Federigo to be dead. Pantalone then renews his vow to marry Clarice to Federigo. Silvio threatens to fight any who would prevent him from marrying Clarice, and then he and his father storm out.

Clarice declares that she would rather marry an executioner than Federigo and also storms out. Angered by her behavior, Pantalone chases after her. Beatrice stops him and says that Clarice will calm down. She then suggests that they go over their business accounts. They set a time to go over everything later, and then Beatrice speaks privately with Brighella, thanking him for not revealing her ruse. Beatrice tells the innkeeper that Federigo is indeed dead, killed in a duel by her lover, Florindo Aretusi. Beatrice is now parading as her brother in order to wrap up his business matters and collect his money. She then plans to find Florindo, who has since fled in disguise to Venice to avoid prosecution, and escape with him.

Brighella notes that Beatrice if Federigo's legal heir and that the money is rightfully hers in any case. She points out that because she is a woman, Pantalone is more likely to take advantage of her, and Brighella agrees with this observation.

Act 1, Scene 2

Outside Brighella's inn, Truffaldino waits for his master. Florindo appears with a porter carrying his trunk. The porter is too weak to continue, and Truffaldino grabs the trunk and carries it into the inn. Florindo is impressed and hires Truffaldino to be his servant, a job that

Truffaldino accepts despite already being employed (a fact he does not share with Florindo). For his first job as Florindo's servant, Truffaldino is instructed to go to the post office and retrieve his master's letters. On his way, Truffaldino encounters Beatrice, who orders him to retrieve her trunk at the port and bring it to the inn. She also orders him to retrieve the mail from the post office (regardless of whether it is addressed to "him" or to Beatrice) and then goes into the inn.

Truffaldino next encounters Silvio, who orders him to fetch his master. Truffaldino is unsure which master Silvio is referring to, so he brings Florindo out of the inn. He then leaves for the post office. Florindo and Silvio realize there has been a mix-up, but Silvio just assumes he has mistaken Florindo's servant for someone else. Florindo and Silvio become fast friends, though Florindo gives a false name because he is a fugitive. Silvio says he was looking for Federigo in order to kill him for making a claim on Clarice. Florindo is appalled to learn that Federigo is still alive and apparently staying at the same inn. Alone, Florindo acknowledges that he ran from the duel so quickly that he never actually saw Federigo die. Thus, rather than reencounter his old enemy, Florindo decides to return to Turin and look for Beatrice.

Truffaldino returns with a porter carrying Beatrice's trunk. When he sees Florindo, he makes the porter wait around the corner. He then goes to his new master with the post, but he realizes that he has mixed up both of his masters' letters. Unable to read, Truffaldino cannot amend the problem, so he tells Florindo that his servant friend, Pasquale, asked him to retrieve a letter for his own master and that it has gotten mixed with Florindo's mail. Florindo sees that the letter is addressed to Beatrice, and he opens it despite Truffaldino's protests. Florindo learns from the letter that Beatrice is in Venice disguised as a man. Thus, he resolves to stay in town and try to find her. He is also very interested in finding the (imaginary) servant Pasquale, believing that the man will lead him to his beloved. Florindo then returns the letter to Truffaldino and heads toward town.

Truffaldino reseals the letter and calls to the porter. Beatrice comes out of the inn and retrieves her trunk and her letter. When she sees that it has been opened, Truffaldino lies and says he opened it by mistake and cannot read. Beatrice accepts the explanation and reads the letter. She gives

Truffaldino the keys to her trunk and orders him to unpack it. Then she heads to Pantalone's house.

Act 1, Scene 3

At his house, Pantalone is attempting to convince Clarice that she must marry Federigo. Smeraldina comes in to announce Federigo's arrival and she tells her mistress that Clarice is lucky to marry such a handsome man. When Beatrice sees how upset Clarice is, she asks to speak with her privately. When they are alone, Beatrice reveals her true identity but makes Clarice promise to keep it a secret, even from Silvio. Clarice reluctantly agrees, but she is overjoyed at the news that Federigo is indeed dead. The two women hug, but when Pantalone walks in and sees them embracing, he assumes that they have made up and that the wedding plans can go forward. In fact, he intends to have the wedding the very next day. Pantalone sets out to inform Silvio of Clarice's change of heart, and she notes that things have now gone from bad to worse.

Act 2, Scene 1

Silvio and his father are in the courtyard of Pantalone's house. Silvio wishes to confront Pantalone, but Dr. Lombardi wishes to take a more coolheaded approach. He convinces Silvio to let him handle it. Silvio agrees and leaves. Soon after, Pantalone enters the courtyard. He tells Dr. Lombardi that Clarice wishes to marry Federigo. Silvio's father tries to reason with Pantalone, but he eventually grows angry and storms off. Silvio then enters and threatens Pantalone. When he reaches for his sword, Pantalone screams for help. Beatrice enters the courtyard and comes to Pantalone's defense. Silvio and Beatrice fight as Pantalone runs out to the street calling for help. Beatrice bests Silvio and is ready to deliver the fatal blow when Clarice rushes in and stops her.

Beatrice reminds Clarice of her promise, which Silvio interprets as Clarice's agreement to marry Federigo. Beatrice leaves Clarice and Silvio alone and Clarice assures Silvio of her fidelity. But, because she is unable to tell him the nature of her promise, he does not believe her. He declares that he never wants to see her again. Clarice picks up his sword and holds it to her chest, threatening to kill herself. Smeraldina runs in and stops her, admonishing Silvio for not stopping her himself. Even Clarice is appalled by Silvio's indifference. She notes that Silvio will one day realize his mistake and runs off in tears.

Act 2, Scene 2

Truffaldino waits at the inn for his masters. Florindo enters and asks whether his servant has found Pasquale yet. Truffaldino, of course, has not. Florindo then gives Truffaldino the keys to his trunk and goes to find Beatrice. After he leaves, Beatrice enters and tells Truffaldino that Pantalone will be joining them for dinner. A little while later, Truffaldino is carrying the food to Beatrice's room when Florindo enters and asks why Truffaldino is serving dinner before his master has appeared. Truffaldino lies and says he saw Florindo coming from the window. Florindo goes to his room and Truffaldino enlists a waiter to help him as he juggles all the dishes, rushing back and forth between both masters' rooms, and occasionally helping himself to some of the food as well.

Act 2, Scene 3

Clarice has sent Smeraldina to the inn with a secret letter for Beatrice. When Smeraldina learns that Pantalone is there, she asks for Beatrice's servant to come out to the street to retrieve the letter. When Truffaldino sees her, the two servants flirt. Smeraldina tells Truffaldino to give the letter to Federigo. Curious, Truffaldino opens the letter, but neither he nor his new love can read, though both lie about this fact to one another. As they attempt to decipher the letter, Pantalone and Beatrice come outside. Beatrice yells at Truffaldino for opening the letter. Smeraldina attempts to lie about her purpose in going to the inn, but the truth is revealed, and she runs off, with Pantalone chasing after her. Beatrice begins to beat Truffaldino with her walking stick, and then she storms off. From the window, Florindo sees a man beating Truffaldino, but the "man" is gone by the time he makes it outside.

When Florindo asks Truffaldino to explain what happened, the servant says he spat on the man's shoe and that the man beat him for it. Florindo sees Truffaldino's calm acceptance of the beating from a stranger as an act that reflects poorly on his master (that is, Florindo himself). Therefore, Florindo also becomes angry and beats Truffaldino.

Act 3, Scene 1

Beatrice is out, and Florindo is sleeping in his room. Truffaldino decides to unpack his masters' trunks and air out their clothes. He brings both trunks out in the hall and begins to sort through them. In Beatrice's trunk, Truffaldino finds a portrait that bears a strong resemblance to Florindo. The only difference is the man's hair and dress. Florindo calls from his room for Truffaldino, and the servant scrambles to pack the trunks before being discovered. In his haste, though, he mixes up some of their belongings. Florindo comes out and sees both trunks, but Truffaldino says the second trunk belongs to a man who has just arrived at the inn.

Florindo has Truffaldino retrieve his suit for him, but when he puts it on, he finds his own portrait (the one he gave Beatrice) in his pocket. Truffaldino lies and says that the portrait belonged to his old master, who has since died. He says he kept it as a memento and accidentally put it in his new master's trunk. Florindo flees in grief to his room, believing Beatrice to be dead.

Beatrice and Pantalone enter, and Truffaldino tells the same lie that he told Florindo about the second trunk. Beatrice opens her trunk in search of some business papers and comes across a strange book, which contains old letters she wrote to Florindo. Truffaldino repeats his lie about a dead former master, and Beatrice of course assumes that Florindo is dead. She forgets herself and laments the loss of her lover aloud, thus revealing her true identity. She runs to her room in despair, leaving Pantalone and Truffaldino shocked at the revelation that Federigo is actually Beatrice.

Act 3, Scene 2

On the street, Pantalone approaches Dr. Lombardi. Pantalone is extremely apologetic; he attempts to explain the recent turn of events and renew Clarice's engagement to Silvio. However, Dr. Lombardi is so angry that he storms off before Pantalone is able to do so. Silvio comes along, and Pantalone is finally successful in his endeavor. Silvio is ecstatic, and he and Pantalone go to find Clarice.

Act 3, Scene 3

Back at the inn, both Beatrice and Florindo exit their rooms. Each is holding a sword and plans to commit suicide. They are so distraught that it is several moments before they notice one another. Delighted, they both explain that they thought the other was dead and how they came to think this. They both wonder what their respective servants are up to, and they call for them at once. Truffaldino is dragged into the room by Brighella. The innkeeper then goes in search of a second servant, as no one has figured out Truffaldino's ruse. The servant whispers to Florindo that Pasquale is

Beatrice's servant and that all of the mistakes today have been made by Pasquale. He says that all of the lies he has told have been attempts to cover for his errant friend. He even tells Florindo that he will admit to Beatrice that everything was his fault. Truffaldino then whispers a similar story to Beatrice, stating that Florindo's servant is named Pasquale and that Truffaldino has been covering up Pasquale's mistakes all day.

Beatrice and Florindo are satisfied by Truffaldino's explanations, and Beatrice sets off to Pantalone's house to resolve their pending business matters. Truffaldino is ordered to take Florindo there to meet her later. After Beatrice has gone, Truffaldino says that he wishes to marry Smeraldina and asks Florindo to put in a good word with Pantalone.

Act 3, Scene 4

Dr. Lombardi, Silvio, Clarice, Smeraldina, and Pantalone are all at Pantalone's house. Silvio begs Clarice's forgiveness, and she eventually grants it. Brighella comes in and announces Beatrice's arrival. She enters and begs forgiveness for her ruse, and it is granted by all. Silvio and Clarice are happily reunited and are pleased to hear of Beatrice's reunion with Florindo. Smeraldina then announces that she wishes to marry as well. She whispers to Clarice that she wants to marry Beatrice's servant and Clarice promises to speak to Beatrice about this.

Truffaldino then enters with Florindo, who is welcomed heartily. Pantalone agrees to give Beatrice away in her wedding and to resolve all of his business matters with her. However, when Florindo announces that he wishes his servant to marry Smeraldina, Clarice announces that she wishes Beatrice's servant to marry her. Believing that Smeraldina now has two potential husbands, Clarice and Florindo decide that she should marry neither; Florindo and Clarice do not wish to offend one another by pressing their case over the other's. Truffaldino, then, is finally forced to reveal his trickery, to the astonishment of all.

CHARACTERS

Florindo Aretusi

Florindo Aretusi is Beatrice's lover from Turin. Beatrice's brother, Federigo, despised his sister's paramour and incited him to a duel. However, since Florindo killed Federigo in the duel, he was forced to flee Turin in order to escape arrest. Florindo had rushed off as soon as Federigo fell, and it was only later that he learned that his rival had died. In fact, when Florindo arrives in Venice in the hopes of being reunited with Beatrice, he learns that Federigo is alive and staying at the same inn. Florindo is so afraid of meeting with his enemy that he plans to return to Turin straightaway. He decides to stay only after he learns that Beatrice is in Venice.

Florindo is a faithful lover who only hopes to find Beatrice, and even the duel is implied to have been Federigo's fault. Thus, he is a relatively blameless character. However, Federigo reveals his prideful nature when he thinks that Truffaldino has allowed himself to be beaten by a stranger. Florindo believes that this humiliating act reflects poorly on him as Truffaldino's master. Thus, he beats his servant in response to that perceived humiliation.

Clarice Dei Bisognosi

Clarice Dei Bisognosi is Pantalone's daughter. She was promised by her father to his business partner, Federigo, a man Clarice had never met. However, when Federigo died, she became free to marry her lover, Silvio. When her engagement to him has been concluded, Beatrice appears disguised as Federigo, and Pantalone feels compelled to honor his original promise. Though Clarice eventually says she will follow her father's wishes out of obedience to him, it is clear that she cares only for Silvio. Clarice is a steadfast and faithful lover, never wavering in her feelings for Silvio. She is also a faithful friend, keeping Beatrice's secret even when it costs her Silvio's love.

Other events that prove her true nature are her attempted suicide at the thought of losing Silvio and her advocacy for Smeraldina's marriage. In the latter case, Clarice withdraws her advocacy to avoid offending Florindo.

Pantalone Dei Bisognosi

Pantalone Dei Bisognosi is Clarice's father. He is a man of honor, and he feels that he must uphold his original promise to Federigo despite the cost to his daughter. He then endeavors to set things right with Silvio and Dr. Lombardi as soon as he learns that Federigo is Beatrice. Pantalone is also an honorable businessman, upholding his dealings with Beatrice even after her true identity has been revealed. However, he attempts to beat both his daughter and Smeraldina when they defy him. Pantalone's cowardice is further revealed when Silvio attempts to kill him and Pantalone runs away, screaming for help.

Brighella

Brighella is the innkeeper and a friend of Pantalone's. He vouches for Beatrice's false identity and does not reveal her secret. This makes him seem a faithful friend to Beatrice, but less so to Pantalone. Indeed, when Beatrice's identity is revealed and Pantalone calls Brighella to account for vouching for her, Brighella lies and says that he was also fooled by the ruse.

Dr. Lombardi

Dr. Lombardi is Silvio's father. He is constantly quoting legal jargon, which he uses in his attempts to persuade Pantalone of the validity of Silvio's engagement over Federigo's. Indeed, whereas Silvio is angered, Dr. Lombardi keeps a cool head, believing that reason and good sense will prevail. However, when that belief proves false, Dr. Lombardi loses his temper to a degree that exceeds that of his own son. When Pantalone attempts to apologize and renew Clarice's engagement to Silvio, Dr. Lombardi is so angry that he storms out before Pantalone can make peace. However, Silvio, despite having attempted to kill Pantalone, is still willing to hear him out.

Silvio Lombardi

Silvio Lombardi is Clarice's lover and Dr. Lombardi's son. He is a passionate and short-tempered man. He threatens to kill anyone who stands in the way of his marriage to Clarice and very nearly does so. He tries to track down Federigo to kill him, and he also attempts to kill Pantalone, who runs away like a coward. However, when Silvio finally faces Beatrice in a sword fight, she bests him. Only Clarice's intervention saves him from certain death.

Silvio's distrust, however, is revealed in the same scene. He believes that Clarice's promise to Beatrice is one of matrimony and not secrecy. He does not trust his lover's protestations, even as she threatens suicide to prove her love. In fact, he would impassively watch Clarice die if not for Smeraldina's intervention. Later, Silvio must beg his lover's forgiveness, which he does gladly.

Pasquale

Although Pasquale is not an actual person, he does figure into the plot in an integral way. Pasquale, in a sense, becomes Truffaldino's alter ego: the man responsible for mixing up belongings and opening letters. Pasquale is also Truffaldino's scapegoat, the person blamed for any mistakes that may occur as Truffaldino attempts to serve two masters.

Beatrice Rasponi

Beatrice Rasponi is Florindo's lover and Federigo's sister. Even before the duel that precipitates the play's action, Beatrice has a reputation for dressing as a man and living wildly. After Federigo's death, Beatrice travels in disguise as her brother, hoping to collect his business debts and reunite with her lover. Although Beatrice is Federigo's legal heir and can thus claim his money without a disguise, she fears that, as a woman, she will be taken advantage of. Beatrice displays a rather skewed sense of morality as she pretends to pursue Clarice's hand in marriage. Indeed, what Beatrice sees at first as harmless fun leads to the despair of Clarice and the anger of Dr. Lombardi and Silvio. It also leads to Clarice's attempted suicide and Silvio's attempt to murder Pantalone and Beatrice.

Beatrice finally reveals her ruse in the heat of her grief for Florindo when she believes him to be dead. She is a faithful and constant lover, and she also treats Truffaldino fairly well. When she beats him, the act is certainly more justified than when Florindo does so; she punishes him because he has been opening her letters.

Federigo Rasponi

Though Federigo is dead before the play begins, his sister Beatrice spends most of her time masquerading as him. Thus, Federigo plays an important role in everything that occurs throughout the play. The hate he felt for Beatrice's lover, Florindo, precipitated the duel with Florindo and his own death.

Smeraldina

Smeraldina is servant to Clarice and Pantolone. She also falls in love with Truffaldino. Despite being illiterate, Smeraldina is often the only voice of reason apparent in the play. She advises Clarice wisely on the ways of men, love, and marriage. She also admonishes Silvio for being so callous and indifferent as to allow Clarice to take her own life without attempting to stop her. She also displays her wit when she runs away from Pantalone as he attempts to beat her, noting that she is young and fast whereas he is old and slow.

Truffaldino

Truffaldino is the servant of Beatrice and Florindo, and he falls in love with Smeraldina. He is the central character in the play, as all of the action revolves around his antics and misadventures. His position as both Beatrice's and Florindo's servant and the lies he tells to keep them from discovering his dual role set in motion the play's coincidences, misunderstandings, and miscommunications. Truffaldino thus plays the classic role of fool and jester, alternately displaying both stupidity and an unwitting wit. Truffaldino's antics are also largely physical, as is the case when he juggles his masters' plates during the dinner service and mixes up their belongings when unpacking their trunks. However, despite being so foolish as to be caught opening letters (even though he is unable to read) and committing other careless acts, Truffaldino is still clever enough to work for two masters without being caught. He is a consummate and quick liar, able to appease all around him with his stories. Truffaldino admits the truth only when his own lies may prevent him from being able to marry Smeraldina.

THEMES

Social Class

All of the characters in the play, and their interactions, constantly exhibit the nature of class structure. At the beginning of the play, Pantalone immediately bows to the will of Federigo over the will of Silvio and his father. This is because Federigo is a business partner of Pantalone's, and he has more money and influence than the Lombardis. Class is again revealed in the different reactions of Dr. Lombardi and his son. The doctor, an educated man, quotes legal jargon and believes that reason and legality will prevail. Silvio, less educated than his father, instead puts his trust in brute force. However, neither reason nor force proves to be effective.

The most striking example of class structure can be seen in the gap between the upper class and their servants. Because Truffaldino is a mere servant, so little attention is paid to him that he is able to work for two masters without anyone being the wiser. Indeed, when Truffaldino brings out the wrong master upon Silvio's request, Silvio simply assumes he has mistaken one servant for another, as if they are interchangeable. Little critical attention is paid to the lies Truffaldino tells, again showing that his masters accept him as a simple creature incapable of such a clever ruse. The facts that the masters in the play think nothing of beating their servants and that even the servants accept this as a matter of course also reveal the nature of class structure in the play.

TOPICS FOR FURTHER STUDY

- Imagine *The Servant of Two Masters* set in modern times. How would the plot and character interactions change to reflect today's attitudes? Rewrite a scene from the play that addresses this scenario.

- Using the Internet, research society in eighteenth-century Italy. Present your findings to the class in a PowerPoint presentation, and explain how your findings deepen your understanding of the play.

- For a modern, young-adult view of arranged marriages read Bali Rai's *(Un)arranged Marriage.* The book features Manny, a seventeen-year-old British Indian boy, and his resistance to his arranged marriage. In an essay, compare and contrast Manny's experience in *(Un)arranged Marriage* to Clarice's in *The Servant of Two Masters.*

- Stage a scene from *The Servant of Two Masters* and perform it for your class. To explore the nature of physical comedy, try out different approaches to portraying Truffaldino's antics.

Beatrice beats Truffaldino for opening her letters and is at least justified in her anger, but Florindo beats Truffaldino for humiliating him by allowing another man to beat him. Yet Truffaldino does not find either beating to be unjust. Even Smeraldina accepts the justice of being beaten by Pantalone for lying, although she does try to escape her punishment.

Gender

Pantalone chooses Federigo over Silvio even at the cost of his daughter's goodwill and personal happiness. Here, though, another aspect of class structure is revealed. As a man, it is Pantalone's right to promise his daughter to other men and to demand her obedience, a fact that even Clarice acknowledges. Another aspect of the power that men have over women is displayed through Beatrice's decision to pose as her brother. As she tells Brighella, she is afraid that Pantalone will try to cheat her or otherwise take advantage of her if he knew she was a woman. Even Brighella admits that she has a point. More of the power that men have over women is exhibited in the duel between Federigo and Florindo, a fight that takes place over Beatrice and reveals the underlying belief that she is akin to property. The same belief is exhibited by Silvio, who plans to kill his rival and Clarice's father in order to remove the obstacles that prevent him from marrying her. Several of the observations Smeraldina makes about love and marriage also reveal the basic inequities between men and women.

Marriage

Love and the nature of marriage are also explored in the play, largely through the sage advice of Smeraldina. Clarice's love for Silvio is valued as such, yet the importance of her marriage to Federigo as a tool for bolstering a business relationship is valued much more. When Clarice despairs over this turn of events, Smeraldina observes that love is different from marriage. It does not matter who Clarice marries, Smeraldina tells her, as all men possess the same nature and she will experience the same disappointments and heartbreaks with anyone. Silvio's fickle nature largely serves to prove Smeraldina's assertions. His love for Clarice wavers when he believes she has promised herself to Federigo, and he does not believe her despite the fact the she threatens suicide to prove her sincerity. Florindo's love for Beatrice is far more steadfast, and he trusts in her despite learning that she is masquerading as his conquered rival. Smeraldina takes her love for Truffaldino and his love for her at face value. The two exchange only a brief conversation before establishing their desire to wed. Indeed, love and marriage are seen as both separate entities and interchangeable circumstances. The latter aspect can be seen when all three couples are happily united and no recriminations are made by any of the characters for their parts in nearly preventing so happy an outcome.

STYLE

Farce

A farce is a play that features an exaggerated plot and the humorous situations that evolve from it. Characters in disguise and resulting instances of mistaken identity are also mainstays of the farcical drama. Romantic misadventures and physical

Typical commedia performance *(Fine Art Photographic Library / Corbis)*

comedy feature as well. All of these characteristics are apparent in *The Servant of Two Masters*. Although Beatrice's disguise is apparent, Truffaldino's masquerade as a servant to two masters is also a case of mistaken identity. Indeed, both Beatrice and Florindo believe that Truffaldino is their servant and that the other's servant is Pasquale. The physical and situational humor largely stems from Truffaldino's various predicaments, though it can also be seen when Pantalone chases after Smeraldina.

Other aspects of a farce include a fast pace and a central plot twist that generally brings matters to a happy conclusion. These conditions certainly apply to *The Servant of Two Masters*. All of the excitement that occurs between the three pairs of lovers takes place in only one day. Although Truffaldino's mistakes largely serve to keep Florindo and Beatrice apart, they ultimately bring them together and lead to the revelation of Beatrice's true identity. This in turn brings about the happy ending.

Aside

An aside is a dramatic construction in which characters speak aloud to themselves or directly to the audience without any of the other characters on the stage overhearing. Asides are used liberally in *The Servant of Two Masters*, and they generally serve to clue the audience in on a character's secret desires and motives. This device is particularly important in Goldoni's play because the characters persist in a near-constant state of confusion. If audience members were not privy to each character's private feelings and motives, they would also be somewhat confused. For instance, if Beatrice's true identity were not known to the audience, then the humor and hijinks that follow this ruse would be lost on the audience as well.

COMPARE & CONTRAST

- **1700s:** Arranged marriages are exceedingly common and accepted as a way of life. Love is also not viewed as a necessary precursor to marriage.

  Today: Love is generally believed to be an essential prerequisite to marriage, and people largely act accordingly. This is especially true in Westernized countries. However, arranged marriages are still fairly common in India, Africa, and the Middle East.

- **1700s:** Before the invention of the camera, the discovery of fingerprints or DNA, and the widespread use of centralized record keeping, accurately confirming a person's identity is nearly impossible. People rely on letters of introduction and the testimony of mutual acquaintances to establish their identity.

  Today: Government-based record keeping and the use of fingerprinting and DNA are regularly used as methods for incontrovertibly establishing identity. However, the prevalence of electronic documentation also leaves information vulnerable to misuse, and identity theft is increasingly common.

- **1700s:** Duels, while often illegal, are still regularly used as a means for solving disputes, especially in matters of honor and love.

  Today: Duels, in the classic sense of the word, are no longer practiced. However, the modern equivalent of a duel might be a drive-by shooting, in which gang members fight for honor or power.

HISTORICAL CONTEXT

Commedia dell'Arte

The Italian theatrical tradition of commedia dell'arte originated in the fifteenth century and remained popular well into the seventeenth century. Although *The Servant of Two Masters* was written in the eighteenth century, it still remains fully rooted in this tradition. The Italian art form owes its foundation to ancient Roman comedies, which featured stock characters and stock comedic situations. Indeed, commedia dell'arte, which literally means "comedy of art" is characterized by improvisational performance, physical comedy, and the use of recurring characters and plots. Both Pantalone and Brighella are such characters, and they would have been immediately recognizable to an eighteenth-century Venetian audience. Indeed, Pantalone appears throughout Italian comedy as a miserly merchant, and Brighella appears throughout as a self-serving shopkeeper. Notably, Goldoni's portrayals of these characters are somewhat more flattering.

Other traditional aspects of commedia dell'arte include the use of masks and the use of a fool or clown. In fact, the harlequin—a type of clown—stems from this tradition as well. Commedia dell'arte generally plays upon such themes as love and jealousy, and *The Servant of Two Masters* is no exception. Indeed, the traditional plot of parents or authorities preventing two lovers from marrying is a typical convention. The lovers then turn to a servant (perhaps more than one) to aid them in their endeavors, and this servant is generally a major source of the play's comedy. While Beatrice and Florindo do not necessarily turn to Truffaldino for help, the similarities are nevertheless apparent. Notably, despite its ancient roots, the traditions of commedia dell'arte remain apparent in contemporary drama. They are also apparent in the works of William Shakespeare and the French playwright Molière.

The Age of Enlightenment

The Enlightenment spread throughout Europe and the United States in the eighteenth century and was known in Italy as the *Illuminismo*. Modes of thought that characterize the era include the movement towards self-governance and away from established monarchies. This political trend was motivated by the growing philosophical belief in the rights of the individual and their corresponding entitlement to liberty. In addition, principles of reason and science began to take precedence over faith or belief: religious, superstitious, or otherwise. Given this emphasis on reason, the authority of the church was questioned as much as (or perhaps more than) the authority of kings. As the eighteenth century dawned, Italy was comprised of several nation-states, and their governance by either the Catholic Church or Spain was haphazard at best. Thus, as the ideas of the Enlightenment took hold, these powers began to lose their grip. Some such Italian thinkers responsible for bringing this about include the historians Ludovico Antonio Muratori (1672–1750) and Pietro Giannone (1676–1748). Other notable Italian figures during the Enlightenment include Giambattista Vico (1668–1744) and Cesare Beccaria (1738–1794). Notably, the more humanistic principles of the day are reflected in Goldoni's play. His stock characters are portrayed in a more flattering and less stereotypical light than their predecessors, and *The Servant of Two Masters* has thus been credited with introducing an element of naturalism to the commedia dell'arte form.

CRITICAL OVERVIEW

The popular and critical success of *The Servant of Two Masters* is evident from its continued study and performance for more than two and a half centuries. In addition, no critical discussion of the play is complete without acknowledging the physical comedy and slapstick or improvisational variations that continue to keep it alive on the stage. Indeed, according to Oscar G. Brockett in *History of the Theatre*, "Goldoni did much to obliterate the distinctions between commedia and regular comedy. Among Goldoni's commedia plays, perhaps the best is *The Servant of Two Masters*." In a 2007 *Back Stage East* review of the play, Nancy Ellen Shore notes that "the irrepressibly mischievous spirit of Carlo Goldoni...comes winging across the footlights." She also adds that "Goldoni's feverishly funny script easily stands alongside theater's classic farces." Yet more praise is

proffered in a *Sacramento Bee* article by Jim Carnes, who writes, "It's fast, it's funny, it's sexy—and it's more than 250 years old." Carnes also finds that the play is "like Shakespeare's comedies—but with a lot more sight gags and one-liners." He remarks that "the comedy is broad, the thought not deep, but it's a rare kind of entertainment."

CRITICISM

Leah Tieger

Tieger is a freelance writer and editor. In the following essay, she discusses the more serious themes and undertones in Carlo Goldoni's The Servant of Two Masters.

A highly comedic farce, Carlo Goldoni's *The Servant of Two Masters* has remained popular for centuries, specifically for its ability to evoke laughter. Indeed, slapstick comedy and physical and situational humor drive the play, as do its easily recognizable characters and situations. Yet at its heart, *The Servant of Two Masters* is an apt and quite serious commentary on love, the differences between men and women, and class structure. For instance, as Stephanie Chidester remarks in *Insights*, Goldoni's play "is at once charmingly light yet surprisingly complex." Chidester goes on to state that "Goldoni enriches the farcical plot-lines... with themes both humorous and serious. One such theme is self-interest, a force seen not only in the behavior of the characters but also in the play's backdrop of Venetian society. Occasionally, some aspects of this backdrop creep into the foreground of plot-lines—namely, double standards and the callous treatment of women by male guardians and law-makers."

Indeed, both the comedic and serious traits of the play hinge on each character's self-interest. Truffaldino's attempt to collect two paychecks results in much of the play's humor, but it also reveals the plight of the servant. Beatrice's disguise leads to several entertaining missteps, yet the masquerade is maintained for a serious reason: Beatrice's desire to avoid being taken advantage of simply because she is a woman. Dr. Lombardi hilariously spouts nonsensical legal jargon, but he does so because he believes in the power of reason. Pantalone chooses money over his daughter's happiness, but he also shows himself to be sensitive to her plight. For example, when he believes that Clarice has reconciled with Federigo,

WHAT DO I READ NEXT?

- Selected comedies by Goldoni appear in the 2009 reprint edition of *The Comedies of Carlo Goldoni*. The collection is edited by Helen Zimmern and Robert Browning and contains four plays, translated into English: *A Curious Mishap*, *The Beneficent Bear*, *The Fan*, and *The Spendthrift Miser*.

- For a fact-filled exploration of how fingerprinting is used as a means of identification, read Mark R. Hawthorne's 2008 book *Fingerprints: Analysis and Understanding*. The volume includes information on how to correctly take fingerprints and recognize the characteristics used to determine identity. Lifting methods, proper storage, and comparative approaches are also discussed.

- In the 2000 young-adult novel *Counterfeit Son* by Elaine Marie Alphin, fourteen-year-old Cameron struggles to maintain his secret identity. Cameron was raised by his father, a serial killer who kidnapped and killed young boys. When Cameron's father dies, he decides to take the identity of one of his father's victims. He poses as Neil Lacey, a boy kidnapped and killed over six years ago. The Lacey family accepts Cameron as their son, and he is finally able to experience a normal childhood.

- Jhumpa Lahiri's 2003 novel *The Namesake* portrays an Indian family founded on an arranged marriage. This modern, multicultural look at an arranged marriage and the resulting family's struggle to assimilate into American society is appropriate for young-adult readers.

- William Shakespeare's circa 1599 play *As You Like It* is a comedy that features cross-dressing characters and cases of mistaken identity akin to that in Goldoni's play. Indeed, the structure of misadventures and comic situations that arise from the circumstances echo those in *The Servant of Two Masters*. Thus, a comparison between the two plays sheds much light on the essential construction of a classic farce.

- For additional insight into the classic plays that influenced Goldoni and *The Servant of Two Masters*, read the 2003 anthology *Five Comedies from the Italian Renaissance*. The volume, edited by Laura Giannetti and Guido Ruggiero, contains sixteenth-century plays by such dramatists as Bernardo Dovizi de Bibbiena, Niccolo Machiavelli, and Pietro Aretino.

he is overjoyed. He is then overjoyed once more when he learns that Federigo is Beatrice, and his first act is to immediately run to the Lombardis and set things right. Silvio and Clarice are perhaps the least comical of the play's characters, and they are also the least self-interested. On the other hand, as Chidester observes, Silvio's self-interest lies in his love for Clarice and his desire to kill anyone who would prevent him from marrying her. Still, he is rather absurd in his anger, which never finds an outlet, as even Beatrice bests him in a sword fight. Clarice is even less comical than Silvio: she is both the least comical and the least self-interested character in the play. Therefore, the

connection seems clear: the characters' desires and their willingness to act upon them fuel the comedic aspects of the play.

The unwitting wit of the play's characters also belies its more serious themes from the outset, especially those related to love, power, and class. At the end of act 1, scene 1, Brighella comments that Beatrice has gone to rather extreme lengths to be successfully reunited with her love. Beatrice replies "Oh, this is nothing. Love makes people do far worse things than this." What passes for witty repartee between the two characters is in fact a serious observation on the nature of love. Only a few lines later, at the beginning of act 1, scene 2, Truffaldino notes that "when they say we ought to serve our masters with love, they ought to tell the masters to have a little charity toward their servants." Here, the foolish Truffaldino is ostensibly referring to his empty stomach, but instead he observes that love is a two-pronged affair, and that no man can give without receiving.

The servant Smeraldina, the wisest character in the play, and thus the character who makes the most astute statements throughout, shows herself to be prudent in the ways of love and in the ways of men. She is especially attuned to how those dynamics are affected by the power that men have over women. In act 2, scene 1, Smeraldina complains of this very problem and of the short shrift accordingly granted to women. She explains that such circumstances exist "because 'tis men who have made the laws." Still, as Chidester also points out, Smeraldina does not find that women are immune to such bias. For instance, the servant goes on to explain that "if the women had made [the laws], things would be just the other way." Next, in a rather poetic and apt image that is as funny as it is serious, arresting, and beautiful, Smeraldina declares: "If I were a queen, I'd make every man who was unfaithful carry a branch of a tree in his hand, and I know all the towns would look like forests."

Whereas Smeraldina is the wise servant who is occasionally foolish, Truffaldino is the foolish servant who is unwittingly wise. Indeed, Smeraldina reveals herself to be a fool only when she is unable to read her mistress's letter and when Pantalone catches her in a lie. She proves her shrewdness, though, when she observes that Pantalone is old and slow where she is young and quick. In this manner, she avoids a beating by running off, knowing that Pantalone will be unable to capture her. Truffaldino, however, constantly plays the fool. In part, this foolishness allows him to maintain his masters' trust as he deceives them, as neither Beatrice nor Florindo thinks him clever enough to lie. However, unlike Smeraldina, Truffaldino calmly and quietly accepts his beatings, whether they are fair or not. The successive beatings that Truffaldino undergoes in act 2, scene 3 are also an opportunity for the fool's unwitting wit to emerge. Indeed, Truffaldino makes light of his own attempts to collect two paychecks. Alone and sore from his punishments, Truffaldino observes: "Well, there's no mistake about my being the servant of two masters. They have both paid me my wages."

Interestingly, the self-interest Chidester refers to is astutely remarked upon within the play by a waiter at the inn. The waiter, who has observed Truffaldino's attempts to serve both Beatrice and Florindo, remarks that "nobody does anything just for love. Whatever they do, either they are robbing their masters or they are throwing dust in their eyes." In the case of Truffaldino, the latter option is most certainly true. Still, as Chidester comments,

> ultimately, love and kindness triumph over selfishness. Beatrice takes pity on Clarice and reveals her true gender, Clarice forgives Silvio rather than revenging herself by rejecting him, and Truffaldino sacrifices his double meals and wages for the love of Smeraldina.

Indeed, the last lines of the play belong to Truffaldino, who says, "Nobody would ever have found me out, if I had not given myself away for love of this girl here."

Source: Leah Tieger, Critical Essay on *The Servant of Two Masters*, in *Drama for Students*, Gale, Cengage Learning, 2010.

Canberra Times
In the following review of the Australian National University production of The Servant of Two Masters, *the focus is on the acting style.*

The Servant of Two Masters, written in 1753 by Italian Carlo Goldoni, "is a late commedia piece," director Jack Spahr says, "rather than one from the classical commedia [dell'arte] period, which was a couple of centuries earlier."

It marked a turning point in Italian theatre as it was the first of its kind to be written down. "Goldoni scripted this play and it caused a great deal of tension between him and the traditionalists. Commedia dell'arte was always improvised, and not scripted, so there would be set scenarios that actors would follow."

Spahr, a Canberra drama teacher with an interest in commedia dell'arte, has performed in theatre, television commercials, and film. Though the genesis of *The Servant of Two Masters* differed from tradition, the plot is pure commedia, he says. Beatrice (Erin Pugh) disguises herself as a man to track down her brother's killer, not because she wants to bring him to justice, but because she loves him. Truffaldino (Arran McKenna), Beatrice's servant, becomes the unlikely hero of the story after accepting the opportunity to work for a second master, Florindo (Chris Zuber), Beatrice's lover. What follows is an hilarious "chase around farce", full of mistaken identity, three sets of lovers, and an over-committed servant. "So don't bite off more then you can chew because you are bound to come unstuck in the end," Spahr says. Cast member Wayne Shepard says the hero Truffaldino "is a delightfully silly confection of every naughty boy who was ever caught out pinching stuff, telling lies, and covering things over. Whenever he is in trouble he tells another lie which two or three minutes later will somehow rebound on him so he has to tell another lie to cover that."

Celebrating the play's comic potential, Shepard says *The Servant of Two Masters* "seems to have absolutely everything".

There are star-crossed lovers, a murderer hiding, someone trying to find the murderer.

Servants falling in love, double identities, and young thwarted lovers who are being held apart because classic commedia character Pantalone has offered his daughter to someone else.

True to its heritage, *The Servant of Two Masters* is a convoluted adventure. One that, in about 2 hours, "amazingly works out in the end", Shepard says.

A respected form of theatre, commedia dell'arte is characterised by its use of stock characters who are the same in every play, and have become instantly recognisable. Pantalone, the merchant, Il Dottore, the wealthy doctor, and Brighella, the innkeeper, are all characters that have become associated with the form. Masks are traditionally used to signify who is who, and set scenes, called "lazzis", give signposts for the action.

In this production of *The Servant of Two Masters,* by the Australian National University's graduate company Moonlight Theatre, Spahr is presenting "the basics of commedia dell'arte with a necessarily more modern approach in terms of theatre direction". Because it is a turning-point play, masks, for instance, are not used. "It's also not performed on the back of a cart, but a formal stage," he says. For actor and set designer Erin Pugh, commedia dell'arte hits the right nerve. "It is a great form of entertainment," she says.

"It's funny, it's exciting, it's one of the best sorts of humour around. It's so entertaining.

It's slapstick, so there are some really crude bits to it, but it's just funny, quick and very slick. It's like little kids playing on the stage, but the audience wants to be involved as well. There is a great charisma to it."

Pugh says *The Servant of Two Masters* is not a piece to have too many deep thoughts about. "There's no real message, it's just silly characters, they have a lot of fun, they tell their story."

Although interpretation is not essential, some message can be found. Martha Ibrahim (who plays Brighella) says there is normally some form of moral that holds the theatrical tricks and farcical scenes of commedia dell'arte together. *The Servant of Two Masters* is about the problem of stretching one's resources.

"You can't serve two masters fully and completely," she says. "There is almost a biblical parallel there. You can't serve God and mammon [money]. Either you'll love one and hate the other, or begrudge them both. Although I'm not sure that is what Goldoni had in mind when he wrote the script."

Source: "Comic Chase in High Farce," in *Canberra Times,* August 22, 2007.

Theatrical Reflections: Notes on the Form and Practice of Drama

In the following review, the history of commedia dell'arte and Goldoni's stock characters in The Servant of Two Masters *are discussed.*

It is fitting that the Company Store, a professional company made up of graduates of the Hartman Theatre Conservatory, should have opened its premiere season Wednesday night at the Landmark Square Playhouse with an adaptation of *The Servant of Two Masters.* Carlo Goldoni's mid-eighteenth century Italian play, itself a variation on an older French theme, is considered its author's best work in the style of the *commedia dell'arte.* And the *commedia* is as good an example as can be found of total theatre: it tells a story or presents a situation through nearly every physical means available, including masks and mime, acrobatics and tricks, color and spectacle.

The aim is not so much to convey an idea or adopt an attitude as to communicate a feeling for people and things in all their "insignificance," apart from their relation to a "higher absolute." Life is not analyzed or questioned, it is celebrated. So too in Kenneth Cavander's adaptation of *The Servant of Two Masters,* with music and lyrics by Barbara Damashek and direction by Larry Arrick. Not only life itself, but also acting and the life of the actor are celebrated here. From the first, in an exhilarating prologue, we are reminded that the actors on stage are separate from the characters they are playing; we are then moved to think of them as a latter-day *commedia* troupe in search of a paying audience to fill their newfound, makeshift home.

The first offering of these "comedians" for the 1977–1978 season can be construed as a histrionic reaction to the slick, lifeless musicals and pseudo-serious melodramas of Broadway, even as the *commedia dell'arte* in its origins can be seen as a histrionic reaction to the somber mystery and morality plays of the Middle Ages. As such, and as an introduction to the elements of theater, *The Servant of Two Masters* is the perfect prelude to a season of high seriousness in the drama. The Company Store will produce *Yerma, Ribbons* (by David F. Eliet, Associate Director), *Marat/Sade,* and *The Three Sisters* in succession from December to April.

Two things distinguish this production more than anything else—and almost everything about it is distinguished, let me hasten to add. These are Miss Damashek's music and Mr. Arrick's choreography. The whole notion of accompanying much of the action with music and having characters break into song from time to time is in keeping with the concept behind the writing of this play. As Heinz Riedt has pointed out, Goldoni's comedy is musical in structure. Unlike most plays, "Goldoni's best comedies make no introductions in the usual sense." Like themes in music, "his characters are immediately presented, and their main qualities quickly highlighted. In the course of the action we get to know them better and better." Music is pure form intended to embody or evoke an emotion. *The Servant of Two Masters,* then, is pure theatre, a stage in motion to music, intended to do the same.

A "fugue of forms," of body and light, this production might be called, as opposed to the more common "play of ideas." This is where director Arrick comes in, providing a painstakingly detailed "visual score" to complement Miss Damashek's musical one. Much of the suspense or tension on stage derives not from the unfolding of the plot, which is thoroughly predictable from the start, but from the alternation of what the literary historian Richard Alewyn calls "creatural exuberance" and "the most abstract geometry," or energy and mass. The actors are now one huge, frozen, symmetrical tableau, now a study in disarray, with bodies coming, going, and clashing.

The acting in this show is, properly, ensemble. While the play ostensibly concerns Truffaldino, the servant of the title, and the temptation is great to make his performance the *tour de force* that carries the action, I think that Mr. Arrick was wise to blend him into the background as much as possible. It was a practical as well as an artistic move: Stephen Roylance does not bring enough variety or strength to his interpretation of Truffaldino; as he rushed through his action I lost much of this character's calculating shrewdness. But Roylance is winsome nonetheless, and he is ably supported by his fellows, among whom Rosalyn R. Farinella (Pantalone), John Olesen (Rasponi and Lombardi), and Robert S. Eichler (Silvio) deserve special mention.

And those Zanies! They are on stage much of the time, acting (and singing) as one more reminder of the "pure play" of the other characters, and they are quite good. There are performances besides Truffaldino's that lack something—those of Susan Strickler (Clarice), Joy Smith (Beatrice), and Philip Soltanoff (Florindo) come to mind— but the Zanies' sheer exuberance is enough to buy them time. After all, we are not dealing with psychological realism here.

There is no virtuoso singing to be heard in the Landmark Square Playhouse, but, then, none is called for. In fact, if there were virtuoso singing, it would probably take away from the intended effect of the play upon its audience. I was rather heartened myself to hear a voice crack from time to time.

Kenneth Cavender's adaptation of the Goldoni script is of interest chiefly for its unabashed topicality. There is, for example, some rock music in the style of the 1950s, mention of Sherlock Holmes, and a pun on the word "closet" as it is referred to by homosexuals. Dialogue from *Romeo and Juliet* manages to find its way into a romantic scene. All this is one more ingenious way of breaking the "illusion of reality," of directing our attention away from the "boy has girl-boy loses girl-boy gets girl" story line and to the "fugue of forms" I mentioned earlier. The same can be said for the spare set, versatile lighting, and portable costumes. They are fashioned, together with the intimate house, to accent the human form as much as possible, not to create a reasonable facsimile of eighteenth-century Venice on stage.

That the Company Store production of *The Servant of Two Masters* has stimulated me to write this much in analysis and interpretation of it, should be recommendation enough for anyone to see it. If further endorsement were necessary, however, I would go so far as to say, in paraphrase of Brecht, that its art contributes to the greatest art of all: the art of living.

Source: "*The Servant of Two Masters* at the Hartman Theatre," in *Theatrical Reflections: Notes on the Form and Practice of Drama*, November 19, 1977, pp. 201–203.

SOURCES

Baldick, Robert, *The Duel: A History of Duelling*, Spring Books, 1970.

Bates, Alfred, ed., "Carlo Goldoni," in *The Drama: Its History, Literature and Influence on Civilization*, Historical Publishing, 1906, pp. 63–68.

Brockett, Oscar G., *History of the Theatre*, Allyn & Bacon, 1982.

Carnes, Jim, "City Theatre Serves Up Laughs in *Two Masters*," in *Sacramento Bee*, May 4, 2009.

Chidester, Stephanie, "*The Servant of Two Masters*: The Politics of Self-Interest," in *Insights*, 2003, http://www.bard.org/Education/studyguides/theservant/servantpolitics.html (July 13, 2009).

Clark, Barrett H., "Carlo Goldoni (1707–1793)," in *European Theories of the Drama*, Stewart & Kidd, 1918.

Cole, Simon A., *Suspect Identities: A History of Fingerprinting and Criminal Identification*, Harvard University Press, 2002.

Goldoni, Carlo, "The Servant of Two Masters, " in *Servant of Two Masters and Other Italian Classics*, translated by Edward J. Dent, edited by Eric Bentley, Applause Theatre Books, 2000.

Rosenblum, Gail, "Myths and Facts about Arranged Marriage," in *Star Tribune*, February 8, 2008.

Rudlin, John, *Commedia Dell'arte: An Actor's Handbook*, Ebooks Corporation, 1994.

Shore, Nancy Ellen, Review of *The Servant of Two Masters*, in *Back Stage East*, Vol. 48, No. 1, January 4, 2007, p. 40.

Wahnbaeck, Till, *Luxury and Public Happiness in the Italian Enlightenment*, Oxford University Press, 2004.

FURTHER READING

Banham, Martin, *The Cambridge Guide to Theatre*, 2nd ed., Cambridge University Press, 1995.
    This reference work contains entries on the theatrical traditions and history of numerous countries, including Italy. It is an invaluable resource for students of historical drama.

Black, Jeremy, *Eighteenth-Century Europe*, 2nd ed., Palgrave Macmillan, 1999.
    This overview of the time and place in which Goldoni lived and worked provides insight into the playwright and his plays. Topics discussed include social, economic, and cultural issues. Historical and political events are also covered.

Holland, Barbara, *Gentlemen's Blood: A History of Dueling*, Bloomsbury, 2004.
    This book is a fun, fact-filled history of dueling, beginning with the medieval practice of trial by combat and tracing the evolution of dueling since then.

Shakespeare, William, *The Comedies of William Shakespeare*, Modern Library, 1994.
    These comedies undoubtedly influenced Goldoni and his work and are thus essential to any study of the Italian dramatist.

A Streetcar Named Desire

1951

A Streetcar Named Desire is a film released in 1951, based on the play of the same title by Tennessee Williams, which was first produced in 1947. The film is closely based on the play. It is set in a poor section of New Orleans and features four main characters: Blanche DuBois; her sister, Stella; Stella's husband, Stanley Kowalski; and Mitch, a friend of Stanley's. Blanche comes to stay with Stella and Stanley in their cramped apartment. Blanche, a refined but unhappy woman who has been unable to find lasting love, soon comes into conflict with the blunt-spoken and aggressive Stanley. She is briefly courted by Mitch, but the new love does not last, and Blanche ends up losing touch with reality and being sent to an asylum for the insane.

The film was the first ever to win three Academy Awards (also known as Oscars) for acting. British actress Vivien Leigh won the award for Best Actress for her portrayal of Blanche. Kim Hunter as Stella and Karl Malden as Mitch won Oscars for Best Supporting Actress and Best Supporting Actor, and Elia Kazan won in the Best Director category. However, Marlon Brando, whose brilliant performance as Stanley has thrilled moviegoers for over half a century, was not rewarded with an Oscar.

With its ruthless presentation of love and loneliness and its stellar individual performances, *A Streetcar Named Desire* is regarded as one of the best American films ever made. Some of the content of the film was considered controversial at the time, and viewers should be

FILM TECHNIQUE

Black-and-White Film

The film was shot in black and white, and it uses lighting to bring out one of the motifs of the play: Blanche's desire to present herself only in dim light out of fear that daylight would reveal her true age. Symbolically, Blanche's desire for darkness over light suggests her need to maintain illusions at the expense of truth. She keeps her room dark, as in the scene in which she meets Mitch, which takes place half in shadow. It is as if there is a veil spread over Blanche. Mitch has to light a match so that she can read the inscription on the cigarette case he shows her. She then asks Mitch to place a colored paper lantern over the bare bulb in her room, to soften the light, before she will switch it on.

The artful use of lighting to convey this aspect of Blanche's personality occurs again in the scene in which Mitch comes late at night and accuses her of lying to him (chapter 20 in the DVD selections). Blanche's face is half in shadow when she hears the doorbell ringing. The film then cuts to the empty and dark living room, which is partially lit by a flashing neon sign out in the street, suggesting the insistent, harsh light that Blanche tries so hard to keep at bay. ("I like the dark. The dark is comforting to me," she says later in this scene.) The light from the flashing neon sign continues as she lets Mitch in and at intervals during the scene. When Mitch switches one light on, Blanche gives a little gasp and runs for cover like a frightened animal. Mitch rips the lantern off the bulb, and she begs him not to turn the bare bulb on. He cruelly forces her to stand with her face directly under the light so he can see what she is really like. It is a savage moment, symbolically as well as physically. The harsh light of reality is like poison to her, and as she confesses what she has been through in her life and why, the scene plays out in normal lighting. The illusion she tried to preserve is gone, and with it anything that gives her hope. When she returns from the street after following Mitch out, she rushes around, closing the shutters to keep out all the light from the street and turning off all the lights again, as if by doing so she could go back to her comforting world of illusion. Again, her face is seen more than half in shadow. The lighting tells Blanche's story, reinforcing the message conveyed by the words.

Duration of Shots

The length of a shot can also create various effects. In moments when the action moves fast, the shots will tend to be of shorter duration. This technique of quick cutting conveys a sense of dynamism and motion. The pace of the film suddenly picks up. An example is the chaotic scene after Stanley throws the radio out of the window, angrily chases after Blanche, and is pulled back by the other men. As in real life, the eye of the viewer must move quickly to take in such a scene and see who is doing what to whom. Confusion abounds. In contrast, some of the many close-ups in the film are of longer duration; the action slows, and the emotions of the characters are explored. The variation in pace creates the subtle rhythm of the film, in which scenes of reflection and emotional disclosure are followed by explosions of action and movement.

---

aware that some scenes contain intense confrontations between the characters, although the actual violence shown is minimal.

PLOT SUMMARY

The film *A Streetcar Named Desire* begins at a railroad station in New Orleans. Blanche DuBois emerges from the crowd, not sure where to go. She asks directions from a young man who tells her that the streetcar she needs, named Desire, is approaching. She boards the streetcar and arrives at a lively area of the city, where people are out enjoying themselves. She asks a woman for directions to a street called Elysian Fields and is told that she is in it. The woman is Eunice, who lives upstairs in the same building as Blanche's sister, Stella. Stella and her husband, Stanley Kowalski, occupy the downstairs apartment.

Director Elia Kazan works with actors Karl Malden (Mitch) and Vivien Leigh (Blanche) on the set of the film. *(Warner Bros | The Kobal Collection | The Picture Desk, Inc.)*

The film cuts to a bowling alley, where Stella is watching Stanley play. Blanche finds Stella and they embrace. Stella points out her husband, who is seen stirring up a quarrel involving several men. Blanche says she does not want to meet him just yet. They find a quiet corner, and Blanche, who is a schoolteacher, explains that she has been able to come during the school term because the superintendent suggested she take a leave of absence. She was suffering from nervous exhaustion.

The next sequence begins in the Kowalskis' apartment, where Stella is running a bath for Blanche. Stella makes a place for Blanche in the small apartment. Blanche is distressed and needs to have people around her. She asks whether Stanley will like her, and Stella replies that they will get along well; it is clear that Stella and Stanley are in love.

Blanche reproaches Stella for leaving their home in Mississippi and going to New Orleans, while Blanche stayed at Belle Reve, their home, trying to keep it going. This was a burden on her, especially when their parents died. Blanche had to manage on her small teacher's salary, and now the house has been lost. Distressed, Stella runs to another room.

The film cuts to the street, where Stanley returns with his friends Mitch and Steve. Steve quarrels with his wife, Eunice. Blanche introduces herself to the muscular Stanley, who is wearing a tight-fitting, sweat-soaked T-shirt. Stanley offers a drink, but she says (untruthfully) that she rarely drinks. After asking Blanche whether she minds, Stanley removes his shirt and puts on a clean one. As they chat, Stanley discovers that Blanche is going to be staying there. Blanche seems nervous, and Stanley says he guesses she will find him an unrefined character. He also says he was told she had been married once, a remark that upsets Blanche. She says her husband died, and she is troubled by the memory.

In the next scene, Stanley arrives in the apartment with Blanche's trunk. While Blanche is in the bath, Stella tells Stanley her sister is upset over losing the family home. Stanley wants to see documents regarding the sale. Stella knows nothing about it, but Stanley gets angry. He says that under the Napoleonic law that operates in Louisiana, anything that belongs to a wife also belongs to the husband, and he feels that she may have been swindled, which means he has been swindled, too.

He pulls out some expensive-looking clothes from Blanche's trunk, saying that Blanche could never have bought such things on a teacher's salary. Over Stella's protests, he says he will get an expert to appraise the value of the clothes. Then he finds Blanche's jewelry, and says he will get that appraised as well. Exasperated, Stella goes outside to the porch.

Blanche emerges from the bathroom. Going behind the curtain that cordons off her sleeping area, she is disturbed when she sees the ransacked trunk. When she has put on another dress, she asks Stanley to fasten the buttons at the back. Stanley questions her about the stylish clothes, and she says they were gifts from long ago. She keeps trying to get Stanley to compliment her on her appearance, without success. He gets impatient with her attempted flattery and yells at her, which brings Stella in from the porch. Blanche sends her away.

Stanley explains to Blanche about the Napoleonic code, and Blanche insists she has never cheated anyone. She retrieves a box from her trunk, in which she keeps most of her papers. She also pulls out what she says are love letters, and Stanley grabs them. She snatches at them and they get scattered on the floor. She gathers them up, saying they are from her dead husband. Then she gives Stanley the legal papers relating to Belle Reve. She says that several generations of the family squandered their wealth until all that was left was the house and twenty acres of land. Stanley says he will have a lawyer examine them. He also reveals that Stella is pregnant. When Stella returns, Blanche congratulates her and says she smoothed things over with Stanley.

Stella and Blanche go out to dinner, while Stanley's friends Mitch, Steve, and Pablo arrive for a game of poker. The gathering goes on until late at night, and Eunice, Steve's wife, bangs on the ceiling (the floor of their apartment), trying to get him to come home. Steve takes no notice. The men move the table before Eunice can start pouring boiling water through the cracks in the ceiling.

When Stella and Blanche return, Stanley is irritated by their presence and suggests that they go up to see Eunice. He slaps her rear in front of the other men, which angers her. Blanche meets Mitch outside the bathroom, and after Mitch goes to join the other men, Blanche tells Stella that he seems a cut above the others. Blanche inquires further, and Stella tells her that Mitch is single and works in the spare parts company. It is the same company Stanley works for, but Stella says Stanley has a better job.

As Stella passes on gossip about Eunice, the two women laugh. Stanley complains about the noise and then complains again when Blanche switches on the radio. Angry, he comes into Blanche's room and switches it off himself.

Mitch quits the card game, and he and Blanche engage in conversation. Mitch is charmed by Blanche, and she, craving attention, is pleased to accept his interest. She asks him to put a colored paper lantern that she has just purchased over the light bulb. Then she turns the radio on again and waltzes to the music, while Mitch self-consciously imitates her and a bemused Stella looks on.

Furious at the noise, Stanley rushes in, grabs the radio, and hurls it through the window. An angry Stella tries to throw the other men out, and there is a commotion. Stanley chases after Stella and has to be restrained by the other men. Pablo hits him, knocking him unconscious. The men drag him to the shower and put his head under it; the cold water revives him. There is another scuffle as Stanley throws the men off.

Stanley calls out for Stella, who has fled upstairs with Blanche. When he cannot find her, he sobs. He stands outside the building and calls up to Stella to come back. Eunice yells abuse at Stanley, but Stella cannot stay away for long. She returns, and they share a passionate embrace. Contrite, he carries her back to their apartment.

Terrified by the altercation, Blanche descends to the now quiet street, where she encounters Mitch, who tells her not to be frightened because Stanley and Stella are very much in love. Blanche thanks him for being kind.

In the morning, Blanche returns to the apartment. Stella is in bed alone; Stanley has already left to get the car fixed. Blanche goes to comfort her sister, only to discover that Stella is not bothered by the events of the previous night. Stanley has always smashed things, she says. Blanche does not understand why her sister accepts this behavior, and she has a plan for both of them to escape. Stella tells Blanche she does not want to escape her marriage. Outside, the returning Stanley overhears all this. Blanche complains to Stella that Stanley is common, like an animal, with his crude desires. Stella is unmoved by Blanche's criticisms of her husband, but she embraces her sister tenderly. Stanley enters, having overheard every word. Stella rushes to him, and they embrace, while Stanley grins at Blanche.

Eunice is chased down the fire escape by Steve. She shouts that he hit her and she is going to call the police. As Stanley comes in, though, he says she went to the bar first for a drink.

Stanley says he has heard something about Blanche from a man named Shaw, who says he met her in the Hotel Flamingo in her hometown. Unsettled, Blanche replies that the Flamingo is not the sort of place where she would be seen.

After Stanley leaves, Blanche asks Stella what people have been saying about her. She reveals there was some unsavory gossip about her in Auriol, her hometown (called Laurel in the play). Stella gives Blanche a Coke with a shot of whiskey, and Blanche promises Stella she will not be staying long. Blanche is distressed, and some of the drink gets spilled on her dress.

Blanche has been dating Mitch, and he is coming for her at seven that night. Blanche wants to hold Mitch's interest and eventually marry him so she will not have to stay with Stella and Stanley any longer. Stella comforts her.

Blanche is on her own in the house when a young man arrives, collecting money for the evening newspaper. Blanche flirts with him, even kissing him. As the boy leaves, Mitch arrives, carrying roses for Blanche.

Mitch and Blanche dance at an amusement park on the lake. They go outside and talk on the pier, and Mitch asks permission to kiss her. He makes it plain that he likes her a lot. Blanche laughs out of embarrassment. She lights a candle and they sit down at a table. Mitch is proud of how he keeps himself physically fit. He says he weighs 207 pounds and asks her what she weighs. She lets him pick her up and he remarks on how light she is. When he puts her down he tries to kiss her, but she resists, saying she is old-fashioned in that respect. It is an awkward moment, and Mitch

is disappointed. The talk gets around to Stanley, and Mitch says he thinks Stanley does not understand her. Blanche says she thinks he hates her.

As they walk together, Mitch asks her how old she is. He says his mother, who is dying, wants him to settle down, and she wanted to know Blanche's age. The talk turns to loneliness, and Blanche reveals that her husband, whom she married when she was very young, was a sensitive, troubled young man who committed suicide. When they were at a dance one night, he stepped outside and shot himself. Moved by her story, Mitch says they are both lonely. He hopes they can have a life together. Blanche is touched, and they kiss.

The next scene begins in the factory, where several men are restraining Mitch, who wants to attack Stanley. Mitch is forced to calm down.

Later, as Stella and Blanche prepare for Blanche's birthday party, Stanley tells Stella he has found out the details of Blanche's disreputable life in Auriol. She used to live at the sleazy Flamingo Hotel but even that hotel asked her to leave. Stella tries to defend her sister, but Stanley insists he is correct. He says everyone in Auriol regarded Blanche as crazy. He adds that she did not take a leave of absence from her school; she was fired because she became involved with a seventeen-year-old boy. Stanley also tells Stella that Mitch will not be coming to the birthday party, because Stanley has told him about Blanche.

Blanche emerges, fresh after her bath, and knows right away that something is wrong because of the look on Stella's face.

At the birthday supper, Blanche says this is the first time she has ever been stood up, and she starts to tells a joke. She is interrupted by a doorbell ringing upstairs. Then Stella criticizes Stanley for his table manners, which angers Stanley so much that he tells her never to talk like that to him again. He sweeps his cup and saucer to the floor while the two women look down at the table. After he goes outside, Blanche tells Stella she has guessed why Mitch did not come.

Outside, Stella reproaches Stanley for his behavior. Stanley says things will be better when Blanche is gone. Back in the kitchen, Stanley becomes angry again because Blanche calls him a Polack. Stanley then presents Blanche with what he says is a birthday gift. It is an envelope containing a bus ticket to Auriol for the following Tuesday. Blanche is upset and runs to the bathroom. Once again, Stella rebukes Stanley for his cruelty.

Stanley explains that they were happy until Blanche arrived. Stella then feels her baby move and tells Stanley to take her to the hospital.

Blanche is alone when she hears knocking at the door. It is Mitch, who is agitated and speaks roughly to her. When she offers him a drink he refuses, adding that he has been told by Stanley that she has been drinking excessively all summer. Still aggressive, Mitch switches the light on, saying he has never seen her in daylight and has therefore never had a good look at her. Blanche prefers dim lighting, which helps her conceal her age. He sees she is older than he thought she was but says he does not mind that. What he does mind are the stories he has been told about her life. Blanche admits she has had encounters with men she barely knew. She says it was because she was lonely after her husband's suicide. She needed some protection. Mitch is angry and accuses her of lying to him while they were developing their relationship. Blanche protests that she was sincere.

A blind Mexican woman comes to the door selling flowers for the dead. Blanche is upset because the mention of death reminds her of all the deaths of relatives she endured at Belle Reve. Mitch embraces her, and they kiss. She ask him to marry her, but he says he no longer wants to. She tells him to get out, and she follows him, in a scene added to the film that does not appear in the play, screaming into the street. A few men show concern for her, but she rushes back into the house, closing the shutters and turning the lights off. A police officer is called. He hammers on the door, but Blanche refuses to open it. Later, she dresses up in her finest clothes and retreats into a fantasy world of her own.

Stanley returns from the hospital, saying the baby will not arrive until the morning. Blanche lies that she has received an invitation by telegram from an old flame inviting her to join him on a Caribbean cruise. Stanley knows she is lying but goes along with her for a while. Blanche pretends her wealthy friend is a gentleman who wants her not for an affair but for companionship. She also lies that Mitch asked her to forgive him.

Stanley confronts Blanche with her lies, saying he knew from the beginning what she was like. He pushes her down onto the bed and yells at her, and then he storms out of the room. In desperation, Blanche gathers up some clothes and goes outside, but when she sees the Mexican woman again she returns to the house. She tries to make a phone call to get some help, but Stanley emerges from the bathroom and she breaks off the call. Stanley becomes aggressive, and Blanche runs into her bedroom. Stanley follows. Blanche, believing herself to be in danger, grabs a bottle, breaks it on a table and holds it up to him, trying to keep him at bay. He wrests the bottle top from her, and the film cuts to a shattered mirror.

Some time passes. Eunice is looking after Stella's baby while Stanley and his friends are playing cards. Stella tells Eunice she has made arrangements for Blanche to rest in the country, but Blanche still talks about the cruise she is going on. Blanche emerges from the bathroom, and the two women speak gently to her. Blanche is lost in her fantasy world.

A doctor and nurse arrive from a mental institution. When Blanche hears she has a visitor, she thinks it must be the man who is taking her on the cruise. When she sees him, she says he is not the man she has been expecting. She becomes hysterical and collapses on the floor, while the nurse grips her. Mitch is angry and aims a punch at Stanley; the other men pull him away.

The nurse lets go of Blanche, and the doctor takes Blanche's arm and leads her away. Blanche still does not know who he is. Stella speaks sharply to Stanley, telling him never to touch her again. Blanche is driven away in a car. As Stella holds her baby, she says to herself that she is not going back to Stanley. Off-screen, Stanley calls out her name.

The film stays close to the play, although there are a few changes in location, especially at the beginning. This was done in order to open out the movie beyond the simple stage setting of the play, in which the action takes place almost entirely in the Kowalski apartment. The play opens with Stanley returning home, bringing his wife some meat, which he tosses to her. This scene is omitted from the film, which begins by showing Blanche's arrival at the railroad station in New Orleans. Blanche is then directed by Eunice to the bowling alley, where she meets up with Stella and sees Stanley for the first time. In the play, there is no scene set in the bowling alley. Another change occurs in scene 6 of the play, in which Blanche and Mitch are seen returning to the apartment from their evening together. In the film, they are shown during the evening, first dancing together and then going outside the hall to the pier at the lake, where they talk.

CHARACTERS

Blanche DuBois

Blanche DuBois (Vivien Leigh) is an old-fashioned Southern belle who comes from an aristocratic family in Mississippi that has fallen on hard times. She married when she was very young, and her husband, whom she refers to as a "boy," committed suicide. His death still haunts her many years later. After the death of her husband she was never to find love again. She stayed on, a tormented widow, at the family home of Belle Reve, while her family squandered what was left of their wealth and her sister escaped to New Orleans. Blanche survived by taking a job as a teacher of English at a high school, but by this time she was emotionally spent, a fragile, brittle, lonely woman with no one to love and no real purpose to her life. Desperate for love and attention, something to nourish her heart, she started to go downhill, living at a sleazy hotel and entertaining men, always seeking love but never finding it.

The nostalgic Blanche tries to live in a world of high ideals, romance, refinement, and beauty that never really existed, She has fallen in the eyes of the world, but she still thinks of herself as being a member of a higher social class. She lives in a world of nostalgia and illusion. She knows that her beauty is fading, and she desperately wants to reclaim some of the magic of life that she once knew. She needs someone to protect her. By the time she arrives at the home of her sister, she is almost beyond hope. She has been fired from her job as a schoolteacher for having an inappropriate relationship with a seventeen-year-old boy, and she has nowhere else to go. She drinks too much in an effort to blot out the reality of her life, and she still likes to dress in fine clothes and act like the lady she believes she still is. She tries to cover up her past. From the moment she first encounters Stanley, they are in conflict; the longer she stays in the Kowalski apartment, the worse the tension between them grows. After the failure of her brief courtship with Mitch and after Stanley's assault on her, the discrepancy between what she needs and what she is able to get becomes too great, and she slips into madness. The only place left for her is the mental asylum. One of the great tragic figures in American drama, Blanche is an example of a woman who is too emotionally delicate to survive in a world that is populated by men such as Stanley Kowalski.

Vivien Leigh won an Academy Award for Best Actress for her portrayal of Blanche.

Doctor

The doctor (Richard Garrick), an elderly man in a dark suit, comes with the nurse to the Kowalski home to escort Blanche to the mental institution. He treats her gently and offers her his arm as they walk out. Blanche does not know who he is, but she is willing to go with him.

Eunice

Eunice (Peg Hillias) is Steve's wife. She and her husband live in the apartment above the Kowalskis'. Eunice is a forthright woman who knows how to stand up for herself. Steve appears not to treat her very well, but she is unbowed. When the card game downstairs goes on too late, she bangs on the ceiling to get Steve to come home. Then she heats up some boiling water in order to pour it down the cracks in the ceiling. The men know what is coming—she has obviously done this before. On one occasion Eunice rushes out of the house saying her husband has hit her and she is going to call the police, but she never does and is soon reconciled to her husband. However, Eunice has no illusions about the way men are. She appears to dislike Stanley and is not intimidated by him. She gets along well with Stella, looking after the baby, and also speaks kindly to Blanche when Blanche is confused and about to be sent away. Eunice adopts a stoic attitude to life. Whatever has to be endured must be endured. "Life has got to go on," she says near the end of the film. "No matter what happens, you've got to keep on going."

Stanley Kowalski

Stanley Kowalski (Marlon Brando) is Stella's husband. He is between twenty-eight and thirty years old. In World War II he was a master sergeant in the Engineers' Corp, according to Stella, who met him when he was still in uniform. His family is of Polish origin, but he resents it when Blanche brings that up. He prides himself on being an American. Tennessee Williams included the following description of Stanley in the first scene of the stage play:

> Animal joy in his being is implicit in all his movements and attitudes. Since earliest manhood the center of his life has been pleasure with women...not with weak indulgence, dependently, but with the power and pride of a richly feathered male bird among hens.

Stanley is a coarse man; he takes his male superiority for granted and does not accept any challenges to his authority from his wife or Blanche. He drinks and eats with relish and enjoys robust male company. He genuinely loves Stella in his own way and is reduced to sobbing and pleading with her when she flees upstairs to escape him after one of his aggressive outbursts. In that sense he relies on Stella and the love she offers, even though he would probably never admit it or even realize it.

Stanley often takes his aggression out on things rather than people—such as the radio, which he smashes. However, he also can be cruel to others, both mentally and physically. Giving Blanche a bus ticket home as a birthday present is an example of this cruelty. It is like twisting a knife in her heart. Another example of his cruelty is when they are alone in the apartment and he steps over the line and attacks her.

From Stanley's point of view, Blanche represents an intrusion on his happy life with Stella. He can no more understand her than he could understand a cat. She cannot understand him, either, or what Stella would see in him. Stella, however, likes a man who is not afraid to be a man, and that is Stanley Kowalski. He lives his life without reflecting on it, quite unlike Blanche, who is always looking back and wanting life to be something it is not. That would never occur to Stanley. He enjoys the things that life brings him—women, cars, buddies to play poker with, a bottle of beer—and he makes no apology for who he is.

Marlon Brando had played Stanley in the original Broadway play production. This was one of his first film roles. Utterly convincing as Stanley, he made a huge impact on moviegoers. Although the main character in the play is meant to be Blanche, Brando's performance as Stanley was so powerful and riveting that it almost became his film rather than Vivien Leigh's as Blanche. Ever since the film was released, few people can imagine the part of Stanley without seeing Brando in his tight-fitting T-shirt, all muscles and raw masculine power. Countless stage actors since have played the role as, in effect, lesser imitations of Brando.

Stella Kowalski

Stella Kowalski (Kim Hunter) is Stanley Kowalski's wife and Blanche's sister. Blanche pretends that Stella is older, but in fact Stella is younger by about five years. Stella left the family home in Mississippi to move to New Orleans, where she married Stanley. Blanche resents the fact that Stella left their home, leaving her to cope, but Stella has no regrets. She is happily married to Stanley. She loves him, in spite of his bullying and violent temper and despite the fact that he comes from a lower social class than she does. Although sometimes she becomes angry with his crude behavior, in general she does not mind his aggressive nature; in fact, she even admires it because it shows his masculinity. To Stella, a quarrel with Stanley does not mean much; they soon make up, and she knows that in spite of all his boorishness, he loves her. Blanche does not understand how Stella could want to remain in such a marriage, but Stella does not aspire to Blanche's refined, romantic ideas. She is happy where she is, with what she has. It is true that at the end of the film, she swears she will never go back to Stanley because of the way he treated Blanche, but the audience has seen her return to Stanley before after a quarrel, so her protestations that the marriage is over are less than convincing. In the play, Stella and Stanley embrace at the end, leaving no doubt about the nature of their relationship, whatever shocks it has gone through following Blanche's arrival.

Kim Hunter won an Academy Award for Best Supporting Actress for her portrayal of Stella.

Mexican Woman

The Mexican woman (Edna Thomas) is a blind woman who sells flowers to be displayed at funerals and other occasions. Blanche is upset on both occasions when she sees the Mexican woman because she is reminded of death.

Harold "Mitch" Mitchell

Mitch (Karl Malden) is an old friend of Stanley's. They fought in World War II together. Like Stanley, Mitch is about twenty-eight to thirty years old, and he works in the spare parts department at the same factory that employs Stanley. A bachelor, Mitch looks after his dying mother. When he first meets Blanche, he is quite taken with her, and they go out together several times. Treating her with a gentlemanly courtesy, he accepts Blanche at face value as a refined, attractive woman. He says he has never met anyone like her before. Like Blanche, Mitch is lonely, and he thinks the two of them might be able to succeed together. However, all those hopes are dashed when Stanley tells him the stories about Blanche's past. Mitch does not believe the stories until he verifies them for himself. He fails to show up at Blanche's birthday party, but he comes by later and harangues her for not being honest with him. She still hopes that they can marry, but he says he is no longer interested. "You're not clean enough to bring in the house with my mother," are his final words to her.

Karl Malden won an Academy Award for Best Supporting Actor for his portrayal of Mitch.

Nurse

The nurse (Ann Dere) is a middle-aged, severe-looking woman who comes with the doctor to take Blanche to the mental institution. She takes charge of Blanche physically, pinning her arms, and asks the doctor whether they will need a straightjacket.

Pablo

Pablo (Nick Dennis) is a friend of Stanley's and a member of the poker-playing group. In the commotion that follows Stanley's tossing of the radio out of the window, Pablo punches Stanley, but Stanley seems to bear him no ill-will for his action. Near the end of the film, Pablo, along with Steve, stares reproachfully at Stanley because of his bad treatment of Blanche.

Steve

Steve (Rudy Bond) is Eunice's husband and Stanley's friend. Like Stanley, he is a rough-hewn character who often argues with his wife. On one occasion, he is seen chasing her down the fire escape, and she runs away, saying that he hit her and she is going to call the police. Later, however, Steve is shown walking Eunice home with his arm around her. He knows how far he can go and what he has to do to win her back.

Young Collector

The young collector (Wright King) is a young man who comes to the Kowalski apartment collecting newspaper money. He is a shy, respectful individual. He refuses Blanche's offer of a drink because he is not allowed to drink while he is working. Blanche flirts with him and kisses him on the mouth.

Since the film is a very close adaptation of the play, all the characters in the play appear in the film. Their personalities and their interactions with one another remain for the most part the same as they are in the play. The only significant

change is Stella's less forgiving attitude toward Stanley at the end.

THEMES

Loneliness

Blanche arrives in New Orleans without a friend in the world other than her sister, Stella. This is particularly unfortunate for her since she is not the independent type. She needs people, and more especially, she needs love and intimacy in her life. Without it she is helpless and vulnerable. In New Orleans, though, she is an outsider. This is conveyed in the first sequence of the film, when she arrives on the train and wanders across the platform, looking around warily, unsure of herself. She is in an alien environment in which she does not belong, like a fish out of water. She still cherishes her ideals of what life should be like, but she is not likely to find those ideals fulfilled at the Kowalski home, and she is also very conscious of the different social class to which Stanley belongs. This is another thing that sets her apart from her environment. In contrast, Stanley and Stella seem not only to be happy together but to fit into their environment, a lively, poor area of New Orleans that seems to have a sense of community. All the people there belong where they are; it is Blanche who is the rootless one.

It is because Blanche is so lonely that she reaches out to Mitch, hopeful that perhaps he could be her protector. For a short while it even appears possible, since Mitch is the play's other lonely character. He does not quite fit in. In the film, he is slightly better dressed than the other men in the poker game—he wears a tie—and his manners are more refined. His life is restricted because he has to look after his sick mother. She will soon die, leaving him alone. He courts Blanche, hoping that she might end his loneliness. They are thus drawn to each other by strong mutual need.

Reality

The New Orleans that Blanche finds herself in is a gritty, realistic world. People get on with their lives, doing what they have to do to get by, and they find their enjoyments. Blanche cannot survive in the real world. Her life is the story of one loss after another. She lost her husband a long time ago, and then she lost the family home she had tried so hard to maintain. She managed to

READ.
WATCH.
WRITE.

- Read the final scene of the play and then watch the same scene in the film version. How closely does the film keep to the play? Has the dialogue been cut or otherwise altered? Do the filmmakers follow Williams's detailed stage directions? Write an essay in which you discuss the differences.

- Watch chapter 7 of the film in the DVD selections, and write an essay in which you analyze the contrast between how the women, especially Stella and Blanche, are presented and how the poker-playing men are seen. What does this scene tell you about relations between men and women in the film, and the different values they have?

- Why are there so many close-ups in the film and not so many long shots or establishing shots? Why would a director choose a close-up over a longer shot? Select three to five close-ups from the film. For each close-up, write a brief paragraph in which you explain the context of the shot and then explain what the actor or actress is conveying in his or her facial expressions.

- With another student, investigate what might be the main differences between a film and a

play. What possibilities does film present that are not possible on the stage? From the opposite point of view, what advantages might the stage have over a film? Give a class presentation in which you discuss these issues, using *A Streetcar Named Desire* as an example, emphasizing the places where play and film differ.

- Vivien Leigh and Marlon Brando are both famous for their roles in this film. With another student, analyze the scene (chapter 4 in the DVD selections) in which Blanche meets Stanley for the first time. How does Leigh, through facial expression, gesture, and other means, convey what Blanche is feeling? What do these nonverbal elements suggest about Blanche's state of mind, beyond the words that she actually speaks? Analyze Brando's performance in the same way. What is his attitude toward Blanche in this scene, and how does he convey it through facial expression, gesture, and movement? Give a class presentation in which you first show the scene and then analyze it using a PowerPoint presentation.

stay afloat for a while as a schoolteacher, but her loneliness led her into a foolish relationship with a seventeen-year-old boy. She now has no means of making a living. The real world has defeated her, so she falls back on the one thing that she has, or hopes she still has: her ability as a woman to attract a male protector who will shield her from the harshness of life. This depends on maintaining her appearance, but Blanche is aging, and she knows it. She is obsessed with her appearance, always seeking reassurance about it. The reality is that time is slowly robbing Blanche of her beauty, but this is not something she can accept. She wants to keep up the illusion. She tells Stanley, in a moment of honesty and self-revelation, that "a

woman's charm is fifty percent illusion." The more hopeless her life becomes, the more she creates illusions to live by.

When Mitch wants to switch the light on so he can see her properly, she tells him she does not want realism, she wants magic. She wants life transformed, not as it is. She knew love a very long time ago, and it briefly lit up the world for her. She wants to find this transformation again, but it cannot happen. Eventually, her wafer-thin grasp on reality vanishes completely. She retreats into an illusory world in which she is preparing to go on a cruise with a millionaire from Texas. This is her madness: the substitution of a false world for the real one and the inability to tell the difference between the two.

loveless life, which is a kind of death for her, the
negation of everything she desires.

Warner Bros | The Kobal Collection | The Picture Desk, Inc.

Love

Stanley and Stella have a down-to-earth yet passionate relationship that keeps them bound to
each other in a way that Blanche does not understand. As husband and wife, they enjoy a physical
intimacy. Blanche is not interested in a relationship based only on physical attraction. The streetcar she takes to reach the Kowalskis' home is
appropriately called Desire, but for Blanche desire
means the desire for a deeper kind of love, not
merely physical. Tragically for Blanche, her desire
for true love, for deep connection with another
person, is continually being thwarted, and she is
associated with what she tells Mitch is the opposite of desire—death. The central event in her life
was the death of her husband, and she cannot
escape the memory of it. Nor can she forget the
many deaths of her relatives at Belle Reve.
Reminders of death keep cropping up to pin
Blanche back to these dark memories: the inscription on Mitch's cigarette case, for example, given
to him by a dying girl, is a quotation from the poet
Elizabeth Barrett Browning about love and death.
Then the Mexican woman comes to the house
selling flowers for funerals. While Stella and Stanley have found a way to keep the flame of life
burning, the unhappy Blanche leads an empty,

STYLE

Musical Symbolism

The musical score was composed by Alex North,
for which he was nominated for an Academy
Award. North combined the rhythms and harmonies of jazz with classical orchestral music
that has a symphonic dimension. North referred
to the music as "simulated jazz," since as written
music it lacks the spontaneous quality associated
with jazz. (This comment is made by the record
producer Robert Townson in the special feature
"North and the Music of the South" in the DVD
edition of the film.) Townson also comments
that North's intention was to create music that
reflects the psychological conditions of the characters. All the music is in some way related to the
main musical theme that is heard at the beginning of the film. The only exception to this is the
French polka music, which is heard every time
Blanche is reminded of her dead husband, since
this was the tune that the band was playing when
her husband shot himself. In the scene in which
the young man comes to the apartment for newspaper money, for example, the polka music is
heard, which tells the audience, without the need
for words, that the young man reminds Blanche
of her deceased husband.

In composing the music for the film, North
stayed close to the play. Williams, the playwright,
describes the music of the "blue piano," coming
from the Four Deuces bar, as expressing the spirit
of life in that part of New Orleans. The piano
music is also heard at times in conjunction with
brass, drums, and clarinet, according to the changing mood and atmosphere of the play. The opposite of the piano music, which represents life, is the
polka music, also called the Varsouviana music,
which represents death.

Montage

After the opening credits, there is a sequence
known as a montage, a succession of shots following quickly one after the other to create, in
this case, an overall impression of the setting.
These are long shots (shots in which the camera
is at some distance from the objects) that show
the larger environment. First, there is a long shot
from the air looking down on the railroad tracks

and the steam locomotive. This is followed by a shot from ground level as the camera follows the taxi cabs at night as they head for and arrive at the railroad station as the train pulls in. Then there is a busy shot of people emerging from the waiting room to greet arriving travelers. As the camera pans to the left, we see Blanche emerging surrounded by steam from the locomotive. The montage has moved from the general (the busy urban setting) to the particular (the main character) in just a few shots.

Visual Symbolism

Film has an advantage over the stage in that it presents possibilities for creating visual images that tell the story of what happens without words or even showing the action itself. An example of this visual symbolism occurs toward the end of the film. As Stanley approaches Blanche with aggressive intent, the film cuts to a shot of a smashed mirror. This shot suggests, without actually showing it, that Blanche has thrown the broken bottle at Stanley and missed, but more important, it conveys symbolically that Blanche herself is shattered by this last encounter with her brother-in-law. She is as fragile as glass and she eventually breaks. The symbol of the broken mirror tells this story in a few seconds, without words.

CULTURAL CONTEXT

Censorship

When the film was made in 1951, standards of what was considered acceptable for mass entertainment were different from what they are today. Although it was an extremely successful stage play, *A Streetcar Named Desire* also had a reputation for containing some sensational and morally questionable material. When the film was made, it had to be approved by the Motion Picture Production Code, popularly known as the Hays Code, after its founder, Will H. Hays. In order that the film might be deemed suitable for family viewing, several scenes had to be slightly rewritten in order to satisfy the censors. In the play, for example, Blanche's husband commits suicide because he is troubled by his homosexuality and Blanche's negative response to it. In those days, homosexuality was considered a shameful thing, and the filmmakers were not permitted to include any reference to it.

Another change demanded by the censors was that Stanley should be punished for his assault on Blanche at the end of the play. Therefore, in the film, Stella vows that she will never go back to Stanley; however, in the play, Stanley comforts Stella, who is upset over the fact that she has committed Blanche to a mental institution. There is no suggestion that Stanley and Stella will split up.

Other small cuts had to be made to satisfy the Legion of Decency, a Catholic organization that had a rating system for films. Originally, the Legion advised Warner Brothers that *A Streetcar Named Desire* would receive a C rating from them, which meant that it would be deemed a morally unsuitable film for Catholics to see. Not wanting to have people discouraged from seeing the film, Warner was ready to compromise, so twelve more cuts, amounting to four minutes of screen time, were made. These cuts included part of the scene in which Stella descends a staircase to Stanley, who waits below. The close-ups and medium shots of Stella were considered too suggestive of Stella's physical attraction to Stanley—the fact that Stanley and Stella are husband and wife seems not to have made any difference to the Legion—so a long shot was substituted in which the expression on Stella's face could not be seen. The changes mollified the Legion of Decency, which issued the film a B rating. This meant that it had some objectionable material, but the revised rating meant that theaters would not be put off from showing it. The director of the film, Elia Kazan, was not happy with the changes that were forced on him, believing that they compromised the artistic integrity of the film. Tennessee Williams also expressed the idea that the ending of the film was unsatisfactory.

In 1993, some of the material that was cut from the original film was restored. This restored version runs a few minutes longer than the 122 minutes of the 1951 film, and is the version that is commercially available on DVD.

Method Acting

As Stanley Kowalski, Marlon Brando brought a new method of acting to Hollywood. This was Method acting, which Brando had studied at the Dramatic Workshop of the New School in New York City, where he was coached by Stella Adler in the methods of the Russian theater director, Konstanin Stanislavski (1863–1938). Another

AP Images

acting teacher associated with popularizing Method acting in the United States was Lee Strasberg (1901–1982). Method actors sought to gain a new depth, intensity, and authenticity to their work by recalling emotional experiences in their own lives, and using other techniques, to understand and represent the emotions of the characters they were portraying. In *A Streetcar Named Desire*, Brando's Method acting contrasted with that of Vivien Leigh, who was trained in the classical British acting style. Method acting became extremely popular in the United States in the 1940s and 1950s, in part due to the success of Brando and James Dean, another Method actor.

CRITICAL OVERVIEW

A Streetcar Named Desire was an immediate success at the box office, and it also garnered twelve Academy Award nominations. The reviewer for *Look* accurately assesses the quality of the film: "*Streetcar* now seizes a place among Hollywood's rare great movies" (quoted in Philip C. Kolin's *Williams: A Streetcar Named Desire*), although the film was also denounced in some quarters as immoral and shocking.

Now over fifty years old, the film has stood the test of time. A new wave of interest in it was created by the restoration in 1993 of several minutes that had been cut in the original 1951 version. Roger Ebert reviewed the restored version of the film for the *Chicago Sun-Times*. After commenting on how the restored parts are crucial to the play's meaning and that Brando's style

of acting was soon to dominate Hollywood films, Ebert also notes how suitable the film is to black-and-white photography. "Color would have been fatal to the special tone. It would have made the characters seem too real, when we need them exactly like this, black and gray and silver, shadows projected on the screens of their own dreams and needs."

In 2008, when the film was presented as part of a Williams season at London's BFI Southbank, Peter Bradshaw wrote in the London *Guardian* that "Brando is lethally powerful," although he was less impressed with Vivien Leigh's "stagey, mad-eyed performance, often pitilessly inspected in close-up."

In 2007, the film was ranked forty-fifth in a list of the hundred greatest American films by the American Film Institute.

CRITICISM

Bryan Aubrey

Aubrey holds a Ph.D. in English. In this essay on A Streetcar Named Desire, *he discusses the major characters and their relationships and whether Blanche may be considered a tragic heroine.*

Tennessee Williams had a Shakespearean gift for empathizing with his characters regardless of how admirable or otherwise they might seem. He shows them in their complexity, with all their contradictions, their vices and their virtues, their struggles, their little victories and defeats. He is reluctant to condemn, which is why Stanley Kowalski in *A Streetcar Named Desire* cannot be presented as the villain of the play or film, even though over the years many have sought to blame him for Blanche's tragic descent into madness. Stanley, so thrillingly captured by Marlon Brando in the film, embodies a kind of raw masculinity that although crude and violent at times also has a kind of authenticity that many a lesser man (Mitch, for example) might envy. Stanley simply takes pleasure in being alive without reflecting much on it. He lives in his body, not his mind, and if ever his mind troubles him and tells him something is not right, he responds with an animal ferocity to restore his equilibrium. Stanley is the king of his domain and has no intention of allowing anyone to challenge him, especially not Blanche. He is a true descendant of the working-class, uncultured, sensually alive man that English novelist D. H. Lawrence held up as an ideal of masculinity in his novel *Lady Chatterley's Lover*

WHAT DO I SEE NEXT?

- *Cat on a Hot Tin Roof* (1958) is a film adaptation of Tennessee Williams's play of the same title, first produced in 1955. It stars Elizabeth Taylor as Maggie, the "cat" of the title, and Paul Newman as Brick, her troubled ex-football player husband. Set in Mississippi, the story centers on a struggle for the family inheritance. Brick's father, Big Daddy, a wealthy plantation owner, is dying of cancer, although the family refuses to inform him of this fact. Also wanting the inheritance are Big Daddy's other son, Gooper, and his wife. The drama is intense as family secrets gradually come out. Although Williams did not like the film adaptation of his play, it did receive six Academy Award nominations.

- *On the Waterfront* (1954) is another famous film featuring Marlon Brando, as well as Karl Malden, who played Mitch in *A Streetcar Named Desire*. It also was directed by Elia Kazan. Set in Hoboken, New Jersey, it is a story of political corruption, in which a longshoreman (Brando) tries to fight back against the taking over of his union by mobsters. The film won eight Academy Awards, including Best Picture, Best Director, Best Actor (Brando), and Best Writing.

- *East of Eden* (1955) is another film directed by Kazan. It is based on part of the novel by John Steinbeck and is set in California during World War I. The film stars James Dean in his first movie role. Like Brando, Dean made his name as a Method actor. The film focuses on the rivalry between two brothers, Caleb and Adam, as they compete for their father's approval.

- *Gone with the Wind* (1939) is one of the most famous of all American films. Set in Georgia during and immediately after the Civil War, the film is adapted from the 1936 novel of the same title by Margaret Mitchell. It stars Vivien Leigh as Scarlett O'Hara, who falls in love with the charming but roguish Rhett Butler (Clark Gable). The film won ten Academy Awards.

- *The Heiress* (1949) is a film adapted from a 1947 play by Ruth and Augustus Goetz. The play was based on *Washington Square* (1880), a novel by Henry James. The main character, Catherine Sloper (Olivia de Havilland), is jilted by her fiance, who later returns, wanting to marry her, when she has inherited her father's fortune. Catherine pretends to forgive him but has her own plans about how to get her revenge. The film won four Academy Awards, including Best Actress for de Havilland.

- In *Kitty Foyle* (1940), Kitty (Ginger Rogers), a young businesswoman, has to decide whether to marry Mark (James Craig), an earnest young doctor, or take up with Wyn (Dennis Morgan), a wealthy old friend who has recently come back into her life and with whom she has always been in love. She chooses Wyn, but the marriage does not succeed and she eventually returns to Mark.

(1928), a book with which Williams was familiar, and in the novella *The Virgin and the Gypsy* (1930). Like these earthy heroes that Lawrence created, Stanley Kowalski has the masculine power to conquer a woman from a higher social class. When he first met Stella, who of course grew up in the same social circumstances as Blanche, as part of the decaying Southern aristocracy, Stella thought he was common. He won her heart, though, by initiating her into a mutually satisfying physical love that has enriched and sustained their marriage. In this sense, Stella has made a transition that Blanche has failed to make, allowing her to experience a joy in marriage that Blanche can only dream of.

The brutish but authentic Stanley stands in contrast to his old World War II buddy, the more

WILLIAMS SUGGESTS THAT DESPITE A DISREPUTABLE PAST THAT HAD RESULTED IN HER BEING CHASED OUT OF HER HOMETOWN, AND DESPITE HER DELUSIONS AND APPROACHING INSANITY, SHE RETAINS A KIND OF PURITY AND INNOCENCE THAT LINK HER TO THE VIRGIN."

refined but much weaker Mitch. Mitch has rather unkindly been called a mama's boy, but the label is an accurate one. Mitch is morbidly attached to his sick mother and allows her to manipulate him. The poker group cannot play at his house because of his mother; he quits the card game at Stanley's early because his mother cannot go to sleep until he comes home; he cannot enjoy the card game fully because he keeps thinking of her. Stanley, who has a merciless instinct for a person's weak spot, jokes that when Mitch wins money (in quarters) at poker, he will go home and "deposit them one by one in a piggy bank his mother give him for Christmas."

The scene in which Blanche and Mitch go on a date is almost comic in what it reveals about Mitch's awkwardness and inexperience with women. He is the very opposite of Stanley. Although he claims to be proud of his physique, he is also ashamed of the fact that he perspires a lot, and he is reluctant to remove his jacket for that reason. In contrast, Stanley sweats and doesn't care, as the film famously shows. Whereas Brando's Stanley is muscular but unselfconscious about it, Mitch tries to impress Blanche with a ridiculous recitation of his height and weight and his claims to physical fitness. Blanche, seeing Mitch as a possible ticket out of loneliness, carefully feigns interest in the subject, which Mitch goes on about for some time, even though he admits it is not a very interesting subject. When he lifts Blanche up on the pretext of seeing how much she weighs, it is a comic counterpart to the end of the film, when Stanley lifts Blanche up with far more sinister intentions.

Mitch buys into the romantic scenario that Blanche seems to demand. He tries to be gentlemanly and gallant with her, although he does not

seem to be at ease. He asks whether he may kiss her, as if he is requesting a personal favor, and he gets a predictably tart response, "Why do you always ask me if you may?" His reply, "I don't know whether you want me to or not," shows his timidity, his un-Stanley-like lack of confidence with women. It is perhaps not surprising that when Mitch learns from Stanley about Blanche's past, he turns on her. He is angry not only with Blanche but with himself for being fooled. Ironically, when he drops the genteel mask that he put on for her benefit, he becomes a more authentic figure—not an attractive one, but at least a man who is expressing what he truly feels. However, there is once more a contrast with Stanley. When Mitch, shorn of romantic illusions, tries to seduce Blanche, he is easily chased off by the enraged woman. Mitch is not a ruthless man, and he can be fended off. Not so Stanley, as Blanche finds out to her cost just a few hours later that night.

Blanche herself is probably the most famous female character in American drama, much written about and discussed, and her portrayal by Vivien Leigh has been justly celebrated. The film is clearly her story. In the play, Stanley appears before she does, but in the film that is reversed. In the opening sequence of the film, the white-clad Blanche appears out of a cloud of steam from the locomotive, as if she is some heavenly creature who has been deposited by a conjurer's magic into a strange new environment in which she is destined always to be out of place. It is as if Williams wanted to counter the fact that Marlon Brando's riveting performance as Stanley in the stage play had become such a talking point and reaffirm that Blanche is the central character.

As that central character, Blanche is a tortured soul. Neurotic and weak, she holds on to an ideal of love that once lit up the world for her but died with her young husband. Desperate for someone to save her from her loneliness and heartache, she loses all her moral bearings in her hometown of Auriol and ends up as a kind of penniless refugee, dependent on the hospitality of her sister and brother-in-law. Her obsession with bathing—it seems as if she is always in the bathroom—symbolically suggests her desire for purity, her attempt to free herself from the taint of an unwholesome past forced upon her not by some innate depravity but by simple human need. In the end, she finds neither love nor purity but only madness.

Is this the stuff of which tragic heroines are made, and can Blanche be seen as one? In the last scene of the film, as Blanche is led away by the doctor, Vivien Leigh does manage to convey in her character a kind of fragile dignity. As she walks accompanied out of the house Blanche is continuing the journey of the soul that began who knows when and was symbolically continued in the directions she was given to Stella's home: "Take a street-car named Desire, and then transfer to one called Cemeteries, and . . . get off at—Elysian Fields." (In classical mythology, the Elysian Fields were the home of the blessed dead.) Death, as Blanche herself says, is the opposite of desire, and it seems that Blanche passes through many kinds of symbolic death—of hope, of love, even of reason. Might her journey be seen as a process of redemption through suffering, ending in some blessed state known only to her?

This might seem a far-fetched notion until one notices that Williams the playwright has given a great deal of attention to symbolically presenting Blanche as Mary the Virgin, the Queen of Heaven in some Christian traditions. At first this sounds like a kind of sarcastic joke that might have been made by Stanley Kowalski, but the playwright is not joking. The first reference that suggests such an interpretation is certainly light-hearted, but it is there for a reason. Blanche is trying to make conversation with Stanley and she mentions that in astrology, she was born under the sign of Virgo, the Virgin. She contrasts this with Stanley, born under the sign of Capricorn, the goat, thus underlining what she sees as her own purity set against Stanley's more carnal nature. Goats are often used as a symbol of animal lust. (In the movie, the dirty look Stanley flashes at Blanche at this point shows exactly what he thinks of being identified with a goat.) After Mitch's departure, Blanche dresses up in a white satin gown with "scuffed silver slippers with brilliants set in their heels" and a "rhinestone tiara" on her head. According to Henry I. Schvey, in "Madonna at the Poker Night: Pictorial Elements in Tennessee Williams's *A Streetcar Named Desire*," an essay on the color symbolism in the play, "the image of Blanche . . . may be seen as a variation on the familiar image of Mary as Queen of Heaven, portrayed with a crown bearing the twelve stars of the apocalyptic vision (Rev. 12:9)." Later, as she is about to be taken away, Blanche dons a blue jacket and defines the color quite specifically: "It's Della Robbia blue. The blue of the robe in the old Madonna pictures." As Schvey points out, this is a reference to the color associated with the Virgin in Renaissance art.

Other references that reinforce the symbolic association of Blanche and the Virgin include the cathedral bells, which Blanche comments on, and Williams's stage directions describing her as having "a look of sorrowful perplexity as though all human experience shows on her face." The latter may be a reference to the compassionate nature of the Virgin as the sorrowful mother.

With the piling up of these allusions, the playwright is clearly trying to lift Blanche above the pathetic situation in which she finds herself: a shattered, deranged woman about to be taken away, without any awareness on her part, to the state mental asylum. Williams suggests that despite a disreputable past that had resulted in her being chased out of her hometown, and despite her delusions and approaching insanity, she retains a kind of purity and innocence that link her to the Virgin. She has stepped through the minefield of the world with an essential part of her nature intact, perhaps even augmented by the suffering she has been through.

However, even if this should be so, does it make Blanche a tragic heroine? Some (including Schvey) might argue that it does, while others might claim that Blanche lacks an essential quality of the tragic hero or heroine: a new, heightened awareness of the situation she is in and what has brought her to this point. The hero, in Aristotle's classic formulation, goes from ignorance to recognition, or knowledge. Blanche, it would seem, flounders around in delusion and incomprehension. Questions race through her mind as she wonders who these people are who have come to take her away. Knowledge eludes her. And yet, in spite of all this, there is in her final, famous line, "I have always depended on the kindness of strangers," a kind of acceptance of her destiny, a coming to terms with her own helplessness and weakness, her need for a shield in a world too harsh for her delicate sensibilities.

Source: Bryan Aubrey, Critical Essay on *A Streetcar Named Desire*, in *Drama for Students*, Gale, Cengage Learning, 2010.

Christine Geraghty

In the following excerpt, film theorist and critic Andre Bazin's views on the 1951 adaptation of A Streetcar Named Desire *are discussed.*

. . . André Bazin was a highly influential figure in the development of film theory and criticism in the 1940s and 1950s, at the same time that Williams's work in theater and cinema was making him famous. Bazin's work has continued to inform critical debate about adaptations since then. James Naremore chose one of his essays, "Adaptation, or the Cinema as Digest," to open his influential *Film Adaptation* collection, praising its open-minded flexibility and suggesting, as Robert Stam later put it, that he "foreshadowed some of the later structuralist and post-structuralist currents which would indirectly undermine a fidelity discourse in relation to adaptation." Here I will concentrate on Bazin's two essays on theater and cinema that offer an approach that appreciates the differences between the two media without, as Naremore and Stam appreciated, getting mired in questions of faithfulness.

Bazin offers a summary of how the difference between the two media is traditionally explained, an explanation that can still be found in much analysis today and that tends to create a hierarchy in which theater emerges as the more engaging and demanding medium. The differences are rooted in two defining concepts—physical presence and audience activity. In the theater, the audience is in the physical presence of the actors whose performances relate directly to the particular audience in front of them; in the cinema, the actors' performance is recorded and takes place is a different space from that of the audience. Both perform to an audience, but one involves a live performance by actors physically present, the other a mechanical recording of absent actors. This might seem to mean that the audience in the theater is the more readily absorbed by the medium, but it is argued that, unlike the film audience, the theater audience has to work to get engaged; it is not mechanically caught up as the film audience is in the close-ups and editing of mainstream cinema. The theater

audience is envisaged as engaged in a social act that involves thought as well as feeling, while the cinema viewer is described as isolated, overemotional, and voyeuristic. In such a description, cinema's association with the mass media is clear, while theater's different relationship to its audience is deemed more likely to produce work of artistic value. And since this distinction is based on differences in media specificity, the processes of adaptation for the cinema once again seem set for failure.

Bazin does not dispute that there are differences that need to be acknowledged between theater and cinema but shifts the ground so that cinema is not inevitably that inferior form. This means changing a key element of difference, making it not the physical presence of the actor but the organization of space. The difference then is based not on something present in theater but absent from cinema but rather on the different approach to something they both share, the organization of space for an audience. Bazin suggests that theater marks out the stage as a "privileged spot," "an area materially enclosed, limited, circumscribed." It is removed from everyday life and is unsuitable for the "slice of life" realism that is possible in cinema. Cinema's space, by contrast, "denies any frontiers to action," encouraging us to imagine limitless off-screen space rather than the wings to which actors retreat in theater. For Bazin, therefore, the difficulty of filmed theater is centrally the difficulty of "transposing a text written for one dramaturgical system into another." The dramatic force of the text and its performance is lost if cinema techniques are used to make us forget the boundaries of the stage. This is, he argues, a problem of décor, so that cinema, rather than opening up the stage, has to rein itself in so as to present "a space orientated towards an inner dimension only." Neither cinema nor theater should be effaced in this process, but cinema must transform itself, "delve deeper into its own language," in order to effect a successful translation.

Bazin argues that the organization of this defined space is written into the theatrical text and that the play "is unassailably protected by its text." This is not just a matter of retaining the words but recognizing that "the mode and style of production" are "already embodied in the text." Because of this, a film that respects the play—and Bazin argues that adaptations of classics are bound to do so—has to follow "the directions it was supposed to go." This means respecting the primacy that theater gives to words and the exploration of internal dilemmas of "the human soul." Opening up a play (Bazin gives the example of a film of a Molière play set in a real forest) "in order to inject the power of 'cinema' into the theater" actually skews the production "so that the dramatic primacy of the word is thrown off center by the additional dramatization that the camera gives to the setting." This is the more painful because it is done in an attempt to compensate for cinema's "inferiority complex" as if "the 'superiority' of its technique" can lend "aesthetic superiority . . . ."

Although the film does show some streets of the quarter, these too are heavily stylized. Compared with the streets of gangster films and thrillers on which cars race and gunfights break out, these streets are cramped and restricted. The arrival of the car in the front yard of the building confirms the artificiality of the set and the limitations it places on the vehicle's movements. The street scenes are used not so much for realism as to mark the passage of the scenes of the play. And although some scenes are taken out of the confines of the main set they too tend to retain the restrictions of the stage. Blanche's date with Mitch is seen rather than just reported on, but the couple quickly move out of the main restaurant, away from the dancing and the crowds, to sit on their own in the restricted space of an outside landing. As with the main set, there is no sense here of a real "outside." Darkness and mist confine our view to the space occupied by the actors, the water reflects light back on to them, and we have no knowledge of or indeed interest in the offscreen space beyond the landing. The presentation of the set and its restrictions could be compared to the way in which the film of *Henry V* put the play into quotation marks, marking the edges of theatrical space. It marks out the limits of the staging and works within them.

A Streetcar Named Desire also deploys editing strategies that emphasize its origins in theater. The film's editing strategies are not those of classical Hollywood, and in particular they construct a position for the spectator that is different from that created by the classic shot-reverse shot structure. Analysis of the opening sequence and of two early exchanges between Stanley and Stella and then Stanley and Blanche illustrates this. The film's opening shots are accompanied by music appropriate for a thriller as a blonde woman in a light dress is picked out by the camera. She is held in a medium shot until the exchange with the sailor that includes a close-up of him and her in a shot-reverse shot exchange. This is all conventional, but the next shot signals something different. The shot of the streetcar moving to its stop at first seems to be from Blanche's point of view since it is preceded by a close-up of her looking offscreen; however, as the shot is held, she herself enters the frame and boards the streetcar. In a thriller or horror film, this shot would be ascribed to the viewpoint of a hidden watcher to be revealed by the narrative; in this film, it is the viewpoint of the audience.

This subtle reworking of cinema's editing conventions can be seen throughout the film, although the pattern of editing is different for Stella and for Blanche. The first scene for analysis occurs between Stanley and Stella after he has brought in Blanche's trunk, which stands in the middle of the front room. Stella tries to persuade Stanley to be nice to Blanche; Stanley queries the sale of Belle Reve and their rights under the "Napoleonic Code" and pulls apparently expensive clothes out of the trunk, while Stella tries to tidy up around him. The two actors continually move, but there is no looking/reverse cutting between them; the dominant shot is a two-shot in which the two are either parallel with each other or in a diagonal line with one closer to the camera. In a scene of four and a half minutes, there are only five cuts, and reframing occurs not through cutting but as the camera follows an actor (normally the one who is speaking) into a different space, establishing a different relationship with the other actor and with objects in the apartment (the trunk, the sink, and the refrigerator). The effect of this is twofold. First, the spectator is not cut into the space of the action by being invited by editing to share the viewpoint of either character. Instead, we observe the action from outside in a manner that preserves the distance of the theater audience while lending it the closeness of cinema. Through the use of the moving camera, we are inside the proscenium arch, as if on the stage, but we are not implicated with the viewpoint of either character. The second effect is to give a physical rhythm to our understanding of the relationship between these two characters. They are conducting an argument, but their movements and the framing indicate a complete harmony between them. As if in a dance, they move together and away, weaving an elaborate pattern around each other. Stella has spoken to Blanche about how she "can't stand it" when Stanley is away; here we see the relationship between them given physical form, through space and movement, but are not invited to share it.

After Stella leaves, Blanche enters fresh from bathing, and the subsequent scene between her and Stanley also revolves around the trunk and the sale of Belle Reve. In this scene, too, there is an emphasis on two-shots, on changing the framing through movement rather than cutting as, for example, when the camera follows Blanche as she attempts to retrieve the love letters. However, the scene is also marked by the use of a wider range of editing strategies, including the exchange of looks between the characters through reverse cutting so the audience takes on the viewpoint of first Stanley and then Blanche as they look at each other. The scene starts with a shot of Blanche at the curtain followed by shots of her view of Stanley, and there are a number of points when we get shot-reverse shot close-ups exchanged between the two, for instance, when Stanley stops Blanche's flirtatious use of perfume. This editing strategy, therefore, while still maintaining the distance associated with the spectator's viewpoint, at various points draws on cinema's more voyeuristic devices to implicate the spectator in the relationship between these two characters. However, most of these close-ups strongly emphasize also the back or profile of the character who is looking so that, to amend Bazin's comment on Cocteau's framing, "the purpose of the shot is to show not that [they are] looking, not even [their] gaze, it is to *see* [*them*] *actually looking*." In this way, while overall the spatial distance of theater is maintained, it is interwoven with the cutting characteristic of Hollywood cinema. Far from simply recording the play by recreating the proscenium arch, this editing, which indicates the different relationships between the characters and binds the audience into watching them watching, confirms that the film is "staging a play by means of cinema."

So far I have emphasized patterns of movement and looking in this analysis of the organization of space through editing in the 1951 *Streetcar*. But speech is also an issue in filmed theater. Sarah Kozloff's valuable book *Overhearing Film Dialogue*

reminds us that the common assertion, which Kazan himself upheld, that film emphasizes image and theater dialogue is unhelpful. The point is more that, as Bazin argued, theater and film dialogue is written for different spaces and different audience positions. The editing patterns of cinema tend to suit the exchange of dialogue, and the long speeches that are a dramatic focal point in much theater can cause problems in the translation to cinema precisely because they are "inherited from theatrical practice." Emphasizing the theatricality of such speech would seem to follow Bazin's logic, but Kazan takes a rather different route of maintaining the wholeness of the speeches but refusing the full visual dramatization that cutting and lighting might give. So, the speech in which Blanche tells Mitch about the suicide of her husband is visually downplayed. It starts with a medium close-up with Mitch in profile watching Blanche, who looks ahead with soft light on her face. The shot is held for over a minute with one brief two-shot intercut for a change of angle. Blanche, then, rises on the phrase describing her husband as "crying like a baby" but turns her back to the camera as she continues so that the audience is refused access to her face. She finally faces the camera in a restrained medium shot to describe the dance and the suicide, and the speech concludes with a shot of them both in long shot on a diagonal that Mitch breaks as he moves to embrace her. The language and length of the speech indicates its theatrical origins, but there is little use of the dramatic powers of close-up and lighting to reinforce its rhetoric....

Source: Christine Geraghty, "Tennessee Williams on Film: Space, Melodrama, and Stardom," in *Now a Major Motion Picture: Film Adaptations of Literature and Drama*, Rowman & Littlefield, 2008, pp. 75–81.

Erin Gabbard

In the following excerpt, Gabbard illustrates how the performance of Brando is an aspect of jazz improvisation.

...The story of jazz overlaps at several points with the development of the Hollywood cinema. Both art forms are uniquely American, and both began to develop and mature dramatically after 1900. According to Mary Carbine, black jazz artists were improvising in orchestra pits during the screening of presound films in African-American neighborhoods in Chicago in the 1920s (28–29). African-American participation at some point in the production and exhibition of the first feature films was, of course, an anomaly. As with most American

BRANDO ONCE WANTED TO BE A JAZZ
DRUMMER. AS LATE AS THE BROADWAY
PRODUCTION OF *STREETCAR* IN 1947, HE WAS STILL
KEEPING A JAZZ DRUMMER'S TRAP SET BACKSTAGE
ALONG WITH HIS BONGOS AND BARBELLS."

institutions at the beginning of the twentieth century, blacks were excluded from virtually all aspects of the film industry, with the notable exception of a handful of independent filmmakers, such as Oscar Micheaux, who worked outside the mainstream film industry. The omnipresence of white actors in blackface in D. W. Griffith's *Birth of a Nation* (1914) is the most striking example of Hollywood's long history of relying upon myths about African-Americans to forge fundamental narratives and ideologies while harshly limiting the actual presence of black actors, directors, writers, and technicians.

The radically different racial orientations of jazz and cinema did not, however, prevent either from being considered low culture during the early decades of the century. The guardians of America's moral, sexual, and religious health launched similar attacks on both. The two art forms became somewhat more sedate in the 1930s with the rise of superego forces, specifically the Production Code, which made movies safe for children, and the success of white swing bands, which made jazz safe for Middle Americans. In the 1950s, new bugbears appeared to make jazz and film seem less disreputable. Rock and roll replaced jazz just as television replaced movies as the explanation for the corruption of America's youth and the lowering of standards of taste. Coincidentally, as Bernard Gendron has argued, claims that jazz and Hollywood films could be "art" first surfaced at about this time in the late 1940s and early 1950s. By the 1980s, after several decades of experimentation, both jazz and cinema fell back into periods of what might be called "recuperation": while some welcomed a return to more classical, more accessible models, others believed that the exhilarating evolution of vital art forms had stopped. At any rate, by the 1990s both jazz and film had begun to acquire the status of elite entertainment.

At New York's Lincoln Center, a ticket to a jazz concert cost as much as a ticket to an opera or a ballet. Across the street, at the Lincoln Plaza Cinemas, moviegoers could purchase gourmet food and espresso in the lobby while Baroque music played in the auditoriums before each screening.

At least a few critics have speculated about the specific ways in which jazz has actually influenced the movies. Stanley Crouch has made a provocative claim for the centrality of Afrocentric practices in American culture, pointing to the call and response dialogue that African-American preachers improvised with their congregations and that eventually became the basis for the interaction between blues singers and their audiences and between the brass and reed sections in arrangements played by black jazz orchestras in the 1920s and 1930s. Crouch argues that Hollywood's shot-reverse shot editing is also an appropriation of call and response (82).

Crouch has almost certainly exaggerated the actual impact of African-American practices on an industry that was much more invested in white mythologies of blackness. Clear evidence of the influence of jazz improvisation in Hollywood is also minimal, especially in the industry's "prestige" products where a small army of producers and technicians oversees each step in a film's deliberate progress to the big screen. Nevertheless, there may have been a substantial—if highly mediated—exchange between jazz improvisation and film in the 1950s. Both jazz and the Method acting that made its way into American cinema at this time were part of a modernist mix that also included a romance with psychoanalysis, new forms of racial imitation, the development of postwar masculinities, and a fascination with improvisation. *A Streetcar Named Desire* had a revolutionary jazz inflected score by Alex North, it was based on the play by Tennessee Williams, who was obsessed with masculine performance; and it was directed by Elia Kazan, who was obsessed with psychoanalysis. All of these strains came together in an aesthetic of jazz improvisation that resonates most powerfully in the performance of the youthful Brando....

Brando once wanted to be a jazz drummer. As late as the Broadway production of *Streetcar* in 1947, he was still keeping a jazz drummer's trap set backstage along with his bongos and barbells. In high school, Brando briefly led a few bands of his own at the same time that he was tormenting his school band director by playing Gene Krupa riffs in the middle of Sousa marches. The Krupa connection is revealing. After starring with the Benny Goodman band in the mid-thirties, the white drummer broke away to form his own band in 1938. Krupa was arrested on a widely reported drug charge in 1943 and forced out of the music business for several months. For many, the drummer's dangerous romance with proscribed substances only increased his glamour. Even before Krupa's arrest, however, his band had a certain subversive appeal. In 1941, the new "girl singer" in Krupa's orchestra was Anita O'Day, who projected a more sexually experienced persona than did most of the demure white women who sang with the big bands. O'Day raised many eyebrows when she refused to wear the prom dresses common among girl singers, choosing instead to wear a blazer like the men in the band. Also in 1941, Krupa hired the black trumpeter Roy Eldridge and prominently featured his improvised solos *and* his singing. The band had a hit with "Let Me Off Uptown" in which Eldridge sang with O'Day. The interracial romance implied in the couple's double entendres was especially daring for 1941. The patter begins with O'Day asking Eldridge if he has been "uptown" and concludes with her urging him, "Well, blow, Roy, blow!" The veiled invitation to interracial oral sex was not lost on the hipsters in the audience. The gender and racial titillation in which Krupa's band specialized may have been as important for the young Brando as Krupa's drumming.

In films such as *Hollywood Hotel* (1938), *Ball of Fire* (1941), *Beat the Band* (1947), and *The Glenn Miller Story* (1954), Krupa can be observed flamboyantly performing his sexuality and masculinity, surely as part of an attempt to re-create what he found most fascinating about black men and their music. Anyone who has watched the revered African-American drummer Jo Jones in a film such as *Jammin' the Blues* (1944) has witnessed an artist who seems, by contrast, to inhabit his exuberance without affectation. I would speculate that Krupa saw and heard sexual power in the improvisations of black drummers like Jones and created his own style of bringing it to the surface in hopes of projecting that same power. At some point in his early life, Brando may have been using Krupa as a transitional object in his appropriation of black masculinity, just as Beiderbecke first discovered black music through the

white artists of the ODJB and NORK. Identifying a parallel phenomenon, Eric Lott has written that imitators of Elvis Presley play out their fascination with black male sexuality safely at one remove by trying to inhabit the body of Presley as he appeared in the 1950s, "as though such performance were a sort of second order blackface, in which, blackface having for the most part disappeared, the figure of Elvis himself is now the apparently still necessary signifier of white ventures into black culture—a signifier to be adopted bodily if one is to have success in achieving the intimacy with 'blackness' that is crucial to the adequate reproduction of Presley's show" ("All the King's Men," 205).

In 1969, Brando attended a meeting to raise money for the Poor People's March on Washington, sponsored by the Southern Christian Leadership Conference in the wake of the assassination of Martin Luther King Jr. The meeting was attended by other Hollywood celebrities, including Barbra Streisand, Harry Belafonte, Natalie Wood, and Jean Seberg, who brought along the man to whom she was married at the time, the French novelist Romain Gary. In his autobiographical novel, *White Dog,* Gary contemptuously describes the behavior of Brando at the event. After stressing the need for a steering committee to continue the work of raising money for the poor, Brando asked for volunteers. In a crowd of approximately three hundred, thirty hands went up: "He glares at the audience and at the thirty raised hands. He braces himself, balances his shoulders in that famous half-roll, then the chin goes up. He is acting. Or rather overacting, for the sudden violence in his voice and the tightening of his facial muscles and of the jaws bears no relation whatsoever to the situation." According to Gary, Brando then said, "those who didn't raise their hands, get the hell out of here!" (172)....

Source: Erin Gabbard, "Improvisation and Imitation: Marlon Brando as Jazz Actor," in *The Other Side of Nowhere: Jazz, Improvisation, and Communities in Dialogue,* edited by Daniel Fischlin and Ajay Heble, Wesleyan University Press, 2004, pp. 299–307.

SOURCES

"AFI's 100 Years . . . The Complete Lists," in *American Film Institute*, http://connect.afi.com/site/PageServer?pagename=100YearsList (accessed June 22, 2009).

Bradshaw, Peter, Review of *A Streetcar Named Desire*, in *Guardian* (London, England), November 14, 2008, http://www.guardian.co.uk/film/2008/nov/14/streetcar-named-desire-film-review (accessed June 22, 2009).

Ebert, Roger, Review of *A Streetcar Named Desire*, in *Chicago Sun-Times*, November 12, 1993, http://rogerebert.suntimes.com/apps/pbcs.dll/article?AID = /19931112/REVIEWS/311120304/102 3 (accessed June 22, 2009).

Kolin, Philip C., *Williams: A Streetcar Named Desire*, Cambridge University Press, 2000, p. 151.

Schvey, Henry I., "Madonna at the Poker Night: Pictorial Elements in Tennessee Williams's *A Streetcar Named Desire*," in *Tennessee Williams's "A Streetcar Named Desire,"* edited and with an introduction by Harold Bloom, Chelsea House, 1988, p. 108.

Williams, Tennessee, *A Streetcar Named Desire*, New American Library, 1947.

The Trojan Women

EURIPIDES

415 BCE

Euripides' *The Trojan Women* is acknowledged to be among the greatest surviving pieces of Greek tragedy. Although it won only second place in the City Dionysia, a dramatic festival, when it premiered in 415 BCE, it endured throughout antiquity in learned literary anthologies that helped to educate taste and reinforce Greek identity. Though it fell into disfavor during the Renaissance because of its flawed form, it has become one of the most commonly staged and adapted Greek dramas in the twentieth century because of its antiwar sentiment (often greatly exaggerated in modern productions and adaptations, such as that by Jean-Paul Sartre).

The Trojan Women tells the story of the women who survived the Greek capture of their city at the end of the Trojan War. They were destined to become the slaves of the victorious Greeks because the women's husbands, brothers, and fathers had all been slaughtered by their conquerors. Its very subject matter is subversive of the Greek heroic ideals expressed in Homer's *Iliad*, the great epic of the Trojan War. There are four main characters: Hecuba, who dominates the entire play, and her daughter and daughters-in-law, each of whom takes the lead in one act of the play. The first of these is the Trojan princess Cassandra, who is driven mad by the gods. Next is Andromache, who is forced to become the concubine to the Greek hero Neoptolemus, the son of Achilles, who had killed her husband Hector in battle. Third is Helen, who is condemned to death

Euripides (The Library of Congress)

drawn from the comedic plays of Aristophanes, in which Euripides sometimes appears as a character. This situation is typical of many ancient authors. In the case of Euripides, all of the surviving material has been collected and translated into English by David Kovacs in *Euripdea*.

His family background is obscure, but he either was wealthy himself or could secure wealthy patrons to produce his plays. He began to compete in the annual Athenian dramatic festival of the City Dionysia in 456 BCE; he entered in twenty-two different years but won the first prize only four times (and once more posthumously). Posterity was kinder to him, however. All three of the surviving tragedians wrote about a hundred plays, but of Euripides' works, eighteen tragedies and one satyr play still exist, compared with seven tragedies each for Aeschylus and Sophocles. The tetralogy (a set of three dramas and a satyr play) of which *The Trojan Women* was a part premiered in 415 BCE and took second place. His other notable plays include *Medea* (431 BCE), *Electra* (420 BCE), and the posthumously produced *Bacchae* (405 BCE). Supposedly, Euripides became disenchanted with his popular and critical failure in Athens, and in 408 BCE he accepted an invitation to join the court of Archelaus, the king of Macedonia, in northern Greece. Euripides died in 406 BCE, about a year after he moved there. The sources provide various elaborate means of his death (for example, being poisoned by rival poets jealous of his talent), but since Euripides was by then seventy-four years old, his death requires no fantastic explanation.

Euripides explored to an unparalleled degree the ideas of science, philosophy, and rhetoric that dominated the intellectual life of fifth-century BCE Athens. For this reason, the sources make him a close associate of such famous philosophers as Anaxagoras, Protagoras, Prodicus, and even Socrates, but that list could just as well be a selection of figures approximately Euripides' age. In any case, Euripides' plays are certainly an exceptional component of the intellectual and cultural achievement of classical Athens.

for adultery but is pardoned because of her beauty and, in Euripides' version, for her clever sophistic arguments. Finally, the Trojan queen Hecuba, present throughout the play, is left alone at the end to bury her infant grandson, whom the Greeks had murdered out of fear of the vengeance he might one day take if he grew to manhood. With its deep concern for injustice and impiety, *The Trojan Women* also reveals the stresses on Athens as it prepared to renew the Peloponnesian War at the end of the Peace of Nicias.

AUTHOR BIOGRAPHY

It is thought that Euripides was born in Athens in 480 BCE. Knowledge of his life is based on an anonymous biography that is sometimes attached to manuscripts of his plays and that was probably composed hundreds of years after his death. A few other sources of information are contained in even later Byzantine (medieval) encyclopedias. These sources are often contradictory, and there is little way of establishing an accurate version of his biography. Much of the material in these sources is actually reworked from Euripides' plays, as if they were autobiographical; other material is

PLOT SUMMARY

Greek tragedies were divided into episodes in which the actors sing and speak, advancing the plot, and *stasima* (choral odes) in which the

MEDIA ADAPTATIONS

- In 1824, the French poet Casimir Delavigne prepared a version of Euripides' *The Trojan Women* for singing as a cantata.

- In 1954, the French composer Paul Danblon composed an oratorio, *Les Troyennes*, based on Euripedes' drama, with a French libretto (lyrics) by Jean Le Paillot.

- In 1971, Michael Cacoyannis directed *The Trojan Women*, a film adaptation starring Katharine Hepburn, Vanessa Redgrave, Brian Blessed, and Patrick Magee. It was released on DVD by Kino Video in 2004.

- Elizabeth Swados composed a 1974 opera, *The Trojan Women*, loosely based on Euripides' original.

- The Greek composer Eleni Karaindrou composed incidental music for *The Trojan Women* in 2001.

---

chorus dances and sings, usually commenting on the development of the plot in the preceding episode.

Prologue, Lines 1–97

The play begins with a conversation between the gods Poseidon and Athene. Although no stage directions are given in the original manuscripts, it is probable that the gods were lowered onto the stage by cranes, symbolizing their heavenly nature. Poseidon is the first to appear. He names himself as the patron of Troy's people and laments that his city has been destroyed by Athene. He establishes the scene of the play as a hill overlooking Troy (also known as Ilium), which was probably visible in the background as scenery painting. He briefly describes the end of the siege, beginning with the deception of the Trojan Horse, and centering on the acts of impiety committed by the victorious Greeks (frequently called Achaeans) that have left the gods' temples empty and defiled. He starts with the murder of Priam, the king of Troy, who

sought sanctuary at the altar of Zeus. According to Greek sacred law, Priam ought to have been safe as long as his hand was on the altar, but the Greeks broke that compact and killed him on the altar. More fundamentally, Poseidon points out that the destruction of Troy ends the very considerable worship that the gods received from Troy in the form of frequent sacrifices and the divine treasuries stored in the city's temples.

Poseidon explains that the war is over. The Greek ships are loaded with the sacred and public treasures of Troy, and the last thing to go on board will be the Trojan women, together with their children. Now enslaved, they are all that is left of the people of Troy since all adult men have been killed. The women are even now being assigned to individual Greek masters while they wait in an encampment of tents. Poseidon mentions by name Helen, the cause of the war, and Hecuba, the queen of Troy. He also mentions in particular two of the daughters of Hecuba and Priam: Polyxena, who has already been killed as a human sacrifice at the tomb of Achilles (the greatest Greek hero, who nevertheless died in battle a few months before the end of the war), and Cassandra, whom the god Apollo has driven mad. Poseidon laments that Troy has been destroyed because just as the Greeks overcame the Trojans, the will of Hera and especially that of the warrior goddess Athene overcame his own.

Athene appears and surprises Poseidon by asking him to help her punish the Greeks by sending storms to wreck their fleet on the homeward voyage across the Aegean Sea. She wishes to do this because the Greeks allowed the hero Ajax to pull Cassandra away from the temple of Athene, where she had sought sanctuary, thus committing sacrilege and insulting her. Naturally, Poseidon agrees.

Parodos, Lines 98–234

The chorus dances onto the stage through the doors in the *skene*, or backdrop to the action. The scene begins with Hecuba already on stage, that is, in the open air of the Trojan women's camp where she had slept during the night. It is now dawn. She sings a song lamenting that Helen ever came to Troy and her own consequent reversal of fortune (typical of tragic plots) from queen of Troy to slave groveling before the smoldering city. She tells the chorus, composed of the other captive Trojan women, that she cannot bear to see Cassandra, since she has been driven mad on top of all her other suffering. She also informs them that the Greeks have decided to take the women as spoils and leave Troy that very day, rather than slaughtering them as they had the men, a fate some of the women feared. The other women echo Hecuba's lament, hoping that they at least do not have to go to Sparta and serve the hated Helen. (Helen's husband, Menelaus, is the king of Sparta.)

First Episode, Lines 235–510

The Greek herald Talthybius now enters the stage, accompanied by some of the soldiers guarding the camp. He delivers the news that each of the Trojan women has been allotted individually as a slave to one of the Greeks. He reveals that Cassandra has been given to Agamemnon as his concubine. Hecuba laments that this as an act of impiety, since her daughter was devoted to lifelong virginity in the service of Apollo. Hecuba asks about her other daughter, Polyxena. Talthybius hints at the truth, but Hecuba perhaps does not wish to understand. She changes the subject to Andromache, who has been given to Achilles' son Neoptolemus. Hecuba herself has been allotted to Odysseus. This is the worst news for her yet, since she especially hates Odysseus as the deviser of Troy's defeat. She laments:

> To be given as slave to that vile, that
>   slippery man,
> right's enemy, brute, murderous beast,
> that mouth of lies and treachery, that
>   makes void
> faith in things promised.

The chorus leader (*coryphaeus*) asks what will become of all the other Trojan women, but no answer is ever given. Their fate is the anonymity of slavery.

Talthybius orders the guards to get Cassandra from her tent, taking her first because she is the property of Agamemnon, who rules over all the other Greeks. As they go to get her, however, she lights a torch inside her tent. This panics Talthybius because he fears the women plan to burn themselves to death rather than become slaves. He asks, "Have they set themselves aflame / in longing for death?" Before the guards can act, Cassandra dances out of the tent, performing the kind of hymn appropriate to a wedding and hence carrying a torch. Since she is by no means going to be properly married to Agamemnon, Hecuba and the others take this as a sign of her madness.

However, Cassandra goes on singing and reveals that she is happier than any bride because she will be able to take revenge for her family and city by murdering Agamemnon, a perfectly rational and honorable wish in the ancient Greek context (other versions of this myth more often make Agamemnon's wife, Clytemnestra, the murderer of Agamemnon and Cassandra). She insists that although the Trojans died honorably fighting in defense of their city, the Greeks have actually suffered more since they lost thousands of soldiers merely to reclaim Helen, who willingly committed adultery, and Agamemnon himself had to sacrifice his own daughter, Iphigenia, before the gods would let the Greek armada set sail at the beginning of the war. This very clear threat and well-reasoned analysis of the Greek situation Talthybius dismisses as evidence of her madness, perhaps because admitting these truths would be unthinkable to him. Cassandra finally turns to prophecy and reveals that Apollo has told her Hecuba will die before leaving Troy and that Odysseus will be doomed to wander through ten more years of suffering before returning home. Hecuba ends the episode with a long lament for her reversal of fortune, finishing with the famous final line: "Of all who walk in bliss / call not one happy, until the man is dead."

First Choral Ode, Lines 511–576

As the chorus dances, its song recalls how happy the women had been when it had seemed the war was over, how they celebrated as the Trojan Horse (supposedly a gift) was brought into the city to be dedicated at the temple of Athene, but then how Odysseus and his Greeks crept out of the Horse and brought about the fall of the city and all its attendant disasters.

Second Episode, Lines 577–798

Andromache and her son, Astyanax, are brought on stage in a wagon containing the arms of her husband, Hector, and other spoils of war. She finally reveals to Hecuba that Polyxena was sacrificed at Achilles' tomb, as she herself witnessed. Andromache tells Hecuba that Polyxena is better off, for the dead experience nothing, while she herself must now betray her dead husband while at the same hating Neoptolemus, the man who will father more children on her. Hecuba advises Andromache that instead she ought love her new master and make him love her, for in that way it might someday become possible for Astyanax (who is the rightful king of Troy) or his son to return to Troy and rebuild the city. That is the only thing they can hope for, however unlikely. Talthybius returns and announces to the two women that he must tell them something so horrible it wishes he did not have the duty to speak it. The Greeks, persuaded by Odysseus, have decided to kill Astyanax by throwing him down from the walls of Troy. Only in this way can they be sure that he will not take revenge against them once he has grown up. When Talthybius moves to take the child, he urges Andromache not to resist and not to curse the Greeks, lest they go even further and leave the child unburied and without the religious rites for the dead.

Second Choral Ode, Lines 799–859
As the chorus again goes into its dance, its song recalls the myth in which Hercules and Telamon (father of Ajax and uncle of Achilles) sacked Troy in the time of Laomedon, Priam's father. They recall also that the gods once loved Troy; that Zeus took his cupbearer, Ganymede, from Troy; and that Eos, the goddess of the dawn, married the Trojan Tithonus, but now the gods have abandoned the city to destruction.

Third Episode, Lines 860–1059
Menelaus, the king of the Greek city of Sparta and legal husband of Helen, now comes to take his wife from the camp. He says that he has little interest in her, but he came to Troy to take revenge on Paris, who violated his hospitality in stealing her away, although that debt has long since been paid by Paris' death and now again by the destruction of Troy. He intends to take her back to Greece and execute her for the blood of all the Greeks spilled because of her adultery. As his soldiers bring Helen out of her tent, Hecuba urges Menelaus to instead execute her at once:

> Kill your wife, Menelaus, and I will
>   bless your name.
> But keep your eyes away from her.
>   Desire will win.
> She looks enchantment, and where she
>   looks homes are set fire;
> she captures cities as she captures the
>   eyes of men.

Told what her husband intends, Helen demurely asks permission to argue for her life. Menelaus agrees, and he also agrees to let Hecuba give a prosecution speech. The two women go over the facts of the case in the rhetorical language of the law courts, and Helen, in particular, argues in the manner of the sophists, actually echoing the arguments of the sophist Gorgias's demonstration speech in defense of Helen. The chorus responds to her with the charge typically leveled against sophists by more conservative elements of Greek society, that she is using the persuasive power of clever rhetoric to advance unjust and immoral arguments. Hecuba, however, persuades Menelaus that Helen indeed deserves to die for her crimes, and he leads her off to his ships in the expectation of having her stoned to death once they return to Greece.

Third Choral Ode, Lines 1060–1122
As the chorus dances, its members sing a lament that Zeus, in dooming Troy to destruction by the Greeks, has brought about the end of his own worship in the rich cults of the city, that they will never be able to bury their husbands and give their graves the religious service demanded by tradition, and finally that, while they themselves will be slaves in an alien land, they hope that the ship bearing Helen will be wrecked at sea and drown her before she can resume her life as queen of Sparta.

Exodos, Lines 1123–1322
The performance of the text becomes more musical, and eventually the chorus and actors dance off the stage, back through the skene. Talthybius returns, bearing the body of Astyanax. He gives it to Hecuba for burial, together with Hector's shield to serve as casket. She cleans and dresses the corpse and buries it, lamenting in song her sad fate and that of her family and nation. The only balm to her grief is the fact that her family will surely be remembered in song in later ages, a reference to the whole Homeric cycle of the Trojan War, but surely also to Euripides' own play. As he leads Hecuba and the other women away to their Greek masters, Talthybius gives the orders for the city of Troy to be set fire for its final destruction (this may have been shown as some kind of special effect on stage). Hecuba tries to throw herself into the flames but is restrained by her guards.

CHARACTERS

Tragedies were performed by three actors, who took all of the parts in turn. *The Trojan Women* is unusual in that the first actor (*protagonist*) played a single character, Hecuba, who is never off stage. The second actor (*deuteragonist*) probably played Poseidon, Cassandra, Andromache, and Helen, while the third actor (*tritagonist*) probably played Athene, Talthybius, and Menelaus.

Andromache

By virtue of being the widow of the Trojan prince Hector, Andromache is the daughter-in-law of Hecuba and mother of Astyanax. She is the main character of the second episode of the play. Euripides presents her as the epitome of the Greek conception of female virtue. She spent her days in the house engaged in domestic labor, such as weaving, and demurely submitted to her husband in all but household affairs. However tempted she was to learn of the world through education or experience, she sacrificed that desire to keep her good name, not even leaving the house to get water at a well. The Greek audience would understand that this kept her safe from the suspicion of adultery, the charge most shameful to Greek women and their husbands. Her purity was so great that it became known to the Greeks and caused her to be selected as concubine by Neoptolemus, the son of Achilles, who killed Hector. The most hateful part of the prospect before her is that she now must betray her husband, to whom she wishes to remain loyal even after he has died. Hecuba advises her that she must ingratiate herself with her new master for the sake of her son. However, when the news comes that Astyanax is to be killed, she is left without even that hope.

Astyanax

Astyanax is the son of Andromache and grandson of Hecuba. He is the rightful king of Troy after the death of his father, Hector, and his grandfather, Priam. (His name means "king of the city.") He is murdered by the Greeks on the advice of Odysseus because "a hero's son could not be allowed to live" and someday take vengeance against any of those who destroyed his city and family. Astyanax is certainly no older than two years and is a nonspeaking role. Whether he was represented on stage by an actual child or by some sort of dummy is unknown.

Athene

Athene (also spelled Athena) is the goddess who stirred up the Trojan War out of rivalry with the goddess Aphrodite over which was the fairest. Originally, Athene had helped the Greeks to attack the Trojans, because Aphrodite had given Helen to the Trojan prince, Paris, in return for judging Aphrodite's beauty superior. However, by the beginning of *The Trojan Women*, the Greeks had offended Athene by desecrating her temple in Troy, and she plots with Poseidon to take revenge on them.

Cassandra

Cassandra is the last surviving daughter of Priam and Hecuba. She is the main character of the first episode of the play. Poets had considerable leeway in how to portray relatively minor characters like this. Euripides presents her as a priestess of Apollo who had been dedicated to perpetual virginity (an extremely rare situation in ancient religions), but "whom Agamemnon, in despite of the gods' will / and all religion, will lead by force to his bed." Apollo possessed her shortly before the beginning of the play. In Greek thought, possession did not entail a spirit entering the victim's body. Instead, the god merely touched her and she was driven mad. Other treatments of Cassandra have her give true prophecies of the future that are not believed. She does this too in *The Trojan Women*, with respect to Odysseus's wanderings. However, Euripides also gives her a similar role when she presents her concise analysis of the Greek situation, pointing out that they suffered more in their victory than the Trojans did in defeat. The Greeks reject this analysis as irrational, although it is all too plausible.

Hecuba

Hecuba was formerly the queen of Troy and is the mother of Polyxena and Cassandra, mother-in-law of Andromache (through her son Hector, killed during the war by the Greek hero Achilles), and grandmother of Andromache's son Astyanax. She is the main character of the play. As queen, she suffers the greatest reversal of fortune and the greatest suffering through the loss of her family and city and, especially, through the fates of her daughters and grandson. Hecuba is completely overwhelmed by the enormity of her loss and can attempt to discharge her grief only through hostility toward those she perceives as responsible for it, such as Odysseus and Helen.

Throughout the play, whenever Talthybius delivers some horrible news, Hecuba puts the best possible interpretation on it, so that through a dialectical discussion with the herald, the full extent of the new misfortune is only gradually revealed. This builds up tension and fear in the audience, who must wonder what will eventually be revealed. For instance, when Hecuba is told that her daughter Cassandra will become Agamemnon's slave, she first imagines that Cassandra will be a maid to the king's wife, Clytemnestra (itself a horrible fate because she is sister of the hated Helen), only to be told that she will become Agamemnon's concubine, an act of sacrilege and so an even greater outrage. She frequently feels herself so utterly powerless that there is nothing left for her to do but cry out, "Tear face, beat bosom," referring to stylized acts of public grieving in Greek culture.

In her debate with Helen, Hecuba is capable of making her own references to the philosophy of fifth-century BCE Athens. When she invokes Zeus, she follows the teachings of the philosopher Anaxagoras, suggesting that Zeus may be a physical principle or natural law, rather than an anthropomorphic (human-like) deity.

Helen

Helen, the most beautiful woman in the world, was offered to Paris by Aphrodite as a bribe for judging Aphrodite more beautiful than Athene and Hera, setting in motion the events that led to the Trojan War. Menelaus, her legitimate husband, recovers his wife after the war and determines to execute her for adultery. However, as the main character of the third episode of the play, she engages in a sort of legal process whereby she defends herself against the capital charge, and Hecuba acts as the prosecutor. Euripides uses the device to make Helen, the worst transgressor of proper social roles because of her adultery, a symbol of sophistry, which many Greeks felt was a more fundamental transgression of social norms of right and justice, because of its duplicitous use of rhetoric. Helen's speech is filled with the technical legal language created by the sophists: "Think what this means, and all the consequence. . . . You will all say this is nothing to the immediate charge. . . . I have witnesses."

After Helen is finished, the coryphaeus accuses her in terms typical of the criticism directed at sophists: "She speaks / well, and has done wickedly. This is dangerous." But Helen and Hecuba both use the same technique that was the essential ingredient in ancient rhetorical discourse and especially in the teaching of the sophists: the appeal to plausibility. They both present facts, and even agree on many points of fact, but each insists that her own interpretation is the more plausible.

Helen begins by saying that Hecuba herself and Priam are the true cause of Troy's destruction because they had received clear prophecy that if they let their infant son Paris live, he would destroy the city, and yet they spared his life twice (this had been the subject of *Alexander*, the first play in Euripides' trilogy of 415 BCE, which the audience would have seen earlier in the morning of the day they saw *The Trojan Women*). She reminds Menelaus that if Paris had picked either Hera or Athene in the goddesses' contest, Paris might not have kidnapped her, but the gods would have given the Trojans the power to conquer Greece, so he was actually injured less by her adultery than if she had remained faithful. Next, Euripides has Helen echo the arguments put forth in the play *Helen* of the sophist Gorgias, the defense speech he had publicly delivered to demonstrate his rhetorical skill for arguing in favor of so obviously an indefensible case. Like Gorgias, she claims she was compelled to leave with Paris by force, that she was powerless to resist the gods who wished her to go.

Hecuba replies to Helen that the talk of goddesses being subject to vanity is so much nonsense, as is Aphrodite aiding Paris in his abduction of her. The only 'Aphrodite' (who represents love) involved had been Helen's own desire. That is what persuaded her to betray her husband. Moreover, she had preferred to be a princess in Troy, a state far richer than the cities controlled by Menelaus. Hecuba bears witness that once the siege began, Helen had tormented Paris with jealously by threatening to slip over the wall and return to Menelaus. Indeed, Hecuba herself had offered to help Helen leave, but she did not. She certainly made no effort to kill herself, which is what Greek morality demanded of a woman in her position. Hecuba persuades Menelaus, who, acting as judge, condemns her to be publicly stoned to death, but back in Greece. The audience, however, knows, from the *Odyssey* (and the chorus suspects) that Helen will still be alive ten years later, with Menelaus once more submissively in love with her beauty.

Menelaus

Menelaus is the husband of Helen, whose adultery led to the Trojan War. Once he recovers her after the war from among the other Trojan women, he condemns her to death for her betrayal. Although he remains resolved on this throughout the play, other mythic sources, such as the *Odyssey*, suggest that Hecuba is correct in thinking he will eventually relent, being again captivated by her beauty.

Poseidon

Poseidon, god of the sea, begins the play with a prologue that describes the Greek capture of Troy. He laments the acts of sacrilege committed by the Greeks and the consequent failure of worship the gods will receive from Troy. When Athene proposes that they should join together to punish Greek impiety, he is highly suspicious of her because until that moment she had been on the Greek side, but nevertheless he eagerly joins in her plan.

Talthybius

Talthybius is the Greeks' herald, charged with communicating their decisions to the Trojan women. He was evidently chosen for this task because he had been known at the Trojan court before the war. He frequently laments that he has no taste for delivering the cruel and horrible news that he must tell Hecuba time after time, suggesting that even an ordinary Greek can be disgusted by the excesses they are forced to commit by war.

THEMES

Catharsis

The earliest critics of Greek tragedy were two philosophers who lived in the generation after its peak, Plato and Aristotle. Both agreed that the function of tragedy was to arouse intense emotions. Plato feared that this process would tend to degrade the emotional life of the audience members and cause them to become worse people. He regretted that he could find little alternative to giving up tragedy. Aristotle, in the *Poetics*, was more pragmatic and viewed tragedy in a very different light.

Aristotle believed that tragedy derived its emotional power from the imitation of events in real life, particularly because it did not show the audience the most pleasant aspects of existence but rather forced them to consider the most unpleasant aspects. Paradoxically, "though the objects themselves may be painful to see, we delight to view the most realistic representations of them in art." Tragedy achieved this goal through showing "incidents arousing pity and fear, wherewith to accomplish its

TOPICS FOR FURTHER STUDY

- Read through the Greek myths retold for young audiences in *D'Aulaires' Book of Greek Myths*. Select one of them and write a brief dramatic scene based on part of it. Perform the scene for your class, with some of your classmates reading the various parts.

- Euripides most likely had in mind the wars his city was involved in when he wrote *The Trojan Women*. Find an interesting news story about events in Iraq or Afghanistan. Write an interpretation of the event, or a reaction to it, in the form of a brief dramatic scene.

- Helen is the most scandalous figure in Greek mythology. Research, write, and read for your class a defense or prosecution speech for a famous figure from American history, such as Marilyn Monroe (a sex symbol whose popularity did not stop her falling into depression and suicide) or Victoria Woodhull (a leading Spiritualist medium and the first woman to run for U.S. president in 1876). Do not limit yourself to a legal context, but consider how the life of the chosen figure conflicted with morality of her period.

- Herodotus and Thucydides, historians contemporary with Euripides, began their works with extensive treatments of the Trojan War and of Helen in particular. How do their presentations of Helen differ or agree? How do they compare with Euripides' in *The Trojan Women*? Research these questions and present your findings to your class in the form of a PowerPoint presentation.

catharsis of such emotions." Catharsis means "cleansing," and it was the Greek word for the then common method of treating illness by forcing the patient to vomit. Aristotle means that the drama serves to heighten these emotions and thereby discharge them, so that the viewer experiences a pleasurable release of tension. Few dramas present a greater object of pity than Hecuba in *The Trojan Women*; she sees all of her sons killed in battle, witnesses the murder of her husband as he seeks sanctuary at a divine altar, and falls from the status of a queen to that of a slave. The audience naturally shares her fear when each new announcement in the course of the play brings news that one of her daughters has been raped, murdered, or sent off into slavery, and finally watches her bury the corpse of her last remaining grandson with her own hands.

Injustice

In the oldest dramatic productions in the early fifth century BCE, it was customary for all three plays to deal with the same event in a more extended fashion. The only trilogy of this type that survives is Aeschylus' *Oresteia*, which concerns Agamemnon's son Orestes having to take revenge on his own mother, who had murdered his father. By the late fifth century BCE, it was more typical to have the three plays deal with different mythical episodes, but in 415 Euripides produced a trilogy that better corresponded to the older type. The three plays all treat material that comes from the mythical cycle of the Trojan War. Although they are not bound in the sense of telling parts of the same story, they all concern acts of injustice. The first is *Alexander*, which concerns the efforts of the brothers of the Trojan prince Paris (who was also called Alexander) to prevent him receiving his rightful inheritance and status. The second is *Palamedes*; it is the story of a Greek hero on whom Odysseus takes personal revenge by framing him for plotting to betray the Greeks to the Trojans, resulting in him being unjustly stoned to death. The third (and the only one whose text survives) is *The Trojan Women*, which concerns many acts of moral injustice inherent in the legal enslavement of the women, but in particular it is about the unjust murder of the child Astyanax to prevent him trying to take revenge on the Greek heroes when he grows up. The plot of the accompanying satyr play, *Sisyphus*, is unknown, but its main surviving fragment is a logical exposition of atheism.

Persuasive Literature

Sophists (the name means "wise men" or "sophisticated men"), such as Gorgias and Protagoras, were teachers of rhetoric, or the art of public speaking, in fifth-century BCE Greece. They especially congregated in Athens, where the democracy fostered their activities. Before the existence of print or any other kind of mass media, when

citizens would have to defend themselves or undertake prosecutions in court without the aid of a lawyer, and where a speech well delivered in the council could persuade other citizens to accept or reject an idea and shape the course of state policy, the ability to persuade through words that sophists taught was of paramount importance. However, as the sophists analyzed what kinds of appeals could persuade people, they came to the opinion that all beliefs and moral standards were relative, changing from city to city and time to time, and therefore, such institutions as religion and law or concepts of right and wrong were social conventions created by people. They concluded not that these could be ignored, but that they could be exploited; an audience's beliefs could be used to make audience members come to the conclusion desired by a skilled speaker. For these reasons, as much as they were highly sought out as teachers, they were hated by philosophers and intellectuals, especially the writers of tragedy and comedy, as well as the general public. To their critics, the sophists seemed to make the worse argument the better: that is, they made the less persuasive argument seem more persuasive and the morally inferior argument seem superior, or at least expedient. Sophists were sometimes prosecuted for impiety or atheism (which were crimes in ancient Athens, where the state and religion were indistinguishable). In traditional Greek thought, impiety arose from the inability to tell right from wrong and so would naturally be associated with sophistic rhetoric. Anaxagoras, for instance, was prosecuted for attempting to explain astronomy in mechanistic rather than mythological terms, and one of the chief factors in the conviction of the philosopher Socrates was his association in the popular mind with the sophistic movement. The sophist Gorgias delivered a public speech in praise of Helen of Troy, claiming that she was completely free of guilt, a shocking supposition in an Athenian society nearly paranoid about adultery, where the honor of men depended on their ability to control the behavior of the female members of their families. In *The Trojan Women*, Euripides engages many sophistic themes about the nature of justice and religion, and his character Helen gives a speech defending herself. Euripides also engaged the sophists on much more serious matters. In his lost *Sisyphus*, the satyr play produced in 415 BCE together with *The Trojan Women*, Euripides has the title character speak the most extreme statement of atheism in Greek literature:

Katharine Hepburn as Queen Hecuba in the 1971 film version of The Trojan Women *(Archive Photos / Hulton Archive / Getty Images)*

Then, when the laws were preventing men from doing violence openly, but they did it in secret, that was the moment I think when . . . some shrewdly intelligent and clever man invented for mankind fear of gods, so that there might be something to frighten bad men even if they do or say or think something in secret. From that time therefore he introduced belief in gods.

The satirical point of the play perhaps came when Sisyphus (famously condemned for attempting to deceive the gods by forever having to push an enormous boulder up a hill in the underworld, only to have it roll back down when he reaches the top) discovers the reality of divine punishment. Sophistic themes of atheism and impiety are hotly contested in a more serious vein in *The Trojan Women* itself, for example, during the debate between Hecuba and Helen.

STYLE

Greek Drama

Religious festivals in which actors represent characters in mythological scenes have been part of many cultures, but drama as it is known in the modern West began in Classical Athens, a period often considered a cultural high point in art, literature, and philosophy. Tragedy started out as part of the festival of the City Dionysia (celebrated in worship of the god Dionysus) in which a chorus of men would dance while singing a hymn. The choruses competed against each other for the honor of a prize. The word *tragedy* is formed from the Greek words for "goat" and "song," perhaps suggesting that the victorious *coryphaeus*, or leader of a chorus, was awarded a goat. By the late sixth and early fifth centuries BCE, these performances had become extended so that lengthy scenes from myth were enacted in great detail by the chorus in conjunction with up to three actors, who performed additional dialogue that made complete stories. There were three types of drama: tragedy, which dealt with mythological themes in a serious manner; satyr plays, which gave burlesque versions of myth (hence the modern word satire); and fantastic and surreal comedies.

The City Dionysia was held each year in late March or early April. The main part of the celebration was the presentation of a series of dramatic cycles over three days. Each of the tragedies retold a familiar Greek myth in the form of a play. On the first day, there was a parade in honor of the god to the theater of Dionysus at the foot of the Acropolis (a hill), ending with the performance of dances by each of the three competing choruses (who would later also appear in the dramas). Next came the sacrifice of bulls to Dionysus in the theater. Over the following three days, each of the competing dramatists presented a trilogy of three tragedies and one satyr play, to make up a tetralogy. Each dramatist not only wrote the plays but paid for the production from his own resources (or from those of a patron), meaning that only aristocrats could compete. The audience consisted of about 20,000 adult male Athenian citizens. Women were not generally permitted in the theater. The performances began in the morning and lasted all day. Three audience members were chosen at random to act as judges. On the final day of the festival, five comedies would be presented, each by a different comedian. Aristophanes was the most prominent comedian.

Tragedy

The most important tragedians (and the only ones with plays that still exist in their complete form) were Aeschylus, Sophocles, and Euripides. In later periods, their work was constantly edited and republished so much that they became part of the core identity of the entire Greek and Roman world, in the same way that Shakespeare is essential to the identity of English-speaking cultures. Dramas would receive only a single official performance, but popular plays from the past would often be performed after the annual competition was completed.

The plays alternated dialogue among the actors with choral odes in which the entire chorus (about fifty dancers) would come out and sing and dance in the *orchestra*, or circular dancing floor nearest the audience. A backdrop was provided by the skene, an architectural screen that could also contain painted scenery. The plays were necessarily set in one location and in real time (there were no changes of scenery or breaks between acts), as if the audience were witnessing an event as it unfolded. However, actors might go into the skene, particularly if they had to carry out some gruesome act such as murder, which was not allowed to be shown on stage. The actors and chorus could exit and enter the stage through the skene or from the wings on either side. In some cases, characters could enter from the wings on a cart (*ekkyklema*), either to represent a chariot or other wheeled vehicle, or because they were dead or dying. When gods appeared in a play, they would be lowered from the top of the skene by a crane (the famous *deus ex machina* literally "god from a machine"). The actors wore masks fixed in the predominant emotion of the characters they portrayed (though the masks might be changed while the character was offstage). The masks contained megaphones that would amplify their voices to the audience. The actors wore buskins (boots) or stilts more than a foot tall and their costumes consisted of long flowing robes that trailed on the ground. Three actors performed all the roles (and therefore played more than one part), and all actors were male, even if they portrayed female characters. While not fully sung, the actors' lines were probably not spoken, but chanted in some way, though little is known about this. Medieval plain chant might suggest something of the way the dialogue was performed, although some of the longer speeches, such as Cassandra's in *The Trojan Women*, were clearly sung in a more complex manner. There is almost no surviving record of what the music in tragedy was like. The music, however, was also composed by the playwright. The subject matter of tragedy was drawn mostly from the Homeric epics or from other legends

concerning the kings of Greece in the mythical period around the Bronze Age.

In the aftermath of the defeat of Athens in the Peloponnesian War, the best writers, such as Menander, shifted to new comedy realistically depicting everyday life, and the art of tragedy declined. Revivals became more important than new work. Dramas composed in the Roman Empire, such as those by Seneca, were mostly intended to be read rather than performed. This kind of work was more directly influential on Renaissance dramatists such as Shakespeare and the French playwright Racine. However, once Greek drama was rediscovered in the Renaissance, the performance of these works became immensely popular and led to the birth of opera as an art form. Although the music of Greek plays was not as extensive or complex as that of opera, the essential unity of tragedy and opera was defended as late as the era of the opera composer Richard Wagner and the philosopher Friedrich Nietzsche in the nineteenth century, especially in the latter's book *The Birth of Tragedy*.

HISTORICAL CONTEXT

Trojan War

The Trojan War and the return of its Greek heroes from Troy is the subject matter of the Homeric poems the *Iliad* and the *Odyssey*. These are the final records of an oral tradition of poetry that had flourished in Greece for centuries before the introduction of writing. In the generations after their publication, many other works were composed, the so-called Epic Cycle, which filled in details of the war left out of the two great poems. These probably also reflected traditional material. Aristotle mentions in the *Poetics* that *The Trojan Women*, like many tragedies, expands material that is mentioned in one of these works, the now lost *Little Iliad*, which told the story of the Trojan Horse and the capture of the city.

The Trojan War began when a golden apple inscribed "To the fairest" was cast into the divine court on Mount Olympus by the goddess Eris (who represents strife). Three goddesses—Hera, Athene, and Aphrodite—disagreed over which one should receive it. They selected the Trojan prince Paris (also known as Alexander) to decide the issue. Each bribed him—Hera with the rule

COMPARE & CONTRAST

- **Bronze Age:** The Greek society presented by Homer is monarchic, ruled by kings whose authority depends on their family lineages.

  Fifth Century BCE: Athens governs itself by the most radical democracy that has ever held power, in which every aspect of state policy is determined by a majority vote of qualified voters, and most officials are chosen randomly.

  Today: Both the United States and Greece are examples of modern democracy. The United States is a representative democracy (also known as a republic) in which most decisions are made by elected officials without direct consultation of the popular will. Greece is a parliamentary democracy.

- **Bronze Age:** The complete destruction of cities by war (including the mass murder of civilians) is common; the archaeological record of the end of the Bronze Age is marked by a layer of destruction in almost every city in Greece, as well as Troy.

  Fifth Century BCE: The destruction of cities (including the murder and enslavement of the civilian population) remains common, as marked by the Athenian destruction of Melos.

  Today: The mass slaughter of civilians is recognized as genocide, and while still all too common, is outlawed as a war crime.

- **Bronze Age:** The characters in literature set during the Bronze Ages by Homer or Euripides live in close contact with the divine world.

  Fifth Century BCE: Religion is inextricably bound up with social and political life and is a main public concern of citizens and the state, even though some intellectuals question the logical and metaphysical foundations of religion.

  Today: Religion is a matter of personal, private conscience, and the political and social realms are largely or entirely secular, a division never imagined in antiquity.

over the whole world and Athene with invincibility in battle—but Paris preferred Aphrodite's bribe, to take Helen, the most beautiful woman in the world, as his wife. Helen, however, was already married to Menelaus, the king of Sparta, so Paris visited Menelaus as a guest and kidnapped Helen, taking her back to Troy. Before Helen's original marriage, her hand had been sought by every prince in Greece. Odysseus decided the issue in favor of Menelaus by trickery, in exchange for being given Helen's sister Penelope as his own bride. Each one of Helen's suitors had sworn to guarantee the marriage with military force if necessary, so Menelaus and his brother Agamemnon (king of the chief Greek city of Mycenae) led an army composed of contingents of all the Greek states to Troy. After a siege that lasted ten years, Odysseus devised a ruse whereby the Greeks pretended

they were admitting the futility of the war and sailing away, but left behind a large wooden statue of a horse as an offering. The Trojans took this inside their city to dedicate it in Athene's temple. That night, while the people of Troy were distracted by celebrating their deliverance from war, Odysseus and a squad of men who were hidden in the horse crept forth to open the city gates and admit the Greek army, which had returned. After Troy fell to the Greeks in this way, the stage was set for Euripides' *The Trojan Women.*

Peloponnesian War

The Peloponnesian War was a conflict between Greek city-states that grew from rivalry between the two leading cities, Sparta and Athens. The principal source of information about the war is the contemporary Athenian historian Thucydides.

A performance in the Theater of Epidaurus, 1954 *(© Bettmann / Corbis)*

After the defeat of the Persian attempt to conquer Greece in 480–479 BCE, Sparta, because of its superior infantry force, was the most powerful Greek state. However, Athens possessed the most powerful navy and was in control of the Delian League, an alliance of Greek city-states devoted to liberating Greek cities still occupied by Persia in Ionia (the Aegean coast of modern Turkey). As this goal was accomplished, Athens increasingly became an imperial power controlling its allies, and it was growing far more powerful than any other Greek state. Sparta protected its preeminent position by organizing the Peloponnesian League (named after the southern peninsula of Greece). The inevitable war between the two alliances lasted from 431 to 404 BCE. The first part of the conflict is generally known as the Archidamian War; in it, Sparta annually invaded Attica, ravaging the countryside around Athens and forcing the population to take shelter within the city walls of Athens, which the relatively primitive

military technology of the Spartans could not attack. Athens was provided with food by sea. However, in 430 BCE, a serious plague broke out, killing more than thirty thousand Athenian citizens, including the leading politician Pericles. Athens maintained its naval supremacy, so both sides were essentially unable to attack the other. Military operations were also carried out elsewhere in Greece, and eventually, in the battle of Spachteria in 425 BCE, a group of about 300 Spartan soldiers were captured by the Athenians, a revolutionary event, since no Spartan had ever surrendered before. The Athenians threatened to execute these soldiers if the Spartans invaded Attica again. By 421 BCE, a truce between the two alliances, supposed to last for fifty years, was negotiated by the Athenian general Nicias.

Athens took advantage of the Peace of Nicias to strengthen itself by gaining new territory not allied with Sparta and therefore unaffected by the truce. In 416 BCE, Athens conquered and annexed the Aegean island of Melos. However, in 415 BCE, the year Euripides' *The Trojan Women* premiered, Athens undertook to conquer the island of Sicily in the western Mediterranean. However, the Sicilian expedition, led by the generals Nicias and Alcibiades, ended in disaster and the complete loss of the Athenian forces in Sicily. During the campaign, Alcibiades was prosecuted for impiety and defected to the Spartan side. On his advice, the Spartans seized and fortified the Attic village of Deceleia in 413 BCE, disrupting Attica as thoroughly as they had with their previous campaigns but at a fraction of the effort. This began the second phase of the war, known as the Decelean War. Surprisingly, Athens recovered from the Sicilian disaster, but it suffered civil war between democratic and oligarchic factions. Sparta began to receive money for the war from the Persian Empire, which it used to construct its own fleet. In 405 BCE, the Spartan commander Lysander caught the main Athenian battle fleet hauled up onto the beach at Aegospotami (on the Chersoneses straits, between Europe and Asia) and destroyed it. After this, the Athenians had no choice but to give their unconditional surrender, ending the war and Athens's position as a great power in 404 BCE.

CRITICAL OVERVIEW

The first criticism of Euripides' *The Trojan Women* was delivered in 415 BCE by the judges of the City Dionysia; they awarded it only second place, behind the plays of the now largely unknown dramatist Xenocles. A generation later, Aristotle in the *Poetics* gives hints that Euripides suffered from the disconnection between popular and sophisticated taste. Aristotle reports that Euripides' rival playwright Sophocles "said that he drew men as they ought to be, and Euripides as they are," implying that audiences do not like to see men as they are. Aristotle adds his own comment that the popular criticism of Euripides for also dwelling on the reversal of fortune was mistaken. Aristotle had realized that suffering was paradoxically the key to the beauty of tragedy, and in no other tragedy is the heroines' suffering so intense and sustained.

Gilbert Murray, the great classicist and translator of the first half of the twentieth century, suggests in *Euripides and His Age* that "Euripides must have been brooding on the crime of Melos

during the autumn and winter" of 416 BCE; Murray thus argues for the first time a link between the Athenian defeat of Melos and Euripides' play of 415 BCE. In the introduction to his translation *Greek Tragedies*, Richmond Lattimore is one of the staunchest defenders of the Melos connection, but he cautions that although it may have inflamed patriotic feeling at the time, *The Trojan Women* was directed not against Athenian imperialism so much as against war in general. However, even this supposition has been questioned, since Greeks of the fifth century BCE did not think of permanent peace as an attainable or even desirable condition. Therefore, more recent critics, such as Casey Dué in *The Captive Woman's Lament in Greek Tragedy*, tend to think of *The Trojan Women* as similar to Aristophanes' peace comedies as arguing for an end to a particular war, namely the Peloponnesian War, which, although it had brought Athens considerable strategic advantage, had also left the Attic countryside ravaged and a large proportion of the Athenian population reduced to refugee status, sheltering inside the city walls. Barbara Goff suggests that the connection to contemporary events is far from implausible but that it would have been made, or not made, by each individual audience member in 415 BCE.

Murray also deals with the other main theme of modern criticism, the play's form. He observes that the structure of *The Trojan Women* is unlike any other drama and is subversive of any ordinary Greek use of myth:

> But it tells the old legend in a peculiar way.
> Slowly, reflectively, with little stir of the blood,
> we are made to look at the great glory until we
> see not glory at all but shame and blindness and
> a world swallowed up in night.

Later critics point out many ways in which *The Trojan Women* violates the tenets of tragedy. For instance, although there is a reversal of fortune in Hecuba and other noble Trojan women becoming slaves, there is no moment of self-discovery in which a hero, such as Oedipus or Agamemnon in other plays, who thought himself happy realizes that his true condition is pitiable and wretched, as Judith Mossman points out in her article in *A Companion to Greek Tragedy*. It has often been observed that, as Goff puts it, the play is liable to "charges of excessive emotionalism, and lack of movement and development." Whatever the character of its antiwar message and whatever its formal defects, *The Trojan Women* was mostly ignored before the twentieth century and Murray's

> PERHAPS THE GREATEST SUFFERING THE TROJAN WOMEN ENDURE, GREATER THAN ANY INSULT FROM THE GREEKS, IS TO HAVE THE FAITHFUL HONOR THEY SHOWED TO THE GODS CAST ASIDE AS NOTHING."

championing of it. In the last century, though, it has generally been acknowledged as among the best of the tragedies; it is among the most performed and the most frequently adapted, always to give it a more straightforward antiwar message.

CRITICISM

Bradley A. Skeen

Skeen is a classics professor. In this essay, Skeen examines impiety (irreverence) as the neglected main theme of The Trojan Women.

Euripides' *The Trojan Women* explores the limits of human suffering as its characters witness their whole civilization being extinguished in the aftermath of war. The Trojan women have already seen their husbands and fathers killed, and Hecuba and Andromache must also face the murder of the infant Astyanax. They must see injustice triumph over justice when Helen, in their view the cause of all their ills, escapes punishment. Seeing these events on stage elicits fear and pity from the audience (which Aristotle identified as the main purpose of tragedy), perhaps to a greater degree than any other play. This very success raises the question of what purposes Euripides has in the play besides the emotional release that *The Trojan Women* shares with all tragedy.

The obvious conclusion is that *The Trojan Women* carries a message against war. Certainly, that is the message that has most often been read in the play during the last hundred years. Modern adapters from Sartre to Osofisan have felt the need to change the text to make the play speak about a specific war going on as they wrote. Sometimes classicists, starting with Murray a century ago, have read the original in that

WHAT DO I READ NEXT?

- *D'Aulaires' Book of Greek Myths*, by Ingri and Edgar D'Aulaire, first published in 1961 and frequently reprinted since, gives short versions of the Greek myths as an introduction for younger readers unfamiliar with the material.

- The Nigerian playwright Femi Osofisan composed a play, *Women of Owu*, based on Euripides' *The Trojan Women*. It was first performed in 2004 and published in 2006. The setting is early modern Nigeria, but the play rather transparently criticizes the Second Gulf War.

- The foundational 1983 collection of essays, *Images of Women in Antiquity*, edited by Averil Cameron and Amélie Kuhrt, presents a range of studies about the lives of women in antiquity, covering settings from ancient Mesopotamia to medieval Celtic society but firmly anchored in the Greco-Roman world.

- In a 2006 book intended for a general audience, *The Trojan War: A New History*, Barry Strauss surveys the representation of the war in the *Iliad* that serves as the background to *The Trojan Women* in conjunction with the archaeological record of the Greek Bronze Age, which sometimes tells a story quite different from Homer's.

- In his 1997 study *The Fall of Troy in Early Greek Poetry and Art*, Michael J. Anderson demonstrates the importance of the fall of Troy not only in Greek literature but, for the first time, in Greek vase painting.

- Henry Treece's 1967 novel for young adults, *The Windswept City*, is set during the last days of the Trojan War.

- The French existentialist philosopher Jean-Paul Sartre wrote a play also called *Trojan Women* in 1965 that was translated into English in 1976. It is more of a comment on Euripides than a translation, and its message is decidedly against the postcolonial wars then raging around the globe, particularly the French conflict in Algeria.

way too, linking it to the conflicts of 416 BCE. A few months before the premiere of *The Trojan Women*, Athens destroyed the island city of Melos, killing all the adult men and selling the surviving women and children into slavery. Thucydides' account of this event finds no parallel in all of Greek historical writing. He sharply stops the flow of his narrative and inserts text formatted like a drama, with the name of the speaker followed by dialogue. The two actors represent not individuals but the Melians and Athenians. What the dialogue contains is far from any historical speech that might have been made at the time. The form is adopted, the characters agree, so that the truth can be told plainly, without the need to "deceive the ears of the multitude by seductive arguments." In other words, they will speak the truth, not engage in the deceptions of sophistic argument. What this truth amounts to is that Athens must pursue its interest no matter whom it destroys. Because its empire is based on force and fear, it is better that Athens cause destruction sometimes to raise fear. Nevertheless, the Athenians will let the Melians submit if they will. But the Melians will not submit, because it is not just. The Athenians succeed merely because they are strong. Far from stripping away sophistry as the Athenians claim, they show that it is the way of the world for the strong, not the just, to prosper. Nowhere does Thucydides come so close to veering from what Aristotle viewed as the role of the historian to that of the tragedian: "The distinction between historian and poet . . . consists really in this, that the one describes the thing that has been, and the other a kind of thing that might be."

But perhaps it is Thucydides' treatment that looks more like *The Trojan Women* than the historical events the report both reveals and conceals. The concern for a truth destroyed by clever argument is a clear point of contact with Euripides, not something that would likely have been discussed on Melos. Sophistry is really only a special case in which the strong overcome the just—a clever speaker persuades the hearers against a speaker who is in the right—and the fear that is the way of the world is central to Thucydides' exposition, and perhaps also to that of Euripides. The fate of Troy is not necessarily based on the fate of Melos. For a defeated city to have all the male citizens killed and its women and children sold as slaves was all too common in the Greek world. At the beginning of the Peloponnesian War, for example, in 429–448

BCE, Sparta had captured the Plataea, a city allied to Athens, and treated it in just that way. The difference was that at the beginning of the siege of the town, the Spartan king, Archidamus, made a public proclamation to Hera, the patron goddess of the city, that the Spartans were acting only because the Plataeans had violated their sacred oaths. After the city's destruction, the Spartans built a large shrine to Hera over the ruins, together with facilities for receiving pilgrims from all over Greece, and they devoted the surrounding farmland to fund the shrine. In short, when Plataea was destroyed, the conquerors took special care not to outrage the gods. Agamemnon and Odysseus showed no such concern for religion.

It is not hard to read *The Trojan Women*, not as a play against war (Greeks commonly believed that the normal condition of a state was to be at war, and one does not find much praise of peace as an absolute virtue in Greek thought), nor even as a criticism of the Peloponnesian War in particular (Euripides, who had composed a victory song to celebrate Alcibiades' first-place finish in the chariot race at the Olympic games, was closely connected to the democratic faction that supported the war), but rather as a play against impiety—disrespect for the gods—in a surprisingly old-fashioned tone. It is surprising because Euripides moved in the circles of sophists and philosophers at the forefront of Athenian intellectual culture. Nevertheless, the fact that the other three plays in the tetralogy produced by Euripides in 415 BCE all took various forms of injustice and impiety as their themes strongly suggests that this is the case also with *The Trojan Women*.

Impiety was sown in Athens from the dislocations of the war. In the first years of the siege of Athens, the city was visited by a plague. This is understandable, rationally, since the city was overcrowded with tens of thousands of refugees from the countryside. However, plague was traditionally seen as a punishment for impiety visited upon humans from the gods, and in the midst of the disaster it was difficult for even the most brazen freethinker not to view it in that light. Moreover, Greek religion was a form of exchange, based on the reciprocity between men that was the dominant feature of Greek life. Human beings gave gifts to the gods in the form of sacrifice and worship, while the gods gave gifts to humanity in the form of the fertility of the land and the other good things to be enjoyed in life. If humanity broke the cycle of reciprocity, it became guilty of impiety and could expect punishment rather than blessings. During the war, the cycle of exchange was forcibly broken. The rites for the fertility of the fields could not be performed inside the city, or if they were, they could not be performed correctly, and that too was impious; the dead could not buried and tended with their rites in family cemeteries, and so on. Whatever the Athenians did, the oracle of Apollo at Delphi (the greatest religious institution in Greece and staunchly Spartan in sympathy) rebuked them. The greatest disruption of this kind came from the interruption of the celebration of the mysteries of Demeter and Kore at the suburb of Eleusis, the most important cult in Athens. When the Spartans destroyed the goddesses' temple, its priests were quick to blame their own government for starting the war in the first place and formed one of the most powerful factions for peace in Athens. In the first months of 415 BCE, Alcibiades profaned the mysteries of Eleusis by performing them at private dinner parties. This was a capital crime, and the motive of Alcibiades and his closest followers is hard to reconstruct. Certainly they did it because they could, because they had a sense that they could not be punished for their crimes. This was another symptom of the breakdown of cohesion in Athenian society occasioned by the war. It is very likely that it would have been known to Euripides, since it was the subject of the play *The Baptists*, a comedy by Eupolis that premiered at the City Dionysia in 415 BCE, a few days after *The Trojan Women*. When it came to the notice of the state that Alcibiades' profanation was a fact rather than the fantastic plot of a play, the profanation was interpreted as a call to revolution and brought about Alcibiades' political downfall.

At the beginning of *The Trojan Women* Poseidon and Athene set out to punish the Greeks for impiety, promising to rain down on them all the misfortunes described in the *Odyssey* and in the plays of Aeschylus' *Oresteia* trilogy: shipwreck, murder, and worse. This seems to follow a very traditional model. The Greeks have broken the cycle of reciprocity between themselves and the gods by acts of impiety and will be punished. Not only have the Greeks murdered suppliants at altars and murdered innocents unjustly, they have also brought the worship offered by the Trojans to the gods to an end. Poseidon complains:

> So I must leave my altars and great Ilium,
> since once a city sinks into sad desolation
> the gods' state sickens also, and their worship fades.

Euripides seems to leave little doubt that he is referring to acts of impious destruction, like those the Athenians carried out at Melos, in his warning against following the Greek example at Troy:

> The mortal who sacks fallen cities is a fool,
> who gives the temples and the tombs, the hollowed places
> of the dead to desolation. His own turn must come.

The Greeks at Troy, and perhaps the Athenians, Euripides suggests, doom themselves by their impieties. But it is impiety that is to be avoided, not war.

If Athene and Poseidon were the patrons of the Greeks and Trojans during the war and had plans and desires opposed to each other, Zeus, who made the final decisions, was an impartial judge. His judgment against Troy brings about the loss of worship that Poseidon complains of, and thereby breaks the cycle of reciprocity between mortals and immortals, which the chorus of Trojan women recalls their city kept intact:

> Thus, O Zeus you betrayed all
> to the Achaeans: your temple
> in Ilium, your misted altar,
> the flame of the clotted sacraments,
> the smoke of the skying incense . . .
> Gone are your sacrifices, the choirs'
> glad voices singing to the gods
> night long, deep into darkness;
> gone the images, gold on wood laid.

Perhaps the greatest suffering the Trojan women endure, greater than any insult from the Greeks, is to have the faithful honor they showed to the gods cast aside as nothing. One could argue that the Trojans brought about their own downfall with their own impiety when Priam spared the life of his son Paris, who was prophesied to be the doom of Troy, and when he received him with his adulterous, kidnapped bride in an affront to Zeus, the guarantor of human hospitality. However, those events had very little meaning to those Trojans who faithfully carried out the worship of Zeus. Certainly there was nothing they could have done about them. The suffering of the Trojan women begins to suggest that the innocent suffer, even that the pious suffer, a truth that points in the direction of the birth of Stoic philosophy a century after Euripides. The playwright and even the gods can offer no answer to the plight of the Trojan women.

A few years after Euripides' death, when the Spartan general Lysander finally captured Athens at the end of the Peloponnesian War, the suggestion was made by some of his advisors that all the male Athenians should be killed and the women and children sold as slaves, but one of the members of the council of war sang the opening of a chorus from Euripides' *Electra*. After that, no one could vote to destroy a city that had created such beauty. If Euripides failed in 415 BCE to dissuade the Athenians from returning to a war whose impious result led to their own ultimate defeat, he at least persuaded another audience not to exceed the bounds of justice in victory.

Source: Bradley Skeen, Critical Essay on *The Trojan Women*, in *Drama for Students*, Gale, Cengage Learning, 2010.

Lee A. Jacobus
In the following essay, Jacobus provides biographical information on Euripides and discusses his influences.

Euripides (c. 485–c. 406 B.C.), last of the great Greek tragedians, did not enjoy the personal popularity accorded Aeschylus and Sophocles, possibly because his work criticized Athenian politics and society. Moreover, he was not highly regarded because he broke away from the formality of language and theme of his predecessors.

Euripides was raised in Salamis, the island from which the Greeks decisively defeated the Persians in 480 B.C. This victory heralded the Periclean Age (c. 460–404 B.C.), when Athens enjoyed its greatest power. During that time, however, the Athenians spent almost three decades fighting the Peloponnesian Wars (431–404 B.C.), which drained their energies and treasury. Eventually, they were forced to relinquish their dominance to Sparta. In such an environment, the officials and patriots of Athens were not happy with the work

of someone who reminded them of their mistakes and questioned their values.

Euripides is especially noted for shifting the focus of dramatic events from the gods to humans. He valued individual human beings and the working of their wills. Influenced by the teaching of the Sophists, wandering professors who taught argument and philosophy, he agreed with Protagoras's principle "Man is the measure of all things." The ancients sometimes referred to Euripides as the philosopher of the stage.

One aspect of his dramatic critique of Greek culture was an unusual emphasis on women. Medea is the first thoroughly developed female character in Greek drama. She is treated as an independent woman, not as Jason's wife or as someone's mother. She is herself. Athenians, intolerant of foreigners and women, felt both groups to be inferior to Greek aristocratic men. It is no wonder that of the twenty plays Euripides produced at the feasts of Dionysus only five won prizes.

Of his ninety-two plays, eighteen survive—more than twice as many as survive from any other Greek tragedian: *Alcestis* (438), *Medea* (431), *The Children of Heracles* (c. 430), *Hippolytus* (428), *Andromache* (426?), *Hecuba* (c. 424), *Cyclops* (c. 423), *The Suppliants* (c. 422), *Electra* (c. 417), *Heracles* (c. 417), *The Trojan Women* (415), *Helen* (412), *Iphigenia in Taurus* (c. 412), *The Phoenician Women* (c. 412–408), *Ion* (c. 411), *Orestes* (408), *The Bacchae* (405), and *Iphigenia in Aulis* (405). Another play, *Rhesus*, long attributed to Euripides, is now thought to have been written by an anonymous fourth-century B.C. playwright. Ten of Euripides' remaining plays place women at their center.

Euripides continued Aeschylus's innovations in his use of the *skene*. Instead of representing the front of a palace, the *skene* in Euripides' plays sometimes represented a peasant's hut, a rural shrine, or other common structure. He was interested in theatrical devices, especially machines that gave him the opportunity to achieve dramatic effects. He often used the *mekane*—a crane or derrick that lifted actors in or out of the play—to resolve his dramas when his characters found themselves in impossible situations. His choral odes, although beautiful, are sometimes considered detachable from the episodes of dramatic action. Moreover, his dialogue is more colloquial—closer to everyday speech—than is the dialogue found in other Greek tragedies. All these deviations from the dramatic norm emphasize the humanity in his plays and elevate human values over those of the gods.

Eighteen months before his death, Euripides left Athens for the court of King Archelaus in Macedon. His departure may have signaled his dissatisfaction with the politics of Athens, or it may have been prompted by the indifference of Athens to his talents. In any event, his works were performed long after his death, and, ironically, his posthumous popularity dwarfed that of the other tragic playwrights.

Source: Lee A. Jacobus, "Euripides," in *Bedford Introduction to Drama*, Bedford/St. Martin's, 2005, pp. 133–34.

B. E.

In the following review, B. E. describes the 1974 LaMama production of The Trojan Women *and the avant-garde techniques used.*

The Trojan Women is the most recently developed of three unrelated pieces that were performed as a trilogy on 18 October 1974 to inaugurate the LaMama Annex in New York City. (*Medea* was created at LaMama in 1972; *Electra* was created for the Festival Octobre a Bordeaux, the Festival d'Automne, and LaMama E.T.C. in Paris in 1973.)

The development of *The Trojan Women* spans five months. It was conceived in a workshop at the II Festival Nacional de Teatro in Brazil. After rehearsal at LaMama in New York, an enlarged company performed an hour-long version of the three pieces called *Fragments*. In September, *The Trojan Women* was performed with *Electra* at Sarah Lawrence College.

Euripedes' text is used as the basis for the action. The hour and twenty minute performance is sung and chanted in a collection of ancient languages—Greek, Mayan, Nahuatl, Enochian, etc. Therefore, meaning is conveyed by the pitch and rhythm of sounds rather than words. Dialog chanting is punctuated with percussion. Group chants that emerge as songs are scored with horn, clarinet, recorder, flute, conch, bells, drums, and a gamelon made of round metal saw blades.

The new LaMama Annex is 100 feet long, 48 feet wide, and 30 feet tall. The space was formerly used for filming. A 28 x 20 proscenium is at the far end of the space. Each of the lengthwise walls has two walkways, which are used for both spectators and performing. One of these walkways is at near ground level, the other approximately eight feet above. The musicians are on ground level to the left of the proscenium.

A steep ramp leads to an acting space above and to the left of the entrance.

The program describes *The Trojan Women* as "an Epic Opera composed by Elizabeth Swados; conceived and directed by Andrei Serban." Here, Epic refers to an interpretation of Brechtian dialectics. The whole is the sum of parts in opposition.

The first part is conceived of as the enslavement of the Trojan women by the soldiers. The eleven men, eleven women, five children, and three musicians enter the lobby singing a homage to Troy. They move through the audience and lead them to the first performance area in the hall, which is divided by a black curtain. In the center of this space, the women huddle on a small platform encircled by soldiers and surrounded by the audience. In response to the soldiers' threatening song, the women defiantly sing "Dios Limna," which signals the end of the first section. The audience watches the enslavement as it if were in their midst.

The second section is a ritual that the audience observes with detachment. As the program notes indicate, "The audience is invited to follow the action of the play by moving together from one area to another where the action takes place, and by taking a seat when the actors so indicate." After the next three scenes, separately concerning Cassandra, Andromache, and Helen, the audience is directed to sit on the side platforms. From here, they observe the final movements of the play.

In the Cassandra scene, which follows the enslavement, an actress is spotlighted left of the proscenium, brandishing a torch. As she prophesies, she is approached by a soldier who slips a noose over her head and violently drags her off.

The Andromache scene begins on the high platform by the entrance. Andromache bathes her child, who then crowns himself the last king of Troy. Soldiers appear carrying a wooden cage, force the child into it, and bear him off. Andromache leaps from the platform into the crowd and is lead away by the soldiers.

The scene of Helen's desecration takes place in the center of the hall. She is forced into a cage and taunted by women and soldiers alike. This is the only time in the performance that women and soldiers unite. Helen has been their mutual nemesis. As she pleads and rants, the actors strip her and throw mud and straw at her. Her wig is ripped off and her shaved head is exposed. An actor costumed as an enormous bear is lead into the cage where he symbolically rapes her. Finally, as the hall fills with smoke, Helen, naked, is carried off to the highest place, where she is destroyed, represented by a loud explosion.

Euripedes' tale is complete. What follows is Serban's addition. As the smoke settles and the audience finds seats, three children holding candles sing a lament. The body of the child/king is carried aloft in funeral procession and laid on a large rug. A weaving woman carries her loom up the ramp, stabs herself, and gently, slowly slides down to the bottom. Blue light on a sheet of mylar gives an eerie reflexion to complete the representation of her drowning.

In the next action, a woman is separated from the chorus of women and given to a god/demon, who is at the top of the ramp. The actor representing the god/demon wears a headdress of black cloth strips and pieces of fur. At the completion of this symbolic rape, a messenger bearing a torch enters. The men beat the women down as they attempt to scramble up the ramp in mock assault. Following the last woman down, the men herd the women into a circle where they are chained. The Trojan women whisper the "Dios Limna" as the soldiers lead the procession out through the proscenium. The performance is over.

The most important element in *The Trojan Women* is vocal sound. Swados and Serban prepared the text without regard to literal meaning. The libretto of ancient languages is transliterated in Roman syllables. The newcomers learn the sounds without pitch or rhythm from experienced company members who have learned it from Swados. When pronunciation is mastered, the sounds are orchestrated, using harmony and a variety of parts. At this point, Serban stages the movement.

Source: B. E., "*The Trojan Women* at LaMama," in *Drama Review: TDR*, Vol. 18, No. 4, December 1974, pp. 112–13.

Raymond Anselment

In the following essay, Anselment examines the three unities of time, place, and action in The Trojan Women.

The Trojan Women, like much Euripidean drama, defies conventional notions of Greek tragedy. The panorama of suffering comprises a series of episodes which appears to lack precise focus. The Trojan women who pass across the foreground of gutted Troy in a tableau of unrelieved horror are the helpless, communal victims

> **DEPRIVED OF TRADITIONAL VALUES AND IMMERSED IN AN ATMOSPHERE OF NEGATION, THE AUDIENCE IS DRAWN TO AND PSYCHICALLY INVOLVED WITH THE ONE CHARACTER WHO, UNBOWED BY SUFFERING, CONTINUES THE QUEST FOR MEANINGFUL ORDER."**

of uncontrollable forces. Even Hecuba, who emerges from the pageant as the dominant figure, neither initiates nor determines the course of events. Yet the dramatic impact, far from being a spectacle of shamelessly exploited pathos, is a striking, even overwhelming recreation of human suffering. *The Trojan Women* combines the senselessness and the anguish of war into a unified tragic experience which is simultaneously a great dramatic indictment of war and a moving study in individual heroism.

The play's forcefulness, it is generally suggested, stems primarily from the tension generated in its linear, unlocalized movement. Characters are intentionally simplistic because they assume supporting roles in a collective indictment of war's horror. The Trojan women—Cassandra, Polyxena, Andromache, Hecuba, and finally Troy herself—comprise a crescendo of sorrow dramatized in successive episodes which accentuate mounting suffering as feeble hopes are tauntingly promised and then cruelly frustrated. But the emotional power of *The Trojan Women* cannot be attributed solely to this dramatic "law of increasing tension." While the rhythmic movement of suffering undoubtedly influences the audience's emotional involvement, it does not determine the nature of the dramatic experience. In fact merely emphasizing an increasing progression of horrors could easily undercut its dramatic effectiveness, since human emotions are easily jaded and excessively frustrated sorrow is dangerously laughable. Moreover, focus on the victims' collective suffering disregards the individuals and minimizes the scope of their experience. "Pathos," "pathetic," "pity"—all frequently employed terms—underrate the complexity of the experience and imply a detachment which misrepresents the actual dramatic involvement.

The play avoids becoming an exhibition of pathos because Euripides creates a tension much more complex than the visceral appeal of unrelieved suffering. He achieves a psychic involvement through a double perspective which structures the plight of the Trojan women. The perspectives are the dramatic realization of the play's fundamental postulate: war is irrational and hence absurd. Seen from one perspective war is totally incomprehensible; it inverts fundamental values and defies rational understanding. The other perspective, however, unrelentingly asserts that war, whatever its fantastical nature, is inescapably real. The perspectives juxtaposed establish a form of reciprocal reenforcement. The absurdity, in denying any rationale for war, increases the horror of a very immediate and pointless suffering. In turn the vivid reality of war makes the insidious absurdity more graphically and poignantly apparent. The audience, caught between these two perspectives, cannot easily maintain a detached passivity; Euripides involves them in a dramatic experience which demands that they try to tolerate the paradoxically meaningful and meaningless void.

The initial absurdity and the play's fundamental inversion are quickly established in the prologue. Poseidon, who ignores the prostrate figure of Hecuba, surveys the ravaged remains of Troy and places the ten years of battle in perspective. Gone is the splendid city he and Phoebus Apollo once built; in its place are desolation and death. The extent of the destruction, emotionally summarized in Poseidon's elegiac lament, is further developed in his exchange with Athene. Troy and her inhabitants are not the only losers; "after ten years' harvests wasted here," the expectant Greek victors will now endure further storm-tossed terror in "a most unhappy coming home." In this apparently fickle world, destruction seems to have no termination and war promises only hollow victory; attempts to comprehend or order the inherent absurdity are futile. Athene's justification of the Greeks' punishment for desecrating the fallen city is lost in bitter irony. In a fit of jealousy the goddess had forced the Greeks to destroy Troy; now she proposes to destroy the Greeks because they have "outraged my temple and shamed me." In both instances the retributive penalties are inordinately disproportionate, and the argument of petty spite mocks rational comprehension.

It is from this point of view that subsequent action must then be reassessed. As the gods leave

and Hecuba lifts her physically and spiritually enervated body from the ground, her opening lament to changing fortune gains new dimension. She and the chorus of Trojan women who unite in communal suffering express the bittersweet memories of former happiness and the growing fears of future misery which make the immediate anguish even more unbearable. And the future, as the messenger Talthybius confirms, holds still greater sorrow. For the moment, Hecuba reels under the new knowledge that the wife of noble Priam must become the slave of Odysseus, the most despicable of Greeks; unaware of Talthybius' cryptic revelation of Polyxena's death, her cry "O wretched, given/the worst lot of all" is premature. The dramatic irony inherent in her specific situation is in turn reenforced by the more general, pervasive irony of the absurd. If the great suffering apparent in the opening movement of the play could be justified in any way, it might be more tolerable; but the perspective established in the prologue renders everything empty and meaningless. Some consolation might arise from the knowledge that the Greeks too will suffer greatly, but even this is negative; because the Trojan fate is now tied to that of the Greeks, no alleviation is possible. An immediate, moving situation is thus simultaneously made distant and paradoxically even more forceful.

The emotional potential is further increased by a pattern of imagery which extends the dimension of the implicit perspectives. As the vanquished queen painfully struggles to her feet, she falters:

O head, O temples
and sides; sweet, to shift,
let the tired spine rest
weight eased by the sides alternate,
against the strain of the tears' song
where the stricken people find music yet
in the song undanced of their
wretchedness.
(ll. 115–121)

The dance imagery in Hecuba's opening lines is striking in part because it has been prefigured. In the opening lines of *The Trojan Women* Poseidon, almost incidentally, begins his long speech with the introductory remark,

I am Poseidon. I come from the Aegean
depths
of the sea beneath whose waters Nereid
choirs evolve

the intricate bright circle of their dancing
    feet.
(ll. 1–3)

The allusion to the graceful Mediterranean nymphs is more than mere ornament; Euripides juxtaposes the divine dance of joy and the human dance of misery. His intention is clearly apparent in the conclusion to Hecuba's opening lament:

And I, as among winged birds
the mother, lead out
the clashing cry, the song; not that song
wherein once long ago,
when I held the scepter of Priam,
my feet were queens of the choir and led
the proud dance to the gods of Phrygia.
(ll. 146–152)

The great discrepancy between past and present perspectives, like that between the divine and the human, dramatizes the inversion. The dance, conventionally a symbol of harmony and joy, is now transformed into a symbol of agonizing sorrow and rampant destruction. Once in blissful ignorance, the chorus later says, the Trojans welcomed the peace offering of the wooden horse:

and all Troy singing, and girls'
light feet pulsing the air
in the kind dance measures;
indoors, lights everywhere,
torchflares on black
to forbid sleep's onset.
(ll. 545–550)

Then the dance hideously and ironically mocked their premature joy; now the dance aptly describes their new suffering. The "song undanced of their wretchedness," an appropriate gathering metaphor for the entire play, structures the complex procession of horrors which informs *The Trojan Women*.

Cassandra's appearance, which immediately follows the disclosure of Hecuba's fate, clearly illustrates the emotional involvement produced by this unique polarization. Garbed as a stage Fury, with her whirling torch she bursts onto the stage before the grief-stricken Hecuba in frenzied dance:

Dance, Mother, dance, laugh; lead; let
    your feet
wind in the shifting pattern and follow
    mine,
keep the sweet step with me,
cry out the name Hymenaeus

and the bride's name in the shrill
and the blessed incantation.
O you daughters of Phrygia robed
    in splendor,
dance for my wedding,
for the lord fate appointed to lie beside
    me.
(ll. 332–340)

Cassandra's startling words and dance, which Hecuba dismisses as the incoherent raving of a "crazed, passionate" daughter, at first seem the heavily ironic expression of a distraught virgin betrayed into captivity. As such her dramatic entrance, initially an abrupt departure from the oppressive atmosphere, vividly increases the emotional tension. But the full effect of Cassandra's scene is even more complicated. The whirling torch and insane dance, later reenacted in other circumstances, symbolize the suffering associated with war. But from another perspective the "wedding" dance, an expression of passionate feeling, promises a form of inverted bliss; and the apparently incomprehensible dance of madness becomes a dance of unrestrained joy. Doomed to tell the truth yet not to be believed, Cassandra sees that her inescapable servitude to the victorious Agamemnon offers an unexpected satisfaction. The forced sexual union will afford Agamemnon neither fulfillment nor new life in its offspring; his reward will be death at the hands of his jealous wife Clytemnestra.

> Cassandra's dance, a contrast to the joyous torchlight dance of the Trojan girls, prefigures the final outrage committed against the Trojan women, the burning of Troy.

This new knowledge, understood only by the audience, creates another dimension of horror. As Cassandra continues to look beyond the apparent chaos and suffering, she sees the irony and emptiness of the Greek victory; in her unwavering logic, Troy's "fate is blessed beside the Achaeans'." Agamemnon, who earns the sarcastic epithet "clever man," had sacrificed his own child for his brother's worthless wife; he also led a nation into futile war in the name of the guest law. But the very principle used to justify the war was meaningless; no one had threatened to take the Greek lands, and the war actually subverted the very ideal it hoped to affirm:

Those the War God caught
never saw their sons again, nor were
    they laid to rest

decently in winding sheets by their
    wives' hands, but lie
buried in alien ground; while all went
    wrong at home
as the widows perished, and barren cou-
    ples raised and nursed
the children of others, no survivor left to
    tend
the tombs, and what is left there, with
    blood sacrificed.
For such success as this congratulate the
    Greeks.
(ll. 376–383)

The vanquished are then ultimately victorious, for they died for their country, "that glory
which is loveliest," and they were honorably buried
by the people they loved. In an irrational world
devoid of absolutes, Cassandra forces the audience
to ponder, "Then was Hector's fate so sad?"

However, the question implies a relative
answer which the play refuses to concede. Cassandra's arguments, although they rationally suggest the paradoxical victory of the defeated, offer
scant consolation; only the dead—and Cassandra
must die to fulfill the revenge promised—find grim
and ultimately meaningless satisfaction. For the
living, as Andromache the next captive in the
tableau of Trojan women illustrates, the prospect
is only further pain. A vivid emblem of war's aftermath, her arrival with her son on a wagon heaped
with plunder from ravaged Troy dispels any
thoughts of final victory. The processional appearance of Hector's helpless wife and son, a striking
parody of the dignified entrances traditionally
accorded tragic figures of royal stature, evokes
from both the chorus and Hecuba a heightened
recognition of the life they have lost and the horrors they now must face alone. But the full effect
of the suffering is yet to come. Andromache's
announcement of Polyxena's death shatters Hecuba's illusions about her daughter's safety and
increases the intolerable anguish. The oppressive
suffering is extended in Andromache's long denunciation of her misfortunes.

Much more than an emotional cry of
woe, Andromache's assertions unrelentingly and
rationally assault fundamental values. The basis of
her plea is a desire for death:

Death, I am sure, is like never being
    born, but death
is better thus by far than to live a life of
    pain,

since the dead with no perception of evil
    feel no grief,
while he who was happy once, and then
    unfortunate,
finds his heart driven far from the old
    lost happiness.
(ll. 636–640)

Denied the oblivion of death, Andromache
must accept a disordered world in which former
happiness can only remain a source of taunting
pain. In this absurd existence honor and honesty
become futile values which offer only greater
suffering. As she pointedly asserts, her life exemplified the virtues of an ideal wife. Although her
role demanded sacrifice, she willingly curbed her
feminine wishes and defined her life according to
her husband's will. Yet ironically her virtues
have only enhanced her value as a captive and
increased her present dilemma:

If I dash back the beloved memory of
    Hector
and open wide my heart to my new lord,
    I shall be
a traitor to the dead love, and know it; if
    I cling
faithful to the past, I win my master's
    hatred. Yet
they say one night of love suffices to
    dissolve
a woman's aversion to share the bed of
    any man.
(ll. 661–666)

Reduced to this wretched state her desire for
death, a denial of the life force so crucial to the
Greek vision, becomes a logical conclusion. War
has destroyed and overturned all values; "That
one thing left / always while life lasts, hope, is not
for me" (ll. 680–681).

Andromache's conclusions receive no via-
ble rebuttal. Hecuba can only counsel endurance in the hope of some future joy: "On some
far day the children of your children might /
come home, and build. There still may be
another Troy" (ll. 704–705). But this chimerical
hope is rudely and immediately dashed with
the announcement that her son Astyanax must
die. Stripped of her one comforting delusion,
Andromache accepts reality:

O darling child I loved too well for
    happiness,
your enemies will kill you and leave
    your mother forlorn.

Your own father's nobility, where
   others found
protection, means your murder now.
   (ll. 740–743)

Again the inescapable inversion of great values is magnified; in a world where love and nobility are rewarded with unhappiness and murder she can only realize frustration and "Vanity in the end." Devoid of hope and emotionally exhausted, Andromache's final defiance before the wagon carries her away to the ship is a violent curse against the one tangible source of her hardships, Helen.

The transvaluation apparent throughout Andromache's scene is only fully realized with the entrance of Helen, the next woman in the procession of captives. Her appearance, although it seems to break the continuity of suffering Trojan women, actually is structurally sound. Her status as a Trojan wife for the last ten years justifies her presence in the line of prisoners; her position in the sequence of events, more importantly, fulfills the contrast implicit in Andromache's speech. Euripides willingly ignores the emotional tension inherent in the mounting sorrows of the Trojan women, because he can achieve a much greater effect; by balancing the wife of Hector and good mother with the wife of Menelaus and good whore, he accentuates the ironic futility of rational, moral conduct.

Helen's struggle for life, unlike Andromache's desire for death, introduces an aura of detachment. The legalistic confrontation with its brittle, rhetorical qualities seems strangely removed from the unrelenting reality of suffering. Yet paradoxically the "trial" of Helen should be very immediate, for it is another attempt to give coherent meaning to the aftermath of war. Hecuba, in fact, underlines the importance of the scene with her prefatory plea:

O power, who mount the world, wheel
   where the world rides,
O mystery of man's knowledge, whoso-
   ever you be,
Zeus named, nature's necessity or mortal mind,
I call upon you; for you walk the path
   none hears
yet bring all human action back to right
   at last.
(ll. 884–888)

The urgency of this desire, which finds its counterpart throughout Greek drama, is quickly frustrated in the events that follow. Although the ordered, rational processes of "mortal mind" are employed, the result is a sham.

Helen's facile defense, essentially a denial of all personal responsibility, is quickly demolished in Hecuba's denunciation. The effect should be a gratifying vindication of justice: if Andromache must suffer for her loyalty, at least Helen will pay the ultimate penalty of death for her treachery. But even this qualified reassurance is nothing more than a mockery. The audience knows that justice will never be fulfilled and that Helen will use her feminine wiles to escape death and to live a long, prosperous life. Hecuba and the chorus of Trojan women also sense the inevitable outcome. Despite Menelaus' somewhat doubtful reassurances that he will punish his wife, the women fear and even anticipate Helen's eventual triumph. Reason may have judged Helen guilty, but reason has no effective place in the world of nonreason.

The dislocation is fully revealed in the conclusion to Helen's scene. Although she is led off to the ship which will supposedly take her to a just punishment, the choral ode which visualizes her journey bitterly questions this futile hope:

I am cut from my country;
as she holds the golden mirror
in her hands, girls' grace,
she, God's daughter. (ll. 1106–09)

This explicit recognition of life's inequity is followed by an event which recalls and reenforces a far greater injustice. Helen's place on the stage is now occupied by the body of Astyanax; the comparison between the two women is tacitly complete.

Astyanax's broken body, carried on the shield of Hector, is emblematic of the total dramatic experience in *The Trojan Women*. The dead boy and the captured shield suggest the father and son united now both in death and in defeat. For the Trojan women who helplessly watch and mourn, the procession signifies the final recognition of the end of present and future expectations. The burning of Troy is thus almost anticlimactic, for there are now no men to attempt a future rebuilding. But more than a termination of hopes, the impromptu bier mutely emphasizes the real victims of war. Like the intimate domestic scene in *The Iliad* when Astyanax reacts with fright to his father's awesome helmet, this scene similarly juxtaposes Hector's son and an instrument of terror. But no trace of humor lessens the implications of the contrast. More relentlessly than *The Iliad*, Euripides' play asserts that the women and the children bear the brunt of war's horror.

Yet in dramatizing the plight of the innocent, Euripides does not cheapen the emotional impact. The death of the child, even more than the suffering of the women, offers great potential pathos; but again the complex perspective heightens rather than diminishes the emotional involvement. Hecuba, understandably affected by the new sorrow, does not languish in her intensified suffering; instead she tries to comprehend the reasons for her grandson's death. But her efforts are futile, and at best she can conclude:

> What shall the poet say,
> What words will he inscribe upon your
>   monument?
> *Here lies a little child the Argives killed,*
>   *because*
> *they were afraid of him.* (ll. 1188–91)

This epitaph to the victors' shame is also an acknowledgement of reason's further extension into the realm of absurdity. Odysseus, traditionally recognized among the Greeks for his clever reasoning, is the mastermind behind the death of Astyanax. From his vantage point the scheme seems prudent; in the larger context of traditional values, however, the accomplished deed denies easy comprehension. The audience, emotionally responsive to the suffering, is further involved in the dramatic paradox. Odysseus can rationally justify his action, and Hecuba can understandably denounce his "mind unreasoning." The inclination is to respond to Hecuba's position, yet logic favors Odysseus' callousness. Caught between these two perspectives, reason must finally be denied, for it has no meaning in the realm of the absurd.

The frustration of meaningful value is compounded in the scene's terminal speech. Just before the Greeks remove Astyanax's body, Hecuba gropes for a semblance of order which might give purpose to their suffering:

> The gods meant nothing except to make
>   life hard for me,
> and of all cities they chose Troy to hate.
>   In vain
> we sacrificed. And yet had not the very
>   hand
> of God gripped and crushed this city
>   deep in the ground,
> we should have disappeared in dark-
>   ness, and not given
> a theme for music, and the songs of men
>   to come.
> (ll. 1240–45)

The vanity is then confirmed in the play's last dance, the burning of Troy. But the consolation Hecuba seeks seems small compensation. The destruction of Troy should be remembered as a timeless exemplum of the inhumanity and senselessness of military conquest; yet the Athenians who perpetuated the saga of Troy in their literature nevertheless also reenacted the same horrors in their actions. Euripides, a master of the ironic, may have intended an irony in Hecuba's consolation; certainly a modern audience cannot ignore the irony of human short-sightedness as history blindly pursues the absurd.

Yet the vision of *The Trojan Women* is not totally negative or nihilistic; in a world without conventional ordering forces one character provides a semblance of stability crucial to the tragic unity and the "theme for music, and the songs of men to come." Although her dramatic nature does not readily conform to conventional notions about the tragic character, Hecuba deserves comparison with the heroic figures traditionally dramatized in Greek tragedy. Studies which minimize her stature do so perhaps in part out of the misguided notion that all tragedy involves a demonstrable *hamartia*. Hecuba, of course, is not responsible for the relentless suffering inflicted upon her, and she approximates none of the *hubris* too often ascribed to Greek tragic heroes. As a victim of circumstances totally beyond her control, she is the central representative of the drama's communal suffering. However, she is more than the paradigm of innocent suffering whose presence throughout the drama gives continuity to the series of episodes. Unlike the sketchy, monochromatic character too often presented in critical evaluations, Euripides' Hecuba manifests a personal, quite unpretentious yet nevertheless moving heroism. In refusing to yield to the physically and spiritually devastating onslaught, Hecuba achieves a self-definition and wisdom well within the rhythm of Greek tragedy.

Hecuba's distinction (although perhaps partly associated with some quantitative measure of experienced anguish) depends primarily upon the manner with which she confronts her experience. Near the end of the play Hecuba summarizes the "song undanced" which she has painfully realized:

> That mortal is a fool who, prospering,
>   thinks his life
> has any strong foundation; since our
>   fortune's course
> of action is the reeling way a madman
>   takes,

and no one person is ever happy all the
time.
(ll. 1203–06)

Other characters in the play share similar
knowledge acquired through unrelieved suffering, but only Hecuba struggles with the full
impact of her sorrow. Cassandra, for example,
transcends her immediate suffering with a divine
madness that sees future revenge, while Andromache bitterly and despondently yields an existence
of insuperable frustrations. Hecuba at first also
experiences this very human reaction; when her
initial suffering is compounded by the appearance of Cassandra, her spirit is almost broken:

What hope? What use?
Guide these feet long ago so delicate in
    Troy,
a slave's feet now, to the straw sacks laid
    on the ground
and the piled stones; let me lay down my
    head and die
in an exhaustion of tears. Of all who
    walk in bliss
call not one happy yet, until the man is
    dead.
(ll. 505–510)

But Hecuba never totally succumbs to despair.
Her tenacious spirit, though at times greatly weakened, finds strength in the role she must play.
Although no longer queen and matriarch of
Troy, Hecuba refuses to relinquish her communal
responsibility. Near the end of the opening lament
in which she defines her misery and isolation,
Hecuba concludes she is "among winged birds /
the mother" (ll. 146–147). This self-characteriza-
tion, sustained in her continual references to the
chorus and other Trojan women as "my children,"
is manifest in her actions. Initially the paralyzing
shock of her own suffering saps her spirit, and she
can only tell others to lighten their hearts as she
herself slips into growing despondency. Cassandra's totally incomprehensible actions only increase
this despair; it is Andromache's plight, however,
that produces a significant change. When the
grief-stricken woman expresses a desire for death,
Hecuba who just before her appearance had
uttered the same wish briefly asserts, "Child, no.
No life, no light is any kind of death, / since death
is nothing, and in life the hopes live still" (ll. 632–
633). This advice, although sudden and contradictory, is readily understood as an instinctively
maternal response. In meeting someone even
more helpless and sorrowful than herself, Hecuba

momentarily forgets her own wretchedness and
reaches out to comfort and to protect. Her gesture,
an affirmation of life, is symbolically appropriate;
as a mother, the source of life, she gropes for
meaningful purpose in life.

Hecuba's assertion of self does not approach
the magnitude of an Oedipus or an Electra,
for the pervasive vision of the absurd frustrates
her efforts. The fleeting consolation given to
Andromache, the uncompromising judgment of
Helen, and the mournful dirge for Astyanax all
are positive, hopeful actions; however, in each
case external events relentlessly deny their fulfillment. While the dramatic thrust naturally emphasizes this steady accumulation of misfortunes,
Hecuba's commitment should not be minimized.
Her voice of protest, which becomes increasingly
apparent, is no longer primarily concerned with
the magnitude of her suffering. The aggressive
accusations hurled against Helen's perfidious
conduct and the Greeks' senseless murder of
Astyanax are tinged with personal bitterness,
but they extend beyond self-concern. In questioning the basis of their actions, Hecuba is struggling
for an elemental ordering force which might
relieve the engulfing chaos. No answers are
found and no code of conduct is suggested, yet
Hecuba achieves a form of wisdom that completes her character.

In the senseless world of war Hecuba learns
that the only certain verities are life and death;
death attractively offers escape and life promises
only further suffering. Accepting life on these
terms demands an act of faith, and this Hecuba
ultimately understands. From her experiences
she gains more than knowledge of war's horrors;
she gains the more valuable knowledge that
despite pain and deprivation life may be meaningful. In part the consolation has no greater
support than her realization that a valueless life
still has potential while "death is nothing." More
positively, however, she realizes man's ability to
endure in unpretentious, ennobling dignity when
no other alternative to defeat is possible. This
modest affirmation, if only tenuously set forth, is
completed in her exit. After she hears the fate of
Troy, the last of the Trojan women, she still finds
compassion in the midst of her own suffering:
"Come, aged feet; make one last weary struggle,
that I / may hail my city in its affliction"
(ll. 1275–76). Her final dirge culminates one
phase of the endless suffering, and Hecuba now
faces the future:

O
shaking, tremulous limbs,
this is the way. Forward:
into the slave's life. (ll. 1327–30)

In contrast to the lethargic, prostrate Hecuba in the opening scenes of the play, this final effort is significant. Although her unsteady steps are those of a captive, Hecuba's spirit remains unvanquished. Movement forward, if only into captivity, implies purpose. Hecuba has achieved an heroic wisdom similar to the knowledge of all Greek heroes—the acceptance and the assertion of the life force. She has met overwhelming suffering and endured.

This is the understated heroism which emerges forcefully in the course of the play to complete its tragic unity. Through the play's multiple perspectives, Euripides jolts the audience out of its detachment and involves them in the omnipresent suffering. Deprived of traditional values and immersed in an atmosphere of negation, the audience is drawn to and psychically involved with the one character who, unbowed by suffering, continues the quest for meaningful order. The ultimate nature of the dramatic experience of *The Trojan Women* becomes then an answer to the question:

What's Hecuba to him or he to her,
That he should weep for her?

Source: Raymond Anselment, "Discordia Concors: Unity in Euripides' *The Trojan Women*," in *Educational Theatre Journal*, Vol. 21, No. 4, December 1969, pp. 403–14.

SOURCES

Aristotle, *Poetics*, in *The Complete Works of Aristotle: The Revised Oxford Translation*, Vol. 2, Bollingen Series LXXI, edited by Jonathan Barnes, Princeton University Press, 1995, pp. 2315–20.

Dué, Casey, *The Captive Woman's Lament in Greek Tragedy*, University of Texas Press, 2006.

Euripides, *Fragments*, Vols. VII–VIII, Loeb Classical Library, translated by Christopher Collard and Martin Cropp, Harvard University Press, 2008.

———, *The Trojan Women*, translated by Richmond Lattimore, in *Greek Tragedies*, Vol. 2, edited by David Greene and Richmond Lattimore, University of Chicago Press, 1958, pp. 247–95.

Furley, William D., *Andokides and the Herms: A Study of Crisis in Fifth-Century Athenian Religion*, Bulletin of the Institute of Classical Studies Supplement 65, University of London, 1996.

Goff, Barbara, *Euripides: Trojan Women*, Duckworth Companions to Greek and Roman Tragedy, Duckworth, 2009.

Goldhill, Simon, "The Language of Tragedy: Rhetoric and Communication," in *The Cambridge Companion to Greek Tragedy*, edited by P. E. Easterling, Cambridge University Press, 1997, pp. 127–50.

Gorgias, "Encomium of Helen," in *The Norton Anthology of Theory and Criticism*, edited by Vincent B. Leitch, W. W. Norton, 2001, pp. 30–33.

Green, Peter, *Armada from Athens*, Doubleday, 1970.

Grene, David, and Richmond Lattimore, eds., Introduction to *Greek Tragedies*, University of Chicago Press, 1960.

Guthrie, W. K. C., *The Sophists*, Cambridge University Press, 1971.

Kagan, Donald, *The Peloponnesian War*, Viking, 2003.

Kovacs, David, *Euripdea*, Mnemosyne Supplement No. 132, E. J. Brill, 1994.

Lefkowitz, Mary L., "'Impiety' and 'Atheism' in Euripides' Dramas," in *Classical Quarterly*, Vol. 39, 1989, pp. 70–82.

Mossman, Judith, "Women's Voices," in *A Companion to Greek Tragedy*, edited by Justina Gregory, Duckworth, 2005, pp. 352–65.

Murray, Gilbert, *Euripides and His Age*, Henry Holt, 1913, pp. 128–39.

Nietzsche, Friedrich, *The Birth of Tragedy*, translated by Douglas Smith, Oxford University Press, 2000.

Thucydides, *The Peloponnesian War*, translated by Richard Crawley, Modern Library, 1982.

Vickers, Brian, *Towards Greek Tragedy: Drama, Myth, Society*, Longman, 1973.

Yunis, Harvey, *A New Creed: Fundamental Religious Beliefs in the Athenian Polis and Euripidean Drama*, Hypomnemata, No. 91, Vandenhoeck & Ruprecht, 1988.

FURTHER READING

Bushnell, Rebecca, ed., *A Companion to Tragedy*, Blackwell, 2005.

> The essays in this volume deal with ancient tragedy, its renaissance, and its modern reception.

Croally, N. T., *Euripidean Polemic: "The Trojan Women" and the Function of Greek Tragedy*, Cambridge University Press, 1994.

> Croally focuses on *The Trojan Women* to argue that the purpose of tragedy in Athenian society was to question tradition through the Socratic method.

Euripides, *Trojan Women*, translated by Diskin Clay, Focus, 2005.

> This recent translation focuses on stage performance by inserting extensive stage directions suitable for a modern production.

McDonald, Marianne, *The Living Art of Greek Tragedy*, Indiana University Press, 2003.

This is a survey of Greek drama with a special emphasis on modern productions and modern adaptations rather than merely translations.

Seneca, Lucius Annaeus, *Trojan Women*, translated by Frederick Ahl, Cornell University Press, 1986.

This is an English translation of the play by the Roman playwright, philosopher, and politician Seneca. His version takes a very different approach from that of Euripides.

Urinetown

GREG KOTIS
MARK HOLLMANN

2001

Urinetown by Greg Kotis, who wrote the book and lyrics, and Mark Hollmann, who wrote the music and lyrics, is a modern classic of the American musical stage, rising quickly from off-off-Broadway (it was performed by Theater of the Apes at the New York International Fringe Festival in 1999) to off-Broadway (American Theater for Actors opened it on May 6, 2001) to the Henry Miller's Theater on Broadway. It was scheduled to open on September 13, 2001, but the terrorist attacks on the World Trade Center two days earlier postponed the opening. It did open on September 20, with some lines that would have been considered in poor taste after the attacks removed, and went on to be nominated for ten Tony awards. It played on Broadway for 965 performances.

The plot of the play concerns a nightmarish town of the future that has coped with a twenty-year drought by outlawing private toilets. People are forced to pay whatever fee Urine Good Company, the company that runs the public amenities, wants to charge. A love affair develops between the daughter of the company's owner and the son of a poor man who cannot pay the fee and is taken away for punishment to the mysterious "Urinetown." What ensues is a parody that pokes fun at all involved: greedy capitalists and angry rabble-rousers, insipid lovers and hard-boiled survivors, dishonest labor leaders and corrupt politicians. With songs mimicking genres from Broadway romances to spirituals to labor

Mark Hollmann, left, and Greg Kotis accept the Tony Award for best original score for Urinetown.
(AP Images)

anthems, *Urinetown* is filled with insights about modern society, packaged in what one character acknowledges is an awful title. The off-Broadway run won a Lortel Award for Outstanding Musical and Choreography, and the Broadway production won three Tony Awards (Best Director, Best Original Score, Best Book of a Musical).

AUTHOR BIOGRAPHY

The book for *Urinetown* and some of the song lyrics were written by Kotis, who attended the University of Chicago, earning a bachelor of arts degree in political science. He graduated from University of Chicago in 1985. While there, he became involved in the improvisation group, Cardiff Giant Theatre Company, where he coauthored six plays. He was also involved with the Neo-Futurists, an experimental theater company, and was a performer and writer on their long-running performance piece *Too Much Light Makes the Baby Go Blind*, which premiered

in 1988. After attending an international theater festival in Transylvania with the Neo-Futurists, Kotis traveled across Europe, finding himself with limited funds in Paris, where many of the public restrooms charge a fee, and from this came the idea of a totalitarian society that has turned the basic process of urinating into a commodity, leading him to write *Urinetown*. After returning to the United States, he moved to New York City, became active in the theater scene, and worked on the play for three years. In that time he married Ayun Halliday, another member of the Neo-Futurist troupe; they have two children. After *Urinetown*, Kotis wrote *Pig Farm*, which premiered in 2006, and *The Truth about Santa*, which premiered in 2008.

Hollmann wrote the music and some of the lyrics for the play. Hollmann was born in Belleville, Illinois, a southern Illinois town near St. Louis, Missouri, in 1963. He attended the University of Chicago to get a law degree, with the idea of going into politics, but he switched to studying English, and then music, while he was there. He graduated from the University of Chicago in 1985. He and Kotis met when they were both members of Cardiff Giant in the 1980s. Hollmann, a talented musician, also played trombone for Maestro Subgum and the Whole, an art-rock band based in Chicago, and played piano for the famed Second City improvisation theater's national touring company. He was trained at the Making Tuners Workshop at the New Tuners Theatre in Chicago and at the BMI Lehman Engel Musical Theatre in New York, where he currently lives with his wife and son. In 2009, the musical *Wild Goats*, for which Hollmann wrote the music, premiered in Chicago.

MEDIA ADAPTATIONS

- The soundtrack audio CD *Urinetown*, featuring the original cast from the play's off-Broadway run, was produced by RCA Victor Broadway in 2001. It includes all of the songs from the Broadway production, with differences in just a few lines. Performers include John Cullum, David Beach, Jeff McCarthy, Ken Jennings, and Jennifer Laura Thompson.

PLOT SUMMARY

Act 1, Scene 1

The first scene of *Urinetown* begins outside of Public Amenity Number Nine, a public urinal in the poorest and dirtiest area of an unnamed city. Poor people line up to pay their money to Penelope Pennywise, who runs this facility, so that they can go inside and urinate. Hope Cladwell passes through on the way to her first day of work at her father's company, Urine Good Company.

A problem arises when Old Man Strong, whose son, Bobby, works at Public Amenity Number Nine, arrives without enough money to pay the entrance fee. Ms. Pennywise refuses him admittance. When he cannot hold his urine any longer, Old Man Strong undoes his pants and urinates against the wall of the building. Officer Lockstock and Officer Barrel immediately show up to arrest him and take him away.

Act 1, Scene 2

The second scene takes place in the executive offices of Urine Good Company. Senator Fipp has come to collect bribe money from the company's president, Caldwell B. Cladwell. Fipp feels that he has completed his service to the company by pushing a bill through Congress that will allow Urine Good Company, or UGC, to raise the rates on people wishing to use the public toilet. Cladwell does not want to pay Fipp until the vote has been taken and the measure has passed. Cladwell's daughter, Hope, arrives to start working at her father's company, and Fipp comments on how beautiful she is until Cladwell tells him to stop his comments. Cladwell introduces Hope to his employees. He explains how he built the

company after a drought, which began twenty years earlier, forced society to ration flush toilets. The employees sing a song praising Cladwell for his money-making ways.

Act 1, Scene 3

On a street corner at night, Little Sally, a poor little girl who is counting her pennies until she has enough to use the public urinal, talks with Officer Lockstock about the drought, raising the question about why the only public action against the drought seems to be rationing toilets, and not something to do with hydraulics that might solve the water shortage. When she leaves, Officer Barrel arrives and says that he has sent Old Man Strong down to Urinetown, screaming all the way. The policemen sing about how all violators of the law who try to get around the use of the public urinals are sent for punishment to Urinetown.

Hope Cladwell and Bobby Strong arrive on stage. When the policemen leave, Hope tells him that he should listen to his heart. During the song "Follow Your Heart," they listen to each other's hearts and find out they are in love with one another.

Act 1, Scene 4

Mr. McQueen, the assistant to Mr. Cladwell, announces the new rate increase to the people waiting to use Public Amenity Number Nine. The poor people gathered around are flabbergasted at the news. When Bobby Strong arrives he tells the people that they should rise up against UGC and refuse to pay to use the urinal anymore.

Act 1, Scene 5

As Senator Fipp is preparing to leave for Rio, Lockstock, Barrel, and Pennywise enter with news about the uprising at the Public Amenity. Hope is shocked to hear that the revolt is being led by Bobby Strong. Cladwell orders the policemen to use violence to stop the protesters, and he leads the cast in the song "Don't Be the Bunny," about the cruel, competitive nature of the world.

Act 1, Scene 6

When the police and the UGC board members arrive at Public Amenity Number Nine, the poor people involved in the rebellion talk about running away, but Bobby Strong encourages them to stay and hold their ground. Faced with guns, the revolutionaries seem poised to be killed until Bobby grabs Hope Cladwell by the arm. He and his supporters take Hope as their hostage, and as scene 6 ends everyone begins running in slow motion.

Act 2, Scene 1

Act 2 begins with a scene in the secret hideout of the revolutionary movement, which is marked with a sign that says "Secret Hideout" hanging above the stage. The poor people are nervous because Bobby Strong has gone out to negotiate with Cladwell and has not returned.

At the UGC headquarters, Officer Lockstock tells Cladwell that the police have searched all over the city for his daughter, and that she is probably being held in the sewers. Cladwell threatens to send everyone off to Urinetown if they will not cooperate.

On the street, Bobby Strong and his mother, Josephine, promise to keep up the fight against the corporation. Lockstock catches Little Sally, a member of the revolution, and offers to send her to "the nice part of Urinetown" if she will cooperate, but she refuses and escapes.

Act 2, Scene 2

Back at the Secret Hideout, Hot Blades Harry and Little Becky Two-Shoes discuss how much satisfaction they would derive from killing Hope, their hostage, and they sing the song "Snuff That Girl." Bobby Strong returns to the hideout and stops them before they kill her. Ms. Pennywise, who is affiliated with the UGC, arrives to encourage Bobby to go and meet with Cladwell, promising

that a peaceful resolution can be found. Hope encourages him to go and talk to her father.

Act 2, Scene 3

At the Urine Good Company offices, Cladwell talks with Bobby. He offers him a suitcase full of cash if he will call off the revolution and tell the people to pay the new fee, but Bobby says his conscience will not let him aid in the oppression of the people. Cladwell tells the police to take Bobby off to Urinetown: Ms. Pennywise reminds him that the revolutionaries are holding his daughter and have promised to harm her if Bobby is harmed, but Cladwell says he does not care. He tells McQueen to prepare all of the police in the city for a battle. Ms. Pennywise and Senator Fipp feel betrayed by Cladwell, as Officers Lockstock and Barrel take Bobby Strong away to "Urinetown." It turns out that "Urinetown" is not a place: "a trip to Urinetown" just means being thrown off of a building's roof.

Act 2, Scene 4

Little Sally arrives at the Secret Hideout with the news that the police have thrown Bobby Strong off of a roof. Before they can take their revenge against Hope, though, Little Sally says that she heard Bobby's dying words, which were about his love for Hope and his understanding that everyone, including the people leading the revolt, are guilty in this situation, but that he envisions a better future.

Before the poor people can harm Hope, Ms. Pennywise reveals that she is actually Hope's mother, from a love affair she had with Cladwell long ago, before he had built his financial empire. Hope tells the poor people that they can kill her and let the rebellion die, or they can follow her and she will lead the rebellion that Bobby began.

Act 2, Scene 5

The revolutionaries go after the representatives of the established order. They catch Mrs. Millennium, an executive with UGC, as she is planning to leave the country with Senator Fipp, and kill them both. Hope and a band of her followers confront Cladwell about his plan to leave her to die. Cladwell is thrown off of a roof, and his assistant McQueen is given a chance to join the revolution.

Officer Lockstock comes onstage to narrate what happened after the revolution. Hope took over her father's company and made the public toilets free for everyone once more. This led to an exhaustion of the available water supply, just as Cladwell had warned it would. Another revolution in the future ended up with Hope suffering the same fate that befell her father, while Mr. McQueen became rich by moving to Brasília and opening a bottling plant, selling the water of the Amazon River. With the town depleted, the people realized that their town itself was Urinetown.

CHARACTERS

Officer Barrel

Officer Barrel is one of two policemen featured in the play. He is less often noticed than Officer Lockstock, the other featured policeman, because Officer Lockstock is also the play's narrator.

Officer Barrel seems to be in a subservient position to Officer Lockstock. He appears once with a shovel and a mop, and is told at another time to go and get the shovel and mop: the implication is that it is Officer Barrel's responsibility to clean up the body after someone has been thrown off of a roof.

In scene 5 of the second act, Officer Barrel blurts out that he loves Officer Lockstock. Lockstock is unresponsive and leaves, uncomfortably, but Barrel is dense enough to believe that his confession of love, though ignored, went well.

Little Becky Two-Shoes

One of the poor people in the town, Little Becky Two-Shoes proves to be aggressive once the revolution begins. Even before hearing that Bobby Strong has been killed by the police, she supports killing their hostage, Hope Cladwell, for no better reason than that killing would feel good.

Dr. Billeaux

Dr. Billeaux is a member of the board of Urine Good Company. He is the head of their research department.

Caldwell B. Cladwell

Mr. Cladwell is the play's villain. He is the president and owner if the Urine Good Company, which owns all of the town's toilets that are available for public use. Cladwell is a self-made millionaire. Years earlier, when the drought first affected the land, he was a poor but ambitious

man. At that time, he had an affair with Penelope Pennywise and had a daughter with her, Hope. Cladwell raised the girl himself. He built the Urine Good Company to force people to pay for a necessary function, urinating. In business dealings, he has proven unscrupulous. The way that Cladwell's employees speak to and of him in only the most glowing terms indicates that he is not willing to tolerate even the slightest hint of disagreement from them.

When his daughter, Hope, is kidnapped by the revolutionaries, Cladwell orders the police to prepare a crackdown, even though it might mean Hope's death. Even his employees who think of him as a ruthless businessman are shocked by how heartless he is. He dies unrepentant, claiming that all that he did that was evil was justified because it conserved water. In the epilogue, Officer Lockstock reveals that Cladwell was right, and that his methods actually were the only thing that delayed an ecological disaster for years.

Hope Cladwell

Hope is the daughter of Caldwell B. Cladwell, the president of Urine Good Company. She has recently graduated from the Most Expensive University in the World, and is starting at her father's company, working in faxing and copying. On the way to her job, she wanders into the poor part of town, where she meets Bobby Strong, who becomes a leader of the revolution against her father's company. They fall in love.

When the revolutionaries are confronted by the police, they take Hope captive. She finds out that her father ordered Bobby executed, thereby killing the boy she loves and taking the chance that the revolutionaries would murder Hope in retaliation. Hope becomes the leader of the revolution, taking control of UGC and opening it up to everyone for free.

Cladwell's Secretary

Like all employees of Urine Good Company, Caldwell B. Cladwell's secretary fears him and speaks only with glowing praise to him.

Senator Fipp

Fipp is a corrupt senator who has been bribed by Caldwell B. Cladwell to push a bill through the Senate that will allow Urine Good Company to raise the rates they charge for using their toilets. Fipp plans to take the bribe money and escape to Rio, but when the revolt begins Cladwell tells him that he has to wait until it is all settled before he can leave. Later, when the revolution is in full blossom, Fipp is again planning to leave for Rio when he is stopped by Mrs. Millennium, who says that Cladwell has forbidden him to leave. He bribes her by offering to take her with him, but the revolutionaries catch them and kill them both.

Hot Blades Harry

Harry is one of the poor people who is involved with the revolution against UGC. He is one of the leading supporters of killing their hostage, Hope Cladwell.

Officer Lockstock

In addition to being a character in *Urinetown*, Officer Lockstock serves as the play's narrator. Within the play he and his partner, Officer Barrel, are the only two policemen identified by name. They are both corrupt, taking their orders from the Urine Good Company and arresting or even killing citizens at the command of UGC's president, Caldwell B. Cladwell. At one point in act 2, scene 5, Officer Lockstock admits that his conscience sometimes bothers him, but that he is motivated to act illegally by his concerns for the health and safety of the community.

As the play's narrator, Officer Lockstock sets up the premise, telling audiences about the water shortage and resultant rationing of toilet facilities. He banters with Little Sally, outside of the bounds of the story, about the shape of the play and its title. Officer Lockstock resumes his narration at the end of the first act, the beginning of the second act, and at the end of the play, when he tells the audience what was to occur in the years to come.

Mr. McQueen

Mr. McQueen is Caldwell Cladwell's second in command at UGC. He is a shameless sycophant who praises every word out of Cladwell's mouth.

Mrs. Millennium

Mrs. Millennium is an executive with UGC.

Penelope Pennywise

Ms. Pennywise, often referred to in the play as "Penny," is the proprietor of Public Amenity Number Nine, which is the filthiest urinal in the poorest part of town. She heartlessly refuses anyone who lacks the entry fee the opportunity to use her facilities, no matter how desperate

they may be. Often, when Ms. Pennywise speaks to her employee, Bobby Strong, she refers to his good looks and strength, implying that she has some degree of sexual attraction to him.

In the second act, Penny tries to aid the poor people in their revolution against the corporate/government establishment. It turns out that she has a vested interest in seeing that the revolution ends peacefully: not only does she care about Bobby, but the revolutionaries' hostage, Hope Cladwell, is actually Penny's daughter, a fact that no one in the play previously knew. Ms. Pennywise remembers the heartless Caldwell B. Cladwell from a time before he was wealthy, back when they were both social equals and had an affair.

Little Sally

Along with Officer Lockstock, Little Sally is one of the characters who is sometimes aware that they exist in a play: she talks to him while he is narrating directly to the audience, referring to theatrical conventions that are or are not being followed. When she is not talking outside of the boundaries of the play, Little Sally is a little girl who is saving her money in order to use the public toilet. She is constantly counting her pennies, to see if she has enough.

At the start of act 2, scene 4, it is Little Sally who brings news of Bobby Strong's death to the people in the Secret Hideout. She sings a song that relates his last words, even though she knows how unlikely it sounds that a man thrown off of a roof could have said so much.

Bobby Strong

Bobby is the play's central figure. In the beginning, he is a dutiful employee of Urine Good Company, building a good future for himself while working for his boss, Penelope Pennywise. His perspective starts changing when he sees his own father, Joseph Strong, turned away from Public Amenity Number Nine because he does not have enough money to pay for his admission. What really changes Bobby, though, is when he meets Hope Cladwell and she tells him to listen to his heart. As a result of listening to his heart, he leads the people in a revolt against the company Hope's father owns. After he is killed by the police, Bobby, appearing in the form of a ghost, comes to realize that the poor people are just as guilty as the rich people who control the town, and his ghost warns both sides that they have to work together.

Josephine Strong

Josephine is Bobby Strong's mother and Joseph Strong's wife.

Old Man Strong

"Old Man" Strong, also known as Joseph Strong, only appears in the first scene. He needs to use the public toilet, but Ms. Pennywise refuses to admit him because he does not have enough money, and she tells Strong's son, Bobby, to refuse him admittance too. Desperate, Strong urinates against the side of the building. The police come and take him away. The next time one of the policemen, Officer Barrel, appears on stage, he is carrying a shovel and a mop, indicating that Strong was taken and thrown off a building.

Soupy Sue

One of the poor people who participates in the revolution.

Tiny Tom

Tiny Tom is one of the poor people of the town. Whenever "Old Man" Joseph Strong's ghost comes back and repeats that he does not have the money to enter the urinal because he is "a little short," Tiny Tom gives the same punch line that he gave when Strong said those words the first time: "No shorter than yesterday. Unless I've grown."

THEMES

Class Conflict

The situation established at the beginning of *Urinetown* only really turns into a plot when Bobby Strong decides to lead the poor people who frequent Public Amenity Number Nine in a rebellion against the powerful forces that control their society. Bobby works for the Public Amenity and is therefore a part of the social hierarchy at the beginning of the play. Two things happen, though, to drive him toward rebellion. First, he watches his own father, who is too poor to pay to use the restroom, forced to break the law, and then Bobby sees the police take Joseph Strong away for punishment or death. The second thing to make Bobby declare class warfare is that Hope Cladwell teaches him how to listen to his heart, and in doing so he finds out how much he hates the prevailing social system.

TOPICS FOR FURTHER STUDY

- The song "Follow Your Heart" claims that people can be led to a true path by following what their heart tells them. Research the origins of the common understanding of the "heart" as an organ associated with compassion. Create a timeline that shows how the role of the heart has evolved in common discourse over the centuries.

- Examine the way that the state controls all aspects of society in George Orwell's classic novel *Animal Farm* (1945), and compare it with the way that the Urine Good Company controls society in *Urinetown*. Lead a class discussion about which has more effective techniques and which method would be able to outlast the other.

- In the song "Don't Be the Bunny," Caldwell B. Cladwell warns his daughter to not be weak, or life will take advantage of her. Write a similar song that uses a different animal as a metaphor to represent some advice that you want to impart to the next generation.

- Watch the 1999 movie *Cradle Will Rock*, in which a theater company during the Great Depression works on staging a musical by real-life playwright Marc Blitzstein. Make a short film montage of scenes that you think Kotis and Hollmann might have had in mind when they were writing *Urinetown*. When you show your work to your class, explain at least one scene that you think they should have copied, and explain why it would have benefited them.

- In the play, Officer Lockstock tells the audience that "Urinetown" is "kind of a mythical place... a bad place... it's filled with symbolism and things like that." Choose a geographic location near where you live and write an explanation for the symbolic elements that it could be used to represent.

Led by Bobby, the poor people, who are the only ones forced to use a decrepit, filthy toilet like Public Amenity Number Nine, wrest control of the facility from Urine Good Company, claiming that they have an inherent right to it. The class struggle expands when Caldwell B. Cladwell and his board members come to the site of the protest. The police, who theoretically should be neutral in the matter, side with the wealthy property owners and threaten the poor people, who then kidnap Cladwell's daughter in their own defense.

The play follows through with its class conflict theme by presenting Cladwell as someone who values money over family ties and is willing to accept the death of his own daughter if it will help him quell the revolution. The revolutionaries sacrifice any claim they have to moral ideals when they talk about killing Hope: doing so would certainly hurt their revolution and drive their cause backwards, but some of them want to kill her simply for the thrill of killing. This kind of thinking is certain to bring stronger repression from those in power, continuing the class divide.

Freedom

The word "freedom" is used often in *Urinetown*. On one level, the play is sincere in showing a group of oppressed people who yearn to be free. The poor people in this play are held at a financial disadvantage by the rich, forced to pay whatever fees the Urine Good Company can bribe the corrupt legislation to let them charge, and they are punished by the law if they will not or cannot pay.

On another level, though, the playwrights use the word "freedom" as something that has almost no meaning, mocking it as the sort of noble-sounding word that is used to stir up emotions with no real context. An example of this is the song "Run, Freedom, Run" in the second scene of act 2. Put into the context of a rousing song, "freedom" seems inspiring, but the song does not really say anything about being free: freedom is spoken to as if it were a person and is told to run away from the challenges it faces. When one character admits to being afraid of freedom, Bobby Strong responds with more noble-sounding but empty rhetoric: "Freedom is scary; it's a blast of cool wind that burns your face and wakes you up."

On its surface, *Urinetown* resembles stories that tell of oppressed people struggling for their freedom. In reality, though, it often treats "freedom" as a meaningless word that people use but do not understand.

The cast of Urinetown *appears on stage during the 58th Annual Tony Awards in 2004.*
(Frank Micelotta / Getty Images)

Corruption

Urinetown begins with a situation that is already corrupt, and then the play looks backward to show how that corruption came to be. In the beginning, Caldwell B. Cladwell, who is easily the most corrupt character in the play, having made his fortune by taking advantage of the intrinsic need to urinate, appears to be nothing more than greed personified. As the story progresses, audiences learn more about how he became that way. Penelope Pennywise recalls her affair with Cladwell before he was rich, implying that he once was a man who could love, who could appreciate the thrill of the struggle for life that he found energizing when he was poor, back during the early years of the drought. Cladwell himself explains his corruption in the song "Don't Be the Bunny," telling Hope that the world is hard and unforgiving to people who do not do harm first. Cladwell is a bad, greedy man, but the play shows audiences that social circumstances corrupted him, forcing him to be the way he is.

Other characters in the play show how a bad situation like the twenty-year drought can lead to corruption. At one point, Officer Lockstock claims that he loves the people of the town, but his actions show anything but love: he is ruled by the money paid to him by the privately owned Urine Good Company. Even the poor people themselves show that they are only uncorrupted when they have no power: once Hope Cladwell is their prisoner, they consider murdering her, simply because they can. The power they have over her is a corruptive influence.

In the end, the play takes a position that corruption is not the terrible thing that it might seem to be. Although he has been motivated by greed, Cladwell turns out to have been the town's savior. By cloaking his greed in a social policy meant to make it seem positive, he actually did help conserve the little water that was left. In this way, *Urinetown* shows corruption to be a part of the natural order, not a diversion from it.

STYLE

Parody

Urinetown has an original story, but many distinct elements of its story are parodies, or humorous variations on other works. For the most part, it parodies works from the musical theater tradition. In his introduction to the book, Hollmann acknowledges that he had in mind the works of the German playwright Bertolt Brecht and the German-born composer Kurt Weill, who wrote musicals about class struggle in the early twentieth century, in writing several tunes for this play, including "It's a Privilege to Pee." Hollmann also acknowledged that he was trying to capture the mood of a traditional hymn in "I See a River," and "a typical second-act musical-comedy gospel tune" in "Run, Freedom, Run." Critics have also noted that the musical style and choreography of the song "Snuff That Girl" is a parody of the song "Cool," by Leonard Bernstein and Stephen Sondheim, presented on Broadway in 1957 in *West Side Story*.

The romance between Bobby Strong and Hope Cladwell in this play is a direct parody of the romantic element that is traditionally forced into Broadway musicals, whether relevant to the story being told or not. They come from opposite sides of two warring factions, a tradition going back at least as far as William Shakespeare's *Romeo and Juliet*. Their ideas about hearts intertwining and hearts speaking to each other are clichés, but Hollmann and Kotis poke fun at these clichés by having the characters acknowledge them once in a while, such as questioning how much a heart is speaking or crossing the line from the metaphoric "heart" to the one that has veins and aortas.

Narrator Role

Plays do not always have a narrator, letting their characters present their stories onstage and trusting the audiences to pick up necessary information from what is presented. In *Urinetown*, there is a narrator, Officer Lockstock. He stands at the front of the stage before the action begins in the first act and tells audiences what the situation is, and he stands there at the end of the play to tell them about the events that occurred in the years after the actions they have witnessed. He also comes forward to speak as the narrator at the end of act 1 and the beginning of act 2. As a character in the play, Officer Lockstock is limited in what he knows, but as the narrator, his knowledge is unlimited.

When Little Sally talks to Officer Lockstock as he is narrating, the two of them banter in a way that not only shows that they are aware of being in a musical play, but that also reflects on the traditions of such musical plays. They talk about the title, *Urinetown*; they talk about the commercial drawbacks of having a narrator reveal too much directly to an audience in exposition, and of how unpopular a musical with a sad ending is destined to be. They are aware of their existence as characters at a theater, standing in front of an audience, but then they instantly join the characters within the play and lose their awareness of the world outside of the world in which they live.

HISTORICAL CONTEXT

The original date scheduled for *Urinetown*'s premier on Broadway was Thursday, September 13, 2001. After the terrorist attacks on New York and Washington, D.C., that occurred two days earlier, on September 11, that date was considered impossible to meet. In the months after the attacks, much

Jeff McCarthy and Spencer Kayden during the curtain call for the closing of Urinetown
(Peter Kramer / Getty Images)

changed in American life, including serious doubts about whether the Broadway theater tradition would be able to survive the social upheaval at all.

On the morning of September 11, 2001, New York City was thrown into chaos when American Airlines Boston-to-Los Angeles flight 11 that had been taken over by armed hijackers crashed into the north tower of the World Trade Center in lower Manhattan at 8:46 a.m. The plane, filled with jet fuel for the cross-continent flight, exploded and began a fire. Seventeen minutes later, as rescue teams raced to help those trapped in the north tower, hijacked United Airlines Boston-to-Los Angeles flight 175 crashed into the matching south tower. Within eighty-five minutes, both 110-story towers had collapsed, creating a deafening roar that shook the entire metropolitan area and released a plume of dust that was large enough to be seen from space. Though the terrorists' plot focused on Manhattan, where it was most successful in terms of carnage caused and in

attracting media attention, there were two other planes hijacked that morning. An American Airlines plane flying out of Washington, D.C., Dulles Airport was crashed into the Pentagon Building, and a plane flying out of Newark, New Jersey, was probably being taken to crash into the U.S. Capitol, but it was forced down in a field in Pennsylvania when passengers heard news of the New York attacks and fought back against their hijackers. Approximately 2,600 people died in the destruction of the World Trade Center, and 125 died at the Pentagon: the passengers and crew on all four hijacked planes raised the death rate another 246.

The attacks shocked the world, leading governments across the globe to reassess the measures they would be willing to use against terrorists. Financially, the airline industry suffered immense losses, as all commercial air traffic in the United States was halted for several days and then, when planes were allowed to fly again, many would-be travelers avoided air travel because of what they had witnessed. The United States tourism industry dropped precipitously, as travelers from other countries cancelled vacation plans, fearing that the United States would not be safe. Lower Manhattan has traditionally been a center for the banking industry in the United States, and many major banks had their headquarters in the World Trade Center, or nearby: records became inaccessible if not lost, and key personnel were killed in the attacks.

Broadway, the country's home of legitimate theater, is just a few miles from where the World Trade Center fell. The decision was made by 10:30 on the morning of September 11 to cancel all Broadway performances for the next few days. Performances were also cancelled in Washington. In both cities, performers and crew were devastated, hit closely by deaths of loved ones. Shows were also cancelled in cities across the country, such as Chicago, Los Angeles, and Houston, that had not been directly hit by the terrorist attacks. In addition, other diversions, such as Major League Baseball, which had not been suspended since the height of World War II, were put on hold for a few days. In the confused days following the attacks, it would have seemed callous to go on with entertainment programs. People were frightened, angry, and sad: they were not in the mood to be entertained.

Theaters reopened later that week, but the Broadway theater scene was to feel the effects of the attack for a long time. Ticket sales were down roughly 50 percent, much of it due to the loss of tourists who shunned Manhattan. Four shows that had been struggling before the attacks closed immediately, and several others closed within a month. Performers and crews took pay cuts of 25 percent to 50 percent to keep their shows open. When *Urinetown* opened a week later, on September 20, it had good sales, but it took more than a year for Broadway theater in general to regain the position it had lost.

CRITICAL OVERVIEW

Urinetown has been popular with audiences, moving quickly from its 1999 premier at the New York International Fringe Festival to its off-Broadway premier two years later, and then moving up to a legitimate Broadway theater in less than a year. In part, audiences seem to have

responded to its general silliness and its lack of pretension. As Nancy Franklin noted in the *New Yorker*:

> [The] show is a terrifically spirited sendup of musicals and their conventions—just the thing for older audiences who have endured some pretty bad serious musicals on Broadway in recent years and for younger audiences who may be more inclined to spend their money on software or shoes than on a Broadway show.

Mark Steyn made a similar point in his review in the *New Criterion*, dismissing those who might find the subject matter distasteful.

> A musical about urine...is still a cut above musicals about musicals, musicals about operetta, musicals about Hollywood, and all the other lame parodies parodying things most of us only know from other parodies."

The show's lack of substance, however, left some critics unimpressed. John Simon, for example, writing in *New York* magazine, found that it lacked even the rudimentary sense of originality that is the mark of a good play. "The originality of *Urinetown*," he wrote,

> if it has any, lies in the equal contempt for the rich and the poor, and in what would be a tragic ending if persiflage could yield to pathos. But if anything makes a show ridiculous rather than entertaining, it is an anything-goes attitude: The thrown-in kitchen sink always lands with a thud.

Robert Brustein agreed, noting in his review in the *New Republic*, that "the tone of the evening is so ambivalent and uncommitted and frivolous that ultimately you don't care about the fates of any of the characters."

In addition to critics who found *Urinetown* not-so-bad and those who found it not-good-enough, there were those critics who actually liked it. Richard Zoglin, for example, wrote a review in *Time* magazine that included the play with two others that he considered better than *The Producers*, the runaway hit from the same year that was widely credited with no less than reviving the energy and commercial interest of the Broadway musical theater tradition. After noting that *The Producers* was great but not groundbreaking, Zoglin went on to praise *Urinetown* for its audacity: "The vest-pocket production has outsize energy, as does the terrific, beefy Kurt Weill-like score by Mark Hollmann and Greg Kotis. They aim for comic-operatic heights and keep the audience soaring."

CRITICISM

David Kelly

Kelly is a writer and an instructor of creative writing and literature. In the following essay, he explores why some critics enjoy Urinetown *but others find the play unengaging.*

When critics favor Greg Kotis and Mark Hollmann's musical *Urinetown*, it is generally because they admire the playwrights' willingness to stick to their own convictions of silliness: unlike traditional Broadway musicals, this play does not spare any character or situation from savage mockery in order to please its audiences. When critics dislike the play, however, it is generally for the same reason, though they see it with different results: they find the entire production difficult to care about, lacking as it is in any serious emotion. Each side is right, of course. *Urinetown* does steer clear of the standard pattern by refusing to provide even one character that audiences might want to identify with. It takes place in a parody world of its authors' creation, one where people are either motivated by greed and cowardice or, if not, they can be expected to be, after they have wised up, given in to corruption, and dropped their simplistic delusions.

Books, plays, and movies often let their audiences see through the attractive coating that is wrapped around the social order, showing them an ugly, hardened reality that they then present as being the way things really work. What marks *Urinetown* as a particularly cynical piece is the way that Kotis and Hollmann keep tearing off layer after layer of veneer until they reach the social core, passing through levels of idiocy and hypocrisy but never finding any layer that they can present as good or true. There is no hope that would make the world of this work a worthwhile place, not even from the one sweet, well-meaning character whose name is actually "Hope." The play ends with a sense of futility that the playwrights then invite audiences to join them in laughing about, a shared sense of doom that usually does not sell out Broadway houses or win Tony Awards.

Most of the characters in the play are simply terrible at heart, lacking any redeeming features. This is most obviously the case with Caldwell B. Cladwell, the mogul so ruthless that he sings a song about killing bunny rabbits to illustrate his point about Darwinian survival and then later

> KOTIS AND HOLLMANN SEEM TO LIKE THEIR CHARACTER, AND THEY WANT AUDIENCES TO LIKE HIM TOO, BUT IN THE END THEY ARE NOT WILLING TO SPARE HIM THE SAME SATIRIC BLADE THAT THEY USE TO DISSECT THE RICH AND MIGHTY CHARACTERS."

provokes the rebels who hold his daughter hostage, because bowing to their demands would be bad for his corporation. Cladwell is surrounded by sycophants and flunkies, including one senator, who might question his wisdom and in fact do later express their regret about having listened to him, but who would never dare challenge his authority out loud.

Greedy corporations, the executives who run them, and the cowardly functionaries (including corrupt politicians) who keep them alive have been pretty standard targets for comedy throughout the ages. Humor takes many forms, but one of its principal tenets is the reversal of expectations. People need to believe that the society they live in has a core of intelligence and competence and is in the hands of others who are at least somewhat concerned with the general good. Satire has therefore, through the ages, earned laughs by showing a world where those who should care are in fact uncaring, where those who are good are so only because they are dolts. Not even the most demanding critic could fault the writers of *Urinetown* for mining such a rich vein of satire as corporations and politicians for laughs. The basic premise of the play is that corporations and politicians are making money off of one of the most intrinsic functions of the human body: a critic who proclaims that it is a "cynical" play is merely stating the obvious.

Usually, though, playwrights will anchor an absurd premise around one or more "normal" characters who exist in the world of the artistic work but have the moral sensibilities of contemporary society. These characters can see the craziness that the audience members see. The character coming closest to this description in *Urinetown* is Bobby Strong, who decides to make a stand against the totalitarian

WHAT DO I READ NEXT?

- When *Urinetown* opened on Broadway, the biggest original show in town was the stage adaptation of Mel Brooks's *The Producers*, which won twelve Tony Awards. The book for the play, which Brooks wrote with Tom Meehan, is available in a deluxe illustrated edition from Roundtable Press, published in 2001.

- A show that carries on the satirical spirit of *Urinetown* is *Avenue Q*, which opened on Broadway in July 2003. Based on the visual style of the television show *Sesame Street*, *Avenue Q* puts puppets in real-life situations, coping with prostitution, drug use, and race. The book, with text by Zachary Pincus-Roth, is available from Hyperion, published in 2006.

- One of the most identifiable sources being parodied in this play is *Mahogany* by Bertolt Brecht and Kurt Weill (sometimes known as *The Little Mahogany* or by its original German title, *Aufstieg und Fall der Stadt Mahagonny*). An experimental opera about the struggle between the working class and the leisure class, it was originally staged in 1927, and the script can be found in book form as *The Rise and Fall of the City of Mahogany*, published in 1975 by Oxford University Press.

- Jeanne DuPrau's novel *The City of Ember* is a dark story written for young adults that takes a serious look at the situation made fun of in *Urinetown*: it takes place in a futuristic world with diminishing natural resources, where people are assigned their life's occupations at an early age and are expected to quietly follow the dictates of corporations. Published in 2003 by Random House, this book has already spawned several sequels.

- The circumstances in *Urinetown* are more realistic than many people like to acknowledge. In *Water Wars: Drought, Flood, Folly, and the Politics of Thirst*, Diane Raines Ward examines the complex ecological situation that is making water scarcer in some parts of the globe. This comprehensive book was published in 2002 by Riverhead Books.

- Nineteenth-century author Thomas Malthus, who is mentioned in the play's final lines, is known for his hard, unsentimental look at how population growth will one day make life on this planet unsustainable. His *An Essay on the Principle of Population*, published in 1798 and available in book form in a 2007 Dover Press edition, lays out a theory of humankind's growing struggle that has influenced economists and social planners for centuries.

---

control of the play's Urine Good Company, costing him his job, and, eventually, his life. Bobby works as an appropriate surrogate for the audience members in several ways. For one thing, he is poor. This is generally not an attribute of most theater patrons, but it does help draw a clear contrast between Bobby's values and the values of the members of the Urine Good Company board. Audience members, disgusted with the wealthy people in this play, identify with the poor more plainly than with the rich they see onstage. Another reason audience members relate to Bobby is that he is an idealist, which also might not describe the average audience

member until they start to identify themselves in contrast to the play's many immoral characters. Finally, Bobby still has enough enthusiasm in him to fall in love at first sight—if this is not a trait that most audience members have, it is certainly a trait that everyone would like to imagine that they possess.

In the end, though, Bobby dies the death of a fool, not the death of a hero, and audiences detach themselves from him immediately. He is tossed off of a roof by two lowly policemen, and his dying words, at first inspirational, drag on and on until their initial nobility becomes nothing more than a joke. Kotis and Hollmann seem to like their character, and they want audiences to like him too, but in the end they are not willing to spare him the same satiric blade that they use to dissect the rich and mighty characters. Audience members and critics end up feeling betrayed to find that there is no more nobility in Bobby Strong's idealism than there is in corruption.

After Bobby's death, the play's one chance for an emotional connection with its audience is Hope Cladwell. From the moment when she first comes onstage, Hope is presented as being sweet but clueless, somewhat vacant: not only is she the spoiled child, educated at the "Most Expensive University in the World" to take a soft position as "a fax/copy girl," but she blurts out her sentimental enthusiasms too readily. She changes after Bobby dies, though. She takes charge of his revolution against the company that she is meant to inherit. She opens the toilets up for free use by the public. She has her father and his underlings killed. She is poised to fit the role of the play's inspirational leader, even bearing some shadings of a born-again religious archetype.

That all ends, though, when the narrator, Officer Lockstock, tells the audience that Hope's well-intentioned meddling was to lead to a hastening of the environmental destruction that her father's self-serving rationing helped stave off. Hidden in the middle of the narrator's synopsis of the years to come is the fact that the poor people Hope led forward with compassion are to eventually rise up and kill her out of resentment.

This is surely where the critics' animosity comes from. Hope, who seemed to be the one character to develop a working conscience, dies as an afterthought, her death so crude a joke that the story has no place for it onstage, resorting to having this unpleasantness told but not dramatized. Anyone who hoped that some good might come of this situation must be disappointed: Kotis and Hollmann kill hope, in both senses of the word. In the last few lines of the play, the mirror world presented in *Urinetown* turns out to be not funny and sad, just sad. The humorous reversal of finding out that Hope cannot fix her society's ills with kindness alone is good for one laugh, but after it has been played, audiences exit with the message that those who care about anything that has happened over the course of the past two hours are suckers.

Comedies exist to amuse their audiences, and tragedies exist to warn against the fates of those who are careless or unlucky. There is nothing inherent in either genre that requires that characters should maintain their dignity. This, at least, seems to be the premise that the authors of *Urinetown* would hold up in their defense, if ever called to face the fact that some viewers find their play to be funny but insubstantial. Tens of thousands of audience members have agreed over the years: this play has a thought-provoking premise, fiendishly clever lyrics, and enough elements of the traditional Broadway musical to show that it is breaking those traditions consciously. To others, though, a joke is just a joke, and, in the end, nothing more. To them, *Urinetown* has nothing to say about what is good in this world, only about what is not.

Source: David Kelly, Critical Essay on *Urinetown*, in *Drama for Students*, Gale, Cengage Learning, 2010.

Julia Katz and Erin Spangler
In the following review, Urinetown, *a popular production for universities and high schools, is critiqued by two high school students.*

Sometimes art really does mirror life.

Albert Einstein High School's musical *Urinetown* boldly takes on a recessionary economy, the mismanagement of greedy corporations, rapidly deteriorating natural resources, the stark differences between Wall Street and Main Street—and potty humor. In a solid farce, Einstein students certainly kept in touch with the times—while still laughing at the absurdity of it all.

One day, playwright-lyricist Greg Kotis really, really had to go, but found himself at a toilet with a fee attached. Collaborating with Mark Hollmann, Kotis turned this odd experience into the Tony Award-winning *Urinetown*, a Broadway production poking fun at politics and the typical American musical.

Set in a drought-ridden fictional town where it soon becomes clear that "It's a Privilege to Pee" when the government mandates pay-per-use public potties, run by wealthy Caldwell Cladwell's Urine Good Co., to conserve water. But Cladwell's optimistic daughter Hope inadvertently encourages frustrated worker Bobby Strong by telling him to "Follow Your Heart" and start a revolution.

Malika Cherifi, mesmerizing from her first appearance through the final curtain, led the company as witty policewoman—and narrator—Officer

Lockstock. Excelling in a classically male role is no easy feat, but spot-on characterization and a lush alto range made Cherifi's performance a hit.

Cherifi's wacky gestures and swift wisecracks were shared with Awate Serequeberhan's tough-guy cop, Officer Barrel, a smaller part that made a huge difference in Einstein's production. Serequeberhan's New York accent and comic range garnered significant laughter throughout the show, as did Tracey Gearhart's precocious portrayal of Little Sally. With her persistent curious questions, Gearhart showcased a witty nature and rarely strayed from her adorable character.

As archetypal hero Bobby Strong and ingenue lover Hope Cladwell, Dan Patrick Leano and Madeleine Grewell each succeeded in difficult roles. Leano's melodic voice rang true in songs such as "Run Freedom, Run," while Grewell's cutesy voice and frivolous movements perfectly suited her character.

Many of the Rebel Poor were an energetic, fun ensemble, such as happy-go-lucky Tiny Tom (Aaron Fellows) and Hot Blades Harry (Milton D. Garcia). A few missteps in musical and comic timing left some songs and gags seeming lackluster.

Standout technical elements at Einstein included the innovative lighting design by Matt Jones, who creatively placed many lights on the stage itself. These were used with more traditional spotlights and beams, all of which were cued flawlessly with the help of crew members Minh Pham, Alexandra Christie, Molly Moses, Ben Sudbrink and Joanne Conelley. The set was also commendable, with different levels and urinal-like pieces on each side that aided actors through many jokes, often a pleasant distraction from screechy microphone quality.

With all the economic issues plaguing Americans today, it seems that we're in what Einstein students might call "The Stink Years." But though the amusing comedy *Urinetown* is by no means a happy musical, let's hope that our story will have a brighter ending—and a slightly more appealing title.

Julia Katz

McLean High School

What musical combines satire of capitalistic society, reverse pantomime and a whole lot of bathroom humor? Over the weekend, the answer to this question was found in the weird farce that was Albert Einstein High School's production of *Urinetown*.

Urinetown: The Musical was created by playwright Greg Kotis after a vacation in Europe, where the existence of "pay to pee" bathrooms inspired him to write the story. The narrative follows the unlikely romance between a cutesy bourgeois daughter of the president of the Urine Good Co. (UGC) and a rebellious amenity worker. After a showing at the New York International Fringe Festival, the musical comedy eventually made it to Broadway, where it earned Tony Awards for best director, best original score and best book of a musical.

Albert Einstein's production was anchored by its ensembles both big and small. The supporting actors were able to significantly add to the performances of the leads with little character details that made the whole production quite believable.

Malika Cherifi, as the tongue-in-cheek narrator Officer Lockstock, had perfect physicality and delivery in her many humorous lines and sang with a clear and pleasant voice. She worked flawlessly with Awate Serequeberhan, who played Officer Barrel. Serequeberhan pulled off a very convincing New York accent and was able to commit entirely to his character, even in improvised bits before the overture and during the intermission.

The strength of the Rebel Poor ensemble, UGC staff ensemble and other supporting characters made up for any deficiencies with more major characters. Although some of the actors were a bit wooden, the movement and dancing of the ensembles were intricate and in sync, especially in the show-stopping satire of "Run, Freedom, Run."

Urinetown requires a great range in vocals, and although many actors had trouble keeping on pitch, Elizabeth Ebron as Penelope Pennywise had strong and spectacular range. Tracey Gearhart, as the philosophical Little Sally, depicted a Cindy Lou Who-esque innocence that was committed and gutsy—not awkward or nervous.

The production was generally technically solid. Matt Jones's lights were very well designed and executed, especially the use of flashlights in "The Cop Song." Although some technical aspects detracted slightly from the performance, making the timing confusing or the actors hard to hear, the sets, including huge urinals, were interesting and funny in of themselves.

Although silly and slapstick, *Urinetown* brings to light the paradox that is modern politics and makes its audience think of ways to refine the problems presented in this unhappy musical. Einstein's production was generally a privilege to watch, just as much as it was a "privilege to pee" for the characters onstage.

Erin Spangler

West Potomac High School

Source: Julia Katz and Erin Spangler, "A Relevant Musical for a Country with an Economy in the Toilet," in *Washington Post*, March 26, 2009, p. GZ17.

Rebecca Stone Thornberry
In the following review, Thornberry covers everything from acting to production values in a major regional production of Urinetown.

In 1989, musical theatre performers with disabilities created The Physically Handicapped Actors and Musical Artists League (PHAMALy), a Denver-based not-for-profit theatre, to establish a venue in which their disabilities would be treated as part of the given circumstances of the production process. Company members live with a wide range of disabilities: some are blind, for example, while others are of short stature, hard of hearing, use wheelchairs, or have conditions such as Parkinson's, cerebral palsy, or bipolar disorder. PHAMALy's entertaining, provocative productions educate audiences and the theatrical community about performers' capabilities, focus, and determination, as well as the creative uses to which disability can be put onstage.

PHAMALy's production of Kotis and Hollman's *Urinetown, The Musical!* aggressively confronted issues of difference by casting performers with physical and developmental disabilities. Artistic director Steve Wilson's clever production, mounted at the Denver Center's 550-seat Space Theatre from 27 July to 19 August 2007, drew enthusiastic audience response. Merged with surprising design elements, his tongue-in-cheek, if not always successful, direction created a deft, funny, and moving production characterized by capable, irreverent performances. *Urinetown,* about a drought-stricken society whose citizens must relieve themselves in corporate pay toilets or face banishment, was an excellent vehicle for these artists, who are known for ingeniously reframing conditions that many producers might deem insurmountable. This production's in-your-face performance style, energy, and dark sense of humor destabilized disability—more often constructed as something to be hidden or spoken of in hushed, serious tones.

The director effectively mined the play's humor and kept an appropriately fast pace throughout. Taking full advantage of the intimate, arena-style theatre, he surprised the audience by rapidly shifting focus between levels, even employing the grid as the rooftop from which the corrupt Officer Lockstock, and his sidekick Barrel catapult hero Bobby Strong. One of Wilson's most intriguing uses of disability highlighted a central theme of the play: the blindness of the wealthy and powerful to the suffering of the disenfranchised. Wilson's casting of blind actors as the corporate drones of Urine Good Company, owner of the city's public toilets, proved an amusing intellectual concept, but the joke lacked adequate variety over the multiple scenes in which these characters appear. Wilson's decision to place blind performers in a synchronized chorus line during the song "Mr. Cladwell," for instance, was a laudably bold choice—we do not expect blind actors who are not necessarily trained dancers to venture into Rockette territory. However, the moment was undercut, not because the dancers could not see, but because the execution lacked the degree of precision expected from such choreography. Wilson admirably staged and executed the script's swift transitions, and the term "ensemble" acquired new meaning as performers took responsibility for helping one another enter, exit, and change position on the dimly lit stage. For example, a cast member in a wheelchair helped guide blind actors offstage: grasping the wheelchair's handles, they were led safely past open traps as the stage picture shifted.

Juliet Vila and Andrew Caldwell delivered engaging performances as Hope Cladwell and Bobby Strong. Vila, who is blind, is a gifted comedienne, with a sweet, clear soprano singing voice and an understanding of both Hope's love for Bobby and her seemingly inborn quest for power. She employed a gentle, singsong voice and a tentative smile to portray Hope as a naive supporter of Bobby and his revolution. After Bobby's death, she markedly changed her vocal and physical choices, employing a gruffer intonation and a maniacal grin, to reveal Hope as even more grasping and conniving than her father. Caldwell, a likeable leading man, made Bobby strong, centered, and believable. Vila and Caldwell's interplay became particularly interesting where physical touch replaced eye contact as their primary means of communication.

As Penelope Pennywise, who presides over one of the city's public toilets, Kathleen Traylor conveyed both the character's aggressive exterior and her heart of gold. From her wheelchair, Traylor, a double-amputee, played Pennywise as a pragmatic graduate of the school of hard knocks who wasted little time on sympathy. Mallory Kay Nelson's costume design, employed to full comedic effect by Traylor, incorporated a tight-fitting bustier and, most surprisingly, a removable plunger and mop as Pennywise's prosthetic legs.

Scenic designers Charles Packard and Jennifer Orf ingeniously solved a particular difficulty of staging *Urinetown* in the round: a number of scenes revolve around a public pay toilet. After considering sight-line issues, the designers forwent a standing unit and instead painted two traps as manhole covers with prominent wheelchair logos. When entering the "public amenity," performers simply stood on or, in the case of those in wheelchairs, rolled over the traps. They were then lowered approximately three feet and bravely mimed relieving themselves in partial view of the audience—a shrewd comment on the privacy concerns of some with physical disabilities. In a playful statement about the daily reality of some people with disabilities, an actor in a wheelchair emptied his colostomy bag into this unusual lavatory.

Urinetown's lyrics acquired additional significance when framed as references to stigmatization and disability. When Traylor's Pennywise growled, "You're no different, then, from lowly me," while glaring up from her wheelchair, the line resonated as a comment on the social construction of disability. In this world, Pennywise clearly retained control despite an otherwise disadvantageous physical condition. In "We're Not Sorry," the ensemble sang a phrase that epitomizes PHAMALy's spirit and could easily serve as the company's motto: "We're not sorry, hey that's life."

Although PHAMALy's focus remains musical theatre, it has performed works such as Thornton Wilder's *Our Town* (January 2007) and Dale Wasserman's *One Flew Over the Cuckoo's Nest* (January 2008), adapted from Ken Kesey's novel. In June 2008, PHAMALy will restage its controversial, critically acclaimed 1999 production of Henry Krieger and Bill Russell's musical *Side Show* about the stigmatization of those whose bodies challenge conventional expectations of the human form. The company will undoubtedly bring its inventive humor and unique, affecting perspective to that work as well.

Source: Rebecca Stone Thornberry, Review of *Urinetown: The Musical*, in *Theatre Journal*, Vol. 60, No. 2, May 2008, pp. 278–80.

Robert Cushman

In the following review, Cushman summarizes the musical numbers and the success of the Hollmann/Kotis team in a Toronto production of Urinetown.

I wouldn't want to give away the beginning. Still, I have to say, even before the overture is played, *Urinetown* is hysterically funny. The overture itself is hilarious; it's a parody, with every taut dissonance in place, of the opening music from *The Threepenny Opera*. Then comes the first song; and that's great, too. In fact, for its first 10 minutes, *Urinetown* is musical-comedy heaven.

That first number is delivered by a loquacious cop named Lockstock. (It later transpires he has a comparatively silent partner called Barrel.) Lockstock is here to tell us about "Urinetown the musical. Not the place." We won't see the place, he informs us, until Act Two, though he does warn us: "It's filled with symbolism and things like that."

Lockstock is assisted in his narrative duties by Little Sally, a presumably orphaned waif who feeds him questions like "Is this where you tell the audience about the water shortage?" Lockstock shushes her: "You're too young to understand it now, but nothing can kill a show like too much exposition." The title of the number is "Too Much Exposition."

Urinetown is a satire on matters political and environmental. It is also a satire on the idea of doing a musical satire in the first place. This higher or self-referential level provides most of the jokes. Or rather, most of the joke, because the show keeps making the same one in different words. I laughed heartily to begin with, but less heartily as the idea—"the central conceit," to quote Lockstock slightly out of context—kept coming back for more. But I have to confess that when it comes around the last time it does so with a twist that justifies most of what has gone before. Urinetown (The Musical) plainly thinks it's very clever and very funny. It overrates itself on the second count but is absolutely accurate on the first.

At the risk of burdening this review with too much exposition: The water shortage became a drought, and this gave the government the excuse to hand over all toilet facilities to a private corporation, the Urine Good Company, which runs them on a fee-for-use basis at a handsome profit. Any citizen found hoarding (though that may not be the right expression) is consigned to the dreaded Urinetown, the musical theatre's answer to Room 101.

The corporation is run by the ruthless Caldwell B. Cladwell, who has a corrupt senator in his pay. (Senators in musicals are always corrupt. This is an inviolable tradition that may have originated in Ancient Rome.) He also has a daughter, whom he was unwise enough to christen Hope. Hope is a college graduate and an idealist. She believes in love. She takes an upstanding but confused young man named Bobby Strong, and, by having him listen closely to her beating heart, turns him into a hero. He leads a rebellion. This being a musical, it succeeds. This being, as it is at pains to assure us, an unconventional musical, the revolution has consequences undreamed of in most shows, even the ones that keep singing at us that dreaming is all-important.

According to Little Sally (and if you haven't heard it from her, you'll have heard it from *Urinetown*'s abundant pre-publicity) another item that could kill a show is a bad title. She's obviously right. Look at *Les Miserables*. This show has *Les Mis* in its sights from the get-go, though it only closes with it toward the end. In *Urinetown,* as not in *Les Mis,* we are actually told why the people are revolting.

It cannot, however, avoid taking on board some of its target's deficiencies. The actual narrative, as heroes and villains and attendant rabble are manoeuvred into position, tends to trundle. The fact that it's being played for laughs rather than sentiment makes less difference than you might think.

Greg Kotis had the idea, which is inspired, and wrote the book, which sometimes isn't. (Give it credit: It is, in the circumstances, remarkably un-scatological. That's a relief.) He also, with composer Mark Hollmann, wrote the lyrics. These have both point and point of view, and they are, when not cramming in too many syllables to be comprehensible, decent. But there is no special joy in them; even I, who love to quote lyrics, feel no urge to quote any of these. Cladwell's big cynical number, "Don't Be the

Bunny," might be better for an occasional change of animal.

The show does have three great and glittering weapons: the music, the staging and the performance. Hollmann's score is super-pastiche; it takes in the styles of just about every musical in circulation while maintaining its own delighted voice. The opening *Threepenny Opera* strains are its Ground Zero, though its greater debt is to the next Brecht-Weill piece, that classic among dystopian musicals, *Mahagonny*. (Actually, *Urinetown* is better satire than *Mahagonny*. For one thing, it makes sense.) The music also draws on sunnier sources like *Bye Bye Birdie* and *The Music Man;* at least I can't think of any better analogue for the rapped-out "Cop Song" than the latter show's "Ya Got Trouble," Urinetown (The Place) being River City with the river dried up. One song, "Run Freedom Run," sort of mutates, starting out by mocking Broadway's idea of country and finishing by crucifying its notion of gospel. The audience claps along as if it were the real thing, leaving you wondering on whom is the joke. A late anthem, "Tell Her I Love Her," impales French musical epics in all their pomposity, while the finale, "I See a River," is a wonderfully vacuous piece of sturdy uplift.

John Rando's direction and John Caraffa's choreography, both imported from the 2001 New York production, supply a great, zany commentary. It's a delight to see a staircase wheeled into position so that Hope and Bobby may serenade one another, Tony-and-Maria-style. Indeed, one of the great joys of the show comes in seeing the insufferably virtuous romantic leads taken down a lot of pegs. Bobby meets just the fate you would want for him. As for Hope, whose divided loyalties make her both heroine and hostage: It was presumably the script's idea to have her spend most of Act Two gagged and bound to a chair, but I imagine it was the production's to have her contributing enthusiastically to one of the numbers from that position.

There is much fun, too, in the staging of the insurrection, when the mob have Cladwell on the run and Lockstock over a Barrel. Suddenly everyone starts walking in slow motion. It's about this time, too, that Little Sally makes an unexplained and unexpected appearance on roller skates. And just as the show begins before its beginning, so too it continues after its close with the company twirling around in a celebratory dance that looks like something left over from *Fiddler on the Roof*. Come to think of it, Cladwell has earlier executed some melismatic cadenzas that outdo "If I Were a Rich Man." Which is fair, because he really is.

The actors maintain the high standards we are coming to expect from homegrown casts in American musicals. David Keeley as Lockstock is butter-smooth, as genial as he is sinister; as Miss Pennywise, the unappetizing proprietress of the even less appetizing Public Amenity No. 9, Mary Ann McDonald reveals a gratifying talent for tuneful overacting; Stephen Patterson and Cara Leslie are straight-faced star-crossed carollers; Frank Moore is an efficient Mr. Big; and Jennifer Walser's Sally is everything you would imagine an omniscient moppet to be. As for the downtrodden poor, they are deeply unsavoury and spend most of their time in a sewer. What else would you expect?

Source: Robert Cushman, "You Gotta Go," in *National Post* (Canada), May 31, 2004, p. AL2.

Toronto Star

The following review describes a perspective on the Broadway production of the musical before New York ticket sales were affected by 9/11.

The New York theatre season really gets going Thursday night with the Broadway opening of a show that arrives with so much positive press and popular buzz that it seems to have "Number 1" built into its very title.

Say hello to *Urinetown*.

It all began when Greg Kotis and Mark Hollmann—the 30-something authors of this piece of sardonic musical merriment—failed to place their brainchild in dozens of conventional regional theatres.

Even with hindsight, it isn't hard to understand why their initial attempts failed to generate much enthusiasm. The show is a savage satire on our society, set in a not-too-distant future when a monopoly controls all public washrooms and makes everyone plunk down a fee to use them.

Or, as the grasping Penelope Pennywise sings in one of the show's first numbers:

"I run the only toilet
In this part of town, you see.
So if you've got to go,
You've got to go through me.
It's a privilege to pee."

Is it any wonder most theatres chose to do *Forever Plaid* instead?

In desperation, Kotis and Hollmann snagged a place in the 1999 New York International Fringe Festival. The show was an instant hit with fringe audiences. Pulitzer Prize-winning playwright David Auburn (*Proof*) liked it as well and persuaded some producers to catch its last performance.

Nearly two years of rewriting and recasting followed, and the show acquired one of New York's hottest directors, John Rando (*The Dinner Party*). It finally debuted last May off-Broadway to an ecstatic critical response and sold-out houses.

And now it's opening at Henry Miller's Theatre for what everyone hopes will be a long and successful run.

I caught the show last spring and was blown away like my critical colleagues. Any initial scepticism vanished during a cheeky opening dialogue between a hardbitten cop, Officer Lockstock (of course, his partner is Officer Barrel), and a streetwise urchin named Little Sally.

Sally is busy explaining the plot to the audience, but Lockstock reminds her "Nothing can kill a show like too much exposition."

She's got a ready answer: "How about bad subject matter? Or a bad title? That could kill a show pretty good."

The rest of the book by Kotis keeps that sly double standard going, and although it droops a bit near the end of Act II, well, so does *The Producers*.

The music by Hollmann is solidly melodic as well as breezily eclectic, suggesting a crossbreeding of Kurt Weill and Cy Coleman in the jaunty numbers and offering up ballads that sound like a shotgun marriage between Stephen Sondheim and the British mega-musicals. (If you can't get down to Manhattan, you can still savour the score on the delightful RCA-Victor recording, or visit the show's amusing Web site: www.urinetownthemusical.com).

Rando has staged it all with great inventiveness (the actors roam throughout the theatre), and the singing voices of the 16-member company can't be bettered.

Broadway veteran and TV star (*Northern Exposure*) John Cullum anchors the proceedings as the venal Caldwell B. Cladwell who runs this pay-for-pee operation, stopping the show with his exhortation to avoid playing the victim, "Don't Be The Bunny."

Urinetown is actually a funkier, feistier riff on that other smash, *The Producers*. Both of them exult in the form of the musical, and celebrate it in high style even while they're deconstructing it with manic glee.

And at bottom, they both have serious things in mind—about society, authority and the cupidity of human nature—although you wouldn't suspect it at first because of the jubilation they generate in the theatre.

The triumph of *Urinetown* made me think about the Toronto Fringe Cinderella, *The Drowsy Chaperone*—a mindless spoof of 1930s musicals—and the similarities and differences it shared with its Gotham cousin.

Both shows opened in the summer of 1999 and proved immediate hits in their alternative venues. But the next step revealed the differences.

Urinetown threw out the entire creative team that had done it at the fringe except for one actor. The authors realized that if their work was to triumph on a broader canvas, they needed all the A-level support they could get. Then they had a series of private readings and workshops, added a savvy production team, and launched off-Broadway nearly two years later.

Only when it succeeded there did they think of moving it to Broadway.

The Drowsy Chaperone, however, rushed five months after the fringe festival into our own version of off-Broadway, a run at Theatre Passe Muraille, marginally expanded, with the original cast and creators largely intact. It was still successful, but a carping note was sounded by some critics (myself included) who found this wafer-thin romp was already wearing out its welcome.

However, the Mirvish organization (which is as close as we get to Broadway up here) picked it up and announced it for its next subscription season, some 18 months down the line.

They hired a director (Daniel Brooks) who had never done a musical, kept some of the old cast, rewrote a bit, and opened at the Winter Garden in June. The reviews by now were decidedly mixed, and although the show was no flop, it didn't exactly set the world on fire. I doubt you'll be seeing it move to Broadway in the near (or distant) future.

Why did *Urinetown* go on to glory while the *Chaperone* still drowses in obscurity?

Several reasons.

The creators of *Chaperone* weren't ruthless enough. They had a fringe hit and thought all it needed was a little tweaking to make the big time. By the time they decided to make changes, they were the wrong ones, and they came too late in the game.

But there's another more important difference. In the end, *The Drowsy Chaperone* was sheer fluff with absolutely nothing to say. As Gertrude Stein once observed about Los Angeles, "There's no there, there."

On the other hand, *Urinetown* is as savage in its own way about the world we live in as *The Threepenny Opera,* and it's that savagery that holds up the spoofery, giving it substance.

You can get away with a one-joke show if that joke is really about something.

Urinetown is the wave of the future. And if that wave is bright yellow, then so be it.

Source: "*Urinetown* Enjoys a Flush of Success," in *Toronto Star,* September 8, 2001, p. J06.

SOURCES

Brustein, Robert, "Varieties of Musical Experience," in *New Republic*, December 10, 2001, pp. 26–27.

Franklin, Nancy, "The Curtain Rises," in *New Yorker*, October 1, 2001, p. 118–19.

Gould, Lance, "Diversions Defer to Disaster," in *New York Daily News*, September 12, 2001, p. 56.

Kean, Thomas H., et al., *The 9/11 Commission Report*, http://govinfo.library.unt.edu/911/report/911Report.pdf (accessed July 28, 2009).

Kotis, Greg, and Mark Hollmann, *Urinetown: The Musical,* Faber & Faber, 2003.

Lines, Andy, "War on Terror: Nation Mourns: Broadway Shut Fears," in *Mirror*, September 19, 2001, p. 17.

Simon, John, "Yellow Peril," in *New York*, September 17, 2001, p. 53.

Steyn, Mark, "Loveless Renderings," in *New Criterion*, October 2001, pp. 34–38.

Zoglin, Richard, "Better Than *The Producers*," in *Time*, July 2, 2001, p. 64.

FURTHER READING

Barbour, David, "Out of the Water Closet: Costume Design for Musical Urinetown," in *Entertainment Design*, November 2001, p. 6.

Barbour examines the choices that costumers Gregory Gale and Jonathan Bixby made in designing the costumes for the play's Broadway run.

Boal, Augusto, *Theatre of the Oppressed*, Theatre Communications Group, 1993.
Boal is a Brazilian artist and social philosopher who views the theater in terms of class struggle. His well-documented book shows the history of serious theatrical movements that are parodied in this play.

Grant, Mark N., *The Rise and Fall of the Broadway Musical*, Northeastern University Press, 2004.
Urinetown is only mentioned in passing in the course of Grant's study, but his study of the history of the Broadway musical provides a context for the musical tradition that is being parodied here.

Heinberg, Richard, *Peak Everything: Waking Up to the Century of Declines*, New Society Publishers, 2007.
The premise of this book is that social decline is unavoidable as important natural resources become unavailable. It is a strongly debatable idea, but it does illustrate the situation in this play very clearly.

West Side Story

**ARTHUR LAURENTS
STEPHEN SONDHEIM
LEONARD BERNSTEIN
JEROME ROBBINS**

1957

West Side Story is a well-known groundbreaking Broadway musical based loosely on William Shakespeare's famous tragedy *Romeo and Juliet*. The musical is noteworthy for its introduction of the serious themes of youth violence and bigotry into a genre usually noted for its lightheartedness. It also broke new ground through its use of dissonant music and through its extensive use of dance as an integral part of the story.

The original idea for the musical came in 1949 from the choreographer and director Jerome Robbins, who thought of updating the Romeo and Juliet story about the feuding Montagues and Capulets by making it a tale of Jewish-Catholic tensions on New York City's East Side; the original title was going to be *East Side Story*. Robbins began working with the playwright Arthur Laurents and the composer-conductor Leonard Bernstein, but the original idea failed to work. Several years later, in 1954 or 1955, Bernstein and Laurents had the idea of transforming the story into a conflict between teenage gangs, one Puerto Rican and the other "American," set on the West Side of New York City. They invited Stephen Sondheim to write the lyrics, and the new version, now called *West Side Story*, opened on Broadway on September 26, 1957, and ran for 732 performances to mixed reviews. In 1958, it began a more successful run in London; meanwhile, a recording of the music from the show, released in 1957, became a hit, with several songs becoming popular, including "Tonight," "Maria," "I Feel Pretty,"

Leonard Bernstein (*AP Images*)

and "Somewhere." A 1961 film version won ten Academy Awards, including the award for Best Picture.

Although objections have sometimes been raised to the portrayal of Puerto Ricans in the musical and to the use of bigoted language by some of the characters (the language also includes mild profanity and sexual innuendo), and although some have objected to what they see as a glorification of gang violence, *West Side Story* has long been considered a classic. It returned to Broadway in 1960 and was revived there again in 1964, 1968, 1980, and 2009. It has also been performed around the world by both professional companies and amateur groups.

AUTHOR BIOGRAPHY

All four of the collaborators on *West Side Story* were born into Jewish families, three of them in New York City (Bernstein was born in Lawrence, Massachusetts), and three of them in 1918: Laurents on July 14, Bernstein on August 25, Robbins on October 11. Sondheim was born on March 22, 1930. The three older collaborators were involved in liberal or left-wing politics and

were investigated for Communist affiliations by the House Un-American Activities Committee (HUAC) in the early 1950s. All four of the collaborators were gay or bisexual, and according to Mary E. Williams, in *Readings on West Side Story*, the collaborators' experience as members of ethnic, political, and sexual minorities influenced the content of *West Side Story*.

Arthur Laurents worked as a writer for television, the Broadway stage, and film. He became known for writing about social outcasts, beginning his career with a play about anti-Semitism called *Home of the Brave* (1945). In 1948, he worked on the screenplay for Alfred Hitchcock's movie *Rope*. After *West Side Story*, he worked on the musicals *Gypsy* (1959) and *Hallelujah, Baby!* (1967), which won a Tony Award for Best Musical. He wrote the screenplays for *The Way We Were* (1973) and *The Turning Point* (1977) and was nominated for an Academy Award for the latter. In 2009, he directed a Broadway revival of *West Side Story* that was notable for its translation of some of the Puerto Ricans' dialogue and songs into Spanish.

Stephen Sondheim had his first career success as the lyricist for *West Side Story*; he next wrote the lyrics for *Gypsy* (1959), but he always considered himself a composer as well as a lyricist. His later career saw him win Tony Awards as the composer and lyricist for such musicals as *Company* (1971), *Follies* (1972), *A Little Night Music* (1973), and *Sweeney Todd* (1979). In 1976, a recording by Judy Collins of his "Send in the Clowns" won the Grammy for Song of the Year. In 1991, he won an Academy Award for Best Original Song for "Sooner or Later" from the film *Dick Tracy*. In 2008 he received a special Tony Award for Lifetime Achievement in the Theatre.

Leonard Bernstein pursued a career in both classical and popular music. He became assistant conductor of the New York Philharmonic Orchestra in 1943 and served as the orchestra's musical director from 1958 until 1969. He also composed classical music, but as a composer he is better known for his work in musical theater; besides *West Side Story*, he wrote the music for *On the Town* (1944) and *Wonderful Town* (1953), which received a Tony Award for Best Musical. He also won numerous Grammy Awards for albums of classical music. He died in New York on October 14, 1990, of a heart attack brought on by lung disease.

Jerome Robbins (born Jerome Rabinowitz) began as a dancer, then became a choreographer and director of Broadway shows. In 1949, he was named associate artistic director of the New York City Ballet. He worked with Bernstein on a ballet called *Fancy Free*, which later became the musical *On the Town* (1944). He also did the choreography for *The King and I* (1953) and *Peter Pan* (1954). His choreography for *West Side Story* earned him a Tony Award, one of five he won during his career. He also shared the Academy Award for Best Director for the film version of *West Side Story*. He died of a stroke in New York on July 29, 1998.

PLOT SUMMARY

Act 1, Scene 1

West Side Story begins with an evening street scene in which two rival gangs, the "American" Jets and the Puerto Rican Sharks engage in a dance version of a fight. The Jets are in possession of the area, but the Sharks threaten their control, and the main casualty is a Jet named A-rab, who has his ear pierced or branded by Bernardo, the leader of the Sharks.

A policeman's whistle sounds, and two policemen arrive to end the fight, at which point the rival gangs close ranks against the intrusion. Both gangs speak insolently to the police, and the Jets refuse to reveal who injured A-rab; in fact, they say it was probably done by a policeman.

The Sharks and the police leave, and the Jets discuss the situation. One of them makes a bigoted remark about Puerto Ricans, blaming them for his father's bankruptcy, prompting a skeptical response from another Jet, who, however, backs down when challenged. A girl named Anybodys, who wants to join the Jets, shows up, but the Jets do not let her stay; the gang is for males only.

The Jets decide they need to have an all-out fight with the Sharks to establish their territorial rights. Riff, the Jets' leader, says he will speak to the Sharks' leader to arrange things, and he will take his lieutenant, Tony, along. One of the other Jets objects that Tony has been missing for over a month, but Riff says Tony, his longtime friend, will come through for them. This leads to the "Jet Song," in which Riff proclaims that a Jet is a Jet till his dying day. The other Jets finish the song by saying how great it is to be a Jet.

Act 1, Scene 2

In this scene, Riff tries to convince Tony to rejoin the Jets and help out against the Sharks. Tony is initially reluctant, saying he no longer gets a kick out of being a member. He seems more interested in painting a new sign for his boss, Doc, who owns a drugstore. He also talks of looking forward to something, though he cannot say what exactly, and he sings of this anticipation in "Something's Coming." However, Riff does convince him to show up to talk to the Sharks at a neighborhood dance that night.

Act 1, Scene 3

Two Puerto Rican girls, the young and naïve Maria, Bernardo's sister, and the more experienced Anita, Bernardo's girlfriend, prepare for the dance. Maria says she is not interested in Chino, the boy Bernardo wants her to marry. She also wants to wear a sexier dress.

Act 1, Scene 4

The two gangs and their girls show up at the dance, still competitive but now in dancing rather than fighting. A well-meaning adult, Glad Hand, tries to organize the teenagers so that Jets and Sharks mingle, but though they pretend to go along, they actually ensure that they remain in their separate groups, still competing with each other.

At this point Tony arrives. He and Maria catch sight of each other and are instantly captivated. They walk toward each other, dance, and then kiss. This annoys Bernardo, who does not want an "American" paying attention to his sister. However, Maria is already lost in love for Tony and does not care what gang or ethnic group he belongs to. Bernardo sends her home with Chino.

Tony calls out to Maria, prompting Bernardo to approach him, but Riff intercepts Bernardo to talk to him about the proposed fight. They agree to talk further at Doc's drugstore. The gangs prepare to go there, but Tony lingers to sing longingly about Maria in the song of that name.

Act 1, Scene 5

Tony enters, still singing about Maria. He sees her at the window of her house above a fire escape, and the two of them express their love in a scene generally said to parallel the balcony scene in *Romeo and Juliet*.

Tony wants to spend more time with Maria, but her parents are calling to her to come away from the window. Before she goes back inside, though, the two of them sing "Tonight," in which they celebrate the "miracle" that has brought them together.

Tony and Maria leave the scene as Bernardo, Anita, and other Sharks arrive. Bernardo expresses concern about Maria's interest in an "American," which leads to a discussion of the situation of Puerto Ricans in America, with Anita mocking Bernardo's complaints about discrimination. Bernardo and the male Sharks exit in disgust, and the Shark girls sing "America," in which one Shark girl, Rosalia, praises Puerto Rico. In response, Anita satirically criticizes Puerto Rico, calling it an island of tropical diseases, and she and the other girls instead praise the United States, though their praise contains some ironic criticisms.

Act 1, Scene 6

The Jets arrive first at the "war council" between the gangs at the drugstore at midnight and wait impatiently for the Sharks. Anybodys tries again to be part of the gang, but the boys dismiss her. Doc disapproves of the whole idea of a big fight, but the gang dismisses him, especially when he starts to say "When I was your age. . . . " One of the gang members says he was never their age, and attacks all "creeps" who say things like that or who call them hoodlums, as Doc does.

Some of the other Jet girls arrive, but Riff says they will have to leave when the war council begins. The Jet boys become a little excited and aggressive, and Riff sings a song about cooling it.

The Sharks arrive, and the Jet girls leave, including Anybodys, who does so reluctantly. Riff and Bernardo negotiate the terms of the "rumble" while the gang members exchange racial insults. The main discussion is about weapons. As they start suggesting everything from sticks to bricks, Tony comes in. Although no one has mentioned knives or guns, Tony does, then calls the gang members chicken for wanting to fight at a distance instead of close up. He convinces them to stage a "fair fight," that is, a fistfight between two gang members, one from each side. This is agreed to just as Lieutenant Schrank of the police shows up. The gang members instantly pretend that nothing is going on.

After forcing the Sharks to leave, and making derogatory remarks about them, Schrank makes a long speech to the Jets about how he will help them get rid of their rivals. But the Jets will have none of it, so he gets angry at them and calls them names.

Act 1, Scene 7

At the bridal shop where they both work, Maria asks Anita why the boys fight. Anita says it is just to get rid of their excess feelings. As Anita leaves, Tony shows up, and he tells Maria that they are untouchable now. Maria, however, is worried about the fight, even if it is only a fistfight. She asks Tony to stop it, and he agrees.

Tony and Maria then act out a mock wedding ceremony with the bridal shop dummies and say that even death will not part them now.

Act 1, Scene 8

The Jets, the Sharks, Anita, Maria, and Tony all wait expectantly for night. The two gangs are looking forward to their fight; Anita is looking forward to being with Bernardo afterward; and Maria and Tony are also looking forward to being together. The various groups all sing the song "Tonight" at the same time, but almost at cross purposes.

Act 1, Scene 9

Night has arrived, and the fight is about to take place, but Tony shows up to stop it. However, his intervention merely turns the one-on-one fistfight planned between Bernardo and the Jet named Diesel into a knife fight between Riff and Bernardo. Tony again attempts to stop things, but once again his intervention merely makes things worse: Riff is distracted by him, allowing Bernardo to stab him. As he falls, Tony grabs his knife and stabs Bernardo.

A police whistle sounds; the gangs flee; and Tony is left standing over the dead bodies of Bernardo and Riff, calling out in anguish for Maria. Anybodys then helps him to flee.

Act 2, Scene 1

Unaware of what has happened at the fight, the Shark girls, including Maria, talk about their plans for the rest of the evening. Maria says it is her wedding night, which makes the others think she is crazy. In high spirits, Maria then sings "I Feel Pretty."

Chino comes in with his clothes all torn and dirty. He explains what happened at the fight. Maria is horrified. She calls Chino a liar, then prays, then asks to die.

Tony comes in through the window. Maria beats his chest in anger, calling him a killer, but they end up embracing and she tells him not to leave her. She says everything around them is the problem, so Tony says they will find someplace where nothing can get to them. This leads to a fantasy sequence in which the walls of the city disappear, giving way to sun and space and air. The gang members in this fantasy cease fighting, and walk together in a friendly procession; meanwhile an offstage voice sings the song "Somewhere."

But the fantasy fades away, replaced by a nightmare re-enactment of the knife fight.

Act 2, Scene 2

Two of the remaining members of the Jets confer about what to do. They are scared by what has happened, but they put on a brave front when Officer Krupke shows up asking questions. They first mock him, then run away.

The two fleeing Jets meet up with the rest of their gang, except Tony, and they all act out a satire against the judicial system, the police, social workers, and psychiatrists for the way they handle so-called juvenile delinquents. This is all part of the song, "Gee, Officer Krupke." They treat us as if we are juvenile delinquents, says one of the Jets, so that is what we give them.

Anybodys appears after the song and tells the boys she has found out that Chino is planning on getting Tony. The gang members this time are grateful to Anybodys and run off to try to find and protect Tony.

Act 2, Scene 3

Tony and Maria are asleep in her bedroom. Anita knocks on the door, and Tony sneaks out, telling Maria to meet him at Doc's.

Anita comes in and, realizing Tony has been there, speaks furiously to Maria, telling her Tony is one of "them," someone who killed her brother and Anita's boyfriend. Maria responds that she loves Tony and must stand by him. This debate takes place as part of the song "A Boy Like That," and by the end of it Maria has convinced Anita that when love is strong, there is no right or wrong.

Anita tells Maria that Chino is after Tony with a gun. Maria seems ready to kill Chino if he harms Tony.

Lieutenant Schrank comes in, wanting to ask Maria questions, but she lies to protect Tony and cleverly sends off a message for Tony via Anita

without Schrank's understanding what she is doing.

Act 2, Scene 4

The Jets gather in the drugstore, where Tony is hiding in the cellar with Doc. Anita comes in to give her message, but the Jets insult her and stop her from going down to the cellar. She says she wants to help Tony, but they do not believe her and begin a savage dance around her, stopping only when Doc comes upstairs.

Very upset, Anita passes on a false message, saying that Maria has been killed by Chino.

Act 2, Scene 5

Tony tells Doc how wonderful Maria is and how they are planning to raise a family. Doc at first is angry about the killings, and asks Tony how he can kill. Then he tells Tony that Maria is dead. Distraught, Tony rushes out into the street, calling out for Chino to shoot him.

Act 2, Scene 6

Anybodys tries to get Tony off the street, but he keeps calling out for Chino to come get him and tells Anybodys that this is no longer a game.

Maria emerges, and Tony runs to her, but there is a gunshot and Tony falls. Chino has shot him. Maria takes his hand as if to urge him back to life; he even sings a line with her from the "Somewhere" song, but he falls back, dead.

Maria takes Chino's gun and threatens to kill everybody, saying "We all killed him." But she cannot bring herself to shoot. Instead, she throws the gun away, and as the police and the other adult characters arrive, she gets the Sharks and the Jets to carry Tony's body away in one joint procession, reminiscent of the procession in the fantasy sequence. Maria joins them sadly but triumphantly, leaving the adults behind, "useless."

CHARACTERS

Action

Action, the most aggressive of the Jets, is eager to fight and to take over Tony's role in his absence.

Anita

Anita, the girlfriend of Bernardo, the leader of the Sharks, acts as Maria's confidant, playing a

MEDIA ADAPTATIONS

- *West Side Story*, directed by Jerome Robbins and Robert Wise and starring Natalie Wood, Rita Moreno, and Richard Beymer, won the Academy Award for Best Picture for 1961, along with ten other Academy Awards. It was produced by the Mirisch Corporation.

- *Leonard Bernstein Conducts West Side Story* is a 1985 television documentary showing Bernstein conducting a performance of the musical.

- *West Side Story Symphonic Dances* is a set of instrumental versions of the songs from the musical prepared by Bernstein and originally released in 1961.

- *West Side Story (Original Broadway Cast)* is the soundtrack to the original production on Broadway, starring Carol Lawrence, Chita Rivera, and Larry Kert. It was released by Columbia in October 1957.

- *West Side Story Suite* is a ballet based on the music from the show, choreographed by Robbins. It premiered with the New York City Ballet in 1995.

role parallel to that of the Nurse in *Romeo and Juliet*. Where Maria is the inexperienced newcomer to America, Anita is much more knowing. In particular, while Maria is either puzzled or aghast at the thought of gang fighting, Anita is accepting of it and even presents a quasi-psychological explanation for it, saying the boys need to get rid of their excess feeling; in fact, she almost seems to approve of the fighting, saying that it makes Bernardo more passionate with her afterwards.

Anita is not one to shy away from the realities of life, whether those be the violent fights of the young men around her or the difficulties encountered by Puerto Ricans in America. On the latter subject, she does not share the views of Rosalia, who seems to want to return to Puerto

Rico. Nor does she have patience for Bernardo's complaints about discrimination. Her attitude seems to be that one should get on with living one's life; Puerto Rico was no paradise, she says, calling it an island of tropical diseases when Rosalia calls it an island of tropical breezes; and rather than complaining about American treatment of Puerto Ricans, her aim seems to be simply to become American herself. She tells Bernardo that she is an American girl now and thus will not simply obey what he says. She also has no patience for attempts to keep Maria and Tony apart; Bernardo's warnings to Maria, she says, simply put ideas into her head.

At the same time, Anita does not want Maria to wear too sexy a dress, and when Tony ends up killing Bernardo, her first reaction is to retreat to an us-versus-them attitude in relation to the "American" Tony. Similarly, when taunted and attacked by the Jets, she becomes defensive. But free of those extreme situations, her attitude is one of openness to experience.

Anybodys

Anybodys is a tomboy and hanger-on of the Jets who is repeatedly rebuffed in her attempts to join the gang. At the end, she discovers that Chino is out to get Tony, and her warning about this to the Jets helps precipitate the final catastrophe.

A-rab

A-rab, a member of the Jets who takes nothing seriously, pretends to be an airplane in the opening fight and has his ear pierced by Bernardo.

Baby John

Baby John is the youngest of the Jets and the most easily frightened, especially after the deaths in the rumble.

Bernardo

Bernardo, the leader of the Sharks, is described in the stage directions as being handsome but with a chip on his shoulder, presumably about the situation of Puerto Ricans in America, about which he complains. He is very protective of his sister, Maria; it is at his urging that Anita will not allow Maria to wear a sexy dress, and he is completely opposed to Maria having anything to do with the "American" Tony. He has arranged for Maria to marry a sweet Puerto Rican boy, Chino.

Bernardo's role is parallel to that of Tybalt in *Romeo and Juliet*. Tybalt kills Mercutio,

Romeo's friend in Shakespeare's play, and is in turn killed by Romeo. In *West Side Story* Bernardo kills Riff, Tony's friend, and Tony, the musical's Romeo, in turn kills Bernardo.

Chino

Chino, described in the stage directions as shy, gentle, and sweet-faced, is the boy Bernardo has chosen for his sister, Maria, but Maria is not interested in him. His role is parallel to that of Paris, Juliet's unwanted suitor in *Romeo and Juliet*, except that whereas in Shakespeare's version, Paris is killed by Romeo, in *West Side Story* it is the other way around. Chino, in revenge for the killing of Bernardo, shoots Tony.

Consuelo

Consuelo is one of the Shark girls. She is described as being a bleached-blond, bangled beauty.

Diesel

Diesel is the member of the Jets designated by Riff to represent them in the "fair fight" against the Sharks, in a one-on-one fistfight with Bernardo.

Doc

Doc, the drugstore owner, and one of the few adult characters in the musical, resembles Friar Laurence, Romeo's advisor in *Romeo and Juliet*, though his comments tend to be more negative than those of the friar.

Glad Hand

Glad Hand is an adult character who tries to get the gangs to mingle with each other at the dance.

Officer Krupke

Described in the stage directions as a big goon-like cop, Officer Krupke is one of two police officers in the play who continually try to keep the gangs in line and prevent their planned "rumble." After the rumble, when he tries unsuccessfully to interrogate the Jets, they mock him in the song "Gee, Officer Krupke."

Maria

Maria, the Juliet of *West Side Story*, is described in the stage directions as a very young girl with the strength and awareness of a woman. She has recently arrived from Puerto Rico with her parents and is staying with her brother, Bernardo. Even before she meets Tony, she is hoping to have a wonderful time at the dance; to her it will be the beginning of being a young lady in America. Once she sees Tony, she is as smitten as he is, but she does not indulge quite as much in his optimistic approach to their relationship. When he says they are magic, she notes that there is such a thing as black magic, and she is generally worried about what will happen; she is particularly worried about the planned fight. On the other hand, she is tremendously loyal to Tony, putting her love for him ahead of her association with the Sharks or even her feelings for her brother.

Commentators, such as Scott Miller in his article "An Examination of *West Side Story*'s Plot and Musical Motifs," see Maria as developing at the end, after the tragedy, when she blames everyone, threatens to shoot indiscriminately, but then manages to unify the two gangs, as if transcending violence. Unlike her prototype in *Romeo and Juliet*, she does not kill herself, even though she becomes quite distraught. Perhaps this is because she is practical and resourceful, something demonstrated in the scene in which she manages to send a message to Tony despite the presence of Lieutenant Schrank. Or perhaps it is that, as the stage directions say, she has the strength of a woman.

The love that strikes Maria makes her feel so buoyant that she sings the exuberant song "I Feel Pretty." Craig Zadan reports that some commentators, including even Stephen Sondheim, the song's creator, have said the song is out of character.

Riff

Riff is the leader of the Jets. The stage directions describe him as glowing, driving, intelligent, and slightly wacky. He also seems like a calming influence on his followers, at least until the big fight. He is good friends with Tony and has been living with Tony's family for four and a half years. He and Tony celebrate their friendship and indicate its enduring nature by using the catchphrases "Womb to tomb" and "Sperm to worm." His main aim is to preserve the territory of the Jets and resist the encroachments of the Sharks, but he does so coolly; he is the one who sings the song "Cool."

His role is parallel to that of Mercutio in *Romeo and Juliet*. He is the friend of Tony, as Mercutio is the friend of Romeo; both Mercutio and Riff are killed in an encounter arising from the feud going on in their respective plays.

Rosalia

Rosalia is the somewhat slow-witted Shark girl who sings the praises of Puerto Rico, prompting the mockery of Anita and the other Puerto Rican girls.

Lieutenant Schrank

Schrank, a plainclothes policeman seeking to clean up the neighborhood by putting an end to the gangs' violence, is hard on both gangs, but he is much harder on the Puerto Rican Sharks, making derogatory remarks about them and offering to help the Jets against them.

Snowboy

Snowboy is the Jet who imitates Officer Krupke in "Gee, Officer Krupke."

Tony

Tony, a good-looking, sandy-haired boy, according to the stage directions, works for the druggist, Doc, and is the Romeo of the play. He is a member of the Jets, but he has not taken part in their activities for some time. When the play begins, he is seeking something, but he doesn't know what, and at the dance he finds it in the person of Maria. He falls so much in love with her that he is willing to try to stop the fistfight agreed to by the war council of the two gangs simply because Maria asks him to. Once he falls in love, he becomes dreamily romantic and perhaps naïve, repeatedly telling Maria that they have nothing to fear, that they are untouchable because of their love. However, his revenge killing of Bernardo leads inexorably to the catastrophe at the end.

Unlike Romeo, who has a girlfriend before he meets Juliet, Tony is not in love with anyone else before meeting Maria, but at the end of the play, when he hears that Maria is dead and rushes out to seek his own death, he is like Romeo, who commits suicide when he believes Juliet to be dead.

TOPICS FOR FURTHER STUDY

- Write an essay comparing *West Side Story* with the more recent novel *The Tequila Worm* by Viola Canales. Compare the situation of Puerto Ricans in New York as presented in the musical with the situation of Mexican Americans in Texas as presented in the novel.

- Put together a ten-minute video including dance and singing about some aspect of teenage life today. Topics might include dating and relationships, bullying in schools, substance abuse.

- Create a PowerPoint presentation that focuses on the situation of Puerto Ricans in New York today. Points to ponder include the number of immigrants, language barriers, lifestyle. To what extent does it differ from the portrayal of their situation in the musical?

- Organize a classroom debate about the pros and cons of belonging to a gang. Are there any good aspects to belonging? Are there different sorts of gangs? Are some gangs more like nonviolent social clubs than criminal organizations?

- Complete a Venn diagram that compares and contrasts *Romeo and Juliet* with *West Side Story*.

- Watch one of the youth movies of the 1950s (e.g., *Rebel without a Cause* or *The Wild One*) and write an essay that compares the themes in the movie with those in *West Side Story*.

THEMES

Juvenile Delinquency

Quite unusually for a Broadway musical, *West Side Story* focuses on serious themes, including juvenile delinquency and gang violence. The song "Gee, Officer Krupke" even includes a mocking survey of various approaches to dealing with the problem, referring to the ideas then current among social workers, psychiatrists, and

the courts. In mocking these ideas, the musical may be suggesting either that there are no simple solutions to the problem or that it is not that big a problem in the first place.

Coming of Age

Related to the issue of juvenile delinquency is the larger issue of growing up. Maria is looking forward to her first love, and so is Tony. Tony is moving on from the adolescent gang by taking a job at the drugstore, and he looks forward to raising a family. The musical can be seen as a story about life transitions, though in this case a failed transition.

Generation Gap

Another youth-related theme in the play is the generation gap between the young gang members and the adult characters. The only thing that can unite the rival gangs, besides Tony's death at the end, is the meddling of the adults, especially the police. The hostility between the Jets and the Sharks seems almost secondary compared to the disgust the Jets express for Officer Krupke and the whole adult world, even Doc.

Prejudice

Another serious theme in *West Side Story* is the issue of prejudice, mostly in connection with the Puerto Rican characters. The "American" characters, notably Lieutenant Schrank, but also some of the Jets, make derogatory remarks about Puerto Ricans, who in turn use an ethnic slur about Tony to refer to his Polish origins. The ethnic division between whites and Puerto Ricans deepens the antagonism between the gangs, though it is probably not essential to it, and it helps create a sense of a generally antagonistic, hostile urban environment.

Immigration

Connected to the theme of prejudice is the issue of immigration. The Puerto Rican characters are recent immigrants who are grappling with their new life in America; they have to deal with discrimination and also simply with being in a society that is different, a society more prosperous but also more commercial than the land they came from. Their responses range from nostalgia for Puerto Rico to complaining about discrimination to acceptance of American ways.

Urban Life and the American Dream

West Side Story paints a harsh picture of urban life, focused on alleyways, fire escapes, and tenement buildings, and dominated by gang conflicts. Although the Puerto Rican girls sing the praises of their new country in "America," highlighting the material prosperity usually associated with the American dream, the overall atmosphere of the musical is fairly bleak as a result of the settings and the gang conflict.

Utopian Escape

As a counterpoint to the harsh urban landscape and the gang conflict, Tony and Maria, with the song

Stephen Sondheim (Fred R. Conrad / New York Times Co. / Getty Images)

"Somewhere" playing in the background, imagine a sunny, utopian escape into a fantasy world where the gangs forget their antagonisms and dance together. Maria had been complaining that everything around them was against them, referring to the gang conflict and the deaths that have resulted, and Tony responds by saying they should find somewhere else to be. The suggestion is that only in some fantasy world can their problems be solved.

Love

Like its Shakespearean model, *West Side Story* is, at least in part, a love story, a portrayal of pure, ideal love. Three of the best-known songs from the musical, "Maria," "Tonight," and "I Feel Pretty," express the ecstasy of young, new love, but even more so than in *Romeo and Juliet*, the love plays out against a grim background that makes it seem doomed from the start.

Gender Roles

A secondary theme in the musical focuses on Anybodys, the girl who wants to join the Jets.

The boys in the gang reject her because she is a girl; the message is that gangs are for boys only.

STYLE

Setting

The place in which the musical is set, the alleys and tenements of New York, helps create its ominous atmosphere, as does the time of day: every scene takes place in the evening or at night, in darkness or as darkness falls. Two major scenes take place at midnight. The sun appears only in the fantasy scene about escaping from the city.

Slang

Arthur Laurents invented such slang words for the musical as "kiddando" and "frabbajabba" to create a sense of a different youth world separate from the adults. The different ways the adults and the adolescents talk is underlined in the scene in which one of the Jets tells Doc he needs to "get hip to" how different the young people are from him if he wants to "dig" them, to which Doc replies by saying he will "dig" their early graves. Doc is deliberately punning, but the effect is still to stress the different language and different sensibility as between youth and age.

Dance and Song

West Side Story is known for its extended dance numbers, which are melded into the story rather than standing apart. Similarly, its songs are notable for being extensions of the action rather than set pieces. It is also notable that the songs and dances are restricted to the adolescent characters, being another way, in addition to their language, in which they are distinguished from the adult characters. That the action, including the fighting, is done in a choreographed, balletic way suggests as well that there is something gamelike about it. Several commentators also note that the dancing compensates for the inarticulateness of the characters.

Dramatic Irony

The second act of the musical begins with an extended scene of dramatic irony, in which the audience knows something the characters do not. In this scene, Maria, supported by her friends, sings ecstatically about her new love in "I Feel Pretty." What none of them knows is that Maria's new lover has just killed her brother, setting events on a course for an even greater disaster. Since the audience does know this, the scene has an ominous, horrifying edge to it, perhaps indicating the hopelessness of the sort of ideal love Maria is singing about.

Satire

Although most of *West Side Story* is serious and tragic, it does have two notable moments of satire, first when the Puerto Rican girls sing "America," in which they mock idealized views of both Puerto Rico and America in a way that brings out the nature of the immigrant experience; that is, they are mostly happy to have left Puerto Rico, but they are not entirely satisfied in their new country. The second satirical song is "Gee, Officer Krupke," in which the Jets mock adult views of juvenile delinquency, bringing out one of the major themes of the musical.

Figures of Speech and Imagery

West Side Story is not primarily metaphorical, and the odd thing about its occasional use of metaphors, similes, and other figures of speech, along with its imagery, is that they tend to undercut the ostensible message of the scenes they appear in. As Wilfrid Mellers notes, Tony's song, "Something's Coming," though ostensibly a positive anticipation of something good, talks of something "cannonballin'" at him, suggesting the dangers that lie ahead. Similarly, the metonymy used by Tony and Riff to express their enduring friendship, the phrases "Womb to tomb" and "Sperm to Worm," in which words associated with birth and death stand in for them, seems darker than the characters intend because of the death associations; this figurative claim by Riff and Tony also seems clearly wrong because they have known each other only four and a half years, not since birth or before. Tony also seems wrong when he figuratively claims that he and Maria are "out of this world," as if they are safe from tragedy. Even the delicate imagery of the song "Tonight" seems somehow wrong. How can the nighttime world of Tony and Maria be "full of light" or have "suns and moons all over the place"? And if their world has become a star, as they claim in the song, how can they live in it?

Shakespearean Parallels and Contrasts

West Side Story is known to be based on Shakespeare's *Romeo and Juliet*, following most of its main outlines. In both stories, young lovers are divided by a feud, a family feud in Shakespeare's version, gang conflict in *West Side Story*. In both stories, the conflicts lead to deaths, and in *Romeo and Juliet* both lovers die. One of the major differences in the two stories is that Maria, the Juliet figure in *West Side Story*, survives and is able to lead a reconciliation between the gangs, something Keith Garebian, in his *The Making of West Side Story*, finds unconvincing. Another difference, following on from the updating of Shakespeare's story, is the introduction of social themes, most notably concerning prejudice and immigration. Some Shakespearean elements are present in modernized form, for instance the famous balcony scene, which here becomes a love song on a fire escape. One other major difference is that whereas in *Romeo and Juliet* the feud encompasses family elders as well as youths, in *West Side Story* the gang conflict solely involves adolescents, another way in which the musical sets its young people apart from adults.

HISTORICAL CONTEXT

Juvenile Delinquency

Juvenile delinquency and gang violence predate the 1950s, but in that decade there was an increasing concern with the problem, typified by a number of films, including *Rebel without a Cause*, starring James Dean as an insolent youth; *The Wild One*, a motorcycle gang movie starring Marlon Brando; and *Blackboard Jungle*, about adults cowed by rebellious high school students. Actual youth violence did also seem to be on the rise, or at least was being reported on more. According to James S. Olson, in his *Historical Dictionary of the 1950s*, the FBI reported in the early 1950s that youths under eighteen were committing approximately half of all car thefts and burglaries and, as reported by Keith Garebian in *The Making of West Side Story*, the inspiration for *West Side Story* with its gang warfare theme was a headline in the *Los Angeles Times* about Hispanic gang wars, which Bernstein and Laurents saw while they were meeting at the Beverly Hills Hotel.

Puerto Rican Immigration

Puerto Rican immigration to the United States, predominantly to New York City, began in the

nineteenth century. After the island became an American territory at the beginning of the twentieth century and still more after Puerto Ricans were granted U.S. citizenship in 1917, immigration increased. But the biggest wave of immigration took place after World War II, especially in the 1950s, when large numbers of Puerto Ricans arrived as the result of the dislocation caused by the Puerto Rican government's industrialization project known as Operation Bootstrap. Once in New York, the Puerto Ricans, who had come in search of jobs and a better life, suffered from discrimination in employment, housing, and services.

HUAC and the Cold War

After World War II, and perhaps most especially in the 1950s, American life became dominated by the Cold War with the Soviet Union, including a nuclear arms race and threatened conflicts over the situations in Berlin and Hungary. At home, fear of Communism and the Soviet Union led to investigations of suspected radicals, who were asked to name fellow radicals before such bodies as the House Un-American Activities Committee (HUAC). Three of the creators of *West Side Story* were investigated during this period, and one of them (Robbins) named names. The worries of the Jets over what weapons the Sharks might have may reflect American concerns over Soviet weaponry, and to Lily Phillips, in her article "Blue Jeans, Black Leather Jackets, and a Sneer," the focus on juvenile delinquency, the fear of teenage gangs, found in so many artistic works of the 1950s, may itself reflect the paranoia of the Cold War.

Teenagers

Although there have always been young people, the concept of the teenager was an invention of the 1940s in America, when adolescents were singled out as a potential market for consumer goods. The spread of high school education meant that instead of entering the labor market, teenagers became a group in waiting and the teen years became a time described by Thomas Hine in *The Rise and Fall of the American Teenager* as "a period of preparation and self-definition, a period of indulgence and unfocused energy." In the 1950s, in addition to being looked to as potential consumers, some teenagers were looked on as dangers to society, as rebels against convention with their new rock- and-roll music, or even as juvenile delinquents.

COMPARE & CONTRAST

- **1957:** Massive Puerto Rican immigration to New York City is underway. The arriving immigrants face poverty and discrimination.

  Today: The Puerto Rican population in New York has declined, with some of those who are better off having left for the suburbs. Some of those remaining still suffer from poverty, but discrimination has at least officially disappeared; the 2009 Puerto Rican Parade in New York drew hundreds of thousands of attendees; and in 2009 a Puerto Rican New Yorker, Sonia Sotomayor, is nominated to serve on the U.S. Supreme Court.

- **1957:** Youth gangs become enough of an issue that there are movies made about juvenile delinquents, and newspaper headlines feature gang violence.

  Today: There is disagreement over whether the gang situation is worse or just reported on more. Drug wars and violence are common among the various ethnic gangs.

- **1957:** Gender roles are fairly strictly observed, and girls who want to join boys and their gangs are rebuffed as tomboys.

  Today: Although gangs remain largely male, with the general loosening of gender roles, there is an increasing number of girls in gangs. Though female crime remains largely nonviolent, there are instances of female assaults and even murder.

- **1957:** At the height of the Cold War, fear of Communism swept the United States, leading to blacklisting of entertainers and harassment of those suspected of having radical associations.

  Today: With the Cold War over, the fear of Communism is a thing of the past, but the 9/11 attack and the war in Iraq have led to new fears that in some cases have led to the curtailing of civil liberties. One notable example of a sort of blacklisting was the cancellation of a television show after its host, Bill Maher, made controversial remarks about the 9/11 attack; but there was no widespread blacklisting as in the 1950s.

CRITICAL OVERVIEW

In September 1957, after receiving good reviews in Washington, D.C., and lukewarm ones in Philadelphia, *West Side Story* opened to mixed reviews in New York City. Henry Hewes, in his review "*West Side Story* Brilliantly Expresses the Character of Teenage Gangs," praises it for its realistic portrayal of gangs and says it is "the best treatment of the juvenile-delinquency problem in our theatre to date." But it was criticized by Wolcott Gibbs, in his review "The Plot of *West Side Story* Is Implausible," for a lack of "real emotional content." Some said it presented a stereotyped view of Puerto Ricans, while others praised its sympathetic portrayal of minorities. Some were shocked to see gang violence on stage; in fact, the musical had problems finding

financial backers because potential supporters found it too violent and angry.

In later years, however, the idea of a musical tragedy won high praise. Perhaps the turning point was the run in London, where Kenneth Tynan, as quoted in Keith Garebian's *The Making of West Side Story*, praised it for being a "rampaging ballet." Another British reviewer cited by Garebian compared it to Georges Bizet's much admired opera *Carmen*. Much later it would be compared, by Wilfrid Mellers, in his article "The Narrative and Thematic Significance of Music in *West Side Story*," to George Gershwin's *Porgy and Bess*. And it won praise from Denny Martin Flinn in his article "The Significance of Dance and Song in *West Side Story*," for "pushing the envelope of American musical theatre" by introducing a tragic

Rita Moreno as Anita in the 1961 film version of West Side Story *(AP Images)*

story and also by integrating the dancing so much into the story.

Another turning point may have been the release of the cast recording (1957) or of the Academy Award-winning film (1967). Eventually, it became so revered that some critics began to say it was superior to its source material, Shakespeare's *Romeo and Juliet*, because it included a social dimension (about prejudice) missing from Shakespeare and because it provided better motivation (also connected to prejudice) for some of the events of the story rather than relying on chance as Shakespeare had.

By the end of the twentieth century, *West Side Story* was being treated like a classic and was widely performed in the theaters and in schools, but it could still stir up controversy. For instance, in the 1990s it was banned in one high school because of its portrayal of Puerto Ricans and its supposed glorification of gangs. But in general it remained in favor, with revivals

on Broadway in 1960, 1968, 1980, and 2009, and two books devoted entirely to it. Keith Garebian, the author of one of those books, *The Making of West Side Story*, calls it "a landmark musical." Mary Williams, the editor of the other book, *Readings on West Side Story*, says that *West Side Story* was ahead of its time, but came to be "quite influential," setting "a bold new standard for American musicals."

CRITICISM

Sheldon Goldfarb

Goldfarb is a specialist in Victorian literature who has published two academic books on William Makepeace Thackeray as well as a novel for young adults set in Victorian times. In this essay, he explores the conflict between youth and age in West Side Story.

WHAT DO I READ NEXT?

- For an account of a production of *West Side Story* in which one of the gangs was played by deaf students, see *Deaf Side Story* by Mark Rigney (2003).

- For a study of the portrayal of immigrants in American popular culture, including a chapter on *West Side Story*, see *Immigration and American Popular Culture: An Introduction* by Rachel Rubin and Jeffrey Paul Melnick (2006).

- For a study of the Jewish immigrant experience in America, the experience of the families of the four creators of *West Side Story*, see Irving Howe's *World of Our Fathers* (1976).

- For a coming-of-age novel written by a teenage girl, see S. E. Hinton's *The Outsiders*, published in 1967, about two rival groups of characters from broken homes.

- For a gritty account of gang life, read *Inside the Crips: Life inside L.A.'s Most Notorious Gang* by Colton Simpson, with Ann Pearlman (2005).

- For a classic novel about gang warfare in a futuristic setting, read *A Clockwork Orange* by Anthony Burgess (1962).

In transforming William Shakespeare's *Romeo and Juliet*, the creators of *West Side Story* chose to set it in the midst of gang conflict and to introduce the issues of prejudice and immigration. In doing so, it is generally accepted that they added a social dimension to a love story, even if at least one critic (Stanley Kauffmann, in his article "An Exceptional Yet Disappointing Film Musical") finds the social commentary in it, or at least in the film version of it, "facile." Mary E. Williams, in her essay "*West Side Story* and Its Creators," declares that in *West Side Story* "the disastrous fate of [the] principal characters is a result of hatred and prejudice—society itself possesses the tragic

> IN ADDITION TO THE LOVE STORY FROM *ROMEO AND JULIET*, AND THE OVERT SOCIAL COMMENTARY INSERTED BY LAURENTS, THERE IS YET ANOTHER LEVEL TO THE STORY IN ITS MODERNIZED FORM. ONE CAN SEE IT AS A THWARTED COMING-OF-AGE STORY."

flaw." The most extreme version of this view can be found in Scott Miller's article "An Examination of *West Side Story*'s Plot and Musical Motifs," in which he says: "Everything in *West Side Story* happens as a result of racial prejudice." In addition to the love story from *Romeo and Juliet*, and the overt social commentary inserted by Laurents, there is yet another level to the story in its modernized form. One can see it as a thwarted coming-of-age story.

Though Miller's claim seems extravagant, he can point to the views of one of the show's creators, Arthur Laurents, who was the one chiefly responsible for the details of the plot. Laurents, as reported by Garebian, described the theme of *West Side Story* as "young love destroyed by a violent world of prejudice." Elsewhere, in his book *Original Story By: A Memoir of Broadway and Hollywood*, he spoke of the "world of violence and prejudice" in *West Side Story*, adding that when he came to write it, he "had more than enough anger at prejudice to fuel and fire the musical."

Within the musical itself, there is plenty of evidence of the social dimension Laurents said he wanted to introduce. Both the police and the Jets make derogatory remarks about Puerto Ricans, Bernardo complains about discrimination, and the reason Anita fails to deliver an accurate message to Tony at the end has much to do with the taunts and racial epithets hurled her way by the other Jets.

Following on this notion of prejudice as central to the musical is the sense that the tragedy is inevitable. Given the nature of society, given the prejudice and hatred, Tony and Maria's love is doomed. As Garebian puts it, they live "in the wrong time and in the wrong place"; he emphasizes the inevitability of it all by speaking of "conditioned responses and provocations." Or, as Miller says, "Here was a musical with the unheard of message that love not only *will not* triumph over all, but *cannot.*"

The lovers themselves share this view. "...it's not us!" says Maria. "It's everything around us." Tony later says, "They won't let us be." And the Jets and Doc argue about whether the gangs make the world "lousy" or whether it was that way before, leaving the audience with a choice between blaming the youth gangs and blaming adult society.

But what if the whole question is being posed the wrong way? What if the problem is not to find out who made the world lousy, but to stop and ask if the world is really as lousy as is being suggested. One might, of course, look at the gangs with their "rumbles" and their knives and guns, and say, Of course, the world is lousy, and it is because of the gangs. One might look at the tenements, the darkness, the discrimination, and say society is to blame.

Now, it is certainly true that the gangs end up using guns and knives, but it may be interesting to see how in the musical they end up doing so. And though the landscape of the musical is certainly bleak, the young lovers at first seem able to transcend it. What, then, goes wrong?

The answer may perhaps be found by looking more closely at the differences between *West Side Story* and its Shakespearean original, especially the differences between Romeo and Tony.

Romeo and Juliet ends tragically too, of course. The blame may be Fate's, or it may be Romeo's. Romeo certainly acts rashly at times, rushing eventually to his death when he falsely believes Juliet to be dead, somewhat as Tony rushes to his death at the end. However, there are some key differences between Romeo and Tony.

At the beginning of *West Side Story*, Tony is already halfway out of the gang. He has been absent for a month or more and has taken a job for Doc at the drugstore. Romeo, like Tony, misses the first fight of the story, but he is not absent because he is trying to leave the Montagues or because he is tired of feuding. Nor has he got a new job. It seems almost silly to say that, but it raises an important point. By shifting the story to twentieth-century America, the creators of *West Side Story* introduced a very

specific social situation. In Shakespeare's version of the story, in contrast, Romeo hardly seems situated at all; he is more a depiction of love incarnate, mad passionate love that burns itself out through premature death.

Tony is not like that. Tony is an American teenager who is growing up. As one of the Jets says in "Gee, Officer Krupke" about an imaginary youth, "The trouble is he's growing." Or as another gang member says, "The trouble is he's grown!" Tony is growing up, leaving the phase of gangs behind him, taking a job, and also searching for something else, as he says in "Something's Coming," though he is at first unsure what that something might be.

When he meets Maria at the dance, Tony becomes certain about what it is he has been searching for. It is Maria, or love, or marriage, or even a family with children. As he tells Doc near the end, "Doc, you know what we're going to do in the country, Maria and me? We're going to have kids and we'll name them all after you...."

This is an interesting difference: Romeo's plans do not extend beyond marrying Juliet and evading the consequences of his banishment for killing Tybalt. For Romeo, everything is focused on the romance itself and the obstacles that must be overcome to consummate it. Tony, in contrast, is looking farther ahead, looking toward the sort of respectable middle-class family that was the 1950s ideal.

In addition to the love story from *Romeo and Juliet*, and the overt social commentary inserted by Laurents, there is yet another level to the story in its modernized form. One can see it as a thwarted coming-of-age story, with Tony moving from teenage gang member into respectable family man.

The question is, Why is it thwarted? And here the answer may require a re-examination of the lovers' claims at the end of *West Side Story*. Maybe Maria is exactly wrong when she says "...it's not us! It's everything around us." Maybe it is Maria and Tony who are to blame.

It seems perfectly natural for Tony to progress from gang member to drugstore employee and serious lover of Maria and, eventually, a family man. What seems less natural is his attempt in the play to go back to his old gang to try and stop them from carrying out their normal gang activities, that is, fighting. And why does he do this? He does it because of

Maria, who is horrified at the very notion of fighting and wants Tony to prevent even a fistfight.

Now, the interesting thing is that it was Tony who convinced the gangs to conduct a fistfight rather than use more dangerous weapons. In doing so, Tony is perhaps adopting something of a parental role, and channeling the energies of the Jets and Sharks into a fairly innocuous fistfight seems like a good thing.

Even at that stage, though, Tony has almost become too much the adult, a bit like cantankerous Doc. He arrives on the scene while the gangs are discussing weapons and immediately exaggerates the dangers of the proposed fight. The gangs have been suggesting using bats or clubs or bricks, but when Tony arrives, he starts talking as if they had been planning to use guns or knives. Having set up that phony extreme, invented by himself, he then proposes a more moderate alternative. It is a reasonable alternative, and yet he somehow seems to have manipulated the gangs into it by distorting what they were originally proposing, like some sort of meddling outsider. Tony by this time—indeed, from the very beginning of the play—is no longer a true gang member or adolescent but is approaching events from a different perspective.

This perspective might be characterized as an adult perspective, as something more mature than an adolescent perspective, but it does seem almost out of place in the "war council" between two teenage gangs. Still, the result—an innocuous fistfight—seems positive.

But then Tony intervenes again, at Maria's urging, to stop even the fistfight. The result of that is catastrophe. His attempt leads to a fight with knives between Riff and Bernardo, and when he tries to stop that, he merely distracts Riff enough to let Bernardo kill him, after which Tony kills Bernardo.

It is a disaster, and it clearly seems to be caused by the quasi-adult Tony trying to stop the fight, trying to stop a fairly harmless and natural expression of youthful energies. Anita has a quite different attitude to such a fight than does Tony or Maria. Maria, angry about the fighting, asks the reason for it, and Anita says: "You saw how they dance: like they have to get rid of something, quick. That's how they fight." Anita respects the imperatives of youth, especially the urges that motivate young males. She even celebrates these, for the energies expressed

in a fight, in her view, carry over afterward, so she expects Bernardo to be very "healthy" after the rumble when he joins her.

But Maria, expressing perhaps the horror of a child, or perhaps that of a wife-to-be, will have none of this. The fight must be stopped, even if it is only a fistfight. But if we accept Anita's analysis of young males, Maria's view may be a terrible mistake. To suppress natural energies, to drive them underground, to try and prevent a fairly innocuous fight, may be to cause those energies to erupt in a much less innocuous form, which is exactly what happens. The attempt to suppress a fistfight leads to something much worse, something much more deadly, than a fistfight.

Thus it may not be mad passion, as in *Romeo and Juliet*, that causes the tragedy. It also may not be primarily prejudice and ethnic hatred that are to blame. The blame may be linked to an attempt to suppress the natural energies of youth, an attempt carried out by someone (Tony) moving out of the youth phase and into the adult phase of life.

What may be lurking beneath the love story and the social document, in other words, may be another story about the conflict between teenagers and adults. In this context, the comic song "Gee, Officer Krupke," which some see as out of place in a tragic story like this one, seems to fit in perfectly. In the Officer Krupke song, the Jets mock a whole range of adult approaches to the supposed problem of juvenile delinquency. Judges, social workers, policemen, and psychiatrists all get their comeuppance, and at the end one is left thinking, What fools these adults are, meddling with youths who, after all, at the beginning of the play seem relatively harmless.

At the beginning of *West Side Story*, the Jets seem almost like innocent little boys. They want to hang a sign saying "Visitors forbidden" and they will have none of the girl Anybodys joining them. It is like boys in a clubhouse saying "No Girls Allowed." Even in the first fight, A-rab goes zooming around like a make-believe airplane, like a boy playing a game. It is true, he then gets cut by the Sharks, but it still seems like kid stuff—so much so that when the police ask about it, the Jets clam up entirely. In general, though the police try to work with the Jets against the Sharks, the Jets repeatedly refuse. It is as if the true enemy is not the Sharks, not the Puerto Ricans—though, granted, the Jets do make some conventional derogatory remarks about Puerto Ricans. The true enemy is the police force and, by extension, all adults: those social workers and psychiatrists who think they can "cure" the teenagers of their supposed problems.

But what if the teenagers have no real problem, except the problem that adults keep meddling with them? What if the Jets and Sharks were allowed to do as they please, engaging in a few rumbles and a fistfight? Perhaps they would never have progressed to serious weapons and deaths. Certainly, some of the Jets seem quite uneasy at the prospect of serious weapons. Tony's notion that the Jets are eager to use guns and knives seems quite wrong. When Baby John hears talk about zip guns, his response is the nervous one of "Zip guns... Gee!" And when Snowboy says, "But if they say knives or guns," Baby John comments: "I say let's forget the whole thing."

Riff the leader does say he will get a switchblade if it is required, but it is significant that he would have to "get" it. It is not something he already has. Meanwhile, with the war council looming, Snowboy goes off to the movies, and when talk turns once more to weapons A-rab says nervously that he hopes it will not be more than rubber hoses.

Near the very end of the play, after two killings and the false rumor about Maria's death, Tony calls out: "It's not playing any more!" He is quite distraught over Maria and is looking for death, but it is interesting that he suggests that at one time it was playing. At the beginning of the story it was playing. In the "Jet Song," what the Jets look forward to is being the "top cat in town, ... the gold-medal kid / With the heavyweight crown." They are imagining themselves in a boxing match and winning a medal.

It is as if the Jets and the Sharks are preparing for some sort of athletic contest, a football game perhaps, and the adults around them refuse to let it go on. The adults do not simply try to put limits on the game; they try to suppress it entirely, and that way lies disaster.

The underlying message of *West Side Story*, therefore, is not so much that prejudice and hatred are bad, though they are, nor that true love is doomed because it must exist in a violent, hostile world, but that boys should be allowed to be boys, that teenagers should be allowed to have their "rumbles," and that if only adults stayed out of the way, things would have a chance to work out.

Carolann M. Sanita as Maria and Ryan Silverman as Tony in a 2004 production of West Side Story *at the German Opera in Berlin* (AP Images)

Source: Sheldon Goldfarb, Critical Essay on *West Side Story*, in *Drama for Students*, Gale, Cengage Learning, 2010.

Christopher Morley

In the following review, Morley notes the reactions to West Side Story *productions, then and now.*

Leonard Bernstein's *West Side Story* hit the world stage in New York's Winter Garden Theatre on September 26, 1957. Its impact was astonishing.

With audiences brought up on the cosy, chocolate-box happy-ever-after operetta and musical—even the brutal *Carousel* ends with a redemption in Heaven—the show hit hard in its depiction of inner-city gang warfare and racial tension.

Though it ends in reconciliation between rival tribes, we remain wondering how fragile this truce is. And, of course, its subject-matter remains painfully relevant today.

Its *Romeo and Juliet* story-line had occurred to the choreographer Jerome Robbins as far back as 1949, when he conceived an East Side Story depicting a love-story between members of the Catholic and Jewish faiths in an America where anti-Semitic feelings were running high.

But tensions between young Los Angeleans and Mexican immigrants during the early 1950s sparked the idea of Latin-American dance-rhythms in Bernstein's mind and the action was shifted to New York with its element of proud, sassy Puerto Ricans among its population. Amazingly and brilliantly, Robbins kept the casts of the rival Jets and Sharks gangs apart during rehearsals for the show's opening run, raising the simmering rivalry to boiling-point by the time they met onstage.

The Shakespearean background to the subject-matter has become almost a cliché, as expressed in John Godber's hilarious play *Teechers,* written for Hull Truck Theatre Company in 1987:

> NIXON (drama teacher): I think it would be a very good thing for us to start with a very important person in the world of drama. Mr William Shakespeare. And in particular a play that you've probably seen but don't realize it. *Romeo and Juliet.*
> (GAIL and HOBBY groan.) Which is a tragedy.
> GAIL: And it's the basis for *West Side Story,* and it's about neighbours arguing.
> HOBBY: We've done it. . . .

But never mind such dismissiveness, *West Side Story* remains one of the most important works ever written for the stage. It opened the doors for musicals which dealt with the most serious of subjects, from the Passion of Jesus Christ to the Vietnam War, from the French Revolution to the Cold War.

And to achieve this stature it needed a composer of the utmost integrity and versatility, one who could turn his hand to a variety of styles but who could also boast intimate involvement with the greatest examples of "classical music".

That man was Leonard Bernstein, already an acclaimed composer of symphonic music and a world-renowned orchestral and operatic conductor (he had conducted the American premiere of Britten's *Peter Grimes* at Tanglewood in 1946 and the world premiere of Messiaen's immense *Turangalila-Symphonie* in Boston in 1948). He later became music director of the famous New York Philharmonic Orchestra, a successor down the line to the mighty Gustav Mahler who had held the position in the early 1900s.

On the most unforgettable evening of my life, one August night in 1968, I stood backstage in the wings at the Teatro La Fenice in Venice to hear and watch Bernstein conducting his NYPO in Mahler's *Fifth Symphony*.

Afterwards, in such a gracious and kind meeting, Bernstein told me how, had he been born 50 years earlier, he was sure he would have composed a work in exactly the same vein (Mahler and he were both composer-conductors, both Jewish, both exiles from their homeland).

So Bernstein's musical pedigree was immaculate, and it certainly shows in *West Side Story* with ensembles of operatic vibrancy, such as "A Boy Like That" and the wonderful Balcony Scene in which Tony and Maria express their new young love across the racial divide.

Later on in the action, the "Tonight" which they have sung to each other becomes the core of an amazing five-part ensemble in which different characters express vastly differing emotions, as brilliantly built as any of the great setpieces by Mozart or Verdi.

Bernstein uses his "classical" experience in such subtle ways, one example being the fugue he introduces into "Cool," the musical material here derived from Beethoven's awesome "Grosse Fuge." Godber's Mr Nixon might well have told his unruly pupils that they'd been listening to late-period Beethoven without realising it.

But there are several kinds of "American" music in the score, too, with the many famous examples of various Latin-American dance rhythms, the ballet sequence depicting a "Somewhere" as wide-eyed and innocent as Copland's "Appalachian Spring," and the uproarious vaudeville of "Gee, Officer Krupke" with its brazenly witty lyrics by Stephen Sondheim.

Bernstein and Sondheim were present for the European premiere of *West Side Story* at the Manchester Opera House in December 1958. As was Bert Hackett, until recently the much-loved cartoonist Gemini on the *Birming-ham Post,* and at that time working for the *Manchester Evening News.*

"In those days I used to read *Time* and *Life* magazines, to keep up with what was happening in America," he remembers.

"The show got rave reviews, so when I learned it was coming to Manchester, I booked up for it.

"I was really excited about it, and found it electrifying. It was a grand gala occasion, and both Lenny Bernstein and Stephen Sondheim were there.

"The reaction of the audience was interesting.

"There were a lot of elderly bluerinse women, who at first expressed disappointment, and then anger. They'd been expecting to see something along the lines of *The Sound of Music,* the traditional American musical coming over to England, which had been a big success.

"But the younger elements in the audience were so excited and so moved by the energy and relevance of the show." Just a little postscript. Before I was appointed classical music correspondent of the *Birmingham Post* on April Fool's Day 1988, I used to do a lot of conducting. I was persuaded out of retirement in 1992 to wield the baton in a week-long run of *West Side Story* at Dudley Castle.

It rained every night. To protect the instruments, they put the orchestra into a dungeon with banks of closed-circuit television screens, with a camera upon me; I insisted upon staying in full contact with the stage, protected by a little tented kiosk like an ice-cream-seller's.

The dancers risked their limbs on that rain-sodden staging, the audience shivered in their cagoules. But Lenny, I'm sure, was up there, blessing and smiling, and I felt I was paying him back for that magical evening 24 years earlier.

Source: Christopher Morley, "Classic That's Still Ready to Rumble," in *Birmingham Post,* April 15, 2009, p. 18.

Martin Samuel

In the following review, Samuel emphasizes the relevancy of West Side Story *to modern audiences as the show celebrates its 50th anniversary.*

When Jerome Robbins, the director and choreographer of *West Side Story* and, as such, the man who transformed modern musical theatre, called his friend Leonard Bernstein, the composer, on January 6, 1949, with the concept of an

> LEAVING THE THEATRE WE KNOW THAT THIS SCENARIO WILL BE PLAYED OUT TIME AND AGAIN, MERELY WITH DIFFERENT CADENCES, MOTIVATIONS AND BACKDROPS."

updated version of *Romeo and Juliet,* he did not mention Sharks and Jets, or even young Americans and Puerto Ricans. The divided clans that Robbins proposed were Jews and Catholics.

The setting was still the New York slums, and the theme of love versus hate would not alter in the long years between that first conversation and opening night, but the backdrop to the racial, religious tension was going to be the Easter and Passover celebrations, Juliet was to be a Jew and her Romeo a Roman Catholic. It took more than eight years for the project to reach the stage, by which time it, and the city in which it was based, had changed greatly, with the arrival of almost 600,000 immigrants from a single north Caribbean island. "We have abandoned the whole Jewish-Catholic premise as not very fresh," wrote Bernstein on August 25, 1955, "and have come up with what I think is going to be it: two teenage gangs, one the warring Puerto Ricans, the other self-styled 'Americans'. Suddenly it all springs to life. I hear rhythms and pulses and, most of all, I can feel the form."

Certainly, it is impossible to imagine *West Side Story* without its sultry and exotic flavours, its mambos and hemiolas, but while these elements and Stephen Sondheim's brilliant words tie the work and its characters to a specific time and place, its message is timeless. More than five decades on from its first performance in Washington, *West Side Story* remains as relevant as ever; some may argue more so. Its revival at Sadler's Wells, on the 50th anniversary of its debut in the West End, which opened last week to excellent reviews, confirms it as one of the great artistic achievements of the 20th century, with an enduring significance.

In London, a city that has had 70 murders this year, many teenagers of first or second-generation immigrant parentage, a tale of angry, edgy young men, their misdirected sense of self-worth tragically reliant on violent and dangerous gang culture says more about our world than many newer productions or commentaries; and they don't have Bernstein's tunes or Sondheim's delicious wordplay, either. *West Side Story* was written at a time when restaurants displayed signs barring dogs and Puerto Ricans (Porto Ricans, to the gang of whites known as the Jets), a distrust that will be familiar to some members of modern immigrant communities. These new citizens feel victimised and shunned and see insularity as the sole means of protection from the spite of the natives, displaying the same cynicism and contempt that Maria's brother Bernardo had for the American dream. This West Side could be any city in Britain on any day of the week and this Story does not need extensive modernising when one considers how little society has progressed in half a century.

The librettist Arthur Laurents and Sondheim as lyricist were limited only by the conventions of their time. Their gang members could not swear, nor could director Robbins douse the stage in spilt blood. Zip guns were mentioned because real guns were harder for juveniles to come by. Times change, sadly. Laurents intends to correct this with a revival scheduled to start at the National Theatre, Washington, in December, transferring to Broadway in February, which will be improved by rewritten exchanges in Spanish. "This show will be radically different from any production of *West Side Story* ever done," he promises. "The musical theatre and cultural conventions of 1957 made it next to impossible for the characters to have authenticity. Every member of both gangs was always a potential killer even then. Now they actually will be. Only Tony and Maria try to live in a different world." Laurents's desire to refashion his work is noble, but to some extent unnecessary. We got the point anyway. The production at Sadler's Wells would be termed conventional by comparison but, despite this, Laurents's original statement that the currency of hatred, and of gang life, is murder is clear. The deaths of Bernardo, Riff and Tony do not have to be made visceral to reach a modern audience. The action and the language, while very much of its time, speak a universal truth.

Although the narrative of *West Side Story* was not new to Laurents, the same could be said of *Romeo and Juliet* to Shakespeare. Matteo Bandello, an Italian poet and novelist, is credited with the first version of the tale, translated by Arthur Brooke as *The Tragical History of Romeus and Juliet* in 1562 and reprinted in 1587, ten years before Shakespeare's play was performed. There was also a prose version, published as one of 60 stories contained in a book, *The Palace of Pleasure,* written by William Painter in 1582. Yet the mission of *West Side Story* was not to overhaul Elizabethan poetry, but to challenge the conventions of musical theatre without, as Bernstein put it, falling into the operatic trap. "A musical that tells a tragic story in musical-comedy terms, using only musical-comedy techniques," he wrote. "If it can work, it's the first." And it was. The year that *West Side Story* opened was part of a golden age for musicals. Bernstein and Sondheim's piece did not even win the 1958 Tony, which went to *The Music Man* by Meredith Willson, another stunning show, innovative, evocative and rich in language and melody (and currently revived in Chichester, coincidentally). In *The Music Man,* however, love triumphs, the conman Harold Hill deciding to stay with his sweetheart and face the wrath of the small Iowa community that he has swindled, rather than skipping town with his ill-gotten loot. By contrast, *West Side Story* ends with the violent death of its hero, following the equally senseless murder of two young men, and only the enormity of these events brings the cycle of violence to an end: for now. Leaving the theatre we know that this scenario will be played out time and again, merely with different cadences, motivations and backdrops.

Not that *The Music Man* is of little consequence by comparison. On the contrary, Willson's score is highly original, making use of everything from barbershop quartets to piano tutorials and the rhythmic sound of a moving train, and he was right confident enough in his achievement to refuse to compromise when studio boss Jack L. Warner wanted to replace leading man and Tony winner Robert Preston with Frank Sinatra or Cary Grant when casting the film role. *The Music Man* is a wonderful musical; go and see it, or rent the movie. But it isn't *West Side Story*; because nothing is.

West Side Story's choreography alone sets it apart (Robbins did win a Tony for that at least), because so much of its emotion is expressed through dance. Creating these scenes was a monumental task because Bernstein thought like a composer, not a hoofer. Rita Moreno, who played

Anita in the film, explained that dancers work in counts of four, six and eight. "Then along comes Leonard Bernstein with his 5/4 time, his 6/8 time, his 25/6 time: it was crazy," she recalled. "It was very difficult to dance to that kind of music, because it doesn't make dancer sense." (There have been few British hit singles written in 5/4 time, one being "Take Five" by Dave Brubeck, the other "Living in the Past" by Jethro Tull, for the simple reason that you can't dance to it without looking like a drunk at a wedding with an inner-ear complication.) The DVD of the film contains an extra segment that makes apparent the achievement of Robbins's choreography. He rehearsed for three months, revised everything on location, and his instructions were so demanding that no scene was filmed all the way through. Some dancers suffered injury, some collapsed through exhaustion, he would have gang members scaling high fences, bare-handed, and jumping down to a playground, all in time. This was new, and it still is.

Watch a conventional chorus line in action to understand the radical nature of the movement in *West Side Story*. "What are they dancing about?" asked Robbins of his juvenile delinquents, and then answered his question with an opening sequence that perfectly sets up the bravado, the roll, the sneer, the pure physical power and arrogant grace of being in a gang. And he says it all, at first, with something as simple as finger snaps and a walk.

Robbins's choreography is so good that it is sometimes possible to overlook Bernstein's immense score, which has such density that when it was first performed at the Winter Garden Theatre in New York, the orchestra could not fit into the pit, and the woodwind section had to play multiple instruments.

Much has been made of the fact that in the film version, the singing of the two lead roles were dubbed, but what is rarely offered as mitigation is how few musicals call for the principal actor to hit the extended high B-flat that concludes "Maria," a song as close to an aria as anything heard in popular music.

Indeed, so aspirational was Bernstein's score that Marni Nixon, who provided the voice of Maria for Natalie Wood, also had to assist Moreno as Anita, and in some parts of the song "Tonight" ends up in a duet with herself. (Nixon was also Deborah Kerr's voice in certain songs in *The King And I*, sung all of Audrey Hepburn's parts in *My Fair Lady* and did the top notes of

"Diamonds Are a Girl's Best Friend" for Marilyn Monroe. At the age of 78, she is appearing in the US revival of *My Fair Lady* as Mrs Higgins. A bit of a trouper, you might say.) Even in the original stage production, Bernstein eschewed experienced singers, wanting the raw kid quality that an untrained voice would bring. He then took those kids and introduced them to something called five-part counterpoint. This is why *West Side Story* continues to matter. Artistically, it was heroically ambitious for its time, and in a world in which a musical is now a repackaged compilation of Boney M's hits, a safe, dumbed-down, populist money-grab, offering nothing new and taking no chances, it remains the standard of what it is possible to achieve.

Equally, its message is tragically untroubled by time. The best live action short film at the 2007 Oscars was *West Bank Story,* a 21-minute parody of the work, set among warring Israeli and Palestinian falafel stands, directed by Ari Sandel. There is not a city in the world in which *West Side Story* does not have resonance and, in London, its moral is more urgent than ever.

Bernstein said it best. "Alas, the materials of the work have not become dated," he mused. "Would that they had, for the sake of our world."

Source: Martin Samuel, "The Fight's Still On," in *Times* (London), July 31, 2008, p. 4.

SOURCES

Flinn, Denny Martin, "The Significance of Dance and Song in *West Side Story*," in *Readings on West Side Story*, edited by Mary E. Williams, Greenhaven Press, 2001, pp. 64–65.

Garebian, Keith, *The Making of West Side Story*, ECW Press, 1995, pp. 9, 35, 39–40, 71, 75–76, 79–80, 140.

Gibbs, Wolcott, "The Plot of *West Side Story* Is Implausible," in *Readings on West Side Story*, edited by Mary E. Williams, Greenhaven Press, 2001, p. 115.

Hewes, Henry, "*West Side Story* Brilliantly Expresses the Character of Teenage Gangs," in *Readings on West Side Story*, edited by Mary E. Williams, Greenhaven Press, 2001, p. 120.

Hine, Thomas, *The Rise and Fall of the American Teenager*, Harper Perennial, 2000, http://www.thomashine.com/the_rise_and_fall_of_the_american_teenager_3432.htm (accessed August 25, 2009).

Kauffmann, Stanley, "An Exceptional Yet Disappointing Film Musical," in *Readings on West Side Story*, edited by Mary E. Williams, Greenhaven Press, 2001, p. 126.

Laurents, Arthur, *Original Story by Arthur Laurents: A Memoir of Broadway and Hollywood*, Knopf, 2000, p. 349.

———, Stephen Sondheim, Leonard Bernstein, and Jerome Robbins, *West Side Story: A Musical* , new ed., Heinemann, 1972.

Mellers, Wilfrid, "The Narrative and Thematic Significance of Music in *West Side Story*," in *Readings on West Side Story*, edited by Mary E. Williams, Greenhaven Press, 2001, pp. 67, 70.

Miller, Scott, "An Examination of *West Side Story*'s Plot and Musical Motifs," in *Readings on West Side Story*, edited by Mary E. Williams, Greenhaven Press, 2001, pp. 78, 81.

Olson, James S., *Historical Dictionary of the 1950s*, Greenwood Press, 2000, p.149.

Phillips, Lily, "Blue Jeans, Black Leather Jackets, and a Sneer: The Iconography of the 1950s Biker and Its Translation Abroad," in *International Journal of Motorcycle Studies*, March 2005, http://ijms.nova.edu/March2005/IJMS_ArtclPhilips0305.html (accessed August 25, 2009).

Williams, Mary E., ed., "Introduction" to *Readings on West Side Story*, Greenhaven Press, 2001, p. 12.

———, "*West Side Story* and Its Creators," in *Readings on West Side Story*, Greenhaven Press, 2001, pp. 15, 20.

Zadan, Craig, "The Creative Process behind *West Side Story*," in *Readings on West Side Story*, edited by Mary E. Williams, Greenhaven Press, 2001, p. 52.

FURTHER READING

Ayala, César J., and Rafael Bernabe, *Puerto Rico in the American Century: A History since 1898*, University of North Carolina Press, 2007.
> Ayala and Bernabe present a history of Puerto Rico under American rule and also discuss the situation of Puerto Ricans on the American mainland, especially in New York.

McGee, Mark Thomas, and R. J. Robertson, *The J. D. Films: Juvenile Delinquency in the Movies*, McFarland, 1982.
> The authors present an informative survey of movies treating juvenile delinquency, including the movie version of *West Side Story*.

Palladino, Grace, *Teenagers: An American History*, Basic Books, 1997.
> Palladino presents a history of the rise of the concept of the teenager, discussing everything from rock and roll to *Seventeen* magazine.

Shoemaker, Donald J., *Juvenile Delinquency*, Rowman & Littlefield, 2009.
> After presenting a historical overview of juvenile delinquency, Shoemaker examines the issue from a variety of perspectives, discussing drug use, female delinquency, schools, religion, family, race, and class.

Glossary of Literary Terms

A

Abstract: Used as a noun, the term refers to a short summary or outline of a longer work. As an adjective applied to writing or literary works, abstract refers to words or phrases that name things not knowable through the five senses. Examples of abstracts include the *Cliffs Notes* summaries of major literary works. Examples of abstract terms or concepts include "idea," "guilt" "honesty," and "loyalty."

Absurd, Theater of the: See *Theater of the Absurd*

Absurdism: See *Theater of the Absurd*

Act: A major section of a play. Acts are divided into varying numbers of shorter scenes. From ancient times to the nineteenth century plays were generally constructed of five acts, but modern works typically consist of one, two, or three acts. Examples of five-act plays include the works of Sophocles and Shakespeare, while the plays of Arthur Miller commonly have a three-act structure.

Acto: A one-act Chicano theater piece developed out of collective improvisation. *Actos* were performed by members of Luis Valdez's Teatro Campesino in California during the mid-1960s.

Aestheticism: A literary and artistic movement of the nineteenth century. Followers of the movement believed that art should not be mixed with social, political, or moral teaching.

The statement "art for art's sake" is a good summary of aestheticism. The movement had its roots in France, but it gained widespread importance in England in the last half of the nineteenth century, where it helped change the Victorian practice of including moral lessons in literature. Oscar Wilde is one of the best-known "aesthetes" of the late nineteenth century.

Age of Johnson: The period in English literature between 1750 and 1798, named after the most prominent literary figure of the age, Samuel Johnson. Works written during this time are noted for their emphasis on "sensibility," or emotional quality. These works formed a transition between the rational works of the Age of Reason, or Neoclassical period, and the emphasis on individual feelings and responses of the Romantic period. Significant writers during the Age of Johnson included the novelists Ann Radcliffe and Henry Mackenzie, dramatists Richard Sheridan and Oliver Goldsmith, and poets William Collins and Thomas Gray. Also known as Age of Sensibility

Age of Reason: See *Neoclassicism*

Age of Sensibility: See *Age of Johnson*

Alexandrine Meter: See *Meter*

Allegory: A narrative technique in which characters representing things or abstract ideas are used to convey a message or teach a lesson. Allegory is typically used to teach moral, ethical, or religious lessons but is sometimes used for satiric or political purposes. Examples of allegorical works include Edmund Spenser's *The Faerie Queene* and John Bunyan's *The Pilgrim's Progress.*

Allusion: A reference to a familiar literary or historical person or event, used to make an idea more easily understood. For example, describing someone as a "Romeo" makes an allusion to William Shakespeare's famous young lover in *Romeo and Juliet.*

Amerind Literature: The writing and oral traditions of Native Americans. Native American literature was originally passed on by word of mouth, so it consisted largely of stories and events that were easily memorized. Amerind prose is often rhythmic like poetry because it was recited to the beat of a ceremonial drum. Examples of Amerind literature include the autobiographical *Black Elk Speaks,* the works of N. Scott Momaday, James Welch, and Craig Lee Strete, and the poetry of Luci Tapahonso.

Analogy: A comparison of two things made to explain something unfamiliar through its similarities to something familiar, or to prove one point based on the acceptedness of another. Similes and metaphors are types of analogies. Analogies often take the form of an extended simile, as in William Blake's aphorism: "As the caterpillar chooses the fairest leaves to lay her eggs on, so the priest lays his curse on the fairest joys."

Angry Young Men: A group of British writers of the 1950s whose work expressed bitterness and disillusionment with society. Common to their work is an anti-hero who rebels against a corrupt social order and strives for personal integrity. The term has been used to describe Kingsley Amis, John Osborne, Colin Wilson, John Wain, and others.

Antagonist: The major character in a narrative or drama who works against the hero or protagonist. An example of an evil antagonist is Richard Lovelace in Samuel Richardson's *Clarissa,* while a virtuous antagonist is Macduff in William Shakespeare's *Macbeth.*

Anthropomorphism: The presentation of animals or objects in human shape or with human characteristics. The term is derived from the Greek word for "human form." The fables of Aesop, the animated films of Walt Disney, and Richard Adams's *Watership Down* feature anthropomorphic characters.

Anti-hero: A central character in a work of literature who lacks traditional heroic qualities such as courage, physical prowess, and fortitude. Anti-heros typically distrust conventional values and are unable to commit themselves to any ideals. They generally feel helpless in a world over which they have no control. Anti-heroes usually accept, and often celebrate, their positions as social outcasts. A well-known anti-hero is Yossarian in Joseph Heller's novel *Catch-22.*

Antimasque: See *Masque*

Antithesis: The antithesis of something is its direct opposite. In literature, the use of antithesis as a figure of speech results in two statements that show a contrast through the balancing of two opposite ideas. Technically, it is the second portion of the statement that is defined as the "antithesis"; the first portion is the "thesis." An example of antithesis is found in the following portion of Abraham Lincoln's "Gettysburg Address"; notice the opposition between the verbs "remember" and "forget" and the phrases "what we say" and "what they did": "The world will little note nor long remember what we say here, but it can never forget what they did here."

Apocrypha: Writings tentatively attributed to an author but not proven or universally accepted to be their works. The term was originally applied to certain books of the Bible that were not considered inspired and so were not included in the "sacred canon." Geoffrey Chaucer, William Shakespeare, Thomas Kyd, Thomas Middleton, and John Marston all have apocrypha. Apocryphal books of the Bible include the Old Testament's Book of Enoch and New Testament's Gospel of Peter.

Apollonian and Dionysian: The two impulses believed to guide authors of dramatic tragedy. The Apollonian impulse is named after Apollo, the Greek god of light and beauty and the symbol of intellectual order. The Dionysian impulse is named after Dionysus, the Greek god of wine and the symbol of the unrestrained forces of nature. The Apollonian impulse is to create a rational, harmonious world, while the Dionysian is to express the irrational forces of personality.

Friedrich Nietzche uses these terms in *The Birth of Tragedy* to designate contrasting elements in Greek tragedy.

Apostrophe: A statement, question, or request addressed to an inanimate object or concept or to a nonexistent or absent person. Requests for inspiration from the muses in poetry are examples of apostrophe, as is Marc Antony's address to Caesar's corpse in William Shakespeare's *Julius Caesar*: "O, pardon me, thou bleeding piece of earth, That I am meek and gentle with these butchers! . . . Woe to the hand that shed this costly blood! . . . "

Archetype: The word archetype is commonly used to describe an original pattern or model from which all other things of the same kind are made. This term was introduced to literary criticism from the psychology of Carl Jung. It expresses Jung's theory that behind every person's "unconscious," or repressed memories of the past, lies the "collective unconscious" of the human race: memories of the countless typical experiences of our ancestors. These memories are said to prompt illogical associations that trigger powerful emotions in the reader. Often, the emotional process is primitive, even primordial. Archetypes are the literary images that grow out of the "collective unconscious." They appear in literature as incidents and plots that repeat basic patterns of life. They may also appear as stereotyped characters. Examples of literary archetypes include themes such as birth and death and characters such as the Earth Mother.

Argument: The argument of a work is the author's subject matter or principal idea. Examples of defined "argument" portions of works include John Milton's *Arguments* to each of the books of *Paradise Lost* and the "Argument" to Robert Herrick's *Hesperides*.

Aristotelian Criticism: Specifically, the method of evaluating and analyzing tragedy formulated by the Greek philosopher Aristotle in his *Poetics*. More generally, the term indicates any form of criticism that follows Aristotle's views. Aristotelian criticism focuses on the form and logical structure of a work, apart from its historical or social context, in contrast to "Platonic Criticism," which stresses the usefulness of art. Adherents of New Criticism including John Crowe Ransom and Cleanth Brooks utilize and value the basic ideas of Aristotelian criticism for textual analysis.

Art for Art's Sake: See *Aestheticism*

Aside: A comment made by a stage performer that is intended to be heard by the audience but supposedly not by other characters. Eugene O'Neill's *Strange Interlude* is an extended use of the aside in modern theater.

Audience: The people for whom a piece of literature is written. Authors usually write with a certain audience in mind, for example, children, members of a religious or ethnic group, or colleagues in a professional field. The term "audience" also applies to the people who gather to see or hear any performance, including plays, poetry readings, speeches, and concerts. Jane Austen's parody of the gothic novel, *Northanger Abbey,* was originally intended for (and also pokes fun at) an audience of young and avid female gothic novel readers.

Avant-garde: A French term meaning "vanguard." It is used in literary criticism to describe new writing that rejects traditional approaches to literature in favor of innovations in style or content. Twentieth-century examples of the literary *avant-garde* include the Black Mountain School of poets, the Bloomsbury Group, and the Beat Movement.

B

Ballad: A short poem that tells a simple story and has a repeated refrain. Ballads were originally intended to be sung. Early ballads, known as folk ballads, were passed down through generations, so their authors are often unknown. Later ballads composed by known authors are called literary ballads. An example of an anonymous folk ballad is "Edward," which dates from the Middle Ages. Samuel Taylor Coleridge's "The Rime of the Ancient Mariner" and John Keats's "La Belle Dame sans Merci" are examples of literary ballads.

Baroque: A term used in literary criticism to describe literature that is complex or ornate in style or diction. Baroque works typically express tension, anxiety, and violent emotion. The term "Baroque Age" designates a period in Western European literature beginning in the late sixteenth century and ending about one hundred years later. Works of this period often mirror the qualities of works more generally associated with the label "baroque" and sometimes feature elaborate conceits. Examples of Baroque works include John Lyly's *Euphues: The Anatomy of Wit*, Luis de Gongora's *Soledads*, and William Shakespeare's *As You Like It*.

Baroque Age: See *Baroque*

Baroque Period: See *Baroque*

Beat Generation: See *Beat Movement*

Beat Movement: A period featuring a group of American poets and novelists of the 1950s and 1960s—including Jack Kerouac, Allen Ginsberg, Gregory Corso, William S. Burroughs, and Lawrence Ferlinghetti—who rejected established social and literary values. Using such techniques as stream of consciousness writing and jazz-influenced free verse and focusing on unusual or abnormal states of mind—generated by religious ecstasy or the use of drugs—the Beat writers aimed to create works that were unconventional in both form and subject matter. Kerouac's *On the Road* is perhaps the best-known example of a Beat Generation novel, and Ginsberg's *Howl* is a famous collection of Beat poetry.

Black Aesthetic Movement: A period of artistic and literary development among African Americans in the 1960s and early 1970s. This was the first major African-American artistic movement since the Harlem Renaissance and was closely paralleled by the civil rights and black power movements. The black aesthetic writers attempted to produce works of art that would be meaningful to the black masses. Key figures in black aesthetics included one of its founders, poet and playwright Amiri Baraka, formerly known as LeRoi Jones; poet and essayist Haki R. Madhubuti, formerly Don L. Lee; poet and playwright Sonia Sanchez; and dramatist Ed Bullins. Works representative of the Black Aesthetic Movement include Amiri Baraka's play *Dutchman*, a 1964 Obie award-winner; *Black Fire: An Anthology of Afro-American Writing*, edited by Baraka and playwright Larry Neal and published in 1968; and Sonia Sanchez's poetry collection *We a BaddDDD People*, published in 1970. Also known as Black Arts Movement.

Black Arts Movement: See *Black Aesthetic Movement*

Black Comedy: See *Black Humor*

Black Humor: Writing that places grotesque elements side by side with humorous ones in an attempt to shock the reader, forcing him or her to laugh at the horrifying reality of a disordered world. Joseph Heller's novel *Catch-22* is considered a superb example of the use of black humor. Other well-known authors who use black humor include Kurt Vonnegut, Edward Albee, Eugene Ionesco, and Harold Pinter. Also known as Black Comedy.

Blank Verse: Loosely, any unrhymed poetry, but more generally, unrhymed iambic pentameter verse (composed of lines of five two-syllable feet with the first syllable accented, the second unaccented). Blank verse has been used by poets since the Renaissance for its flexibility and its graceful, dignified tone. John Milton's *Paradise Lost* is in blank verse, as are most of William Shakespeare's plays.

Bloomsbury Group: A group of English writers, artists, and intellectuals who held informal artistic and philosophical discussions in Bloomsbury, a district of London, from around 1907 to the early 1930s. The Bloomsbury Group held no uniform philosophical beliefs but did commonly express an aversion to moral prudery and a desire for greater social tolerance. At various times the circle included Virginia Woolf, E. M. Forster, Clive Bell, Lytton Strachey, and John Maynard Keynes.

Bon Mot: A French term meaning "good word." A *bon mot* is a witty remark or clever observation. Charles Lamb and Oscar Wilde are celebrated for their witty *bon mots*. Two examples by Oscar Wilde stand out: (1) "All women become their mothers. That is their tragedy. No man does. That's his." (2) "A man cannot be too careful in the choice of his enemies."

Breath Verse: See *Projective Verse*

Burlesque: Any literary work that uses exaggeration to make its subject appear ridiculous, either by treating a trivial subject with profound seriousness or by treating a dignified subject frivolously. The word "burlesque" may also be used as an adjective, as in "burlesque show," to mean "striptease act." Examples of literary burlesque include the comedies of Aristophanes, Miguel de Cervantes's *Don Quixote*, Samuel Butler's poem "Hudibras," and John Gay's play *The Beggar's Opera*.

C

Cadence: The natural rhythm of language caused by the alternation of accented and unaccented syllables. Much modern poetry—notably free verse—deliberately manipulates cadence to create complex rhythmic effects. James Macpherson's "Ossian poems" are richly cadenced, as is the poetry of the Symbolists, Walt Whitman, and Amy Lowell.

Caesura: A pause in a line of poetry, usually occurring near the middle. It typically corresponds to a break in the natural rhythm or sense of the line but is sometimes shifted to create special meanings or rhythmic effects. The opening line of Edgar Allan Poe's "The Raven" contains a caesura following "dreary": "Once upon a midnight dreary, while I pondered weak and weary...."

Canzone: A short Italian or Provencal lyric poem, commonly about love and often set to music. The *canzone* has no set form but typically contains five or six stanzas made up of seven to twenty lines of eleven syllables each. A shorter, five- to ten-line "envoy," or concluding stanza, completes the poem. Masters of the *canzone* form include Petrarch, Dante Alighieri, Torquato Tasso, and Guido Cavalcanti.

Carpe Diem: A Latin term meaning "seize the day." This is a traditional theme of poetry, especially lyrics. A *carpe diem* poem advises the reader or the person it addresses to live for today and enjoy the pleasures of the moment. Two celebrated *carpe diem* poems are Andrew Marvell's "To His Coy Mistress" and Robert Herrick's poem beginning "Gather ye rosebuds while ye may...."

Catharsis: The release or purging of unwanted emotions—specifically fear and pity—brought about by exposure to art. The term was first used by the Greek philosopher Aristotle in his *Poetics* to refer to the desired effect of tragedy on spectators. A famous example of catharsis is realized in Sophocles' *Oedipus Rex,* when Oedipus discovers that his wife, Jacosta, is his own mother and that the stranger he killed on the road was his own father.

Celtic Renaissance: A period of Irish literary and cultural history at the end of the nineteenth century. Followers of the movement aimed to create a romantic vision of Celtic myth and legend. The most significant works of the Celtic Renaissance typically present a dreamy, unreal world, usually in reaction against the reality of contemporary problems. William Butler Yeats's *The Wanderings of Oisin* is among the most significant works of the Celtic Renaissance. Also known as Celtic Twilight.

Celtic Twilight: See *Celtic Renaissance*

Character: Broadly speaking, a person in a literary work. The actions of characters are what constitute the plot of a story, novel, or poem. There are numerous types of characters, ranging from simple, stereotypical figures to intricate, multifaceted ones. In the techniques of anthropomorphism and personification, animals—and even places or things—can assume aspects of character. "Characterization" is the process by which an author creates vivid, believable characters in a work of art. This may be done in a variety of ways, including (1) direct description of the character by the narrator; (2) the direct presentation of the speech, thoughts, or actions of the character; and (3) the responses of other characters to the character. The term "character" also refers to a form originated by the ancient Greek writer Theophrastus that later became popular in the seventeenth and eighteenth centuries. It is a short essay or sketch of a person who prominently displays a specific attribute or quality, such as miserliness or ambition. Notable characters in literature include Oedipus Rex, Don Quixote de la Mancha, Macbeth, Candide, Hester Prynne, Ebenezer Scrooge, Huckleberry Finn, Jay Gatsby, Scarlett O'Hara, James Bond, and Kunta Kinte.

Characterization: See *Character*

Chorus: In ancient Greek drama, a group of actors who commented on and interpreted the unfolding action on the stage. Initially the chorus was a major component of the presentation, but over time it became less significant, with its numbers reduced and its role eventually limited to commentary between acts. By the sixteenth century the chorus—if employed at all—was typically a single person who provided a prologue and an epilogue and occasionally appeared between acts to introduce or underscore an important event. The chorus in William Shakespeare's *Henry V* functions in this way. Modern dramas rarely feature a chorus, but T. S. Eliot's *Murder in the Cathedral* and Arthur Miller's *A View from the Bridge* are notable exceptions. The Stage Manager in Thornton Wilder's *Our Town* performs a role similar to that of the chorus.

Chronicle: A record of events presented in chronological order. Although the scope and level of detail provided varies greatly among the chronicles surviving from ancient times, some, such as the *Anglo-Saxon Chronicle,* feature vivid descriptions and a lively recounting of events. During the Elizabethan Age, many dramas—appropriately called "chronicle plays"—were based on material from chronicles. Many of William Shakespeare's dramas of English history as well as Christopher Marlowe's *Edward II* are based in part on Raphael Holinshead's *Chronicles of England, Scotland, and Ireland.*

Classical: In its strictest definition in literary criticism, classicism refers to works of ancient Greek or Roman literature. The term may also be used to describe a literary work of recognized importance (a "classic") from any time period or literature that exhibits the traits of classicism. Classical authors from ancient Greek and Roman times include Juvenal and Homer. Examples of later works and authors now described as classical include French literature of the seventeenth century, Western novels of the nineteenth century, and American fiction of the mid-nineteenth century such as that written by James Fenimore Cooper and Mark Twain.

Classicism: A term used in literary criticism to describe critical doctrines that have their roots in ancient Greek and Roman literature, philosophy, and art. Works associated with classicism typically exhibit restraint on the part of the author, unity of design and purpose, clarity, simplicity, logical organization, and respect for tradition. Examples of literary classicism include Cicero's prose, the dramas of Pierre Corneille and Jean Racine, the poetry of John Dryden and Alexander Pope, and the writings of J. W. von Goethe, G. E. Lessing, and T. S. Eliot.

Climax: The turning point in a narrative, the moment when the conflict is at its most intense. Typically, the structure of stories, novels, and plays is one of rising action, in which tension builds to the climax, followed by falling action, in which tension lessens as the story moves to its conclusion. The climax in James Fenimore Cooper's *The Last of the Mohicans* occurs when Magua and his captive Cora are pursued to the edge of a cliff by Uncas. Magua kills Uncas but is subsequently killed by Hawkeye.

Colloquialism: A word, phrase, or form of pronunciation that is acceptable in casual conversation but not in formal, written communication. It is considered more acceptable than slang. An example of colloquialism can be found in Rudyard Kipling's *Barrack-room Ballads:* When 'Omer smote 'is bloomin' lyre He'd 'eard men sing by land and sea; An' what he thought 'e might require 'E went an' took—the same as me!

Comedy: One of two major types of drama, the other being tragedy. Its aim is to amuse, and it typically ends happily. Comedy assumes many forms, such as farce and burlesque, and uses a variety of techniques, from parody to satire. In a restricted sense the term comedy refers only to dramatic presentations, but in general usage it is commonly applied to nondramatic works as well. Examples of comedies range from the plays of Aristophanes, Terrence, and Plautus, Dante Alighieri's *The Divine Comedy,* Francois Rabelais's *Pantagruel* and *Gargantua,* and some of Geoffrey Chaucer's tales and William Shakespeare's plays to Noel Coward's play *Private Lives* and James Thurber's short story "The Secret Life of Walter Mitty."

Comedy of Manners: A play about the manners and conventions of an aristocratic, highly sophisticated society. The characters are usually types rather than individualized personalities, and plot is less important than atmosphere. Such plays were an important aspect of late seventeenth-century English comedy. The comedy of manners was revived in the eighteenth century by Oliver Goldsmith and Richard Brinsley Sheridan, enjoyed a second revival in the late nineteenth century, and has endured into the twentieth century. Examples of comedies of manners include William Congreve's *The*

Way of the World in the late seventeenth century, Oliver Goldsmith's *She Stoops to Conquer* and Richard Brinsley Sheridan's *The School for Scandal* in the eighteenth century, Oscar Wilde's *The Importance of Being Earnest* in the nineteenth century, and W. Somerset Maugham's *The Circle* in the twentieth century.

Comic Relief: The use of humor to lighten the mood of a serious or tragic story, especially in plays. The technique is very common in Elizabethan works, and can be an integral part of the plot or simply a brief event designed to break the tension of the scene. The Gravediggers' scene in William Shakespeare's *Hamlet* is a frequently cited example of comic relief.

Commedia dell'arte: An Italian term meaning "the comedy of guilds" or "the comedy of professional actors." This form of dramatic comedy was popular in Italy during the sixteenth century. Actors were assigned stock roles (such as Pulcinella, the stupid servant, or Pantalone, the old merchant) and given a basic plot to follow, but all dialogue was improvised. The roles were rigidly typed and the plots were formulaic, usually revolving around young lovers who thwarted their elders and attained wealth and happiness. A rigid convention of the *commedia dell'arte* is the periodic intrusion of Harlequin, who interrupts the play with low buffoonery. Peppino de Filippo's *Metamorphoses of a Wandering Minstrel* gave modern audiences an idea of what *commedia dell'arte* may have been like. Various scenarios for *commedia dell'arte* were compiled in Petraccone's *La commedia dell'arte, storia, technica, scenari*, published in 1927.

Complaint: A lyric poem, popular in the Renaissance, in which the speaker expresses sorrow about his or her condition. Typically, the speaker's sadness is caused by an unresponsive lover, but some complaints cite other sources of unhappiness, such as poverty or fate. A commonly cited example is "A Complaint by Night of the Lover Not Beloved" by Henry Howard, Earl of Surrey. Thomas Sackville's "Complaint of Henry, Duke of Buckingham" traces the duke's unhappiness to his ruthless ambition.

Conceit: A clever and fanciful metaphor, usually expressed through elaborate and extended comparison, that presents a striking parallel between two seemingly dissimilar things—for example, elaborately comparing a beautiful woman to an object like a garden or the sun. The conceit was a popular device throughout the Elizabethan Age and Baroque Age and was the principal technique of the seventeenth-century English metaphysical poets. This usage of the word conceit is unrelated to the best-known definition of conceit as an arrogant attitude or behavior. The conceit figures prominently in the works of John Donne, Emily Dickinson, and T. S. Eliot.

Concrete: Concrete is the opposite of abstract, and refers to a thing that actually exists or a description that allows the reader to experience an object or concept with the senses. Henry David Thoreau's *Walden* contains much concrete description of nature and wildlife.

Concrete Poetry: Poetry in which visual elements play a large part in the poetic effect. Punctuation marks, letters, or words are arranged on a page to form a visual design: a cross, for example, or a bumblebee. Max Bill and Eugene Gomringer were among the early practitioners of concrete poetry; Haroldo de Campos and Augusto de Campos are among contemporary authors of concrete poetry.

Confessional Poetry: A form of poetry in which the poet reveals very personal, intimate, sometimes shocking information about himself or herself. Anne Sexton, Sylvia Plath, Robert Lowell, and John Berryman wrote poetry in the confessional vein.

Conflict: The conflict in a work of fiction is the issue to be resolved in the story. It usually occurs between two characters, the protagonist and the antagonist, or between the protagonist and society or the protagonist and himself or herself. Conflict in Theodore Dreiser's novel *Sister Carrie* comes as a result of urban society, while Jack London's short story "To Build a Fire" concerns the protagonist's battle against the cold and himself.

Connotation: The impression that a word gives beyond its defined meaning. Connotations may be universally understood or may be significant only to a certain group. Both "horse" and "steed" denote the same animal, but "steed" has a different connotation, deriving from the chivalrous or romantic narratives in which the word was once often used.

Consonance: Consonance occurs in poetry when words appearing at the ends of two or more verses have similar final consonant sounds but have final vowel sounds that differ, as with "stuff" and "off." Consonance is found in "The curfew tolls the knells of parting day" from Thomas Grey's "An Elegy Written in a Country Church Yard." Also known as Half Rhyme or Slant Rhyme.

Convention: Any widely accepted literary device, style, or form. A soliloquy, in which a character reveals to the audience his or her private thoughts, is an example of a dramatic convention.

Corrido: A Mexican ballad. Examples of *corridos* include "Muerte del afamado Bilito," "La voz de mi conciencia," "Lucio Perez," "La juida," and "Los presos."

Couplet: Two lines of poetry with the same rhyme and meter, often expressing a complete and self-contained thought. The following couplet is from Alexander Pope's "Elegy to the Memory of an Unfortunate Lady": 'Tis Use alone that sanctifies Expense, And Splendour borrows all her rays from Sense.

Criticism: The systematic study and evaluation of literary works, usually based on a specific method or set of principles. An important part of literary studies since ancient times, the practice of criticism has given rise to numerous theories, methods, and "schools," sometimes producing conflicting, even contradictory, interpretations of literature in general as well as of individual works. Even such basic issues as what constitutes a poem or a novel have been the subject of much criticism over the centuries. Seminal texts of literary criticism include Plato's *Republic,* Aristotle's *Poetics,* Sir Philip Sidney's *The Defence of Poesie,* John Dryden's *Of Dramatic Poesie,* and William Wordsworth's "Preface" to the second edition of his *Lyrical Ballads.* Contemporary schools of criticism include deconstruction, feminist, psychoanalytic, poststructuralist, new historicist, postcolonialist, and reader-response.

D

Dactyl: See *Foot*

Dadaism: A protest movement in art and literature founded by Tristan Tzara in 1916. Followers of the movement expressed their outrage at the destruction brought about by World War I by revolting against numerous forms of social convention. The Dadaists presented works marked by calculated madness and flamboyant nonsense. They stressed total freedom of expression, commonly through primitive displays of emotion and illogical, often senseless, poetry. The movement ended shortly after the war, when it was replaced by surrealism. Proponents of Dadaism include Andre Breton, Louis Aragon, Philippe Soupault, and Paul Eluard.

Decadent: See *Decadents*

Decadents: The followers of a nineteenth-century literary movement that had its beginnings in French aestheticism. Decadent literature displays a fascination with perverse and morbid states; a search for novelty and sensation—the "new thrill"; a preoccupation with mysticism; and a belief in the senselessness of human existence. The movement is closely associated with the doctrine Art for Art's Sake. The term "decadence" is sometimes used to denote a decline in the quality of art or literature following a period of greatness. Major French decadents are Charles Baudelaire and Arthur Rimbaud. English decadents include Oscar Wilde, Ernest Dowson, and Frank Harris.

Deconstruction: A method of literary criticism developed by Jacques Derrida and characterized by multiple conflicting interpretations of a given work. Deconstructionists consider the impact of the language of a work and suggest that the true meaning of the work is not necessarily the meaning that the author intended. Jacques Derrida's *De la grammatologie* is the seminal text on deconstructive strategies; among American practitioners of this method of criticism are Paul de Man and J. Hillis Miller.

Deduction: The process of reaching a conclusion through reasoning from general premises to a specific premise. An example of deduction is present in the following syllogism: Premise: All mammals are animals. Premise: All whales are mammals. Conclusion: Therefore, all whales are animals.

Denotation: The definition of a word, apart from the impressions or feelings it creates in the reader. The word "apartheid" denotes a political and economic policy of segregation by race, but its connotations—oppression, slavery, inequality—are numerous.

Denouement: A French word meaning "the unknotting." In literary criticism, it denotes the resolution of conflict in fiction or drama. The *denouement* follows the climax and provides an outcome to the primary plot situation as well as an explanation of secondary plot complications. The *denouement* often involves a character's recognition of his or her state of mind or moral condition. A well-known example of *denouement* is the last scene of the play *As You Like It* by William Shakespeare, in which couples are married, an evildoer repents, the identities of two disguised characters are revealed, and a ruler is restored to power. Also known as Falling Action.

Description: Descriptive writing is intended to allow a reader to picture the scene or setting in which the action of a story takes place. The form this description takes often evokes an intended emotional response—a dark, spooky graveyard will evoke fear, and a peaceful, sunny meadow will evoke calmness. An example of a descriptive story is Edgar Allan Poe's *Landor's Cottage*, which offers a detailed depiction of a New York country estate.

Detective Story: A narrative about the solution of a mystery or the identification of a criminal. The conventions of the detective story include the detective's scrupulous use of logic in solving the mystery; incompetent or ineffectual police; a suspect who appears guilty at first but is later proved innocent; and the detective's friend or confidant—often the narrator—whose slowness in interpreting clues emphasizes by contrast the detective's brilliance. Edgar Allan Poe's "Murders in the Rue Morgue" is commonly regarded as the earliest example of this type of story. With this work, Poe established many of the conventions of the detective story genre, which are still in practice. Other practitioners of this vast and extremely popular genre include Arthur Conan Doyle, Dashiell Hammett, and Agatha Christie.

Deus ex machina: A Latin term meaning "god out of a machine." In Greek drama, a god was often lowered onto the stage by a mechanism of some kind to rescue the hero or untangle the plot. By extension, the term refers to any artificial device or coincidence used to bring about a convenient and simple solution to a plot. This is a common device in melodramas and includes such fortunate circumstances as the sudden receipt of a legacy to save the family farm or a last-minute stay of execution. The *deus ex machina* invariably rewards the virtuous and punishes evildoers. Examples of *deus ex machina* include King Louis XIV in Jean-Baptiste Moliere's *Tartuffe* and Queen Victoria in *The Pirates of Penzance* by William Gilbert and Arthur Sullivan. Bertolt Brecht parodies the abuse of such devices in the conclusion of his *Threepenny Opera*.

Dialogue: In its widest sense, dialogue is simply conversation between people in a literary work; in its most restricted sense, it refers specifically to the speech of characters in a drama. As a specific literary genre, a "dialogue" is a composition in which characters debate an issue or idea. The Greek philosopher Plato frequently expounded his theories in the form of dialogues.

Diction: The selection and arrangement of words in a literary work. Either or both may vary depending on the desired effect. There are four general types of diction: "formal," used in scholarly or lofty writing; "informal," used in relaxed but educated conversation; "colloquial," used in everyday speech; and "slang," containing newly coined words and other terms not accepted in formal usage.

Didactic: A term used to describe works of literature that aim to teach some moral, religious, political, or practical lesson. Although didactic elements are often found in artistically pleasing works, the term "didactic" usually refers to literature in which the message is more important than the form. The term may also be used to criticize a work that the critic finds "overly didactic," that is, heavy-handed in its delivery of a lesson. Examples of didactic literature include John Bunyan's *Pilgrim's Progress,* Alexander Pope's *Essay on Criticism,* Jean-Jacques Rousseau's *Emile,* and Elizabeth Inchbald's *Simple Story*.

Dimeter: See *Meter*

Dionysian: See *Apollonian and Dionysian*

Discordia concours: A Latin phrase meaning "discord in harmony." The term was coined by the eighteenth-century English writer Samuel Johnson to describe "a combination of dissimilar images or discovery of occult resemblances in things apparently unlike." Johnson created the expression by reversing a phrase by the Latin poet Horace. The metaphysical poetry of John Donne, Richard Crashaw, Abraham Cowley, George Herbert, and Edward Taylor among others, contains many examples of *discordia concours.* In Donne's "A Valediction: Forbidding Mourning," the poet compares the union of himself with his lover to a draftsman's compass: If they be two, they are two so, As stiff twin compasses are two: Thy soul, the fixed foot, makes no show To move, but doth, if the other do; And though it in the center sit, Yet when the other far doth roam, It leans, and hearkens after it, And grows erect, as that comes home.

Dissonance: A combination of harsh or jarring sounds, especially in poetry. Although such combinations may be accidental, poets sometimes intentionally make them to achieve particular effects. Dissonance is also sometimes used to refer to close but not identical rhymes. When this is the case, the word functions as a synonym for consonance. Robert Browning, Gerard Manley Hopkins, and many other poets have made deliberate use of dissonance.

Doppelganger: A literary technique by which a character is duplicated (usually in the form of an alter ego, though sometimes as a ghostly counterpart) or divided into two distinct, usually opposite personalities. The use of this character device is widespread in nineteenth- and twentieth-century literature, and indicates a growing awareness among authors that the "self" is really a composite of many "selves." A well-known story containing a *doppelganger* character is Robert Louis Stevenson's *Dr. Jekyll and Mr. Hyde,* which dramatizes an internal struggle between good and evil. Also known as The Double.

Double Entendre: A corruption of a French phrase meaning "double meaning." The term is used to indicate a word or phrase that is deliberately ambiguous, especially when one of the meanings is risque or improper. An example of a *double entendre* is the Elizabethan usage of the verb "die," which refers both to death and to orgasm.

Double, The: See *Doppelganger*

Draft: Any preliminary version of a written work. An author may write dozens of drafts which are revised to form the final work, or he or she may write only one, with few or no revisions. Dorothy Parker's observation that "I can't write five words but that I change seven" humorously indicates the purpose of the draft.

Drama: In its widest sense, a drama is any work designed to be presented by actors on a stage. Similarly, "drama" denotes a broad literary genre that includes a variety of forms, from pageant and spectacle to tragedy and comedy, as well as countless types and subtypes. More commonly in modern usage, however, a drama is a work that treats serious subjects and themes but does not aim at the grandeur of tragedy. This use of the term originated with the eighteenth-century French writer Denis Diderot, who used the word *drame* to designate his plays about middle-class life; thus "drama" typically features characters of a less exalted stature than those of tragedy. Examples of classical dramas include Menander's comedy *Dyscolus* and Sophocles' tragedy *Oedipus Rex.* Contemporary dramas include Eugene O'Neill's *The Iceman Cometh,* Lillian Hellman's *Little Foxes,* and August Wilson's *Ma Rainey's Black Bottom.*

Dramatic Irony: Occurs when the audience of a play or the reader of a work of literature knows something that a character in the work itself does not know. The irony is in the contrast between the intended meaning of the statements or actions of a character and the additional information understood by the audience. A celebrated example of dramatic irony is in Act V of William Shakespeare's *Romeo and Juliet,* where two young lovers meet their end as a result of a tragic misunderstanding. Here, the audience has full knowledge that Juliet's apparent "death" is merely temporary; she will regain her senses when the mysterious "sleeping potion" she has taken wears off. But Romeo, mistaking Juliet's drug-induced trance for true death, kills himself in grief. Upon awakening, Juliet discovers Romeo's corpse and, in despair, slays herself.

Dramatic Monologue: See *Monologue*

Dramatic Poetry: Any lyric work that employs elements of drama such as dialogue, conflict, or characterization, but excluding works that are intended for stage presentation. A monologue is a form of dramatic poetry.

Dramatis Personae: The characters in a work of literature, particularly a drama. The list of characters printed before the main text of a play or in the program is the *dramatis personae*.

Dream Allegory: See *Dream Vision*

Dream Vision: A literary convention, chiefly of the Middle Ages. In a dream vision a story is presented as a literal dream of the narrator. This device was commonly used to teach moral and religious lessons. Important works of this type are *The Divine Comedy* by Dante Alighieri, *Piers Plowman* by William Langland, and *The Pilgrim's Progress* by John Bunyan. Also known as Dream Allegory.

Dystopia: An imaginary place in a work of fiction where the characters lead dehumanized, fearful lives. Jack London's *The Iron Heel,* Yevgeny Zamyatin's *My,* Aldous Huxley's *Brave New World,* George Orwell's *Nineteen Eighty-four,* and Margaret Atwood's *Handmaid's Tale* portray versions of dystopia.

E

Eclogue: In classical literature, a poem featuring rural themes and structured as a dialogue among shepherds. Eclogues often took specific poetic forms, such as elegies or love poems. Some were written as the soliloquy of a shepherd. In later centuries, "eclogue" came to refer to any poem that was in the pastoral tradition or that had a dialogue or monologue structure. A classical example of an eclogue is Virgil's *Eclogues,* also known as *Bucolics.* Giovanni Boccaccio, Edmund Spenser, Andrew Marvell, Jonathan Swift, and Louis MacNeice also wrote eclogues.

Edwardian: Describes cultural conventions identified with the period of the reign of Edward VII of England (1901-1910). Writers of the Edwardian Age typically displayed a strong reaction against the propriety and conservatism of the Victorian Age. Their work often exhibits distrust of authority in religion, politics, and art and expresses strong doubts about the soundness of conventional values.

Writers of this era include George Bernard Shaw, H. G. Wells, and Joseph Conrad.

Edwardian Age: See *Edwardian*

Electra Complex: A daughter's amorous obsession with her father. The term Electra complex comes from the plays of Euripides and Sophocles entitled *Electra,* in which the character Electra drives her brother Orestes to kill their mother and her lover in revenge for the murder of their father.

Elegy: A lyric poem that laments the death of a person or the eventual death of all people. In a conventional elegy, set in a classical world, the poet and subject are spoken of as shepherds. In modern criticism, the word elegy is often used to refer to a poem that is melancholy or mournfully contemplative. John Milton's "Lycidas" and Percy Bysshe Shelley's "Adonais" are two examples of this form.

Elizabethan Age: A period of great economic growth, religious controversy, and nationalism closely associated with the reign of Elizabeth I of England (1558–1603). The Elizabethan Age is considered a part of the general renaissance—that is, the flowering of arts and literature—that took place in Europe during the fourteenth through sixteenth centuries. The era is considered the golden age of English literature. The most important dramas in English and a great deal of lyric poetry were produced during this period, and modern English criticism began around this time. The notable authors of the period—Philip Sidney, Edmund Spenser, Christopher Marlowe, William Shakespeare, Ben Jonson, Francis Bacon, and John Donne—are among the best in all of English literature.

Elizabethan Drama: English comic and tragic plays produced during the Renaissance, or more narrowly, those plays written during the last years of and few years after Queen Elizabeth's reign. William Shakespeare is considered an Elizabethan dramatist in the broader sense, although most of his work was produced during the reign of James I. Examples of Elizabethan comedies include John Lyly's *The Woman in the Moone,* Thomas Dekker's *The Roaring Girl, or, Moll Cut Purse,* and William Shakespeare's *Twelfth Night.* Examples of Elizabethan tragedies include William Shakespeare's *Antony and Cleopatra,* Thomas Kyd's *The Spanish*

Tragedy, and John Webster's *The Tragedy of the Duchess of Malfi.*

Empathy: A sense of shared experience, including emotional and physical feelings, with someone or something other than oneself. Empathy is often used to describe the response of a reader to a literary character. An example of an empathic passage is William Shakespeare's description in his narrative poem *Venus and Adonis* of: the snail, whose tender horns being hit, Shrinks backward in his shelly cave with pain. Readers of Gerard Manley Hopkins's *The Windhover* may experience some of the physical sensations evoked in the description of the movement of the falcon.

English Sonnet: See *Sonnet*

Enjambment: The running over of the sense and structure of a line of verse or a couplet into the following verse or couplet. Andrew Marvell's "To His Coy Mistress" is structured as a series of enjambments, as in lines 11-12: "My vegetable love should grow/Vaster than empires and more slow."

Enlightenment, The: An eighteenth-century philosophical movement. It began in France but had a wide impact throughout Europe and America. Thinkers of the Enlightenment valued reason and believed that both the individual and society could achieve a state of perfection. Corresponding to this essentially humanist vision was a resistance to religious authority. Important figures of the Enlightenment were Denis Diderot and Voltaire in France, Edward Gibbon and David Hume in England, and Thomas Paine and Thomas Jefferson in the United States.

Epic: A long narrative poem about the adventures of a hero of great historic or legendary importance. The setting is vast and the action is often given cosmic significance through the intervention of supernatural forces such as gods, angels, or demons. Epics are typically written in a classical style of grand simplicity with elaborate metaphors and allusions that enhance the symbolic importance of a hero's adventures. Some well-known epics are Homer's *Iliad* and *Odyssey,* Virgil's *Aeneid,* and John Milton's *Paradise Lost.*

Epic Simile: See *Homeric Simile*

Epic Theater: A theory of theatrical presentation developed by twentieth-century German playwright Bertolt Brecht. Brecht created a type of drama that the audience could view with complete detachment. He used what he termed "alienation effects" to create an emotional distance between the audience and the action on stage. Among these effects are: short, self-contained scenes that keep the play from building to a cathartic climax; songs that comment on the action; and techniques of acting that prevent the actor from developing an emotional identity with his role. Besides the plays of Bertolt Brecht, other plays that utilize epic theater conventions include those of Georg Buchner, Frank Wedekind, Erwin Piscator, and Leopold Jessner.

Epigram: A saying that makes the speaker's point quickly and concisely. Samuel Taylor Coleridge wrote an epigram that neatly sums up the form: What is an Epigram? A Dwarfish whole, Its body brevity, and wit its soul.

Epilogue: A concluding statement or section of a literary work. In dramas, particularly those of the seventeenth and eighteenth centuries, the epilogue is a closing speech, often in verse, delivered by an actor at the end of a play and spoken directly to the audience. A famous epilogue is Puck's speech at the end of William Shakespeare's *A Midsummer Night's Dream.*

Epiphany: A sudden revelation of truth inspired by a seemingly trivial incident. The term was widely used by James Joyce in his critical writings, and the stories in Joyce's *Dubliners* are commonly called "epiphanies."

Episode: An incident that forms part of a story and is significantly related to it. Episodes may be either self-contained narratives or events that depend on a larger context for their sense and importance. Examples of episodes include the founding of Wilmington, Delaware in Charles Reade's *The Disinherited Heir* and the individual events comprising the picaresque novels and medieval romances.

Episodic Plot: See *Plot*

Epitaph: An inscription on a tomb or tombstone, or a verse written on the occasion of a person's death. Epitaphs may be serious or humorous. Dorothy Parker's epitaph reads, "I told you I was sick."

Epithalamion: A song or poem written to honor and commemorate a marriage ceremony.

Famous examples include Edmund Spenser's "Epithalamion" and e. e. cummings's "Epithalamion." Also spelled Epithalamium.

Epithalamium: See *Epithalamion*

Epithet: A word or phrase, often disparaging or abusive, that expresses a character trait of someone or something. "The Napoleon of crime" is an epithet applied to Professor Moriarty, arch-rival of Sherlock Holmes in Arthur Conan Doyle's series of detective stories.

Exempla: See *Exemplum*

Exemplum: A tale with a moral message. This form of literary sermonizing flourished during the Middle Ages, when *exempla* appeared in collections known as "example-books." The works of Geoffrey Chaucer are full of *exempla*.

Existentialism: A predominantly twentieth-century philosophy concerned with the nature and perception of human existence. There are two major strains of existentialist thought: atheistic and Christian. Followers of atheistic existentialism believe that the individual is alone in a godless universe and that the basic human condition is one of suffering and loneliness. Nevertheless, because there are no fixed values, individuals can create their own characters—indeed, they can shape themselves—through the exercise of free will. The atheistic strain culminates in and is popularly associated with the works of Jean-Paul Sartre. The Christian existentialists, on the other hand, believe that only in God may people find freedom from life's anguish. The two strains hold certain beliefs in common: that existence cannot be fully understood or described through empirical effort; that anguish is a universal element of life; that individuals must bear responsibility for their actions; and that there is no common standard of behavior or perception for religious and ethical matters. Existentialist thought figures prominently in the works of such authors as Eugene Ionesco, Franz Kafka, Fyodor Dostoyevsky, Simone de Beauvoir, Samuel Beckett, and Albert Camus.

Expatriates: See *Expatriatism*

Expatriatism: The practice of leaving one's country to live for an extended period in another country. Literary expatriates include English poets Percy Bysshe Shelley and John Keats in Italy, Polish novelist Joseph Conrad in England, American writers Richard Wright, James Baldwin, Gertrude Stein, and Ernest Hemingway in France, and Trinidadian author Neil Bissondath in Canada.

Exposition: Writing intended to explain the nature of an idea, thing, or theme. Expository writing is often combined with description, narration, or argument. In dramatic writing, the exposition is the introductory material which presents the characters, setting, and tone of the play. An example of dramatic exposition occurs in many nineteenth-century drawing-room comedies in which the butler and the maid open the play with relevant talk about their master and mistress; in composition, exposition relays factual information, as in encyclopedia entries.

Expressionism: An indistinct literary term, originally used to describe an early twentieth-century school of German painting. The term applies to almost any mode of unconventional, highly subjective writing that distorts reality in some way. Advocates of Expressionism include dramatists George Kaiser, Ernst Toller, Luigi Pirandello, Federico Garcia Lorca, Eugene O'Neill, and Elmer Rice; poets George Heym, Ernst Stadler, August Stramm, Gottfried Benn, and Georg Trakl; and novelists Franz Kafka and James Joyce.

Extended Monologue: See *Monologue*

F

Fable: A prose or verse narrative intended to convey a moral. Animals or inanimate objects with human characteristics often serve as characters in fables. A famous fable is Aesop's "The Tortoise and the Hare."

Fairy Tales: Short narratives featuring mythical beings such as fairies, elves, and sprites. These tales originally belonged to the folklore of a particular nation or region, such as those collected in Germany by Jacob and Wilhelm Grimm. Two other celebrated writers of fairy tales are Hans Christian Andersen and Rudyard Kipling.

Falling Action: See *Denouement*

Fantasy: A literary form related to mythology and folklore. Fantasy literature is typically set in non-existent realms and features supernatural beings. Notable examples of fantasy literature are *The Lord of the Rings* by J. R. R. Tolkien and the Gormenghast trilogy by Mervyn Peake.

Farce: A type of comedy characterized by broad humor, outlandish incidents, and often vulgar subject matter. Much of the "comedy" in film and television could more accurately be described as farce.

Feet: See *Foot*

Feminine Rhyme: See *Rhyme*

Femme fatale: A French phrase with the literal translation "fatal woman." A *femme fatale* is a sensuous, alluring woman who often leads men into danger or trouble. A classic example of the *femme fatale* is the nameless character in Billy Wilder's *The Seven Year Itch,* portrayed by Marilyn Monroe in the film adaptation.

Fiction: Any story that is the product of imagination rather than a documentation of fact. characters and events in such narratives may be based in real life but their ultimate form and configuration is a creation of the author. Geoffrey Chaucer's *The Canterbury Tales,* Laurence Sterne's *Tristram Shandy,* and Margaret Mitchell's *Gone with the Wind* are examples of fiction.

Figurative Language: A technique in writing in which the author temporarily interrupts the order, construction, or meaning of the writing for a particular effect. This interruption takes the form of one or more figures of speech such as hyperbole, irony, or simile. Figurative language is the opposite of literal language, in which every word is truthful, accurate, and free of exaggeration or embellishment. Examples of figurative language are tropes such as metaphor and rhetorical figures such as apostrophe.

Figures of Speech: Writing that differs from customary conventions for construction, meaning, order, or significance for the purpose of a special meaning or effect. There are two major types of figures of speech: rhetorical figures, which do not make changes in the meaning of the words, and tropes, which do. Types of figures of speech include simile, hyperbole, alliteration, and pun, among many others.

Fin de siecle: A French term meaning "end of the century." The term is used to denote the last

decade of the nineteenth century, a transition period when writers and other artists abandoned old conventions and looked for new techniques and objectives. Two writers commonly associated with the *fin de siecle* mindset are Oscar Wilde and George Bernard Shaw.

First Person: See *Point of View*

Flashback: A device used in literature to present action that occurred before the beginning of the story. Flashbacks are often introduced as the dreams or recollections of one or more characters. Flashback techniques are often used in films, where they are typically set off by a gradual changing of one picture to another.

Foil: A character in a work of literature whose physical or psychological qualities contrast strongly with, and therefore highlight, the corresponding qualities of another character. In his Sherlock Holmes stories, Arthur Conan Doyle portrayed Dr. Watson as a man of normal habits and intelligence, making him a foil for the eccentric and wonderfully perceptive Sherlock Holmes.

Folk Ballad: See *Ballad*

Folklore: Traditions and myths preserved in a culture or group of people. Typically, these are passed on by word of mouth in various forms—such as legends, songs, and proverbs—or preserved in customs and ceremonies. This term was first used by W. J. Thoms in 1846. Sir James Frazer's *The Golden Bough* is the record of English folklore; myths about the frontier and the Old South exemplify American folklore.

Folktale: A story originating in oral tradition. Folktales fall into a variety of categories, including legends, ghost stories, fairy tales, fables, and anecdotes based on historical figures and events. Examples of folktales include Giambattista Basile's *The Pentamerone,* which contains the tales of Puss in Boots, Rapunzel, Cinderella, and Beauty and the Beast, and Joel Chandler Harris's Uncle Remus stories, which represent transplanted African folktales and American tales about the characters Mike Fink, Johnny Appleseed, Paul Bunyan, and Pecos Bill.

Foot: The smallest unit of rhythm in a line of poetry. In English-language poetry, a foot is typically one accented syllable combined with one or two unaccented syllables. There are many different types of feet. When the accent is on the second syllable of a two syllable word (con-*tort*), the foot is an "iamb"; the reverse accentual pattern (*tor* -ture) is a "trochee." Other feet that commonly occur in poetry in English are "anapest," two unaccented syllables followed by an accented syllable as in in-ter-*cept*, and "dactyl," an accented syllable followed by two unaccented syllables as in *su*-i- cide.

Foreshadowing: A device used in literature to create expectation or to set up an explanation of later developments. In Charles Dickens's *Great Expectations,* the graveyard encounter at the beginning of the novel between Pip and the escaped convict Magwitch foreshadows the baleful atmosphere and events that comprise much of the narrative.

Form: The pattern or construction of a work which identifies its genre and distinguishes it from other genres. Examples of forms include the different genres, such as the lyric form or the short story form, and various patterns for poetry, such as the verse form or the stanza form.

Formalism: In literary criticism, the belief that literature should follow prescribed rules of construction, such as those that govern the sonnet form. Examples of formalism are found in the work of the New Critics and structuralists.

Fourteener Meter: See *Meter*

Free Verse: Poetry that lacks regular metrical and rhyme patterns but that tries to capture the cadences of everyday speech. The form allows a poet to exploit a variety of rhythmical effects within a single poem. Free-verse techniques have been widely used in the twentieth century by such writers as Ezra Pound, T. S. Eliot, Carl Sandburg, and William Carlos Williams. Also known as *Vers libre.*

Futurism: A flamboyant literary and artistic movement that developed in France, Italy, and Russia from 1908 through the 1920s. Futurist theater and poetry abandoned traditional literary forms. In their place, followers of the movement attempted to achieve total freedom of expression through bizarre imagery and deformed or newly invented words. The Futurists were self-consciously modern artists who attempted to incorporate the appearances and sounds of modern life into their work. Futurist writers include Filippo Tommaso Marinetti, Wyndham Lewis, Guillaume Apollinaire, Velimir Khlebnikov, and Vladimir Mayakovsky.

G

Genre: A category of literary work. In critical theory, genre may refer to both the content of a given work—tragedy, comedy, pastoral— and to its form, such as poetry, novel, or drama. This term also refers to types of popular literature, as in the genres of science fiction or the detective story.

Genteel Tradition: A term coined by critic George Santayana to describe the literary practice of certain late nineteenth- century American writers, especially New Englanders. Followers of the Genteel Tradition emphasized conventionality in social, religious, moral, and literary standards. Some of the best-known writers of the Genteel Tradition are R. H. Stoddard and Bayard Taylor.

Gilded Age: A period in American history during the 1870s characterized by political corruption and materialism. A number of important novels of social and political criticism were written during this time. Examples of Gilded Age literature include Henry Adams's *Democracy* and F. Marion Crawford's *An American Politician.*

Gothic: See *Gothicism*

Gothicism: In literary criticism, works characterized by a taste for the medieval or morbidly attractive. A gothic novel prominently features elements of horror, the supernatural, gloom, and violence: clanking chains, terror, charnel houses, ghosts, medieval castles, and mysteriously slamming doors. The term "gothic novel" is also applied to novels that lack elements of the traditional Gothic setting but that create a similar atmosphere of terror or dread. Mary Shelley's *Frankenstein* is perhaps the best-known English work of this kind.

Gothic Novel: See *Gothicism*

Great Chain of Being: The belief that all things and creatures in nature are organized in a hierarchy from inanimate objects at the bottom to God at the top. This system of belief was popular in the seventeenth and eighteenth centuries. A summary of the concept of the great chain of being can be found in the first epistle of Alexander Pope's *An Essay on Man,* and more recently in Arthur O. Lovejoy's *The Great Chain of Being: A Study of the History of an Idea.*

Grotesque: In literary criticism, the subject matter of a work or a style of expression characterized by exaggeration, deformity, freakishness, and disorder. The grotesque often includes an element of comic absurdity. Early examples of literary grotesque include Francois Rabelais's *Pantagruel* and *Gargantua* and Thomas Nashe's *The Unfortunate Traveller,* while more recent examples can be found in the works of Edgar Allan Poe, Evelyn Waugh, Eudora Welty, Flannery O'Connor, Eugene Ionesco, Gunter Grass, Thomas Mann, Mervyn Peake, and Joseph Heller, among many others.

H

Haiku: The shortest form of Japanese poetry, constructed in three lines of five, seven, and five syllables respectively. The message of a *haiku* poem usually centers on some aspect of spirituality and provokes an emotional response in the reader. Early masters of *haiku* include Basho, Buson, Kobayashi Issa, and Masaoka Shiki. English writers of *haiku* include the Imagists, notably Ezra Pound, H. D., Amy Lowell, Carl Sandburg, and William Carlos Williams. Also known as *Hokku.*

Half Rhyme: See *Consonance*

Hamartia: In tragedy, the event or act that leads to the hero's or heroine's downfall. This term is often incorrectly used as a synonym for tragic flaw. In Richard Wright's *Native Son,* the act that seals Bigger Thomas's fate is his first impulsive murder.

Harlem Renaissance: The Harlem Renaissance of the 1920s is generally considered the first significant movement of black writers and artists in the United States. During this period, new and established black writers published more fiction and poetry than ever before, the first influential black literary journals were established, and black authors and artists received their first widespread recognition and serious critical appraisal. Among the major writers associated with this period are Claude McKay, Jean Toomer, Countee Cullen, Langston Hughes, Arna Bontemps, Nella Larsen, and Zora Neale Hurston. Works representative of the Harlem Renaissance include Arna Bontemps's poems "The Return" and "Golgotha Is a Mountain," Claude McKay's novel *Home to Harlem,* Nella Larsen's novel *Passing,* Langston Hughes's poem "The Negro Speaks of Rivers," and the journals *Crisis* and *Opportunity,* both founded during this period. Also known as Negro Renaissance and New Negro Movement.

Harlequin: A stock character of the *commedia dell'arte* who occasionally interrupted the action with silly antics. Harlequin first appeared on the English stage in John Day's *The Travailes of the Three English Brothers.* The San Francisco Mime Troupe is one of the few modern groups to adapt Harlequin to the needs of contemporary satire.

Hellenism: Imitation of ancient Greek thought or styles. Also, an approach to life that focuses on the growth and development of the intellect. "Hellenism" is sometimes used to refer to the belief that reason can be applied to examine all human experience. A cogent discussion of Hellenism can be found in Matthew Arnold's *Culture and Anarchy.*

Heptameter: See *Meter*

Hero/Heroine: The principal sympathetic character (male or female) in a literary work. Heroes and heroines typically exhibit admirable traits: idealism, courage, and integrity, for example. Famous heroes and heroines include Pip in Charles Dickens's *Great Expectations,* the anonymous narrator in Ralph Ellison's *Invisible Man,* and Sethe in Toni Morrison's *Beloved.*

Heroic Couplet: A rhyming couplet written in iambic pentameter (a verse with five iambic feet). The following lines by Alexander Pope are an example: "Truth guards the Poet, sanctifies the line,/ And makes Immortal, Verse as mean as mine."

Heroic Line: The meter and length of a line of verse in epic or heroic poetry. This varies by language and time period. For example, in English poetry, the heroic line is iambic pentameter (a verse with five iambic feet); in French, the alexandrine (a verse with six iambic feet); in classical literature, dactylic hexameter (a verse with six dactylic feet).

Heroine: See *Hero/Heroine*

Hexameter: See *Meter*

Historical Criticism: The study of a work based on its impact on the world of the time period in which it was written. Examples of postmodern historical criticism can be found in the work of Michel Foucault, Hayden White, Stephen Greenblatt, and Jonathan Goldberg.

Hokku: See *Haiku*

Holocaust: See *Holocaust Literature*

Holocaust Literature: Literature influenced by or written about the Holocaust of World War II. Such literature includes true stories of survival in concentration camps, escape, and life after the war, as well as fictional works and poetry. Representative works of Holocaust literature include Saul Bellow's *Mr. Sammler's Planet,* Anne Frank's *The Diary of a Young Girl,* Jerzy Kosinski's *The Painted Bird,* Arthur Miller's *Incident at Vichy,* Czeslaw Milosz's *Collected Poems,* William Styron's *Sophie's Choice,* and Art Spiegelman's *Maus.*

Homeric Simile: An elaborate, detailed comparison written as a simile many lines in length. An example of an epic simile from John Milton's *Paradise Lost* follows: Angel Forms, who lay entranced Thick as autumnal leaves that strow the brooks In Vallombrosa, where the Etrurian shades High over-arched embower; or scattered sedge Afloat, when with fierce winds Orion armed Hath vexed the Red-Sea coast, whose waves o'erthrew Busiris and his Memphian chivalry, While with perfidious hatred they pursued The sojourners of Goshen, who beheld From the safe shore their floating carcasses And broken chariot-wheels. Also known as Epic Simile.

Horatian Satire: See *Satire*

Humanism: A philosophy that places faith in the dignity of humankind and rejects the medieval perception of the individual as a weak, fallen creature. "Humanists" typically believe in the perfectibility of human nature and view reason and education as the means to that end. Humanist thought is represented in the works of Marsilio Ficino, Ludovico Castelvetro, Edmund Spenser, John Milton, Dean John Colet, Desiderius Erasmus, John Dryden, Alexander Pope, Matthew Arnold, and Irving Babbitt.

Humors: Mentions of the humors refer to the ancient Greek theory that a person's health and personality were determined by the balance of four basic fluids in the body: blood, phlegm, yellow bile, and black bile. A dominance of any fluid would cause extremes in behavior. An excess of blood created a sanguine person who was joyful, aggressive, and passionate; a phlegmatic person was shy, fearful, and sluggish; too much yellow bile led to a choleric temperament characterized by impatience, anger, bitterness, and stubbornness; and excessive black bile created melancholy, a state of laziness, gluttony, and lack of motivation. Literary treatment of the humors is exemplified by several characters in Ben Jonson's plays *Every Man in His Humour* and *Every Man out of His Humour.* Also spelled Humours.

Humours: See *Humors*

Hyperbole: In literary criticism, deliberate exaggeration used to achieve an effect. In William Shakespeare's *Macbeth,* Lady Macbeth hyperbolizes when she says, "All the perfumes of Arabia could not sweeten this little hand."

I

Iamb: See *Foot*

Idiom: A word construction or verbal expression closely associated with a given language. For example, in colloquial English the construction "how come" can be used instead of "why" to introduce a question. Similarly, "a piece of cake" is sometimes used to describe a task that is easily done.

Image: A concrete representation of an object or sensory experience. Typically, such a representation helps evoke the feelings associated with the object or experience itself. Images are either "literal" or "figurative." Literal images are especially concrete and involve little or no extension of the obvious meaning of the words used to express them. Figurative images do not follow the literal meaning of the words exactly. Images in literature are usually visual, but the term "image" can also refer to the representation of any sensory experience. In his poem "The Shepherd's

Hour," Paul Verlaine presents the following image: "The Moon is red through horizon's fog;/ In a dancing mist the hazy meadow sleeps." The first line is broadly literal, while the second line involves turns of meaning associated with dancing and sleeping.

Imagery: The array of images in a literary work. Also, figurative language. William Butler Yeats's "The Second Coming" offers a powerful image of encroaching anarchy: Turning and turning in the widening gyre The falcon cannot hear the falconer; Things fall apart....

Imagism: An English and American poetry movement that flourished between 1908 and 1917. The Imagists used precise, clearly presented images in their works. They also used common, everyday speech and aimed for conciseness, concrete imagery, and the creation of new rhythms. Participants in the Imagist movement included Ezra Pound, H. D. (Hilda Doolittle), and Amy Lowell, among others.

In medias res: A Latin term meaning "in the middle of things." It refers to the technique of beginning a story at its midpoint and then using various flashback devices to reveal previous action. This technique originated in such epics as Virgil's *Aeneid.*

Induction: The process of reaching a conclusion by reasoning from specific premises to form a general premise. Also, an introductory portion of a work of literature, especially a play. Geoffrey Chaucer's "Prologue" to the *Canterbury Tales,* Thomas Sackville's "Induction" to *The Mirror of Magistrates,* and the opening scene in William Shakespeare's *The Taming of the Shrew* are examples of inductions to literary works.

Intentional Fallacy: The belief that judgments of a literary work based solely on an author's stated or implied intentions are false and misleading. Critics who believe in the concept of the intentional fallacy typically argue that the work itself is sufficient matter for interpretation, even though they may concede that an author's statement of purpose can be useful. Analysis of William Wordsworth's *Lyrical Ballads* based on the observations about poetry he makes in his "Preface" to the second edition of that work is an example of the intentional fallacy.

Interior Monologue: A narrative technique in which characters' thoughts are revealed in a way that appears to be uncontrolled by the author. The interior monologue typically aims to reveal the inner self of a character. It portrays emotional experiences as they occur at both a conscious and unconscious level. images are often used to represent sensations or emotions. One of the best-known interior monologues in English is the Molly Bloom section at the close of James Joyce's *Ulysses.* The interior monologue is also common in the works of Virginia Woolf.

Internal Rhyme: Rhyme that occurs within a single line of verse. An example is in the opening line of Edgar Allan Poe's "The Raven": "Once upon a midnight dreary, while I pondered weak and weary." Here, "dreary" and "weary" make an internal rhyme.

Irish Literary Renaissance: A late nineteenth- and early twentieth-century movement in Irish literature. Members of the movement aimed to reduce the influence of British culture in Ireland and create an Irish national literature. William Butler Yeats, George Moore, and Sean O'Casey are three of the best-known figures of the movement.

Irony: In literary criticism, the effect of language in which the intended meaning is the opposite of what is stated. The title of Jonathan Swift's "A Modest Proposal" is ironic because what Swift proposes in this essay is cannibalism—hardly "modest."

Italian Sonnet: See *Sonnet*

J

Jacobean Age: The period of the reign of James I of England (1603-1625). The early literature of this period reflected the worldview of the Elizabethan Age, but a darker, more cynical attitude steadily grew in the art and literature of the Jacobean Age. This was an important time for English drama and poetry. Milestones include William Shakespeare's tragedies, tragi-comedies, and sonnets; Ben Jonson's various dramas; and John Donne's metaphysical poetry.

Jargon: Language that is used or understood only by a select group of people. Jargon may refer to terminology used in a certain profession, such as computer jargon, or it may refer to any nonsensical language that is not understood by most people. Literary examples of jargon are Francois Villon's *Ballades en jargon,* which is composed in the secret language of the *coquillards,* and Anthony Burgess's *A Clockwork Orange,* narrated in the fictional characters' language of "Nadsat."

Juvenalian Satire: See *Satire*

K

Knickerbocker Group: A somewhat indistinct group of New York writers of the first half of the nineteenth century. Members of the group were linked only by location and a common theme: New York life. Two famous members of the Knickerbocker Group were Washington Irving and William Cullen Bryant. The group's name derives from Irving's *Knickerbocker's History of New York.*

L

Lais: See *Lay*

Lay: A song or simple narrative poem. The form originated in medieval France. Early French *lais* were often based on the Celtic legends and other tales sung by Breton minstrels—thus the name of the "Breton lay." In fourteenth-century England, the term "lay" was used to describe short narratives written in imitation of the Breton lays. The most notable of these is Geoffrey Chaucer's "The Minstrel's Tale."

Leitmotiv: See *Motif*

Literal Language: An author uses literal language when he or she writes without exaggerating or embellishing the subject matter and without any tools of figurative language. To say "He ran very quickly down the street" is to use literal language, whereas to say "He ran like a hare down the street" would be using figurative language.

Literary Ballad: See *Ballad*

Literature: Literature is broadly defined as any written or spoken material, but the term most often refers to creative works. Literature includes poetry, drama, fiction, and many kinds of nonfiction writing, as well as oral, dramatic, and broadcast compositions not necessarily preserved in a written format, such as films and television programs.

Lost Generation: A term first used by Gertrude Stein to describe the post-World War I generation of American writers: men and women haunted by a sense of betrayal and emptiness brought about by the destructiveness of the war. The term is commonly applied to Hart Crane, Ernest Hemingway, F. Scott Fitzgerald, and others.

Lyric Poetry: A poem expressing the subjective feelings and personal emotions of the poet. Such poetry is melodic, since it was originally accompanied by a lyre in recitals. Most Western poetry in the twentieth century may be classified as lyrical. Examples of lyric poetry include A. E. Housman's elegy "To an Athlete Dying Young," the odes of Pindar and Horace, Thomas Gray and William Collins, the sonnets of Sir Thomas Wyatt and Sir Philip Sidney, Elizabeth Barrett Browning and Rainer Maria Rilke, and a host of other forms in the poetry of William Blake and Christina Rossetti, among many others.

M

Mannerism: Exaggerated, artificial adherence to a literary manner or style. Also, a popular style of the visual arts of late sixteenth-century Europe that was marked by elongation of the human form and by intentional spatial distortion. Literary works that are self-consciously high-toned and artistic are often said to be "mannered." Authors of such works include Henry James and Gertrude Stein.

Masculine Rhyme: See *Rhyme*

Masque: A lavish and elaborate form of entertainment, often performed in royal courts, that emphasizes song, dance, and costumery. The Renaissance form of the masque grew out of the spectacles of masked figures common in medieval England and Europe. The masque reached its peak of popularity and development in seventeenth-century England, during the reigns of James I and, especially, of Charles I. Ben Jonson, the most significant masque writer, also created the "antimasque," which incorporates elements of humor and the grotesque into the traditional masque and achieved greater dramatic quality. Masque-like interludes appear in Edmund Spenser's *The Faerie Queene* and in William Shakespeare's *The Tempest.* One of the best-known English masques is John Milton's *Comus.*

Measure: The foot, verse, or time sequence used in a literary work, especially a poem. Measure is often used somewhat incorrectly as a synonym for meter.

Melodrama: A play in which the typical plot is a conflict between characters who personify extreme good and evil. Melodramas usually end happily and emphasize sensationalism. Other literary forms that use the same techniques are often labeled "melodramatic." The term was formerly used to describe a combination of drama and music; as such, it was synonymous with "opera." Augustin Daly's *Under the Gaslight* and Dion Boucicault's *The Octoroon, The Colleen Bawn,* and *The Poor of New York* are examples of melodramas. The most popular media for twentieth-century melodramas are motion pictures and television.

Metaphor: A figure of speech that expresses an idea through the image of another object. Metaphors suggest the essence of the first object by identifying it with certain qualities of the second object. An example is "But soft, what light through yonder window breaks?/ It is the east, and Juliet is the sun" in William Shakespeare's *Romeo and Juliet.* Here, Juliet, the first object, is identified with qualities of the second object, the sun.

Metaphysical Conceit: See *Conceit*

Metaphysical Poetry: The body of poetry produced by a group of seventeenth-century English writers called the "Metaphysical Poets." The group includes John Donne and Andrew Marvell. The Metaphysical Poets made use of everyday speech, intellectual analysis, and unique imagery. They aimed to portray the ordinary conflicts and contradictions of life. Their poems often took the form of an argument, and many of them emphasize physical and religious love as well as the fleeting nature of life. Elaborate conceits are typical in metaphysical poetry. Marvell's "To His Coy Mistress" is a well-known example of a metaphysical poem.

Metaphysical Poets: See *Metaphysical Poetry*

Meter: In literary criticism, the repetition of sound patterns that creates a rhythm in poetry. The patterns are based on the number of syllables and the presence and absence of accents. The unit of rhythm in a line is called a foot. Types of meter are classified according to the number of feet in a line. These are the standard English lines: Monometer, one foot; Dimeter, two feet; Trimeter, three feet; Tetrameter, four feet; Pentameter, five feet; Hexameter, six feet (also called the Alexandrine); Heptameter, seven feet (also called the "Fourteener" when the feet are iambic). The most common English meter is the iambic pentameter, in which each line contains ten syllables, or five iambic feet, which individually are composed of an unstressed syllable followed by an accented syllable. Both of the following lines from Alfred, Lord Tennyson's "Ulysses" are written in iambic pentameter: Made weak by time and fate, but strong in will To strive, to seek, to find, and not to yield.

Mise en scene: The costumes, scenery, and other properties of a drama. Herbert Beerbohm Tree was renowned for the elaborate *mises en scene* of his lavish Shakespearean productions at His Majesty's Theatre between 1897 and 1915.

Modernism: Modern literary practices. Also, the principles of a literary school that lasted from roughly the beginning of the twentieth century until the end of World War II. Modernism is defined by its rejection of the literary conventions of the nineteenth century and by its opposition to conventional morality, taste, traditions, and economic values. Many writers are associated with the concepts of Modernism, including Albert Camus, Marcel Proust, D. H. Lawrence, W. H. Auden, Ernest Hemingway, William Faulkner, William Butler Yeats, Thomas Mann, Tennessee Williams, Eugene O'Neill, and James Joyce.

Monologue: A composition, written or oral, by a single individual. More specifically, a speech given by a single individual in a drama or other public entertainment. It has no set length, although it is usually several or more lines long. An example of an "extended monologue"—that is, a monologue of great length and seriousness—occurs in the one-act, one-character play *The Stronger* by August Strindberg.

Monometer: See *Meter*

Mood: The prevailing emotions of a work or of the author in his or her creation of the work. The mood of a work is not always what might be expected based on its subject matter. The poem "Dover Beach" by Matthew Arnold offers examples of two different moods originating from the same experience: watching the ocean at night. The mood of the first three lines—The sea is calm tonight The tide is full, the moon lies fair Upon the straights.... is in sharp contrast to the mood of the last three lines— And we are here as on a darkling plain Swept with confused alarms of struggle and flight, Where ignorant armies clash by night.

Motif: A theme, character type, image, metaphor, or other verbal element that recurs throughout a single work of literature or occurs in a number of different works over a period of time. For example, the various manifestations of the color white in Herman Melville's *Moby Dick* is a "specific" *motif,* while the trials of star-crossed lovers is a "conventional" *motif* from the literature of all periods. Also known as *Motiv* or *Leitmotiv.*

Motiv: See *Motif*

Muckrakers: An early twentieth-century group of American writers. Typically, their works exposed the wrongdoings of big business and government in the United States. Upton Sinclair's *The Jungle* exemplifies the muckraking novel.

Muses: Nine Greek mythological goddesses, the daughters of Zeus and Mnemosyne (Memory). Each muse patronized a specific area of the liberal arts and sciences. Calliope presided over epic poetry, Clio over history, Erato over love poetry, Euterpe over music or lyric poetry, Melpomene over tragedy, Polyhymnia over hymns to the gods, Terpsichore over dance, Thalia over comedy, and Urania over astronomy. Poets and writers traditionally made appeals to the Muses for inspiration in their work. John Milton invokes the aid of a muse at the beginning of the first book of his *Paradise Lost:* Of Man's First disobedience, and the Fruit of the Forbidden Tree, whose mortal taste Brought Death into the World, and all our woe, With loss of Eden, till one greater Man Restore us, and regain the blissful Seat, Sing Heav'nly Muse, that on the secret top of Oreb, or of Sinai, didst inspire That Shepherd, who first taught the chosen Seed, In the Beginning how the Heav'ns and Earth Rose out of Chaos....

Mystery: See *Suspense*

Myth: An anonymous tale emerging from the traditional beliefs of a culture or social unit. Myths use supernatural explanations for natural phenomena. They may also explain cosmic issues like creation and death. Collections of myths, known as mythologies, are common to all cultures and nations, but the best-known myths belong to the Norse, Roman, and Greek mythologies. A famous myth is the story of Arachne, an arrogant young girl who challenged a goddess, Athena, to a weaving contest; when the girl won, Athena was enraged and turned Arachne into a spider, thus explaining the existence of spiders.

N

Narration: The telling of a series of events, real or invented. A narration may be either a simple narrative, in which the events are recounted chronologically, or a narrative with a plot, in which the account is given in a style reflecting the author's artistic concept of the story. Narration is sometimes used as a synonym for "storyline." The recounting of scary stories around a campfire is a form of narration.

Narrative: A verse or prose accounting of an event or sequence of events, real or invented. The term is also used as an adjective in the sense "method of narration." For example, in literary criticism, the expression "narrative technique" usually refers to the way the author structures and presents his or her story. Narratives range from the shortest accounts of events, as in Julius Caesar's remark, "I came, I saw, I conquered," to the longest historical or biographical works, as in Edward Gibbon's *The Decline and Fall of the Roman Empire,* as well as diaries, travelogues, novels, ballads, epics, short stories, and other fictional forms.

Narrative Poetry: A nondramatic poem in which the author tells a story. Such poems may be of any length or level of complexity. Epics such as *Beowulf* and ballads are forms of narrative poetry.

Narrator: The teller of a story. The narrator may be the author or a character in the story through whom the author speaks. Huckleberry Finn is the narrator of Mark Twain's *The Adventures of Huckleberry Finn.*

Naturalism: A literary movement of the late nineteenth and early twentieth centuries.

The movement's major theorist, French novelist Emile Zola, envisioned a type of fiction that would examine human life with the objectivity of scientific inquiry. The Naturalists typically viewed human beings as either the products of "biological determinism," ruled by hereditary instincts and engaged in an endless struggle for survival, or as the products of "socioeconomic determinism," ruled by social and economic forces beyond their control. In their works, the Naturalists generally ignored the highest levels of society and focused on degradation: poverty, alcoholism, prostitution, insanity, and disease. Naturalism influenced authors throughout the world, including Henrik Ibsen and Thomas Hardy. In the United States, in particular, Naturalism had a profound impact. Among the authors who embraced its principles are Theodore Dreiser, Eugene O'Neill, Stephen Crane, Jack London, and Frank Norris.

Negritude: A literary movement based on the concept of a shared cultural bond on the part of black Africans, wherever they may be in the world. It traces its origins to the former French colonies of Africa and the Caribbean. Negritude poets, novelists, and essayists generally stress four points in their writings: One, black alienation from traditional African culture can lead to feelings of inferiority. Two, European colonialism and Western education should be resisted. Three, black Africans should seek to affirm and define their own identity. Four, African culture can and should be reclaimed. Many Negritude writers also claim that blacks can make unique contributions to the world, based on a heightened appreciation of nature, rhythm, and human emotions—aspects of life they say are not so highly valued in the materialistic and rationalistic West. Examples of Negritude literature include the poetry of both Senegalese Leopold Senghor in *Hosties noires* and Martiniquais Aime-Fernand Cesaire in *Return to My Native Land.*

Negro Renaissance: See *Harlem Renaissance*

Neoclassical Period: See *Neoclassicism*

Neoclassicism: In literary criticism, this term refers to the revival of the attitudes and styles of expression of classical literature. It is generally used to describe a period in European history beginning in the late seventeenth century and lasting until about 1800. In its purest form, Neoclassicism marked a return to order, proportion, restraint, logic, accuracy, and decorum. In England, where Neoclassicism perhaps was most popular, it reflected the influence of seventeenth-century French writers, especially dramatists. Neoclassical writers typically reacted against the intensity and enthusiasm of the Renaissance period. They wrote works that appealed to the intellect, using elevated language and classical literary forms such as satire and the ode. Neoclassical works were often governed by the classical goal of instruction. English neoclassicists included Alexander Pope, Jonathan Swift, Joseph Addison, Sir Richard Steele, John Gay, and Matthew Prior; French neoclassicists included Pierre Corneille and Jean-Baptiste Moliere. Also known as Age of Reason.

Neoclassicists: See *Neoclassicism*

New Criticism: A movement in literary criticism, dating from the late 1920s, that stressed close textual analysis in the interpretation of works of literature. The New Critics saw little merit in historical and biographical analysis. Rather, they aimed to examine the text alone, free from the question of how external events—biographical or otherwise—may have helped shape it. This predominantly American school was named "New Criticism" by one of its practitioners, John Crowe Ransom. Other important New Critics included Allen Tate, R. P. Blackmur, Robert Penn Warren, and Cleanth Brooks.

New Negro Movement: See *Harlem Renaissance*

Noble Savage: The idea that primitive man is noble and good but becomes evil and corrupted as he becomes civilized. The concept of the noble savage originated in the Renaissance period but is more closely identified with such later writers as Jean-Jacques Rousseau and Aphra Behn. First described in John Dryden's play *The Conquest of Granada,* the noble savage is portrayed by the various Native Americans in James Fenimore Cooper's "Leatherstocking Tales," by Queequeg, Daggoo, and Tashtego in Herman Melville's *Moby Dick,* and by John the Savage in Aldous Huxley's *Brave New World.*

O

Objective Correlative: An outward set of objects, a situation, or a chain of events corresponding to an inward experience and evoking this experience in the reader. The term frequently appears in modern criticism in discussions of authors' intended effects on the emotional responses of readers. This term was originally used by T. S. Eliot in his 1919 essay "Hamlet."

Objectivity: A quality in writing characterized by the absence of the author's opinion or feeling about the subject matter. Objectivity is an important factor in criticism. The novels of Henry James and, to a certain extent, the poems of John Larkin demonstrate objectivity, and it is central to John Keats's concept of "negative capability." Critical and journalistic writing usually are or attempt to be objective.

Occasional Verse: poetry written on the occasion of a significant historical or personal event. *Vers de societe* is sometimes called occasional verse although it is of a less serious nature. Famous examples of occasional verse include Andrew Marvell's "Horatian Ode upon Cromwell's Return from England," Walt Whitman's "When Lilacs Last in the Dooryard Bloom'd"—written upon the death of Abraham Lincoln—and Edmund Spenser's commemoration of his wedding, "Epithalamion."

Octave: A poem or stanza composed of eight lines. The term octave most often represents the first eight lines of a Petrarchan sonnet. An example of an octave is taken from a translation of a Petrarchan sonnet by Sir Thomas Wyatt: The pillar perisht is whereto I leant, The strongest stay of mine unquiet mind; The like of it no man again can find, From East to West Still seeking though he went. To mind unhap! for hap away hath rent Of all my joy the very bark and rind; And I, alas, by chance am thus assigned Daily to mourn till death do it relent.

Ode: Name given to an extended lyric poem characterized by exalted emotion and dignified style. An ode usually concerns a single, serious theme. Most odes, but not all, are addressed to an object or individual. Odes are distinguished from other lyric poetic forms by their complex rhythmic and stanzaic patterns. An example of this form is John Keats's "Ode to a Nightingale."

Oedipus Complex: A son's amorous obsession with his mother. The phrase is derived from the story of the ancient Theban hero Oedipus, who unknowingly killed his father and married his mother. Literary occurrences of the Oedipus complex include Andre Gide's *Oedipe* and Jean Cocteau's *La Machine infernale,* as well as the most famous, Sophocles' *Oedipus Rex.*

Omniscience: See *Point of View*

Onomatopoeia: The use of words whose sounds express or suggest their meaning. In its simplest sense, onomatopoeia may be represented by words that mimic the sounds they denote such as "hiss" or "meow." At a more subtle level, the pattern and rhythm of sounds and rhymes of a line or poem may be onomatopoeic. A celebrated example of onomatopoeia is the repetition of the word "bells" in Edgar Allan Poe's poem "The Bells."

Opera: A type of stage performance, usually a drama, in which the dialogue is sung. Classic examples of opera include Giuseppi Verdi's *La traviata*, Giacomo Puccini's *La Boheme,* and Richard Wagner's *Tristan und Isolde.* Major twentieth- century contributors to the form include Richard Strauss and Alban Berg.

Operetta: A usually romantic comic opera. John Gay's *The Beggar's Opera*, Richard Sheridan's *The Duenna*, and numerous works by William Gilbert and Arthur Sullivan are examples of operettas.

Oral Tradition: See *Oral Transmission*

Oral Transmission: A process by which songs, ballads, folklore, and other material are transmitted by word of mouth. The tradition of oral transmission predates the written record systems of literate society. Oral transmission preserves material sometimes over generations, although often with variations. Memory plays a large part in the recitation and preservation of orally transmitted material. Breton lays, French *fabliaux,* national epics (including the Anglo- Saxon *Beowulf,* the Spanish *El Cid,* and the Finnish *Kalevala*), Native American myths and legends, and African folktales told by plantation slaves are examples of orally transmitted literature.

Oration: Formal speaking intended to motivate the listeners to some action or feeling. Such public speaking was much more common before the development of timely printed communication such as newspapers. Famous examples of oration include Abraham Lincoln's "Gettysburg Address" and Dr. Martin Luther King Jr.'s "I Have a Dream" speech.

Ottava Rima: An eight-line stanza of poetry composed in iambic pentameter (a five-foot line in which each foot consists of an unaccented syllable followed by an accented syllable), following the abababcc rhyme scheme. This form has been prominently used by such important English writers as Lord Byron, Henry Wadsworth Longfellow, and W. B. Yeats.

Oxymoron: A phrase combining two contradictory terms. Oxymorons may be intentional or unintentional. The following speech from William Shakespeare's *Romeo and Juliet* uses several oxymorons: Why, then, O brawling love! O loving hate! O anything, of nothing first create! O heavy lightness! serious vanity! Mis-shapen chaos of well-seeming forms! Feather of lead, bright smoke, cold fire, sick health! This love feel I, that feel no love in this.

P

Pantheism: The idea that all things are both a manifestation or revelation of God and a part of God at the same time. Pantheism was a common attitude in the early societies of Egypt, India, and Greece—the term derives from the Greek *pan* meaning "all" and *theos* meaning "deity." It later became a significant part of the Christian faith. William Wordsworth and Ralph Waldo Emerson are among the many writers who have expressed the pantheistic attitude in their works.

Parable: A story intended to teach a moral lesson or answer an ethical question. In the West, the best examples of parables are those of Jesus Christ in the New Testament, notably "The Prodigal Son," but parables also are used in Sufism, rabbinic literature, Hasidism, and Zen Buddhism.

Paradox: A statement that appears illogical or contradictory at first, but may actually point to an underlying truth. "Less is more" is an example of a paradox. Literary examples include Francis Bacon's statement, "The most corrected copies are commonly the least correct," and "All animals are equal, but some animals are more equal than others" from George Orwell's *Animal Farm*.

Parallelism: A method of comparison of two ideas in which each is developed in the same grammatical structure. Ralph Waldo Emerson's "Civilization" contains this example of parallelism: Raphael paints wisdom; Handel sings it, Phidias carves it, Shakespeare writes it, Wren builds it, Columbus sails it, Luther preaches it, Washington arms it, Watt mechanizes it.

Parnassianism: A mid nineteenth-century movement in French literature. Followers of the movement stressed adherence to well-defined artistic forms as a reaction against the often chaotic expression of the artist's ego that dominated the work of the Romantics. The Parnassians also rejected the moral, ethical, and social themes exhibited in the works of French Romantics such as Victor Hugo. The aesthetic doctrines of the Parnassians strongly influenced the later symbolist and decadent movements. Members of the Parnassian school include Leconte de Lisle, Sully Prudhomme, Albert Glatigny, Francois Coppee, and Theodore de Banville.

Parody: In literary criticism, this term refers to an imitation of a serious literary work or the signature style of a particular author in a ridiculous manner. A typical parody adopts the style of the original and applies it to an inappropriate subject for humorous effect. Parody is a form of satire and could be considered the literary equivalent of a caricature or cartoon. Henry Fielding's *Shamela* is a parody of Samuel Richardson's *Pamela*.

Pastoral: A term derived from the Latin word "pastor," meaning shepherd. A pastoral is a literary composition on a rural theme. The conventions of the pastoral were originated by the third-century Greek poet Theocritus, who wrote about the experiences, love affairs, and pastimes of Sicilian shepherds. In a pastoral, characters and language of a courtly nature are often placed in a simple setting. The term pastoral is also used to classify dramas, elegies, and lyrics that exhibit the use of country settings and shepherd characters. Percy Bysshe Shelley's "Adonais" and John Milton's "Lycidas" are two famous examples of pastorals.

Pastorela: The Spanish name for the shepherds play, a folk drama reenacted during the Christmas season. Examples of *pastorelas* include Gomez Manrique's *Representacion del nacimiento* and the dramas of Lucas Fernandez and Juan del Encina.

Pathetic Fallacy: A term coined by English critic John Ruskin to identify writing that falsely endows nonhuman things with human intentions and feelings, such as "angry clouds" and "sad trees." The pathetic fallacy is a required convention in the classical poetic form of the pastoral elegy, and it is used in the modern poetry of T. S. Eliot, Ezra Pound, and the Imagists. Also known as Poetic Fallacy.

Pelado: Literally the "skinned one" or shirtless one, he was the stock underdog, sharp-witted picaresque character of Mexican vaudeville and tent shows. The *pelado* is found in such works as Don Catarino's *Los effectos de la crisis* and *Regreso a mi tierra*.

Pen Name: See *Pseudonym*

Pentameter: See *Meter*

Persona: A Latin term meaning "mask." *Personae* are the characters in a fictional work of literature. The *persona* generally functions as a mask through which the author tells a story in a voice other than his or her own. A *persona* is usually either a character in a story who acts as a narrator or an "implied author," a voice created by the author to act as the narrator for himself or herself. *Personae* include the narrator of Geoffrey Chaucer's *Canterbury Tales* and Marlow in Joseph Conrad's *Heart of Darkness*.

Personae: See *Persona*

Personal Point of View: See *Point of View*

Personification: A figure of speech that gives human qualities to abstract ideas, animals, and inanimate objects. William Shakespeare used personification in *Romeo and Juliet* in the lines "Arise, fair sun, and kill the envious moon,/ Who is already sick and pale with grief." Here, the moon is portrayed as being envious, sick, and pale with grief—all markedly human qualities. Also known as *Prosopopoeia*.

Petrarchan Sonnet: See *Sonnet*

Phenomenology: A method of literary criticism based on the belief that things have no existence outside of human consciousness or awareness. Proponents of this theory believe that art is a process that takes place in the mind of the observer as he or she contemplates an object rather than a quality of the object itself. Among phenomenological critics are Edmund Husserl, George Poulet, Marcel Raymond, and Roman Ingarden.

Picaresque Novel: Episodic fiction depicting the adventures of a roguish central character ("picaro" is Spanish for "rogue"). The picaresque hero is commonly a low-born but clever individual who wanders into and out of various affairs of love, danger, and farcical intrigue. These involvements may take place at all social levels and typically present a humorous and wide-ranging satire of a given society. Prominent examples of the picaresque novel are *Don Quixote* by Miguel de Cervantes, *Tom Jones* by Henry Fielding, and *Moll Flanders* by Daniel Defoe.

Plagiarism: Claiming another person's written material as one's own. Plagiarism can take the form of direct, word-for-word copying or the theft of the substance or idea of the work. A student who copies an encyclopedia entry and turns it in as a report for school is guilty of plagiarism.

Platonic Criticism: A form of criticism that stresses an artistic work's usefulness as an agent of social engineering rather than any quality or value of the work itself. Platonic criticism takes as its starting point the ancient Greek philosopher Plato's comments on art in his *Republic*.

Platonism: The embracing of the doctrines of the philosopher Plato, popular among the poets of the Renaissance and the Romantic period. Platonism is more flexible than Aristotelian Criticism and places more emphasis on the supernatural and unknown aspects of life. Platonism is expressed in the love poetry of the Renaissance, the fourth book of Baldassare Castiglione's *The Book of the Courtier,* and the poetry of William Blake, William Wordsworth, Percy Bysshe Shelley, Friedrich Holderlin, William Butler Yeats, and Wallace Stevens.

Play: See *Drama*

Plot: In literary criticism, this term refers to the pattern of events in a narrative or drama. In its simplest sense, the plot guides the author in composing the work and helps the reader follow the work. Typically, plots exhibit causality and unity and have a beginning, a middle, and an end. Sometimes, however, a plot may consist of a series of disconnected events, in which case it is known as an "episodic plot." In his *Aspects of the Novel,* E. M. Forster distinguishes between a story, defined as a "narrative of events arranged in their time- sequence," and plot, which organizes the events to a "sense of causality." This definition closely mirrors Aristotle's discussion of plot in his *Poetics.*

Poem: In its broadest sense, a composition utilizing rhyme, meter, concrete detail, and expressive language to create a literary experience with emotional and aesthetic appeal. Typical poems include sonnets, odes, elegies, *haiku,* ballads, and free verse.

Poet: An author who writes poetry or verse. The term is also used to refer to an artist or writer who has an exceptional gift for expression, imagination, and energy in the making of art in any form. Well-known poets include Horace, Basho, Sir Philip Sidney, Sir Edmund Spenser, John Donne, Andrew Marvell, Alexander Pope, Jonathan Swift, George Gordon, Lord Byron, John Keats, Christina Rossetti, W. H. Auden, Stevie Smith, and Sylvia Plath.

Poetic Fallacy: See *Pathetic Fallacy*

Poetic Justice: An outcome in a literary work, not necessarily a poem, in which the good are rewarded and the evil are punished, especially in ways that particularly fit their virtues or crimes. For example, a murderer may himself be murdered, or a thief will find himself penniless.

Poetic License: Distortions of fact and literary convention made by a writer—not always a poet—for the sake of the effect gained. Poetic license is closely related to the concept of "artistic freedom." An author exercises poetic license by saying that a pile of money "reaches as high as a mountain" when the pile is actually only a foot or two high.

Poetics: This term has two closely related meanings. It denotes (1) an aesthetic theory in literary criticism about the essence of poetry or (2) rules prescribing the proper methods, content, style, or diction of poetry. The term poetics may also refer to theories about literature in general, not just poetry.

Poetry: In its broadest sense, writing that aims to present ideas and evoke an emotional experience in the reader through the use of meter, imagery, connotative and concrete words, and a carefully constructed structure based on rhythmic patterns. Poetry typically relies on words and expressions that have several layers of meaning. It also makes use of the effects of regular rhythm on the ear and may make a strong appeal to the senses through the use of imagery. Edgar Allan Poe's "Annabel Lee" and Walt Whitman's *Leaves of Grass* are famous examples of poetry.

Point of View: The narrative perspective from which a literary work is presented to the reader. There are four traditional points of view. The "third person omniscient" gives the reader a "godlike" perspective, unrestricted by time or place, from which to see actions and look into the minds of characters. This allows the author to comment openly on characters and events in the work. The "third person" point of view presents the events of the story from outside of any single character's perception, much like the omniscient point of view, but the reader must understand the action as it takes place and without any special insight into characters' minds or motivations. The "first person" or "personal" point of view relates events as they are perceived by a single character. The main character "tells" the story and may offer opinions about the action and characters which differ from those of the author. Much less common than omniscient, third person, and first person is the "second person" point of view, wherein the author tells the story as if it is happening to the reader. James Thurber employs the omniscient point of view in his short story "The Secret Life of Walter Mitty." Ernest Hemingway's "A Clean, Well-Lighted Place" is a short story told from the third person point of view. Mark Twain's novel *Huck Finn* is presented from the first person viewpoint. Jay McInerney's *Bright Lights, Big City* is an example of a novel which uses the second person point of view.

Polemic: A work in which the author takes a stand on a controversial subject, such as abortion or religion. Such works are often extremely argumentative or provocative. Classic examples of polemics include John Milton's *Aeropagitica* and Thomas Paine's *The American Crisis.*

Pornography: Writing intended to provoke feelings of lust in the reader. Such works are often condemned by critics and teachers, but those which can be shown to have literary value are viewed less harshly. Literary works that have been described as pornographic include Ovid's *The Art of Love,* Margaret of Angouleme's *Heptameron,* John Cleland's *Memoirs of a Woman of Pleasure; or, the Life of Fanny Hill,* the anonymous *My Secret Life,* D. H. Lawrence's *Lady Chatterley's Lover,* and Vladimir Nabokov's *Lolita.*

Post-Aesthetic Movement: An artistic response made by African Americans to the black aesthetic movement of the 1960s and early '70s. Writers since that time have adopted a somewhat different tone in their work, with less emphasis placed on the disparity between black and white in the United States. In the words of post-aesthetic authors such as Toni Morrison, John Edgar Wideman, and Kristin Hunter, African Americans are portrayed as looking inward for answers to their own questions, rather than always looking to the outside world. Two well-known examples of works produced as part of the post-aesthetic movement are the Pulitzer Prize-winning novels *The Color Purple* by Alice Walker and *Beloved* by Toni Morrison.

Postmodernism: Writing from the 1960s forward characterized by experimentation and continuing to apply some of the fundamentals of modernism, which included existentialism and alienation. Postmodernists have gone a step further in the rejection of tradition begun with the modernists by also rejecting traditional forms, preferring the anti-novel over the novel and the anti-hero over the hero. Postmodern writers include Alain Robbe-Grillet, Thomas Pynchon, Margaret Drabble, John Fowles, Adolfo Bioy-Casares, and Gabriel Garcia Marquez.

Pre-Raphaelites: A circle of writers and artists in mid nineteenth-century England. Valuing the pre-Renaissance artistic qualities of religious symbolism, lavish pictorialism, and natural sensuousness, the Pre-Raphaelites cultivated a sense of mystery and melancholy that influenced later writers associated with the Symbolist and Decadent movements. The major members of the group include Dante Gabriel Rossetti, Christina Rossetti, Algernon Swinburne, and Walter Pater.

Primitivism: The belief that primitive peoples were nobler and less flawed than civilized peoples because they had not been subjected to the tainting influence of society. Examples of literature espousing primitivism include Aphra Behn's *Oroonoko: Or, The History of the Royal Slave,* Jean-Jacques Rousseau's *Julie ou la Nouvelle Heloise,* Oliver Goldsmith's *The Deserted Village,* the poems of Robert Burns, Herman Melville's stories *Typee, Omoo,* and *Mardi,* many poems of William Butler Yeats and Robert Frost, and William Golding's novel *Lord of the Flies.*

Projective Verse: A form of free verse in which the poet's breathing pattern determines the lines of the poem. Poets who advocate projective verse are against all formal structures in writing, including meter and form. Besides its creators, Robert Creeley, Robert Duncan, and Charles Olson, two other well-known projective verse poets are Denise Levertov and LeRoi Jones (Amiri Baraka). Also known as Breath Verse.

Prologue: An introductory section of a literary work. It often contains information establishing the situation of the characters or presents information about the setting, time period, or action. In drama, the prologue is spoken by a chorus or by one of the principal characters. In the "General Prologue" of *The Canterbury Tales,* Geoffrey Chaucer describes the main characters and establishes the setting and purpose of the work.

Prose: A literary medium that attempts to mirror the language of everyday speech. It is distinguished from poetry by its use of unmetered, unrhymed language consisting of logically related sentences. Prose is usually grouped into paragraphs that form a cohesive whole such as an essay or a novel. Recognized masters of English prose writing include Sir Thomas Malory, William Caxton, Raphael

Holinshed, Joseph Addison, Mark Twain, and Ernest Hemingway.

Prosopopoeia: See *Personification*

Protagonist: The central character of a story who serves as a focus for its themes and incidents and as the principal rationale for its development. The protagonist is sometimes referred to in discussions of modern literature as the hero or anti-hero. Well-known protagonists are Hamlet in William Shakespeare's *Hamlet* and Jay Gatsby in F. Scott Fitzgerald's *The Great Gatsby*.

Protest Fiction: Protest fiction has as its primary purpose the protesting of some social injustice, such as racism or discrimination. One example of protest fiction is a series of five novels by Chester Himes, beginning in 1945 with *If He Hollers Let Him Go* and ending in 1955 with *The Primitive*. These works depict the destructive effects of race and gender stereotyping in the context of interracial relationships. Another African American author whose works often revolve around themes of social protest is John Oliver Killens. James Baldwin's essay "Everybody's Protest Novel" generated controversy by attacking the authors of protest fiction.

Proverb: A brief, sage saying that expresses a truth about life in a striking manner. "They are not all cooks who carry long knives" is an example of a proverb.

Pseudonym: A name assumed by a writer, most often intended to prevent his or her identification as the author of a work. Two or more authors may work together under one pseudonym, or an author may use a different name for each genre he or she publishes in. Some publishing companies maintain "house pseudonyms," under which any number of authors may write installations in a series. Some authors also choose a pseudonym over their real names the way an actor may use a stage name. Examples of pseudonyms (with the author's real name in parentheses) include Voltaire (Francois-Marie Arouet), Novalis (Friedrich von Hardenberg), Currer Bell (Charlotte Bronte), Ellis Bell (Emily Bronte), George Eliot (Maryann Evans), Honorio Bustos Donmecq (Adolfo Bioy-Casares and Jorge Luis Borges), and Richard Bachman (Stephen King).

Pun: A play on words that have similar sounds but different meanings. A serious example of the pun is from John Donne's "A Hymne to God the Father": Sweare by thyself, that at my death thy sonne Shall shine as he shines now, and hereto fore; And, having done that, Thou haste done; I fear no more.

Pure Poetry: poetry written without instructional intent or moral purpose that aims only to please a reader by its imagery or musical flow. The term pure poetry is used as the antonym of the term "didacticism." The poetry of Edgar Allan Poe, Stephane Mallarme, Paul Verlaine, Paul Valery, Juan Ramoz Jimenez, and Jorge Guillen offer examples of pure poetry.

Q

Quatrain: A four-line stanza of a poem or an entire poem consisting of four lines. The following quatrain is from Robert Herrick's "To Live Merrily, and to Trust to Good Verses": Round, round, the root do's run; And being ravisht thus, Come, I will drink a Tun To my *Propertius*.

R

Raisonneur: A character in a drama who functions as a spokesperson for the dramatist's views. The *raisonneur* typically observes the play without becoming central to its action. *Raisonneurs* were very common in plays of the nineteenth century.

Realism: A nineteenth-century European literary movement that sought to portray familiar characters, situations, and settings in a realistic manner. This was done primarily by using an objective narrative point of view and through the buildup of accurate detail. The standard for success of any realistic work depends on how faithfully it transfers common experience into fictional forms. The realistic method may be altered or extended, as in stream of consciousness writing, to record highly subjective experience. Seminal authors in the tradition of Realism include Honore de Balzac, Gustave Flaubert, and Henry James.

Refrain: A phrase repeated at intervals throughout a poem. A refrain may appear at the end of each stanza or at less regular intervals. It may be altered slightly at each appearance. Some refrains are nonsense expressions—as with "Nevermore" in Edgar Allan Poe's "The Raven"—that seem to take on a different significance with each use.

Renaissance: The period in European history that marked the end of the Middle Ages. It began in Italy in the late fourteenth century. In broad terms, it is usually seen as spanning the fourteenth, fifteenth, and sixteenth centuries, although it did not reach Great Britain, for example, until the 1480s or so. The Renaissance saw an awakening in almost every sphere of human activity, especially science, philosophy, and the arts. The period is best defined by the emergence of a general philosophy that emphasized the importance of the intellect, the individual, and world affairs. It contrasts strongly with the medieval worldview, characterized by the dominant concerns of faith, the social collective, and spiritual salvation. Prominent writers during the Renaissance include Niccolo Machiavelli and Baldassare Castiglione in Italy, Miguel de Cervantes and Lope de Vega in Spain, Jean Froissart and Francois Rabelais in France, Sir Thomas More and Sir Philip Sidney in England, and Desiderius Erasmus in Holland.

Repartee: Conversation featuring snappy retorts and witticisms. Masters of *repartee* include Sydney Smith, Charles Lamb, and Oscar Wilde. An example is recorded in the meeting of "Beau" Nash and John Wesley: Nash said, "I never make way for a fool," to which Wesley responded, "Don't you? I always do," and stepped aside.

Resolution: The portion of a story following the climax, in which the conflict is resolved. The resolution of Jane Austen's *Northanger Abbey* is neatly summed up in the following sentence: "Henry and Catherine were married, the bells rang and every body smiled."

Restoration: See *Restoration Age*

Restoration Age: A period in English literature beginning with the crowning of Charles II in 1660 and running to about 1700. The era, which was characterized by a reaction against Puritanism, was the first great age of the comedy of manners. The finest literature of the era is typically witty and urbane, and often lewd. Prominent Restoration Age writers include William Congreve, Samuel Pepys, John Dryden, and John Milton.

Revenge Tragedy: A dramatic form popular during the Elizabethan Age, in which the protagonist, directed by the ghost of his murdered father or son, inflicts retaliation upon a powerful villain. Notable features of the revenge tragedy include violence, bizarre criminal acts, intrigue, insanity, a hesitant protagonist, and the use of soliloquy. Thomas Kyd's *Spanish Tragedy* is the first example of revenge tragedy in English, and William Shakespeare's *Hamlet* is perhaps the best. Extreme examples of revenge tragedy, such as John Webster's *The Duchess of Malfi,* are labeled "tragedies of blood." Also known as Tragedy of Blood.

Revista: The Spanish term for a vaudeville musical revue. Examples of *revistas* include Antonio Guzman Aguilera's *Mexico para los mexicanos,* Daniel Vanegas's *Maldito jazz,* and Don Catarino's *Whiskey, morfina y marihuana* and *El desterrado.*

Rhetoric: In literary criticism, this term denotes the art of ethical persuasion. In its strictest sense, rhetoric adheres to various principles developed since classical times for arranging facts and ideas in a clear, persuasive, appealing manner. The term is also used to refer to effective prose in general and theories of or methods for composing effective prose. Classical examples of rhetorics include *The Rhetoric of Aristotle,* Quintillian's *Institutio Oratoria,* and Cicero's *Ad Herennium.*

Rhetorical Question: A question intended to provoke thought, but not an expressed answer, in the reader. It is most commonly used in oratory and other persuasive genres. The following lines from Thomas Gray's "Elegy Written in a Country Churchyard" ask rhetorical questions: Can storied urn or animated bust Back to its mansion call the fleeting breath? Can Honour's voice provoke the silent dust, Or Flattery soothe the dull cold ear of Death?

Rhyme: When used as a noun in literary criticism, this term generally refers to a poem in which words sound identical or very similar and appear in parallel positions in two or more lines. Rhymes are classified into different types according to where they fall in a line or stanza or according to the degree of similarity they exhibit in their spellings and sounds. Some major types of rhyme are "masculine" rhyme, "feminine" rhyme, and "triple" rhyme. In a masculine rhyme, the rhyming sound falls in a single accented syllable, as with "heat" and "eat." Feminine rhyme is a rhyme of two syllables, one stressed and one unstressed, as with "merry" and "tarry." Triple rhyme matches the sound of the accented syllable and the two unaccented syllables that follow: "narrative" and "declarative." Robert Browning alternates feminine and masculine rhymes in his "Soliloquy of the Spanish Cloister": Gr-r-r—there go, my heart's abhorrence! Water your damned flower-pots, do! If hate killed men, Brother Lawrence, God's blood, would not mine kill you! What? Your myrtle-bush wants trimming? Oh, that rose has prior claims—Needs its leaden vase filled brimming? Hell dry you up with flames! Triple rhymes can be found in Thomas Hood's "Bridge of Sighs," George Gordon Byron's satirical verse, and Ogden Nash's comic poems.

Rhyme Royal: A stanza of seven lines composed in iambic pentameter and rhymed *ababbcc.* The name is said to be a tribute to King James I of Scotland, who made much use of the form in his poetry. Examples of rhyme royal include Geoffrey Chaucer's *The Parlement of Foules,* William Shakespeare's *The Rape of Lucrece,* William Morris's *The Early Paradise,* and John Masefield's *The Widow in the Bye Street.*

Rhyme Scheme: See *Rhyme*

Rhythm: A regular pattern of sound, time intervals, or events occurring in writing, most often and most discernably in poetry. Regular, reliable rhythm is known to be soothing to humans, while interrupted, unpredictable, or rapidly changing rhythm is disturbing. These effects are known to authors, who use them to produce a desired reaction in the reader. An example of a form of irregular rhythm is sprung rhythm poetry; quantitative verse, on the other hand, is very regular in its rhythm.

Rising Action: The part of a drama where the plot becomes increasingly complicated. Rising action leads up to the climax, or turning point, of a drama. The final "chase scene" of an action film is generally the rising action which culminates in the film's climax.

Rococo: A style of European architecture that flourished in the eighteenth century, especially in France. The most notable features of *rococo* are its extensive use of ornamentation and its themes of lightness, gaiety, and intimacy. In literary criticism, the term is often used disparagingly to refer to a decadent or over-ornamental style. Alexander Pope's "The Rape of the Lock" is an example of literary *rococo.*

Roman à clef: A French phrase meaning "novel with a key." It refers to a narrative in which real persons are portrayed under fictitious names. Jack Kerouac, for example, portrayed various real-life beat generation figures under fictitious names in his *On the Road.*

Romance: A broad term, usually denoting a narrative with exotic, exaggerated, often idealized characters, scenes, and themes. Nathaniel Hawthorne called his *The House of the Seven Gables* and *The Marble Faun* romances in order to distinguish them from clearly realistic works.

Romantic Age: See *Romanticism*

Romanticism: This term has two widely accepted meanings. In historical criticism, it refers to a European intellectual and artistic movement of the late eighteenth and early nineteenth centuries that sought greater freedom of personal expression than that allowed by the strict rules of literary form and logic of the eighteenth-century neoclassicists. The Romantics preferred emotional and imaginative expression to rational analysis. They considered the individual to be at the center of all experience and so placed him or her at the center of their art. The Romantics believed that the creative imagination reveals nobler truths—unique feelings and attitudes—than those that could be discovered by logic or by scientific examination. Both the natural world and the state of childhood were important sources for revelations of "eternal truths." "Romanticism" is also used as a general term to refer to a type of sensibility found in all periods of literary history and usually considered to be in opposition to the principles of classicism. In this sense, Romanticism signifies any work or philosophy in which the exotic or dreamlike figure strongly, or that is devoted to individualistic expression, self-analysis, or a pursuit of a higher realm of knowledge than can be discovered by human reason. Prominent Romantics include

Jean-Jacques Rousseau, William Wordsworth, John Keats, Lord Byron, and Johann Wolfgang von Goethe.

Romantics: See *Romanticism*

Russian Symbolism: A Russian poetic movement, derived from French symbolism, that flourished between 1894 and 1910. While some Russian Symbolists continued in the French tradition, stressing aestheticism and the importance of suggestion above didactic intent, others saw their craft as a form of mystical worship, and themselves as mediators between the supernatural and the mundane. Russian symbolists include Aleksandr Blok, Vyacheslav Ivanovich Ivanov, Fyodor Sologub, Andrey Bely, Nikolay Gumilyov, and Vladimir Sergeyevich Solovyov.

S

Satire: A work that uses ridicule, humor, and wit to criticize and provoke change in human nature and institutions. There are two major types of satire: "formal" or "direct" satire speaks directly to the reader or to a character in the work; "indirect" satire relies upon the ridiculous behavior of its characters to make its point. Formal satire is further divided into two manners: the "Horatian," which ridicules gently, and the "Juvenalian," which derides its subjects harshly and bitterly. Voltaire's novella *Candide* is an indirect satire. Jonathan Swift's essay "A Modest Proposal" is a Juvenalian satire.

Scansion: The analysis or "scanning" of a poem to determine its meter and often its rhyme scheme. The most common system of scansion uses accents (slanted lines drawn above syllables) to show stressed syllables, breves (curved lines drawn above syllables) to show unstressed syllables, and vertical lines to separate each foot. In the first line of John Keats's *Endymion,* "A thing of beauty is a joy forever:" the word "thing," the first syllable of "beauty," the word "joy," and the second syllable of "forever" are stressed, while the words "A" and "of," the second syllable of "beauty," the word "a," and the first and third syllables of "forever" are unstressed. In the second line: "Its loveliness increases; it will never" a pair of vertical lines separate the foot ending with "increases" and the one beginning with "it."

Scene: A subdivision of an act of a drama, consisting of continuous action taking place at a single time and in a single location. The beginnings and endings of scenes may be indicated by clearing the stage of actors and props or by the entrances and exits of important characters. The first act of William Shakespeare's *Winter's Tale* is comprised of two scenes.

Science Fiction: A type of narrative about or based upon real or imagined scientific theories and technology. Science fiction is often peopled with alien creatures and set on other planets or in different dimensions. Karel Capek's *R.U.R.* is a major work of science fiction.

Second Person: See *Point of View*

Semiotics: The study of how literary forms and conventions affect the meaning of language. Semioticians include Ferdinand de Saussure, Charles Sanders Pierce, Claude Levi-Strauss, Jacques Lacan, Michel Foucault, Jacques Derrida, Roland Barthes, and Julia Kristeva.

Sestet: Any six-line poem or stanza. Examples of the sestet include the last six lines of the Petrarchan sonnet form, the stanza form of Robert Burns's "A Poet's Welcome to his love-begotten Daughter," and the sestina form in W. H. Auden's "Paysage Moralise."

Setting: The time, place, and culture in which the action of a narrative takes place. The elements of setting may include geographic location, characters' physical and mental environments, prevailing cultural attitudes, or the historical time in which the action takes place. Examples of settings include the romanticized Scotland in Sir Walter Scott's "Waverley" novels, the French provincial setting in Gustave Flaubert's *Madame Bovary,* the fictional Wessex country of Thomas Hardy's novels, and the small towns of southern Ontario in Alice Munro's short stories.

Shakespearean Sonnet: See *Sonnet*

Signifying Monkey: A popular trickster figure in black folklore, with hundreds of tales about this character documented since the 19th century. Henry Louis Gates Jr. examines the history of the signifying monkey in *The Signifying Monkey: Towards a Theory of Afro-American Literary Criticism,* published in 1988.

Simile: A comparison, usually using "like" or "as," of two essentially dissimilar things, as in "coffee as cold as ice" or "He sounded like a broken record." The title of Ernest Hemingway's "Hills Like White Elephants" contains a simile.

Slang: A type of informal verbal communication that is generally unacceptable for formal writing. Slang words and phrases are often colorful exaggerations used to emphasize the speaker's point; they may also be shortened versions of an often-used word or phrase. Examples of American slang from the 1990s include "yuppie" (an acronym for Young Urban Professional), "awesome" (for "excellent"), wired (for "nervous" or "excited"), and "chill out" (for relax).

Slant Rhyme: See *Consonance*

Slave Narrative: Autobiographical accounts of American slave life as told by escaped slaves. These works first appeared during the abolition movement of the 1830s through the 1850s. Olaudah Equiano's *The Interesting Narrative of Olaudah Equiano, or Gustavus Vassa, The African* and Harriet Ann Jacobs's *Incidents in the Life of a Slave Girl* are examples of the slave narrative.

Social Realism: See *Socialist Realism*

Socialist Realism: The Socialist Realism school of literary theory was proposed by Maxim Gorky and established as a dogma by the first Soviet Congress of Writers. It demanded adherence to a communist worldview in works of literature. Its doctrines required an objective viewpoint comprehensible to the working classes and themes of social struggle featuring strong proletarian heroes. A successful work of socialist realism is Nikolay Ostrovsky's *Kak zakalyalas stal* (*How the Steel Was Tempered*). Also known as Social Realism.

Soliloquy: A monologue in a drama used to give the audience information and to develop the speaker's character. It is typically a projection of the speaker's innermost thoughts. Usually delivered while the speaker is alone on stage, a soliloquy is intended to present an illusion of unspoken reflection. A celebrated soliloquy is Hamlet's "To be or not to be" speech in William Shakespeare's *Hamlet*.

Sonnet: A fourteen-line poem, usually composed in iambic pentameter, employing one of several rhyme schemes. There are three major types of sonnets, upon which all other variations of the form are based: the "Petrarchan" or "Italian" sonnet, the "Shakespearean" or "English" sonnet, and the "Spenserian" sonnet. A Petrarchan sonnet consists of an octave rhymed *abbaabba* and a "sestet" rhymed either *cdecde, cdccdc,* or *cdedce.* The octave poses a question or problem, relates a narrative, or puts forth a proposition; the sestet presents a solution to the problem, comments upon the narrative, or applies the proposition put forth in the octave. The Shakespearean sonnet is divided into three quatrains and a couplet rhymed *abab cdcd efef gg.* The couplet provides an epigrammatic comment on the narrative or problem put forth in the quatrains. The Spenserian sonnet uses three quatrains and a couplet like the Shakespearean, but links their three rhyme schemes in this way: *abab bcbc cdcd ee.* The Spenserian sonnet develops its theme in two parts like the Petrarchan, its final six lines resolving a problem, analyzing a narrative, or applying a proposition put forth in its first eight lines. Examples of sonnets can be found in Petrarch's *Canzoniere,* Edmund Spenser's *Amoretti,* Elizabeth Barrett Browning's *Sonnets from the Portuguese,* Rainer Maria Rilke's *Sonnets to Orpheus,* and Adrienne Rich's poem "The Insusceptibles."

Spenserian Sonnet: See *Sonnet*

Spenserian Stanza: A nine-line stanza having eight verses in iambic pentameter, its ninth verse in iambic hexameter, and the rhyme scheme ababbcbcc. This stanza form was first used by Edmund Spenser in his allegorical poem *The Faerie Queene.*

Spondee: In poetry meter, a foot consisting of two long or stressed syllables occurring together. This form is quite rare in English verse, and is usually composed of two monosyllabic words. The first foot in the following line from Robert Burns's "Green Grow the Rashes" is an example of a spondee: Green grow the rashes, O.

Sprung Rhythm: Versification using a specific number of accented syllables per line but disregarding the number of unaccented syllables that fall in each line, producing an irregular rhythm in the poem. Gerard Manley Hopkins, who coined the term "sprung rhythm," is the most notable practitioner of this technique.

Stanza: A subdivision of a poem consisting of lines grouped together, often in recurring patterns of rhyme, line length, and meter. Stanzas may also serve as units of thought in a poem much like paragraphs in prose. Examples of stanza forms include the quatrain, *terza rima, ottava rima,* Spenserian, and the so-called *In Memoriam* stanza from Alfred, Lord Tennyson's poem by that title. The following is an example of the latter form: Love is and was my lord and king, And in his presence I attend To hear the tidings of my friend, Which every hour his couriers bring.

Stereotype: A stereotype was originally the name for a duplication made during the printing process; this led to its modern definition as a person or thing that is (or is assumed to be) the same as all others of its type. Common stereotypical characters include the absent-minded professor, the nagging wife, the troublemaking teenager, and the kindhearted grandmother.

Stream of Consciousness: A narrative technique for rendering the inward experience of a character. This technique is designed to give the impression of an ever-changing series of thoughts, emotions, images, and memories in the spontaneous and seemingly illogical order that they occur in life. The textbook example of stream of consciousness is the last section of James Joyce's *Ulysses.*

Structuralism: A twentieth-century movement in literary criticism that examines how literary texts arrive at their meanings, rather than the meanings themselves. There are two major types of structuralist analysis: one examines the way patterns of linguistic structures unify a specific text and emphasize certain elements of that text, and the other interprets the way literary forms and conventions affect the meaning of language itself. Prominent structuralists include Michel Foucault, Roman Jakobson, and Roland Barthes.

Structure: The form taken by a piece of literature. The structure may be made obvious for ease of understanding, as in nonfiction works, or may obscured for artistic purposes, as in some poetry or seemingly "unstructured" prose. Examples of common literary structures include the plot of a narrative, the acts and scenes of a drama, and such poetic forms as the Shakespearean sonnet and the Pindaric ode.

Sturm und Drang: A German term meaning "storm and stress." It refers to a German literary movement of the 1770s and 1780s that reacted against the order and rationalism of the enlightenment, focusing instead on the intense experience of extraordinary individuals. Highly romantic, works of this movement, such as Johann Wolfgang von Goethe's *Gotz von Berlichingen,* are typified by realism, rebelliousness, and intense emotionalism.

Style: A writer's distinctive manner of arranging words to suit his or her ideas and purpose in writing. The unique imprint of the author's personality upon his or her writing, style is the product of an author's way of arranging ideas and his or her use of diction, different sentence structures, rhythm, figures of speech, rhetorical principles, and other elements of composition. Styles may be classified according to period (Metaphysical, Augustan, Georgian), individual authors (Chaucerian, Miltonic, Jamesian), level (grand, middle, low, plain), or language (scientific, expository, poetic, journalistic).

Subject: The person, event, or theme at the center of a work of literature. A work may have one or more subjects of each type, with shorter works tending to have fewer and longer works tending to have more. The subjects of James Baldwin's novel *Go Tell It on the Mountain* include the themes of father-son relationships, religious conversion, black life, and sexuality. The subjects of Anne Frank's *Diary of a Young Girl* include Anne and her family members as well as World War II, the Holocaust, and the themes of war, isolation, injustice, and racism.

Subjectivity: Writing that expresses the author's personal feelings about his subject, and which may or may not include factual information about the subject. Subjectivity is demonstrated in James Joyce's *Portrait of the Artist as a Young Man,* Samuel Butler's *The Way of All Flesh,* and Thomas Wolfe's *Look Homeward, Angel.*

Subplot: A secondary story in a narrative. A subplot may serve as a motivating or complicating force for the main plot of the work, or it may provide emphasis for, or relief from, the main plot. The conflict between the Capulets and the Montagues in William Shakespeare's *Romeo and Juliet* is an example of a subplot.

Surrealism: A term introduced to criticism by Guillaume Apollinaire and later adopted by Andre Breton. It refers to a French literary and artistic movement founded in the 1920s. The Surrealists sought to express unconscious thoughts and feelings in their works. The best-known technique used for achieving this aim was automatic writing—transcriptions of spontaneous outpourings from the unconscious. The Surrealists proposed to unify the contrary levels of conscious and unconscious, dream and reality, objectivity and subjectivity into a new level of "super-realism." Surrealism can be found in the poetry of Paul Eluard, Pierre Reverdy, and Louis Aragon, among others.

Suspense: A literary device in which the author maintains the audience's attention through the buildup of events, the outcome of which will soon be revealed. Suspense in William Shakespeare's *Hamlet* is sustained throughout by the question of whether or not the Prince will achieve what he has been instructed to do and of what he intends to do.

Syllogism: A method of presenting a logical argument. In its most basic form, the syllogism consists of a major premise, a minor premise, and a conclusion. An example of a syllogism is: Major premise: When it snows, the streets get wet. Minor premise: It is snowing. Conclusion: The streets are wet.

Symbol: Something that suggests or stands for something else without losing its original identity. In literature, symbols combine their literal meaning with the suggestion of an abstract concept. Literary symbols are of two types: those that carry complex associations of meaning no matter what their contexts, and those that derive their suggestive meaning from their functions in specific literary works. Examples of symbols are sunshine suggesting happiness, rain suggesting sorrow, and storm clouds suggesting despair.

Symbolism: This term has two widely accepted meanings. In historical criticism, it denotes an early modernist literary movement initiated in France during the nineteenth century that reacted against the prevailing standards of realism. Writers in this movement aimed to evoke, indirectly and symbolically, an order of being beyond the material world of the five senses. Poetic expression of personal emotion figured strongly in the movement, typically by means of a private set of symbols uniquely identifiable with the individual poet. The principal aim of the Symbolists was to express in words the highly complex feelings that grew out of everyday contact with the world. In a broader sense, the term "symbolism" refers to the use of one object to represent another. Early members of the Symbolist movement included the French authors Charles Baudelaire and Arthur Rimbaud; William Butler Yeats, James Joyce, and T. S. Eliot were influenced as the movement moved to Ireland, England, and the United States. Examples of the concept of symbolism include a flag that stands for a nation or movement, or an empty cupboard used to suggest hopelessness, poverty, and despair.

Symbolist: See *Symbolism*

Symbolist Movement: See *Symbolism*

Sympathetic Fallacy: See *Affective Fallacy*

T

Tale: A story told by a narrator with a simple plot and little character development. Tales are usually relatively short and often carry a simple message. Examples of tales can be found in the work of Rudyard Kipling, Somerset Maugham, Saki, Anton Chekhov, Guy de Maupassant, and Armistead Maupin.

Tall Tale: A humorous tale told in a straightforward, credible tone but relating absolutely impossible events or feats of the characters. Such tales were commonly told of frontier adventures during the settlement of the west in the United States. Tall tales have been spun around such legendary heroes as Mike Fink, Paul Bunyan, Davy Crockett, Johnny Appleseed, and Captain Stormalong as well as the real-life William F. Cody and Annie Oakley. Literary use of tall tales can be found in Washington Irving's *History of New York*, Mark Twain's *Life on the Mississippi*, and in the German R. F. Raspe's *Baron Munchausen's Narratives of His Marvellous Travels and Campaigns in Russia*.

Tanka: A form of Japanese poetry similar to *haiku*. A *tanka* is five lines long, with the lines containing five, seven, five, seven, and seven syllables respectively. Skilled *tanka* authors include Ishikawa Takuboku, Masaoka Shiki, Amy Lowell, and Adelaide Crapsey.

Teatro Grottesco: See *Theater of the Grotesque*

Terza Rima: A three-line stanza form in poetry in which the rhymes are made on the last word of each line in the following manner: the first and third lines of the first stanza, then the second line of the first stanza and the first and third lines of the second stanza, and so on with the middle line of any stanza rhyming with the first and third lines of the following stanza. An example of *terza rima* is Percy Bysshe Shelley's "The Triumph of Love": As in that trance of wondrous thought I lay This was the tenour of my waking dream. Methought I sate beside a public way Thick strewn with summer dust, and a great stream Of people there was hurrying to and fro Numerous as gnats upon the evening gleam, . . .

Tetrameter: See *Meter*

Textual Criticism: A branch of literary criticism that seeks to establish the authoritative text of a literary work. Textual critics typically compare all known manuscripts or printings of a single work in order to assess the meanings of differences and revisions. This procedure allows them to arrive at a definitive version that (supposedly) corresponds to the author's original intention. Textual criticism was applied during the Renaissance to salvage the classical texts of Greece and Rome, and modern works have been studied, for instance, to undo deliberate correction or censorship, as in the case of novels by Stephen Crane and Theodore Dreiser.

Theater of Cruelty: Term used to denote a group of theatrical techniques designed to eliminate the psychological and emotional distance between actors and audience. This concept, introduced in the 1930s in France, was intended to inspire a more intense theatrical experience than conventional theater allowed. The "cruelty" of this dramatic theory signified not sadism but heightened actor/audience involvement in the dramatic event. The theater of cruelty was theorized by Antonin Artaud in his *Le Theatre et son double* (*The Theatre and Its Double*), and also appears in the work of Jerzy Grotowski, Jean Genet, Jean Vilar, and Arthur Adamov, among others.

Theater of the Absurd: A post-World War II dramatic trend characterized by radical theatrical innovations. In works influenced by the Theater of the Absurd, nontraditional, sometimes grotesque characterizations, plots, and stage sets reveal a meaningless universe in which human values are irrelevant. Existentialist themes of estrangement, absurdity, and futility link many of the works of this movement. The principal writers of the Theater of the Absurd are Samuel Beckett, Eugene Ionesco, Jean Genet, and Harold Pinter.

Theater of the Grotesque: An Italian theatrical movement characterized by plays written around the ironic and macabre aspects of daily life in the World War I era. Theater of the Grotesque was named after the play *The Mask and the Face* by Luigi Chiarelli, which was described as "a grotesque in three acts." The movement influenced the work of Italian dramatist Luigi Pirandello, author of *Right You Are, If You Think You Are*. Also known as *Teatro Grottesco*.

Theme: The main point of a work of literature. The term is used interchangeably with thesis. The theme of William Shakespeare's *Othello*—jealousy—is a common one.

Thesis: A thesis is both an essay and the point argued in the essay. Thesis novels and thesis plays share the quality of containing a thesis which is supported through the action of the story. A master's thesis and a doctoral dissertation are two theses required of graduate students.

Thesis Play: See *Thesis*

Three Unities: See *Unities*

Tone: The author's attitude toward his or her audience may be deduced from the tone of the work. A formal tone may create distance or convey politeness, while an informal tone may encourage a friendly, intimate, or intrusive feeling in the reader. The author's attitude toward his or her subject matter may also be deduced from the tone of the words he or she uses in discussing it. The tone of John F. Kennedy's speech which included the appeal to "ask not what your country can do for you" was intended to instill feelings of camaraderie and national pride in listeners.

Tragedy: A drama in prose or poetry about a noble, courageous hero of excellent character who, because of some tragic character flaw or *hamartia*, brings ruin upon him- or herself. Tragedy treats its subjects in a dignified and serious manner, using poetic language to help evoke pity and fear and bring about catharsis, a purging of these emotions. The tragic form was practiced extensively by the ancient Greeks. In the Middle Ages, when classical works were virtually unknown, tragedy came to denote any works about the fall of persons from exalted to low conditions due to any reason: fate, vice, weakness, etc. According to the classical definition of tragedy, such works present the "pathetic"—that which evokes pity—rather than the tragic. The classical form of tragedy was revived in the sixteenth century; it flourished especially on the Elizabethan stage. In modern times, dramatists have attempted to adapt the form to the needs of modern society by drawing their heroes from the ranks of ordinary men and women and defining the nobility of these heroes in terms of spirit rather than exalted social standing. The greatest classical example of tragedy is Sophocles' *Oedipus Rex*. The "pathetic" derivation is exemplified in "The Monk's Tale" in Geoffrey Chaucer's *Canterbury Tales*. Notable works produced during the sixteenth century revival include William Shakespeare's *Hamlet, Othello,* and *King Lear*. Modern dramatists working in the tragic tradition include Henrik Ibsen, Arthur Miller, and Eugene O'Neill.

Tragedy of Blood: See *Revenge Tragedy*

Tragic Flaw: In a tragedy, the quality within the hero or heroine which leads to his or her downfall. Examples of the tragic flaw include Othello's jealousy and Hamlet's indecisiveness, although most great tragedies defy such simple interpretation.

Transcendentalism: An American philosophical and religious movement, based in New England from around 1835 until the Civil War. Transcendentalism was a form of American romanticism that had its roots abroad in the works of Thomas Carlyle, Samuel Coleridge, and Johann Wolfgang von Goethe. The Transcendentalists stressed the importance of intuition and subjective experience in communication with God. They rejected religious dogma and texts in favor of mysticism and scientific naturalism. They pursued truths that lie beyond the "colorless"

realms perceived by reason and the senses and were active social reformers in public education, women's rights, and the abolition of slavery. Prominent members of the group include Ralph Waldo Emerson and Henry David Thoreau.

Trickster: A character or figure common in Native American and African literature who uses his ingenuity to defeat enemies and escape difficult situations. Tricksters are most often animals, such as the spider, hare, or coyote, although they may take the form of humans as well. Examples of trickster tales include Thomas King's *A Coyote Columbus Story*, Ashley F. Bryan's *The Dancing Granny* and Ishmael Reed's *The Last Days of Louisiana Red*.

Trimeter: See *Meter*

Triple Rhyme: See *Rhyme*

Trochee: See *Foot*

U

Understatement: See *Irony*

Unities: Strict rules of dramatic structure, formulated by Italian and French critics of the Renaissance and based loosely on the principles of drama discussed by Aristotle in his *Poetics*. Foremost among these rules were the three unities of action, time, and place that compelled a dramatist to: (1) construct a single plot with a beginning, middle, and end that details the causal relationships of action and character; (2) restrict the action to the events of a single day; and (3) limit the scene to a single place or city. The unities were observed faithfully by continental European writers until the Romantic Age, but they were never regularly observed in English drama. Modern dramatists are typically more concerned with a unity of impression or emotional effect than with any of the classical unities. The unities are observed in Pierre Corneille's tragedy *Polyeuctes* and Jean-Baptiste Racine's *Phedre*. Also known as Three Unities.

Urban Realism: A branch of realist writing that attempts to accurately reflect the often harsh facts of modern urban existence. Some works by Stephen Crane, Theodore Dreiser, Charles Dickens, Fyodor Dostoyevsky, Emile Zola, Abraham Cahan, and Henry Fuller feature urban realism. Modern examples include Claude Brown's *Manchild in the*

Promised Land and Ron Milner's *What the Wine Sellers Buy.*

Utopia: A fictional perfect place, such as "paradise" or "heaven." Early literary utopias were included in Plato's *Republic* and Sir Thomas More's *Utopia,* while more modern utopias can be found in Samuel Butler's *Erewhon,* Theodor Herzka's *A Visit to Freeland,* and H. G. Wells' *A Modern Utopia.*

Utopian: See *Utopia*

Utopianism: See *Utopia*

V

Verisimilitude: Literally, the appearance of truth. In literary criticism, the term refers to aspects of a work of literature that seem true to the reader. Verisimilitude is achieved in the work of Honore de Balzac, Gustave Flaubert, and Henry James, among other late nineteenth-century realist writers.

Vers de societe: See *Occasional Verse*

Vers libre: See *Free Verse*

Verse: A line of metered language, a line of a poem, or any work written in verse. The following line of verse is from the epic poem *Don Juan* by Lord Byron: "My way is to begin with the beginning."

Versification: The writing of verse. Versification may also refer to the meter, rhyme, and other mechanical components of a poem. Composition of a "Roses are red, violets are blue" poem to suit an occasion is a common form of versification practiced by students.

Victorian: Refers broadly to the reign of Queen Victoria of England (1837-1901) and to anything with qualities typical of that era. For example, the qualities of smug narrowmindedness, bourgeois materialism, faith in social progress, and priggish morality are often considered Victorian. This stereotype is contradicted by such dramatic intellectual developments as the theories of Charles Darwin, Karl Marx, and Sigmund Freud (which stirred strong debates in England) and the critical attitudes of serious Victorian writers like Charles Dickens and George Eliot. In literature, the Victorian Period was the great age of the English novel, and

the latter part of the era saw the rise of movements such as decadence and symbolism. Works of Victorian literature include the poetry of Robert Browning and Alfred, Lord Tennyson, the criticism of Matthew Arnold and John Ruskin, and the novels of Emily Bronte, William Makepeace Thackeray, and Thomas Hardy. Also known as Victorian Age and Victorian Period.

Victorian Age: See *Victorian*

Victorian Period: See *Victorian*

W

Weltanschauung: A German term referring to a person's worldview or philosophy. Examples of *weltanschauung* include Thomas Hardy's view of the human being as the victim of fate, destiny, or impersonal forces and circumstances, and the disillusioned and laconic cynicism expressed by such poets of the 1930s as W. H. Auden, Sir Stephen Spender, and Sir William Empson.

Weltschmerz: A German term meaning "world pain." It describes a sense of anguish about the nature of existence, usually associated with a melancholy, pessimistic attitude. *Weltschmerz* was expressed in England by George Gordon, Lord Byron in his *Manfred* and *Childe Harold's Pilgrimage,* in France by Viscount de Chateaubriand, Alfred de Vigny, and Alfred de Musset, in Russia by Aleksandr Pushkin and Mikhail Lermontov, in Poland by Juliusz Slowacki, and in America by Nathaniel Hawthorne.

Z

Zarzuela: A type of Spanish operetta. Writers of *zarzuelas* include Lope de Vega and Pedro Calderon.

Zeitgeist: A German term meaning "spirit of the time." It refers to the moral and intellectual trends of a given era. Examples of *zeitgeist* include the preoccupation with the more morbid aspects of dying and death in some Jacobean literature, especially in the works of dramatists Cyril Tourneur and John Webster, and the decadence of the French Symbolists.

Cumulative
Author/Title Index

Numerical

36 Views (Iizuka): V21
84, Charing Cross Road (Hanff): V17

A

Abe Lincoln in Illinois (Sherwood, Robert E.): V11
Abe, Kobo
    The Man Who Turned into a Stick: V14
Accidental Death of an Anarchist (Fo): V23
Ackermann, Joan
    Off the Map: V22
The Advertisement (Ginzburg): V14
Aeschylus
    Agamemnon: V26
    Prometheus Bound: V5
    Seven Against Thebes: V10
Agamemnon (Aeschylus): V26
Ajax (Sophocles): V8
Albee, Edward
    The American Dream: V25
    A Delicate Balance: V14
    Seascape: V13
    Three Tall Women: V8
    Tiny Alice: V10
    Who's Afraid of Virginia Woolf?: V3
    The Zoo Story: V2
The Alchemist (Jonson): V4
Alison's House (Glaspell): V24
All My Sons (Miller): V8
Amadeus (Shaffer): V13
The Amen Corner (Baldwin): V11
American Buffalo (Mamet): V3
The American Dream (Albee): V25

Anderson, Maxwell
    Both Your Houses: V16
    Winterset: V20
Angels Fall (Wilson): V20
Angels in America (Kushner): V5
Anna Christie (O'Neill): V12
Anna in the Tropics (Cruz): V21
Anonymous
    Arden of Faversham: V24
    Everyman: V7
    The Second Shepherds' Play: V25
Anouilh, Jean
    Antigone: V9
    Becket, or the Honor of God: V19
    Ring Around the Moon: V10
Antigone (Anouilh): V9
Antigone (Sophocles): V1
Arcadia (Stoppard): V5
Arden, John
    Serjeant Musgrave's Dance: V9
Arden of Faversham (Anonymous): V24
Aria da Capo (Millay): V27
Aristophanes
    Lysistrata: V10
Arms and the Man (Shaw): V22
Arsenic and Old Lace (Kesselring): V20
Art (Reza): V19
Artaud, Antonin
    The Cenci: V22
As Bees in Honey Drown (Beane): V21
The Au Pair Man (Leonard): V24
Auburn, David
    Proof: V21
Ayckbourn, Alan
    A Chorus of Disapproval: V7

B

The Bacchae (Euripides): V6
The Balcony (Genet): V10
The Bald Soprano (Ionesco, Eugène): V4
Baldwin, James
    The Amen Corner: V11
    One Day, When I Was Lost: A Scenario: V15
The Baptism (Baraka): V16
Baraka, Amiri
    The Baptism: V16
    Dutchman: V3
    Slave Ship: V11
The Barber of Seville (de Beaumarchais): V16
Barnes, Peter
    The Ruling Class: V6
Barrie, J(ames) M.
    Peter Pan: V7
Barry, Philip
    The Philadelphia Story: V9
The Basic Training of Pavlo Hummel (Rabe): V3
Beane, Douglas Carter
    As Bees in Honey Drown: V21
The Bear (Chekhov): V26
Beautiful Señoritas (Prida): V23
Becket, or the Honor of God (Anouilh): V19
Beckett, Samuel
    Endgame: V18
    Krapp's Last Tape: V7
    Waiting for Godot: V2
Behan, Brendan
    The Hostage: V7

Behn, Aphra
    The Forc'd Marriage: V24
    The Rover: V16
Beim, Norman
    The Deserter: V18
The Belle's Stratagem (Cowley): V22
Bent (Sherman): V20
Bernstein, Leonard
    West Side Story: V27
Beyond the Horizon (O'Neill): V16
Biloxi Blues (Simon): V12
The Birthday Party (Pinter): V5
Blank, Jessica
    The Exonerated: V24
Blessing, Lee
    Eleemosynary: V23
    A Walk in the Woods: V26
Blood Relations (Pollock): V3
Blood Wedding (García Lorca): V10
Blue Room (Hare): V7
Blue Surge (Gilman): V23
Blues for an Alabama Sky (Cleage):
    V14
Boesman & Lena (Fugard): V6
Bolt, Robert
    A Man for All Seasons: V2
Bond, Edward
    Lear: V3
    Saved: V8
Bonner, Marita
    The Purple Flower: V13
Both Your Houses (Anderson): V16
The Boys in the Band (Crowley): V14
Brand (Ibsen): V16
Brecht, Bertolt
    The Good Person of Szechwan: V9
    *Mother Courage and Her
        Children:* V5
    The Threepenny Opera: V4
Brighton Beach Memoirs (Simon): V6
Brooks, Mel
    The Producers: V21
The Browning Version (Rattigan): V8
Buero Vallejo, Antonio
    The Sleep of Reason: V11
Buried Child (Shepard): V6
Burn This (Wilson): V4
Bus Stop (Inge): V8
Bye-Bye, Brevoort (Welty): V26

C

Calderón de la Barca, Pedro
    Life Is a Dream: V23
Calm Down Mother (Terry): V18
Capek, Josef
    The Insect Play: V11
Capek, Karel
    The Insect Play: V11
    R.U.R.: V7
Carballido, Emilio
    I, Too, Speak of the Rose: V4

The Caretaker (Pinter): V7
Cat on a Hot Tin Roof (Williams): V3
The Cenci (Artaud): V22
The Chairs (Ionesco, Eugène): V9
The Changeling (Middleton): V22
Chase, Mary
    Harvey: V11
A Chaste Maid in Cheapside
    (Middleton): V18
Chayefsky, Paddy
    Marty: V26
Chekhov, Anton
    The Bear: V26
    The Cherry Orchard: V1
    The Seagull: V12
    The Three Sisters: V10
    Uncle Vanya: V5
The Cherry Orchard (Chekhov): V1
Children of a Lesser God (Medoff):
    V4
The Children's Hour (Hellman): V3
Childress, Alice
    Florence: V26
    Trouble in Mind: V8
    The Wedding Band: V2
    Wine in the Wilderness: V14
A Chorus of Disapproval
    (Ayckbourn): V7
Christie, Agatha
    The Mousetrap: V2
Churchill, Caryl
    Cloud Nine: V16
    Light Shining in Buckinghamshire:
        V27
    Serious Money: V25
    Top Girls: V12
Clark, John Pepper
    The Raft: V13
Cleage, Pearl
    Blues for an Alabama Sky: V14
    Flyin' West: V16
Cloud Nine (Churchill): V16
Coburn, D. L.
    The Gin Game: V23
The Cocktail Party (Eliot): V13
Cocteau, Jean
    Indiscretions: V24
Come Back, Little Sheba (Inge): V3
Congreve, William
    Love for Love: V14
    The Way of the World: V15
Connelly, Marc
    The Green Pastures: V12
Copenhagen (Frayn): V22
Corneille, Pierre
    Le Cid: V21
Coward, Noel
    Hay Fever: V6
    Private Lives: V3
Cowley, Hannah
    The Belle's Stratagem: V22
Crimes of the Heart (Henley): V2

Cristofer, Michael
    The Shadow Box: V15
The Critic (Sheridan): V14
Crossroads (Solórzano): V26
Crouse, Russel
    State of the Union: V19
Crowley, Mart
    The Boys in the Band: V14
The Crucible (Miller): V3
The Crucible (Motion picture): V27
Cruz, Migdalia
    Telling Tales: V19
Cruz, Nilo
    Anna in the Tropics: V21
Curse of the Starving Class
    (Shepard): V14
Cyrano de Bergerac (Rostand): V1

D

Da (Leonard): V13
Dancing at Lughnasa (Friel): V11
de Beaumarchais, Pierre-Augustin
    The Barber of Seville: V16
    The Marriage of Figaro: V14
de Hartog, Jan
    The Fourposter: V12
Death and the King's Horseman
    (Soyinka): V10
Death and the Maiden (Dorfman): V4
Death of a Salesman (Miller): V1
Delaney, Shelagh
    A Taste of Honey: V7
A Delicate Balance (Albee): V14
The Deserter (Beim): V18
Desire under the Elms (O'Neill): V27
The Desperate Hours (Hayes): V20
Detective Story (Kingsley): V19
The Diary of Anne Frank
    (Goodrichand Hackett): V15
Dinner with Friends (Margulies): V13
Dirty Blonde (Shear): V24
Doctor Faustus (Marlowe): V1
Dogg's Hamlet, Cahoot's Macbeth
    (Stoppard): V16
A Doll's House (Ibsen): V1
Dorfman, Ariel
    Death and the Maiden: V4
Doubt (Shanley): V23
Driving Miss Daisy (Uhry): V11
The Duchess of Malfi (Webster): V17
Duffy, Maureen
    Rites: V15
The Dumb Waiter (Pinter): V25
Duras, Marguerite
    India Song: V21
Dutchman (Baraka): V3

E

Edgar, David
    *The Life and Adventures of
        Nicholas Nickleby:* V15

Edson, Margaret
  Wit: V13
Edward II: The Troublesome Reign and Lamentable Death of Edward the Second, King of England, with the Tragical Fall of Proud Mortimer (Marlowe): V5
The Effect of Gamma Rays on Man-in-the-Moon Marigolds (Zindel): V12
Electra (Sophocles): V4
Electra (von Hofmannsthal): V17
Eleemosynary (Blessing): V23
The Elephant Man (Pomerance): V9
Eliot, T. S.
  The Cocktail Party: V13
  Murder in the Cathedral: V4
The Emperor Jones (O'Neill): V6
Endgame (Beckett): V18
An Enemy of the People (Ibsen): V25
Ensler, Eve
  Necessary Targets: V23
Entertaining Mr. Sloane (Orton): V3
Ephron, Nora
  Imaginary Friends: V22
Equus (Shaffer): V5
Euripides
  The Bacchae: V6
  Hippolytus: V25
  Iphigenia in Taurus: V4
  Medea: V1
  The Trojan Women: V27
Everyman (Anonymous): V7
The Exonerated (Blank and Jensen): V24

F

Fabulation; or, The Re-Education of Undine (Nottage): V25
Feeding the Moonfish (Wiechmann): V21
Fefu and Her Friends (Fornes): V25
Fences (Wilson): V3
Fiddler on the Roof (Stein): V7
Fierstein, Harvey
  Torch Song Trilogy: V6
The Firebugs (Frisch): V25
Fires in the Mirror (Smith): V22
Fletcher, Lucille
  Sorry, Wrong Number: V26
The Flies (Sartre): V26
Florence (Childress): V26
Flyin' West (Cleage): V16
Fo, Dario
  Accidental Death of an Anarchist: V23
Fool for Love (Shepard): V7
Foote, Horton
  The Young Man from Atlanta: V20
for colored girls who have considered suicide/when the rainbow is enuf (Shange): V2

For Services Rendered (Maugham): V22
The Forc'd Marriage (Behn): V24
Ford, John
  'Tis Pity She's a Whore: V7
The Foreigner (Shue): V7
Fornes, Marie Irene
  Fefu and Her Friends: V25
The Fourposter (de Hartog): V12
Frayn, Michael
  Copenhagen: V22
Friel, Brian
  Dancing at Lughnasa: V11
Frisch, Max
  The Firebugs: V25
The Front Page (Hecht and MacArthur): V9
Frozen (Lavery): V25
Fugard, Athol
  Boesman & Lena: V6
  A Lesson from Aloes: V24
  "Master Harold"... and the Boys: V3
  Sizwe Bansi is Dead: V10
Fuller, Charles H.
  A Soldier's Play: V8
Funnyhouse of a Negro (Kennedy): V9

G

Gale, Zona
  Miss Lulu Bett: V17
García Lorca, Federico
  Blood Wedding: V10
  The House of Bernarda Alba: V4
Gardner, Herb
  I'm Not Rappaport: V18
  A Thousand Clowns: V20
Gems, Pam
  Stanley: V25
Genet, Jean
  The Balcony: V10
Gerstenberg, Alice
  Overtones: V17
The Ghost Sonata (Strindberg): V9
Ghosts (Ibsen): V11
Gibson, William
  The Miracle Worker: V2
Gilman, Rebecca
  Blue Surge: V23
Gilroy, Frank D.
  The Subject Was Roses: V17
The Gin Game (Coburn): V23
Ginzburg, Natalia
  The Advertisement: V14
Glaspell, Susan
  Alison's House: V24
  Trifles: V8
  The Verge: V18
The Glass Menagerie (Williams): V1
Glengarry Glen Ross (Mamet): V2

Gogol, Nikolai
  The Government Inspector: V12
Golden Boy (Odets): V17
Goldman, James
  The Lion in Winter: V20
Goldoni, Carlo
  The Servant of Two Masters: V27
Goldsmith, Oliver
  She Stoops to Conquer: V1
The Good Person of Szechwan (Brecht): V9
Goodnight Desdemona (Good Morning Juliet) (MacDonald): V23
Goodrich, Frances
  The Diary of Anne Frank: V15
Gorki, Maxim
  The Lower Depths: V9
The Governess (Simon): V27
The Government Inspector (Gogol): V12
The Great God Brown (O'Neill): V11
The Great White Hope (Sackler): V15
The Green Pastures (Connelly): V12
Greenberg, Richard
  Take Me Out: V24
Guare, John
  The House of Blue Leaves: V8
  Six Degrees of Separation: V13

H

Habitat (Thompson): V22
Hackett, Albert
  The Diary of Anne Frank: V15
The Hairy Ape (O'Neill): V4
Hammerstein, Oscar II
  The King and I: V1
Hanff, Helene
  84, Charing Cross Road: V17
Hansberry, Lorraine
  A Raisin in the Sun: V2
Hare, David
  Blue Room: V7
  Plenty: V4
  The Secret Rapture: V16
Harris, Bill
  Robert Johnson: Trick the Devil: V27
Hart, Moss
  Once in a Lifetime: V10
  You Can't Take It with You: V1
Harvey (Chase): V11
Havel, Vaclav
  The Memorandum: V10
Hay Fever (Coward): V6
Hayes, Joseph
  The Desperate Hours: V20
Heather Raffo's 9 Parts of Desire (Raffo): V27
Hecht, Ben
  The Front Page: V9

Hedda Gabler (Ibsen): V6

Heggen, Thomas
  Mister Roberts: V20

The Heidi Chronicles (Wasserstein): V5

Hellman, Lillian
  The Children's Hour: V3
  The Little Foxes: V1
  Watch on the Rhine: V14

Henley, Beth
  Crimes of the Heart: V2
  Impossible Marriage: V26
  The Miss Firecracker Contest: V21

Henrietta (Jones Meadows): V27

Highway, Tomson
  The Rez Sisters: V2

Hippolytus (Euripides): V25

Hollmann, Mark
  Urinetown: V27

The Homecoming (Pinter): V3

The Hostage (Behan): V7

Hot L Baltimore (Wilson): V9

The House of Bernarda Alba (GarcíaLorca, Federico): V4

The House of Blue Leaves (Guare): V8

How I Learned to Drive (Vogel): V14

Hughes, Langston
  Mulatto: V18
  Mule Bone: V6

Hurston, Zora Neale
  Mule Bone: V6

Hwang, David Henry
  M. Butterfly: V11
  The Sound of a Voice: V18

I

I Am My Own Wife (Wright): V23

I Hate Hamlet (Rudnick): V22

I Never Saw Another Butterfly (Raspanti): V27

I, Too, Speak of the Rose (Carballido): V4

Ibsen, Henrik
  Brand: V16
  A Doll's House: V1
  An Enemy of the People: V25
  Ghosts: V11
  Hedda Gabler: V6
  The Master Builder: V15
  Peer Gynt: V8
  The Wild Duck: V10

The Iceman Cometh (O'Neill): V5

An Ideal Husband (Wilde): V21

Idiot's Delight (Sherwood): V15

Iizuka, Naomi
  36 Views: V21

Ile (O'Neill): V26

I'm Not Rappaport (Gardner): V18

Imaginary Friends (Ephron): V22

The Imaginary Invalid (Molière): V20

The Importance of Being Earnest (Wilde): V4

Impossible Marriage (Henley): V26

Inadmissible Evidence (Osborne): V24

India Song (Duras): V21

Indian Ink (Stoppard): V11

Indians (Kopit): V24

Indiscretions (Cocteau): V24

Inge, William
  Bus Stop: V8
  Come Back, Little Sheba: V3
  Picnic: V5

Inherit the Wind (Lawrence and Lee): V2

The Insect Play (Capek): V11

Into the Woods (Sondheim and Lapine): V25

Ionesco, Eugène
  The Bald Soprano: V4
  The Chairs: V9
  Rhinoceros: V25

Iphigenia in Taurus (Euripides): V4

J

J. B. (MacLeish): V15

Jarry, Alfred
  Ubu Roi: V8

Jensen, Erik
  The Exonerated: V24

Jesus Christ Superstar (Webber and Rice): V7

The Jew of Malta (Marlowe): V13

Joe Turner's Come and Gone (Wilson): V17

Jones, LeRoi
  see Baraka, Amiri

Jones Meadows, Karen
  Henrietta: V27

Jonson, Ben(jamin)
  The Alchemist: V4
  Volpone: V10

K

Kaufman, George S.
  Once in a Lifetime: V10
  You Can't Take It with You: V1

Kaufman, Moisés
  The Laramie Project: V22

Kennedy, Adrienne
  Funnyhouse of a Negro: V9

The Kentucky Cycle (Schenkkan): V10

Kesselring, Joseph
  Arsenic and Old Lace: V20

The King and I (Hammerstein and Rodgers): V1

Kingsley, Sidney
  Detective Story: V19
  Men in White: V14

Kopit, Arthur
  Indians: V24
  Oh Dad, Poor Dad, Mamma's Hung You in the Closet and I'm Feelin' So Sad: V7
  Y2K: V14

Kotis, Greg
  Urinetown: V27

Kramm, Joseph
  The Shrike: V15

Krapp's Last Tape (Beckett): V7

Kushner, Tony
  Angels in America: V5

Kyd, Thomas
  The Spanish Tragedy: V21

L

Lady Windermere's Fan (Wilde): V9

Lapine, James
  Into the Woods: V25

The Laramie Project (Kaufman): V22

Larson, Jonathan
  Rent: V23

The Last Night of Ballyhoo (Uhry): V15

Laurents, Arthur
  West Side Story: V27

Lavery, Bryony
  Frozen: V25

Lawrence, Jerome
  Inherit the Wind: V2
  The Night Thoreau Spent in Jail: V16

Le Cid (Corneille): V21

Lear (Bond): V3

Lee, Robert E.
  Inherit the Wind: V2
  The Night Thoreau Spent in Jail: V16

Leight, Warren
  Side Man: V19

Leonard, Hugh
  The Au Pair Man: V24
  Da: V13

Lessing, Doris
  Play with a Tiger: V20

A Lesson from Aloes (Fugard): V24

The Life and Adventures of Nicholas Nickleby (Edgar): V15

A Life in the Theatre (Mamet): V12

Life Is a Dream (Calderón de la Barca): V23

Light Shining in Buckinghamshire (Churchill): V27

Lindsay, Howard
  State of the Union: V19

The Lion in Winter (Goldman): V20

The Little Foxes (Hellman): V1

Lonergan, Kenneth
  This Is Our Youth: V23

Long Day's Journey into Night
  (O'Neill): V2
Look Back in Anger (Osborne):
  V4
Lost in Yonkers (Simon): V18
Love for Love (Congreve): V14
Love! Valour! Compassion!
  (McNally): V19
The Lower Depths (Gorki): V9
Luce, Clare Boothe
  The Women: V19
Luther (Osborne): V19
Lysistrata (Aristophanes): V10

M

M. Butterfly (Hwang): V11
Ma Rainey's Black Bottom (Wilson):
  V15
MacArthur, Charles
  The Front Page: V9
MacDonald, Ann-Marie
  *Goodnight Desdemona (Good
    Morning Juliet):* V23
Machinal (Treadwell): V22
MacLeish, Archibald
  J. B.: V15
Major Barbara (Shaw): V3
Mamet, David
  American Buffalo: V3
  Glengarry Glen Ross: V2
  A Life in the Theatre: V12
  Reunion: V15
  Speed-the-Plow: V6
Man and Superman (Shaw): V6
A Man for All Seasons (Bolt): V2
The Man Who Turned into a Stick
  (Abe): V14
Marat/Sade (Weiss): V3
Margulies, Donald
  Dinner with Friends: V13
Marlowe, Christopher
  Doctor Faustus: V1
  *Edward II: The Troublesome Reign
    and Lamentable Death of
    Edward the Second, King of
    England, with the Tragical Fall
    of Proud Mortimer:* V5
  The Jew of Malta: V13
  Tamburlaine the Great: V21
The Marriage of Figaro (de
  Beaumarchais): V14
Martin, Steve
  WASP: V19
Marty (Chayefsky): V26
The Master Builder (Ibsen): V15
Master Class (McNally): V16
"Master Harold": . . . and the Boys
  (Fugard): V3
The Matchmaker (Wilder): V16
Maugham, Somerset
  For Services Rendered: V22

McCullers, Carson
  The Member of the Wedding: V5
  The Square Root of Wonderful:
    V18
McNally, Terrence
  Love! Valour! Compassion!: V19
  Master Class: V16
Medea (Euripides): V1
Medoff, Mark
  Children of a Lesser God: V4
The Member of the Wedding
  (McCullers): V5
The Memorandum (Havel): V10
Men in White (Kingsley): V14
Middleton, Thomas
  The Changeling: V22
  A Chaste Maid in Cheapside: V18
Millay, Edna St. Vincent
  Aria da Capo: V27
Miller, Arthur
  All My Sons: V8
  The Crucible: V3
  The Crucible (Motion picture): V27
  Death of a Salesman: V1
Miller, Jason
  That Championship Season: V12
The Miracle Worker (Gibson): V2
The Misanthrope (Molière): V13
The Miss Firecracker Contest
  (Henley): V21
Miss Julie (Strindberg): V4
Miss Lulu Bett (Gale): V17
Mister Roberts (Heggen): V20
Molière
  The Imaginary Invalid: V20
  The Misanthrope: V13
  Tartuffe: V18
A Month in the Country (Turgenev):
  V6
Mother Courage and Her Children
  (Brecht): V5
The Mound Builders (Wilson): V16
Mountain Language (Pinter): V14
Mourning Becomes Electra (O'Neill):
  V9
The Mousetrap (Christie): V2
Mrs. Warren's Profession (Shaw): V19
Mulatto (Hughes): V18
Mule Bone (Hurston and Hughes):
  V6
Murder in the Cathedral (Eliot): V4

N

Necessary Targets (Ensler): V23
Nicholson, William
  Shadowlands: V11
'night, Mother (Norman): V2
The Night of the Iguana (Williams):
  V7
The Night Thoreau Spent in Jail
  (Lawrence and Lee): V16

No Exit (Sartre, Jean-Paul): V5
Norman, Marsha
  'night, Mother: V2
Nottage, Lynn
  *Fabulation; or, The Re-Education
    of Undine:* V25
Novio Boy (Soto): V26

O

O'Casey, Sean
  Red Roses for Me: V19
The Odd Couple (Simon): V2
Odets, Clifford
  Golden Boy: V17
  Rocket to the Moon: V20
  Waiting for Lefty: V3
Oedipus Rex (Sophocles): V1
Off the Map (Ackermann): V22
*Oh Dad, Poor Dad, Mamma's Hung
  You in the Closet and I'm Feelin'
  So Sad* (Kopit): V7
On Golden Pond (Thompson): V23
Once in a Lifetime (Hart): V10
Once in a Lifetime (Kaufman): V10
*One Day, When I Was Lost: A
  Scenario* (Baldwin): V15
O'Neill, Eugene
  Anna Christie: V12
  Beyond the Horizon: V16
  Desire under the Elms: V27
  The Emperor Jones: V6
  The Great God Brown: V11
  The Hairy Ape: V4
  The Iceman Cometh: V5
  Ile: V26
  Long Day's Journey into Night: V2
  Mourning Becomes Electra: V9
  Strange Interlude: V20
Orpheus Descending (Williams): V17
Orton, Joe
  Entertaining Mr. Sloane: V3
  What the Butler Saw: V6
Osborne, John
  Inadmissible Evidence: V24
  Look Back in Anger: V4
  Luther: V19
Othello (Shakespeare): V20
The Other Shore (Xingjian): V21
Our Town (Wilder): V1
Overtones (Gerstenberg): V17

P

Parks, Suzan-Lori
  Topdog/Underdog: V22
Patrick, John
  The Teahouse of the August Moon:
    V13
Peer Gynt (Ibsen): V8
Peter Pan (Barrie): V7
The Petrified Forest (Sherwood):
  V17

The Philadelphia Story (Barry): V9
The Piano Lesson (Wilson): V7
Picnic (Inge): V5
Pinter, Harold
    The Birthday Party: V5
    The Caretaker: V7
    The Dumb Waiter: V25
    The Homecoming: V3
    Mountain Language: V14
Pirandello, Luigi
    *Right You Are, If You Think You
        Are:* V9
    *Six Characters in Search of an
        Author:* V4
Play with a Tiger (Lessing): V20
The Playboy of the Western World
    (Synge): V18
Plenty (Hare): V4
Pollock, Sharon
    Blood Relations: V3
Pomerance, Bernard
    The Elephant Man: V9
The Post Office (Tagore): V26
Prida, Dolores
    Beautiful Señoritas: V23
The Prisoner of Second Avenue
    (Simon): V24
Private Lives (Coward): V3
The Producers (Brooks): V21
Prometheus Bound (Aeschylus): V5
Proof (Auburn): V21
The Purple Flower (Bonner): V13
Pygmalion (Shaw): V1

R

R.U.R. (Capek): V7
Rabe, David
    *The Basic Training of Pavlo
        Hummel:* V3
    Sticks and Bones: V13
    Streamers: V8
Raffo, Heather
    Heather Raffo's 9 Parts of Desire:
        V27
The Raft (Clark): V13
A Raisin in the Sun (Hansberry): V2
Raspanti, Celeste
    I Never Saw Another Butterfly:
        V27
Rattigan, Terence
    The Browning Version: V8
The Real Thing (Stoppard): V8
Rebeck, Theresa
    Spike Heels: V11
Red Roses for Me (O'Casey): V19
Rent (Larson): V23
Reunion (Mamet): V15
The Rez Sisters (Highway): V2
Reza, Yasmina
    Art: V19
Rhinoceros (Ionesco): V25

Rice, Elmer
    Street Scene: V12
Rice, Tim
    Jesus Christ Superstar: V7
Right You Are, If You Think You Are
    (Pirandello): V9
Ring Around the Moon (Anouilh):
    V10
Rites (Duffy): V15
The Rivals (Sheridan): V15
The River Niger (Walker): V12
Robbins, Jerome
    West Side Story: V27
Robert Johnson: Trick the Devil
    (Harris): V27
Rocket to the Moon (Odets): V20
Rodgers, Richard
    The King and I: V1
Romeo and Juliet (Shakespeare): V21
Rose, Reginald
    Twelve Angry Men: V23
The Rose Tattoo (Williams): V18
*Rosencrantz and Guildenstern Are
    Dead* (Stoppard): V2
Rostand, Edmond
    Cyrano de Bergerac: V1
The Rover (Behn): V16
Rudnick, Paul
    I Hate Hamlet: V22
The Ruling Class (Barnes): V6

S

Sackler, Howard
    The Great White Hope: V15
Saint Joan (Shaw): V11
Salome (Wilde): V8
Saroyan, William
    The Time of Your Life: V17
Sartre, Jean-Paul
    The Flies: V26
    No Exit: V5
Saved (Bond): V8
Schary, Dore
    Sunrise at Campobello: V17
Schenkkan, Robert
    The Kentucky Cycle: V10
School for Scandal (Sheridan): V4
The Seagull (Chekhov): V12
Seascape (Albee): V13
The Second Shepherds' Play
    (Anonymous): V25
The Secret Rapture (Hare): V16
Serious Money (Churchill): V25
Serjeant Musgrave's Dance (Arden):
    V9
The Servant of Two Masters
    (Goldoni): V27
Seven Against Thebes (Aeschylus):
    V10
The Shadow Box (Cristofer): V15
Shadowlands (Nicholson): V11

Shaffer, Anthony
    Sleuth: V13
Shaffer, Peter
    Amadeus: V13
    Equus: V5
Shakespeare, William
    Othello: V20
    Romeo and Juliet: V21
Shange, Ntozake
    *for colored girls who have
        considered suicide/when the
        rainbow is enuf:* V2
Shanley, John Patrick
    Doubt: V23
Shaw, George Bernard
    Arms and the Man: V22
    Major Barbara: V3
    Man and Superman: V6
    Mrs. Warren's Profession: V19
    Pygmalion: V1
    Saint Joan: V11
She Stoops to Conquer (Goldsmith):
    V1
Shear, Claudia
    Dirty Blonde: V24
Shepard, Sam
    Buried Child: V6
    Curse of the Starving Class: V14
    Fool for Love: V7
    True West: V3
Sheridan, Richard Brinsley
    The Critic: V14
    The Rivals: V15
    School for Scandal: V4
Sherman, Martin
    Bent: V20
Sherwood, Robert E.
    Abe Lincoln in Illinois: V11
    Idiot's Delight: V15
    The Petrified Forest: V17
The Shrike (Kramm): V15
Shue, Larry
    The Foreigner: V7
Side Man (Leight): V19
Simon, Neil
    Biloxi Blues: V12
    Brighton Beach Memoirs: V6
    The Governess: V27
    Lost in Yonkers: V18
    The Odd Couple: V2
    The Prisoner of Second Avenue:
        V24
The Sisters Rosensweig
    (Wasserstein): V17
Six Characters in Search of an Author
    (Pirandello): V4
Six Degrees of Separation (Guare): V13
Sizwe Bansi is Dead (Fugard): V10
The Skin of Our Teeth (Wilder): V4
Slave Ship (Baraka): V11
The Sleep of Reason (Buero Vallejo):
    V11

Sleuth (Shaffer): V13
Smith, Anna Deavere
    Fires in the Mirror: V22
    Twilight: Los Angeles, 1992: V2
A Soldier's Play (Fuller, Charles H.):
    V8
Solórzano, Carlos
    Crossroads: V26
Sondheim, Stephen
    Into the Woods: V25
    West Side Story: V27
Sophocles
    Ajax: V8
    Antigone: V1
    Electra: V4
    Oedipus Rex: V1
    Women of Trachis: Trachiniae:
    V24
Sorry, Wrong Number (Fletcher):
    V26
Soto, Gary
    Novio Boy: V26
The Sound of a Voice (Hwang):
    V18
Soyinka, Wole
    Death and the King's Horseman:
    V10
    The Trials of Brother Jero: V26
The Spanish Tragedy (Kyd): V21
Speed-the-Plow (Mamet): V6
Spike Heels (Rebeck): V11
The Square Root of Wonderful
    (McCullers): V18
Stanley (Gems): V25
State of the Union (Crouse and
    Lindsay): V19
Stein, Joseph
    Fiddler on the Roof: V7
Sticks and Bones (Rabe): V13
Stoppard, Tom
    Arcadia: V5
    Dogg's Hamlet, Cahoot's
    Macbeth: V16
    Indian Ink: V11
    The Real Thing: V8
    Rosencrantz and Guildenstern Are
    Dead: V2
    Travesties: V13
Strange Interlude (O'Neill): V20
Streamers (Rabe): V8
Street Scene (Rice): V12
A Streetcar Named Desire
    (Williams): V1
A Streetcar Named Desire (Motion
    picture): V27
Strindberg, August
    The Ghost Sonata: V9
    Miss Julie: V4
The Subject Was Roses (Gilroy): V17
Sunrise at Campobello (Schary): V17
Sweeney Todd: The Demon Barber of
    Fleet Street (Wheeler): V19

Sweet Bird of Youth (Williams): V12
Synge, J. M.
    The Playboy of the Western
    World: V18

T

Tagore, Rabindranath
    The Post Office: V26
Take Me Out (Greenberg): V24
Talley's Folly (Wilson): V12
Tamburlaine the Great (Marlowe):
    V21
Tartuffe (Molière): V18
A Taste of Honey (Delaney): V7
The Teahouse of the August Moon
    (Patrick): V13
Telling Tales (Cruz): V19
Terry, Megan
    Calm Down Mother: V18
That Championship Season (Miller):
    V12
This Is Our Youth (Lonergan): V23
Thompson, Ernest
    On Golden Pond: V23
Thompson, Judith
    Habitat: V22
A Thousand Clowns (Gardner): V20
The Three Sisters (Chekhov): V10
Three Tall Women (Albee): V8
The Threepenny Opera (Brecht): V4
The Time of Your Life (Saroyan):
    V17
Tiny Alice (Albee): V10
'Tis Pity She's a Whore (Ford): V7
Topdog/Underdog (Parks): V22
Top Girls (Churchill): V12
Torch Song Trilogy (Fierstein): V6
The Tower (von Hofmannsthal): V12
Travesties (Stoppard): V13
Treadwell, Sophie
    Machinal: V22
The Trials of Brother Jero (Soyinka):
    V26
Trifles (Glaspell): V8
The Trojan Women (Euripides): V27
Trouble in Mind (Childress): V8
True West (Shepard): V3
Turgenev, Ivan
    A Month in the Country: V6
Twelve Angry Men (Rose): V23
Twilight: Los Angeles, 1992 (Smith):
    V2
Two Trains Running (Wilson): V24

U

Ubu Roi (Jarry): V8
Uhry, Alfred
    Driving Miss Daisy: V11
    The Last Night of Ballyhoo: V15
Uncle Vanya (Chekhov): V5
Urinetown (Hollmann, Kotis): V27

V

Valdez, Luis*Zoot Suit:* V5
The Verge (Glaspell): V18
Vidal, Gore
    Visit to a Small Planet: V2
Visit to a Small Planet (Vidal): V2
Vogel, Paula
    How I Learned to Drive: V14
Volpone (Jonson, Ben(jamin)): V10
von Hofmannsthal, Hugo
    Electra: V17
    The Tower: V12

W

Waiting for Godot (Beckett): V2
Waiting for Lefty (Odets): V3
A Walk in the Woods (Blessing): V26
Walker, Joseph A.
    The River Niger: V12
WASP (Martin): V19
Wasserstein, Wendy
    The Heidi Chronicles: V5
    The Sisters Rosensweig: V17
Watch on the Rhine (Hellman): V14
The Way of the World (Congreve):
    V15
Webber, Andrew Lloyd
    Jesus Christ Superstar: V7
Webster, John
    The Duchess of Malfi: V17
    The White Devil: V19
The Wedding Band (Childress): V2
Weiss, Peter
    Marat/Sade: V3
Welty, Eudora
    Bye-Bye, Brevoort: V26
West Side Story (Laurents,
    Sondheim, Bernstein,
    Robbins): V27
What the Butler Saw (Orton): V6
Wheeler, Hugh
    Sweeney Todd: The Demon Barber
    of Fleet Street: V19
The White Devil (Webster): V19
Who's Afraid of Virginia Woolf?
    (Albee): V3
Wiechmann, Barbara
    Feeding the Moonfish: V21
The Wild Duck (Ibsen): V10
Wilde, Oscar
    An Ideal Husband: V21
    The Importance of Being Earnest:
    V4
    Lady Windermere's Fan: V9
    Salome: V8
Wilder, Thornton
    The Matchmaker: V16
    Our Town: V1
    The Skin of Our Teeth: V4
Williams, Tennessee
    Cat on a Hot Tin Roof: V3

The Glass Menagerie: V1
The Night of the Iguana: V7
Orpheus Descending: V17
The Rose Tattoo: V18
A Streetcar Named Desire: V1
A Streetcar Named Desire:
  (Motion picture): V27
Sweet Bird of Youth: V12
Wilson, August
  Fences: V3
  Joe Turner's Come and Gone: V17
  Ma Rainey's Black Bottom: V15
  The Piano Lesson: V7
  Two Trains Running: V24
Wilson, Lanford
  Angels Fall: V20
  Burn This: V4

Hot L Baltimore: V9
The Mound Builders: V16
Talley's Folly: V12
Wine in the Wilderness (Childress):
  V14
Winterset (Anderson): V20
Wit (Edson): V13
The Women (Luce): V19
Women of Trachis: Trachiniae
  (Sophocles): V24
Wright, Doug
  I Am My Own Wife: V23

X

Xingjian, Gao
  The Other Shore: V21

Y

Y2K (Kopit): V14
You Can't Take It with You (Hart):
  V1
You Can't Take It with You
  (Kaufman): V1
The Young Man from Atlanta
  (Foote): V20

Z

Zindel, Paul
  *The Effect of Gamma Rays on
    Man-in-the-Moon Marigolds:*
    V12
The Zoo Story (Albee): V2
Zoot Suit (Valdez): V5

Cumulative
Nationality/Ethnicity Index

Anonymous
  Everyman: V7

African American
Baldwin, James
  The Amen Corner: V11
  One Day, When I Was Lost: A
    Scenario: V15
Baraka, Amiri
  The Baptism: V16
  Dutchman: V3
  Slave Ship: V11
Bonner, Marita
  The Purple Flower: V13
Childress, Alice
  Florence: V26
  Trouble in Mind: V8
  The Wedding Band: V2
  Wine in the Wilderness: V14
Cleage, Pearl
  Blues for an Alabama Sky: V14
  Flyin' West: V16
Fuller, Charles H.
  A Soldier's Play: V8
Hansberry, Lorraine
  A Raisin in the Sun: V2
Harris, Bill
  Robert Johnson: Trick the Devil:
    V27
Hughes, Langston
  Mulatto: V18
  Mule Bone: V6
Hurston, Zora Neale
  Mule Bone: V6
Jones Meadows, Karen
  Henrietta: V27

Kennedy, Adrienne
  Funnyhouse of a Negro: V9
Nottage, Lynn
  Fabulation; or, The Re-Education
    of Undine: V25
Shange, Ntozake
  for colored girls who have
    considered suicide/when the
    rainbow is enuf: V2
Smith, Anna Deavere
  Twilight: Los Angeles, 1992: V2
Wilson, August
  Fences: V3
  Joe Turner's Come and Gone: V17
  Ma Rainey's Black Bottom: V15
  The Piano Lesson: V7
  Two Trains Running: V24

American
Albee, Edward
  The American Dream: V25
  A Delicate Balance: V14
  Seascape: V13
  Three Tall Women: V8
  Tiny Alice: V10
  Who's Afraid of Virginia Woolf?: V3
  The Zoo Story: V2
Anderson, Maxwell
  Both Your Houses: V16
  Winterset: V20
Auburn, David
  Proof: V21
Baldwin, James
  The Amen Corner: V11
  One Day, When I Was Lost: A
    Scenario: V15

Baraka, Amiri
  The Baptism: V16
  Dutchman: V3
  Slave Ship: V11
Barry, Philip
  The Philadelphia Story: V9
Beane, Douglas Carter
  As Bees in Honey Drown: V21
Beim, Norman
  The Deserter: V18
Bernstein, Leonard
  West Side Story: V27
Blank, Jessica
  The Exonerated: V24
Blessing, Lee
  Eleemosynary: V23
  A Walk in the Woods: V26
Bonner, Marita
  The Purple Flower: V13
Brooks, Mel
  The Producers: V21
Chase, Mary
  Harvey: V11
Chayefsky, Paddy
  Marty: V26
Childress, Alice
  Florence: V26
  Trouble in Mind: V8
  The Wedding Band: V2
  Wine in the Wilderness: V14
Cleage, Pearl
  Blues for an Alabama Sky: V14
  Flyin' West: V16
Coburn, D. L.
  The Gin Game: V23
Connelly, Marc
  The Green Pastures: V12

Cristofer, Michael
   The Shadow Box: V15
Crouse, Russel
   State of the Union: V19
Crowley, Mart
   The Boys in the Band: V14
Cruz, Migdalia
   Telling Tales: V19
Cruz, Nilo
   Anna in the Tropics: V21
Edson, Margaret
   Wit: V13
Eliot, T. S.
   The Cocktail Party: V13
   Murder in the Cathedral: V4
Ensler, Eve
   Necessary Targets: V23
Ephron, Nora
   Imaginary Friends: V22
Fierstein, Harvey
   Torch Song Trilogy: V6
Fletcher, Lucille
   Sorry, Wrong Number: V26
Foote, Horton
   The Young Man from Atlanta:
      V20
Fornes, Maria Irene
   Fefu and Her Friends: V25
Fuller, Charles H.
   A Soldier's Play: V8
Gale, Zona
   Miss Lulu Bett: V17
Gardner, Herb
   I'm Not Rappaport: V18
   A Thousand Clowns: V20
Gerstenberg, Alice
   Overtones: V17
Gibson, William
   The Miracle Worker: V2
Gilman, Rebecca
   Blue Surge: V23
Gilroy, Frank D.
   The Subject Was Roses: V17
Glaspell, Susan
   Alison's House: V24
   Trifles: V8
   The Verge: V18
Goldman, James
   The Lion in Winter: V20
Goodrich, Frances
   The Diary of Anne Frank: V15
Greenberg, Richard
   Take Me Out: V24
Guare, John
   The House of Blue Leaves: V8
   Six Degrees of Separation: V13
Hackett, Albert
   The Diary of Anne Frank: V15
Hammerstein, Oscar II
   The King and I: V1
Hanff, Helene
   84, Charing Cross Road: V17

Hansberry, Lorraine
   A Raisin in the Sun: V2
Harris, Bill
   Robert Johnson: Trick the Devil:
      V27
Hart, Moss
   Once in a Lifetime: V10
   You Can't Take It with You: V1
Hayes, Joseph
   The Desperate Hours: V20
Hecht, Ben
   The Front Page: V9
Heggen, Thomas
   Mister Roberts: V20
Hellman, Lillian
   The Children's Hour: V3
   The Little Foxes: V1
   Watch on the Rhine: V14
Henley, Beth
   Crimes of the Heart: V2
   Impossible Marriage: V26
   The Miss Firecracker Contest:
      V21
Hollmann, Mark
   Urinetown: V27
Hughes, Langston
   Mulatto: V18
Hurston, Zora Neale
   Mule Bone: V6
Hwang, David Henry
   M. Butterfly: V11
   The Sound of a Voice: V18
Iizuka, Naomi
   36 Views: V21
Inge, William
   Bus Stop: V8
   Come Back, Little Sheba: V3
   Picnic: V5
Jensen, Erik
   The Exonerated: V24
Jones Meadows, Karen
   Henrietta: V27
Kaufman, George S.
   Once in a Lifetime: V10
   You Can't Take It with You: V1
Kesselring, Joseph
   Arsenic and Old Lace: V20
Kingsley, Sidney
   Detective Story: V19
   Men in White: V14
Kopit, Arthur
   Indians: V24
   *Oh Dad, Poor Dad, Mamma's
      Hung You in the Closet and I'm
      Feelin' So Sad:* V7
   Y2K: V14
Kotis, Greg
   Urinetown: V27
Kramm, Joseph
   The Shrike: V15
Kushner, Tony
   Angels in America: V5

Lapine, James
   Into the Woods: V25
Larson, Jonathan
   Rent: V23
Laurents, Arthur
   West Side Story: V27
Lawrence, Jerome
   Inherit the Wind: V2
   The Night Thoreau Spent in Jail:
      V16
Lee, Robert E.
   Inherit the Wind: V2
   The Night Thoreau Spent in Jail:
      V16
Leight, Warren
   Side Man: V19
Lindsay, Howard
   State of the Union: V19
Lonergan, Kenneth
   This Is Our Youth: V23
Luce, Clare Boothe
   The Women: V19
MacArthur, Charles
   The Front Page: V9
MacLeish, Archibald
   J. B.: V15
Mamet, David
   American Buffalo: V3
   Glengarry Glen Ross: V2
   A Life in the Theatre: V12
   Reunion: V15
   Speed-the-Plow: V6
Margulies, Donald
   Dinner with Friends: V13
Martin, Steve
   WASP: V19
McCullers, Carson
   The Member of the Wedding: V5
   The Square Root of Wonderful: V18
McNally, Terrence
   Love! Valour! Compassion!: V19
   Master Class: V16
Medoff, Mark
   Children of a Lesser God: V4
Millay, Edna St. Vincent
   Aria da Capo: V27
Miller, Arthur
   All My Sons: V8
   The Crucible: V3
   The Crucible (Motion picture):
      V27
   Death of a Salesman: V1
Miller, Jason
   That Championship Season: V12
Norman, Marsha
   'night, Mother: V2
Nottage, Lynn
   *Fabulation; or, The Re-Education
      of Undine:* V25
O'Neill, Eugene
   Anna Christie: V12
   Beyond the Horizon: V16

Desire under the Elms: V27
The Emperor Jones: V6
The Great God Brown: V11
The Hairy Ape: V4
The Iceman Cometh: V5
Ile: V26
Long Day's Journey into Night: V2
Mourning Becomes Electra: V9
Strange Interlude: V20
Odets, Clifford
Golden Boy: V17
Rocket to the Moon: V20
Waiting for Lefty: V3
Parks, Suzan-Lori
Topdog/Underdog: V22
Patrick, John
The Teahouse of the August Moon:
V13
Pomerance, Bernard
The Elephant Man: V9
Rabe, David
*The Basic Training of Pavlo
Hummel:* V3
Sticks and Bones: V13
Streamers: V8
Raffo, Heather
Heather Raffo's 9 Parts of Desire: V27
Raspanti, Celeste
I Never Saw Another Butterfly: V27
Rebeck, Theresa
Spike Heels: V11
Rice, Elmer
Street Scene: V12
Robbins, Jerome
West Side Story: V27
Rodgers, Richard
The King and I: V1
Rose, Reginald
Twelve Angry Men: V23
Rudnick, Paul
I Hate Hamlet: V22
Sackler, Howard
The Great White Hope: V15
Saroyan, William
The Time of Your Life: V17
Schary, Dore
Sunrise at Campobello: V17
Schenkkan, Robert
The Kentucky Cycle: V10
Shange, Ntozake
*for colored girls who have
considered suicide/when the
rainbow is enuf:* V2
Shanley, John Patrick
Doubt: V23
Shear, Claudia
Dirty Blonde: V24
Shepard, Sam
Buried Child: V6
Curse of the Starving Class: V14
Fool for Love: V7
True West: V3

Sherman, Martin
Bent: V20
Sherwood, Robert E.
Abe Lincoln in Illinois: V11
Idiot's Delight: V15
The Petrified Forest: V17
Shue, Larry
The Foreigner: V7
Simon, Neil
Biloxi Blues: V12
Brighton Beach Memoirs: V6
The Governess: V27
Lost in Yonkers: V18
The Odd Couple: V2
The Prisoner of Second Avenue:
V24
Smith, Anna Deavere
Fires in the Mirror: V22
Twilight: Los Angeles, 1992: V2
Soto, Gary
Novio Boy: V26
Sondheim, Stephen
Into the Woods: V25
West Side Story: V27
Stein, Joseph
Fiddler on the Roof: V7
Terry, Megan
Calm Down Mother: V18
Thompson, Ernest
On Golden Pond: V23
Treadwell, Sophie
Machinal: V22
Uhry, Alfred
Driving Miss Daisy: V11
The Last Night of Ballyhoo:
V15
Valdez, Luis
Zoot Suit: V5
Vidal, Gore
Visit to a Small Planet: V2
Vogel, Paula
How I Learned to Drive: V14
Walker, Joseph A.
The River Niger: V12
Wasserstein, Wendy
The Heidi Chronicles: V5
The Sisters Rosensweig: V17
Welty, Eudora
Bye-Bye, Brevoort: V26
Wiechmann, Barbara
Feeding the Moonfish: V21
Wilder, Thornton
The Matchmaker: V16
Our Town: V1
The Skin of Our Teeth: V4
Williams, Tennessee
Cat on a Hot Tin Roof: V3
The Glass Menagerie: V1
The Night of the Iguana: V7
Orpheus Descending: V17
The Rose Tattoo: V18
A Streetcar Named Desire: V1

A Streetcar Named Desire (Motion
picture): V27
Sweet Bird of Youth: V12
Wilson, August
Fences: V3
Joe Turner's Come and Gone: V17
Ma Rainey's Black Bottom: V15
The Piano Lesson: V7
Two Trains Running: V24
Wilson, Lanford
Angels Fall: V20
Burn This: V4
Hot L Baltimore: V9
The Mound Builders: V16
Talley's Folly: V12
Wright, Doug
I Am My Own Wife: V23
Zindel, Paul
*The Effect of Gamma Rays on
Man-in-the-Moon Marigolds:*
V12

Argentinian

Dorfman, Ariel
Death and the Maiden: V4

Asian American

Hwang, David Henry
M. Butterfly: V11
The Sound of a Voice: V18

Austrian

von Hofmannsthal, Hugo
Electra: V17
The Tower: V12

Bohemian (Czechoslovakian)

Capek, Karel
The Insect Play: V11

Canadian

Highway, Tomson
The Rez Sisters: V2
MacDonald, Ann-Marie
*Goodnight Desdemona (Good
Morning Juliet):* V23
Pollock, Sharon
Blood Relations: V3
Thompson, Judith
Habitat: V22

Chilean

Dorfman, Ariel
Death and the Maiden: V4

Chinese

Xingjian, Gao
The Other Shore: V21

Cuban

Cruz, Nilo
  Anna in the Tropics: V21
Fornes, Maria Irene
  Fefu and Her Friends: V25
Prida, Dolores
  Beautiful Señoritas: V23

Cuban American

Cruz, Nilo
  Anna in the Tropics: V21

Czechoslovakian

Capek, Joseph
  The Insect Play: V11
Capek, Karel
  The Insect Play: V11
  R.U.R.: V7
Havel, Vaclav
  The Memorandum: V10
Stoppard, Tom
  Arcadia: V5
  Dogg's Hamlet, Cahoot's
    Macbeth: V16
  Indian Ink: V11
  The Real Thing: V8
  Rosencrantz and Guildenstern Are
    Dead: V2
  Travesties: V13

Dutch

de Hartog, Jan
  The Fourposter: V12

English

Anonymous
  Arden of Faversham: V24
  The Second Shepherds' Play: V25
Arden, John
  Serjeant Musgrave's Dance: V9
Ayckbourn, Alan
  A Chorus of Disapproval: V7
Barnes, Peter
  The Ruling Class: V6
Behn, Aphra
  The Forc'd Marriage: V24
  The Rover: V16
Bolt, Robert
  A Man for All Seasons: V2
Bond, Edward
  Lear: V3
  Saved: V8
Christie, Agatha
  The Mousetrap: V2
Churchill, Caryl
  Cloud Nine: V16
  Light Shining on Buckinghamshire:
    V27
  Serious Money: V25
  Top Girls: V12

Congreve, William
  Love for Love: V14
  The Way of the World: V15
Coward, Noel
  Hay Fever: V6
  Private Lives: V3
Cowley, Hannah
  The Belle's Stratagem: V22
Delaney, Shelagh
  A Taste of Honey: V7
Duffy, Maureen
  Rites: V15
Edgar, David
  The Life and Adventures of
    Nicholas Nickleby: V15
Ford, John
  'Tis Pity She's a Whore: V7
Frayn, Michael
  Copenhagen: V22
Gems, Pam
  Stanley: V25
Goldsmith, Oliver
  She Stoops to Conquer: V1
Hare, David
  Blue Room: V7
  Plenty: V4
  The Secret Rapture: V16
Jonson, Ben(jamin)
  The Alchemist: V4
  Volpone: V10
Kyd, Thomas
  The Spanish Tragedy: V21
Lavery, Bryony
  Frozen: V25
Lessing, Doris
  Play with a Tiger: V20
Marlowe, Christopher
  Doctor Faustus: V1
  Edward II: The Troublesome Reign
    and Lamentable Death of
    Edward the Second, King of
    England, with the Tragical Fall
    of Proud Mortimer: V5
  The Jew of Malta: V13
  Tamburlaine the Great: V21
Maugham, Somerset
  For Services Rendered: V22
Middleton, Thomas
  The Changeling: V22
  A Chaste Maid in Cheapside: V18
Nicholson, William
  Shadowlands: V11
Orton, Joe
  Entertaining Mr. Sloane: V3
  What the Butler Saw: V6
Osborne, John
  Inadmissible Evidence: V24
  Look Back in Anger: V4
  Luther: V19
Pinter, Harold
  The Birthday Party: V5
  The Caretaker: V7

  The Dumb Waiter: V25
  The Homecoming: V3
  Mountain Language: V14
Rattigan, Terence
  The Browning Version: V8
Rice, Tim
  Jesus Christ Superstar: V7
Shaffer, Anthony
  Sleuth: V13
Shaffer, Peter
  Amadeus: V13
  Equus: V5
Shakespeare, William
  Othello: V20
  Romeo and Juliet: V21
Stoppard, Tom
  Arcadia: V5
  Dogg's Hamlet, Cahoot's Mac
    beth: V16
  Indian Ink: V11
  The Real Thing: V8
  Rosencrantz and Guildenstern Are
    Dead: V2
  Travesties: V13
Webber, Andrew Lloyd
  Jesus Christ Superstar: V7
Webster, John
  The Duchess of Malfi: V17
  The White Devil: V19
Wheeler, Hugh
  Sweeney Todd: The Demon Barber
    of Fleet Street: V19

French

Anouilh, Jean
  Antigone: V9
  Becket, or the Honor of God: V19
  Ring Around the Moon: V10
Artaud, Antonin
  The Cenci: V22
Beckett, Samuel
  Endgame: V18
  Krapp's Last Tape: V7
  Waiting for Godot: V2
Cocteau, Jean
  Indiscretions: V24
Corneille, Pierre
  Le Cid: V21
de Beaumarchais, Pierre-Augustin
  The Barber of Seville: V16
  The Marriage of Figaro: V14
Duras, Marguerite
  India Song: V21
Genet, Jean
  The Balcony: V10
Ionesco, Eugène
  The Bald Soprano: V4
  The Chairs: V9
  Rhinoceros: V25
Jarry, Alfred
  Ubu Roi: V8

Molière
    The Imaginary Invalid: V20
    The Misanthrope: V13
    Tartuffe: V18
Reza, Yasmina
    Art: V19
Rostand, Edmond
    Cyrano de Bergerac: V1
Sartre, Jean-Paul
    The Flies: V26
    No Exit: V5

German

Brecht, Bertolt
    The Good Person of Szechwan: V9
    *Mother Courage and Her
        Children:* V5
    The Threepenny Opera: V4
Weiss, Peter
    Marat/Sade: V3

Greek

Aeschylus
    Agamemnon: V26
    Prometheus Bound: V5
    Seven Against Thebes: V10
Aristophanes
    Lysistrata: V10
Euripides
    The Bacchae: V6
    Hippolytus: V25
    Iphigenia in Taurus: V4
    Medea: V1
    The Trojan Women: V27
Sophocles
    Ajax: V8
    Antigone: V1
    Electra: V4
    Oedipus Rex: V1
    Women of Trachis: Trachiniae: V24

Guatemalan

Solórzano, Carlos
    Crossroads: V26

Hispanic

Cruz, Nilo
    Anna in the Tropics: V21
Fornes, Maria Irene
    Fefu and Her Friends: V25
Valdez, Luis
    Zoot Suit: V5

Indian

Tagore, Rabindranath
    The Post Office: V26

Indochinese

Duras, Marguerite
    India Song: V21

Irish

Beckett, Samuel
    Endgame: V18
    Krapp's Last Tape: V7
    Waiting for Godot: V2
Behan, Brendan
    The Hostage: V7
Friel, Brian
    Dancing at Lughnasa: V11
Leonard, Hugh
    The Au Pair Man: V24
    Da: V13
O'Casey, Sean
    Red Roses for Me: V19
Shaw, George Bernard
    Arms and the Man: V22
    Major Barbara: V3
    Man and Superman: V6
    Mrs. Warren's Profession: V19
    Pygmalion: V1
    Saint Joan: V11
Sheridan, Richard Brinsley
    The Critic: V14
    The Rivals: V15
    School for Scandal: V4
Synge, J. M.
    Playboy of the Western World: V18
Wilde, Oscar
    An Ideal Husband: V21
    The Importance of Being Earnest: V4
    Lady Windermere's Fan: V9
    Salome: V8

Italian

Fo, Dario
    Accidental Death of an Anarchist: V23
Ginzburg, Natalia
    The Advertisement: V14
Goldoni, Carlo
    The Servant of Two Masters: V27
Pirandello, Luigi
    *Right You Are, If You Think You
        Are:* V9
    *Six Characters in Search of an
        Author:* V4

Japanese

Abe, Kobo
    The Man Who Turned into a Stick:
        V14
Iizuka, Naomi
    36 Views: V21

Jewish

Bernstein, Leonard
    West Side Story: V27
Chayefsky, Paddy
    Marty: V26
Gardner, Herb
    A Thousand Clowns: V20

Laurents, Arthur
    West Side Story: V27
Mamet, David
    Reunion: V15
Odets, Clifford
    Rocket to the Moon: V20
Robbins, Jerome
    West Side Story: V27
Sherman, Martin
    Bent: V20
Simon, Neil
    Biloxi Blues: V12
    Brighton Beach Memoirs: V6
    The Governess: V27
    Lost in Yonkers: V18
    The Odd Couple: V2
    The Prisoner of Second Avenue: V24
Sondheim, Stephen
    Into the Woods: V25
    West Side Story: V27
Uhry, Alfred
    Driving Miss Daisy: V11
    The Last Night of Ballyhoo: V15

Mexican

Carballido, Emilio
    I, Too, Speak of the Rose: V4
Solórzano, Carlos
    Crossroads: V26
Soto, Gary
    Novio Boy: V26

Native Canadian

Highway, Tomson
    The Rez Sisters: V2

Nigerian

Clark, John Pepper
    The Raft: V13
Soyinka, Wole
    Death and the King's Horseman: V10
    The Trials of Brother Jero: V26

Norwegian

Ibsen, Henrik
    Brand: V16
    A Doll's House: V1
    An Enemy of the People: V25
    Ghosts: V11
    Hedda Gabler: V6
    The Master Builder: V15
    Peer Gynt: V8
    The Wild Duck: V10

Romanian

Ionesco, Eugène
    The Bald Soprano: V4
    The Chairs: V9
    Rhinoceros: V25

Russian

Chekhov, Anton
  The Bear: V26
  The Cherry Orchard: V1
  The Seagull: V12
  The Three Sisters: V10
  Uncle Vanya: V5
Gogol, Nikolai
  The Government Inspector: V12
Gorki, Maxim
  The Lower Depths: V9
Turgenev, Ivan
  A Month in the Country: V6

Scottish

Barrie, J(ames) M.
  Peter Pan: V7

South African

Fugard, Athol
  Boesman & Lena: V6
  A Lesson from Aloes: V24
  "Master Harold" . . . and the Boys:
    V3
  Sizwe Bansi is Dead: V10

Spanish

Buero Vallejo, Antonio
  The Sleep of Reason: V11
Calderón de la Barca, Pedro
  Life Is a Dream: V23
García Lorca, Federico
  Blood Wedding: V10
  The House of Bernarda Alba:
    V4

Swedish

Strindberg, August
  The Ghost Sonata: V9
  Miss Julie: V4

Swiss

Frisch, Max
  The Firebugs: V25

Ukrainian

Chayefsky, Paddy
  Marty: V26

Venezuelan

Kaufman, Moisés
  The Laramie Project: V22

Subject/Theme Index

Numerical

1930s (Decade)
  Robert Johnson: Trick the Devil:
    178, 180
1950s (Decade)
  The Crucible: 38–39
1970s (Decade)
  The Governess: 81–82
1980s (Decade)
  Henrietta: 116

A

Abandonment
  Henrietta: 120
Absurdity
  The Trojan Women: 251, 253,
    255, 256
Acceptance
  The Crucible: 37
  The Trojan Women: 257
Adultery
  The Crucible: 26, 27, 29, 30, 32–33,
    35, 37, 39, 42, 44, 46
  Desire under the Elms: 49, 53, 55
  Heather Raffo's 9 Parts of Desire:
    97
  The Trojan Women: 235
African American culture
  Robert Johnson: Trick the Devil:
    180–181, 187–191
African American history
  Robert Johnson: Trick the Devil:
    178, 180
African Americans
  Robert Johnson: Trick the Devil:
    178, 180

Aggression (Psychology)
  A Streetcar Named Desire: 216
Allegories
  Aria da Capo: 1
Allusions
  A Streetcar Named Desire: 224
  The Trojan Women: 252
Ambiguity
  Henrietta: 127–130
Ambition
  Urinetown: 263
Ambivalence
  Henrietta: 124
American culture
  Heather Raffo's 9 Parts of Desire:
    97–98, 100
  West Side Story: 289
American dream
  West Side Story: 288, 294, 299
Anger
  The Crucible: 33
  Robert Johnson: Trick the Devil:
    183–184
  The Servant of Two Masters: 200
  A Streetcar Named Desire: 212, 214
  West Side Story: 293
Animals
  Desire under the Elms: 71
Apathy
  Aria da Capo: 1, 6, 8–9
Appearance *vs.* reality
  A Streetcar Named Desire: 218
Arab Americans
  Heather Raffo's 9 Parts of Desire:
    113–114
Archetypes
  Desire under the Elms: 61

Art
  Heather Raffo's 9 Parts of Desire:
    100, 101
Atheism
  The Trojan Women: 239–240
Attachment
  Henrietta: 120, 121
Authenticity
  A Streetcar Named Desire: 221, 222
Authority
  The Governess: 78–80
  Light Shining in Buckinghamshire:
    151, 160
Autobiographical fiction
  The Governess: 91

B

Beauty
  Desire under the Elms: 51, 52, 55,
    56, 58, 71
  The Trojan Women: 237, 238
Betrayal
  The Crucible: 34
  The Trojan Women: 234, 236
Blank verse
  Aria da Capo: 10
  Robert Johnson: Trick the Devil: 178

C

Capitalism
  Aria da Capo: 13–16
  Urinetown: 259
Catharsis
  The Trojan Women: 238–239
Chaos
  The Trojan Women: 252, 253, 256

Characterization
  Desire under the Elms: 68, 70–72
  Heather Raffo's 9 Parts of Desire:
    105–108
  Henrietta: 127–130
  Light Shining in Buckinghamshire:
    168–169
  Robert Johnson: Trick the Devil:
    183–185, 187–191
  A Streetcar Named Desire:
    221–224
  Urinetown: 270–272
Choice (Psychology)
  Henrietta: 122
Christianity
  The Crucible: 37–38
  Light Shining in Buckinghamshire:
    155, 156, 158–159
Circularity
  Desire under the Elms: 58–59
Civil war
  Light Shining in Buckinghamshire:
    151, 158–159, 164–165
Class conflict
  Aria da Capo: 15–16
  Light Shining in Buckinghamshire:
    160
  Urinetown: 265–266
  *Urinetown:*Humor 271
Coincidence
  The Servant of Two Masters:
    193, 199
Cold War
  West Side Story: 290
Comedy
  The Servant of Two Masters:
    193, 203
Coming of age
  West Side Story: 287–288,
    294–296
Commedia dell'arte
  Aria da Capo: 4, 6, 9–10, 12
  The Servant of Two Masters: 193,
    202, 205–207
Compassion
  The Governess: 92
  The Trojan Women: 256
Confession
  The Crucible: 26, 28–31, 34
  Robert Johnson: Trick the Devil:
    184, 188
Confidence
  Heather Raffo's 9 Parts of Desire:
    100, 102
Confinement
  Henrietta: 122
Conflict
  Aria da Capo: 1, 6–7, 16
  Desire under the Elms: 61
  Henrietta: 124
  Robert Johnson: Trick the Devil:
    177

  The Servant of Two Masters: 209
  A Streetcar Named Desire: 215
  West Side Story: 286, 290, 293
Confusion
  Henrietta: 129, 130
Consolation
  The Trojan Women: 256
Contentment
  Aria da Capo: 13
Contradiction
  Henrietta: 120, 127, 129
Control (Psychology)
  Henrietta: 119, 121
Cooperation
  Urinetown: 264
Corruption
  Urinetown: 259, 263, 264,
    266–267, 270
  *Urinetown:*Humor 276
Cowardice
  Robert Johnson: Trick the Devil:
    184
  The Servant of Two Masters: 198
  *Urinetown:*Humor 270
Creativity
  I Never Saw Another Butterfly: 140
Cruelty
  Desire under the Elms: 69
  The Governess: 77, 79–81, 84,
    86, 87
  A Streetcar Named Desire:
    213, 216
Cultural identity
  Heather Raffo's 9 Parts of Desire:
    99, 101, 113–114
  Robert Johnson: Trick the Devil:
    189–190
Culture
  I Never Saw Another Butterfly: 142
Cynicism
  Aria da Capo: 6

D

Dance
  The Trojan Women: 251–252
  West Side Story: 289, 299–300
Death
  Aria da Capo: 1, 13
  The Crucible: 30
  Desire under the Elms: 60, 62
  I Never Saw Another Butterfly:
    134
  A Streetcar Named Desire: 211,
    214–216, 219, 224
  The Trojan Women: 253, 255
  West Side Story: 284, 290
Defiance
  The Crucible: 45
  The Trojan Women: 254
Delusions
  The Trojan Women: 253

Depression (Psychology)
  Light Shining in Buckinghamshire:
    164
Desire
  The Crucible: 34, 39, 41, 45
  Desire under the Elms: 49, 52,
    56–57, 64, 69
Despair
  I Never Saw Another Butterfly:
    134
Destruction
  The Trojan Women: 235, 246, 251,
    252, 255
Devil
  The Crucible: 41–42
  Robert Johnson: Trick the Devil:
    170, 173–175, 184, 187,
    188, 191
Dignity
  A Streetcar Named Desire:
    224
Discrimination. *See* Prejudice
Disguise
  The Servant of Two Masters: 193,
    195, 199, 201
Disillusionment
  Light Shining in Buckinghamshire:
    156
Doubt
  Henrietta: 130
Duty
  The Crucible: 34

E

Economics
  The Governess: 83, 85, 86
Embarrassment
  Henrietta: 116, 118
Emotions
  Robert Johnson: Trick the Devil:
    177
  The Trojan Women: 238–239, 244,
    251, 255
  West Side Story: 299
Endurance
  The Trojan Women: 253, 257
English history
  Light Shining in Buckinghamshire:
    151, 158–160, 162–165
English literature, 1558-1603
    (Elizabethan)
  West Side Story: 289–290
Enlightenment (Cultural movement)
  The Servant of Two Masters:
    202–203
Equality
  Light Shining in Buckinghamshire:
    153, 155
Exploitation
  The Governess: 78, 84, 87
  Robert Johnson: Trick the Devil:
    174, 189

F

Faith
  Desire under the Elms: 57–58
  I Never Saw Another Butterfly: 149
  The Trojan Women: 256
Family
  Henrietta: 120, 121
Family life
  The Governess: 89
Farce
  The Governess: 80–81, 84
  The Servant of Two Masters:
    200–201, 203, 206
  *Urinetown:*Humor 272
Fate
  Desire under the Elms: 62, 68
Father-child relationships
  Desire under the Elms: 55–56, 63
Fear
  Aria da Capo: 13, 16
  The Crucible: 31, 45, 47
  Heather Raffo's 9 Parts of Desire:
    99
  I Never Saw Another Butterfly:
    136, 149
  Robert Johnson: Trick the Devil:
    177, 184
  The Trojan Women: 236, 239, 246
Female-male relations
  The Servant of Two Masters: 200,
    203, 205
  A Streetcar Named Desire: 222
Femininity
  Aria da Capo: 17
  Desire under the Elms: 64–67
Feminism
  Aria da Capo: 16
  Light Shining in Buckinghamshire:
    162–165, 168–169
Fidelity
  The Servant of Two Masters: 199
Flashbacks
  I Never Saw Another Butterfly:
    140, 144
Folk culture
  Robert Johnson: Trick the Devil: 189
Forgiveness
  The Crucible: 30, 34
  The Servant of Two Masters: 198
Freedom
  Desire under the Elms: 52
  Heather Raffo's 9 Parts of Desire:
    98, 99
  Henrietta: 116, 121, 122, 131
  I Never Saw Another Butterfly:
    137–138, 140
  Light Shining in Buckinghamshire:
    151, 154, 158
  Urinetown: 266
Friendship
  Aria da Capo: 13

Henrietta: 131
  West Side Story: 286
Frustration
  Henrietta: 116
  Robert Johnson: Trick the Devil:
    183–184
  The Trojan Women: 255, 256
Futility
  The Trojan Women: 251, 253–255
  Urinetown: 270

G

Generation gap
  West Side Story: 288
God
  Desire under the Elms: 57–59, 68, 71
  Light Shining in Buckinghamshire:
    156, 158–159
Good and evil
  The Crucible: 40
Goodness
  The Crucible: 32, 33
Great Depression
  Robert Johnson: Trick the Devil: 180
Greed
  Aria da Capo: 5
  The Crucible: 32, 33
  Desire under the Elms: 49
  Urinetown: 259, 266
  *Urinetown:*Humor 270, 272
Greek drama
  Desire under the Elms: 59–64,
    67–70
  The Trojan Women: 231, 238–241,
    248–251, 255
Greek history (Ancient)
  The Trojan Women: 241–244, 246
Greek mythology
  Desire under the Elms: 64
  The Trojan Women: 244, 246–247
Grief
  The Trojan Women: 235–237, 256
Guilt (Psychology)
  The Crucible: 34
  Robert Johnson: Trick the Devil:
    177

H

Hatred
  Desire under the Elms: 55, 63
  West Side Story: 293, 298
Helplessness
  The Governess: 84
  A Streetcar Named Desire: 224
  The Trojan Women: 254
Heritage
  Heather Raffo's 9 Parts of Desire:
    113–114
  Robert Johnson: Trick the Devil: 190
Heroes
  *Urinetown:*Humor 276

Heroines
  A Streetcar Named Desire: 223–224
  The Trojan Women: 244
Heroism
  The Trojan Women: 250, 255, 257
Hispanic American culture
  West Side Story: 298
Hispanic Americans
  West Side Story: 285
History
  Heather Raffo's 9 Parts of Desire:
    106
Holocaust
  I Never Saw Another Butterfly:
    134–136, 138–149
Homelessness
  Henrietta: 116, 118
Honesty
  The Governess: 84
Honor
  The Crucible: 30
  The Trojan Women: 247
Hope
  Heather Raffo's 9 Parts of Desire:
    101
  I Never Saw Another Butterfly:
    134, 137, 140, 149
  The Trojan Women: 253, 254, 256
Hostility
  The Crucible: 33
Human behavior
  Desire under the Elms: 61
Human condition
  Desire under the Elms: 68
  The Governess: 92–93
Human nature
  Desire under the Elms: 61
Humanity
  Henrietta: 131–132
Humiliation
  The Servant of Two Masters: 198,
    200
Humor
  The Governess: 93
  Henrietta: 127, 131–132
  The Servant of Two Masters: 201,
    203, 205–206
  Urinetown: 270
Hypocrisy
  Light Shining in Buckinghamshire:
    168
  Robert Johnson: Trick the Devil: 184
Hysteria
  The Crucible: 31, 32, 34–36, 39, 42,
    46

I

Identity
  Henrietta: 124
  The Servant of Two Masters: 193,
    195–197, 201

Ideology
    Aria da Capo: 15–16
    Light Shining in Buckinghamshire:
        156, 168
Ignorance (Theory of knowledge)
    The Crucible: 36
Imagery (Literature)
    Desire under the Elms: 64, 67,
        70–72
    The Trojan Women: 251
    West Side Story: 289
Immigrant life
    West Side Story: 288, 290, 293,
        298–299
Impiety
    The Trojan Women: 232, 238–240,
        246–248
Independence
    Heather Raffo's 9 Parts of Desire:
        99
    Robert Johnson: Trick the Devil:
        174
Indifference. *See* Apathy
Individualism
    The Crucible: 43
    Light Shining in Buckinghamshire:
        158
Inferiority
    The Governess: 76, 85
Influence (Psychology)
    Henrietta: 128–129
Inheritance
    Desire under the Elms: 51–52, 55
Inhumanity
    The Trojan Women: 255
Injustice
    The Crucible: 30, 44, 46
    Desire under the Elms: 55
    The Governess: 78, 80, 86, 87
    The Trojan Women: 232, 239, 245,
        254
Innocence
    Aria da Capo: 13
    The Governess: 74, 77, 78, 80
    The Trojan Women: 248, 255
Insecurity
    The Crucible: 32
    Henrietta: 124
Integrity
    The Crucible: 34
Intelligence
    The Crucible: 34
    Robert Johnson: Trick the Devil:
        174
Intolerance
    The Crucible: 25, 40–44, 46
Iraqi culture
    Heather Raffo's 9 Parts of Desire:
        97, 101, 113–114
Iraqi history
    Heather Raffo's 9 Parts of Desire:
        95, 100, 101, 103–107, 109–112

Irony
    Aria da Capo: 12, 22, 23
    The Crucible: 37, 45
    Desire under the Elms: 71
    The Governess: 78, 81
    The Trojan Women: 251, 254, 255
    West Side Story: 289
Islamic culture
    Heather Raffo's 9 Parts of Desire:
        95
Isolation
    Desire under the Elms: 49, 66, 68,
        71
    Henrietta: 129
    Robert Johnson: Trick the Devil:
        174, 178
    The Trojan Women: 256

J

Jazz
    A Streetcar Named Desire:
        227–229
Jealousy
    The Crucible: 33
    Desire under the Elms: 52
    Henrietta: 122
    Robert Johnson: Trick the Devil:
        187
Jewish culture
    The Governess: 89, 93
Judaism
    I Never Saw Another Butterfly:
        147–149
Judgment
    The Trojan Women: 247, 256
Justice
    Desire under the Elms: 69–70
    The Servant of Two Masters: 200
Justification
    The Trojan Women: 255
Juvenile delinquency
    West Side Story: 287, 289–291

K

Kindness
    The Servant of Two Masters:
        205
    A Streetcar Named Desire: 215
Knowledge
    The Governess: 85
    The Trojan Women: 256

L

Language and languages
    Desire under the Elms: 58, 70–72
    Light Shining in Buckinghamshire:
        159
    Robert Johnson: Trick the Devil:
        177–178, 188, 189
    West Side Story: 289

Life and death
    Heather Raffo's 9 Parts of Desire:
        103
    The Trojan Women: 256
Light and darkness
    The Crucible: 36–37
Loneliness
    Desire under the Elms: 55, 57–58,
        66, 71
    Henrietta: 124, 131
    I Never Saw Another Butterfly:
        149
    A Streetcar Named Desire: 213,
        216–218, 223
Loss (Psychology)
    Henrietta: 124
    A Streetcar Named Desire: 217
Love
    Aria da Capo: 5
    The Crucible: 30, 32–34, 37, 46
    Desire under the Elms: 49, 53–54,
        58, 63, 67
    Heather Raffo's 9 Parts of Desire:
        97, 99, 101, 102, 107, 111
    I Never Saw Another Butterfly:
        137, 149
    The Servant of Two Masters:
        198–200, 203–206
    A Streetcar Named Desire: 211,
        212, 215, 216, 219, 223
    The Trojan Women: 254
    Urinetown: 259, 263
    *Urinetown:*Humor 276
    West Side Story: 282–283,
        286–288, 293, 294, 298
Lower class
    The Governess: 78, 85–87
Loyalty
    The Crucible: 46
    Heather Raffo's 9 Parts of Desire:
        99, 102
    The Trojan Women: 236, 254
    West Side Story: 286
Lust
    The Crucible: 35

M

Madness
    The Crucible: 34–35
    Henrietta: 130–131
    The Servant of Two Masters: 209
    A Streetcar Named Desire: 214,
        215, 218, 223
    The Trojan Women: 234, 236,
        256
Manipulation
    The Crucible: 34
    Henrietta: 129
    Light Shining in Buckinghamshire:
        168
    A Streetcar Named Desire: 223

Marginalization
    Aria da Capo: 18
    Light Shining in Buckinghamshire:
        164–165
Marriage
    The Servant of Two Masters:
        195–197, 200
    A Streetcar Named Desire: 222
    The Trojan Women: 242
Masculinity
    A Streetcar Named Desire:
        215–216, 221–222, 228–229
Materialism
    The Crucible: 33
McCarthyism
    The Crucible: 25, 38–39, 46, 47
    West Side Story: 290
Meaninglessness
    The Trojan Women: 252, 253
Memory
    Heather Raffo's 9 Parts of Desire:
        101, 106
    I Never Saw Another Butterfly:
        138–140, 143–144, 148–149
    The Trojan Women: 251
Mental disorders
    Henrietta: 116, 119, 121, 130–131
Metaphors
    Desire under the Elms: 71–72
    Heather Raffo's 9 Parts of Desire:
        111
    Robert Johnson: Trick the Devil:
        184, 185
    West Side Story: 289
Middle class
    Aria da Capo: 19–21
Middle class values
    West Side Story: 294
Middle Eastern culture
    Heather Raffo's 9 Parts of Desire:
        105–107
Misery
    The Trojan Women: 252, 256
Misfortunes
    The Trojan Women: 256
Mistakes
    The Crucible: 32–33
    The Servant of Two Masters: 195, 198
Misunderstanding
    The Servant of Two Masters: 193,
        199
Modern life
    Urinetown: 260
Modernism (Literature)
    Aria da Capo: 16–21
Monarchy
    Light Shining in Buckinghamshire:
        154–155
Morality
    The Crucible: 36, 38
    Desire under the Elms: 69–70
    The Trojan Women: 239, 254

Mother-child relationships
    Henrietta: 122
    A Streetcar Named Desire: 223
Motherhood
    The Trojan Women: 256
Murder
    Desire under the Elms: 49, 54,
        59–60, 63, 67
    The Trojan Women: 254
Music
    Aria da Capo: 9
    Robert Johnson: Trick the Devil:
        170, 172, 173, 175, 177, 183,
        184, 186–187
    A Streetcar Named Desire: 219,
        227–229
    West Side Story: 289, 297–300
Mystery
    Desire under the Elms: 67, 70–72
Mysticism
    Desire under the Elms: 68, 71
Mythology
    Robert Johnson: Trick the Devil:
        175, 180–181, 183–185, 187–191

N

Narrators
    Urinetown: 267
Nature
    Desire under the Elms: 64–67,
        70–71
Nobility
    The Trojan Women: 254
Northeastern United States
    The Crucible: 44
    Desire under the Elms: 49, 51
    West Side Story: 290, 298

O

Oedipus complex
    Desire under the Elms: 59–60,
        63–65, 68
Onomatopoeia
    Desire under the Elms: 72
Oppression (Politics)
    The Governess: 78–79, 84–85
    Heather Raffo's 9 Parts of Desire:
        101
    Light Shining in Buckinghamshire:
        168
    Urinetown: 262, 266
Order
    The Trojan Women: 256–257

P

Pacifism
    Aria da Capo: 1, 11–12
    The Trojan Women: 244–245, 250
Pain
    The Governess: 86

Paradoxes
    The Trojan Women: 251, 253–255
    *Urinetown:*Humor 273–274
Paranoia
    The Crucible: 40, 43, 46, 47
Parodies
    Urinetown: 259, 267, 270
Passion
    Heather Raffo's 9 Parts of Desire:
        97, 102
Past
    Heather Raffo's 9 Parts of Desire:
        101, 106
    Robert Johnson: Trick the Devil:
        183
    The Trojan Women: 252
Pastoral literature
    Aria da Capo: 4, 13
Pathos
    The Trojan Women: 250–251, 255
Perception
    The Governess: 79–80
    Henrietta: 129–130
Perfection
    Light Shining in Buckinghamshire:
        156
Personification
    Desire under the Elms: 72
Persuasive literature
    The Trojan Women: 239–240
Politics
    Heather Raffo's 9 Parts of Desire:
        101
    *Urinetown:*Humor 273–274
Positivism
    Desire under the Elms: 67, 68
Possessiveness
    Desire under the Elms: 55, 56–57,
        65–67
Poverty
    Robert Johnson: Trick the Devil:
        190
Power (Philosophy)
    The Crucible: 42
    Desire under the Elms: 63, 65
    The Governess: 84
    Light Shining in Buckinghamshire:
        154–155, 160, 164
    The Servant of Two Masters: 204,
        205
    Urinetown: 267
    *Urinetown:*Humor 274
Prejudice
    The Crucible: 42
    West Side Story: 285, 288, 290,
        293
Pride
    Desire under the Elms: 55, 66, 71
Protest
    The Governess: 81–82
    Heather Raffo's 9 Parts of Desire:
        97

Psychoanalysis
  Desire under the Elms: 60–61, 63, 68
Psychology
  Desire under the Elms: 60–61, 67
Punishment
  The Crucible: 30, 38, 42
  Henrietta: 122–124
  The Servant of Two Masters: 199, 200
  The Trojan Women: 235, 238, 246, 247, 251
  Urinetown: 259, 266
Puritanism
  The Crucible: 34–37, 40–42, 44–46
Purity
  The Crucible: 37, 38
  A Streetcar Named Desire: 223, 224
  The Trojan Women: 236

R

Race relations
  Robert Johnson: Trick the Devil: 174, 175, 177, 178, 180–181, 188–189
  West Side Story: 296
Racism
  The Crucible: 42
  Robert Johnson: Trick the Devil: 184
Reality
  A Streetcar Named Desire: 217–218
  The Trojan Women: 253
  West Side Story: 285
Reason
  The Crucible: 32, 35–37
  The Servant of Two Masters: 198, 203
  The Trojan Women: 254
Rebellion
  Light Shining in Buckinghamshire: 153–154, 156–158, 160, 162–165, 168
  Urinetown: 263
  Urinetown:Humor 276
Reciprocity
  The Trojan Women: 246–247
Reconciliation
  The Crucible: 37
  Desire under the Elms: 67
Redemption
  A Streetcar Named Desire: 224
Regret
  The Crucible: 32
Religion
  The Crucible: 37–38, 43
  Desire under the Elms: 57–58, 71
Religious beliefs
  Light Shining in Buckinghamshire: 158–159

Religious reform
  Light Shining in Buckinghamshire: 160
Religious tolerance
  I Never Saw Another Butterfly: 147–149
Repetition
  Desire under the Elms: 58–59
Repression (Psychology)
  The Crucible: 27, 34, 36, 39, 44
Resentment
  Desire under the Elms: 51, 55
Resistance
  I Never Saw Another Butterfly: 143–144
Respect
  I Never Saw Another Butterfly: 149
Responsibility
  The Crucible: 42
  The Trojan Women: 256
Retribution. *See* Revenge
Revelation
  The Servant of Two Masters: 197
Revenge
  The Crucible: 44
  Desire under the Elms: 55, 66, 69
  Light Shining in Buckinghamshire: 164
  Robert Johnson: Trick the Devil: 187
  The Trojan Women: 234, 235, 251, 253, 256
  West Side Story: 287
Reversal of fortune
  Desire under the Elms: 60
  The Trojan Women: 233, 236, 244
Right and wrong
  The Crucible: 38, 40
Rigidity (Psychology)
  The Crucible: 40–41
Rituals
  The Crucible: 43
Rivalry
  West Side Story: 297
Roman Catholicism
  I Never Saw Another Butterfly: 147–149
Romanticism
  Robert Johnson: Trick the Devil: 187, 189, 190
Rural life
  Desire under the Elms: 49, 51
  Robert Johnson: Trick the Devil: 177–178

S

Sacrifice
  The Trojan Women: 253
Satire
  The Governess: 74
  Urinetown:Humor 270, 275
  West Side Story: 289

Scapegoating
  The Crucible: 42, 45
Self identity
  Light Shining in Buckinghamshire: 154, 163–164
Self image
  The Crucible: 33
Self interest
  The Servant of Two Masters: 203–204
Selfishness
  The Governess: 86
  The Servant of Two Masters: 205
Sensitivity
  Desire under the Elms: 55
  The Governess: 92
Sentimentality
  Aria da Capo: 17–21
Servitude
  The Trojan Women: 252
Setting (Literature)
  A Streetcar Named Desire: 226
  West Side Story: 289
Sex roles
  Light Shining in Buckinghamshire: 162–165
  West Side Story: 288–289
Sexuality
  The Crucible: 44, 45
Shame
  The Trojan Women: 255
Similes
  Desire under the Elms: 71–72
  West Side Story: 289
Simplicity
  Aria da Capo: 13
Sin
  The Crucible: 40–41
  Light Shining in Buckinghamshire: 155
Slavery
  The Trojan Women: 233–235, 244, 246, 249
Social class
  The Crucible: 42
  The Governess: 78, 84–87
  Light Shining in Buckinghamshire: 153, 155, 159, 160
  The Servant of Two Masters: 199–200, 203, 204
  A Streetcar Named Desire: 216, 217, 221, 222
Social commentary
  The Governess: 84
  West Side Story: 293, 294
Social identity
  Light Shining in Buckinghamshire: 151
Social realism
  Henrietta: 116

Social satire
    *Urinetown:*Humor 277, 278
Social welfare
    Henrietta: 125–126
Socialism
    Aria da Capo: 13–136
Sophism
    The Trojan Women: 235, 237,
        239–240, 246
Sorrow
    The Trojan Women: 251, 252,
        254–256
Southern United States
    Robert Johnson: Trick the Devil:
        170, 173, 175, 177–178, 180,
        185, 187, 190
    A Streetcar Named Desire: 217
Stereotypes (Psychology)
    The Governess: 84
Stoicism
    A Streetcar Named Desire: 215
    The Trojan Women: 248
Storytelling
    Robert Johnson: Trick the Devil:
        185, 190
Strength
    Desire under the Elms: 55
    I Never Saw Another Butterfly:
        136, 137
    Robert Johnson: Trick the Devil:
        174
    The Trojan Women: 246
Struggle
    Aria da Capo: 6–7
    Desire under the Elms: 65
    The Trojan Women: 256
Submission
    The Governess: 78, 85
Success
    Henrietta: 122
Suffering
    Desire under the Elms: 57
    The Governess: 86
    Heather Raffo's 9 Parts of Desire:
        104, 107
    A Streetcar Named Desire: 224
    The Trojan Women: 244, 245, 247,
        248, 250–252, 254–257
Superiority
    Desire under the Elms: 66
    The Governess: 86
    A Streetcar Named Desire: 216
Supernatural
    The Crucible: 28, 31, 40, 44
    Desire under the Elms: 69
    Robert Johnson: Trick the Devil:
        175, 184
Survival
    Heather Raffo's 9 Parts of Desire:
        101–102, 106, 108
    I Never Saw Another Butterfly:
        134, 136, 137, 142

Suspicion
    Aria da Capo: 3, 5, 7, 13, 16
    The Crucible: 30–31, 34, 41
Symbolism
    Aria da Capo: 7
    The Crucible: 25, 36–38
    Desire under the Elms: 64
    Heather Raffo's 9 Parts of Desire:
        100, 102–103
    I Never Saw Another Butterfly:
        140
    A Streetcar Named Desire: 219,
        223
    The Trojan Women: 252, 256

T

Temptation
    The Crucible: 34
Tension
    The Crucible: 33, 37, 47
    Robert Johnson: Trick the Devil:
        174
    The Trojan Women: 236, 250,
        254
Totalitarianism
    Urinetown: 270–271
Tradition
    Robert Johnson: Trick the Devil:
        190
Tragedies (Drama)
    Aria da Capo: 5, 22
    Desire under the Elms: 59–65,
        67–71
    The Trojan Women: 231, 238–241,
        244–245, 248–251, 255
    West Side Story: 280, 286,
        291–292, 299
Tragic heroes
    Desire under the Elms: 60, 62
Transcendence
    Light Shining in Buckinghamshire:
        168
    The Trojan Women: 256
    West Side Story: 286
Transformation
    The Crucible: 42
    Desire under the Elms: 67
    A Streetcar Named Desire: 218
Trickery
    The Governess: 74
    Robert Johnson: Trick the Devil:
        170, 174, 175
    The Servant of Two Masters: 197
Trust (Psychology)
    Aria da Capo: 5
    The Governess: 77, 78, 80
Truth
    The Crucible: 32, 33, 37, 38,
        46, 47
    The Governess: 84

    Robert Johnson: Trick the Devil:
        174, 177, 184, 188, 191
    The Trojan Women: 246, 252
Tyranny
    Light Shining in Buckinghamshire:
        15–155

U

Understanding
    The Trojan Women: 256
Unfairness. *See* Injustice
Unhappiness
    Desire under the Elms: 57–58
    The Trojan Women: 254
Unity
    The Trojan Women: 257
Universality
    The Crucible: 43
    The Governess: 93
    Robert Johnson: Trick the Devil:
        175
Upper class
    The Governess: 87
    Light Shining in Buckinghamshire:
        159
Urban life
    West Side Story: 288–290,
        298–299

V

Values (Philosophy)
    The Trojan Women: 254, 255
    *Urinetown:*Humor 271
Vanity
    Aria da Capo: 4
    The Governess: 85
    The Trojan Women: 255
Victimization
    The Governess: 84
    I Never Saw Another Butterfly:
        134
    The Trojan Women: 254
Violence
    West Side Story: 283–286, 291,
        296, 299
Virtue
    The Crucible: 32
    The Trojan Women: 236, 253

W

Warning
    West Side Story: 285
Wars
    Aria da Capo: 23
    Heather Raffo's 9 Parts of Desire:
        98–104, 107
    Light Shining in Buckinghamshire:
        155, 168
    The Trojan Women: 231, 241–245,
        249–250, 252–256

Weakness
  A Streetcar Named Desire: 223,
    224
Wealth
  Aria da Capo: 13–16
  The Governess: 74
  Urinetown: 263
  *Urinetown:*Humor 273–274
Western culture
  Heather Raffo's 9 Parts of Desire:
    105

Wisdom
  The Servant of Two Masters:
    205
  The Trojan Women: 256, 257
Witchcraft
  The Crucible: 26, 28–31, 46
  Light Shining in Buckinghamshire:
    164
Working class
  Aria da Capo: 15–16
  The Governess: 78, 85

  A Streetcar Named Desire:
    221
World War I, 1914-1918
  Aria da Capo: 10–12

Y

Yearning. *See* Desire
Youth
  West Side Story: 289, 290,
    294–296, 298–299

$107.35   5/20/10

LONGWOOD PUBLIC LIBRARY
800 Middle Country Road
Middle Island, NY 11953
(631) 924-6400
mylpl.net

LIBRARY HOURS

Monday-Friday	9:30 a.m. - 9:00 p.m.
Saturday	9:30 a.m. - 5:00 p.m.
Sunday (Sept-June)	1:00 p.m. - 5:00 p.m.